A·HISTORY·OF
WORLD·SOCIETIES

THIS BOOK WAS FUNDED BY THE
CUNY STUDENT FINANCIAL AID
TEXTBOOK INITIATIVE, 2009/2010.

Timeline

A HISTORY O
A BRIEF OVERVIEW

	1500	1600	1700
Africa	Portugal dominates East Africa, ca. 1500–1650 Height of Kanem-Bornu, 1571–1603	Dutch West India Co. supplants Portuguese in West Africa, ca. 1630 Dutch settle Cape Town, 1651	Rise of Ashanti Empire, ca. 1700
The Americas	Mesoamerican and South American holocaust, ca. 1500–1600 First African slaves brought to Americas, ca. 1510 Cortés arrives in Mexico, 1519; Aztec Empire falls, 1521 Pizarro reaches Peru, conquers Incas, 1531	British settle Jamestown, 1607; first plantations established Champlain founds Quebec, 1608 Dutch found New Amsterdam, 1624	Silver production quadruples in Mexico and Peru, ca. 1700–1800 Spain's defeat in War of the Spanish Succession results in colonial dependence on Spanish goods, ca. 1700–1800
Asia and Oceania	Babur defeats Delhi sultanate, 1526–1527; founds Mughal Empire Christian missionaries active in China and Japan, ca. 1550–1650 Akbar expands Mughal Empire, 1556–1605 Unification of Japan, 1568–1600 Spain conquers Philippines, 1571	Tokugawa Shogunate, 1600–1867 Height of Mughal Empire, 1628–1658 Japan expels all Europeans, 1637 Manchus establish Qing Dynasty, 1644–1911 British found Calcutta, 1690	Height of Edo urban culture in Japan, ca. 1700 Decline of Mughal Empire, ca. 1700–1800 Persian invaders loot Delhi, 1739 French and British fight for control of India, 1740–1763
Europe	Luther's Ninety-five Theses, 1517 Charles V elected Holy Roman emperor, 1519 English Reformation begins, 1532 Council of Trent, 1545–1563 Dutch declare independence, 1581 Spanish Armada, 1588	Thirty Years' War, 1618–1648 English civil war, 1642–1649 Growth of absolutism in central and eastern Europe, ca. 1680–1790 The Enlightenment, ca. 1680–1800 Ottomans besiege Vienna, 1683 Revocation of Edict of Nantes, 1685 Glorious Revolution in England, 1688	War of the Spanish Succession, 1701–1713 Peace of Utrecht, 1713 Cabinet system develops in England, 1714–1742
Middle East	Safavid Empire in Persia, 1501–1722 Peak of Ottoman power under Suleiman, 1520–1566 Battle of Lepanto, 1571 Height of Safavid Empire under Shah Abbas, 1587–1629		Decline of Safavid Empire under Nadir Shah, 1737–1747

1970	**1980**	**1990**	**2000**

Nelson Mandela: Mohamed Loures/Gamma

	South African president Frederik de Klerk legalizes African National Congress, 1989	Growth of Islamic fundamentalism, 1990 to present	AIDS epidemic, 2000 to present
	Nelson Mandela freed, 1990	Nelson Mandela elected president of South Africa, 1994	Civil war and genocide in Darfur, 2003 to present
		Rwandan genocide, 1994	Zimbabwean President Robert Mugabe increases violence against opponents after losing election, 2008

Military coup in Chile, 1973	U.S. military buildup, 1980–1988	Canada, Mexico, and United States form free-trade area (NAFTA), 1994	Terrorist attack on United States, September 11, 2001
U.S. Watergate scandal, 1974	Argentina restores civilian rule, 1983	Haiti establishes democratic government, 1994	Space shuttle *Columbia* explodes, 2003
Revolutions in Nicaragua and El Salvador, 1979		Permanent extension of Treaty on the Non-Proliferation of Nuclear Weapons, 1995	Hurricanes Katrina and Rita ravage Gulf Coast of U.S., 2005
			Raúl Castro succeeds his ailing brother Fidel as president of Cuba, 2008

India-Pakistan war, 1971	Japanese foreign investment surge, 1980–1992	Economic growth and political repression in China, 1990 to present	China joins WTO, 2001
Communist victory in Vietnam War, 1975	Sikh nationalism in India, 1984 to present	Vietnam embraces foreign investment, 1990 to present	India and Pakistan come close to all-out war, 2002
China pursues modernization, 1976 to present	China crushes democracy movement, 1989	U.S. military bases closed in Philippines, 1991	Tsunami in Southeast Asia, 2004
Chinese invade Vietnam, 1979		Hong Kong returns to Chinese rule, 1997	North Korea dismantles nuclear facilities, 2007
			Cyclone Nargis in Myanmar (Burma), 2008
			8.0 magnitude earthquake in Sichuan Province, China, 2008

Chinese students in 1989: Erika Lansner/stockphoto.com

Helsinki Accord on human rights, 1975	Soviet reform under Gorbachev, 1985–1991	Maastricht treaty proposes monetary union, 1990	Euro note enters circulation, 2002
Soviet invasion of Afghanistan, 1979	Communism falls in eastern Europe, 1989–1990	Conservative economic policies, 1990s	Madrid train bombing, 2004
		End of Soviet Union, 1991	Chechen terrorists take Russian schoolchildren hostage, 2004
		Civil war in Bosnia, 1991–1995	London subway and bus bombing, 2005
		Creation of European Union, 1993	

"Yom Kippur War," 1973	Iran-Iraq War, 1980–1988	Growth of Islamic fundamentalism, 1990 to present	Israel begins construction of West Bank barrier, 2003
Islamic revolution in Iran, 1979		Iraq driven from Kuwait by United States and allies, 1991	Wars in Iraq and Afghanistan, 2003 to present
Camp David Accords, 1979		Israel and Palestinians sign peace agreement, 1993	Iran advances nuclear energy program, 2004 to present
		Assassination of Israeli prime minister Yitzak Rabin, 1995	Benazir Bhutto assassinated, 2007

A·HISTORY·OF
WORLD·SOCIETIES

Volume C 3
From 1775 to the Present

eighth edition

John P. McKay
University of Illinois at Urbana-Champaign

Bennett D. Hill
Late of Georgetown University

John Buckler
University of Illinois at Urbana-Champaign

Patricia Buckley Ebrey
University of Washington

Roger B. Beck
Eastern Illinois University

Clare Haru Crowston
University of Illinois at Urbana-Champaign

Merry E. Wiesner-Hanks
University of Wisconsin–Milwaukee

BEDFORD / ST. MARTIN'S
Boston • New York

FOR BEDFORD/ST. MARTIN'S

Publisher for History: Mary Dougherty
Executive Editor for History: Traci Mueller
Director of Development for History: Jane Knetzger
Executive Marketing Manager: Jenna Bookin Barry
Copyeditor: Sybil Sosin
Proofreader: Angela Hoover Morrison
Text Design and Page Layout: Janet Theurer
Photo Research: Carole Frohlich
Indexer: Leoni McVey
Cover Design: Donna Lee Dennison
Cover Art: Diego Rivera (1886–1957), *Cuca Bustamente,* 1946. Museum of Modern Art, Mexico/Gianni Dagli Orti/The Art Archive. Copyright 2008 Banco de Mexico, Trustees of the Diego Rivera & Frida Kahlo Museums Trust, Av. Cinco de Mayo No. 2, Col. Centro, Del Cuauhtemoc 06059, Mexico D. F.
Cartography: Charlotte Miller/GeoNova
Composition: NK Graphics
Printing and Binding: R.R. Donnelley & Sons Company

President: Joan E. Feinberg
Editorial Director: Denise B. Wydra
Director of Marketing: Karen R. Soeltz
Director of Editing, Design, and Production: Marcia Cohen
Assistant Director of Editing, Design, and Production: Elise S. Kaiser
Managing Editor: Elizabeth M. Schaaf

Library of Congress Control Number: 2008933879

In this age of a global environment and global warming, of a global economy and global banking, of global migration and rapid global travel, of global sports and global popular culture, the study of world history becomes more urgent. Surely, an appreciation of other, and earlier, societies helps us to understand better our own and to cope more effectively in pluralistic cultures worldwide. The large numbers of Turks living in Germany, of Italians, Hungarians, and Slavic peoples living in Australia, of Japanese living in Peru and Argentina, and of Arabs, Mexicans, Chinese, and Filipinos living in the United States—to mention just a few obvious examples—represent diversity on a global scale. The movement of large numbers of peoples from one continent to another goes back thousands of years, at least as far back as the time when peoples migrated from Asia into the Americas. Swift air travel and the Internet have accelerated these movements, and they testify to the incredible technological changes the world has experienced in the last half of the twentieth century and beginning of the twenty-first.

For most peoples, the study of history has traditionally meant the study of their own national, regional, and ethnic pasts. Fully appreciating the great differences among various societies and the complexity of the historical problems surrounding these cultures, we have wondered if the study of local or national history is sufficient for people who will spend their lives in the twenty-first century on one small interconnected planet. The authors of this book believe the study of world history in a broad and comparative context is an exciting, important, and highly practical pursuit. It is our conviction, based on considerable experience in introducing large numbers of students to the broad sweep of world history, that a book reflecting current trends can excite readers and inspire an enduring interest in the long human experience. Our strategy has been twofold.

First, we have made social history the core element of our work. We not only incorporate recent research by social historians but also seek to re-create the life of ordinary people in appealing human terms. A strong social element seems especially appropriate in a world history text, for identification with ordinary men and women of the past allows today's reader to reach an empathetic understanding of different cultures. At the same time we have been mindful of the need to give great economic, political, intellectual, and

cultural developments the attention they deserve. We want to give individual students and instructors a balanced, integrated perspective so that they can pursue on their own or in the classroom those themes and questions that they find particularly exciting and significant.

Second, we have made every effort to strike an effective global balance. We are acutely aware of the great drama of our times—the passing of the era of Western dominance and the increasing complexity in lines of political, economic, and cultural power and influence. Today the whole world interacts, and to understand that interaction and what it means for today's citizens, we must study the whole world's history. Thus we have adopted a comprehensive yet manageable global perspective. We study all geographical areas, conscious of the separate histories of many parts of the world, particularly in the earliest millennia of human development. We also stress the links among cultures, political units, and economic systems, for it is these connections and interactions that have made the world what it is today.

Changes in the Eighth Edition

In preparing the Eighth Edition of this book, we have worked hard to keep our book up-to-date and to strengthen our distinctive yet balanced approach.

Organizational Changes

Responding to the wishes of many of the faculty who use this book, we have shortened the text significantly. The narrative has been tightened in each chapter, and the consolidations improve the overall global balance of our work.

In addition, several chapters have been extensively reorganized. Merry Wiesner-Hanks from the University of Wisconsin-Milwaukee and Clare Crowston from the University of Illinois joined the author team with this edition, taking responsibility for Chapters 7, 10, 13, and 14 and Chapters 15–17 and 21, respectively. Chapter 7, "Europe and Western Asia, ca. 350–850," has a broader geographic focus, with more material on the Byzantine Empire and the various migrating peoples. Former Chapter 13 on the Americas has been brought into the story earlier as new Chapter 10, and the chapter has been rewritten to reflect the newest scholarship on early cultures of North America, Mesoamerica, and South America. Discussion of the Thirty Years' War has been integrated into Chapter 16, allowing a better assessment of its impact on state-building, along with broader coverage of economic and demographic trends. Other chapters have been restructured as well. Chapter 19, "The Islamic World Powers, ca. 1400–1800," has been completely reorganized to highlight parallels among the Ottoman, Safavid, and Mughal Empires in terms of political, cultural, and economic developments. Reflecting current understandings of the connections around the Atlantic world, Chapter 21 includes extensive discussion of the Haitian Revolution along with the American and French Revolutions. Chapter 26, "Nation Building in the Western Hemisphere and Australia," contains a new section that places the nations in comparative perspective. In addition, former chapters 33 and 34 are now combined as a new and streamlined Chapter 33, "A New Era in World History." The new chapter focuses on global political and economic issues (such as the United Nations, terrorism, globalization and its consequences, and vital resources), plus global issues that affect individuals (such as poverty, disease, urbanization, and education), and shows how they evolved over the course of the twentieth century. "The Middle East in Today's World," a supplement to later printings of the seventh edition, has been updated to reflect recent developments in the Middle East, and is now the Epilogue.

Geographical and Gender Issues

In previous editions we added significantly more discussion of groups and regions that are often shortchanged in the general histories of world civilizations, and we have continued to do so in this new revision. This expanded scope reflects the renewed awareness within the historical profession of the enormous diversity of the world's peoples. Examples include more material on the Etruscans in Chapter 5, the Huns in Chapter 7, and the Turks in Chapter 8. Chapter 10 includes increased discussion of the Hohokam, Hopewell, and Mississippian peoples in North America and of pre-Inca cultures in Peru. Study of the Mongols and other peoples of Central Asia has exploded in the past several years, which has shaped the changes in Chapter 11. Chapter 17 includes a new discussion of new ideas about race during the Enlightenment. Chapter 21 has considerable new material on the Haitian Revolution. Overall, an expanded treatment of non-European societies and cultures has been achieved.

In addition, we have continued to include updated and expanded material relating to gender in nearly every chapter, incorporating insights from women's history, the history of sexuality, the history of the family, and the new history of masculinities. Chapter 4 includes revised coverage of Greek sexuality and the family, with new focus in Chapter 7 on the role of women in barbarian society, Chapter 8 on women in classical Islamic society, Chapter 12 on women's lives in Song China, Chapter 14 on gender hierarchies in Renaissance Europe and on the Reformation and marriage, Chapter 18 on women, marriage, and work in early modern Africa, Chapter 22 on the sexual division of labor in the Industrial Revolution, and Chapter 33 on women's rights and feminist movements. In addition to "Individuals in Society" features from previous editions that focus on the lives of specific women, several new ones have been added: the feature in Chapter 1 focuses on the Egyptian monarch Nefertiti, in Chapter 7 on Empress Theodora of Constantinople, in Chapter 13 on the Christian abbess Hildegard of Bingen, and in Chapter 16 on the Jewish merchant and diarist Glückel of Hameln. Chapter 8 includes a new "Listening to the Past" feature on the etiquette of marriage in the Islamic world.

Cross-Cultural Comparisons and Connections

In this edition we have continued to expand our comparative coverage to help students see and understand the cross-cultural connections of world history. Chapter 2 offers expanded discussion of trading networks in early India, and both Chapters 5 and 6 provide enhanced discussion of the Silk Road. Chapter 7 includes a reframed discussion of the barbarian migrations into Europe. Chapter 8 addresses new questions such as "How were the Muslim lands governed and what new challenges did they face?" and "What social distinctions were important in Muslim society?" Updated treatment of the trans-Saharan trade appears in Chapter 9, and Chapter 10 now discusses trade along the rivers and lakes of North America. Chapter 15 has been extensively rewritten, with a new section on global economies, forced migrations, and cultural encounters. Chapter 24 addresses the important question "What were the global consequences of European industrialization between 1800 and 1914?"

Incorporation of Recent Scholarship

As in previous revisions we have made a serious effort to keep our book fresh and up-to-date by incorporating new and important scholarship throughout the Eighth Edition. Chapter 4 includes new findings about the role of women in religious movements in the ancient world, including Christianity. Chapter 7 highlights the continuing significance of the Byzantines and the transformations brought through barbarian migrations. Chapter 10 features innovative research on agricultural communities in the Americas and the connections among them. New sections on popular religion and social hierarchies appear in Chapters 13 and 14. Chapters 14 and 17 include sections derived from the new scholarship on changing conceptions of race. Chapter 17 also draws upon new work about the emergence of the public sphere in Enlightenment Europe to discuss the political and social implications of intellectual change. Chapter 20 features new treatment of maritime East Asia. Chapter 26 includes a new comparative discussion of the incorporation of the nations of the Americas into the world economy. Material in the final three chapters and the Epilogue has been updated to ensure a clear account of contemporary world history. Thus, the text includes discussion of such events as the unfolding war in Iraq, the worsening crisis in Afghanistan, Hezbollah's revival in Lebanon, moves toward peace in Israel, elections in Zimbabwe, charges of genocide against the Sudanese president, China and Tibet and the 2008 Olympics, and North Korea's dismantling of its nuclear facilities. In sum, we have tried hard to bring new research and interpretation into our global history, believing it essential to keep our book stimulating, accurate, and current for students and instructors.

Revised Full-Color Art and Map Program

Finally, the illustrative component of our work has been carefully revised. We have added many new illustrations to our extensive art program, which includes over three hundred color reproductions, thus highlighting the connections among art, material culture, events, and social changes. Illustrations have been selected to support and complement the text, and, wherever possible, illustrations are contemporaneous with the textual material discussed. Considerable research went into many of the captions in order to make them as informative as possible. We have reflected on the observation that "there are more valid facts and details in works of art than there are in history books," and we would modify it to say that art is "a history book." Artwork remains an integral part of our book; the past can speak in pictures as well as in words. The maps have been completely redesigned and revised in this edition to be more dynamic, engaging, and relevant than ever before. The use of full color serves to clarify the maps and graphs and to enrich the textual material. The maps and map captions have been updated to correlate directly to the text.

Distinctive Features

Distinctive features from earlier editions guide the reader in the process of historical understanding. Many of these features also show how historians sift through and evaluate evidence. Our goal is to suggest how historians actually work and think. We want the reader to think critically and to realize that history is neither a list of cut-and-dried facts nor a senseless jumble of conflicting opinions.

"Individuals in Society" Feature

The Eighth Edition presents eight new short studies of a fascinating woman or man, which are carefully integrated into the main discussion of the text. This "Individuals in Society" feature grew out of our long-standing focus on people's lives and the varieties of historical experience, and we believe that readers will empathize with these flesh-and-blood human beings as they themselves seek to define their own identities today. The spotlighting of individuals, both famous and obscure, carries forward the greater attention to cultural and intellectual developments that we have used to invigorate our social history, and it reflects changing interests within the historical profession as well as the development of "micro history."

The men and women included in the Eighth Edition represent a wide range of careers and personalities. Several are renowned historical or present-day figures, such as Plutarch, the Greek historian and biographer (Chapter 5); Amda Siyon, probably the most important ruler of Ethiopia's Solomonic dynasty (Chapter 9); Giuseppe Garibaldi, the flamboyant, incorruptible popular hero of Italy's national unification (Chapter 23); and the Dalai Lama, exiled spiritual leader of a captive nation (Chapter 33). Two individuals were brilliant writers who testified to tragedy and calamitous destruction: Vera Brittain, an English nurse on the frontlines in World War I (Chapter 27); and Primo Levi, an Italian Jewish chemist who survived the Holocaust and probed the horrors of the death camps (Chapter 30). Others are lesser-known individuals, yet highly accomplished in their own societies and time, such as the Ban family from China, who were influential in the military, government, and literary fields (Chapter 6); Bhaskara, the Indian astronomer and mathematician who published many books in those fields (Chapter 11); Tan Yunxian, a Chinese female doctor who devoted her practice to the treatment of women (Chapter 20); and José Rizal, a Philippine nationalist and author (Chapter 25).

"Listening to the Past" Feature

A two-page excerpt from a primary source concludes each chapter. This signature feature, entitled "Listening to the Past," extends and illuminates a major historical issue considered in the chapter. Each primary source opens with a problem-setting introduction and closes with "Questions for Analysis" that invite students to evaluate the evidence as historians would. Drawn from a range of writings addressing a variety of social, cultural, political, and intellectual issues, these sources promote active involvement and critical interpretation. Selected for their interest and importance and carefully fitted into their historical context, these sources do indeed allow the student to "listen to the past" and to observe how history has been shaped by individual men and women, some of them great aristocrats, others ordinary folk.

"Global Trade" Feature

In the form of two-page essays that focus on a particular commodity, this popular feature explores the world trade, social and economic impact, and cultural influence of that commodity. Each essay is accompanied by a detailed map showing the trade routes of the commodity. Retaining the seven essays of the previous edition on pottery, silk, tea, slaves, indigo, oil, and arms, we added one on spices in Chapter 11. We believe that careful attention to all of these essays will enable the student to appreciate the complex ways in which trade has connected and influenced the various parts of the world.

Improved Pedagogy

To help make the narrative accessible to students, we have put a number of pedagogical features in the text. At the start of each chapter, an outline of the major section titles provides students with a brief preview of the chapter coverage. Also at the beginning of each chapter, we pose specific historical questions to help guide the reader toward understanding. These questions are then answered in the course of the chapter, and each chapter concludes with a concise summary of its findings. All of the questions and summaries have been re-examined and frequently revised in order to maximize their usefulness.

Throughout the chapter we have highlighted in boldface the major terms with which a student should become familiar. These Key Terms are then listed at the conclusion of the chapter. The student may use these terms to test his or her understanding of the chapter's material. A complete list of the Key Terms and definitions is also provided on the student website, along with electronic flashcards that allow students to quiz themselves on their mastery of the terms.

In addition to posing chapter-opening questions and presenting more problems in historical interpretation, we have quoted extensively from a wide variety of primary sources in the narrative, demonstrating in our use of these quotations how historians evaluate evidence. Thus primary sources are examined as an integral part of the narrative as well as presented in extended form in the "Listening to the Past" chapter feature. We believe that such an extensive program of both integrated and separate primary source excerpts will help readers learn to interpret and think critically.

Each chapter concludes with a Summary section and carefully selected suggestions for further reading. These suggestions are briefly described to help readers know where to turn to continue thinking and learning about the world. Also, chapter bibliographies have been thoroughly revised and updated to keep them current with the vast amount of new work being done in many fields.

Revised Timelines

To better present the flow of critical developments, the comparative timelines of earlier editions have been converted into chapter chronologies in each chapter. The extended comparative timeline has been moved to the front of the book and is now a perforated foldout poster. Comprehensive and easy to locate, this useful timeline poster allows students to compare simultaneous political, economic, social, cultural, intellectual, and scientific developments over the centuries.

Flexible Format

World history courses differ widely in chronological structure from one campus to another. To accommodate the various divisions of historical time into intervals that fit a two-quarter, three-quarter, or two-semester period, *A History of World Societies* is published in three versions that embrace the complete work:

- One-volume hardcover edition: *A History of World Societies* (Chapters 1–33 and Epilogue)
- Two-volume paperback edition: *Volume I: To 1715* (Chapters 1–16); and *Volume II: Since 1500* (Chapters 15–33 and Epilogue)
- Three-volume paperback edition: *Volume A: From Antiquity to 1500* (Chapters 1–13); *Volume B: From 800 to 1815* (Chapters 10–21); and *Volume C: From 1775 to the Present* (Chapters 21–33 and Epilogue)

Overlapping chapters in two-volume and three-volume editions facilitate matching the appropriate volume with the opening and closing dates of a specific course. In addition, this title is available as an e-Book.

Ancillaries

We are pleased to introduce a full ancillary package that will help students in learning and instructors in teaching:

- *Student website*
- *Instructor website*
- *Electronic Testing (powered by Diploma™)*
- *Online Instructor's Resource Manual*
- *PowerPoint maps and images*
- *PowerPoint questions for personal response systems*
- *Blackboard® and WebCT® course cartridges*

The student website features a wide array of resources to help students master the subject matter including learning objectives, chapter outlines, pre-class quizzes and other self-testing material like interactive flashcards, chronological ordering exercises, and more. Students can also find additional text resources such as an online glossary, audio chapter summaries, and an audio pronunciation guide.

The instructor website features all of the material on the student site plus additional password-protected resources for teaching the course such as an electronic version of the *Instructor's Resource Manual* and *PowerPoint* slides.

Electronic Testing (powered by *Diploma*) offers instructors a flexible and powerful tool for test generation and test management. Supported by the Brownstone Research Group's market-leading *Diploma* software, this new version of *Electronic Testing* significantly improves on functionality and ease of use by offering all of the tools needed to create, author, deliver, and customize multiple types of tests. *Diploma* is currently in use at thousands of college and university campuses throughout the United States and Canada.

The online *Instructor's Resource Manual,* prepared by John Reisbord of Vassar College and updated for the Eighth Edition by Jason Stratton of Bakersfield College, contains advice on teaching the world history course, instructional objectives, chapter outlines, lecture suggestions, paper and class activity topics, primary source and map activities, and suggestions for cooperative learning.

We are pleased to offer a collection of world history *PowerPoint* maps and images for use in classroom presentations. This collection includes all of the photos and maps in the text, as well as numerous other images from our world history titles. *PowerPoint* questions and answers for use with personal response system software are also offered to adopters free of charge.

Graded homework questions have been developed to work with the *Blackboard* and *WebCT* course management systems. Instructors can choose to use the content as is, modify it, or even add their own.

In addition, instructors have numerous options for packaging Bedford/St. Martin's titles with *A History of World Societies.* Based on the popular "World History Matters" websites produced by the Center for History and New Media at George Mason University, the print resource *World History Matters: A Student Guide to World History Online* provides an illustrated and annotated guide to 150 of the most useful and reliable websites for student research in world history as well as advice on evaluating and using Internet sources. This title, edited by Kristin Lehner, Kelly Schrum, and T. Mills Kelly, is available free when packaged with the textbook. Over 100 titles in the *Bedford Series in History and Culture* combine first-rate scholarship, historical narrative, and important primary documents for undergraduate courses. Each book is brief, inexpensive, and focused on a specific topic or period. Package discounts are available. Trade books published by sister companies Farrar, Straus and Giroux; Henry Holt and Company; Hill and Wang;

Picador; St. Martin's Press; and Palgrave Macmillan are available at a 50 percent discount when packaged with Bedford/St. Martin's textbooks. For more information, visit **bedfordstmartins.com/tradeup**.

Acknowledgments

It is a pleasure to thank the many instructors who have read and critiqued the manuscript throughout its development:

Wayne Ackerson
Salisbury University

Edward M. Anson
University of Arkansas at Little Rock

Beau Bowers
Central Piedmont Community College

Eric Dorn Brose
Drexel University

Erwin F. Erhardt III
Thomas More College

Dolores Grapsas
New River Community College

Candace Gregory-Abbott
California State University, Sacramento

Roger Hall
Allan Hancock College

John Jovan Markovic
Andrews University

Christopher E. Mauriello
Salem State College

Michael G. Murdock
Brigham Young University

Phyllis E. Pobst
Arkansas State University

Thomas Saylor
Concordia University

Jason M. Stratton
Bakersfield College

Ruth Smith Truss
University of Montevallo

Claude Welch
State University of New York at Buffalo

It is also a pleasure to thank our editors for their efforts over many years. To Christina Horn, who guided production, and to Tonya Lobato, our development editor, we express our admiration and special appreciation. And we thank Carole Frohlich for her contributions in photo research and selection.

Many of our colleagues at the University of Illinois, University of Washington, Eastern Illinois University, and the University of Wisconsin–Milwaukee continue to provide information and stimulation, often without even knowing it. We thank them for it.

Each of us has benefited from the criticism of his or her coauthors, although each of us assumes responsibility for what he or she has written. John Buckler has written Chapters 1, 4, and 5. Patricia Buckley Ebrey has written or updated Chapters 2–3, 6, 8, 11–12, 19–20, and 25–26. Bennett Hill originally conceived the narrative for Chapters 7–9, 12–15, 18–20, and 26; since his untimely death his coauthors have taken on his chapters. In this edition new coauthor Merry Wiesner-Hanks handled Chapters 7, 10, 13, and 14; and new coauthor Clare Crowston handled Chapters 15–17 and 21. Roger Beck contributed to Chapters 9 and 18 and handled Chapters 27–33 in this edition. Roger Beck also wrote the Epilogue. John McKay originally wrote the narrative for Chapters 16–17, 21–24, and 27–30, and he continues to take responsibility for Chapters 22–24 in this edition. Finally, we continue to welcome the many comments and suggestions that have come from our readers, for they have helped us greatly in this ongoing endeavor.

J.P.M.

J.B.

P.B.E.

R.B.B.

C.H.C.

M.W-H.

Brief Contents

Contents

Chapter 21

THE REVOLUTION IN POLITICS, 1775–1815   610

Chapter 22

THE INDUSTRIAL REVOLUTION IN EUROPE, CA. 1780–1860   642

Chapter 23

THE TRIUMPH OF NATIONALISM IN EUROPE, 1815–1914   674

Maps

Listening to the Past

Individuals in Society

About the Authors

JOHN P. McKAY Born in St. Louis, John P. McKay received his B.A. from Wesleyan University (1961), his M.A. from the Fletcher School of Law and Diplomacy (1962), and his Ph.D. from the University of California, Berkeley (1968). He began teaching history at the University of Illinois in 1966 and became a Professor there in 1976. John won the Herbert Baxter Adams Prize for his book *Pioneers for Profit: Foreign Entrepreneurship and Russian Industrialization, 1885–1913* (1970). He has also written *Tramways and Trolleys: The Rise of Urban Mass Transport in Europe* (1976) and has translated Jules Michelet's *The People* (1973). His research has been supported by fellowships from the Ford Foundation, the Guggenheim Foundation, the National Endowment for the Humanities, and IREX. He has written well over a hundred articles, book chapters, and reviews, which have appeared in numerous publications, including *The American Historical Review, Business History Review, The Journal of Economic History,* and *Slavic Review.* He contributed extensively to C. Stewart and P. Fritzsche, eds., *Imagining the Twentieth Century* (1997).

BENNETT D. HILL A native of Philadelphia, Bennett D. Hill earned an A.B. from Princeton (1956) and advanced degrees from Harvard (A.M., 1958) and Princeton (Ph.D., 1963). He taught history at the University of Illinois, where he was department chair from 1978 to 1981. He published *English Cistercian Monasteries and Their Patrons in the Twelfth Century* (1968), *Church and State in the Middle Ages* (1970), and articles in *Analecta Cisterciensia, The New Catholic Encyclopaedia, The American Benedictine Review, and The Dictionary of the Middle Ages.* His reviews appeared in *The American Historical Review, Speculum, The Historian,* the *Journal of World History,* and *Library Journal.* He was one of the contributing editors to *The Encyclopedia of World History* (2001). He was a Fellow of the American Council of Learned Societies and served on the editorial board of *The American Benedictine Review,* on committees of the National Endowment for the Humanities, and as vice president of the American Catholic Historical Association (1995–1996). A Benedictine monk of St. Anselm's Abbey in Washington, D.C., he was also a Visiting Professor at Georgetown University.

JOHN BUCKLER Born in Louisville, Kentucky, John Buckler received his Ph.D. from Harvard University in 1973. In 1980 Harvard University Press published his *Theban Hegemony, 371–362 B.C.* He published *Philip II and the Sacred War* (Leiden 1989) and also edited *BOIOTIKA: Vorträge vom 5. Internationalen Böotien-Kolloquium* (Munich 1989). In 2003 he published *Aegean Greece in the Fourth Century B.C.* In the following year appeared his editions of W. M. Leake, *Travels in the Morea* (three volumes), and Leake's *Peloponnesiaca.* Cambridge University Press published his *Central Greece and the Politics of Power in the Fourth Century BC,* edited by Hans Beck, in 2008.

PATRICIA BUCKLEY EBREY Born in Hasbrouck Heights, New Jersey, Patricia Ebrey received her A.B. from the University of Chicago in 1968 and her Ph.D. from Columbia University in 1975. She taught Asian history and culture at the University of Illinois for twenty years before moving to the University of Washington in 1997. Her research has been supported by fellowships from the American Council of Learned Societies, the National Endowment for the Humanities, the Guggenheim Foundation, and the Chiang Ching-Kuo Foundation. Probably the best known of her many books are *Chinese Civilization: A Sourcebook* (1981, 1993), *The Inner Quarters: Marriage and the Lives of Chinese Women in the Sung Period* (1993) (which won the Levenson Prize of the Association for Asian Studies), and *The Cambridge Illustrated History of China* (1996). *East Asia: A Cultural, Social, and Political History,* coauthored with Anne Walthall and James Palais, is now in its second edition.

ROGER B. BECK An Indiana native, Roger B. Beck received his B.A. from the University of Evansville (1969), and an M.S. in social studies education (1977), M.A. in history (1979), and Ph.D. in African history (1987) from Indiana University. He taught history at international schools in Paris, Tokyo, and London for six years and was a visiting lecturer at the University of Cape Town in 1981. He has taught at Eastern Illinois University since 1987, where he is Distinguished Professor of African, World, and Twentieth-century World History. His publications include *The History of South Africa* (2000), a translation of P. J. van der Merwe's *The Migrant Farmer in the History of the Cape Colony, 1657–1842,* and more than seventy-five articles, book chapters, and reviews. He is a senior consultant to McDougal Littell's widely used high school text *World History: Patterns of Interaction,* now in its third edition. He is the recipient of two Fulbright fellowships. He has been an active member of the World Hisvtory Association for nearly twenty years, including serving a term on the executive council and as treasurer for six years.

CLARE HARU CROWSTON Born in Cambridge, Massachusetts, and raised in Toronto, Clare Haru Crowston received her B.A. in 1985 from McGill University and her Ph.D. in 1996 from Cornell University. Since 1996, she has taught at the University of Illinois, where she has served as associate chair and Director of Graduate Studies, and is currently Associate Professor of history. She is the author of *Fabricating Women: The Seamstresses of Old Regime France, 1675–1791* (Duke University Press, 2001), which won two awards, the Berkshire Prize and the Hagley Prize. She edited two special issues of the *Journal of Women's History* (vol. 18, nos. 3 and 4) and has published numerous articles and reviews in journals such as *Annales: Histoire, Sciences Sociales, French Historical Studies, Gender and History,* and the *Journal of Economic History.* Her research has been supported with grants from the National Endowment for the Humanities, the Mellon Foundation, and the Bourse Châteaubriand of the French government. She is a past president of the Society for French Historical Studies and a former chair of the Pinkney Prize Committee.

MERRY E. WIESNER-HANKS Having grown up in Minneapolis, Merry E. Wiesner-Hanks received her B.A. from Grinnell College in 1973 (as well as an honorary doctorate some years later), and her Ph.D. from the University of Wisconsin–Madison in 1979. She taught first at Augustana College in Illinois, and since 1985 at the University of Wisconsin–Milwaukee, where she is currently UWM Distinguished Professor in the department of history. She is the co-editor of the *Sixteenth Century Journal* and the author or editor of nineteen books and many articles that have appeared in English, German, Italian, Spanish, and Chinese. These include *Early Modern Europe, 1450–1789* (Cambridge, 2006), *Women and Gender in Early Modern Europe* (Cambridge, 3d ed., 2008), and *Gender in History* (Blackwell, 2001). She currently serves as the Chief Reader for Advanced Placement World History and has also written a number of source books for use in the college classroom, including *Discovering the Western Past* (Houghton Mifflin, 6th ed, 2007) and *Discovering the Global Past* (Houghton Mifflin, 3d. ed., 2006), and a book for young adults, *An Age of Voyages, 1350–1600* (Oxford 2005).

ARCTIC OCEAN

80°N

Arctic Ci

60°N

ALASKA RANGE

ROCKY MOUNTAINS

CANADIAN SHIELD

NORTH AMERICA

40°N

NORTH PACIFIC OCEAN

Mississippi R.

APPALACHIAN MTS.

NORTH ATLANTIC OCEAN

Rio Grande R.

Tropic of Cancer

20°N

0° Equator

Amazon R.

SOUTH AMERICA

20°S

ANDES MOUNTAINS

Tropic of Capricorn

SOUTH PACIFIC OCEAN

SOUTH ATLANTIC OCEAN

40°S

Cape Horn

60°S

Antarctic Circle

80°S

180°

Sea ice
Ice cap
Tundra
Forest
Grassland
Desert
Mountains

180° 160°W 140°W 120°W 100°W 80°W 60°W 40°W 20°W

ARCTIC OCEAN

80°N

60°N

URAL MTS.

Ob R.

Volga R.

EUROPE

ASIA

GOBI

40°N

HINDU KUSH

HIMALAYA MTS.

Indus R.

Ganges R.

Tropic of Cancer

20°N

SYRIAN
DESERT

AFRICA

Nile R.

SAHARA

DECCAN
PLATEAU

PACIFIC OCEAN

0°

INDIAN OCEAN

NAMIB DESERT

KALAHARI
DESERT

Cape of
Good Hope

GREAT
SANDY
DESERT

20°S

Tropic of Capricorn

AUSTRALIA

0   1,000   2,000 Km.

0   1,000   2,000 Mi.

60°S

Antarctic Circle

ANTARCTICA

80°S

180°

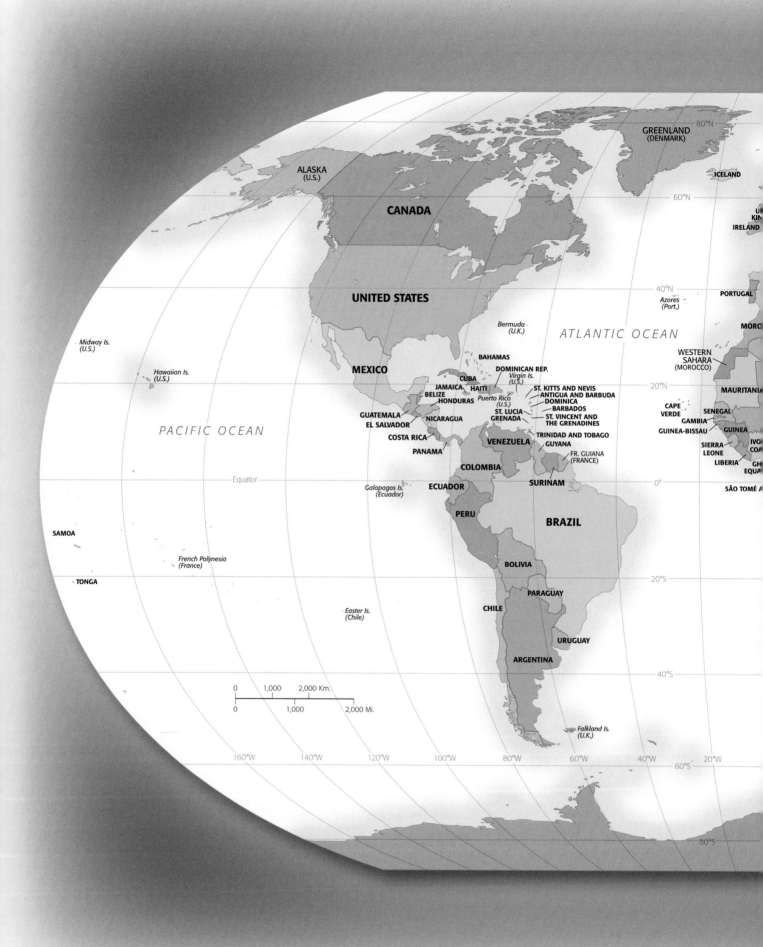

GREENLAND
(DENMARK)

ICELAND

ALASKA
(U.S.)

CANADA

UNITED
KING...

IRELAND

UNITED STATES

PORTUGAL

Bermuda
(U.K.)

ATLANTIC OCEAN

Azores
(Port.)

MORO...

Midway Is.
(U.S.)

BAHAMAS

MEXICO

WESTERN
SAHARA
(MOROCCO)

Hawaiian Is.
(U.S.)

CUBA

DOMINICAN REP.

Virgin Is.
(U.S.)

JAMAICA
HAITI

BELIZE
HONDURAS

Puerto Rico
(U.S.)

ST. KITTS AND NEVIS
ANTIGUA AND BARBUDA
DOMINICA
BARBADOS

ST. LUCIA
GRENADA

ST. VINCENT AND
THE GRENADINES

CAPE
VERDE

MAURITANIA

SENEGAL

GUATEMALA
EL SALVADOR

NICARAGUA

GAMBIA

GUINEA-BISSAU

GUINEA

COSTA RICA

TRINIDAD AND TOBAGO

SIERRA
LEONE

IVO...
COA...

PACIFIC OCEAN

PANAMA

VENEZUELA

GUYANA

LIBERIA

GH...

FR. GUIANA
(FRANCE)

EQUA...

COLOMBIA

SÃO TOMÉ A...

Galapagos Is.
(Ecuador)

ECUADOR

SURINAM

Equator

PERU

BRAZIL

SAMOA

French Polynesia
(France)

BOLIVIA

TONGA

PARAGUAY

Easter Is.
(Chile)

CHILE

URUGUAY

ARGENTINA

0   1,000   2,000 Km.

0   1,000   2,000 Mi.

Falkland Is.
(U.K.)

160°W   140°W   120°W   100°W   80°W   60°W   40°W   20°W

80°N

60°N

40°N

20°N

0°

20°S

40°S

60°S

80°S

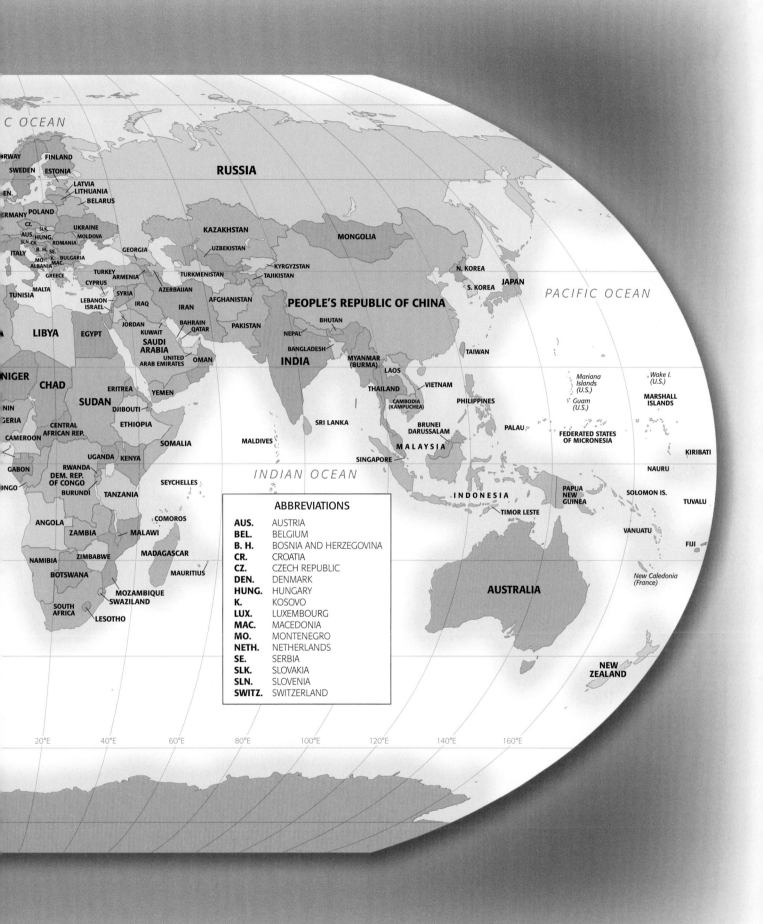

C OCEAN

RWAY FINLAND
SWEDEN ESTONIA
EN. LATVIA
LITHUANIA
BELARUS
RMANY POLAND
CZ.
AUS. SLK.
SLN. CR. HUNG.
ITALY B. H. SE. ROMANIA
MO. K. BULGARIA
ALBANIA MAC.
GREECE

RUSSIA

KAZAKHSTAN

MONGOLIA

N. KOREA
S. KOREA JAPAN

PACIFIC OCEAN

TURKEY ARMENIA
CYPRUS
TUNISIA
MALTA
LEBANON
ISRAEL
SYRIA
IRAQ
JORDAN
GEORGIA
AZERBAIJAN
UZBEKISTAN
KYRGYZSTAN
TAJIKISTAN
TURKMENISTAN
AFGHANISTAN
IRAN

PEOPLE'S REPUBLIC OF CHINA

LIBYA EGYPT
KUWAIT
BAHRAIN
QATAR
SAUDI
ARABIA
UNITED
ARAB EMIRATES
OMAN
PAKISTAN
NEPAL
BHUTAN
BANGLADESH
INDIA
MYANMAR
(BURMA)
TAIWAN

NIGER CHAD
SUDAN
ERITREA
YEMEN
DJIBOUTI
LAOS
THAILAND
VIETNAM

Mariana
Islands
(U.S.)

Wake I.
(U.S.)

MARSHALL
ISLANDS

NIN
GERIA
CENTRAL
AFRICAN REP.
ETHIOPIA
CAMBODIA
(KAMPUCHEA)
PHILIPPINES
Guam
(U.S.)

CAMEROON
SOMALIA
SRI LANKA
BRUNEI
DARUSSALAM
PALAU
FEDERATED STATES
OF MICRONESIA

KIRIBATI

MALDIVES
MALAYSIA
SINGAPORE

GABON
UGANDA KENYA
RWANDA
DEM. REP.
OF CONGO
NGO
BURUNDI
TANZANIA
SEYCHELLES

INDIAN OCEAN

NAURU

COMOROS

INDONESIA
PAPUA
NEW
GUINEA
TIMOR LESTE
SOLOMON IS.

TUVALU

ANGOLA
ZAMBIA
MALAWI
MADAGASCAR
MAURITIUS

VANUATU

FIJI

NAMIBIA
ZIMBABWE
BOTSWANA

New Caledonia
(France)

MOZAMBIQUE
SWAZILAND
SOUTH
AFRICA
LESOTHO

AUSTRALIA

ABBREVIATIONS

AUS.	AUSTRIA
BEL.	BELGIUM
B. H.	BOSNIA AND HERZEGOVINA
CR.	CROATIA
CZ.	CZECH REPUBLIC
DEN.	DENMARK
HUNG.	HUNGARY
K.	KOSOVO
LUX.	LUXEMBOURG
MAC.	MACEDONIA
MO.	MONTENEGRO
NETH.	NETHERLANDS
SE.	SERBIA
SLK.	SLOVAKIA
SLN.	SLOVENIA
SWITZ.	SWITZERLAND

NEW
ZEALAND

20°E   40°E   60°E   80°E   100°E   120°E   140°E   160°E

Liberty. The figure of Liberty bears a copy of the Declaration of the Rights of Man in one hand and a pike to defend them in the other, in this painting by the female artist Nanine Vallain. The painting hung in the Jacobin Club until its fall from power. *(Musée de la Revolution Française, Vizille/The Bridgeman Art Library)*

chapter

21 THE REVOLUTION IN POLITICS, 1775–1815

Chapter Preview

Background to Revolution
• What social, political, and economic factors formed the background to the French Revolution?

Revolution in Metropole and Colony (1789–1791)
• What were the immediate events and ideas that sparked the Revolution in France and its Caribbean colony of Saint-Domingue?

World War and Republican France (1791–1799)
• How and why did the Revolution take a radical turn at home and in the colonies?

The Napoleonic Era (1799–1815)
• What factors explain the rise and fall of Napoleon Bonaparte and his loss of the colony of Saint-Domingue?

The last years of the eighteenth century were a time of great upheaval. A series of revolutions and revolutionary wars challenged the old order of monarchs and aristocrats. The ideas of freedom and equality, ideas that continue to shape the world, flourished and spread. The revolutionary era began in North America in 1775. Then in 1789 France, the most influential country in Europe, became the leading revolutionary nation. It established first a constitutional monarchy, then a radical republic, and finally a new empire under Napoleon. Inspired by both the ideals of the Revolution and internal colonial conditions, the slaves of Saint-Domingue rose up in 1791. Their rebellion led to the creation of the new independent nation of Haiti in 1805.

The armies of France violently exported revolution beyond the nation's borders in an effort to establish new governments throughout much of Europe. The world of modern domestic and international politics was born.

BACKGROUND TO REVOLUTION

What social, political, and economic factors formed the background to the French Revolution?

The origins of the French Revolution have been one of the most debated topics in history. In order to understand the path to revolution, numerous interrelated factors must be taken into account. These include deep social changes in France, a long-term political crisis that eroded monarchical legitimacy, the impact of new political ideas derived from the Enlightenment, the emergence of a "public sphere" in which such opinions were formed and shared, and, perhaps most important, a financial crisis created by France's participation in expensive overseas wars.

Legal Orders and Social Change

As in the Middle Ages, France's 25 million inhabitants were still legally divided into three orders, or estates—the clergy, the nobility, and everyone else. As the nation's first estate, the clergy numbered about one hundred thousand and had important privileges, including exemption from regular taxes and the ability to tax landowners. The second estate consisted of some four hundred thousand nobles who owned about 25 percent of the land in France. The nobility also enjoyed special privileges associated with their exalted social position, including lighter taxes, exclusive hunting and fishing rights, monopolies on bread-baking and wine-pressing equipment, and the right to wear swords. The third estate was a conglomeration of very different social groups—prosperous merchants, lawyers, and officials along with poorer peasants, urban artisans, and unskilled day laborers—united only by their shared legal status as distinct from the nobility and clergy.

In discussing the origins of the French Revolution, historians long focused on growing tensions between the nobility and the comfortable members of the third estate, the *bourgeoisie* or upper middle class. In this formulation, the French bourgeoisie eventually rose up to lead the entire third estate in a great social revolution that destroyed feudal privileges and established a capitalist order based on individualism and a market economy.

In recent years, a flood of new research has challenged these accepted views. Above all, revisionist historians have questioned the existence of growing conflict between a capitalistic bourgeoisie and a reactionary feudal nobility in eighteenth-century France. Instead, they see both bourgeoisie and nobility as highly fragmented, riddled with internal rivalries. The ancient sword nobility, for example, was separated from the newer robe nobility by differences in wealth, education, and worldview. Differences within the bourgeoisie—between wealthy financiers and local lawyers, for example—were no less profound. Rather than standing as unified blocs against each other, nobility and bourgeoisie formed two parallel social ladders increasingly linked together at the top by wealth, marriage, and Enlightenment culture.

Revisionist historians note that the nobility and the bourgeoisie shared economic interests. Investment in land and government service were the preferred activities of both groups, and the goal of the merchant capitalist was to gain enough wealth to retire from trade, purchase an estate, and live nobly as a large landowner. At the same time, wealthy nobles often acted as aggressive capitalists, investing especially in mining, metallurgy, and foreign trade. In addition, until the Revolution actually began, key sections of both nobility and bourgeoisie were joined in opposition to the government.

Revisionists have clearly shaken the belief that the bourgeoisie and the nobility were locked in growing conflict before the Revolution. Yet they also make clear that the Old Regime had ceased to correspond with social reality by the 1780s. Legally, society was still based on rigid orders inherited from the Middle Ages. In reality, France had already moved far toward being a society based on wealth and education in which an

● **The Three Estates** In this political cartoon from 1789 a peasant of the third estate struggles under the crushing burden of a happy clergyman and a plumed nobleman. The caption—"Let's hope this game ends soon"—sets forth a program of reform that any peasant could understand. *(Réunion des Musées Nationaux/Art Resource, NY)*

A FAUT ESPERER Q'EU JEU LA FINIRA BEN TOT.

Vtuleur en Campagne Ap. 1789.

emerging elite that included both aristocratic and bourgeois notables was frustrated by a bureaucratic monarchy that continued to claim the right to absolute power.

The Crisis of Political Legitimacy

Overlaying these social changes was a century-long political and fiscal struggle between the monarchy and its opponents that was primarily enacted in the law courts. When Louis XIV died, his successor Louis XV (r. 1715–1774) was only five years old. The high courts of France—the parlements—regained the ancient right to evaluate royal decrees publicly in writing before they were registered and given the force of law. The parlements used this power to prevent the king from imposing taxes after a series of wars plunged France into fiscal crisis. The Parlement of Paris asserted that it was acting as the representative of the entire nation when it checked the king's power to levy taxes.

After years of attempting to compromise, Louis XV roused himself to defend his absolutist inheritance. His chancellor, René de Maupeou, abolished the existing parlements, exiled the vociferous members of the Parlement of Paris to the provinces, and began to tax privileged groups. Public opinion sided with the parlements, however, and there was widespread criticism of "royal despotism." The king also came under attack for his many mistresses and lost the sacred aura of God's anointed on earth.

Despite this progressive **desacralization** of the monarchy, its power was still great enough to quell opposition, and Louis XV would probably have prevailed if he had lived long enough, but he died in 1774. The new king, Louis XVI (r. 1774–1792), a shy twenty-year-old with good intentions, yielded in the face of vehement opposition from France's educated elite. He dismissed chancellor Maupeou and recalled the parlements. Louis also waffled on the economy, dismissing controller general Turgot when his attempts to liberalize the economy drew fire. A weakened but unreformed monarchy now faced a judicial opposition that claimed to speak for the entire French nation. The country was drifting toward renewed financial crisis and political upheaval.

The Impact of the American Revolution

Coinciding with the first years of Louis XVI's reign, the American Revolution had an enormous practical and ideological impact on France. French expenses to support the colonists bankrupted the Crown, while the ideals of liberty and equality provided heady inspiration for political reform.

Like the French Revolution, the American Revolution originated in struggles over taxes. The high cost of the Seven Years' War—fought with little financial contribution from the colonies—doubled the British national debt. When the government tried to recoup its losses in increased taxes on the colonies in 1765, the colonists reacted with anger.

Chronology

1775–1783	American Revolution
1786–1789	Financial crisis in France
1789	Feudalism abolished in France; ratification of U.S. Constitution; storming of the Bastille
1789–1799	French Revolution
1790	Burke, *Reflections on the Revolution in France*
1791	Slave insurrection in Saint-Domingue
1792	Wollstonecraft, *A Vindication of the Rights of Woman*
1793	Execution of Louis XVI
1793–1794	Economic controls to help poor in France; Robespierre's Reign of Terror
1794	Robespierre deposed and executed
1794–1799	Thermidorian reaction
1799–1815	Napoleonic era
1804	Haitian republic declares independence
1812	Napoleon invades Russia
1814–1815	Napoleon defeated and exiled

desacralization *The removal (during the reigns of Louis XV and Louis XVI) of the divine sanction that had undergirded the absolutism of Louis XIV.*

● **Toward Revolution in Boston** The Boston Tea Party was only one of many angry confrontations between British officials and Boston patriots. On January 27, 1774, an angry crowd seized a British customs collector and tarred and feathered him. This French engraving of 1784 commemorates the defiant and provocative action. *(The Granger Collection, New York)*

Primary Source:
The U.S. Declaration of Independence
Read a selection from Jefferson's famous text, which lays out the Enlightenment principles on which the United States was founded.

The key questions were political rather than economic. To what extent could the home government assert its power while limiting the authority of colonial legislatures? Accordingly, who should represent the colonies, and who had the right to make laws for Americans? The British government replied that Americans were represented in Parliament, albeit indirectly (like most British people themselves), and that the absolute supremacy of Parliament throughout the empire could not be questioned. Many Americans felt otherwise.

In 1773 the dispute reignited after the British government awarded a monopoly on Chinese tea to the East India Company, excluding colonial merchants from a lucrative business. In response, Boston men disguised as Indians held a rowdy "tea party" and threw the company's tea into the harbor. This led to extreme measures. The so-called Coercive Acts closed the port of Boston, curtailed local elections, and expanded the royal governor's power. County conventions in Massachusetts urged that the acts be "rejected as the attempts of a wicked administration to enslave America." Other colonial assemblies joined the protest. In September 1774 the First Continental Congress met in Philadelphia, where the more radical members argued successfully against concessions to the Crown. Compromise was also rejected by the British Parliament, and in April 1775 fighting began at Lexington and Concord.

The fighting spread, and the colonists moved slowly toward open rebellion. The uncompromising attitude of the British government and its use of German mercenaries dissolved long-standing loyalties to the home country. Many "Loyalists" who wished to remain within the empire emigrated to the northern colonies of Canada.

On July 4, 1776, the Second Continental Congress adopted the Declaration of Independence. Written by Thomas Jefferson, it boldly listed the tyrannical acts committed by George III (r. 1760–1820) and proclaimed the sovereignty of the American states. It also universalized the traditional rights of English people, stating that "all men are created equal, that they are endowed by their Creator with certain unalienable Rights, that among these are Life, Liberty, and the Pursuit of Happiness." By 1780, all thirteen states had adopted their own written constitutions.

On the international scene, the French wanted revenge for the humiliating defeats of the Seven Years' War. They sympathized with the rebels and supplied guns and gunpowder from the beginning. By 1777 French volunteers were arriving in Virginia, and a dashing young nobleman, the marquis de Lafayette (1757–1834), became one of Washington's most trusted generals. In 1778 the French government offered a formal alliance to the American ambassador in Paris, Benjamin Franklin, and in 1779 and 1780 the Spanish and Dutch declared war on Britain. Catherine the Great of Russia helped organize the League of Armed Neutrality in order to protect neutral shipping rights, which Britain refused to recognize.

Thus by 1780 Great Britain was at war with most of Europe as well as against the thirteen colonies. Outnumbered and suffering severe reverses, a new British government offered peace on generous terms. By the Treaty of Paris of 1783, Britain recognized the independence of the thirteen colonies and ceded vast territory between the

Allegheny Mountains and the Mississippi River to the Americans. In 1787 the Federal Convention met in Philadelphia to draft the new Constitution of the United States.

Europeans who dreamed of a new era were fascinated by the American Revolution. The Americans had begun with a revolutionary defense against tyrannical oppression, and they had been victorious. They had then shown how rational beings could assemble to exercise sovereignty and form a new social contract. All this gave greater reality to the concepts of individual liberty and representative government and reinforced a primary Enlightenment ideal: that a better world was possible.

No country felt the consequences of the American Revolution more directly than France. Hundreds of French officers were inspired by service in America, the marquis de Lafayette chief among them. French intellectuals engaged in passionate analysis of the new federal and state constitutions. Perhaps most importantly, the war's expenses provided the last nail in the coffin for the French treasury.

Financial Crisis

The French Revolution thus had its immediate origins in the king's financial difficulties. Thwarted in its efforts to reform the tax system, the royal government was forced to finance its contribution to the American Revolutionary with borrowed money. As a result, the national debt and the annual budget deficit soared.

By the 1780s, fully 50 percent of France's annual budget went for interest payments on the debt. Another 25 percent went to maintain the military, while 6 percent was absorbed by the king and his court at Versailles. Less than 20 percent of the national budget was available for productive functions, such as transportation and general administration. This was an impossible financial situation.

Louis XVI's minister of finance revived old proposals to impose a general tax on all landed property as well as to form provincial assemblies to administer the tax, and he convinced the king to call an **Assembly of Notables** to gain support for the idea. The notables, mainly important noblemen and high-ranking clergy, opposed the new tax. In exchange for their support, they demanded that control over government spending be given to the provincial assemblies. When the government refused, the notables responded that such sweeping reforms required the approval of the Estates General, the representative body of all three estates, which had not met since 1614.

Assembly of Notables *A consulting body of eminent nobles and clergymen that convened to advise the king of France in 1788 and 1789.*

Facing imminent bankruptcy, the king tried to reassert his authority. He dismissed the notables and established new taxes by decree. The Parlement of Paris promptly declared them null and void. When the king tried to exile the judges, a wave of protest erupted. Frightened investors also refused to advance more loans to the state. Finally, in July 1788, Louis XVI bowed to public opinion and called for a spring session of the Estates General.

REVOLUTION IN METROPOLE AND COLONY (1789–1791)

What were the immediate events and ideas that sparked the Revolution in France and its Caribbean colony of Saint-Domingue?

Although inspired by the ideals of the American Revolution, the French Revolution did not mirror the American example. It was more radical and more complex, more influential and more controversial, more loved and more hated. For Europeans and most of the rest of the world, it was the great revolution of the eighteenth century, *the* revolution that opened the modern era in politics. In turn, the slave insurrection in Saint-Domingue—which ultimately resulted in the second independent republic of the Americas—inspired liberation movements across the world.

The Formation of the National Assembly

Estates General *A legislative body in pre-revolutionary France made up of representatives of each of the three classes, or estates; it was called into session in 1789 for the first time since 1614.*

Once Louis had agreed to hold the **Estates General,** following precedent, he set elections for the three orders. Elected officials from the noble order were primarily conservatives from the provinces, but fully one-third of the nobility's representatives were liberals committed to major changes. The third estate elected lawyers and government officials to represent them, with few delegates representing business or the working poor.

As at previous meetings of the Estates General, local assemblies were to prepare a list of grievances for their representatives to bring to the next electoral level. The petitions for change coming from the three estates showed a surprising degree of consensus. There was general agreement that royal absolutism should give way to a constitutional monarchy in which laws and taxes would require the consent of the Estates General in regular meetings. All agreed that individual liberties should be guaranteed by law and economic regulations loosened. The striking similarities in the grievance petitions of the clergy, nobility, and third estate reflected a shared platform of basic reform among the educated elite.

Yet an increasingly bitter quarrel undermined this consensus: *how* would the Estates General vote, and *who* would lead political reorganization? The Estates General of 1614 had sat as three separate houses. Each house held one vote, despite the fact that the third estate represented the vast majority of France. Given the close ties between them, the nobility and clergy would control all decisions. As soon as the estates were called, the aristocratic Parlement of Paris ruled that the Estates General should once again sit separately. In response to protests from some reform-minded critics, the government agreed that the third estate should have as many delegates as the clergy and the nobility combined but then rendered this act meaningless by upholding voting by separate order.

Meeting in May 1789, the estates were almost immediately deadlocked. Delegates of the third estate refused to transact any business until the king ordered the clergy and nobility to sit with them in a single body. Finally, after a six-week war of nerves, a few parish priests began to go over to the third estate, which on June 17 voted to call itself the **"National Assembly."** On June 20 the delegates of the third estate, excluded from their hall because of "repairs," moved to a large indoor tennis court. There they swore the famous Oath of the Tennis Court, pledging not to disband until they had written a new constitution.

National Assembly *The first French revolutionary legislature, a constituent assembly made up primarily of representatives of the third estate and a few nobles and clergy who joined them, in session from 1789 to 1791.*

The king's response was ambivalent. On June 23 he made a conciliatory speech urging reforms to a joint session, and four days later he ordered the three estates to meet together. At the same time, the vacillating monarch apparently followed the advice of relatives and court nobles who urged him to dissolve the Estates General by force. Belatedly asserting his "divine right" to rule, the king called an army of eighteen thousand troops toward Versailles, and on July 11 he dismissed his finance minister and other liberal ministers.

The Revolt of the Poor and the Oppressed

While delegates of the third estate pressed for political rights, economic hardship gripped the common people. A poor grain harvest in 1788 caused the price of bread to soar, unleashing a classic economic depression of the preindustrial age. Demand for manufactured goods collapsed, and thousands were thrown out of work. By the end of 1789 almost half of the French people were in need of relief. In Paris perhaps 150,000 of the city's 600,000 people were unemployed in July 1789.

Against this background of political and economic crisis, the people of Paris entered decisively onto the revolutionary stage. They believed that they should have steady work and adequate bread at fair prices. They also feared that the dismissal of the king's moderate finance minister would put them at the mercy of aristocratic landowners and grain speculators. As rumors spread that the king's troops would sack the city, angry crowds formed and demanded action. On July 13 the people began to seize arms for the defense of the city, and on July 14 several hundred people marched to the Bastille in search of weapons.

The Bastille, once a medieval fortress, was a detested royal prison. Its panicked governor ordered his men to resist, killing ninety-eight people attempting to enter. Fighting continued until the prison surrendered. The next day a committee of citizens appointed the marquis de Lafayette commander of the city's armed forces. Paris was lost to the king, who was forced to recall the finance minister and disperse his troops. The popular uprising had saved the National Assembly. As the delegates resumed their debates, the countryside sent a radical message. Throughout France peasants began to rise against their lords, ransacking manor houses and burning feudal documents that recorded their obligations. In some areas peasants reinstated traditional village practices, undoing recent enclosures and reoccupying common lands. Fear of vagabonds and outlaws—called the **Great Fear** by contemporaries—seized the countryside and fanned the flames of rebellion. The long-suffering peasants were doing their best to free themselves from manorial rights and exploitation.

Great Fear *In the summer of 1789, the fear of vagabonds and outlaws that seized the French countryside and fanned the flames of revolution.*

In the end, they were successful. On the night of August 4, 1789, the delegates at Versailles agreed to abolish noble privileges—peasant serfdom where it still existed, exclusive hunting rights, fees for justice, village monopolies, and a host of other dues. Thus the French peasantry achieved an unprecedented victory in the early days of revolutionary upheaval. Henceforth, French peasants would seek mainly to protect their achievements. As the Great Fear subsided in the countryside, they became a force for order and stability.

A Limited Monarchy

The National Assembly moved forward. On August 27, 1789, it issued the Declaration of the Rights of Man, which stated, "Men are born and remain free and equal in rights." The declaration also maintained that mankind's natural rights are "liberty, property, security, and resistance to oppression" and that "every man is presumed innocent until he is proven guilty." As for law, "it is an expression of the general will; all citizens have the right to concur personally or through their representatives in its formation. . . . Free expression of thoughts and opinions is one of the most precious rights of mankind: every citizen may therefore speak, write, and publish freely." In short, this clarion call of the liberal revolutionary ideal guaranteed equality before the law, representative government for a sovereign people, and individual freedom. The declaration was disseminated throughout France and Europe and around the world.

Primary Source: The Declaration of Rights of Man and Citizen *This document, drafted by the National Assembly of France, is an Enlightenment cousin of Jefferson's Declaration.*

Moving beyond general principles to draft a constitution proved difficult. The questions of how much power the king should retain and whether he could veto legislation led to another deadlock. Once again the decisive answer came from the poor—in this instance, the poor women of Paris. Women customarily managed poor families' slender resources. The economic crisis worsened after the fall of the Bastille, as aristocrats fled the country and the luxury market collapsed. Foreign markets also shrunk, and unemployment grew.

On October 5 some seven thousand desperate women marched the twelve miles from Paris to Versailles to demand action. This great crowd invaded the Assembly, "armed with scythes, sticks and pikes." One tough old woman defiantly shouted into the debate, "Who's that talking down there? Make the chatterbox shut up. That's not the point: the point is that we want bread."[1] Hers was the genuine voice of the people, essential to any understanding of the French Revolution.

The women invaded the royal apartments, killed some of the royal bodyguards, and searched for the queen, Marie Antoinette, who was widely despised for her frivolous

a Versaille a Versaille. du 5. Octobre 1789.

● **The Women of Paris March to Versailles** On October 5, 1789, a large group of Parisian market women marched to Versailles to protest the price of bread. For the people of Paris, the king was the baker of last resort, responsible for feeding his people during times of scarcity. The crowd forced the royal family to return with them and to live in Paris, rather than remain isolated from their subjects at court. *(Erich Lessing/Art Resource, NY)*

constitutional monarchy *A form of government in which the king retains his position as head of state, while the authority to tax and make new laws resides in an elected body.*

and supposedly immoral behavior. The intervention of Lafayette and the National Guard saved the royal family from harm. But the only way to calm the disorder was for the king to live in Paris, as the crowd demanded.

The National Assembly followed the king to Paris, and the next two years, until September 1791, saw the consolidation of the liberal revolution. The National Assembly abolished the nobility as a legal order and pushed forward with the creation of a **constitutional monarchy,** which Louis XVI reluctantly accepted in July 1790. In the final constitution, the king remained the head of state, but lawmaking power was placed in the hands of the National Assembly. New laws broadened women's rights to seek divorce, to inherit property, and to obtain financial support for illegitimate children from fathers, but women were not allowed to hold political office or even vote. The men of the National Assembly believed that civic virtue would be restored if women focused on child rearing and domestic duties.

The National Assembly replaced the patchwork of historic provinces with eighty-three departments of approximately equal size. The jumble of weights and measures that varied from province to province was reformed, leading to the introduction of the metric system in 1793. Monopolies, guilds, and workers' associations were prohibited, and barriers to trade within France were abolished in the name of economic liberty. Thus the National Assembly applied the critical spirit of the Enlightenment in a thorough reform of France's laws and institutions.

The Assembly also imposed a radical reorganization on the country's religious life. It granted religious freedom to French Jews and Protestants. It nationalized the Catholic Church's property, used it as collateral to guarantee a new paper currency, the *assignats* and then sold the property in an attempt to put the state's finances on a solid footing.

Imbued with Enlightenment rationalism, delegates distrusted popular piety and "superstitious religion." Thus they established a national church with priests chosen by voters. The National Assembly forced the Catholic clergy to take a loyalty oath to the new government. The pope formally condemned these actions, and only half of French priests swore the oath. Many sincere Christians, especially those in the countryside, were upset by these changes. The attempt to remake the Catholic Church, like the Assembly's abolition of guilds and workers' associations, sharpened the conflict between the educated classes and the common people that had been emerging in the eighteenth century.

Revolutionary Aspirations in Saint-Domingue

On the eve of the Revolution, French Saint-Domingue—the most profitable of all Caribbean colonies—was even more rife with social tensions than France itself. The island was composed of a variety of social groups who resented and mistrusted one another. The European population included French colonial officials, wealthy plantation owners and merchants, and poor immigrants. Greatly outnumbering the white population were the colony's five hundred thousand slaves, along with a sizable population of free people of African and mixed African European descent. This last group referred to it members as "free coloreds" or *"free people of color."*

The political turmoil of the 1780s, with its rhetoric of liberty, equality, and fraternity, raised new challenges and possibilities for each group. For slaves, abolitionist agitation in France and the royal government's attempts to rein in the abuses of slavery led to hope that the mother country might grant them freedom. Free people of color found in such rhetoric the principles on which to base claims for legal and political rights. They hoped for political enfranchisement and to regain legal rights that had been rescinded by colonial administrators. The white elite looked to revolutionary ideals of representative government for the chance to gain control of their own affairs, as had the American colonists before them. The meeting of the Estates General and the Declaration of the Rights of Man and Citizen raised these conflicting colonial aspirations to new levels.

The National Assembly, however, frustrated all of their hopes. It allowed each colony to draft its own constitution, with free rein over decisions on slavery and enfranchisement. After dealing this blow to the aspirations of slaves and free coloreds, the committee also reaffirmed French monopolies over colonial trade, thereby angering planters as well.

Following a failed revolt in Saint-Domingue led by Vincent Ogé, a free man of color, the National Assembly attempted a compromise. It granted political rights to free people of color born to two free parents who possessed sufficient property. The white elite of Saint-Domingue was furious, and the colonial governor refused to enact the legislation. Violence now erupted between groups of whites and free coloreds. The liberal revolution had failed to satisfy contradictory ambitions in the colonies.

free people of color *Free people of African or partly African descent living in the French isles of the Caribbean.*

WORLD WAR AND REPUBLICAN FRANCE (1791–1799)

How and why did the Revolution take a radical turn at home and in the colonies?

When Louis XVI accepted the National Assembly's constitution in September 1791, a young provincial lawyer and delegate named Maximilien Robespierre (1758–1794) concluded, "The Revolution is over." Robespierre was both right and wrong. He was right in the sense that the most constructive and lasting reforms were in place. Nothing substantial in the way of liberty and fundamental reform would be gained in the next generation. He was wrong in the sense that a much more radical stage lay ahead.

New heroes and new ideologies were to emerge in revolutionary wars and international conflict in which Robespierre himself would play a central role.

Foreign Reactions and the Beginning of War

Revolution in France produced great excitement and a sharp division of opinion in Europe and the United States. Liberals and radicals saw a mighty triumph of liberty over despotism. In Great Britain especially, they hoped that the French example would undo the landed elite's stronghold over Parliament. Conservative leaders, such as Edmund Burke (1729–1797), were deeply troubled by the Revolution. In 1790 Burke published *Reflections on the Revolution in France,* which defended inherited privileges in general and those of the English monarchy and aristocracy in particular. He predicted that thoroughgoing reform like that occurring in France would lead only to chaos and tyranny. Burke's work sparked much debate.

One passionate rebuttal came from a young writer in London, Mary Wollstonecraft (1759–1797). Incensed by Burke's book, Wollstonecraft wrote a blistering, widely read response, *A Vindication of the Rights of Man* (1790). Then she made a daring intellectual leap, developing for the first time the logical implications of natural-law philosophy in her masterpiece, *A Vindication of the Rights of Woman* (1792). To fulfill the still-unrealized potential of the French Revolution and to eliminate sexual inequality, she demanded that

the Rights of Women be respected . . . [and] JUSTICE for one-half of the human race. . . . It is time to effect a revolution in female manners, time to restore to them their lost dignity, and make them, as part of the human species, labor, by reforming themselves, to reform the world.

Wollstonecraft advocated rigorous coeducation, which would make women better wives and mothers, good citizens, and economically independent. Women could manage businesses and enter politics if only men would give them the chance. Wollstonecraft's analysis testified to the power of the Revolution to inspire outside of France. Paralleling ideas put forth independently in France by Olympe de Gouges (1748–1793), a self-taught writer and woman of the people (see the feature "Listening to the Past: Revolution and Women's Rights" on pages 638–639), Wollstonecraft's work marked the birth of the modern women's movement for equal rights.

European rulers, who had at first welcomed the revolution in France as weakening a competing monarchy, realized that their power was also threatened. In June 1791, Louis XVI and Marie-Antoinette were arrested and returned to Paris after trying unsuccessfully to slip out of France. The shock of this arrest led the monarchs of Austria and Prussia to issue the Declaration of Pillnitz in August 1791. This carefully worded statement declared their willingness to intervene in France in certain circumstances and was expected to prevent revolutionary excesses without causing war.

But the crowned heads of Europe misjudged France's revolutionary spirit. The representative body, known as the Legislative Assembly, that convened in October 1791 had new delegates and a different character. Most of the legislators were still prosperous and well-educated, but they were younger and less cautious than their predecessors. Many belonged to a political club called the **Jacobin club,** after the name of the former monastery in which they met. Such clubs had proliferated in Parisian neighborhoods since the beginning of the Revolution, drawing men and women to debate the burning political questions of the day.

The new Legislative Assembly representatives reacted with patriotic fury against the Declaration of Pillnitz. If the kings of Europe were attempting to incite war against France, then "we will incite a war of people against kings. . . . Ten million Frenchmen, kindled by the fire of liberty, armed with the sword, with reason, with eloquence

Jacobin club *In revolutionary France, a political club whose members were a radical republican group.*

● **The Capture of Louis XVI, June 1791**   This painting commemorates a dramatic turning point in the French Revolution, the midnight arrest of Louis XVI and the royal family as they tried to flee France in disguise and reach counter-revolutionaries in the Austrian Netherlands. Recognized and stopped at Varennes, the royal family was returned to house arrest in Paris. *(Bibliothèque nationale de France)*

would be able to change the face of the world and make the tyrants tremble on their thrones."[2] In April 1792 France declared war on Francis II, the Habsburg monarch.

France's crusade against tyranny went poorly at first. Prussian forces joined Austria against the French, who broke and fled at their first military encounter with this First Coalition. The road to Paris lay open, and it is possible that only conflict between the eastern monarchs over the division of Poland saved France from defeat.

The Legislative Assembly declared the country in danger, and volunteers rallied to the capital. In this supercharged atmosphere, rumors spread of treason by the king and queen. On August 10, 1792, a revolutionary crowd attacked the royal palace at the Tuileries, while the king and his family fled for their lives to the nearby Legislative Assembly. Rather than offering refuge, the Assembly suspended the king from all his functions, imprisoned him, and called for a new National Convention to be elected by universal male suffrage.

The Second Revolution

second revolution *From 1792 to 1795, the second phase of the French Revolution during which the fall of the French monarchy introduced a rapid radicalization of politics.*

Girondists *A group contesting control of the National Convention in France; it was named after a department in southwestern France.*

the Mountain *The radical faction of the National Convention led by Robespierre. So called because its members sat in the uppermost benches on the left side of the assembly hall. The source of the modern division of political ideologies into "Left" and "Right."*

sans-culottes *The name for the laboring poor of Paris, so called because the men wore trousers instead of the knee breeches of the aristocracy and middle class; it came to refer to the militant radicals of the city.*

The fall of the monarchy initiated a rapid radicalization of the Revolution, a phase often called the **second revolution.** Louis's imprisonment was followed by the September Massacres. Wild stories that imprisoned aristocrats and priests were plotting with the allied invaders seized the city. Angry crowds invaded the prisons of Paris and slaughtered half the men and women they found. In late September 1792 the new, popularly elected National Convention proclaimed France a republic.

The republic sought to create a new popular culture, fashioning symbols that broke with the past and glorified the new order. Its new revolutionary calendar eliminated saints' days and renamed the days and the months after the seasons of the year, while also adding secular holidays designed to instill a love of nation. These secular celebrations were less successful in villages, where Catholicism was stronger.

All members of the National Convention were republicans, and at the beginning almost all belonged to the Jacobin club of Paris. But the Jacobins themselves were increasingly divided into two bitterly opposed groups—the **Girondists,** named after a department in southwestern France that was home to several of their leaders, and **the Mountain,** led by Robespierre and another young lawyer, Georges Jacques Danton. In Paris the National Convention was locked in a life-and-death political struggle between the Mountain and the more moderate Girondists. A majority of the indecisive Convention members, seated in the "Plain" below, floated back and forth between the rival factions.

This division emerged clearly after the National Convention overwhelmingly convicted Louis XVI of treason. The Girondists accepted his guilt but did not wish to put the king to death. By a narrow majority, the Mountain carried the day, and Louis was executed on January 21, 1793, on the newly invented guillotine. Both the Girondists and the Mountain were determined to continue the "war against tyranny." The Prussians had been stopped at the Battle of Valmy in September 1792. French armies then invaded Savoy, moved into the German Rhineland, and by November 1792 were occupying the entire Austrian Netherlands (modern Belgium). Everywhere they went French armies of occupation chased the princes, abolished feudalism, and "liberated" the people.

But French armies also lived off the land, requisitioning supplies and plundering local treasures. The liberators looked increasingly like foreign invaders. International tensions mounted. In February 1793 the National Convention, at war with Austria and Prussia, declared war on Britain, Holland, and Spain as well. Republican France was now at war with almost all Europe, a great war that would last almost without interruption until 1815.

Conflict within France added to the turmoil. Peasants in western France revolted against being drafted into the army, and devout Catholics, royalists, and foreign agents encouraged their rebellion. In Paris the National Convention was locked in a life-and-death political struggle between the Girondists and the more moderate Mountain. With the political system bitterly divided, the laboring poor of Paris emerged as the decisive political factor. The laboring poor and the petty traders were often known as the **sans-culottes,** "without breeches," because their men wore trousers instead of the knee breeches of the aristocracy and bourgeoisie. The sans-culottes demanded radical political action to guarantee their daily bread. The Mountain joined with sans-culottes activists in the city government to engineer a popular uprising that forced the Convention to arrest thirty-one Girondist deputies for treason on June 2. All power passed to the Mountain.

The Convention also formed a Committee of Public Safety to deal with the threats to the Revolution. Led by Robespierre, the committee obtained dictatorial power. Moderates in leading provincial cities, such as Lyons and Marseilles, revolted against excessive central control. The peasant revolt also spread, and the republic's armies were driven back on all fronts. By July 1793 only the areas around Paris and on the eastern frontier were firmly held. Defeat seemed imminent.

The French Revolution

May 5, 1789	Estates General convene at Versailles.
June 17, 1789	Third estate declares itself the National Assembly.
June 20, 1789	Oath of the Tennis Court is sworn.
July 14, 1789	Storming of the Bastille occurs.
July–August 1789	Great Fear ravages the countryside.
August 4, 1789	National Assembly abolishes feudal privileges.
August 27, 1789	National Assembly issues Declaration of the Rights of Man.
October 5, 1789	Women march on Versailles and force royal family to return to Paris.
November 1789	National Assembly confiscates church lands.
July 1790	Civil Constitution of the Clergy establishes a national church. Louis XVI reluctantly agrees to accept a constitutional monarchy.
June 1791	Royal family is arrested while attempting to flee France.
August 1791	Austria and Prussia issue the Declaration of Pillnitz. Slave insurrections break out in Saint-Domingue.
April 1792	France declares war on Austria.
August 1792	Parisian mob attacks the palace and takes Louis XVI prisoner.
September 1792	September Massacres occur. National Convention declares France a republic and abolishes monarchy.
January 1793	Louis XVI is executed.
February 1793	France declares war on Britain, Holland, and Spain. Revolts take place in some provincial cities.
March 1793	Bitter struggle occurs in the National Convention between Girondists and the Mountain.
April–June 1793	Robespierre and the Mountain organize the Committee of Public Safety and arrest Girondist leaders.
September 1793	Price controls are instituted to aid the sans-culottes and mobilize the war effort. British troops invade Saint-Domingue.
1793–1794	Reign of Terror darkens Paris and the provinces.
February 1794	National Convention abolishes slavery in all French territories.
Spring 1794	French armies are victorious on all fronts.
July 1794	Robespierre is executed. Thermidorian reaction begins.
1795–1799	Directory rules.
1795	Economic controls are abolished, and suppression of the sans-culottes begins. Toussaint L'Ouverture named brigadier general.
1797	Napoleon defeats Austrian armies in Italy and returns triumphant to Paris.
1798	Austria, Great Britain, and Russia form the Second Coalition against France.
1799	Napoleon overthrows the Directory and seizes power.

*Des Tetes !– du Sang !– la Mort !– à la Lanterne !– à la Guillotine.
– point de Reine !– Je suis la Deesse de la Liberté !– l'egalité !– que
Londres soit brulé !– que Paris soit Libre !– Vive la Guillotine !–*

Miss Mary Stokes delt.

A PARIS BELLE.

Pubd Feby 26.th 1794, by H. Humphrey No.18 Old Bond Street

● **Contrasting Visions of the Sans-Culottes** The woman on the left, with her playful cat and calm simplicity, suggests how the French sans-culottes saw themselves as democrats and virtuous citizens. The ferocious sans-culotte harpy on the right, a creation of wartime England's vivid counter-revolutionary imagination, screams for more blood, more death: "I am the Goddess of Liberty! Long live the guillotine!" *(Bibliothèque nationale de France)*

Total War and the Terror

A year later, in July 1794, the Austrian Netherlands and the Rhineland were once again in the hands of French armies, and the First Coalition was falling apart. This remarkable reversal stemmed from the revolutionary government's success in harnessing, for perhaps the first time in history, the forces of a planned economy, revolutionary terror, and modern nationalism in a total war effort.

Robespierre and the Committee of Public Safety first collaborated with the fiercely patriotic sans-culottes to establish a **planned economy**. Rather than let supply and demand determine prices, the government set maximum allowable prices for key products. The most important was bread. Rationing was introduced, and bakers were permitted to make only the "bread of equality"—a brown bread made of a mixture of all available flours. The poor of Paris may not have eaten well, but at least they ate.

They also worked, mainly to produce arms and munitions for the war effort. The government told craftsmen what to produce, nationalized many small workshops, and requisitioned raw materials and grain. The second revolution and the ascendancy of the sans-culottes had produced an embryonic emergency socialism, which thoroughly frightened Europe's propertied classes and had great influence on the subsequent development of socialist ideology.

planned economy *In response to inflation and high unemployment, Robespierre and the government set maximum prices for products, rather than relying on supply and demand.*

Second, while radical economic measures supplied the poor with bread and the armies with weapons, the **Reign of Terror** (1793–1794) used revolutionary terror to solidify the home front. Special revolutionary courts tried "enemies of the nation" for political crimes. Some forty thousand French men and women were executed or died in prison. Another three hundred thousand suspects were arrested.

The third and perhaps most decisive element in the French republic's victory over the First Coalition was its ability to draw on the explosive power of patriotic dedication to a national mission. An essential part of modern **nationalism,** this commitment was something new in history. With their common identity newly reinforced by the ideas of popular sovereignty and democracy, large numbers of French people were stirred by a common loyalty. They developed an intense emotional commitment to the defense of the nation and saw the war as a life-and-death struggle between good and evil.

The fervor of nationalism combined with the all-out mobilization of resources made the French army virtually unstoppable. After August 1793 all unmarried young men were subject to the draft, resulting in the largest fighting force in the history of European warfare. French armed forces outnumbered their enemies almost four to one.[3] French generals used mass assaults at bayonet point to overwhelm the enemy. "No maneuvering, nothing elaborate," declared the fearless General Hoche. "Just cold steel, passion and patriotism."[4] By spring 1794 French armies were victorious on all fronts. The republic was saved.

Reign of Terror *The period from 1793 to 1794, during which Robespierre used revolutionary terror to solidify the home front of France. Some 40,000 French men and women were killed during this period.*

nationalism *Patriotic dedication to a national state and mission; it was a decisive element in the French republic's victory.*

● **Slave Revolt on Saint-Domingue**   Starting in August 1791 the slaves of Saint-Domingue rose in revolt. *(Giraudon/Art Resource, NY)*

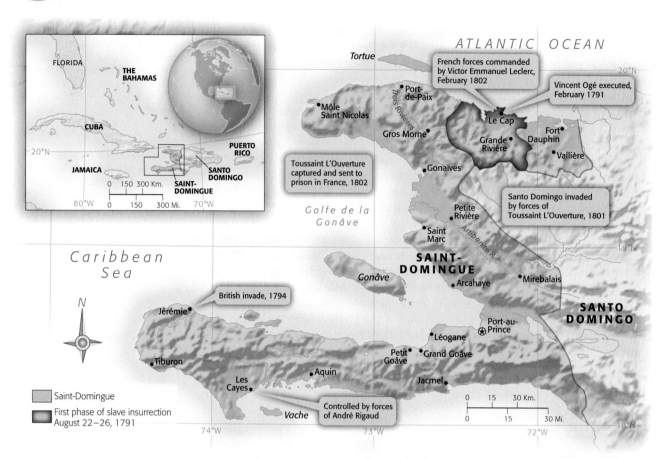

MAP 21.1 **The Haitian Revolution** Neighbored by the Spanish colony of Santo Domingo, Saint-Domingue was the most profitable European colony in the Caribbean. In 1770 the French transferred the capital from Le Cap to Port-au-Prince, which became capital of the newly independent Haïti in 1804. Slave revolts erupted in the north, near Le Cap, in 1791.

Revolution in Saint-Domingue

The second stage of revolution in Saint-Domingue (see Map 21.1) also resulted from decisive action from below. In August 1791 groups of slaves organized a revolt that spread across much of the northern plain. By the end of August the uprising was "10,000 strong, divided into 3 armies, of whom 700 or 800 are on horseback, and tolerably well-armed."[5] During the next month slaves attacked and destroyed hundreds of sugar and coffee plantations.

On April 4, 1792, as war loomed with the European states, the National Assembly issued a decree enfranchising all free blacks and free people of color. This move was intended to gain loyalty against the slave rebellion and stabilize the colony, a vital source of income for the French state.

Less than two years later, on February 4, 1794, the Convention abolished slavery throughout its Caribbean colonies, and in 1795 granted former slaves full political rights. The National Convention was forced to make these concessions when Saint-Domingue came under siege from Spanish and British troops hoping to capture the profitable colony. With former slaves and free colored forces on their side, the French gradually regained control of the island in 1796.

The key leader in the French victory was General Toussaint L'Ouverture (1743–1803), who was named commander of the western province of Saint-Domingue. (See the feature "Individuals in Society: Toussaint L'Ouverture" on page 633.) The increasingly conservative nature of the French government, however, threatened to undo the gains made by former slaves and free people of color. As exiled planters gained a stronger voice in French policymaking, L'Ouverture and other local leaders grew ever more wary of what the future might hold.

The Thermidorian Reaction and the Directory (1794–1799)

With the French army victorious, Robespierre and the Committee of Public Safety relaxed emergency economic controls, but they extended the political Reign of Terror. In March 1794, he wiped out many of his critics as well as long-standing collaborators, including the famous orator Danton. A strange assortment of radicals and moderates in the Convention, knowing that they might be next, organized a conspiracy. They howled down Robespierre when he tried to speak to the National Convention on 9 Thermidor (July 27, 1794). The next day it was Robespierre's turn to face the guillotine.

As Robespierre's closest supporters were also put to death, France unexpectedly experienced a thorough reaction to the violence of the Reign of Terror. In a general way, this **Thermidorian reaction** recalled the early days of the Revolution. The middle-class professionals who had led the liberal revolution of 1789 reasserted their authority, drawing support from their own class, the provincial cities, and the better-off

Thermidorian reaction *The period after the execution of Robespierre in 1794; it was a reaction to the violence of the Reign of Terror.*

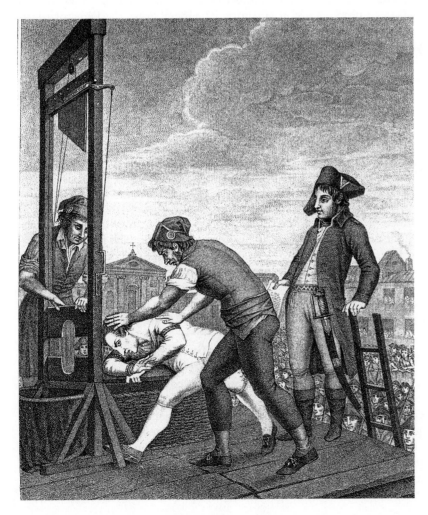

● **The Execution of Robespierre** The guillotine was painted red and was completely wooden except for the heavy iron blade. Large crowds witnessed the executions in a majestic public square in central Paris, then known as the Place de la Revolution and now called the Place de la Concorde (Harmony Square). *(Snark/Art Resource, NY)*

peasants. The National Convention abolished many economic controls, let prices rise sharply, and severely restricted the local political organizations where sans-culottes congregated.

The collapse of economic controls, coupled with runaway inflation, devastated the working poor. After the Convention used the army to suppress protest, the urban poor lost their revolutionary fervor. Excluded and disillusioned, they would have little interest in and influence on politics until 1830. The poor of the countryside turned toward religion as a relief from earthly cares. Rural women, especially, brought back the Catholic Church as the government began to soften its antireligious revolutionary stance.

As for the National Convention, in 1795 its members wrote yet another constitution that they believed would guarantee their economic position and political supremacy. As in previous elections, the mass of the population voted only for electors, whose number was cut back to men of substantial means. Electors then elected the members of a reorganized legislative assembly as well as key officials throughout France. The new assembly also chose a five-man executive—the Directory.

The Directory continued to support French military expansion abroad. War was no longer so much a crusade as a means to meet ever-present, ever-unsolved economic problems. Large, victorious French armies reduced unemployment at home and were able to live off the territories they conquered and plundered.

The unprincipled action of the Directory reinforced widespread disgust with war and starvation. This general dissatisfaction revealed itself clearly in the national elections of 1797, which returned a large number of conservative and even monarchist deputies who favored peace at almost any price. The members of the Directory, fearing for their skins, used the army to nullify the elections and began to govern dictatorially. Two years later Napoleon Bonaparte ended the Directory in a coup d'état and substituted a strong dictatorship for a weak one. The effort to establish stable representative government had failed.

THE NAPOLEONIC ERA (1799–1815)

What factors explain the rise and fall of Napoleon Bonaparte and his loss of the colony of Saint-Domingue?

For almost fifteen years, from 1799 to 1814, France was in the hands of a keen-minded military dictator of exceptional ability. One of history's most fascinating leaders, Napoleon Bonaparte (1769–1821) realized the need to put an end to civil strife in France in order to create unity and consolidate his rule. And he did. But Napoleon saw himself as a man of destiny, and the glory of war and the dream of universal empire proved irresistible. For years he spiraled from victory to victory, but in the end he was destroyed by a mighty coalition united in fear of his restless ambition.

Napoleon's Rule of France

In 1799 when he seized power, young General Napoleon Bonaparte was a national hero. Born in Corsica into an impoverished noble family in 1769, Napoleon left home and became a lieutenant in the French artillery. After a brief and unsuccessful adventure fighting for Corsican independence in 1789, he returned to France as a French patriot and a dedicated revolutionary. Rising rapidly in the new army, Napoleon was placed in command of French forces in Italy and won brilliant victories there in 1796 and 1797. His next campaign, in Egypt, was a failure, but Napoleon returned to France before the fiasco was generally known, and his reputation remained intact.

The Napoleonic Era

November 1799	Napoleon overthrows the Directory.
December 1799	French voters overwhelmingly approve Napoleon's new constitution.
1800	Napoleon founds the Bank of France.
1801	France defeats Austria and acquires Italian and German territories in the Treaty of Lunéville. Napoleon signs the Concordat with the pope.
February 1802	French forces arrive in Saint-Domingue.
March 1802	France signs the Treaty of Amiens with Britain.
August 1802	Napoleon restores slavery in French colonies.
April 1803	Toussaint L'Ouverture dies in France.
January 1804	Jean Jacques Dessalines declares Haitian independence.
March 1804	Napoleonic Code comes into force.
December 1804	Napoleon crowns himself emperor.
May 1805	First Haitian constitution promulgated.
October 1805	Britain defeats the French and Spanish fleet at the Battle of Trafalgar.
December 1805	Napoleon defeats Austria and Russia at the Battle of Austerlitz.
1807	Napoleon redraws the map of Europe in the treaties of Tilsit.
1810	The Grand Empire is at its height.
June 1812	Napoleon invades Russia with 600,000 men.
Fall–Winter 1812	Napoleon makes a disastrous retreat from Russia.
March 1814	Russia, Prussia, Austria, and Britain sign the Treaty of Chaumont, pledging alliance to defeat Napoleon.
April 1814	Napoleon abdicates and is exiled to Elba.
February–June 1815	Napoleon escapes from Elba and rules France until he is defeated at the Battle of Waterloo.

Napoleon soon learned that prominent members of the legislature were plotting against the Directory. Ten years of upheaval and uncertainty had convinced these disillusioned revolutionaries that a strong military ruler was needed to restore order. Together the conspirators and Napoleon organized a takeover. On November 9, 1799, they ousted the Directors, and the following day soldiers disbanded the legislature. Napoleon was named first consul of the republic, and a new constitution consolidating his position was overwhelmingly approved in a plebiscite in December 1799. Republican appearances were maintained, but Napoleon was the real ruler of France.

The essence of Napoleon's domestic policy was to use his great and highly personal powers to maintain order and end civil strife. He did so by working out unwritten agreements with powerful groups in France whereby the groups received favors in return for loyal service. Napoleon's bargain with the solid middle class was codified in the famous Civil Code of 1804, which reasserted two of the fundamental principles of the liberal revolution of 1789: equality of all male citizens before the law and absolute security of wealth and private property. Napoleon and the leading bankers of Paris established the privately owned Bank of France, which served the interests of both the state and the financial oligarchy. Peasants were also appeased when Napoleon defended the gains in land and status they had claimed during the revolution.

At the same time Napoleon perfected a thoroughly centralized state. He consolidated his rule by recruiting disillusioned revolutionaries for the network of ministers, prefects, and centrally appointed mayors that depended on him and came to serve him well. Only former revolutionaries who leaned too far to the left or to the right were excluded.[6] Nor were members of the old nobility slighted. In 1800 and 1802 Napoleon granted amnesty to one hundred thousand émigrés on the condition that they return to France and take a loyalty oath. Members of this returning elite soon occupied many high posts in the expanding centralized state. Napoleon also created a new imperial nobility to reward his most talented generals and officials.

Napoleon applied his diplomatic skills to healing the Catholic Church in France so that it could serve as a bulwark of order and social peace. Napoleon and Pope Pius VII (1800–1823) signed the Concordat of 1801. The pope gained the precious right for French Catholics to practice their religion freely, but Napoleon gained political power: his government now nominated bishops, paid the clergy, and exerted great influence over the church in France.

The domestic reforms of Napoleon's early years were his greatest achievement. Much of his legal and administrative reorganization has survived in France to this day. More generally, Napoleon's domestic initiatives gave the great majority of French people a welcome sense of stability and national unity.

Order and unity had a price: Napoleon's authoritarian rule. Women lost many of the gains they had made in the 1790s. Under the law of the new Napoleonic Code, women were dependents of either their fathers or their husbands, and they could not make contracts or even have bank accounts in their own names. Indeed, Napoleon and his advisers aimed at re-establishing a family monarchy, where the power of the husband and father was as absolute over the wife and the children as that of Napoleon was over his subjects.

Free speech and freedom of the press were continually violated. By 1811 only four newspapers were left, and they were little more than organs of government propaganda. The occasional elections were a farce. Later laws prescribed harsh penalties for political offenses, and people were watched carefully under an efficient spy system. There were about twenty-five hundred political prisoners in 1814.

Napoleon's Expansion in Europe

Napoleon was above all a military man, and a great one. After coming to power in 1799 he sent peace feelers to Austria and Great Britain, the two remaining members of the Second Coalition of 1798. When these overtures were rejected, French armies led by Napoleon decisively defeated the Austrians. In the Treaty of Lunéville (1801), Austria accepted the loss of almost all its Italian possessions, and German territory on the west bank of the Rhine was incorporated into France. The British agreed to the Treaty of Amiens in 1802, allowing France to remain in control of Holland, the Austrian Netherlands, the west bank of the Rhine, and most of the Italian peninsula. The Treaty of Amiens was a diplomatic triumph for Napoleon.

In 1802 Napoleon was secure but driven to expand his power. Aggressively redrawing the map of Germany so as to weaken Austria and encourage the secondary states of southwestern Germany to side with France, Napoleon tried to restrict British trade with all of Europe. He then plotted to attack Great Britain, but his Mediterranean fleet was virtually annihilated by Lord Nelson at the Battle of Trafalgar on October 21, 1805. Invasion of England was henceforth impossible. Renewed fighting had its

● **The Coronation of Napoleon, 1804 (detail)**　In this grandiose painting by Jacques-Louis David, Napoleon prepares to crown his wife, Josephine, in an elaborate ceremony in Notre Dame Cathedral. Napoleon, the ultimate upstart, also crowned himself. Pope Pius VII, seated glumly behind the emperor, is reduced to being a spectator. *(Louvre/Réunion des Musées Nationaux/Art Resource, NY)*

advantages, however, for the first consul used the wartime atmosphere to have himself proclaimed emperor in late 1804.

Austria, Russia, and Sweden joined with Britain to form the Third Coalition against France shortly before the Battle of Trafalgar. Actions such as Napoleon's assumption of the Italian crown had convinced both Alexander I of Russia and Francis II of Austria that Napoleon was a threat to their interests and to the European balance of power. Yet they were no match for Napoleon, who scored a brilliant victory over them at the Battle of Austerlitz in December 1805. Alexander I decided to pull back, and Austria accepted large territorial losses in return for peace as the Third Coalition collapsed.

Napoleon then proceeded to reorganize the German states. In 1806 he abolished many of the tiny German states as well as the ancient Holy Roman Empire and established by decree the German Confederation of the Rhine, a union of fifteen German states minus Austria, Prussia, and Saxony. Naming himself "protector" of the confederation, Napoleon firmly controlled western Germany.

Napoleon's intervention in German affairs alarmed the Prussians, who mobilized their armies after more than a decade of peace with France. Napoleon attacked and won two more brilliant victories in October 1806 at Jena and Auerstädt, where the Prussians were outnumbered two to one. The war with Prussia, now joined by Russia, continued into the following spring. After Napoleon's larger armies won another victory, Alexander I of Russia was ready to negotiate the peace. In the subsequent treaties of Tilsit, Prussia lost half of its population, while Russia accepted Napoleon's reorganization of western and central Europe and promised to enforce Napoleon's economic blockade against British goods.

The War of Haitian Independence

Another strong military leader was emerging in the French colonies. Toussaint L'Ouverture increasingly acted as an independent ruler of the western province of Saint-Domingue. This provoked another general, André Rigaud, to set up his own government in the southern peninsula, which had long been more isolated from France than the rest of the colony. Civil war broke out between the two sides in 1799, when L'Ouverture's forces, led by his lieutenant Jean Jacques Dessalines, invaded the south. Victory over Rigaud gave Toussaint control of the entire colony. (See the feature "Individuals in Society: Toussaint L'Ouverture.")

L'Ouverture's victory was soon challenged, however, by Napoleon's arrival in power. Napoleon intended to re-invigorate the Caribbean plantation economy as a basis for expanding French power. He ordered his brother-in-law General Charles-Victor-Emmanuel Leclerc to crush the new regime. In 1802 Leclerc landed in Saint-Domingue. Although Toussaint L'Ouverture cooperated with the French and turned his army over to them, he was arrested and deported, along with his family, to France, where he died in 1803. Jean Jacques Dessalines united the resistance under his command and led them to a crushing victory over the French forces. Of the fifty-eight thousand French soldiers, fifty thousand were lost in combat and to disease. On January 1, 1804, Dessalines formally declared the creation of the new sovereign nation of Haiti, the name used by the pre-Columbian inhabitants of the island. (France's other Caribbean colonies were not granted independence. Napoleon re-established slavery in 1802, and it remained in force until 1848.)

Haiti, the second independent state in the Americas and the first in Latin America, was thus born from the first successful large-scale slave revolt in history. As one recent historian of the Haitian revolution commented:

The insurrection of Saint-Domingue led to the expansion of citizenship beyond racial barriers despite the massive political and economic investment in the slave system at the time. If we live in a world in which democracy is meant to exclude no one, it is in no small part because of the actions of those slaves in Saint-Domingue who insisted that human rights were theirs too.[7]

The Grand Empire and Its End

Grand Empire *Napoleon's name for the European empire over which he intended to rule. This Grand Empire would consist of France, a number of lesser dependent states ruled by his relations, and several major allied states (Austria, Prussia, and Russia).*

Napoleon resigned himself to the loss of Saint-Domingue, but he still maintained imperial ambitions in Europe. Increasingly, he saw himself as the emperor of Europe and not just of France. The so-called **Grand Empire** he built had three parts. The core was an ever-expanding France, which by 1810 included Belgium, Holland, parts of northern Italy, and much German territory on the east bank of the Rhine. Beyond French borders Napoleon established the second part: a number of dependent satellite kingdoms ruled by members of his large family. The third part comprised the independent but allied states of Austria, Prussia, and Russia. After 1806 both satellites and allies were expected to support Napoleon's continental system and to cease trade with Britain.

The impact of the Grand Empire on the peoples of Europe was considerable. In the areas incorporated into France and in the satellites (see Map 21.2), feudal dues and serfdom were abolished. Yet Napoleon put the prosperity and special interests of France first in order to safeguard his power base. Levying heavy taxes in money and men for his armies, he came to be regarded more as a conquering tyrant than as an enlightened liberator. Thus French rule encouraged the growth of reactive

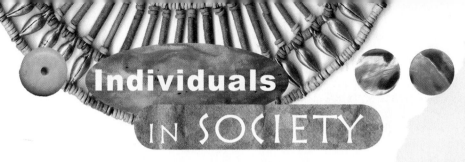

Toussaint L'Ouverture

Little is known of the early life of the brilliant military and political leader Toussaint L'Ouverture. He was born in 1743 on a plantation outside Le Cap owned by the Count de Bréda. According to tradition, Toussaint was the eldest son of a captured African prince from modern-day Benin. Toussaint Bréda, as he was then called, occupied a privileged position among slaves. Instead of performing backbreaking labor in the fields, he served his master as a coachman and livestock keeper. He also learned to read and write French and some Latin, but he was always more comfortable in the Creole dialect.

During the 1770s the plantation manager emancipated Toussaint. After being freed, he leased his own small coffee plantation, worked by slaves. A devout Catholic who led a frugal and ascetic life, L'Ouverture impressed others with his enormous physical energy, intellectual acumen, and air of mystery. He married Suzanne Simone, who already had one son, and the couple had another son during their marriage.

Toussaint L'Ouverture entered history in 1791 when he joined the slave uprisings that swept Saint-Domingue. (At some point he took on the cryptic *nom de guerre* "l'ouverture" meaning "the opening.") Toussaint rose to prominence among rebel slaves allied with Spain and by early 1794 controlled his own army. In 1794 he defected to the French side and led his troops to a series of victories against the Spanish. In 1795 France's National Convention promoted L'Ouverture to brigadier general.

Over the next three years L'Ouverture successively eliminated rivals for authority on the island. First he freed himself of the French commissioners sent to govern the colony. With a firm grip on power in the northern province, Toussaint defeated General André Rigaud in 1800 to gain control in the south. His army then marched on the capital of Spanish Santo Domingo on the eastern half of the island, meeting little resistance. The entire island of Hispaniola was now under his command.

With control of Saint-Domingue in his hands, L'Ouverture was confronted with the challenge of building a post-emancipation society, the first of its kind. The task was made even more difficult by the chaos wreaked by war, the destruction of plantations, and bitter social and racial tensions. For L'Ouverture the most pressing concern was to re-establish the plantation economy. Without revenue to pay his army, the gains of the rebellion could be lost. He there-

Equestrian portrait of Toussaint L'Ouverture. *(Réunion des Musées Nationaux/Art Resource, NY)*

fore encouraged white planters to return and reclaim their property. He also adopted harsh policies toward former slaves, forcing them back to their plantations and restricting their ability to acquire land. When they resisted, he sent troops across the island to enforce submission.

In 1801 L'Ouverture convened a colonial assembly to draft a new constitution that reaffirmed his draconian labor policies. The constitution named L'Ouverture governor for life, leaving Saint-Domingue as a colony in name alone. When news of the constitution arrived in France, an angry Napoleon dispatched General Leclerc to reestablish French control. In June 1802 Leclerc's forces arrested L'Ouverture and took him to France. He was jailed at Fort de Joux in the Jura Mountains near the Swiss border, where he died of pneumonia on April 7, 1803. It was left to his lieutenant, Jean Jacques Dessalines, to win independence for the new Haitian nation.

Questions for Analysis

1. Toussaint L'Ouverture was both slave and slave owner. How did each experience shape his life and actions?

2. Despite their differences, what did Toussaint L'Ouverture and Napoleon Bonaparte have in common? Why did they share a common fate?

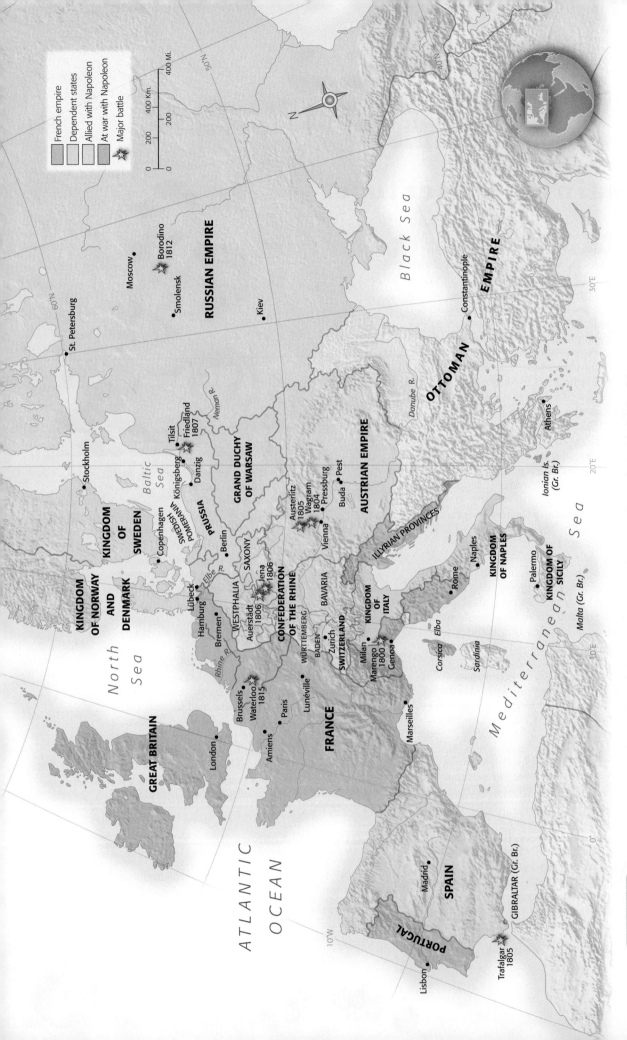

MAP 21.2 Napoleonic Europe in 1810 Only Great Britain remained at war with Napoleon at the height of the Grand Empire. Many British goods were smuggled through Helgoland, a tiny but strategic British possession off the German coast.

French empire
Dependent states
Allied with Napoleon
At war with Napoleon
★ Major battle

ATLANTIC OCEAN

North Sea

Baltic Sea

Black Sea

Mediterranean Sea

GREAT BRITAIN
London

KINGDOM OF NORWAY AND DENMARK
KINGDOM OF SWEDEN
Stockholm
Copenhagen

RUSSIAN EMPIRE
St. Petersburg
Moscow
Borodino 1812 ★
Smolensk
Kiev

Lübeck
Hamburg
Bremen
SWEDISH POMERANIA
Berlin
PRUSSIA
Königsberg
Danzig
Tilsit
Friedland 1807 ★
Neman R.

WESTPHALIA
Auerstädt 1806 ★
Jena 1806 ★
SAXONY
GRAND DUCHY OF WARSAW
Elbe R.
Rhine R.

Brussels
Waterloo 1815 ★
Paris
Amiens
Lunéville

FRANCE

CONFEDERATION OF THE RHINE
BAVARIA
BADEN
WÜRTTEMBERG
Zurich
SWITZERLAND

Vienna
Wagram 1809 ★
Austerlitz 1805 ★
Pressburg
Buda
Pest
AUSTRIAN EMPIRE
Danube R.

ILLYRIAN PROVINCES

KINGDOM OF ITALY
Milan
Marengo 1800 ★
Genoa
Marseilles

Corsica
Sardinia

Rome
Naples
KINGDOM OF NAPLES
Palermo
KINGDOM OF SICILY
Elba
Malta (Gr. Br.)

Ionian Is. (Gr. Br.)
Athens

OTTOMAN EMPIRE
Constantinople

SPAIN
Madrid

PORTUGAL
Lisbon
Trafalgar 1805 ★
GIBRALTAR (Gr. Br.)

0   200   400 Km.
0   200   400 Mi.

N

50°N
60°N
40°N
30°E
20°E
10°E
0°
10°W

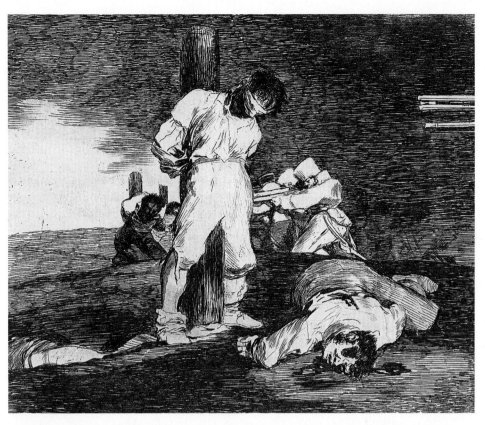

● **The War in Spain**   This unforgettable etching by the Spanish painter Francisco Goya (1746–1828) comes from his famous collection "The Disasters of the War." A French firing squad executes captured Spanish rebels almost as soon as they are captured, an everyday event in a war of atrocities on both sides. Do you think these rebels are "terrorists" or "freedom fighters"? *(Foto Marburg/Art Resource, NY)*

nationalism, for individuals in different lands developed patriotic feelings of their own in opposition to Napoleon's imperialism.

The first great revolt occurred in Spain. In 1808 a coalition of Catholics, monarchists, and patriots rebelled against Napoleon's attempts to make Spain a French satellite with a Bonaparte as its king. Yet Napoleon pushed on, determined to hold his complex and far-flung empire together. In 1810, when the Grand Empire was at its height, Britain still remained at war with France, helping guerrillas in Spain and Portugal. The continental system, organized to exclude British goods from the continent and force that "nation of shopkeepers" to its knees, was a failure. Instead, it was France that suffered economically from Britain's counter-blockade. Perhaps looking for a scapegoat, Napoleon turned on Alexander I of Russia, who in 1811 openly repudiated Napoleon's war of prohibitions against British goods.

Napoleon's invasion of Russia began in June 1812 with a force that eventually numbered 600,000, probably the largest force yet assembled in a single army. Only one-third of this Great Army was French, however; nationals of all the satellites and allies were drafted into the operation. Napoleon reached Smolensk and recklessly pressed on toward Moscow. The great Battle of Borodino that followed was a draw, and the Russians retreated in good order. Alexander ordered the evacuation of Moscow, which then burned in part, and he refused to negotiate. Finally, after five weeks in the abandoned city, Napoleon ordered a retreat, one of the greatest disasters in military history. The Russian army, the Russian winter, and starvation cut Napoleon's army to pieces. When the frozen remnants staggered into Poland and Prussia in December, 370,000 men had died and another 200,000 had been taken prisoner.[8]

Leaving his troops to their fate, Napoleon raced to Paris to raise yet another army. Austria and Prussia deserted Napoleon and joined Russia and Great Britain in the Treaty of Chaumont in March 1814, by which the four powers pledged allegiance to defeat the French emperor. All across Europe patriots called for a "war of liberation" against Napoleon's oppression. Less than a month later, on April 4, 1814, a defeated Napoleon abdicated his throne. The victorious allies granted Napoleon the island of Elba off the coast of Italy as his own tiny state. Napoleon was even allowed to keep his imperial title, and France was required to pay him a yearly income of 2 million francs.

The allies also agreed to the restoration of the Bourbon dynasty under Louis XVIII (r. 1814–1824). The new monarch tried to gain support by issuing the Constitutional Charter, which accepted many of France's revolutionary changes and guaranteed civil liberties. Yet Louis XVIII—old, ugly, and crippled by gout—lacked the glory and magic of Napoleon. Sensing an opportunity, Napoleon staged a daring escape from Elba in February 1815. Landing in France, he issued appeals for support and marched on Paris with a small band of followers. Louis XVIII fled, and once more Napoleon took command. But Napoleon's gamble was a desperate long shot, for the allies were united against him. At the end of a frantic period known as the Hundred Days, they crushed his forces at Waterloo on June 18, 1815, and imprisoned him on the rocky island of St. Helena, off the western coast of Africa. Louis XVIII recommenced his reign. The allies now dealt more harshly with the apparently incorrigible French. As for Napoleon, he took revenge by writing his memoirs, skillfully nurturing the myth that he had been Europe's revolutionary liberator, a romantic hero whose lofty work had been undone by oppressive reactionaries. An era had ended.

Chapter Summary

Key Terms

desacralization
Assembly of Notables
Estates General
National Assembly
Great Fear
constitutional monarchy
free people of color
Jacobin club
second revolution
Girondists
the Mountain
sans-culottes
planned economy
Reign of Terror
nationalism
Thermidorian reaction
Grand Empire

To assess your mastery of this chapter, go to
bedfordstmartins.com/mckayworld

• *What social, political, and economic factors formed the background to the French Revolution?*

The French Revolution was forged by multiple and complex factors. French society had undergone significant transformations during the eighteenth century, which dissolved many economic and social differences among elites without removing the legal distinction between them. These changes were accompanied by political struggles between the monarchy and its officers, particularly in the high law courts. Emerging public opinion focused on the shortcomings of monarchical rule in political and personal terms. With their sacred royal aura severely tarnished, Louis XV and his successor Louis XVI found themselves unable to respond to the financial crises generated by war and public debt. Louis XVI's half-hearted efforts to redress the situation were quickly overwhelmed by demands for fundamental reform.

• *What were the immediate events and ideas that sparked the Revolution in France and its Caribbean colony of Saint-Domingue?*

Forced to call a meeting of the Estates General for the first time since 1614, Louis XVI fell back on the traditional formula of one vote for each of the three orders of society. Debate over the composition of the assembly called forth a bold new paradigm: that the Third Estate in itself constituted the French nation. By 1791 the National Assembly had eliminated Old Regime privileges and had established a constitutional monarchy. Talk in France of liberty, equality, and fraternity raised contradictory aspirations among the wealthy white planters, free people of color, and African slaves of the colony of Saint-Domingue. All looked to the Revolution for a better future, a promise that could not be fulfilled for all.

• How and why did the Revolution take a radical turn at home and in the colonies?

With the execution of the royal couple and the declaration of terror as the order of the day, the French Revolution took an increasingly radical turn from the summer of 1792. Fears of counter-revolutionary conspiracy combined with the outbreak of war convinced many that the Revolution was vulnerable and must be defended against its multiple enemies. In a spiraling cycle of accusations and executions, the Jacobins eliminated political opponents and then factions within their own party. The Directory government that took power after the fall of Robespierre restored political equilibrium at the cost of his platform of social equality. In the colonies, slave revolt and the pressure of war led to the abolition of slavery and the enfranchisement of free people of color and former slaves.

• What factors explain the rise and fall of Napoleon Bonaparte and his loss of the colony of Saint-Domingue?

Wearied by the Directory's weaknesses, conspirators gave Napoleon Bonaparte control of France. His military brilliance, his charisma and determination made him seem ideal to lead France to victory over its enemies. As is so often the case in history, Napoleon's relentless ambitions ultimately led to his downfall. His story is paralleled by that of Toussaint L'Ouverture, another soldier who emerged to the political limelight from the chaos of revolution only to endure exile and defeat.

As complex as its origins are, the legacies of the French Revolution included liberalism, assertive nationalism, radical democratic republicanism, embryonic socialism, self-conscious conservatism, abolitionism, decolonization, and movements for racial and sexual equality. The Revolution also left a rich and turbulent history of electoral competition, legislative assemblies, and even mass politics. Thus the French Revolution presented a range of political options and alternative visions of the future. For this reason, it was truly the revolution in modern European politics.

Suggested Reading

Bell, David A. *The Cult of the Nation in France: Inventing Nationalism, 1680–1800*. 2001. Traces early French nationalism through its revolutionary culmination.

Blanning, T. C. W. *The French Revolutionary Wars (1787–1802)*. 1996. A masterful account of the revolutionary wars that also places the French Revolution in its European context.

Broers, Michael. *Europe Under Napoleon*. 2002. Probes Napoleon's impact on the territories he conquered.

Connelly, Owen. *The French Revolution and Napoleonic Era*. 1991. An excellent introduction to the French Revolution and Napoleon.

Desan, Suzanne. *The Family on Trial in Revolutionary France*. 2004. Studies the effects of revolutionary law on the family, including the legalization of divorce.

Dubois, Laurent. *Avengers of the New World: The Story of the Haitian Revolution*. 2004. An excellent and highly readable account of the revolution that transformed the French colony of Saint-Domingue into the independent state of Haiti.

Englund, Steven. *Napoleon: A Political Life*. 2004. A good biography of the French emperor.

(continued on page 640)

Listening to the PAST

Revolution and Women's Rights

The 1789 Declaration of the Rights of Man was a revolutionary call for legal equality, representative government, and individual freedom that excluded women from its manifesto. Among those who saw the contradiction in granting supposedly universal rights to only half the population was Marie Gouze (1748–1793), known to history as Olympe de Gouges. The daughter of a provincial butcher and peddler, she pursued a literary career in Paris after the death of her husband. De Gouges's great work was her "Declaration of the Rights of Woman" (1791). Excerpted here, it called on males to end their oppression of women and to give women equal rights. A radical on women's issues, de Gouges sympathized with the monarchy and criticized Robespierre in print. Convicted of sedition, she was guillotined in November 1793.

. . . Man, are you capable of being just? . . . Tell me, what gives you sovereign empire to oppress my sex? Your strength? Your talents? Observe the Creator in his wisdom . . . and give me, if you dare, an example of this tyrannical empire. Go back to animals, consult the elements, study plants . . . and distinguish, if you can, the sexes in the administration of nature. Everywhere you will find them mingled; everywhere they cooperate in harmonious togetherness in this immortal masterpiece.

Man alone has raised his exceptional circumstances to a principle. . . . [H]e wants to command as a despot a sex which is in full possession of its intellectual faculties; he pretends to enjoy the Revolution and to claim his rights to equality in order to say nothing more about it.

DECLARATION OF THE RIGHTS OF WOMAN AND THE FEMALE CITIZEN

. . . Mothers, daughters, sisters and representatives of the nation demand to be constituted into a national assembly. Believing that ignorance, omission, or scorn for the rights of woman are the only causes of public

misfortunes and of the corruption of governments, [the women] have resolved to set forth in a solemn declaration the natural, inalienable, and sacred rights of woman. . . .

I. Woman is born free and lives equal to man in her rights. Social distinctions can be based only on the common utility.

II. The purpose of any political association is the conservation of the natural and imprescriptible rights of woman and man; these rights are liberty, property, security, and especially resistance to oppression.

III. The principle of all sovereignty rests essentially with the nation, which is nothing but the union of woman and man. . . .

IV. Liberty and justice consist of restoring all that belongs to others; thus, the only limits on the exercise of the natural rights of woman are perpetual male tyranny; these limits are to be reformed by the laws of nature and reason.

V. Laws of nature and reason proscribe all acts harmful to society. . . .

VI. The law must be the expression of the general will; all female and male citizens must contribute either personally or through their representatives to its formation; it must be the same for all: male and female citizens, being equal in the eyes of the law, must be equally admitted to all honors, positions, and public employment according to their capacity and without other distinctions besides those of their virtues and talents. . . .

IX. Once any woman is declared guilty, complete rigor is [to be] exercised by the law.

X. No one is to be disquieted for his very basic opinions; woman has the right to mount the scaffold; she must equally have the right to mount the rostrum, provided that her demonstrations do not disturb the legally established public order.

XI. The free communication of thoughts and opinions is one of the most precious rights of woman, since that liberty assures the recognition of children by their fathers. Any female citizen thus may say freely, I am the mother of a child which belongs to you, without being forced by a barbarous prejudice to hide the truth. . . .

XIII. For the support of the public force and the expenses of administration, the contributions of woman and man are equal; she shares all the duties . . . and all the painful tasks; therefore, she must have the same share in the distribution of positions, employment, offices, honors, and jobs. . . .

XVI. No society has a constitution without the guarantee of rights and the separation of powers; the constitution is null if the majority of individuals comprising the nation have not cooperated in drafting it.

XVII. Property belongs to both sexes whether united or separate; for each it is an inviolable and sacred right.

Olympe de Gouges in 1784; aquatint by Madame Aubry (1748–1793). *(Musée de la Ville de Paris, Musée Carnavalet, Paris, France/The Bridgeman Art Library)*

Questions for Analysis

1. On what basis did de Gouges argue for gender equality? Did she believe in natural law?

2. What consequences did "scorn for the rights of woman" have for France, according to de Gouges?

3. Did de Gouges stress political rights at the expense of social and economic rights? If so, why?

Source: Olympe de Gouges, "Declaration of the Rights of Woman," in *Women in Revolutionary Paris, 1789–1795: Selected Documents Translated with Notes and Commentary*. Translated with notes and commentary by Darline Gay Levy, Harriet Branson Applewhite, and Mary Durham Johnson. Copyright © 1979 by the Board of Trustees, University of Illinois. Used with permission of the editors and the University of Illinois Press.

Hunt, Lynn. *Politics, Culture and Class in the French Revolution,* 2d ed. 2004. A pioneering examination of the French Revolution as a cultural phenomenon that generated new festivals, clothing, and songs and even a new calendar.

Landes, John B. *Visualizing the Nation: Gender, Representation, and Revolution in Eighteenth-Century France.* 2001. Analyzes images of gender and the body in revolutionary politics.

Schechter, Ronald. *Obstinate Hebrews: Representations of Jews in France, 1715–1815.* An illuminating study of Jews and attitudes toward them in France from Enlightenment to emancipation.

Sutherland, Donald. *France, 1789–1815.* 1986. An overview of the French Revolution that emphasizes its many opponents as well as its supporters.

Tackett, Timothy. *When the King Took Flight.* 2003. An exciting re-creation of the royal family's doomed effort to escape from Paris.

Notes

1. G. Pernoud and S. Flaisser, eds., *The French Revolution* (Greenwich, Conn.: Fawcett, 1960), p. 61.
2. Quoted in L. Gershoy, *The Era of the French Revolution, 1789–1799* (New York: Van Nostrand, 1957), p. 150.
3. T. Blanning, *The French Revolutionary Wars, 1787–1802* (London: Arnold, 1996), pp. 116–128.
4. 10. Quoted ibid., p. 123.
5. Quoted in Laurent Dubois, *Avengers of the New World: The Story of the Haitian Revolution* (Cambridge: Harvard University Press, 2004), p. 97.
6. I. Woloch, *Napoleon and His Collaborators: The Making of a Dictatorship* (New York: W. W. Norton, 2001), pp. 36–65.
7. Quoted in Laurent Dubois, *Avengers of the New World: The Story of the Haitian Revolution* (Cambridge: Harvard University Press, 2004), p. 3.
8. D. Sutherland, France, *1789–1815: Revolution and Counterrevolution* (New York: Oxford University Press, 1986), p. 420.

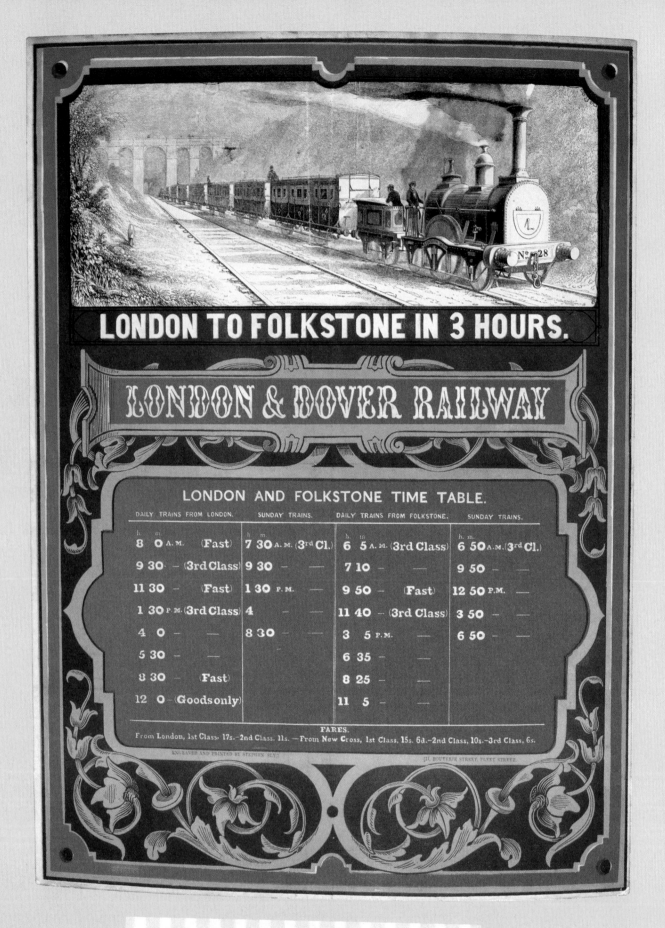

A Colorful Timetable Poster lists the trains from London to Folkstone, the English Channel's gateway port to the European continent, and proudly proclaims the speed of the journey. *(The Bridgeman Art Library)*

chapter

22

THE INDUSTRIAL REVOLUTION IN EUROPE, CA. 1780–1860

Chapter Preview

The Initial Breakthrough in England
• *What were the origins of the Industrial Revolution in England?*

Energy and Transportation
• *What changes in England revolutionized the provision of energy and transportation?*

Industrialization in Continental Europe
• *How after 1815 did continental countries respond to the challenge of industrialization?*

Capital and Labor
• *How did the Industrial Revolution affect social classes, the standard of living, and working conditions?*

While the Revolution in France was opening a new political era, another revolution was transforming economic and social life. The Industrial Revolution, which began in England around the 1780s, started to influence continental Europe and the rest of the world after 1815. Because the Industrial Revolution was less dramatic than the French Revolution, some historians see industrial development as basically moderate and evolutionary. From a long-term global perspective, however, it was rapid and brought about radical changes. Perhaps only the development of agriculture during Neolithic times had a similar impact and significance.

The Industrial Revolution profoundly modified much of human experience. It changed patterns of work, transformed the social class structure, and altered the international balance of political and military power, giving added impetus to ongoing Western expansion into non-Western lands. The Industrial Revolution also helped ordinary people gain a higher standard of living.

Unfortunately, improvement in the European standard of living was quite limited until about 1850, for at least two reasons. First, even in England only a few key industries experienced a technological revolution. Many more industries continued to use old methods, especially on the European continent, and this held down the increase in total production. Second, the increase in Europe's total population, which began in the eighteenth century, continued as the era of the Industrial Revolution unfolded. As a result, the rapid growth in population threatened—quite literally—to eat up the growth in production and to leave individuals poorer than ever. Chapter 23 will examine accompanying changes in urban living, and Chapters 24 and 25 will probe the consequences of industrialization in Europe for world history.

THE INITIAL BREAKTHROUGH IN ENGLAND

What were the origins of the Industrial Revolution in England?

The Industrial Revolution began in England. It was something new in history, and it was quite unplanned. With no models to copy and no idea of what to expect, England had to pioneer not only in industrial technology but also in social relations and urban living. Between 1793 and 1815 almost constant war with France complicated these formidable tasks.

Eighteenth-Century Origins

Although many aspects of the Industrial Revolution are still matters for scholarly debate, it is generally agreed that the industrial changes that did occur grew out of a complex combination of factors. These factors came together in eighteenth-century England and initiated a decisive breakthrough that many place in the 1780s.

In analyzing the causes of the late-eighteenth-century acceleration in the English economy, historians have paid particular attention to dramatic changes in agriculture, foreign trade, technology, energy supplies, and transportation. Although this chapter focuses on those issues, one must first understand that England had other, less conspicuous assets that favored the long process of development that culminated in industrial breakthrough.

Relatively good government was one such asset. The monarchy and the aristocratic oligarchy, which jointly ruled the country after the constitutional settlement of 1688, provided stable and predictable government. Neither civil strife nor invading armies threatened peace. Thus the government let the domestic economy operate fairly freely and with few controls, encouraging personal initiative, technological change, and a free market.

A related asset was an experienced business class with modern characteristics. This business class, which traced its origins to the Middle Ages, eagerly sought to make profits and to accumulate capital. England also had a large class of hired agricultural laborers. These rural wage earners were relatively mobile—compared with village-bound peasants in France and western Germany, for example—and along with cottage workers they formed a potential labor force for capitalist entrepreneurs.

Several other assets supporting English economic growth stand out. First, unlike its rival France as well as most other countries, England had an effective central bank and well-developed credit institutions. Second, although England may seem a rather small country today, it undoubtedly enjoyed the largest effective domestic market in eighteenth-century Europe. In an age when shipping goods by water was much cheaper than shipping goods by land, no part of England was more than twenty miles from navigable water. Beginning in the 1770s a canal-building boom greatly enhanced this natural advantage. Nor were there any tariffs within the country to hinder trade, as there were in France before 1789 and in politically fragmented Germany and Italy. Finally, only in Holland did the lower classes appear to live as well as in England. The ordinary English family did not have to spend almost everything it earned just to buy bread. It could spend more on other items, thereby adding significantly to the growing demand for manufactured goods that was a critical factor in initiating England's industrial breakthrough.

All these factors combined to bring about the **Industrial Revolution,** a term coined in the 1830s by awed contemporaries to describe the burst of major inventions and technical changes that they had witnessed in certain industries. This technical revolution went hand in hand with an impressive quickening in the annual rate of industrial

Industrial Revolution *A term coined in the 1830s to describe the burst of major inventions and technical changes in certain industries.*

growth in England. Thus industry grew at only 0.7 percent per year between 1700 and 1760—before the Industrial Revolution—but it grew at the much higher rate of 3 percent between 1801 and 1831, when industrial transformation was in full swing.[1] The decisive quickening of growth probably came in the 1780s, after the American War of Independence and just before the French Revolution.

The economic and political revolutions that shaped the modern world occurred almost simultaneously. The Industrial Revolution, however, was a longer process. It was not complete in England until about 1850, and it had no real impact on continental European countries until after the Congress of Vienna (see page 676) ended the era of revolutionary wars in Europe in 1815.

The Agricultural Revolution

A gradual but profound revolution in agricultural methods promoted accelerated economic growth. In essence, the **agricultural revolution** eliminated the traditional pattern of village agriculture found in northern and central Europe. It replaced the medieval **open-field system** and the annual fallowing of some fields with a new system of continuous rotation that resulted in more food for humans and their animals. The new agricultural system had profound implications, for it eliminated long-standing **common rights** as well as the fallow. But whereas peasants and rural laborers checked the spread of the new system on the continent of Europe in the eighteenth century, large landowners and powerful market forces overcame such opposition in England.

The new methods of agriculture originated in the Low Countries. The vibrant, dynamic middle-class society of seventeenth-century republican Holland was the most advanced in Europe in many areas of human endeavor, including agriculture. By 1650 intensive farming was well established throughout much of the Low Countries. Enclosed fields, continuous rotation, heavy manuring, and a wide variety of crops—all these innovations were present. Agriculture was highly specialized and commercialized. The Low Countries became "the Mecca of foreign agricultural experts who came . . . to see Flemish agriculture with their own eyes, to write about it and to propagate its methods in their home lands."[2]

The English were the best students. They learned about water control from Dutch experts, who made a great contribution to draining the extensive marshes, or fens, of wet and rainy England. Dutch practice also encouraged improvements in livestock through selective breeding. By 1740 agricultural improvement had become a craze among the English aristocracy.

By the mid-eighteenth century English agriculture was in the process of a radical and technologically desirable transformation. The eventual result was that by 1870 English farmers produced 300 percent more food than they had produced in 1700, although the number of people working the land had increased by only 14 percent. This great surge of agricultural production provided food for England's rapidly growing urban population. It was a remarkable achievement.

Chronology

ca. 1765	Hargreaves invents spinning jenny
1769	Watt creates modern steam engine
1775–1783	American Revolution
1780–1851	Population boom in England
1780s–1850	Industrial Revolution in England
1789–1799	French Revolution
1798	Malthus, *Essay on the Principle of Population*
1799	Combination Acts passed
1810	Strike of Manchester cotton spinners
1812	First Luddite attacks on factories
1824	Combination Acts repealed
1830	Stephenson's *Rocket,* first effective steam locomotive
1833	Factory Act
1842	Mines Act
1844	Engels, *The Condition of the Working Class in England*
1851	Great Exposition held at Crystal Palace

agricultural revolution *A gradual but profound change in agricultural methods that promoted accelerated economic growth.*

open-field system *A system of village farming developed by peasants where the land was divided into several large fields, which were in turn cut into strips.*

common rights *The shared use of agriculture land; it was abolished with the enclosure movement.*

Technological progress in agriculture had a cost. The impetus for enclosing the fields came mainly from the powerful ruling class—the English landowning aristocracy, who benefited directly from higher yields that could support higher rents. The large landowners controlled Parliament, which made the laws. They had Parliament pass hundreds of "enclosure acts," each of which authorized the fencing of open fields in a given village and the division of the common lands in proportion to one's property in the open fields. The division of the heavy legal and surveying costs of **enclosure** among the landowners meant that many peasants who had small holdings had to sell out to pay their share of the expenses. Similarly, landless cottagers lost their age-old access to the common pasture but received no compensation.

enclosure *The enclosing of the individual shares of the pastures as a way of farming more effectively.*

By eliminating common rights and greatly reducing the access of poor men and women to the land, the eighteenth-century enclosure movement marked the completion of two major historical developments in England: the rise of market-oriented estate agriculture and the emergence of a landless proletariat. By 1815 a tiny minority of wealthy English (and Scottish) landowners held most of the land and pursued profits aggressively, leasing their holdings through agents to middle-size farmers at competitive prices. These farmers produced mainly for cash markets and relied on landless laborers for their workforce. In strictly economic terms these landless laborers may have lived as well in 1800 as in 1700, but they had lost that bit of independence and self-respect that common rights had provided. They had become completely dependent on cash wages. In no other European country had this **proletarianization**—this transformation of large numbers of small peasant farmers into landless rural wage earners—gone as far as it had in England by the late eighteenth century. England's village poor found the cost of economic change and technological progress heavy and unjust.

proletarianization *The transformation of large numbers of small peasant farmers into landless rural wage earners.*

The Growth of Foreign Trade

In the eighteenth century Great Britain (formed in 1707 by the union of England and Scotland into a single kingdom) also became the leading maritime power, dominating long-distance trade, particularly intercontinental trade across the Atlantic. This foreign trade stimulated the economy.

Britain's commercial leadership in the eighteenth century had its origins in the mercantilism of the seventeenth century. European **mercantilism** was a system of economic regulations aimed at increasing the power of the state. It rested on the general premise that a nation's power and wealth were determined by its supply of precious metals, which were to be acquired by increasing exports (paid for with gold) and reducing imports to achieve domestic self-sufficiency. What distinguished English mercantilism was the unusual idea that government economic regulations could and should serve the private interests of individuals and groups as well as the public needs of the state.

mercantilism *The prevailing economic theory of European nations in the sixteenth and seventeenth centuries. Mercantilism remained the dominant theory until the Industrial Revelation and articulation of the theory of laissez faire.*

The seventeenth-century Navigation Acts reflected the desire of Great Britain to increase both its military power and its private wealth. The initial target of these instruments of economic warfare was the Netherlands, which was far ahead of the English in shipping and foreign trade in the mid-seventeenth century. By the later seventeenth century, after three Anglo-Dutch wars, the Netherlands was falling behind England in shipping, trade, and colonies. France then stood clearly as England's most serious rival in the competition for overseas empire. Thus from 1701 to 1763 Britain and France were locked in a series of wars to decide, in part, which nation would become Europe's leading maritime power and claim the lion's share of the profits of Europe's overseas expansion.

The first round was the War of the Spanish Succession, which resulted in major gains for Great Britain in the Peace of Utrecht (1713). France ceded Newfoundland, Nova Scotia, and the Hudson Bay territory to Britain. Spain was compelled to give

Britain control of the lucrative West African slave trade—the so-called *asiento*—and to let Britain send one ship of merchandise into the Spanish colonies annually.

The Seven Years' War (1756–1763) was the decisive round in the Franco-British competition for colonial empire. With the Treaty of Paris (1763) France lost all its possessions on the mainland of North America and gave up most of its holdings in India as well. By 1763 Britain had realized its goal of monopolizing a vast trade and colonial empire for its benefit.

This interconnected expansion of trade and empire marked a major step toward the Industrial Revolution, although people could not know it at the time. Protected colonial markets provided a great stimulus for many branches of English manufacturing. The value of the sales of manufactured products to the Atlantic economy—primarily the mainland colonies of North America and the West Indian sugar islands, with an important assist from West Africa and Latin America—soared from 1700 to 1773. English exports of manufactured goods to continental Europe grew hardly at all in these years.

English exports became much more balanced and diversified. To America and Africa went large quantities of metal items—axes to frontiersmen, firearms, chains for slave owners. Also exported were clocks and coaches, buttons and saddles, china and furniture, musical instruments and scientific equipment, and a host of other things. Thus the mercantile system established in the seventeenth century continued to shape trade in the eighteenth century, and the English concentrated in their hands much of the demand for manufactured goods from the growing Atlantic economy. Sales to other "colonies"—Ireland and India—also rose substantially in the eighteenth century. Nor was this all. Demand from the well-integrated home market was also rising. Thus growing demand from home and abroad put intense pressure on the whole system of production.

The First Factories

The pressure to produce more goods for a growing market was directly related to the first decisive breakthrough of the Industrial Revolution—the creation of the world's first large factories in the English cotton textile industry. Technological innovations in the manufacture of cloth led to a whole new pattern of production and social relationships. No other industry experienced such a rapid or complete transformation before 1830.

Although merchant-capitalists "put out" raw materials to cottage workers for processing and payment all across Europe in the late eighteenth century, this pattern of rural industry was most fully developed in England. Thus it was in England, under the pressure of growing demand for more production, that the putting-out system's shortcomings first began to outweigh its advantages—especially in the cottage textile industry after about 1760.

There was always a serious imbalance in this family enterprise: the work of four or five spinners was needed to keep one weaver steadily employed. The wife and the husband had constantly to try to find more thread and more spinners. Widows and unmarried women—"spinsters" who spun for their living—were recruited by the wife. Or perhaps the weaver's son went off on horseback to seek thread.

Deep-seated conflict between workers and employers complicated increased production. In "The Clothier's Delight, or the Rich Men's Joy and the Poor Men's Sorrow," an English popular song written about 1700, a merchant boasts of his countless tricks used to "beat down wages":

We heapeth up riches and treasure great store
Which we get by griping and grinding the poor.
And this is a way for to fill up our purse
Although we do get it with many a curse.[3]

● **Woman Working a Hargreaves's Spinning Jenny** The loose cotton strands on the slanted bobbins passed up to the sliding carriage and then on to the spindles in back for fine spinning. The worker, almost always a woman, regulated the sliding carriage with one hand and with the other she turned the crank on the wheel to supply power. By 1783 one woman could spin by hand a hundred threads at a time on an improved model. *(Mary Evans Picture Library)*

There were constant disputes over the weights of materials and the quality of the cloth. Merchants accused workers of stealing raw materials, and weavers complained that merchants delivered underweight bales. Both were right; each tried to cheat the other, even if only in self-defense.

There was another problem, at least from the merchant-capitalist's point of view. Scattered rural labor was cheap but hard to control. Cottage workers tended to work in spurts. After they got paid on Saturday afternoon, the men in particular tended to drink and carouse for two or three days. By the end of the week the weaver was probably working feverishly to make his quota. But if he did not succeed, there was little the merchant could do. The merchant-capitalist's search for more efficient methods of production intensified.

Attention focused on ways of improving spinning. Many a tinkering worker knew that a better spinning wheel promised rich rewards. It proved hard to spin the traditional raw materials—wool and flax—with improved machines, but cotton was different. Cotton textiles had first been imported into England from India by the East India Company, and by 1760 there was a tiny domestic industry in northern England. After many experiments over a generation, a gifted carpenter and jack-of-all-trades, James Hargreaves, invented his cotton-spinning jenny about 1765. At almost the same moment a barber-turned-manufacturer named Richard Arkwright invented another kind of spinning machine, the water frame. These breakthroughs produced an explosion in the infant cotton textile industry in the 1780s. By 1790 the new machines were producing ten times as much cotton yarn as had been made in 1770.

spinning jenny *A machine, invented by James Hargreaves, that enabled workers to spin cotton.*

Hargreaves's **spinning jenny** was simple and inexpensive. It was also hand operated. In early models from six to twenty-four spindles were mounted on a sliding carriage, and each spindle spun a fine, slender thread. The woman moved the carriage back and forth with one hand and turned a wheel to supply power with the other. Now it was the male weaver who could not keep up with the vastly more efficient female spinner.

Arkwright's **water frame** employed a different principle. It quickly acquired a capacity of several hundred spindles and demanded much more power—waterpower. The water frame thus required large specialized mills, factories that employed as many as one thousand workers from the very beginning. The water frame could spin only coarse, strong thread, which was then put out for respinning on hand-powered cottage jennies. After about 1790, all cotton spinning was gradually concentrated in factories.

water frame *Invented by Richard Arkwright, this machine used waterpower to spin coarse, strong thread in factories.*

The first consequences of these revolutionary developments were more beneficial than is generally believed. Cotton goods became much cheaper, and they were bought and treasured by all classes. In the past only the wealthy could afford the comfort and cleanliness of underwear, which was called **body linen** because it was made from expensive linen cloth. Now millions of poor people, who had earlier worn nothing underneath their coarse, filthy outer garments, could afford to wear cotton slips and underpants as well as cotton dresses and shirts.

body linen *Another term for underwear, so called because it was made from expensive cloth.*

Families using cotton in cottage industry were freed from their constant search for adequate yarn from scattered part-time spinners, for all the thread needed could be spun in the cottage on the jenny or obtained from a nearby factory. The wages of weavers, now hard-pressed to keep up with the spinners, rose markedly until about 1792. Weavers were among the best-paid workers in England. As a result, large numbers of agricultural laborers became hand-loom weavers, while mechanics and capitalists soon sought to invent a power loom to save on labor costs. This Edmund Cartwright achieved in 1785. But the power looms of the factories worked poorly at first, and hand-loom weavers continued to receive good wages until at least 1800.

Until the late 1780s most English factories were in rural areas, where they had access to waterpower. These factories employed a relatively small percentage of all cotton textile workers. Working conditions in the early factories were less satisfactory than the conditions of cottage weavers and spinners, and people were reluctant to work in them. Therefore, factory owners turned to young children who had been abandoned by their parents and put in the care of local officials. These local officials often "apprenticed" such unfortunate orphans to factory owners, who gained over them almost the authority of slave owners.

Both symbolically and substantially, the big new cotton mills marked the beginning of the Industrial Revolution in England. By 1831 the largely mechanized cotton textile industry towered above all others, accounting for fully 22 percent of the country's entire industrial production.

ENERGY AND TRANSPORTATION

What changes in England revolutionized the provision of energy and transportation?

The growth of the cotton textile industry might have been stunted or cut short if water from rivers and streams had remained the primary source of power for the new factories. But this did not occur. Instead, an epoch-making solution was found to the age-old problem of energy and power. The solution to the energy problem permitted continued rapid development in cotton textiles, the gradual generalization of the factory system, and the triumph of the Industrial Revolution in England and Scotland.

The Problem of Energy

Human beings, like all living organisms, require energy. Depending on the individual's level of physical activity, adult men and women need two thousand to four thousand calories (units of energy) daily simply to fuel their bodies, work, and survive.

Prehistoric people relied on plants and plant-eating animals as their sources of energy. With the development of agriculture, early civilizations were able to increase the number of useful plants and thus the supply of energy. Some plants could be fed to domesticated animals, such as the horse. Stronger than human beings, these animals converted the energy in the plants into work.

Human beings have used their toolmaking abilities to construct machines that convert one form of energy into another for their own benefit. In the common era people began to develop water mills to grind their grain and windmills to pump water and drain swamps. More efficient use of water and wind in the sixteenth and seventeenth centuries enabled human beings to accomplish more; intercontinental sailing ships were a prime example. Nevertheless, societies around the world continued to rely mainly on plants for energy, and human beings and animals continued to perform most work.

Lack of power lay at the heart of the poverty that afflicted the large majority of the world's people. The man behind the plow and the woman at the spinning wheel could employ only horsepower and human muscle in their labor. No matter how hard they worked, they could not produce very much.

The shortage of energy had become particularly severe in England by the eighteenth century. Wood was in ever-shorter supply, yet it remained tremendously important. In addition to serving as the primary source of heat for homes and industries and as a basic raw material, processed wood (charcoal) was the fuel that was mixed with iron ore in the blast furnace to produce pig iron. The iron industry's appetite for wood was enormous, and by 1740 the English iron industry was stagnating. Vast forests enabled Russia in the eighteenth century to become the world's leading producer of iron, much of which was exported to England.

The Steam Engine Breakthrough

As this early energy crisis grew worse, England looked toward its abundant and widely scattered reserves of coal as an alternative to its vanishing wood. By 1640 most homes in London were heated with it, and it also provided heat for making beer, glass, soap, and other products. Coal, however, was not used to make iron, to produce mechanical energy, or to power machinery. It was there that coal's potential was enormous, as a simple example shows.

A hard-working miner can dig out five hundred pounds of coal a day using hand tools, the equivalent of about one horsepower-hour of labor. Even an extremely inefficient converter, which transforms only 1 percent of the heat energy in coal into mechanical energy, will produce twenty-seven horsepower-hours of work from that five hundred pounds of coal. Early steam engines were just such inefficient converters.

As more coal was produced, mines were dug deeper and deeper and were constantly filling with water. Mechanical pumps, usually powered by animals walking in circles at the surface, had to be installed. At one mine fully five hundred horses were used in pumping. Such power was expensive and bothersome. In an attempt to overcome these disadvantages Thomas Savery in 1698 and Thomas Newcomen in 1705 invented the first primitive **steam engines.** Both engines burned coal to produce steam, which was then used to operate a pump. Both engines were extremely inefficient, but by the early 1770s hundreds of these steam engines were operating successfully in English and Scottish mines.

In the early 1760s a gifted young Scot named James Watt (1736–1819) was drawn to a critical study of the steam engine. Watt was employed at the time by the University of Glasgow as a skilled craftsman making scientific instruments. Called on to repair a Newcomen engine being used in a physics course, Watt saw that the Newcomen engine's great waste of energy could be reduced by adding a separate condenser. This splendid invention, patented in 1769, greatly increased the efficiency of the steam engine.

steam engines *A breakthrough invention by Thomas Savery in 1698 and Thomas Newcomen in 1705 in which coal was burned to produce steam, which was then used to operate a pump.*

Watt formed a partnership with a wealthy toymaker, who provided risk capital and a manufacturing plant. In England's craft tradition of locksmiths, tinsmiths, and mill-wrights, Watt found skilled mechanics who could install, regulate, and repair his so-phisticated engines. This support and more than twenty years of constant effort allowed him to create and regulate a complex engine. By the late 1780s the steam engine had become a practical and commercial success in England.

The steam engine of Watt and his followers was the Industrial Revolution's most fundamental advance in technology. For the first time in history, humanity had, at least for a few generations and without much serious thought about the environmental consequences, almost unlimited power at its disposal. For the first time inventors and engineers could devise and implement all kinds of power equipment to aid people in their work. For the first time abundance was at least a possibility for the world's ordinary men and women.

The steam engine was quickly put to use in several industries in England. It drained mines and began to replace waterpower in the cotton-spinning mills during the 1780s, contributing greatly to that industry's phenomenal rise. Steam also took the place of waterpower in flour mills, in the malt mills used in breweries, in the flint mills supplying the china industry, and in the mills exported by England to the West Indies to crush sugar cane.

Steam power promoted important breakthroughs in other industries. The English iron industry was radically transformed. The use of powerful steam-driven bellows in blast furnaces helped ironmakers switch over rapidly from limited charcoal to unlimited **coke** (which is made from coal) in the smelting of pig iron after 1770. In the 1780s Henry Cort developed the puddling furnace, which allowed pig iron to be refined in turn with coke. Strong, skilled ironworkers—the puddlers—"cooked" molten pig iron in a great vat, raking off globs of refined iron for further processing. Cort also

● **Manchester, England, 1851** The development of the steam engine enabled industry to concentrate in towns and cities. Manchester mushroomed from a town of 20,000 in 1750 into "Cottonopolis," cotton city, with 400,000 inhabitants in 1850. In this painting the artist contrasts the smoky city and its awesome power with the idealized beauty of the suburbs, where the new rich settled and built their mansions. *(The Royal Collection, © 2007 Her Majesty Queen Elizabeth II)*

coke *A form of coal that was unlimited in supply and therefore easier and better to use.*

● **James Nasmyth's Mighty Steam Hammer** Nasmyth's invention was the forerunner of the modern pile driver, and its successful introduction in 1832 epitomized the rapid development of steam power technology in Britain. In this painting by the inventor himself, workers manipulate a massive iron shaft being hammered into shape at Nasmyth's foundry near Manchester. *(Science & Society Picture Library, London)*

developed heavy-duty steam-powered rolling mills, which were capable of spewing out finished iron in every shape and form.

The economic consequence of these technical innovations was a great boom in the English iron industry. In 1740 annual British iron production was only 17,000 tons. With the spread of coke smelting and the first impact of Cort's inventions, production reached 68,000 tons in 1788, 125,000 tons in 1796, and 260,000 tons in 1806. In 1844 Britain produced 3 million tons of iron. This was a truly amazing expansion. Once scarce and expensive, iron became the cheap, basic, indispensable building block of the economy.

The Coming of the Railroads

Throughout western Europe the second half of the eighteenth century saw extensive construction of hard and relatively smooth roads, particularly in France before the Revolution. Yet it was passenger traffic that benefited most from this construction. Overland shipment of freight, relying solely on horsepower, was still quite limited and frightfully expensive. Shippers used rivers and canals for heavy freight whenever possible. It was logical, therefore, that inventors would try to apply steam power to transportation.

As early as 1800 an American ran a "steam engine on wheels" through city streets. Other experiments followed. In the 1820s English engineers created steam cars capable of carrying fourteen passengers at ten miles an hour—as fast as the mail coach. But the noisy, heavy steam automobiles frightened passing horses and damaged themselves as well as the roads with their vibrations. For the rest of the nineteenth century horses continued to reign on highways and city streets.

The coal industry had long been using plank roads and rails to move coal wagons within mines and at the surface. Thus once a rail capable of supporting a heavy locomotive was developed in 1816, all sorts of experiments with steam engines on rails went forward. In 1825 after ten years of work, George Stephenson built an effective locomotive. In 1830 his *Rocket* sped down the track of the just-completed Liverpool and Manchester Railway at sixteen miles per hour. The world's first important railroad, the line from Liverpool to Manchester was a financial as well as a technical success, and many private companies were quickly organized to build more rail lines. Within twenty years these companies had completed the main trunk lines of Great Britain. Other countries in Europe and North America were quick to follow.

The significance of the railroad was tremendous. The railroad dramatically reduced the cost and uncertainty of shipping freight overland. This advance had many economic consequences. Previously, markets had tended to be small and local. As the barrier of high transportation costs was lowered, markets became larger. These larger markets encouraged larger factories with more sophisticated machinery in a growing number of industries. Such factories could make goods more cheaply, and they gradually subjected most cottage workers and many urban artisans to severe competitive pressures.

In all countries the construction of railroads created a strong demand for unskilled labor and contributed to the growth of a class of urban workers. Many landless farm laborers and poor peasants went to build railroads. After the work was finished, many men drifted to towns in search of work. By the time they sent for their wives and sweethearts to join them, they had become urban workers.

The railroad changed the outlook and values of the entire society. The last and culminating invention of the Industrial Revolution, the railroad dramatically revealed the power and increased the speed of the new age. Racing down a track at sixteen miles per hour or, by 1850, at a phenomenal fifty miles per hour was a new and awesome experience. As a French economist put it after a ride on the Liverpool and Manchester in 1833, "There are certain impressions that one cannot put into words!"

Some great painters, notably Joseph M. W. Turner (1775–1851) and Claude Monet (1840–1926), succeeded in expressing this sense of power and awe. So did the

● **The Saltash Bridge**
Railroad construction presented innumerable challenges, such as the building of bridges to span rivers and gorges. Civil engineers responded with impressive feats, and their profession bounded ahead. This painting portrays the inauguration of I. K. Brunel's Saltash Bridge, where the railroad crosses the Tamar River into Cornwall in southwest England. The high spans allow large ships to pass underneath. *(Elton Collection, Ironbridge Gorge Museum Trust)*

● **The Crystal Palace** The Great Exhibition of 1851 attracted more than 6 million visitors, many of whom journeyed to London on the newly built railroads. Countries and companies from all over the world displayed their products and juries awarded prizes in the strikingly modern Crystal Palace, an architectural marvel built using the cheap iron and glass of the industrial age. In this illustration visitors stroll through the domed hall and peruse the 1,500 exhibits. *(British Museum/Laurie Platt Winfrey, Inc.)*

massive new train stations, the cathedrals of the industrial age. Leading railway engineers, whose tunnels pierced mountains and whose bridges spanned valleys, became public idols—the astronauts of their day. Everyday speech absorbed the images of railroading. After you got up a "full head of steam," you "highballed" along. And if you didn't "go off the track," you might "toot your own whistle." The railroad fired the imagination.

Industry and Population

Crystal Palace *The location of the Great Exhibition in 1851 in London; an architectural masterpiece made entirely of glass and iron, both of which were now cheap and abundant.*

In 1851 London was the site of a famous industrial fair. This Great Exhibition was held in the newly built **Crystal Palace,** an architectural masterpiece made entirely of glass and iron, both of which were now cheap and abundant. For the millions who visited, one fact stood out: the little island of Britain—England, Wales, and Scotland—was the "workshop of the world." It alone produced two-thirds of the world's coal and more than one-half of its iron and cotton cloth. More generally, it has been estimated that in 1860 Britain produced 20 percent of the entire world's output of industrial goods, whereas it had produced only about 2 percent of the world total in 1750.[4] Experiencing revolutionary industrial change, Britain became the first industrial nation (see Map 22.1).

As the British economy significantly increased its production of manufactured goods, the gross national product (GNP) rose roughly fourfold at constant prices between 1780 and 1851. In other words, the British people as a whole increased their wealth and their national income dramatically. At the same time, the population of Great Britain boomed, growing from about 9 million in 1780 to almost 21 million in 1851. Thus average consumption per person increased by only 75 percent between 1780 and 1851, as the growth in the total population ate up a large part of the fourfold increase in GNP in those years.[5]

Many economic historians now believe that rapid population growth in Great Britain was not harmful because it facilitated industrial expansion and provided a more mobile labor force. Contemporaries were much less optimistic. In his famous and influential *Essay on the Principle of Population* (1798), Thomas Malthus (1766–1834) argued that population would always tend to grow faster than the food supply. In Malthus's opinion the only hope of warding off harsh checks to population growth such as war, famine, and disease was "prudential restraint": young men and women

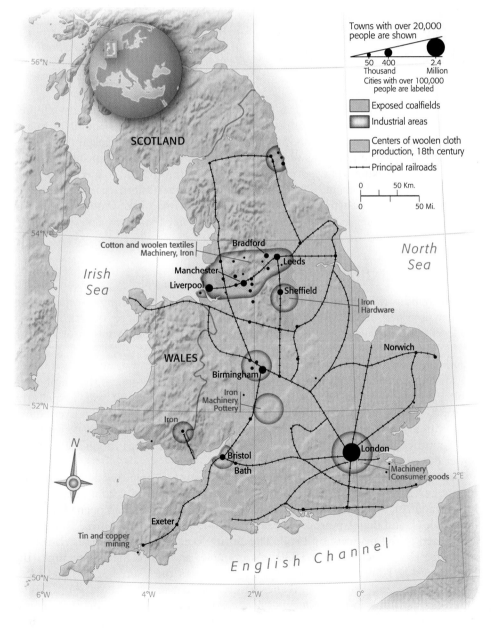

MAP 22.1 **The Industrial Revolution in England, ca. 1850** Industry concentrated in the rapidly growing cities of the north and the Midlands, where rich coal and iron deposits were in close proximity.

had to limit the growth of population by the old tried-and-true means of marrying late in life. But Malthus was not optimistic about this possibility. The powerful attraction of the sexes would cause most people to marry early and have many children.

Wealthy English stockbroker and leading economist David Ricardo (1772–1823) coldly spelled out the pessimistic implications of Malthus's thought. Ricardo's depressing **iron law of wages** posited that because of the pressure of population growth, wages would always sink to subsistence level—that is, wages would be just high enough to keep workers from starving. With Malthus and Ricardo setting the tone, economics was soon dubbed "the dismal science."

There was another problem with early industrialization. Perhaps workers, farmers, and ordinary people did not get their rightful share of the new wealth. Perhaps only the rich got richer while the poor got poorer or made no progress. We will turn to this great issue after looking at the process of industrialization in continental European countries in the nineteenth century.

iron law of wages *The rule that because of the pressure of population growth, wages would always sink to subsistence level, meaning that wages would be just high enough to keep workers from starving.*

INDUSTRIALIZATION IN CONTINENTAL EUROPE

How after 1815 did continental countries respond to the challenge of industrialization?

The new technologies developed in the British Industrial Revolution were adopted rather slowly by businesses in continental Europe, and there were uneven jerks and national (and regional) variations. Scholars are still struggling to explain these variations, especially since good answers may offer valuable lessons in our own time for poor countries seeking to improve their material condition through industrialization and economic development. The latest findings on the Western experience are encouraging. They suggest that there were alternative paths to the industrial world in the nineteenth century and that there was (and is) no need to follow a rigid, predetermined British model.

National Variations

European industrialization, like most economic developments, requires some statistical analysis as part of the effort to understand it. One important set of data compares the level of industrialization on a per capita basis in several countries from 1750 to 1913. These data are presented in Table 22.1 for closer study.

The table is a comparison of how much industrial product was available, on average, to each person in a given country in a given year. Therefore, all the numbers in Table 22.1 are expressed in terms of a single index number of 100, which equals the per capita level of industrial goods in Great Britain (and Ireland) in 1900. Every number is thus a percentage of the 1900 level in Great Britain and is directly comparable. The countries are listed in roughly the order in which they began to use large-scale, power-driven technology.

This quantitative overview of European industrialization confirms the primacy and relative rapidity of Britain's Industrial Revolution. In 1750 the leading countries of Europe and Asia were fairly close together. But by 1800 Britain had opened up a noticeable lead, and that gap progressively widened as the British Industrial Revolution accelerated to full maturity by 1860. The British level of per capita industrialization was twice the French level in 1830, for example, and more than three times the French level in 1860. All other large countries (except the United States) had fallen even further behind Britain than France had at both dates.

Second, variations in the timing and in the extent of industrialization in the continental powers and the United States are also apparent. Belgium, independent in 1831

Table 22.1   Per Capita Levels of Industrialization, 1750–1913

	1750	1800	1830	1860	1880	1900	1913
Great Britain	10	16	25	64	87	100	115
Belgium	9	10	14	28	43	56	88
United States	4	9	14	21	38	69	126
France	9	9	12	20	28	39	59
Germany	8	8	9	15	25	52	85
Austria-Hungary	7	7	8	11	15	23	32
Italy	8	8	8	10	12	17	26
Russia	6	6	7	8	10	15	20
China	8	6	6	4	4	3	3
India	7	6	6	3	2	1	2

Note: All entries are based on an index value of 100, equal to the per capita level of industrialization in Great Britain in 1900. Data for Great Britain are actually for the United Kingdom, thereby including Ireland with England, Wales, and Scotland.

Source: P. Bairoch, "International Industrialization Levels from 1750 to 1980," *Journal of European Economic History* 11 (Fall 1982): 294. Reprinted with permission.

and rich in iron and coal, led in adopting Britain's new technology. France developed factory production more gradually, although its pattern of early industrial growth was relatively good. In general, eastern and southern Europe began the process of modern industrialization later than northwestern and central Europe, as development in Austria-Hungary, Italy, and Russia suggests.

Third, Table 22.1 highlights the explosive rise of the United States and Germany to industrial prominence from 1880 to 1913, which is sometimes called the era of the Second Industrial Revolution. Thus in these years the United States and Germany led in the development of important new industries such as electricity, organic chemicals, petroleum, and automobiles. These new industries allowed the industrialized countries to continue rapid economic development as textiles and railroads became mature and slowed down.

Finally, all European states (as well as the United States, Canada, and Japan) managed to raise per capita industrial levels in the nineteenth century. These continent-wide increases stood in stark contrast to the large decreases that occurred at the same time in most non-Western countries, most notably China and India, as Table 22.1 shows. European countries industrialized to a greater or lesser extent even as most of the non-Western world *de*-industrialized. Thus differential rates of wealth- and power-creating industrial development greatly magnified growing inequalities between Europe and the rest of the world. We shall return to this momentous change in Chapters 24 and 25.

The Challenge of Industrialization

The different patterns of industrial development suggest that the process of industrialization was far from automatic. Indeed, building modern industry was an awesome challenge. When the pace of English industry began to accelerate in the 1780s, continental businesses began to adopt the new methods as they proved their profitability. English industry enjoyed clear superiority, but at first continental Europe was close behind. By 1815, however, the situation was quite different. In spite of wartime difficulties, English industry maintained the momentum of the 1780s and continued to grow and improve between 1789 and 1815. On the continent, the unending political and economic upheavals that began with the French Revolution disrupted trade, created runaway inflation, and impeded continental efforts to use new British machinery and technology. Thus economically and industrially France and the rest of Europe were further behind Britain in 1815 than in 1789.

This widening gap made it more difficult, if not impossible, for other countries to follow the British pattern in energy and industry after peace was restored in 1815. Above all, in the newly mechanized industries British goods were being produced very economically, and these goods had come to dominate world markets completely. Continental European firms had little hope of competing with mass-produced British goods in foreign markets for a long time. In addition, British technology had become so advanced and complicated that very few engineers or skilled technicians outside England understood it. Moreover, the technology of steam power had grown much more expensive. It involved large investments in the iron and coal industries and, after 1830, required the existence of railroads, which were very costly. Continental business people had great difficulty finding the large sums of money the new methods demanded, and there was a shortage of laborers accustomed to working in factories. Landowners and government officials were often so suspicious of the new form of industry and the changes it brought that they did little at first to encourage it. All these disadvantages slowed the spread of modern industry to continental Europe (see Map 22.2).

After 1815, however, continental countries also had at least three important advantages. First, most had a rich tradition of putting-out enterprise, merchant capitalists, and skilled urban artisans. Such a tradition gave firms in continental Europe the ability to adapt and survive in the face of new market conditions. Second, continental capitalists could simply "borrow" the advanced technology already developed in Great Britain, as well as engineers and some of the financial resources these countries lacked. European countries had a third asset that many non-Western areas lacked in the nineteenth century. They had strong independent governments that did not fall under foreign political control. These governments could fashion economic policies to serve their own interests.

Agents of Industrialization

The British realized the great value of their technical discoveries and tried to keep their secrets to themselves. Until 1825 it was illegal for artisans and skilled mechanics to leave Britain; until 1843 the export of textile machinery and other equipment was forbidden. Many talented, ambitious workers, however, slipped out of the country illegally and introduced the new methods abroad.

One such man was William Cockerill, a Lancashire carpenter. He and his sons began building cotton-spinning equipment in French-occupied Belgium in 1799. In 1817 the most famous son, John Cockerill, purchased the old summer palace of the deposed bishops of Liège in southern Belgium. Cockerill converted the palace into a large industrial enterprise that produced machinery, steam engines, and then railway locomotives. He also established modern ironworks and coal mines.

Many skilled British workers came illegally to work for Cockerill, and some went on to found their own companies throughout Europe. Newcomers brought the latest plans and secrets, so Cockerill could boast that ten days after an industrial advance occurred in Britain, he knew all about it in Belgium. Thus British technicians and skilled workers were a powerful force in the spread of early industrialization.

Talented entrepreneurs such as Fritz Harkort, a business pioneer in the German machinery industry, were a second agent of industrialization. Serving in England as a

Prussian army officer during the Napoleonic wars, Harkort concluded that Germany had to match English achievements as quickly as possible. Setting up shop in an abandoned castle in the still-tranquil Ruhr Valley, he felt an almost religious calling to build steam engines and become the "Watt of Germany."

Harkort's basic idea was simple but enormously difficult to carry out. Lacking skilled laborers to do the job, Harkort turned to England for experienced, though expensive, mechanics. He had to import from England the thick iron boilers that he needed at great cost. In spite of these problems, Harkort built and sold engines, winning fame and praise. His ambitious efforts over sixteen years also resulted in large financial losses for himself and his partners, and in 1832 his financial backers forced him out of his company. Harkort's career illustrates both the great efforts of a few important business leaders to duplicate the British achievement and the difficulty of the task.

Less famous entrepreneurs adopted factory technology slowly, and handicraft methods lived on. In France, for example, artisan production of luxury items grew, as the rising income of the international middle class created foreign demand for silk scarves, embroidered needlework, perfumes, and fine wines.

A third force for industrialization was government, which often helped business people in European countries to overcome some of their difficulties. **Tariff protection** was one such support. And after 1815 continental governments bore the cost of building roads and canals to improve transportation. They also bore to a significant

tariff protection *A government's way of supporting and aiding its own economy by laying high tariffs on the cheaper goods imported from another country.*

MAP 22.2 **Continental European Industrialization, ca. 1850** Although continental countries were beginning to make progress by 1850, they still lagged far behind Britain. For example, continental railroad building was still in an early stage, whereas the British rail system was essentially complete.

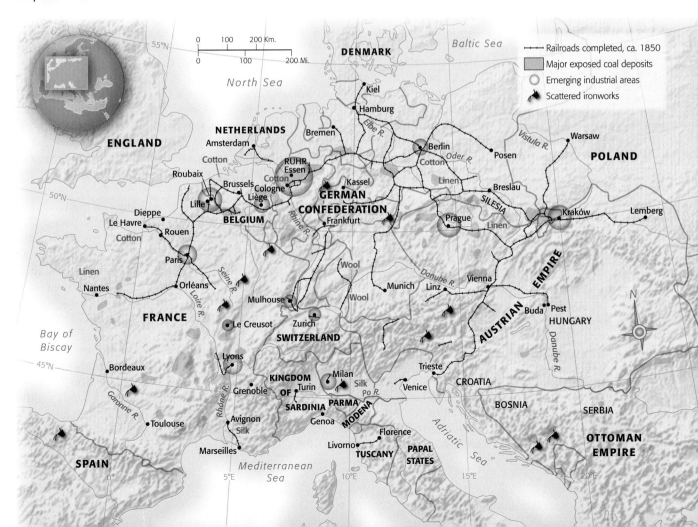

● **A German Ironworks, 1845** This big business enterprise, the Borsig ironworks in Berlin, mastered the new British method of smelting iron ore with coke. Germany, and especially the state of Prussia, was well endowed with both iron and coal, and the rapid exploitation of these resources after 1840 transformed a poor agricultural country into an industrial powerhouse. *(akg-images)*

economic nationalism *The idea that countries should protect and foster their own businesses by imposing high protective tariffs on imported goods as well as eliminating tariffs within the country.*

extent the cost of building railroads, the all-important leading sector in continental industrialization.

The career of German journalist and thinker Friedrich List (1789–1846) reflects government's greater role in industrialization on the European continent than in England. List considered the growth of modern industry of the utmost importance because manufacturing was a primary means of increasing people's well-being and relieving their poverty. Moreover, List was a dedicated nationalist who believed that an agricultural nation was not only poor but also weak, increasingly unable to defend itself and maintain its political independence. To promote industry was to defend the nation.

The practical policies that List focused on were railroad building and the tariff. List supported the formation of a customs union, or *Zollverein*, among the separate German states. Such a tariff union came into being in 1834. It allowed goods to move without tariffs between the German member states. A single uniform tariff was erected against all other nations to help infant industries to develop. List denounced the English doctrine of free trade as little more than England's attempt "to make the rest of the world, like the Hindus, its serfs in all industrial and commercial relations." By the 1840s List's **economic nationalism** had become increasingly popular in Germany, the United States, and elsewhere.

Banks, like governments, also played a larger and more creative role in continental countries than in England. Previously, almost all banks in Europe had been private partnerships. All the active partners were liable for all the debts of the firm. This unlimited liability meant that in the event of a disastrous bankruptcy each partner could lose all of his or her personal wealth. Such banks were content to deal with a few rich clients and a few big merchants. They generally avoided industrial investment as being too risky.

In the 1830s two important Belgian banks pioneered in a new direction, establishing themselves as corporations enjoying limited liability. A stockholder in these two banks could lose only his or her original investment in the bank's common stock. Able to attract many shareholders, large and small, because of the reduced risk, these Belgian banks mobilized impressive resources for investment in big industrial companies. They became industrial banks and successfully promoted industrial development.

Similar corporate banks became important in France and Germany in the 1850s and 1860s. Usually working in collaboration with governments, they established and developed many railroads and many companies working in heavy industry, which were increasingly organized as limited-liability corporations.

The combined efforts of skilled workers, entrepreneurs, governments, and industrial banks meshed successfully between 1850 and the financial crash of 1873. In Belgium, Germany, and France, key indicators of modern industrial development—railway mileage, iron and coal production, and steam-engine capacity—increased at average annual rates ranging from 5 to 10 percent compounded. In the early 1870s Britain was still Europe's most industrial nation, but a select handful of countries was closing the gap that had been opened up by the Industrial Revolution.

· · · · · · · · · · · ·

CAPITAL AND LABOR

How did the Industrial Revolution affect social classes, the standard of living, and working conditions?

Industrial development brought new social relations and intensified long-standing problems between capital and labor. A new group of factory owners and industrial capitalists arose. These men and women and their families strengthened the wealth and size of the middle class, which had previously been made up mainly of merchants and professional people. The nineteenth century became the golden age of the European middle class. Modern industry also created a much larger group: the factory workers. For the first time large numbers of men, women, and children came together under one roof to work with complicated machinery for a single owner or a few partners in large companies.

The growth of new occupational groups in industry stimulated new thinking about social relations. It was argued, with considerable success, that individuals were members of economically determined classes that had conflicting interests. Accordingly, the comfortable, well-educated "public" of eighteenth-century Europe came increasingly to see itself as the backbone of the middle class (or the middle classes), and the "people" gradually transformed themselves into the modern working class (or working classes). The new class interpretation appealed to many because it seemed to explain what was happening. Thus conflicting classes came into being in part because many individuals came to believe that they existed and developed an appropriate sense of class feeling—what Marxists call **class-consciousness**.

class-consciousness *Conflicting classes existed, in part, because many individuals came to believe they existed and developed an appropriate sense of class feeling.*

The New Class of Factory Owners

Early industrialists operated in a highly competitive economic system in which success and large profits were by no means certain. Manufacturers waged a constant battle to cut their production costs and stay afloat. "Dragged on by the frenzy of this terrible life," according to one of the dismayed critics, the struggling manufacturer had "no time for niceties. He must conquer or die, make a fortune or drown himself."[6]

The early industrialists came from a variety of backgrounds. Many, such as Harkort, were from well-established merchant families, but artisans and skilled workers of exceptional ability had unparalleled opportunities. The ethnic and religious groups that had been discriminated against in the traditional occupations controlled by the landed aristocracy jumped at the new chances. Quakers and Scots were tremendously important in England; Protestants and Jews dominated banking in Catholic France.

As factories grew larger, opportunities declined, at least in well-developed industries. It became considerably harder for a gifted but poor young mechanic to end up as a wealthy manufacturer. Formal education became more important as a means of advancement, and formal education at the advanced level was expensive. In England by 1830 and in France and Germany by 1860, leading industrialists were more likely to have inherited their well-established enterprises, and they were financially much more secure than their fathers and grandfathers had been. They also had a greater sense of class-consciousness, fully aware that ongoing industrial development had widened the gap between themselves and their workers.

The wives and daughters of successful businessmen also found fewer opportunities for active participation in Europe's increasingly complex business world. Rather than contributing as vital partners in family-owned enterprises, as so many middle-class women such as Elizabeth Strutt had done (see the feature "Individuals in Society: The Strutt Family"), these women were increasingly valued for their ladylike gentility. By 1850 some influential women writers and most businessmen assumed that middle-class wives and daughters should steer clear of undignified work in offices and factories. Rather, a middle-class lady should protect and enhance her femininity, concentrating on her proper role as wife and mother.

The New Factory Workers

The social consequences of the Industrial Revolution have long been hotly debated. The condition of English workers during the transformation has always generated the most controversy among historians because England was the first country to industrialize and because the social consequences seemed harshest there. Before 1850 other countries had not proceeded very far with industrialization, and almost everyone agrees that the economic conditions of European workers improved after 1850. Thus the experience of English workers to about 1850 deserves special attention. (Industrial growth also promoted rapid urbanization, with its own awesome problems, as will be shown in Chapter 23.)

From the beginning the Industrial Revolution in England had its critics. Among the first were the romantic poets. William Blake (1757–1827) called the early factories "satanic mills" and protested against the hard life of the London poor. William Wordsworth (1770–1850) lamented the destruction of the rural way of life and the pollution of the land and water. Some handicraft workers—notably the **Luddites,** who attacked whole factories in northern England in 1812 and after—smashed the new machines, which they believed were putting them out of work. Doctors and reformers wrote eloquently of problems in the factories and new towns, and Malthus and Ricardo concluded that workers would earn only enough to stay alive.

Friedrich Engels (1820–1895), the future revolutionary and colleague of Karl Marx, accepted and reinforced this pessimistic view. After studying conditions in northern England, this young middle-class German published in 1844 *The Condition of the Working Class in England.* "At the bar of world opinion," he wrote, "I charge the English middle classes with mass murder, wholesale robbery, and all the other crimes in the calendar." The new poverty of industrial workers was worse than the old poverty of cottage workers and agricultural laborers, according to Engels, and the culprit was industrial capitalism. Engels's extremely influential charge of middle-class exploitation and increasing worker poverty was embellished by Marx and later socialists.

Meanwhile, other observers believed that conditions were improving for the working people. Edwin Chadwick, a conscientious government official well acquainted with the problems of the working population, concluded that the "laboring community" was increasingly able "to buy more of the necessities and minor luxuries of life."[7] Nevertheless, if all the contemporary assessments had been counted up, those

Luddites *Followers of Ned Ludd; a social movement in protest against the industrial revolution that began in northern England in 1812. These handicraft workers attacked the new machines being brought in by the factory owners, which they believed were taking their jobs.*

Individuals IN SOCIETY

The Strutt Family

For centuries economic life in Europe revolved around hundreds of thousands of small family enterprises. These family enterprises worked farms, crafted products, and traded goods. They built and operated the firms and factories of the early industrial era, with the notable exceptions of the capital-hungry railroads and a few big banks. Indeed, until late in the nineteenth century, close-knit family groups continued to control most successful businesses, including those organized as corporations.

One successful and fairly well-documented family enterprise began with the marriage of Jedediah Strutt (1726–1797) and Elizabeth Woollat (1729–1774) in Derbyshire in northern England in 1755. The son of a farmer, Jedediah fell in love with Elizabeth when he was apprenticed away from home as a wheelwright and lodged with her parents. Both young people grew up in the close-knit dissenting Protestant community, which did not accept the doctrines of the state-sponsored Church of England, and the well-educated Elizabeth worked in a local school for dissenters and then for a dissenter minister in London. Indecisive and self-absorbed, Jedediah inherited in 1754 a small stock of animals from an uncle and finally married Elizabeth the following year.

Aided by Elizabeth, who was "obviously a very capable woman" and who supplied some of the drive her husband had previously lacked, Jedediah embarked on a new career.* He invented a machine to make handsome, neat-fitting ribbed silk stockings, which had previously been made by hand. He secured a patent, despite strong opposition from competitors, and went into production. Elizabeth helped constantly in the enterprise, which was nothing less than an informal partnership between husband and wife.†

In 1757, for example, when Jedediah was fighting to uphold his patent in the local court, Elizabeth left her son of nine months and journeyed to London to seek a badly needed loan from her former employer.

Jedediah Strutt (ca. 1790), by Joseph Wright of Derby. *(Derby Museum & Art Gallery/The Bridgeman Art Library)*

She also canvassed her London relatives and dissenter friends for orders for stockings and looked for sales agents and sources of capital. Elizabeth's letters reveal a detailed knowledge of ribbed stockings and the prices and quality of different kinds of thread. The family biographers, old-line economic historians writing without a trace of feminist concerns, conclude that her husband "owed much of his success to her energy and counsel." Elizabeth was always "active in the business—a partner in herself."‡ Historians have often overlooked such invaluable contributions from wives like Elizabeth, partly because the legal rights and consequences of partnership were denied to married women in Britain and Europe in the eighteenth and nineteenth centuries.

The Strutt enterprise grew and gradually prospered, but it always retained its family character. The firm built a large silk mill and then went into cotton spinning in partnership with Richard Arkwright, the inventor of the water frame (see page 648). The brothers of both Jedediah and Elizabeth worked for the firm, and their eldest daughter worked long hours in the warehouse. Bearing three sons, Elizabeth fulfilled yet another vital task because the typical family firm looked to its own members for managers and continued success. All three sons entered the business and became cotton textile magnates. Elizabeth never saw these triumphs. The loyal and talented wife in the family partnership died suddenly at age forty-five while in London with Jedediah on a business trip.

Questions for Analysis

1. How and why did the Strutts succeed?
2. What does Elizabeth's life tell us about the role of British women in the early Industrial Revolution?

---

*R. Fitton and A Wadsworth, *The Strutts and the Arkwrights, 1758–1830: A Study of the Early Factory System* (Manchester, England: Manchester University Press, 1958), p. 23.

†See the excellent discussion by C. Hall, "Strains in the 'Firm of Wife, Children and Friends'? Middle-Class Women and Employment in Early Nineteenth-Century England," in P. Hudson and W. Lee, eds., *Women's Work and the Family Economy in Historical Perspective* (Manchester, England: Manchester University Press, 1990), pp. 106–132.

‡Fitton and Wadsworth, *The Strutts,* pp. 110–111.

who thought conditions were getting worse for working people would probably have been the majority.

Scholarly statistical studies have weakened the idea that the condition of the English working class got much worse with industrialization. But more recent studies also confirm the view that the early years of the Industrial Revolution were hard ones for British workers. From about 1780 to about 1820 there was little or no increase in the purchasing power of the average British worker's wages. The years from 1792 to 1815, a period of almost constant warfare with France, were particularly difficult. Food prices rose faster than wages, and the living conditions of the laboring poor declined. Only after 1820, and especially after 1840, did real wages rise substantially. The average worker earned and consumed roughly 50 percent more in real terms in 1850 than in 1770.[8] In short, there was considerable economic improvement for workers throughout Great Britain by 1850, but that improvement was hard won and slow in coming.

At the same time the hours in the average workweek increased. To a large extent, workers earned more simply because they worked more. Thus England nonagricultural workers labored about 250 days per year in 1760 as opposed to 300 days per year in 1830, while the normal workday remained an exhausting eleven hours throughout the entire period. In 1760 nonagricultural workers still observed many religious and public holidays by not working. However, these days of leisure and relaxation declined rapidly after 1760, and by 1830 nonagricultural workers had generally joined landless agricultural laborers in toiling six rather than five days a week.[9]

Another way to consider the workers' standard of living is to look at the goods they purchased. Again the evidence is somewhat contradictory. Speaking generally, workers ate somewhat more food of higher nutritional quality as the Industrial Revolution progressed, except during wartime, and diets became more varied. Clothing improved, but housing for working people probably deteriorated somewhat. In short, per capita use of specific goods supports the position that the standard of living of the English working classes rose, at least moderately, after the long wars with France.

Conditions of Work

What about working conditions? Did workers eventually earn more only at the cost of working longer and harder? Were workers exploited harshly by the new factory owners? The first factories were cotton mills, which began functioning along rivers and streams in the 1770s. Cottage workers were reluctant to work in factories even when they received relatively good wages. In the factory, workers had to keep up with the machine and follow its tempo. They had to show up every day and work long, monotonous hours, adjusting their daily lives to the shrill call of the factory whistle. Cottage workers were not used to that kind of life and discipline. All members of the family worked hard and long, but in spurts, setting their own pace. They could interrupt their work when they wanted to. Women and children could break up their long hours of spinning with other tasks.

Also, early factories resembled English poorhouses, where totally destitute people went to live at public expense. Some poorhouses were industrial prisons where the inmates had to work in order to receive their food and lodging. The similarity between large brick factories and large stone poorhouses increased the cottage workers' fear of factories and their hatred of factory discipline.

It was cottage workers' reluctance to work in factories that prompted the early cotton mill owners to turn to abandoned and pauper children for their labor. These owners contracted with local officials to employ large numbers of these children, who were apprenticed as young as five or six years of age and who were forced by law to labor for their "master" for as many as fourteen years. Housed, fed, and locked up nightly in factory dormitories, the young workers received little or no pay. Hours were appalling—commonly thirteen or fourteen hours a day, six days a week. Harsh

● **Ford Maddox Brown: Work**   This midcentury painting provides a rich visual representation of the new concepts of social class that became common by 1850. The central figures are the colorful laborers, endowed by the artist with strength and nobility. Close by, a poor girl minds her brother and sister for her working mother. On the right, a middle-class minister and a social critic observe and do intellectual work. What work does the couple on horseback perform? *(Birmingham Museums and Art Gallery/The Bridgeman Art Library)*

physical punishment maintained strict discipline. This unprecedented wholesale exploitation ultimately stirred the conscience of reformers and encouraged more humanitarian attitudes toward children and their labor.

By 1790 the early pattern was rapidly changing. The use of pauper apprentices was in decline, and in 1802 it was forbidden by Parliament. Many more factories were being built, mainly in urban areas, where they could use steam power rather than waterpower and attract a workforce more easily than in the countryside. People came from near and far to work in the cities, both as factory workers and as laborers, builders, and domestic servants. Yet as they took these new jobs, working people did not simply give in to a system of labor that had formerly repelled them. Rather, they helped modify the system by carrying over old, familiar working traditions.

For one thing, they often came to the mills and the mines as family units. This was how they had worked on farms and in cottage industry. The mill or mine owner paid the head of the family for the work of the whole family. In the cotton mills children worked for their mothers or fathers, collecting wastes and "piecing" broken threads together. In the mines children sorted coal, mothers pulled coal wagons through narrow tunnels, and fathers hewed with pick and shovel at the face of the seam.

The preservation of the family as an economic unit in the factories from the 1790s on made the new surroundings more tolerable, both in Great Britain and in other countries. Parents disciplined their children and directed their upbringing. The presence of the whole family meant that children and adults worked the same long hours (twelve-hour shifts were normal in cotton mills in 1800). Only when technical changes threatened to place control and discipline in the hands of impersonal managers and foremen did adult workers protest against inhuman conditions in the name of their children.

Some enlightened employers and social reformers in Parliament definitely felt otherwise. They argued that more humane standards were necessary, and they used widely circulated parliamentary reports to influence public opinion. (See the feature "Listening to the Past: The Testimony of Young Mine Workers" on pages 672–673.) For example, Robert Owen (1771–1858), a very successful manufacturer in Scotland, testified in 1816 before an investigating committee on the basis of his experience. He stated that "very strong facts" demonstrated that employing children under ten years of age as factory workers was "injurious to the children, and not beneficial to the proprietors."[10] Workers also provided graphic testimony at such hearings as the reformers pressed Parliament to pass corrective laws. They scored some important successes.

Their first major accomplishment was the **Factory Act of 1833**. It limited the factory workday for children between the ages of nine and thirteen to eight hours and that of adolescents between fourteen and eighteen to twelve hours, although the act made no effort to regulate the hours of work for children at home or in small businesses. The law also prohibited the factory employment of children under nine; they were to be enrolled in the elementary schools that factory owners were required to establish. The employment of children declined rapidly. Thus the Factory Act broke the pattern of whole families working together in the factory.

Factory Act of 1833 *An act that limited the factory workday for children between nine and thirteen years of age to eight hours and that of adolescents between fourteen and eighteen years of age to twelve hours.*

The Sexual Division of Labor

The era of the Industrial Revolution witnessed major changes in the sexual division of labor. In preindustrial Europe certain jobs were traditionally defined by gender—women and girls for milking and spinning, men and boys for plowing and weaving—but many tasks might go to either sex as particular circumstances dictated. Family employment carried over into early factories and subcontracting, but it collapsed as child labor was restricted and new attitudes emerged. A different sexual division of labor gradually arose to take its place. The man emerged as the family's primary wage earner, and the woman found only limited job opportunities. Generally denied good jobs at good wages in the growing urban economy, women were expected to concentrate on unpaid housework, child care, and craftwork at home.

This new pattern of "separate spheres" had several aspects. First, married women were much less likely to work full-time for wages outside the house after the first child arrived, although they often earned small amounts doing putting-out handicrafts at home and taking in boarders. Second, married women who did work for wages outside the house usually came from the poorest families, where the husbands were poorly paid, sick, unemployed, or missing. Third, these poor married (or widowed) women were joined by legions of young unmarried women, who worked full-time but only in certain jobs. Fourth, all women were generally confined to low-paying, dead-end jobs. Virtually no occupation open to women paid a wage sufficient for a person to live independently. Evolving gradually but largely in place by 1850, the new sexual division of labor in Britain constituted a major development in the history of women and of the family.

Although the reorganization of paid work along gender lines is widely recognized, there is as yet no agreement on its causes. One school of scholars sees little connection with industrialization and finds the answer in the deeply ingrained sexist attitudes of a "patriarchal tradition," which predated the economic transformation. These scholars stress the role of male-dominated craft unions in denying women access to good jobs

● **Workers at a Large Cotton Mill**   This 1833 engraving shows adult women operating power looms under the supervision of a male foreman, and it accurately reflects both the decline of family employment and the emergence of a gender-based division of labor in many English factories. The jungle of belts and shafts connecting the noisy looms to the giant steam engine on the ground floor created a constant din. *(Time Life Pictures/Getty Images)*

and relegating them to unpaid housework. Other scholars, stressing that the gender roles of women and men can vary enormously with time and culture, look more to a combination of economic and biological factors to explain the emergence of a sex-segregated division of labor.

Three ideas stand out in this more recent interpretation. First, the new and unfamiliar discipline of the clock and the machine was especially hard on married women. Above all, relentless factory discipline conflicted with child care in a way that labor on the farm or in the cottage had not done. A woman operating ear-splitting spinning machinery could mind a child of seven or eight working beside her (until such work was outlawed), but she could no longer pace herself through pregnancy or breast-feed her baby on the job. Thus a working-class woman had strong incentives to concentrate on child care within her home if her family could afford for her to do so.

Second, running a working-class household in conditions of primitive urban poverty was an extremely demanding job in its own right. There were no supermarkets or public transportation. Everything had to be done on foot. Shopping and feeding the family constituted a never-ending challenge. The woman marched from one tiny shop to another, dragging her tired children and struggling valiantly with heavy sacks and tricky shopkeepers. Yet another brutal job outside the house—a "second shift"—had limited appeal for the average married woman. Thus women might well have accepted the emerging division of labor as the best available strategy for family survival in the industrializing society.[11]

Third, why were the women who did work for wages outside the home segregated and confined to certain "women's jobs"? No doubt the desire of men to monopolize the best opportunities and hold women down provides part of the answer. But as some feminist scholars have argued, sex-segregated employment was also a collective response to the new industrial system. The growth of factories and mines brought unheard-of opportunities for girls and boys to mix on the job, free of familial supervision. Continuing to mix after work, they were "more likely to form liaisons, initiate courtships, and respond to advances."[12] Such intimacy also led to more unplanned pregnancies and fueled the illegitimacy explosion that had begun in Europe in the late eighteenth-century and that gathered force until at least 1850. Thus segregation of jobs by gender was partly an effort by older people to help control the sexuality of working-class youths.

Investigations into the British coal industry before 1842 provide a graphic example of this concern.(See the feature "Listening to the Past: The Testimony of Young Mine Workers" on pages 672–673). The middle-class men leading the inquiry often failed to appreciate the physical effort of the girls and women who dragged the carts of coal along narrow underground passages. But they professed horror at the sight of girls and women working without shirts, which was a common practice because of the heat, and they quickly assumed the prevalence of licentious sex with the male miners, who also wore very little clothing. In fact, most girls and married women worked in the coal mines for related males in a family unit that provided considerable protection and restraint. Yet many witnesses from the working class also stressed particularly the danger of sexual aggression in letting girls work past puberty. As one miner explained, "I consider it a scandal for girls to work in the pits. Till they are 12 or 14 they may work very well but after that it's an abomination. . . . The work of the pit does not hurt them, it is the effect on their morals that I complain of."[13] The **Mines Act of 1842** prohibited underground work for all women as well as for boys under ten.

Some women who had to support themselves protested against being excluded from coal mining, which paid higher wages than most other jobs open to women. But the girls and the women who had worked underground were generally pleased with the law if they were part of families that could manage economically. In explaining her satisfaction in 1844, one mother of four provided real insight into why many women accepted the emerging sexual division of labor:

While working in the pit I was worth to my [miner] husband seven shillings a week, out of which we had to pay 2½ shillings to a woman for looking after the younger children. I used to take them to her house at 4 o'clock in the morning, out of their own beds, to put them into hers. Then there was one shilling a week for washing; besides, there was mending to pay for, and other things. The house was not guided. The other children broke things; they did not go to school when they were sent; they would be playing about, and get ill-used by other children, and their clothes torn. Then when I came home in the evening, everything was to do after the day's labor, and I was so tired I had no heart for it; no fire lit, nothing cooked, no water fetched, the house dirty, and nothing comfortable for my husband. It is all far better now, and I wouldn't go down again.[14]

The Early Labor Movement

Many kinds of employment changed slowly during and after the Industrial Revolution in Great Britain. In 1850 more British people still worked on farms than in any other occupation. The second largest occupation was domestic service, with more than a million household servants, 90 percent of whom were women. Thus many old, familiar

Mines Act of 1842 *The act that prohibited underground work for all women as well as for boys under ten.*

jobs outside industry lived on and provided alternatives for individual workers. This helped ease the transition to industrial civilization.

Within industry itself the pattern of artisans working with hand tools in small shops remained unchanged in many trades, even as technological change revolutionized some others. For example, as in the case of cotton and coal, large-scale capitalist firms completely dominated the British iron industry by 1850. Yet the firms that fashioned iron into small metal goods—such as tools, tableware, and toys—employed on average fewer than ten wage workers, who used time-honored handicraft skills. The survival of small workshops in some handicraft industries gave many workers an alternative to factory employment.

In Great Britain and in other countries later on, workers gradually built a labor movement to improve working conditions and to serve their needs. In 1799, partly in panicked reaction to the French Revolution, Parliament had passed the Combination Acts outlawing unions and strikes. These acts were widely disregarded by workers. Societies of skilled factory workers organized unions, as printers, papermakers, carpenters, and other such craftsmen had long since done. The unions sought to control the number of skilled workers, limit apprenticeship to members' own children, and bargain with owners over wages. They were not afraid to strike; there was, for example, a general strike of adult cotton spinners in Manchester in 1810. In the face of widespread union activity Parliament repealed the Combination Acts in 1824, and unions were tolerated though not fully accepted after 1825.

The next stage in the development of the British trade-union movement was the attempt to create a single large national union. This effort was led not so much by working people as by social reformers such as Robert Owen. Owen, the self-made cotton manufacturer quoted earlier, had pioneered in industrial relations by combining firm discipline with concern for the health, safety, and hours of his workers. After 1815 he experimented with cooperative and socialist communities, including one at New Harmony, Indiana. Then in 1834 Owen organized one of the largest and most visionary of the early national unions, the **Grand National Consolidated Trades Union.** When this and other grandiose schemes collapsed, the British labor movement moved once again after 1851 in the direction of craft unions. The most famous of these "new model unions" was the Amalgamated Society of Engineers. These unions won real benefits for members by fairly conservative means and thus became an accepted part of the industrial scene.

British workers also engaged in direct political activity in defense of their own interests. After the collapse of Owen's national trade union, many working people went into the Chartist movement, whose goal was political democracy. The key Chartist demand—that all men be given the right to vote—became the great hope of millions of aroused people. Workers were also active in campaigns to limit the workday in factories to ten hours and to permit duty-free importation of wheat into Great Britain to secure cheap bread. Thus working people developed a sense of their own identity and played an active role in shaping the new industrial system. Clearly, they were neither helpless victims nor passive beneficiaries.

● **Celebrating Skilled Labor**   This handsome engraving embellished the membership certificate of the British carpenters union, one of the "new model unions" that represented skilled workers effectively after 1850. The upper panel shows carpenters building the scaffolding for a great arch; the lower panel captures the spirit of a busy workshop. *(HIP/Art Resource, NY)*

Grand National Consolidated Trades Union   *Organized by Owen in 1834, this was one of the largest and most visionary early national unions.*

Chapter Summary

Key Terms

Industrial Revolution
agricultural revolution
open-field system
common rights
enclosure
proletarianization
mercantilism
spinning jenny
water frame
body linen
steam engines
coke
Crystal Palace
iron law of wages
tariff protection
economic nationalism
class-consciousness
Luddites
Factory Act of 1833
Mines Act of 1842
Grand National
   Consolidated Trades Union

To assess your mastery of this chapter, go to
bedfordstmartins.com/mckayworld

• *What were the origins of the Industrial Revolution in England?*

England's industrial breakthrough grew out of a long process of economic and social change in which the rise of capitalism, overseas expansion, and the growth of rural industry stood out as critical preparatory developments. Profiting also from stable government, agricultural improvement, a flexible labor force, and a growing demand for its products, England created a new system of factory production for cotton textiles in the 1780s. In doing so, England launched an epoch-making transformation known as the Industrial Revolution.

• *What changes in England revolutionized the provision of energy and transportation?*

Building on Watt's invention and development of the modern steam engine, England obtained abundant energy for the first time in history. Abundant energy encouraged factory production, transformed the iron and coal industries, and powered the railroads that revolutionized transportation. The island of Britain—England, Scotland, and Wales—became the "workshop of the world," producing 20 percent of the world's industrial goods in 1860.

• *How after 1815 did continental countries respond to the challenge of industrialization?*

In 1815 continental European countries lagged well behind Britain in industrialization, and they faced major obstacles to catching up. Only gradually did business initiatives, protective tariffs, economic nationalism, and industrial banks combine to bring major results. Only in the 1840s did railroad construction begin to create the strong demand for iron, coal, and railway equipment that speeded up the process of industrial growth in the 1850s and 1860s.

• *How did the Industrial Revolution affect social classes, the standard of living, and working conditions?*

The rise of modern industry intensified long-standing problems between capital and labor and promoted class feeling. Improvements in the average standard of living came slowly, but they were substantial by 1850. Industrialization fostered new attitudes toward child labor, encouraged protective factory legislation, and called forth an assertive labor movement with a strong sense of class consciousness. The era of industrial transformation also promoted within the family a more rigid division of roles and responsibilities that severely restricted women socially and economically, another gradual but profound change of revolutionary proportions.

Suggested Reading

Cameron, Rondo, and Larry Neal. *A Concise Economic History of the World,* 4th ed. 2003. Provides an introduction to key issues related to global industrialization and has a carefully annotated bibliography.

Davidoff, Leonore, and Catherine Hall. *Family Fortunes: Men and Women of the English Middle Class, 1750–1850,* rev. ed. 2003. Examines both economic and cultural beliefs with great skill.

Fuchs, Rachel G. *Gender and Poverty in Nineteenth Century Europe.* 2005. Provides a broad comparative perspective.

Gaskell, Elizabeth. *Mary Barton.* 1848. Gaskell's famous novel, which offers a realistic contemporary portrayal of social conflicts in the new industrial society.

Goodman, Jordan, and Katrina Honeyman. *Gainful Pursuits: The Making of Industrial Europe, 1600–1914.* 1988. An excellent general treatment of European industrial growth in long-term perspective.

Landes, David. *Dynasties: Fortunes and Misfortunes of the World's Great Family Businesses.* 2006. Fascinating and insightful histories of famous enterprises and leading capitalists in global perspective.

Pomeranz, Kenneth. *The Great Divergence: China, Europe, and the Making of the Modern World Economy.* 2000. A sophisticated reconsideration of why western Europe underwent industrialization and China did not.

Stearns, Peter N. *The Industrial Revolution in World History,* 3d ed. 2007. A helpful short survey.

Valenze, Deborah. *The First Industrial Woman.* 1995. A lively gender study that reinvigorates the debate about the consequences of industrialization for women in Great Britain.

Wrigley, E. A. *Continuity, Chance and Change: The Character of the Industrial Revolution in England.* 1994. An important reconsideration stressing resources and population growth.

Notes

1. N. F. R. Crafts, *British Economic Growth During the Industrial Revolution* (Oxford: Oxford University Press, 1985), p. 32. These estimates are for Great Britain as a whole.

2. B. H. Slicher van Bath, *The Agrarian History of Western Europe, A.D. 500–1850* (New York: St. Martin's Press, 1963), p. 240.

3. Quoted in P. Mantoux, *The Industrial Revolution in the Eighteenth Century* (New York: Harper & Row, 1961), p. 75.

4. P. Bairoch, "International Industrialization Levels from 1750 to 1980," *Journal of European Economic History* 11 (Spring 1982): 269–333.

5. Crafts, *British Economic Growth During the Industrial Revolution,* pp. 45, 95–102.

6. J. Michelet, *The People,* trans. with an introduction by J. P. McKay (Urbana: University of Illinois Press, 1973; original publication, 1846), p. 64.

7. Quoted in W. A. Hayek, ed., *Capitalism and the Historians* (Chicago: University of Chicago Press, 1954), p. 126.

8. Crafts, *British Economic Growth During the Industrial Revolution,* p. 95.

9. H.-J. Voth, *Time and Work in England, 1750–1830* (Oxford: Oxford University Press, 2000), pp. 268–270; also pp. 118–133.

10. Quoted in E. R. Pike, *"Hard Times": Human Documents of the Industrial Revolution* (New York: Praeger, 1966), p. 109.

11. See especially J. Brenner and M. Rama, "Rethinking Women's Oppression," *New Left Review* 144 (March–April 1984): 33–71, and sources cited there.

12. J. Humphries, ". . . 'The Most Free from Objection' . . . : The Sexual Division of Labor and Women's Work in Nineteenth-Century England," *Journal of Economic History* 47 (December 1987): 948.

13. Ibid., p. 941; Pike, *"Hard Times,"* p. 266.

14. Quoted in Pike, *"Hard Times,"* p. 208.

Listening to the PAST

The Testimony of Young Mine Workers

The use of child labor in British industrialization quickly attracted the attention of humanitarians and social reformers. This interest led to investigations by parliamentary commissions, which resulted in laws limiting the hours and the ages of children working in large factories. Designed to build a case for remedial legislation, parliamentary inquiries gave large numbers of workers a rare chance to speak directly to contemporaries and to historians.

The moving passages that follow are taken from testimony gathered in 1841 and 1842 by the Ashley Mines Commission. Interviewing employers and many male and female workers, the commissioners focused on the physical condition of the youth and on the sexual behavior of workers far underground. The subsequent Mines Act of 1842 sought to reduce immoral behavior and sexual bullying by prohibiting underground work for all women (and for boys younger than ten).

Mr. Payne, coal master:

That children are employed generally at nine years old in the coal pits and sometimes at eight. In fact, the smaller the vein of coal is in height, the younger and smaller are the children required; the work occupies from six to seven hours per day in the pits; they are not ill-used or worked beyond their strength; a good deal of depravity exists but they are certainly not worse in morals than in other branches of the Sheffield trade, but upon the whole superior; the morals of this district are materially improving; Mr. Bruce, the clergyman, has been zealous and active in endeavoring to ameliorate their moral and religious education. . . .

Ann Eggley, hurrier, 18 years old:

I'm sure I don't know how to spell my name. We go at four in the morning, and sometimes at half-past four. We begin to work as soon as we get down. We get out after four, sometimes at five, in the evening. We work the whole time except an hour for dinner, and sometimes we haven't time to eat. I hurry [move coal wagons underground] by myself, and have done

so for long. I know the corves [small coal wagons] are very heavy, they are the biggest corves anywhere about. The work is far too hard for me; the sweat runs off me all over sometimes. I am very tired at night. Sometimes when we get home at night we have not power to wash us, and then we go to bed. Sometimes we fall asleep in the chair. Father said last night it was both a shame and a disgrace for girls to work as we do, but there was naught else for us to do. I began to hurry when I was seven and I have been hurrying ever since. I have been 11 years in the pits. The girls are always tired. I was poorly twice this winter; it was with headache. I hurry for Robert Wiggins; he is not akin to me. . . . We don't always get enough to eat and drink, but we get a good supper. I have known my father go at two in the morning to work . . . and he didn't come out till four. I am quite sure that we work constantly 12 hours except on Saturdays. We wear trousers and our shifts in the pit and great big shoes clinkered and nailed. The girls never work naked to the waist in our pit. The men don't insult us in the pit. The conduct of the girls in the pit is good enough sometimes and sometimes bad enough. I never went to a day-school. I went a little to a Sunday-school, but I soon gave it over. I thought it too bad to be confined both Sundays and week-days. I walk about and get the fresh air on Sundays. I have not learnt to read. I don't know my letters. I never learnt naught. I never go to church or chapel; there is no church or chapel at Gawber, there is none nearer than a mile. . . . I have never heard that a good man came into the world who was God's son to save sinners. I never heard of Christ at all. Nobody has ever told me about him, nor have my father and mother ever taught me to pray. I know no prayer; I never pray.

Patience Kershaw, aged 17:

My father has been dead about a year; my mother is living and has ten children, five lads and five lasses; the oldest is about thirty, the youngest is four; three lasses go to mill; all the lads are colliers, two getters and three hurriers; one lives at home and does nothing; mother does nought but look after home.

This illustration of a girl dragging a coal wagon was one of several that shocked public opinion and contributed to the Mines Act of 1842. *(© British Library Board. All rights reserved.)*

All my sisters have been hurriers, but three went to the mill. Alice went because her legs swelled from hurrying in cold water when she was hot. I never went to day-school; I go to Sunday-school, but I cannot read or write; I go to pit at five o'clock in the morning and come out at five in the evening; I get my breakfast of porridge and milk first; I take my dinner with me, a cake, and eat it as I go; I do not stop or rest any time for the purpose; I get nothing else until I get home, and then have potatoes and meat, not every day meat. I hurry in the clothes I have now got on, trousers and ragged jacket; the bald place upon my head is made by thrusting the corves; my legs have never swelled, but sisters' did when they went to mill; I hurry the corves a mile and more under ground and back; they weigh 300; I hurry 11 a day; I wear a belt and chain at the workings to get the corves out; the putters [miners] that I work for are *naked* except their caps; they pull off all their clothes; I see them at work when I go up; sometimes they beat me, if I am not quick enough, with their hands; they strike me upon my back; the boys take liberties with me, sometimes, they pull me about; I am the only girl in the pit; there are about 20 boys and 15 men; all the men are naked; I would rather work in mill than in coal-pit.

Isabel Wilson, 38 years old, coal putter:

When women have children thick [fast] they are compelled to take them down early. I have been married 19 years and have had 10 bairns [children]; seven are in life. When on Sir John's work was a carrier of coals, which caused me to miscarry five times from the strains, and was gai [very] ill after each. Putting is no so oppressive; last child was born on Saturday morning, and I was at work on the Friday night.

Once met with an accident; a coal brake my cheek-bone, which kept me idle some weeks.

I have wrought below 30 years, and so has the guid man; he is getting touched in the breath now.

None of the children read, as the work is no regular. I did read once, but no able to attend to it now; when I go below lassie 10 years of age keeps house and makes the broth or stir-about.

Questions for Analysis

1. To what extent are the testimonies of Ann Eggley and Patience Kershaw in harmony with that of Payne?

2. Describe the work of Eggley and Kershaw. What do you think of their work? Why?

3. What strikes you most about the lives of these workers?

4. The witnesses were responding to questions from middle-class commissioners. What did the commissioners seem interested in? Why?

Source: J. Bowditch and C. Ramsland, eds., *Voices of the Industrial Revolution* (Ann Arbor, Mich.: University of Michigan Press, 1961), pp. 86–90. Copyright © 1961, 1989 by the University of Michigan. Reprinted by permission.

Revolutionaries in Transylvania. Ana Ipatescu was a member of the first group of revolutionaries in Transylvania against Russia, 1848. *(National Historical Museum, Bucharest/The Art Archive)*

chapter

23 THE TRIUMPH OF NATIONALISM IN EUROPE, 1815–1914

Chapter Preview

Peace, Radical Ideas, and Romanticism
• How did the allies make peace in 1815, and what radical ideas emerged between 1815 and 1848?

Reforms and Revolutions (1815–1850)
• Why did revolutions break out in 1848, and why did they fail?

Nation Building in Italy, Germany, and Russia
• How did strong leaders and nation building transform Italy, Germany, and Russia?

Life in Urban Society
• What was the impact of urban growth on cities, social classes, families, and ideas?

The National State and the Socialist Movement (1871–1914)
• How did governments gain popular support and deal with the socialist movement?

Europe's momentous economic and political transformation of modern times began in the late eighteenth century with the Industrial Revolution in England and then the French Revolution. Until about 1815 these economic and political revolutions were separate, involving different countries and activities and proceeding at very different paces. After peace returned in 1815, the situation changed. Economic and political changes tended to fuse, reinforcing each other and bringing about what historian Eric Hobsbawm incisively called the **dual revolution**. For instance, the growth of the industrial middle class encouraged the drive for representative government, and the demands of French workers in 1793 and 1794 eventually inspired socialists in many countries. Gathering strength, the dual revolution transformed Europe and had a powerful impact on the rest of the world.

Revolutionary changes in economics and politics posed a tremendous intellectual challenge. The changes that were occurring fascinated observers and stimulated the growth of new ideas and powerful ideologies. The most important of these were revitalized conservatism and three ideologies of change—liberalism, nationalism, and socialism.

In the midst of the intellectual and economic upheaval after 1815, popular political revolutions welled up again in 1848 throughout most of Europe. These revolutions failed, however, and gave way to more sober—and more successful—nation building in the 1860s. Redrawing the political geography of central Europe and uniting first Italy and then Germany, European political leaders and middle-class nationalists also began to deal effectively with some of the problems posed by the burgeoning of urban society. European leaders also encouraged their peoples to put their faith in a responsive national state. Identification with the national state gradually enlisted widespread support, and in many European countries ordinary citizens developed a sense of belonging to a large and beloved national community. At the same time, the triumph of nationalism promoted bitter rivalries between states and peoples, and in the twentieth century it would bring an era of tragedy and decline in Europe.

dual revolution *The term that historian Eric Hobsbawn used for the economic and political changes that tended to fuse, reinforcing each other.*

Congress of Vienna *The peace settlement that attempted to redraw Europe's political map after the defeat of Napoleonic France.*

Holy Alliance *An alliance formed by Austria, Russia, and Prussia in September 1815 that became a symbol of the repression of liberal and revolutionary movements all over Europe.*

● **Metternich** This portrait by Sir Thomas Lawrence reveals much about Metternich the man. Handsome, refined, and intelligent, Metternich was a great aristocrat who was passionately devoted to the defense of his class and its interests. *(The Royal Collection, © 2007 Her Majesty Queen Elizabeth II)*

PEACE, RADICAL IDEAS, AND ROMANTICISM

How did the allies make peace in 1815, and what radical ideas emerged between 1815 and 1848?

The triumph of revolutionary economic and political forces was by no means certain as the Napoleonic era ended. Quite the contrary. The aristocratic monarchies of Russia, Prussia, Austria, and Great Britain had finally defeated France, and they were determined to reestablish a stable conservative order. This meant holding France in line and preventing political revolutions and radical change. Thus the allies agreed to meet at the **Congress of Vienna** to fashion a general peace settlement and reinforce conservative forces. The allies succeeded in constructing a settlement that did not sow the seeds of another great war, thereby contributing to a century unmarred by destructive generalized war in Europe (see Map 23.1).

Efforts to shore up conservatism were much less successful after 1815. Intellectuals and social observers articulated ideas that still live in today's world. Almost all of these basic ideas were radical. In one way or another they rejected the old conservatism, with its stress on tradition, a hereditary monarchy, and a strong landowning aristocracy. Instead, radicals developed and refined alternative visions—alternative ideologies—and tried to convince society to act on them. With time, they were very successful.

The Peace Settlement

The allied powers were most concerned with the defeated enemy, France. Agreeing to the restoration of the Bourbon dynasty (see page 636), the allies were quite lenient toward France after Napoleon's abdication. France was given the boundaries it possessed in 1792, and France did not have to pay any war reparations. Thus the victorious powers did not foment a spirit of injustice and revenge in the defeated country.

When the four allies of the Quadruple Alliance—Austria, Britain, Prussia, and Russia—met together at the Congress of Vienna, assisted in a minor way by a host of delegates from the smaller European states, they also agreed to raise a number of formidable barriers against renewed French aggression. For example, Prussia received considerably more territory on France's eastern border so as to stand as the "sentinel on the Rhine" against France.

In their moderation toward France, the allies were motivated primarily by self-interest and traditional ideas about the balance of power. To the peacemakers, and especially to Klemens von Metternich, Austria's all-important foreign minister, the European balance of power meant an international equilibrium of political and military forces that would discourage aggression by any single state or any combination of states. Unfortunately for France, in February 1815 Napoleon suddenly escaped from the island of Elba. Yet the peace concluded after Napoleon's final defeat at Waterloo was still relatively moderate toward France.

The rest of the settlement already concluded at the Congress of Vienna was left intact. Of considerable importance, the members of the Quadruple Alliance did agree to meet periodically to discuss their common interests and to consider appropriate measures for the maintenance of peace in Europe. This agreement marked the beginning of the European "congress system," which lasted long into the nineteenth century and peacefully settled many international crises through international conferences and balance-of-power diplomacy.

The domestic side of the peace settlement was much less moderate. In 1815 under Metternich's leadership, Austria, Prussia, and Russia embarked on a crusade against the ideas and politics of the dual revolution. This crusade lasted until Metternich fell from power in 1848. The first step was the **Holy Alliance,** formed by Austria, Prussia, and Russia in September 1815. First proposed by Russia's Alexander I, the alliance soon became a symbol of the repression of liberal and revolutionary movements all over Europe.

Metternich's policies dominated not only Austria and the Italian peninsula but also the entire German Confederation, which the peace settlement of Vienna had called into being (see Map 23.1). The confederation was composed of thirty-eight independent German states and was dominated by Austria, with Prussia a willing junior partner in the planning and execution of repressive measures. It was through the German Confederation that Metternich had the repressive **Carlsbad Decrees** issued in 1819. These decrees required the thirty-eight German member states to root out subversive ideas in their universities and newspapers, while a permanent committee was established to investigate and punish any liberal or radical organizations.

Born into the landed nobility, Metternich was a zealous defender of his class and its privileges. Like many European conservatives of his time, he firmly believed that liberalism, as embodied in revolutionary America and France, had been responsible for a generation of war with untold bloodshed and suffering. He blamed liberal revolutionaries for stirring up the lower classes, which he believed desired nothing more than peace and quiet.

The threat of liberalism appeared doubly dangerous to Metternich because liberals believed that each national group had a right to establish its own independent government. Such national self-determination posed a grave threat to the vast Austrian Empire of the Habsburgs, for it was a dynastic state made up of many national groups. The Germans had long dominated the empire, yet they accounted for only one-fourth of the population. The Magyars (Hungarians), a substantially smaller group, dominated the kingdom of Hungary, though even they did not account for a majority of the population in that part of the Austrian Empire. Czechs formed the third major group. There were also large numbers of Italians, Poles, and Ukrainians as well as smaller groups of Slovenes, Croats, Serbs, Ruthenians, and

Chronology

1790s–1840s	Romantic movement in literature and other arts
1814–1815	Congress of Vienna
1815	Revision of Corn Laws in Britain
1819	Carlsbad Decrees issued by German Confederation
1830–1848	Reign of Louis Philippe in France
1832	Reform Bill in Britain
1840s–1890s	Realism in literature
1845–1851	Great Famine in Ireland
1847	Ten Hours Act in Britain
1848	Revolutions in France, Austria, and Prussia; Marx and Engels, *The Communist Manifesto*
1850–1914	Modernization of cities; condition of working classes improves
1859	Darwin, *On the Origin of Species*
1859–1870	Unification of Italy
1861	Freeing of serfs in Russia
1866–1871	Unification of Germany
1870	France's Third Republic founded
1881	Assassination of Russian tsar Alexander II
1883–1889	Social security laws in Germany
1889–1914	Second Socialist International
1905	Revolution in Russia

Carlsbad Decrees *Issued in 1819, these decrees required the thirty-eight German member states to root out subversive ideas in their universities and newspapers.*

Legend:
- Kingdom of Prussia
- Austrian Empire
- —— Boundary of German Confederation

MAP 23.1 **Europe in 1815** Europe's leaders re-established a balance of political power after the defeat of Napoleon. Prussia gained territory on the Rhine and in Saxony and consolidated its position as a Great Power.

Romanians. Moreover, different ethnic groups often lived in the same provinces and even in the same villages.

The multinational state that Metternich served was both strong and weak. It was strong because of its large population and vast territories; it was weak because of its many and potentially dissatisfied nationalities. In these circumstances, Metternich virtually had to oppose liberalism and nationalism, for Austria was simply unable to accommodate those ideologies of the dual revolution.

In his efforts to hold back liberalism and nationalism Metternich was supported by the Russian Empire and, to a lesser extent, by the Ottoman Empire. Bitter enemies, these far-flung empires were, like Austria, absolutist states with powerful armies and long traditions of expansion and conquest. Both were multinational empires made up of many peoples, languages, and religions, but in each case most of the ruling elite came from a dominant ethnic group—the Orthodox Christian Russians and the Muslim Ottoman Turks. After 1815, both states worked with Austria to preserve their respective conservative orders.

Liberalism

The principal ideas of liberalism—liberty and equality—were by no means defeated in 1815. Liberalism demanded representative government as opposed to autocratic monarchy, equality before the law as opposed to legally separate classes. The idea of liberty also continued to mean specific individual freedoms: freedom of the press, freedom of speech, freedom of assembly, and freedom from arbitrary arrest. In Europe only France with Louis XVIII's Constitutional Charter and Great Britain with its Parliament and historic rights of English men and women had realized much of the liberal program in 1815. Even in those countries, liberalism had not fully succeeded.

Although liberalism retained its cutting edge, many considered it a somewhat duller tool than it had been. The reasons for this opinion were that liberalism faced more radical ideological competitors in the early nineteenth century. Opponents of classical liberalism especially criticized its economic principles, which called for unrestricted private enterprise and no government interference in the economy. This philosophy was popularly known as the doctrine of **laissez faire.** (This form of liberalism is often called "classical" liberalism in the United States to distinguish it sharply from modern American liberalism, which usually favors more government programs to meet social needs and to regulate the economy.)

laissez faire *Economic liberalism that believes in unrestricted private enterprise and no government interference in the economy.*

The idea of a free economy had first been persuasively formulated by Scottish philosophy professor Adam Smith, whose *Inquiry into the Nature and Causes of the Wealth of Nations* (1776) founded modern economics. Smith was highly critical of eighteenth-century mercantilism and its attempt to regulate trade and economic activity. Far preferable, he believed, were free competition and the "invisible hand" of the self-regulating market, which would give all citizens a fair and equal opportunity to do what they did best. Everyone would benefit, not just the rich.

In the early nineteenth century in Britain this economic liberalism was embraced most enthusiastically by business groups and became a doctrine associated with business interests. Businessmen used the doctrine to defend their right to do as they wished in their factories. Labor unions were outlawed because they supposedly restricted free competition and the individual's "right to work."

In the early nineteenth century liberal political ideals also became more closely associated with narrow class interests. Early-nineteenth-century liberals favored representative government, but they generally wanted property qualifications attached to the right to vote. In practice this meant limiting the vote to well-to-do males—aristocratic landowners, substantial businessmen, and successful members of the professions. Workers and peasants as well as the lower middle class of shopkeepers, clerks, and artisans did not own the necessary property and so could not vote.

As liberalism became increasingly identified with the middle class after 1815, some intellectuals and foes of conservatism felt that liberalism did not go nearly far enough. Inspired by memories of the French Revolution and the young American republic, they called for universal voting rights, at least for males, and for democracy. These democrats and republicans were more radical than the liberals.

Nationalism

Nationalism was a second radical idea in the years after 1815—an idea destined to have an enormous influence in the modern world. Early advocates of the "national idea" argued that each people had its own genius and its own *cultural* unity, which manifested itself especially in a common language, history, and territory. In fact, within each ethnic grouping only an elite spoke a standardized written language, and a variety of ethnic groups shared the territory of most states.

Nevertheless, European nationalists usually sought to turn the cultural unity that they perceived into a *political* reality, so that each people lived in an independent nation-state. It was this political goal that made nationalism so explosive in central

● **Building German Nationalism** As popular upheaval in France spread to central Europe in March 1848, Germans from the solid middle classes came together in Frankfurt to draft a constitution for a new united Germany. This colored woodcut commemorates the solemn procession of delegates entering Saint Paul's Cathedral in Frankfurt, where the delegates would have their deliberations. Festivals, celebrations, and parades helped create a feeling of belonging to a large unseen community, a nation binding millions of strangers together. *(akg-images)*

and eastern Europe after 1815, when there were either too few states (Austria, Russia, and the Ottoman Empire) or too many (the Italian peninsula and the German Confederation) and when different peoples overlapped and intermingled.

The nationalist vision, often fitting poorly with existing conditions, triumphed in the long run partly because the epoch-making development of complex industrial and urban society required much better communication between individuals and groups.[1] These communication needs promoted the use of a standardized national language within many countries, creating at least a superficial cultural unity as it eventually encompassed the entire population through mass education.

Nation-states also emerged because those who believed in the new ideology wanted to create "imagined communities," communities seeking to bind millions of strangers together around the abstract concept of an all-embracing national identity. Thus nationalist intellectuals and leaders brought citizens together with emotionally charged symbols and ceremonies, such as ethnic festivals and flag-waving parades, which celebrated the imagined nation of spiritual equals.[2]

Between 1815 and 1850 most people who believed in nationalism also believed in either liberalism or radical, democratic republicanism. A common faith in the creativity and nobility of the people was perhaps the single most important reason for the linking of these two concepts. Liberals and especially democrats saw the people as the ultimate source of all good government.

Early nationalists usually believed that every nation, like every citizen, had the right to exist in freedom and to develop its character and spirit. They were confident that a symphony of free nations would promote the harmony and ultimate unity of all peoples. Thus the liberty of the individual and the love of a free nation overlapped greatly in early-nineteenth-century Europe.

Yet early nationalists also stressed the differences among peoples. Even early nationalism developed a strong sense of "we" and "they," and the "they" was often the enemy. Thus early nationalism in Europe was ambiguous. Its main thrust was liberal and democratic. But below the surface lurked ideas of national superiority and national mission that could lead to aggression and conflict.

Socialism

socialism *A backlash against the emergence of individualism and fragmentation of society, it was a move toward cooperation and a sense of community; the key ideas were planning, greater economic equality, and state regulation of property.*

Socialism, the new radical doctrine after 1815, began in France, despite the fact that France trailed Great Britain in developing modern industry. These French thinkers were acutely aware that the political revolution in France, the rise of laissez faire, and the emergence of factory industry in England were transforming society. They were disturbed because they saw these trends as fomenting selfish individualism and splitting the community into isolated fragments. There was, they believed, an urgent need for a further reorganization of society to establish cooperation and a new sense of community.

Early French socialists believed in economic planning. Inspired by the emergency measures of 1793 and 1794 in France, they argued that the government should rationally organize the economy. Early socialists also shared an intense desire to help the poor. Finally, socialists believed that private property should be strictly regulated by the government or even abolished. Planning, greater economic equality, and state control of property—these were the key ideas of early French socialism and of all socialism since.

One of the most influential early socialist thinkers was Henri de Saint-Simon (1760–1825). Saint-Simon optimistically proclaimed the tremendous possibilities of industrial development: "The age of gold is before us!" The key to progress was proper social organization. Such an arrangement of society required the **parasites**—the court, the aristocracy, lawyers, churchmen—to give way, once and for all, to the **doers**—the leading scientists, engineers, and industrialists. The doers would carefully plan the economy, guide it forward, and improve conditions for the poor.

parasites *In Saint-Simon's thought, these were the social groups that did not contribute directly to the industrial development of the state—the lawyers, clergymen, court, and aristocracy.*

doers *In Saint-Simon's thought, these were the social groups that led the way in the industrial development of the state—the scientists, engineers, and industrialists.*

Charles Fourier (1772–1837), another influential French thinker, envisaged a socialist utopia of self-sufficient communities. An early proponent of the total emancipation of women, Fourier also called for the abolition of marriage, free unions based only on love, and sexual freedom. To many middle-class men and women, these ideas were shocking and immoral and made the socialist program appear doubly dangerous and revolutionary.

The message of French utopian socialists interacted with the experiences of French urban workers. Workers cherished the memory of the French Revolution, and they became violently opposed to laissez-faire laws that denied them the right to organize. Developing a sense of class in the process, workers favored collective action and government intervention in economic life. Thus the aspirations of workers and utopian theorists reinforced each other, and a genuine socialist movement emerged in Paris in the 1830s and 1840s.

It was left to Karl Marx (1818–1883) to establish firm foundations for modern socialism. The son of a Jewish lawyer who had converted to Christianity, the atheistic young Marx had studied philosophy at the University of Berlin before turning to journalism and economics. In 1848 the thirty-year-old Karl Marx and the twenty-eight-year-old Friedrich Engels (1820–1895) published *The Communist Manifesto*, which became the bible of socialism.

**Primary Source:
"Working Men of All Countries, Unite!"**
Read these excerpts from The Communist Manifesto *and find out why "the proletarians have nothing to lose but their chains."*

Early French socialists often appealed to the middle class and the state to help the poor. Marx ridiculed such appeals as naive. He argued that the interests of the middle class and those of the industrial working class were inevitably opposed to each other. Indeed, according to the *Manifesto,* the "history of all previously existing society is the history of class struggles." In Marx's view one class had always exploited the other, and with the advent of modern industry society was split more clearly than ever before: between the middle class (the **bourgeoisie**) and the modern working class (the **proletariat**).

bourgeoisie *A term for well-educated, prosperous, middle-class groups.*

proletariat *The Marxian term for the modern working class.*

Just as the bourgeoisie had triumphed over the feudal aristocracy, the proletariat, Marx predicted, would conquer the bourgeoisie in a violent revolution. While a tiny minority owned the means of production and grew richer, the ever-poorer proletariat was constantly growing in size and in class-consciousness. The critical moment, Marx thought, was very near. "The proletarians have nothing to lose but their chains. They have a world to win. WORKING MEN OF ALL COUNTRIES, UNITE!" So ends *The Communist Manifesto.*

Marx was strongly influenced by England's classical economists, who taught that labor was the source of all value. Marx went on to argue that profits were really wages stolen from the workers. Moreover, Marx incorporated Engels's account of the terrible oppression of the new class of factory workers in England; thus Marx's doctrines seemed to be based on hard facts. Forced to flee Germany after the revolutions of 1848, Marx settled in England and worked tirelessly to build an international socialist movement (see page 708).

Romanticism

Radical concepts of politics and society were accompanied by comparable changes in literature and other arts during the dual revolution. The early nineteenth century marked the acme of the romantic movement, which profoundly influenced the arts and enriched European culture immeasurably. The romantic movement was in part a revolt against classicism and the Enlightenment. The classicists believed that the ancient Greeks and Romans had discovered eternally valid aesthetic rules; that these rules fit with the Enlightenment's belief in rationality, order, and restraint; and that playwrights and painters should continue to follow them.

Forerunners of the romantic movement appeared from about 1750 on. Of these, Rousseau—the passionate advocate of feeling, freedom, and natural goodness—was the most influential. Romanticism then crystallized fully in the 1790s, primarily in England and Germany. The French Revolution kindled the belief that radical reconstruction was also possible in cultural and artistic life, and romanticism gained strength until the 1840s.

Romanticism was characterized by a belief in emotional exuberance, unrestrained imagination, and spontaneity in both art and personal life. In Germany early romantics of the 1770s and 1780s called themselves the **Sturm und Drang** (Storm and Stress), and many romantic artists of the early nineteenth century lived lives of tremendous emotional intensity. Suicide, duels to the death, madness, and strange illnesses were not uncommon among leading romantics. Great individualists, they believed the full development of each person's unique human potential to be the supreme purpose in life.

The French painter Eugène Delacroix (1798–1863) was a romantic master of dramatic, colorful scenes that stirred the emotions. He was fascinated with remote and exotic subjects, whether lion hunts in Morocco or the languishing, sensuous women of a sultan's harem. He was also a passionate spokesman for freedom, celebrating popular revolution in general and revolution in France in particular.

It was in music that romanticism realized most fully and permanently its goals of free expression and emotional intensity. Whereas the composers of the eighteenth century had remained true to well-defined structures, the great romantics used a great range of forms. Romantic composers also transformed the small classical orchestra, tripling its size by adding wind instruments, percussion, and more brass and strings. No composer ever surpassed its first great master, Ludwig van Beethoven (1770–1827). As the contemporary German novelist Ernst Hoffmann (1776–1822) wrote, "Beethoven's music sets in motion the lever of fear, of awe, of horror, of suffering, and awakens just that infinite longing which is the essence of Romanticism."

Nowhere was the break with classicism more apparent than in romanticism's general con-

Sturm und Drang *Literally "Storm and Stress," the German early romantics of the 1770s and 1780s who lived lives of tremendous emotional intensity; suicides, duels, madness, and strange illnesses were common.*

● **Nature and the Meaning of Life** Caspar David Friedrich (1774–1840) was Germany's greatest romantic painter, and his *Traveler Looking over a Sea of Fog* (1815) is a representative masterpiece. Friedrich's paintings often focus on dark silhouetted figures silently contemplating an eerie landscape. Friedrich came to believe that humans were only an insignificant part of an all-embracing higher unity. *(Bildarchiv Preussischer Kulturbesitz/Art Resource, NY)*

ception of nature. Eighteenth-century classicism was not particularly interested in nature. The romantics, in contrast, were enchanted by nature. Sometimes fascinated by its awesome and tempestuous side, at other times they saw nature as a source of spiritual inspiration. Most romantics saw the growth of modern industry as an ugly, brutal attack on their beloved nature and on the human personality.

Fascinated by color and diversity, the romantic imagination turned toward history with a passion. For romantics, history was beautiful and exciting. And it was the art of change over time—the key to a universe that was now perceived to be organic and dynamic. Historical studies supported the development of national aspirations and encouraged entire peoples to seek in the past their special destinies.

Victor Hugo (1802–1885) was France's greatest romantic master in both poetry and prose. His powerful novels exemplified the romantic fascination with fantastic characters, strange settings, and human emotions. The hero of Hugo's famous *Hunchback of Notre Dame* (1831) is the great cathedral's deformed bell-ringer, a "human gargoyle" overlooking the teeming life of fifteenth-century Paris.

In central and eastern Europe, literary romanticism and early nationalism often reinforced each other. Seeking a unique greatness in every people, well-educated romantics plumbed their own histories and cultures. Like modern anthropologists, they turned their attention to peasant life and transcribed the folk songs, tales, and proverbs that the cosmopolitan Enlightenment had disdained. The brothers Jacob and Wilhelm Grimm were particularly successful at rescuing German fairy tales from oblivion. In the Slavic lands romantics played a decisive role in converting spoken peasant languages into modern written languages. The greatest of all Russian poets, Aleksander Pushkin (1799–1837), used his lyric genius to mold the modern literary language of Russia.

REFORMS AND REVOLUTIONS (1815–1850)

Why did revolutions break out in 1848, and why did they fail?

While the romantic movement was developing, liberal, national, and socialist forces battered against the conservatism of 1815. In a few countries change occurred gradually and peacefully. Elsewhere pressure built up like steam in a pressure cooker without a safety valve. Then in 1848 revolutionary political and social ideologies combined with economic crisis and the romantic impulse to produce a vast upheaval. National independence, liberal-democratic constitutions, and social reform—the lofty aspirations of a generation seemed at hand. Yet in the end the revolutions failed, and the lofty aspirations were shattered.

Liberal Reform in Great Britain

Eighteenth-century British society was dominated by the landowning aristocracy, but that class was neither closed nor rigidly defined. Basic civil rights were guaranteed, but only about 8 percent of the population could vote for representatives to Parliament. The French Revolution then threw the British aristocracy into a panic for a generation, and after 1815 it was determined to defend its ruling position.

The first step in this direction began in 1815 with revision of the **Corn Laws** dealing with foreign grain imports. Fearing peace would bring a resumption of imports and lower prices for wheat, the aristocracy rammed through Parliament a new law that prohibited the importation of foreign grain unless the price at home rose to very high levels. More broadly, the landed aristocracy opposed the new manufacturing and

Corn Laws *The laws revised in 1815 that prohibited the importation of foreign grain into Great Britain unless the price at home rose to improbable levels.*

commercial groups that were insisting on a much greater place in the framework of political power and social prestige. Thus the House of Lords successfully blocked the reform of voting rights and representation in Parliament as long as possible. Only in 1832 did a surge of popular protest convince the king and lords to give in.

The Reform Bill of 1832 had profound significance. First, the House of Commons had emerged as the all-important legislative body. Second, the new industrial areas of the country gained representation in the Commons. Third, the number of voters increased by about 50 percent. Comfortable middle-class groups in the urban population, as well as some substantial farmers, received the vote. Thus the pressures building in Great Britain were temporarily released without revolution or civil war.

The principal radical program was embodied in the "People's Charter" of 1838 and the Chartist movement (see page 669), with its core demand for universal male (but not female) suffrage. In three separate campaigns hundreds of thousands of people signed gigantic petitions calling on Parliament to grant all men the right to vote. Parliament rejected the petitions, but the working poor learned a valuable lesson in mass politics.

While calling for universal male suffrage, many working-class people also joined with middle-class manufacturers in the Anti–Corn Law League. Mass participation made possible a popular crusade led by fighting liberals who argued that lower food prices and more jobs in industry depended on repeal of the Corn Laws. After Ireland's potato crop failed in 1845 and famine prices for food seemed likely in England, a minority of Tory aristocrats joined with the Whigs to repeal the Corn Laws in 1846 and allow free imports of grain. England escaped famine.

The following year the Tories passed the Ten Hours Act of 1847, which limited the workday for women and young people in factories to ten hours. Tory aristocrats continued to champion legislation regulating factory conditions. They were competing vigorously with the middle class for the support of the working class. This healthy competition between a still-vigorous aristocracy and a strong middle class was a crucial factor in Great Britain's peaceful evolution in the nineteenth century.

The people of Ireland did not benefit from this political competition. Long ruled as a conquered people, the great mass of the population (outside the northern counties of Ulster, which were partly Presbyterian) were Irish Catholic peasants who rented their land from a tiny minority of Church of England Protestants, many of whom lived in England. Ruthlessly exploited and growing rapidly in numbers, Irish peasants had come to depend on the potato crop.

The potato crop failed in 1845, 1846, 1848, and 1851 in Ireland and throughout much of Europe. Blight attacked the young plants, and the tubers rotted. The general result in Europe was high food prices, widespread suffering, and, frequently, social upheaval. In Ireland the result was widespread starvation and mass fever epidemics. Total losses of population were staggering. Fully 1 million emigrants fled the famine between 1845 and 1851, going primarily to the United States and Great Britain.

Revolutions in France

Louis XVIII's Constitutional Charter of 1814 protected the economic and social gains made by sections of the middle class and the peasantry in the French Revolution, and it permitted great intellectual and artistic freedom. The charter was anything but democratic, however. Only a tiny minority of males had the right to vote for the legislative deputies, who, with the king and his ministers, made the laws of the nation. The old aristocracy, with its pre-1789 mentality, was a minority within the voting population.

It was this situation that Louis's successor, his brother Charles X (r. 1824–1830), could not abide. A true reactionary who wanted to re-establish the old order in France, Charles finally repudiated the Constitutional Charter in an attempted coup in July 1830. He issued decrees stripping much of the wealthy middle class of its voting

● **The Triumph of Democratic Republics** This French illustration constructs a joyous, optimistic vision of the initial revolutionary breakthrough in 1848. The peoples of Europe, joined together around their respective national banners, are achieving republican freedom, which is symbolized by the statue of liberty and the discarded crowns. The woman wearing pants (*front left*)—very radical attire—represents feminist hopes for liberation. (*Archives Charmet/The Bridgeman Art Library*)

rights, and he censored the press. The immediate reaction, encouraged by journalists and lawyers, was an insurrection in the capital by printers, other artisans, and small traders. In "three glorious days" the revolution of 1830 brought down the government. Charles fled. Then the upper middle class skillfully seated Charles's cousin, Louis Philippe, duke of Orléans, on the vacant throne.

Louis Philippe (r. 1830–1848) accepted the Constitutional Charter of 1814 and admitted that he was merely the "king of the French people." Yet the situation in France remained fundamentally unchanged. The vote was extended only from 100,000 to 170,000 citizens. Republicans, democrats, social reformers, and the poor of Paris were bitterly disappointed.

These disappointments in France grew in the 1840s, which were economically hard and politically tense throughout Europe. The government's stubborn refusal to consider electoral reform heightened a sense of class injustice among shopkeepers and urban working people, and it eventually touched off a popular revolt in Paris in February 1848. Barricades went up and Louis Philippe quickly abdicated.

The revolutionaries were firmly committed to a truly popular and democratic republic so that the healthy, life-giving forces of the common people—the peasants and the workers—could reform society with wise legislation. In practice, building such a republic meant giving the right to vote to every adult male, and this was quickly done. Revolutionary compassion and sympathy for freedom were expressed in the freeing of all slaves in French colonies, the abolition of the death penalty, and the establishment of **national workshops** for unemployed workers in Paris.

Yet there were profound differences within the revolutionary coalition in Paris. The moderate liberal republicans of the middle class viewed universal male suffrage as the ultimate reform, and they strongly opposed any further radical social measures. The radical republicans were committed to some kind of socialism. Thus when the French

national workshops *A system established to offer Parisians constant work at fair wages.*

masses went to the election polls for the first time in late April, they elected a majority of moderate republicans to the new Constituent Assembly. Socialism frightened not only the middle and upper classes but also the peasants, many of whom owned land.

After the elections this clash of ideologies—of liberal capitalism and socialism—became a clash of classes and arms. When the government dissolved the national workshops in Paris, workers rose in a spontaneous and violent uprising. Barricades sprang up in the narrow streets of Paris, and a terrible class war began. Working people fought with courage, but the government had the army and the support of peasant France. After three terrible "June Days" and the death or injury of more than ten thousand people, the republican army stood triumphant in a sea of working-class blood and hatred.

The revolution in France thus ended in spectacular failure. The February coalition of the middle and working classes had in four short months become locked in mortal combat. In place of a generous democratic republic, the Constituent Assembly completed a constitution featuring a strong executive. This allowed Louis Napoleon, nephew of Napoleon Bonaparte, to win a landslide victory in the election of December 1848.

Elected to a four-year term, President Louis Napoleon at first shared power with a conservative National Assembly. But in 1851 Louis Napoleon dismissed the Assembly and seized power in a coup d'état. A year later he called on the French to make him hereditary emperor, and 97 percent voted to do so in a national plebiscite. Louis Napoleon—proclaimed Emperor Napoleon III—then ruled France until 1870. Gradually his government became less authoritarian as he liberalized his empire. In 1870, on the eve of a disastrous war with Prussia, Louis Napoleon was still seeking with some success to reconcile a strong national state with universal male suffrage and an independent National Assembly with real power.

The Revolutions of 1848 in Central Europe

Throughout central Europe news of the upheaval in France evoked feverish excitement and eventually revolution. Liberals demanded written constitutions, representative government, and greater civil liberties from authoritarian regimes. When governments hesitated, popular revolts followed. Urban workers and students served as the shock troops, but they were allied with middle-class liberals and peasants. In the face of this united front, monarchs collapsed and granted almost everything. The popular revolutionary coalition then broke down as it had in France. Conflicting national aspirations played a key role. This permitted the traditional forces—the monarchy, the aristocracy, and the regular army—to recover their nerve, reassert their authority, and take back many, though not all, of the concessions. Reaction was everywhere victorious.

The revolution in the Austrian Empire began in Hungary, where nationalistic Hungarians demanded national autonomy, full civil liberties, and universal suffrage. When Viennese students and workers also took to the streets and peasant disorders broke out, the Habsburg emperor capitulated and promised reforms and a liberal constitution. However, the peasants soon lost interest in the political and social questions agitating the cities, for they quickly won a great victory when the monarchy abolished the harsh serfdom that still existed in the Austrian Empire.

Above all, the coalition was weakened and destroyed by conflicting national aspirations. In March the Hungarian revolutionary leaders pushed through an extremely liberal, almost democratic, constitution. But the Hungarian revolutionaries also sought to transform the mosaic of provinces and peoples that was the kingdom of Hungary into a unified, centralized Hungarian nation. To the minority groups that formed half of the population—the Croats, Serbs, and Romanians—such unification was completely unacceptable. Each felt entitled to political autonomy and cultural independence. The Habsburg monarchy in Vienna exploited the fears of the minority groups, and they were soon locked in armed combat with the new Hungarian government. In a somewhat similar way Czech nationalists based in the city of Prague and elsewhere in Bohemia came into conflict with German nationalists.

The monarchy's first breakthrough came in June when the army bombarded Prague and savagely crushed a working-class revolt. Subsequently, the well-equipped, predominantly peasant troops of the regular Austrian army attacked the student and working-class radicals in Vienna and retook the city.. Thus the determination of Austria's aristocracy and the loyalty of its army were the final ingredients in the triumph of reaction and the defeat of revolution.

Finally, another determined conservative, Nicholas I of Russia (r. 1825–1855), obligingly lent his iron hand. In June 1849, 130,000 Russian troops poured into Hungary and subdued the country after bitter fighting. For a number of years the Habsburgs ruled Hungary as a conquered territory.

After Austria, Prussia was the largest and most influential German kingdom. Prior to 1848, the goal of middle-class Prussian liberals had been to transform absolutist Prussia into a liberal constitutional monarchy that would transform the thirty-eight states of the German Confederation into a unified nation. Following the fall of Louis Philippe in France, artisans and factory workers in Berlin exploded in March 1848 and joined with the middle-class liberals in the struggle against the monarchy. The autocratic yet paternalistic Frederick William IV (r. 1840–1861) caved in and promised to grant Prussia a liberal constitution and to merge Prussia into a new national German state.

A self-appointed committee of predominantly middle-class liberals from various German states also began writing a federal constitution for a unified German state. Meeting in Frankfurt, the National Assembly soon became absorbed in a battle with Denmark over the provinces of **Schleswig and Holstein.** The provinces were inhabited primarily by Germans, but the new nationalistic king of Denmark was trying to integrate both provinces into the rest of his state. Hypnotized by this conflict, the National Assembly at Frankfurt finally called on the Prussian army to oppose Denmark in the name of the German nation. Prussia responded and began war with Denmark. As the Schleswig-Holstein issue demonstrated, the national ideal was the crucial factor motivating the German middle classes in 1848.

Schleswig and Holstein
Provinces that were inhabited primarily by Germans, but ruled by the king of Denmark; they revolted at the prospect of being integrated into the Danish state by the new Danish king, Frederick VII.

In March 1849 the slow moving National Assembly finally completed its drafting of a liberal constitution and elected King Frederick William of Prussia emperor of the new German national state. By early 1849, however,. Frederick William had reasserted his royal authority and granted his subjects a conservative constitution. Reasserting that he ruled by divine right, Frederick William contemptuously refused to accept the "crown from the gutter." Preoccupied with nationalist issues, the middle-class revolutionaries in Frankfurt had waited too long and acted too timidly.

When Frederick William tried to get the small monarchs of Germany to elect him emperor with authoritarian power, Austria balked. Supported by Russia, Austria forced Prussia to renounce all its schemes of unification in late 1850. The German Confederation was re-established. Attempts to unite the Germans—first in a liberal national state and then in a conservative Prussian empire—had failed completely.

In conclusion, political, economic, and social pressures building after 1815 exploded in 1848, but the upheavals were abortive, and very few revolutionary goals were realized. The moderate, nationalistic middle classes were unable to consolidate their initial victories in France or elsewhere in Europe. Instead, they drew back when artisans, factory workers, and radical socialists rose up to present their own much more revolutionary demands. This retreat made possible the crushing of Parisian workers by a coalition of solid bourgeoisie and landowning peasantry in France, and it facilitated the efforts of dedicated aristocrats in central Europe. By 1850, a sea of blood and disillusion had washed away the lofty ideals and utopian visions of a generation.

NATION BUILDING IN ITALY, GERMANY, AND RUSSIA

How did strong leaders and nation building transform Italy, Germany, and Russia?

The revolutions of 1848 closed one era in the West and opened another. In thought and culture exuberant romanticism gave way to hardheaded realism. In the Atlantic economy the hard years of the 1840s were followed by good times and prosperity throughout most of the 1850s and 1860s. In international politics the repressive peace and diplomatic stability of Metternich's time were replaced by a period of war and rapid change. Above all, Western society progressively found, for better or worse, a new and effective organizing principle capable of coping with the many-sided challenges of the dual revolution and the emerging urban civilization. That principle was nationalism—dedication to and identification with the nation-state.

The triumph of modern nationalism in Europe was an enormously significant historical development. A powerful force since at least 1789, nationalism became an almost universal faith in Western society after 1850, evolving away from a narrow appeal to predominately middle-class liberals to an intoxicating creed moving the broad masses. Many leaders and peoples throughout the world eventually embraced large parts of the doctrine of nationalism and the nation-state.

Cavour, Garibaldi, and the Unification of Italy

Italy had never been a united nation prior to 1860. Part of Rome's great empire in ancient times, the Italian peninsula was divided in the Middle Ages into competing city-states, and it became a battleground for foreign powers after 1494. Italy was reorganized in 1815 at the Congress of Vienna. The rich northern provinces of Lombardy and Venetia were taken by Metternich's Austria. Sardinia and Piedmont were under the rule of an Italian monarch, and Tuscany shared north-central Italy with several smaller states. Central Italy and Rome were ruled by the papacy. Naples and Sicily were ruled by a branch of the Bourbons. Metternich was not wrong in dismissing Italy as "a geographical expression" (see Map 23.2).

After 1815 the goal of a unified Italian nation captured the imaginations of increasing numbers of Italians, but there was no agreement on how it could be achieved. In 1848, revolutionary efforts to form a democratic Italian republic failed completely, and a thoroughly frightened Pope Pius IX (r. 1846–1878) turned against most modern trends, including a federation of existing Italian states under his presidency. At the same time, the king of independent Sardinia, Victor Emmanuel, retained the moderate liberal constitution granted under duress in March 1848. To the Italian middle classes Sardinia appeared to be a liberal, progressive state ideally suited to achieve the goal of national unification.

Sardinia had the good fortune of being led by a brilliant statesman, Count Camillo Benso di Cavour. Cavour came from a noble family and embraced the economic doctrines and business activities associated with the prosperous middle class. Cavour's national goals were limited and realistic. Until 1859 he sought unity only for the states of northern and perhaps central Italy in a greatly expanded kingdom of Sardinia.

In the 1850s Cavour worked to consolidate Sardinia as a liberal constitutional state capable of leading northern Italy. He worked out a secret diplomatic alliance with Napoleon III, and in July 1858 he goaded Austria into attacking Sardinia. The combined Franco-Sardinian forces were victorious, but Napoleon III decided on a compromise peace with the Austrians in July 1859. Sardinia would receive only Lombardy, the area around Milan. Cavour resigned in a rage.

Popular revolts and Italian nationalism salvaged Cavour's plans. While the war against Austria had raged in the north, dedicated nationalists in central Italy had risen

MAP 23.2 **The Unification of Italy, 1859–1870** The leadership of Sardinia-Piedmont and nationalist fervor were decisive factors in the unification of Italy.

and driven out their rulers. Nationalist fervor seized the urban masses, and the leaders of the nationalist movement called for fusion with Sardinia. Cavour returned to power in early 1860, and the people of central Italy voted overwhelmingly to join a greatly enlarged kingdom of Sardinia. Cavour had achieved his original goal of a north Italian state (see Map 23.2).

For superpatriots such as Giuseppe Garibaldi (1807–1882), the job of unification was still only half done. The son of a poor sailor, Garibaldi personified the romantic revolutionary nationalism of 1848. Leading a corps of volunteers against Austria in 1859, Garibaldi emerged in 1860 as a powerful independent force in Italian politics. (See the feature "Individuals in Society: Giuseppe Garibaldi.")

Secretly supported by Cavour, Garibaldi had a bold plan to "liberate" the kingdom of the Two Sicilies. Landing on the shores of Sicily in May 1860, Garibaldi's guerrilla band of a thousand **Red Shirts** captured the imagination of the Sicilian peasantry. Outwitting the twenty-thousand-man royal army, the guerrilla leader took Palermo, crossed to the mainland, and prepared to attack Rome and the pope. But the wily Cavour quickly sent Sardinian forces to occupy most of the Papal States (but not

Red Shirts *The guerrilla army of Giuseppe Garibaldi, who invaded Sicily in 1860 in an attempt to "liberate" it and won the hearts of the Sicilian peasantry.*

Rome) and to intercept Garibaldi. When Garibaldi and Victor Emmanuel rode through Naples to cheering crowds, they symbolically sealed the union of north and south, of monarch and people.

Cavour had succeeded. He had controlled Garibaldi and had turned popular nationalism in a conservative direction. The new kingdom of Italy, which did not include Venice until 1866 or Rome until 1870, was a parliamentary monarchy under Victor Emmanuel, neither radical nor democratic. Only a small minority of Italian males had the right to vote. Despite political unity, the propertied classes and the common people were divided. A great social and cultural gap separated the progressive industrializing north from the stagnant agrarian south.

Bismarck and German Unification

Primary Source:
Extracts from History of Germany in the Nineteenth Century
A nineteenth-century German historian proclaims a racist and militarist ideology.

In the aftermath of 1848 the German states were locked in a political stalemate. Tension grew between Austria and Prussia as each power sought to block the other within the German Confederation. Stalemate and reaction also prevailed in the domestic politics of the individual German states in the 1850s.

At the same time, powerful economic forces were undermining the political status quo. Modern industry was growing rapidly within the German customs union (*Zollverein*), founded in 1834 to stimulate trade. By the end of 1853 all the German states except Austria had joined the customs union, and a new Germany excluding Austria was becoming an economic reality.

The national uprising in Italy in 1859 made a profound impression in Prussia. Great political change and war—perhaps with Austria, perhaps with France—seemed quite possible. Along with his top military advisers, the tough-minded William I of Prussia (r. 1861–1888) was convinced of the need for major army reforms and wanted to double the size of the regular army. Army reforms meant a bigger defense budget and higher taxes.

Prussia had emerged from 1848 with a parliament of sorts, the Prussian Assembly, which was in the hands of the liberal middle class by 1859. Above all, the middle-class representatives wanted to establish once and for all that the parliament, not the king, had the ultimate political power and that the army was responsible to Prussia's elected representatives. These demands were popular. After the parliament rejected the military budget in 1862, the liberals triumphed completely in new elections. King William then called on Count Otto von Bismarck to head a new ministry and defy the parliament. This was a momentous choice.

The most important figure in German history between Luther and Hitler, Otto von Bismarck (1815–1898) was above all a master of politics. Born into the Prussian landowning aristocracy, Bismarck loved power, but he was also extraordinarily flexible and pragmatic in pursuing his goals.

When Bismarck took office as chief minister in 1862, he declared that the government would rule without parliamentary consent. He lashed out at the middle-class opposition and ordered the Prussian bureaucracy to go on collecting taxes even though the Prussian parliament refused to approve the budget. He reorganized the army. And for four years, from 1862 to 1866, the voters of Prussia supported the opposition and sent large liberal majorities to the parliament.

Opposition at home spurred the search for success abroad. When the Danish king tried again, as in 1848, to bring the provinces of Schleswig and Holstein into a centralized Danish state, Prussia joined Austria in a short and successful war against Denmark in 1864. Then, determined to expel Austria from German politics, Bismarck launched another war of aggression.

The Austro-Prussian War of 1866 lasted only seven weeks. Utilizing railroads to mass troops, the reorganized Prussian army defeated Austria decisively at the Battle of Sadowa in Bohemia. Granting Austria realistic, even generous, peace terms, Bismarck forced Austria to withdraw from German affairs. The mainly Protestant states north

Individuals IN SOCIETY

Giuseppe Garibaldi

Giuseppe Garibaldi, the charismatic leader, shown in an 1856 engraving based on a photograph. *(Corbis)*

When Giuseppe Garibaldi (1807–1882) visited England in 1864, he received the most triumphant welcome ever given to any foreigner. Honored and feted by politicians and high society, he also captivated the masses. An unprecedented crowd of a half-million people cheered his carriage through the streets of London. These ovations were no fluke. In his time, Garibaldi was probably the most famous and most beloved figure in the world.* How could this be?

A rare combination of wild adventure and extraordinary achievement partly accounted for his demigod status. Born in Nice, Garibaldi went to sea at fifteen and sailed the Mediterranean for twelve years. At seventeen his travels took him to Rome, and he was converted in an almost religious experience to the "New Italy, the Italy of all the Italians." As he later wrote in his best-selling *Autobiography*, "The Rome that I beheld with the eyes of youthful imagination was the Rome of the future—the dominant thought of my whole life."

Sentenced to death in 1834 for his part in a revolutionary uprising in Genoa, Garibaldi barely escaped to South America. For twelve years, he led a guerrilla band in Uruguay's struggle for independence from Argentina. "Shipwrecked, ambushed, shot through the neck," he found in a tough young woman, Anna da Silva, a mate and companion in arms. Their first children nearly starved in the jungle while Garibaldi, clad in his long red shirt, fashioned a legend as a fearless freedom fighter.

Returning to Italy in 1848, the campaigns of his patriotic volunteers against the Austrians in 1848 and 1859 mobilized democratic nationalists. The stage was set for his volunteer army to liberate Sicily against enormous odds, astonishing the world and creating a large Italian state. Garibaldi's achievement matched his legend.

A brilliant fighter, the handsome and inspiring leader was an uncompromising idealist of absolute integrity. He never drew any personal profit from his exploits, continuing to milk his goats and rarely possessing more than one change of clothing. When Victor Emmanuel offered him lands and titles after

*Denis Mack Smith, *Garibaldi: A Great Life in Brief* (New York: Alfred A. Knopf, 1956), pp. 136–147; and Denis Mack Smith, "Giuseppe Garibaldi," *History Today,* August 1991, pp. 20–26.

his great victory in 1861, even as the left-leaning volunteers were disbanded and humiliated, Garibaldi declined, saying he could not be bought off. Returning to his farm on a tiny rocky island, he denounced the government without hesitation when he concluded that it was betraying the dream of unification with its ruthless rule in the south. Yet even after a duplicitous Italian government caused two later attacks on Rome to fail, his faith in the generative power of national unity never wavered. Garibaldi showed that ideas and ideals count in history.

Above all, millions of ordinary men and women identified with Garibaldi because they believed that he was fighting for them. They recognized him as one of their own and saw that he remained true to them in spite of his triumphs, thereby ennobling their own lives and aspirations. Welcoming runaway slaves as equals in Latin America, advocating the emancipation of women, introducing social reforms in the south, and pressing for free education and a broader suffrage in the new Italy, Garibaldi the national hero fought for freedom and human dignity. The common people understood and loved him for it.

Questions for Analysis

1. Why was Garibaldi so famous and popular?
2. Nationalism evolved and developed in the nineteenth century. How did Garibaldi fit into this evolution? What kind of a nationalist was he?

North German Confederation *A new government structure created by Bismarck after the Austro-Prussian War of 1866; it put the federal government in control of the army and military affairs, but created a legislature with two houses that shared equally in the making of laws.*

of the Main River were grouped in the new **North German Confederation,** led by an expanded Prussia (see Map 23.3). Each state retained its own local government, but the federal government—William I and Bismarck—controlled the army and foreign affairs. There was also a legislature with delegates to the confederation's lower house elected by universal male suffrage, giving Bismarck the possibility of going over the head of the middle class directly to the people.

Long convinced that the old order should make peace with the liberal middle class and the nationalist movement Bismarck asked the Prussian parliament to approve after the fact all of the government's "illegal" spending between 1862 and 1866. Most of the liberals snatched at the chance to cooperate. With German unity in sight, they repented their "sins" and legalized the government's spending. The constitutional struggle in Prussia was over, and the German middle class was accepting respectfully the monarchical authority and aristocratic superiority that Bismarck represented.

The final act in the drama of German unification followed quickly with a patriotic war with France. The apparent issue—whether a distant relative of Prussia's William I might become king of Spain—was only a diplomatic pretext. By 1870 the French leaders of the Second Empire, alarmed by their powerful new neighbor on the Rhine, had decided on a war to teach Prussia a lesson.

As soon as war against France began in 1870, Bismarck had the wholehearted support of the south German states. With other European governments remaining neutral, German forces under Prussian leadership decisively defeated Louis Napoleon's armies at Sedan on September 1, 1870. Three days later French patriots in Paris proclaimed yet another French republic (the third) and vowed to continue fighting. But after five months, in January 1871, a starving Paris surrendered, and France went on to accept Bismarck's harsh peace terms. By this time the south German states had agreed to join a new German Empire. As in the 1866 constitution, the king of Prussia

● **Proclaiming the German Empire, January 1871** This commemorative painting by Anton von Werner testifies to the nationalistic intoxication in Germany after the victory over France. William I of Prussia stands on a platform surrounded by princes and generals in the famous Hall of Mirrors in the palace of Versailles, while officers from all the units around a besieged Paris cheer and salute him with uplifted swords as emperor of a unified Germany. Bismarck, like a heroic white knight, stands between king and army. *(akg-images)*

MAP 23.3 **The Unification of Germany, 1866–1871** This map deserves careful study. Note how Prussian expansion, Austrian expulsion from the old German Confederation, and the creation of a new German Empire went hand in hand. Austria lost no territory, but Prussia's neighbors in the north suffered grievously or simply disappeared. The annexation of Alsace-Lorraine turned France into a lasting enemy of Germany before 1914.

and his ministers had ultimate power in the new German Empire, and the lower house of the legislature was elected by universal male suffrage.

The Franco-Prussian War, which Europeans generally saw as a test of nations in a pitiless Darwinian struggle for existence, released an enormous surge of patriotic feeling in Germany. Bismarck's genius, the invincible Prussian army, the solidarity of king and people in a unified nation—these and similar themes were trumpeted endlessly during and after the war. The new German Empire had become the most powerful state in Europe, and most Germans were enormously proud, blissfully imagining themselves the fittest and best of the European species. Semi-authoritarian nationalism and a "new conservatism," which was based on an alliance of the propertied classes and sought the active support of the working classes, had triumphed in Germany.

The Modernization of Russia

In 1850, the Russian empire was an enormous multinational state, containing all the ethnic Russians and many other nationalities as well. Russia was also a poor agrarian society with backward agricultural techniques and a rapidly growing population. Serfdom was still the basic social institution. Then the Crimean War of 1853 to 1856, arising out of a dispute with France over who should protect certain Christian shrines in the Ottoman Empire, brought crisis. France and Great Britain, aided by Sardinia and the Ottoman Empire, inflicted a humiliating defeat on Russia.

modernization *The changes that enable a country to compete effectively with the leading countries at a given time.*

Military defeat showed that Russia had fallen behind western Europe in many areas. Russia's leaders realized that they had to embrace the process of **modernization**, defined narrowly as the changes that enable a country to compete effectively with the leading countries at a given time. At the very least, Russia needed railroads, better armaments, and reorganization of the army if it was to maintain its international position. Military disaster thus forced the new tsar, Alexander II (r. 1855–1881), and his ministers along the path of rapid social change and general modernization.

The first and greatest of the reforms was the freeing of the serfs in 1861. Human bondage was abolished forever, and the emancipated peasants received, on average, about half of the land. But the peasants had to pay fairly high prices for their land, which was owned collectively by peasant villages. Thus the effects of the reform were limited. More successful was reform of the legal system, which established independent courts and equality before the law. Education was also liberalized somewhat, and censorship was relaxed but not removed.

Russia made great strides toward economic modernization in the reform era. Rapid railroad construction to 1880 enabled agricultural Russia to export grain and thus earn money for further industrialization. Industrial suburbs grew up around Moscow and St. Petersburg, and a class of modern factory workers began to take shape.

In 1881 a small group of terrorists assassinated Alexander II, and the era of reform came to an abrupt end. Political modernization remained frozen until 1905, but economic modernization sped forward in the massive industrial surge of the 1890s. Nationalism played a decisive role, as it had after the Crimean War. The key leader was Sergei Witte, the energetic minister of finance. Witte subscribed to the economic nationalism of Friedrich List (see page 660) and believed that industrial backwardness was threatening Russia's power and greatness. Under Witte's leadership the government built state-owned railroads rapidly and promoted Russian industry with high protective tariffs.

By 1900 a fiercely independent Russia was catching up with western Europe and expanding its empire in Asia. By 1903 Russia had established a sphere of influence in Chinese Manchuria and was casting greedy eyes on northern Korea. When the diplomatic protests of equally imperialistic Japan were ignored, the Japanese launched a surprise attack in February 1904. To the amazement of self-confident Europeans, Japan scored repeated victories, and Russia was forced in August 1905 to accept a humiliating defeat.

October Manifesto *The result of a great general strike in October 1905, it granted full civil rights and promised a popularly elected Duma (parliament) with real legislative power.*

Military disaster in East Asia brought the revolution of 1905. Beginning in January 1905, a wave of strikes, peasant uprisings, and troop mutinies swept the country. The revolutionary surge culminated in October 1905 in a paralyzing general strike, which forced the government to capitulate. The tsar issued the **October Manifesto**, which granted full civil rights and promised a popularly elected *Duma* (parliament) with real legislative power.

Under the new constitution the tsar retained great powers and the Duma had only limited authority. The middle-class liberals, the largest group in the newly elected Duma, were badly disappointed, and efforts to cooperate with the tsar's ministers soon broke down. In 1907, the tsar and his reactionary advisers rewrote the electoral law to increase greatly the weight of the wealthy classes at the expense of workers, peasants, national minorities, and middle-class professionals.

● **The Fruits of Terrorism**
In the late 1870s a small group of revolutionaries believed that killing the tsar could destroy the Russian state. Succeeding in blowing up the reforming Alexander II after several near misses, the five assassins, including one woman, were quickly caught and hanged. Russia entered an era of reaction and harsh authoritarian rule. *(Visual Connection Archive)*

The new law had the intended effect. With landowners assured half of the seats in the Duma, the government reestablished semi-authoritarian rule. On the eve of World War I, Russia was partially modernized, a conservative constitutional monarchy with a peasant-based but industrializing economy.

LIFE IN URBAN SOCIETY

What was the impact of urban growth on cities, social classes, families, and ideas?

After 1850, as identification with the nation-state was becoming a basic organizing principle of Western society, the growth of towns and cities rushed forward with undiminished force. In 1900 Western society was urban and industrial as surely as it had been rural and agrarian in 1800. This rapid urbanization, both a result of the Industrial Revolution and a key element in its enormous long-term impact, posed pressing practical problems that governments had to deal with. Eventual success with urban problems encouraged people to look to government as a problem solver and put their faith in a responsive national state.

Taming the City

Since the Middle Ages European cities had been centers of government, culture, and large-scale commerce. They had also been congested, dirty, and unhealthy. Nonetheless, as the Industrial Revolution took hold and the steam engine freed industrialists from dependence on the energy of fast-flowing streams and rivers, there was by 1800 a powerful incentive to build new factories in cities, which grew rapidly in Europe in the nineteenth century (see Map 23.4). There were also many hands wanting work in the cities, for cities drew people like a magnet.

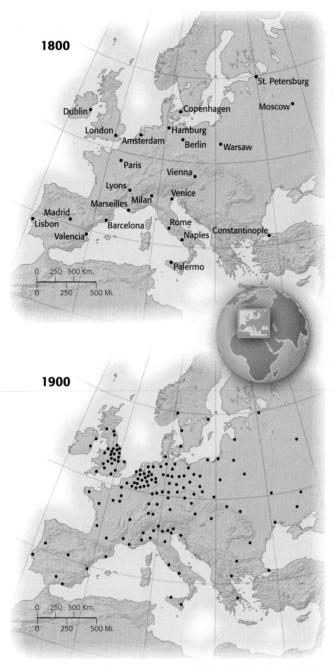

St. Petersburg

Dublin   Copenhagen   Moscow

London   Hamburg
Amsterdam   Berlin   Warsaw

Paris

Vienna

Lyons   Venice
Marseilles   Milan

Madrid   Rome
Lisbon   Barcelona   Naples   Constantinople
Valencia

Palermo

0   250   500 Km.
0   250   500 Mi.

1900

0   250   500 Km.
0   250   500 Mi.

MAP 23.4 **European Cities of 100,000 or More, 1800 and 1900** There were more large cities in Great Britain in 1900 than in all of Europe in 1800. Northwestern Europe was the most urbanized area.

Benthamite *Followers of the radical philosopher Jeremy Bentham, they believed in the "greatest good for the greatest number."*

miasmatic theory *The belief that people contract disease by breathing bad odors and decay and putrefying excrement.*

In the 1820s and 1830s people in Britain and France began to worry about the condition of their cities. Everyone could agree that, except on the outskirts, each town or city was using every scrap of land to the full extent. Parks and open areas were almost nonexistent, and narrow houses were usually built wall to wall in long rows.

These highly concentrated urban populations lived in extremely unsanitary and unhealthy conditions. Open drains and sewers flowed alongside or down the middle of unpaved streets. Toilet facilities were primitive in the extreme. In parts of industrial Manchester as many as two hundred people shared a single outhouse.

The urban challenge eventually brought an energetic response from a generation of reformers. The most famous was Edwin Chadwick, a British official. Chadwick was a good **Benthamite**—that is, a follower of radical British philosopher Jeremy Bentham (1748–1832). Bentham had taught that public problems ought to be dealt with on a rational, scientific basis and according to the "greatest good for the greatest number." Applying these principles, Chadwick became convinced that disease and death actually caused poverty and that disease could be prevented by cleaning up the urban environment. That was his "sanitary idea."

Collecting detailed reports from local officials and publishing his findings in 1842, Chadwick correctly believed that the stinking excrement of communal outhouses could be carried off by water through cheap iron pipes at less than one-twentieth the cost of removing it by hand. In 1848, Britain created a national health board and gave cities broad authority to build modern sanitary systems. The public health movement won dedicated supporters in the United States, France, and Germany from the 1840s on. By the 1860s and 1870s European cities were making real progress toward adequate water supplies and sewerage systems, and city dwellers were beginning to reap the reward of better health.

Early reformers were seriously handicapped by the prevailing **miasmatic theory** of disease—the belief that people contract disease when they breathe the bad odors of decay and putrefying excrement. In the 1840s and 1850s keen observation suggested that contagion was *spread through* filth and not caused by it, thus weakening the miasmatic idea.

The theoretical breakthrough was the development of the **germ theory** of disease by Louis Pasteur (1822–1895), a French chemist who found that the growth of living organisms could be suppressed by heating a beverage—by **pasteurization.** By 1870 the work of Pasteur and others had clearly demonstrated the general connection between germs and disease. When, in the middle of the 1870s, Robert Koch and his German coworkers developed pure cultures of harmful bacteria and described their life cycles, the dam broke. Over the next twenty years researchers identified the organisms responsible for disease after disease. These discoveries led to the development of a number of effective vaccines. Surgeons also applied the germ theory in hospitals, sterilizing not only the wound but also everything—hands, instruments, clothing—that entered the operating room.

The achievements of the bacterial revolution coupled with the ever-more-sophisticated public health movement saved millions of lives, particularly after about 1890. In England, France, and Germany death rates declined dramatically from a range of twenty-one to twenty-seven per thousand inhabitants in the 1860s to a range of fourteen to eighteen per thousand in 1913. The awful death sentences of the past—diphtheria, typhoid, typhus, cholera, yellow fever—became vanishing diseases in the industrializing nations.

More effective urban planning after 1850 also improved the quality of urban life. France took the lead during the rule of Napoleon III (1848–1870), who believed that rebuilding much of Paris would provide employment, improve living conditions, and glorify his empire. In the baron Georges Haussmann (1809–1884), an aggressive, impatient Alsatian whom he placed in charge of Paris, Napoleon III found an authoritarian planner capable of bulldozing both buildings and opposition. In twenty years Paris was transformed by slum clearance, new streets and housing, small neighborhood parks and open spaces, and good fresh water. The rebuilding Paris stimulated modern urbanism throughout Europe, particularly after 1870.

The development of mass public transportation was also of great importance in the improvement of urban living conditions. In the 1870s many European cities authorized private companies to operate horse-drawn streetcars. Then in the 1890s countries in North America and Europe adopted another transit innovation, the electric streetcar. Electric streetcars were cheaper, faster, more dependable, and more comfortable than their horse-drawn counterparts. Service improved dramatically. Millions of riders—workers, shoppers, schoolchildren—hopped on board during the workweek. And on weekends and holidays, streetcars carried city people on happy outings to parks and the countryside, racetracks and music halls.[3] Electric streetcars also gave people of modest means access to improved housing, as the still-crowded city was able to expand and become less congested.

germ theory *The idea, contrary to miasmatic theory, that disease was spread through filth and not caused by it.*

pasteurization *The process developed by Louis Pasteur that suppressed the activity of living organisms in a beverage by heating it.*

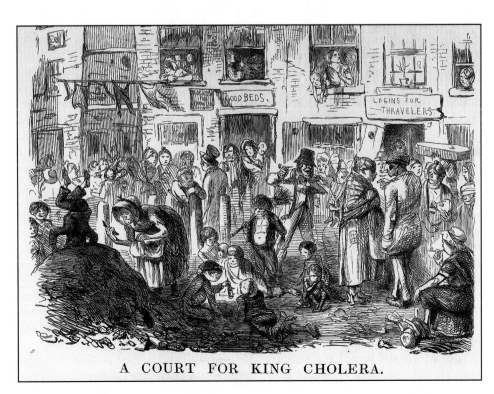

A COURT FOR KING CHOLERA.

● **Filth and Disease** This 1852 drawing from *Punch* tells volumes about the unhealthy living conditions of the urban poor. In the foreground children play with a dead rat and a woman scavenges a dungheap. Cheap rooming houses provide shelter for the frightfully overcrowded population. *(© British Library Board. All rights reserved.)*

Social Structure and the Middle Classes

With general improvements in health and in the urban environment, the almost-completed journey to an urban industrialized world was bringing beneficial consequences for all kinds of people. The first great change was a substantial increase in the standard of living for the average person. The real wages of British workers, for example, almost doubled between 1850 and 1906. Similar increases occurred in continental European countries, reinforcing efforts to improve many aspects of human existence.

However. greater economic rewards for the average person did *not* eliminate hardship and poverty, nor did they significantly narrow the wealth and income gap separating the rich and the poor. In almost every industrialized country around 1900 the richest 20 percent of households received anywhere from 50 to 60 percent of all national income, whereas the bottom 30 percent of households received 10 percent or less of all income. Thus the gap between rich and poor remained enormous in western countries. It was probably almost as great in 1900 as it had been in the age of agriculture and aristocracy before the Industrial Revolution.

The great gap between rich and poor endured, in part, because industrial and urban development made society more diverse and less unified. By no means did society split into two sharply defined opposing classes, as Marx had predicted. Instead, economic specialization created more new social groups than it destroyed. There developed an almost unlimited range of jobs, skills, and earnings; one group or subclass shaded off into another in a complex, confusing hierarchy.

Certainly the diversity and range within the urban middle class were striking at the beginning of the twentieth century. Indeed, it is more meaningful to think of a confederation of middle classes loosely united by occupations requiring primarily mental, rather than physical, skill.

At the top stood the upper middle class, composed mainly of the most successful business families. As people in the upper middle class gained in income and progressively lost all traces of radicalism after the trauma of 1848, they were almost irresistibly drawn toward the aristocratic lifestyle. For although the genuine hereditary aristocracy constituted only a tiny minority in every European country, it retained imposing wealth, unrivaled social prestige, and substantial political influence. Thus the upper middle class purchased lavish country places or built beach houses for weekend and summer use. A large number of servants also indicated wealth and standing, while fancy carriages were sure signs of high social status.

Below the wealthy upper middle class were much larger, much less wealthy, and increasingly diversified middle-class groups. Here one found the moderately successful industrialists and merchants as well as professionals in law and medicine. This was the middle middle class, solid and quite comfortable but lacking great wealth. Below it were independent shopkeepers, small traders, and tiny manufacturers—the lower middle class.

The expansion of industry and technology created a growing demand for experts with specialized knowledge, and the most valuable of the specialties became solid middle-class professions. Engineers, architects, chemists, accountants, and surveyors first achieved professional standing in this period. Management of large public and private institutions also emerged as a kind of profession as governments provided more services and as very large corporations such as railroads came into being.

Industrialization and urbanization also diversified the lower middle class and expanded the number of white-collar employees. White-collar employees were propertyless, but generally they were fiercely committed to the middle class and to the ideal of moving up in society.

Well fed and well served, the middle classes were also well housed by 1900 and were quite clothes conscious. Education was another growing expense, as middle-class parents tried to provide their children with ever-more-crucial advanced education. The keystones of culture and leisure were books, music, and travel.

The middle classes were loosely united by a shared code of expected behavior and morality. Strict and demanding, this code laid great stress on hard work, self-discipline, and personal achievement. Men and women who fell into crime or poverty were generally assumed to be responsible for their own circumstances. In short, the middle-class person was supposed to know right from wrong and to act accordingly.

The Working Classes

About four out of five people belonged to the European working classes at the turn of the twentieth century. Many members of the working classes—that is, people whose livelihoods depended on physical labor and who did not employ domestic servants—were still small landowning peasants and hired farm hands. This was especially true in eastern Europe.

The urban working classes were even less unified and homogeneous than the middle classes. In the first place, economic development and increased specialization expanded the traditional range of working-class skills, earnings, and experiences. In the second place, skilled, semiskilled, and unskilled workers developed widely divergent lifestyles and cultural values, and their differences contributed to a keen sense of social status and hierarchy within the working classes. The result was great variety and limited class unity.

Highly skilled workers, who made up about 15 percent of the working classes, became a real **labor aristocracy**. The most "aristocratic" of the highly skilled workers were construction bosses and factory foremen, men who had often risen from the ranks and were fiercely proud of their achievement. The labor aristocracy also included members of the traditional highly skilled handicraft trades that had not yet been placed in factories, as well as new kinds of skilled workers such as shipbuilders and railway locomotive engineers. Thus the labor elite remained in a state of flux as individuals and whole crafts moved in and out of it.

To maintain this precarious standing, the upper working class adopted distinctive values and strait-laced, almost puritanical behavior. Like the middle classes, the labor aristocracy was strongly committed to the family and to economic improvement. Yet skilled workers viewed themselves primarily not as aspirants to the middle class but as the pacesetters and natural leaders of all the working classes. They practiced self-discipline and generally frowned on heavy drinking and sexual permissiveness.

Below the labor aristocracy stood the complex world of semiskilled and unskilled urban workers. A large number of the semiskilled were factory workers who earned highly variable but relatively good wages and whose relative importance in the labor force was increasing. Below the semiskilled workers was a larger group of unskilled workers that included day laborers such as longshoremen, wagon-driving teamsters, maids, teenagers, and every kind of "helper." Many of these people had real skills and performed valuable services, but they were unorganized and divided, united only by the common fate of meager earnings. The same lack of unity characterized street vendors and market people—self-employed workers who competed savagely with each other and with the established shopkeepers of the lower middle class.

Many a poor wife and mother joined the broad ranks of working women in the "sweated industries." These industries resembled the old putting-out and cottage industries of earlier times. The women normally worked at home and were paid by the piece.

The urban working classes sought fun and recreation, and they found both. Across the face of Europe drinking remained unquestionably the favorite leisure-time activity of working people. Generally, however, heavy "problem" drinking declined in the late nineteenth century as drinking became more public and social. Cafés and pubs became increasingly bright, friendly places.

labor aristocracy *Highly skilled workers who made up about 15 percent of the working classes at the turn of the twentieth century.*

The two other leisure-time passions of the working classes were sports and music halls. A great decline in "cruel sports," such as bullbaiting and cockfighting, led to the rise of modern spectator sports, of which racing and soccer were the most popular. There was a great deal of gambling on sports events. Music halls and vaudeville theaters, the working-class counterparts of middle-class opera and classical theater, were enormously popular throughout Europe.

The Changing Family

Industrialization and the growth of modern cities brought great changes to the lives of European women. These changes were particularly consequential for married women, and most women did marry in the nineteenth century.

After 1850 the work of most wives continued to become increasingly distinct and separate from that of their husbands (see pages 712–714). Husbands became wage earners in factories and offices; wives tended to stay home and manage households and care for children. As economic conditions improved, only married women in poor families tended to work outside the home. The ideal became **separate spheres,** the strict division of labor by sex: the wife as mother and homemaker, the husband as wage earner. This rigid division meant that married women faced great injustice if they tried to move into the men's world of employment outside the home.

separate spheres *A rigid gender division of labor, with the wife as mother and homemaker and the husband as wage earner.*

Middle-class women lacked legal rights and faced severe discrimination in education and employment. Thus organizations founded by middle-class feminists campaigned for legal equality as well as access to higher education and professional employment. In the later nineteenth century middle-class women scored some significant victories, such as the 1882 law giving English married women full property rights. Socialist women leaders usually took a different path. They argued that the liberation of working-class women would come only with the liberation of the entire working class through revolution. In the meantime they championed the cause of working women and won some practical improvements. In a general way these different approaches to women's issues reflected the diversity of classes in urban society.

As the ideology and practice of rigidly separate spheres narrowed women's horizons, their control and influence in the home became increasingly strong throughout Europe in the later nineteenth century. Among the English working classes, for example, it was the wife who generally determined how the family's money was spent. All the major domestic decisions, from the children's schooling and religious instruction to the selection of new furniture or a new apartment, were hers.

The woman's guidance of the household went hand in hand with the increased emotional importance of home and family. The home she ran was idealized as a warm shelter in a hard and impersonal urban world.

Married couples also developed stronger emotional ties to each other. Even in the comfortable classes, marriages in the late nineteenth century were increasingly based on sentiment and sexual attraction as money and financial calculation gradually declined in importance. Affection and eroticism became more central to the couple after marriage. Many French marriage manuals of the late 1800s stressed that women had legitimate sexual needs, such as the "right to orgasm."

One sign of deepening emotional ties within the family was the growing love and concern that mothers gave their tiny infants. Thus whereas the typical mother in preindustrial Western society was frequently indifferent toward her baby because the child was so likely to die, ordinary women became better mothers as the nineteenth century progressed. For example, mothers increasingly breast-fed their infants, which saved lives. The surge of maternal feeling also gave rise to a wave of specialized books on child rearing and infant hygiene.

There was also greater concern for older children and adolescents. They, too, were wrapped in the strong emotional ties of a more intimate and protective family. For one thing, European women began to limit the number of children they bore in order

SUNDAY MORNING
WORKMANS HOME
LEATHER LANE

● **A Working-Class Home, 1875** Emotional ties within ordinary families grew stronger in the nineteenth century. Parents gave their children more love and better care. (*Illustrated London News Library/ Mary Evans Picture Library*)

to care adequately for those they had. Indeed, many parents, especially in the middle classes, probably became *too* concerned about their children. The result was that many children and especially adolescents came to feel trapped and in need of greater independence.

The working classes probably had more avenues of escape from such tensions than did the middle classes. Unlike their middle-class counterparts, who remained economically dependent on their families until a long education was finished or a proper marriage secured, working-class boys and girls went to work when they reached adolescence. Earning wages on their own, they could bargain with their parents for greater independence within the household, or they could leave home to live cheaply as paying lodgers in other working-class homes. Thus the young person from the working classes broke away from the family more easily when emotional ties became oppressive.

Science and Culture

Major changes in Western thought and culture accompanied the emergence of urban society. Two aspects of these complex developments stand out as especially significant. Scientific knowledge expanded rapidly and came to influence the Western worldview more profoundly than ever before. And between about the 1840s and the 1890s, European literature underwent a shift from soaring romanticism to tough-minded realism.

The intellectual achievements of the scientific revolution in the seventeenth century had resulted in few practical benefits, and theoretical knowledge had also played a relatively small role in the Industrial Revolution in England. But breakthroughs in industrial technology enormously stimulated basic scientific inquiry as researchers sought to explain theoretically how such things as steam engines and blast furnaces actually worked. The result from the 1830s onward was an explosive growth of fundamental scientific discoveries that were increasingly transformed into material improvements for the general population.

MR. BERGH TO THE RESCUE.

THE DEFRAUDED GORILLA. "That *Man* wants to claim my Pedigree. He says he is one of my Descendants."
Mr. BERGH. "Now, Mr. DARWIN, how could you insult him so?"

● **Satirizing Darwin's Ideas** The heated controversies over Darwin's theory of evolution also spawned innumerable jokes and cartoons. This cartoon is by Darwin's contemporary, the American Thomas Nast. *(Culver Pictures)*

thermodynamics *A branch of physics built on Newton's laws of mechanics that investigated the relationship between heat and mechanical energy.*

evolution *The idea, applied by thinkers in many fields, that stresses gradual change and continuous adjustment.*

Social Darwinists *A group of thinkers who saw the human race as driven forward to ever-greater specialization and progress by the unending economic struggle, which would determine "the survival of the fittest."*

A perfect example of the translation of better scientific knowledge into practical human benefits was the work of Louis Pasteur and his followers in biology and the medical sciences (see page 696). Another was the development of the branch of physics known as **thermodynamics,** the relationship between heat and mechanical energy. By mid-century physicists had formulated the fundamental laws of thermodynamics, which were then applied to mechanical engineering, chemical processes, and many other fields.

The triumph of science and technology had at least three significant consequences. First, though ordinary citizens continued to lack detailed scientific knowledge, everyday experience and innumerable popularizers impressed the importance of science on the popular mind.

Second, as science became more prominent in popular thinking, the philosophical implications of science formulated in the Enlightenment spread to broad sections of the population. Natural processes appeared to be determined by rigid laws, leaving little room for either divine intervention or human will.

Third, the methods of science acquired unrivaled prestige after 1850. Thus many thinkers tried to apply the objective methods of science to the study of society from the 1830s onward. Leading nineteenth-century social scientists resembled the eighteenth-century philosophes, but they were more all-encompassing and dogmatic. Marx was a prime example (see page 681).

Living in an era of rapid change, nineteenth-century thinkers in Europe were fascinated with the idea of **evolution** and dynamic development. The most influential of all nineteenth-century evolutionary thinkers was Charles Darwin (1809–1882). Darwin came to doubt the general belief in a special divine creation of each species of animal. Instead, he concluded, all life had gradually evolved from a common ancestral origin in an unending "struggle for survival." Darwin's theory is summarized in the title of his work *On the Origin of Species by the Means of Natural Selection* (1859). He argued that chance differences among the members of a given species help some survive while others die. Thus the variations that prove useful in the struggle for survival are selected naturally and spread gradually to the entire species through reproduction.

Darwin's theory had a powerful and many-sided influence on European thought and the European middle classes. His findings reinforced the teachings of secularists such as Marx, who scornfully dismissed religious belief in favor of agnostic or atheistic materialism. Many writers also applied the theory of biological evolution to human affairs. Herbert Spencer (1820–1903), an English philosopher, saw the human race as driven forward to ever-greater specialization and progress by a brutal economic struggle that efficiently determines the "survival of the fittest." According to Spencer and other **Social Darwinists,** the poor are the ill-fated weak, the prosperous the chosen strong.

In literature, the key themes of realism emerged in the 1840s and continued to dominate Western culture and style until the 1890s. Realist writers believed that literature should depict life exactly as it is. Forsaking poetry for prose and the personal, emotional viewpoint of the romantics for strict scientific objectivity, the realists simply observed and recorded—content, they said, to let the facts speak for themselves.

The major realist writers focused their extraordinary powers of observation on contemporary everyday life. Beginning with a dissection of the middle classes, from which most of them sprang, many realists eventually focused on the working classes, especially the urban working classes, which had been neglected in imaginative literature before this time. The realists put a microscope to many unexplored and taboo subjects—sex, strikes, violence, alcoholism—and hastened to report that slums and factories teemed with savage behavior.

The realists' claims of objectivity did not prevent the elaboration of a definite world-view. Unlike the romantics, who had gloried in individual freedom and an unlimited universe, realists such as the famous French novelist Emile Zola (1840–1902) were strict determinists. They believed that human beings, like atoms, are components of the physical world and that all human actions are caused by unalterable natural laws: heredity and environment determine human behavior; good and evil are merely social conventions.

THE NATIONAL STATE AND THE SOCIALIST MOVEMENT (1871–1914)

How did governments gain popular support and deal with the socialist movement?

After 1871 the heartland of Europe was organized into strong national states, and the common themes within that framework were the emergence of mass politics and growing mass loyalty toward the national state. On the borders of Europe—in Ireland and Russia, in Austria-Hungary and the Balkans—the dynamics were different. Subject peoples there were still striving for political unity and independence. National aspirations created tensions, and mass politics often undermined existing states.

There were good reasons why ordinary people—the masses of an industrializing, urbanizing society—felt increasing loyalty to their governments in central and western Europe. More people could vote. By 1914 universal male suffrage had become the rule rather than the exception. This development had as much psychological as political significance. Ordinary men felt that they were becoming "part of the system."

Women also began to demand the right to vote. The women's suffrage movement achieved its first success in the western United States, and by 1913 women could vote in twelve states. In Europe, Norway gave the vote to most women in 1914. Elsewhere women generally failed before 1914, but they prepared the way for the triumph of the women's suffrage movement in many countries immediately after World War I.

As the right to vote spread, politicians and parties in national parliaments usually represented the people more responsively. The multiparty system prevailing in most countries meant that parliamentary majorities were built on shifting coalitions, which gave political parties leverage to obtain benefits for their supporters. Governments also passed laws to alleviate general problems, thereby acquiring greater legitimacy and appearing more worthy of support.

Less positively, governments found that they could manipulate national feeling to create a sense of unity and to divert attention away from the growing socialist movement. Therefore, after 1871 governing elites frequently channeled national sentiment in an antiliberal and militaristic direction, tolerating anti-Semitism and waging wars in nonwestern lands. This policy helped manage domestic conflicts, but only at the expense of increasing the international tensions that erupted in 1914 in cataclysmic war and revolution (see Chapter 27).

The German Empire

Politics in Germany after 1871 reflected many of the general developments. The new German Empire was a federal union of Prussia and twenty-four smaller states. Much of the everyday business of government was conducted by the separate states, but

Reichstag *The popularly elected lower house of government of the new German Empire after 1871.*

Kulturkampf *Bismarck's attack on the Catholic Church within Germany, also known as the "struggle for civilization."*

there was a strong national government with a chancellor—until 1890 Bismarck—and a popularly elected parliament called the **Reichstag**. Although Bismarck refused to be bound by a parliamentary majority, he tried nonetheless to maintain one. This situation gave the political parties opportunities. Until 1878 Bismarck relied mainly on the National Liberals, who had rallied to him after 1866 and represented the solid middle class. They supported legislation useful for further economic and legal unification of the country.

Less wisely, they backed Bismarck's attack on the Catholic Church, the so-called **Kulturkampf**, or "struggle for civilization." Like Bismarck, the middle-class National Liberals were particularly alarmed by Pius IX's declaration of papal infallibility in 1870. That dogma seemed to ask German Catholics to put loyalty to their church above loyalty to their nation. The Kulturkampf had limited success because German Catholics generally voted for the Catholic Center party, which blocked passage of national laws hostile to the church. Finally, in 1878 Bismarck abandoned his attack and entered into an uneasy but mutually advantageous alliance with the Catholic Center party. The reasons on both sides were largely economic.

Bismarck moved to enact high tariffs on cheap grain from the United States, Canada, and Russia, against which less efficient European producers could not compete. This won over not only the Catholic Center, whose supporters were small farmers in western and southern Germany, but also the Protestant Junkers, who had large landholdings in the east. With the tariffs, then, Bismarck won Catholic and conservative support. His use of tariffs was typical of other European governments of the late 1800s, which tried to protect national industries in response to popular pressure.

As for socialism, Bismarck tried to stop its growth in Germany, and in 1878 he forced through a law outlawing the Social Democrats. He genuinely feared their revolutionary language and allegiance to a movement transcending the nation-state. Unable to force socialism out of existence, Bismarck's essentially conservative nation-state pioneered social measures designed to win the support of working-class people. In 1883 he pushed through the Reichstag the first of several modern social security laws to help wage earners. Henceforth sick, injured, and retired workers could look forward to some regular benefits from the state. This national social security system, paid for through compulsory contributions by wage earners and employers as well as grants from the state, was the first of its kind anywhere.

In 1890 the new emperor, the young, idealistic, and unstable William II (r. 1888–1918), opposed Bismarck's attempt to renew the law outlawing the Social Democratic party. Eager to rule in his own right and to earn the support of the workers, William II forced Bismarck to resign. The government did pass new laws to aid workers and to legalize socialist political activity, but German foreign policy changed profoundly and mostly for the worse.

Yet William II was no more successful than Bismarck in getting workers to renounce socialism, and more and more Social Democrats were elected to the Reichstag in the 1890s. Yet the "revolutionary" socialists were actually becoming less and less revolutionary in Germany. In the years before World War I, the Social Democratic party broadened its base and adopted a more patriotic tone. Thus even German socialists identified increasingly with the German state, and they concentrated on gradual social and political reform.

Republican France

Although Napoleon III's reign made some progress in reducing antagonisms between classes, the war with Prussia undid these efforts, and in 1871 France seemed hopelessly divided once again. The patriotic republicans who proclaimed the Third Republic in Paris after the military disaster on the battlefield refused to admit defeat. They defended Paris with great heroism for weeks, living off rats and zoo animals until they were starved into submission by German armies in January 1871. When national elections then sent a large majority of conservatives and monarchists to the National Assembly, the traumatized Parisians exploded in patriotic frustration and proclaimed the Paris Commune in March 1871. Vaguely radical, the leaders of the Commune wanted to govern Paris without interference from the conservative French countryside. The National Assembly, led by aging conservative politician Adolphe Thiers, would hear none of it. The Assembly ordered the French army into Paris and brutally crushed the Commune. Twenty thousand people died in the fighting. As in June 1848, it was Paris against the provinces, French against French.

Out of this tragedy France slowly formed a new national unity before 1914. How is one to account for this? Luck played a part. Until 1875 the monarchists in the "republican" National Assembly had a majority but could not agree about who should be king. Thiers's destruction of the radical Commune and his other firm measures showed the fearful provinces and the middle class that the Third Republic might be moderate and socially conservative. France therefore retained the republic, though reluctantly.

Another stabilizing factor was the skill and determination of the moderate republican leaders in the early years. The most famous of these was Léon Gambetta, the son of an Italian grocer, a warm, easygoing lawyer who had turned professional politician. By 1879 the great majority of members of the upper and lower houses of the National Assembly were republicans, and the Third Republic had firm foundations after almost a decade.

● **Captain Alfred Dreyfus** Leaving an 1899 reconsideration of his original court martial, Dreyfus receives an insulting "guard of dishonor" from soldiers whose backs are turned. Top army leaders were determined to brand Dreyfus as a traitor. *(Roger-Viollet/Getty Images)*

The moderate republicans sought to preserve their creation by winning the hearts and minds of the next generation. Trade unions were fully legalized, and France acquired a colonial empire. More important, a series of laws between 1879 and 1886 established free compulsory elementary education for both girls and boys, thereby greatly reducing the role of parochial Catholic schools that had long been hostile to republics and to much of secular life. In France and elsewhere the general expansion of public education served as a critical nation-building tool in the late nineteenth century.

Many French Catholics rallied to the republic in the 1890s, and tensions between church and state eased. Unfortunately, the **Dreyfus affair** changed all that. Alfred Dreyfus, a Jewish captain in the French army, was falsely accused and convicted of treason. His family never doubted his innocence and fought to reopen the case, enlisting the support of prominent republicans and intellectuals. In 1898 and 1899 the case split France apart. On one side was the army, which had manufactured evidence against Dreyfus, joined by anti-Semites and most of the Catholic establishment. On the other side stood the civil libertarians and most of the more radical republicans.

This battle, which eventually led to Dreyfus's being declared innocent, revived militant republican feeling against the church. Between 1901 and 1905 the government severed all ties between the state and the Catholic Church after centuries of close relations, and the state school system's power of indoctrination was greatly strengthened. In France only the growing socialist movement, with its very different but thoroughly secular ideology, stood in opposition to the dominant faith in patriotic republican nationalism.

Dreyfus affair *A divisive case in which a Jewish captain in the French army was falsely accused and convicted of treason.*

Great Britain and the Austro-Hungarian Empire

The development of Great Britain and Austria-Hungary, two leading but quite different powers, throws a powerful light on the dynamics of nationalism in Europe before 1914. Britain in the late nineteenth century has often been seen as a shining example of peaceful and successful political evolution, where an effective two-party parliament skillfully guided the country from classical liberalism to full-fledged democracy with hardly a misstep. This view of Great Britain is not so much wrong as incomplete. After the right to vote was granted to males of the solid middle class in 1832, opinion leaders and politicians wrestled with the uncertainties of a further extension of the franchise. In 1867 Benjamin Disraeli and the Conservatives extended the vote to all middle-class males and the best-paid workers in the Second Reform bill, in order to broaden the Conservative party's traditional base of aristocratic and landed support. After 1867 English political parties and electoral campaigns became more modern, and the "lower orders" appeared to vote as responsibly as their "betters." Hence the Third Reform Bill of 1884 gave the vote to almost every adult male.

While the House of Commons was drifting toward democracy, the House of Lords, between 1901 and 1910, tried and ultimately failed to reassert itself. Aristocratic conservatism yielded to popular democracy once and for all. The result was that extensive social welfare measures, slow to come to Great Britain, were passed in a spectacular rush between 1906 and 1914. During those years the Liberal party substantially raised taxes on the rich as part of the so-called People's Budget. This income helped the government pay for national health insurance, unemployment benefits, old-age pensions, and a host of other social measures. The state was integrating the urban masses socially as well as politically.

This record of accomplishment was only part of the story, however. On the eve of World War I the question of Ireland brought Great Britain to the brink of civil war. The Irish famine in the 1840s (see page 684) fueled an Irish revolutionary movement. Thereafter the English slowly granted concessions, but refused to give Ireland self-government. After two decades of relative quiet, Irish nationalists in the British Parliament saw their chance. They supported the Liberals in their battle for the People's Budget and in 1913 received a home-rule bill for Ireland in return.

Ireland, however, was composed of two peoples. The Irish Catholic majority in the southern counties wanted home rule, but the Irish Protestants in the northern counties of Ulster vowed to resist it in northern Ireland with a hundred thousand armed volunteers. Ireland and Britain faced the prospect of civil war. Unable to resolve the conflicting nationalisms in Ireland as all Europe was suddenly overtaken by World War I in August 1914, the British government decided to postpone indefinitely the whole question of home rule for Ireland.

The dilemma of conflicting nationalisms in Ireland also helps one appreciate how desperate the situation in the Austro-Hungarian Empire had become by the early twentieth century. In 1849 Magyar nationalism had driven Hungarian patriots to declare an independent Hungarian republic, which was savagely crushed by Russian and Austrian armies (see pages 686–687). Throughout the 1850s Hungary was ruled as a conquered territory, and Emperor Francis Joseph (r. 1848–1916) and his bureaucracy tried hard to centralize the state and Germanize the language and culture of the different nationalities.

Then in the wake of defeat by Prussia in 1866, a weakened Austria was forced to strike a compromise and establish the so-called dual monarchy. The empire was divided in two, and the nationalistic Magyars gained virtual independence for Hungary. The two states were joined only by a shared monarch and common ministries for finance, defense, and foreign affairs. After 1867 the disintegrating force of competing nationalisms continued unabated, for both Austria and Hungary had several "Irelands" within their borders.

In Hungary the Magyar nobility in 1867 restored the constitution of 1848 and used it to dominate both the Magyar peasantry and the minority populations until 1914. Only the wealthiest one-fourth of adult males had the right to vote, making the parliament the creature of the Magyar elite. Laws promoting use of the Magyar (Hungarian) language in schools and government were rammed through and bitterly resented, especially by the Croatians and Romanians. While Magyar extremists campaigned loudly for total separation from Austria, the radical leaders of the subject nationalities dreamed in turn of independence from Hungary. Unlike most major European countries, which harnessed nationalism to strengthen the state after 1871, the Austro-Hungarian Empire was progressively weakened and eventually destroyed by the conflicting national aspirations of its different ethnic groups.

Jewish Emancipation and Modern Anti-Semitism

Revolutionary changes in political principles and the triumph of the nation-state brought equally revolutionary changes in Jewish life in western and central Europe. Beginning in France in 1791, Jews gradually gained their civil rights, although early progress was slow and uneven. In the 1850s and 1860s liberals in Austria, Italy, and Prussia pressed successfully for legal equality. In 1871 the constitution of the new German Empire consolidated the process of Jewish emancipation in central Europe. It abolished all restrictions on Jewish marriage, choice of occupation, place of residence, and property ownership. Exclusion from government employment and discrimination in social relations remained. However, according to one leading historian, by 1871 "it was widely accepted in Central Europe that the gradual disappearance of anti-Jewish prejudice was inevitable."[4]

The process of emancipation presented Jews with challenges and opportunities. Traditional Jewish occupations, such as court financial agent, village moneylender, and peddler, were undermined by free-market reforms, but careers in business, the professions, and the arts were opening to Jewish talent. Many Jews responded energetically and successfully. By 1871 a majority of Jewish people in western and central Europe had improved their economic situations and entered the middle classes. Most Jewish people also identified strongly with their respective nation-states and with good reason saw themselves as patriotic citizens.

Vicious anti-Semitism reappeared after the stock market crash of 1873, beginning in central Europe. Drawing on long traditions of religious intolerance, ghetto exclusion, and periodic anti-Jewish riots and expulsions, this anti-Semitism was also a modern development. It built on the general reaction against liberalism and its economic and political policies. Modern anti-Semitism whipped up resentment against Jewish achievement and Jewish "financial control," while fanatics claimed that the Jewish race (rather than the Jewish religion) posed a biological threat to the German people. Anti-Semitic beliefs were particularly popular among conservatives, extremist nationalists, and people who felt threatened by Jewish competition.

Anti-Semites also created modern political parties to attack and degrade Jews. In 1893, the prewar electoral high point in Germany, small anti-Semitic parties secured 2.9 percent of the votes cast. However, in Austrian Vienna in the early 1890s, Karl Lueger and his "Christian socialists" won striking electoral victories. This spurred a Jewish journalist named Theodor Herzl (1860–1904) to turn from German nationalism and advocate Jewish political nationalism, or **Zionism,** and the creation of a Jewish state. Lueger, the popular mayor of Vienna from 1897 to 1910, combined fierce anti-Semitic rhetoric with municipal ownership of basic services, and he appealed especially to the German-speaking lower middle class—and to an unsuccessful young artist named Adolf Hitler.

Before 1914 anti-Semitism was most oppressive in eastern Europe, where Jews also suffered from terrible poverty. In the Russian empire, where there was no Jewish

Primary Source:
Leo Pinsker, a Jewish Intellectual, Proposes a "Jewish Homeland," 1882
Noting that they are "at home everywhere, and nowhere at home," Pinsker argues that in order to be truly free, Jews need a homeland.

Zionism   *The movement toward Jewish political nationhood started by Theodor Herzl.*

Primary Source:
Ahad Ha-Am's "The Jewish State and the Jewish Problem"
Ha-Ams provides a different, more cautious, perspective on Zionism.

Primary Source:
The Jews' State
The organizer of the first World Zionist Congress argues for the creation of a Jewish state in Palestine.

emancipation and 4 million of Europe's 7 million Jewish people lived in 1880, officials used anti-Semitism to channel popular discontent away from the government and onto the Jewish minority. Russian Jews were denounced as foreign exploiters, and in 1881–1882 a wave of violent pogroms commenced in southern Russia. The police and the army stood aside for days while peasants looted Jewish property and injured and killed many Jewish people. Official harassment and discrimination continued in the following decades. As a result, some Russian Jews turned toward self-emancipation and the vision of a Zionist settlement in the Ottoman province of Palestine. Large numbers also emigrated to western Europe and the United States. About 2.75 million Jews left eastern Europe between 1881 and 1914.

The Socialist Movement

Nationalism served, for better or worse, as a new unifying principle. But what about socialism? Did the rapid growth of socialist parties, which were generally Marxian parties dedicated to an international proletarian revolution, mean that national states had failed to gain the support of workers? This question requires close examination.

Certainly socialism appealed to large numbers of working men and women in the late nineteenth century, and the growth of socialist parties after 1871 was phenomenal. (See the feature "Listening to the Past: The Making of a Socialist" on pages 712–713.) By 1912, the German Social Democratic party, which espoused Marxian ideology, had millions of followers and was the largest party in the Reichstag. Socialist parties also grew in other countries, and Marxian socialist parties were linked together in an international organization.

The bookish Marx showed a rare flair for combining theorization with both lively popular writing and organizational ability. In 1864 he played an important role in founding the First International of socialists, and he used its annual meetings as a means of spreading his realistic, "scientific" doctrines of inevitable socialist revolution.

The First International collapsed, but in 1889 socialist leaders came together to form the Second International, which lasted until 1914. The International had a great psychological impact. Every three years delegates from the different parties met to interpret Marxian doctrines and plan coordinated action by a permanent executive. Many feared and many others rejoiced in the growing power of socialism and the Second International.

Yet socialism was not as radical and revolutionary in these years as it sometimes appeared. Indeed, as socialist parties grew and attracted large numbers of members, they looked more and more toward gradual change and steady improvement for the working class and less and less toward revolution. Workers themselves were progressively less inclined to follow radical programs for several reasons. As workers gained the right to vote and won real benefits, their attention focused more on elections than on revolutions. Workers were also not immune to patriotic education, drum-beating parades, and aggressive foreign policy as they loyally voted for socialists. Nor were workers a unified social group. Perhaps most important of all, workers' standard of living rose gradually but substantially after 1850, and the quality of life improved substantially in urban areas. Thus workers tended to become militantly moderate: they demanded gains, but they were less likely to take to the barricades in pursuit of them.

The growth of labor unions reinforced this trend toward moderation. In the early stages of industrialization modern unions were considered subversive bodies and were generally prohibited by law. In Great Britain new unions formed for skilled workers after 1850 avoided radical politics and concentrated on winning better wages and hours for their members through collective bargaining and compromise. After 1890, unions for unskilled workers developed in Britain.

German unions were not granted important rights until 1869, and until the antisocialist law was repealed in 1890 the government frequently harassed them as socialist fronts. Then, with German industrialization still storming ahead and almost all legal harassment eliminated, union membership skyrocketed from only about 270,000 in 1895 to roughly 3 million in 1912. Genuine collective bargaining, long opposed by socialist intellectuals as a "sellout," was officially recognized as desirable by the German Trade Union Congress in 1899.

The German trade unions and their leaders were in fact, if not in name, thoroughgoing revisionists. **Revisionism** was an important effort by various socialists to update Marxian doctrines to reflect the realities of the time. The socialist Edward Bernstein (1850–1932) argued in 1899 in his *Evolutionary Socialism* that Marx's predictions of ever-greater poverty for workers had been proved false. Therefore, Bernstein suggested, socialists should reform their doctrines and win gradual evolutionary gains for workers through legislation, unions, and further economic development. The Second International denounced these views as heresy. Yet the revisionist, gradualist approach continued to gain the tacit acceptance of many German socialists, particularly in the trade unions.

Moderation found followers elsewhere. In France the great socialist leader Jean Jaurès (1859–1914) formally repudiated revisionist doctrines in order to establish a unified socialist party, but he remained at heart a gradualist. Questions of revolutionary versus gradualist policies split Russian Marxists.

Socialist parties in other countries also had clear-cut national characteristics. Russians and socialists in the Austro-Hungarian Empire tended to be the most radical. In Great Britain the socialist Labour party was non-Marxian and formally committed to gradual reform. In Spain and Italy anarchism, seeking to smash the state rather than the bourgeoisie, dominated radical thought and action. In short, socialist policies and doctrines varied from country to country. Socialism itself was to a large extent "nationalized" behind the imposing façade of international unity. This helps explain why almost all socialist leaders supported their governments when war came in 1914.

● **"Greetings from the May Day Festival"** Workers participated enthusiastically in the annual one-day strike on May 1 to honor internationalist socialist solidarity, as this postcard from a happy woman visitor to her cousin suggests. Speeches, picnics, and parades were the order of the day, and workers celebrated their respectability and independent culture. Picture postcards developed with railroads and mass travel. *(akg-images)*

revisionism *An effort by various socialists to update Marxian doctrines to reflect the realities of the time.*

Chapter Summary

Key Terms

dual revolution
Congress of Vienna
Holy Alliance
Carlsbad Decrees
laissez faire
socialism
parasites
doers
bourgeoisie
proletariat
Sturm und Drang
Corn Laws
national workshops
Schleswig and Holstein
Red Shirts
North German
  Confederation
modernization
October Manifesto
Benthamite
miasmatic theory
germ theory
pasteurization
labor aristocracy
separate spheres
thermodynamics
evolution
Social Darwinists
Reichstag
Kulturkampf
Dreyfus affair
Zionism
revisionism

To assess your mastery of this chapter, go to
bedfordstmartins.com/mckayworld

• How did the allies make peace in 1815, and what radical ideas emerged between 1815 and 1848?

In 1814 the victorious allied powers came together to restore peace and stability in Europe. Dealing moderately with France and wisely settling their own differences, the allies laid the foundations for beneficial international cooperation throughout much of the nineteenth century. Led by Metternich, the conservative powers also sought to prevent the spread of subversive ideas and radical changes in domestic politics. Yet European thought has seldom been more powerfully creative than after 1815, and ideologies of liberalism, nationalism, and socialism all developed to challenge the existing order. The romantic movement reinforced the spirit of change and revolutionary anticipation.

• Why did revolutions break out in 1848, and why did they fail?

All of these forces culminated in the liberal and nationalistic revolutions of 1848, but these upheavals failed to realize their goals. The moderate middle classes were unable to consolidate their initial victories. Instead, they drew back in fear when artisans, factory workers, and radical socialists rose up to present their own much more revolutionary demands. This retreat facilitated a resurgence of conservative forces that crushed revolution all across Europe.

• How did strong leaders and nation building transform Italy, Germany, and Russia?

These conservative forces, led by Cavour in Sardinia and by Bismarck in Prussia, then took the lead in the unification of Italy and of Germany after 1850. In both countries nation building relied on strong rule that was fortified by popular nationalism at critical moments. By 1871 larger, more unified, and more popular states had emerged in the West. Responding to military defeat, Russia also built a stronger country as it modernized partially by freeing the serfs, industrializing rapidly, and establishing a conservative constitutional monarchy after 1905.

• What was the impact of urban growth on cities, social classes, families, and ideas?

As urban civilization also came to prevail in Europe, governments took effective action in public health and developed badly needed urban services. Family life became more stable and more loving, although a sharp separation of gender roles tended to lock women into subordinate and stereotypical roles. While the quality of urban and family life improved, the class structure became more complex and diversified. Urban society featured many distinct social groups, and the complexity of social relations was a favorite theme of realist novelists. More generally, literary realism reflected Western society's growing faith in science, material progress, and evolutionary thinking.

• **How did governments gain popular support and deal with the socialist movement?**

Western society became increasingly nationalistic as well as urban and industrial in the late nineteenth century. Nation-states became more responsive, and they enlisted widespread support as peaceful political participation expanded, educational opportunities increased, and social security systems took shape. More broadly, nation-states may be seen as providing a stabilizing response to the profoundly unsettling challenges of the dual revolution. Even socialism became increasingly national in orientation, gathering strength as a champion of working-class interests in domestic politics. Yet even though nationalism served to unite peoples, it also drove them apart—not only in Austria-Hungary and Ireland but also throughout Europe and the rest of the world. The national faith, which reduced social tensions within states, promoted a bitter, almost Darwinian competition between states and thus threatened the progress and unity it had helped to build, as we shall see in Chapter 27.

Suggested Reading

Anderson, Bonnie S., and Judith P. Zinsser. *A History of Their Own: Women in Europe from Prehistory to the Present,* vol. 2, rev. ed. 2000. An excellent, wide-ranging survey.

Berend, Ivan T. *History Derailed: Central and Eastern Europe in the Long Nineteenth Century.* 2003. Focuses on industrialization and its consequences.

Coontz, Stephanie. *Marriage, A History: From Obedience to Intimacy, or How Love Conquered Marriage.* 2005. A lively inquiry into the historical background to current practice.

Gildea, Robert. *Barricades and Borders: Europe, 1800–1914,* 2d ed. 1996. A recommended general study.

Gottlieb, Beatrice. *The Family in the Western World.* 1993. A wide-ranging synthesis.

Malia, Martin, and Terrence Emmons. *History's Locomotives: Revolutions and the Making of the Modern World.* 2006. An ambitious comparative work of high quality.

Mann, Thomas. *Buddenbrooks.* 1901. A wonderful historical novel that traces the rise and fall of a prosperous German family over three generations.

Rubinstein, W. D. *Britain's Century: Political and Social History, 1815–1905.* 1998. An excellent history with strong coverage of social questions.

Tombs, Robert. *France, 1814–1914,* 1996. An impressive survey with a useful bibliography.

Vital, David. *A People Apart: The Jews in Europe, 1789–1939.* 1999. An engaging and judicious investigation.

Notes

1. E. Gellner, *Nations and Nationalism* (Oxford: Basil Blackwell, 1983), pp. 19–39.
2. B. Anderson, *Imagined Communities: Reflections on the Origins and Spread of Nationalism,* rev. ed. (London/New York: Verso, 1991).
3. J. McKay, *Tramways and Trolleys: The Rise of Urban Mass Transport in Europe* (Princeton, N.J.: Princeton University Press, 1976), p. 81.
4. R. Seltzer, *Jewish People, Jewish Thought: The Jewish Experience in History* (New York: Macmillan, 1980), p. 533.

Listening to the PAST

The Making of a Socialist

Nationalism and socialism appeared locked in bitter competition in Europe before 1914, but they actually complemented each other in many ways. Both faiths were secular as opposed to religious, and both fostered political awareness. A working person who became interested in politics and developed nationalist beliefs might well convert to socialism at a later date.

This was the case for Adelheid Popp (1869–1939), a self-taught working woman who became an influential socialist leader. Born into a desperately poor working-class family in Vienna and remembering only a "hard and gloomy childhood," she was forced by her parents to quit school at age ten to begin full-time work. She struggled with low-paying piecework for years before she landed a solid factory job, as she recounts in the following selection from her widely read autobiography.

Always an avid reader, Popp became the editor of a major socialist newspaper for German working women. She then told her life story so that all working women might share her truth: "Socialism could change and strengthen others, as it did me."

[Finally] I found work again; I took everything that was offered me in order to show my willingness to work, and I passed through much. But at last things became better. [At age fifteen] I was recommended to a great factory which stood in the best repute. Three hundred girls and about fifty men were employed. I was put in a big room where sixty women and girls were at work. Against the windows stood twelve tables, and at each sat four girls. We had to sort the goods which had been manufactured, others had to count them, and a third set had to brand on them the mark of the firm. We worked from 7 A.M. to 7 P.M. We had an hour's rest at noon, half-an-hour in the afternoon. . . . I had never yet been paid so much. . . .

I seemed to myself to be almost rich. . . . [Yet] from the women of this factory one can judge how sad and full of deprivation is the lot of a factory worker. In none of the neighbouring factories were the wages so high; we were envied everywhere. Parents considered themselves fortunate if they could get their daughters of fourteen in there on leaving school. . . . And even

here, in this paradise, all were badly nourished. Those who stayed at the factory for the dinner hour would buy themselves for a few pennies a sausage or the leavings of a cheese shop. . . . In spite of all the diligence and economy, every one was poor, and trembled at the thought of losing her work. All humbled themselves, and suffered the worst injustice from the foremen, not to risk losing this good work, not to be without food. . . .

I did not only read novels and tales; I had begun . . . to read the classics and other good books. I also began to take an interest in public events. . . . I was not democratically inclined. I was full of enthusiasm then for emperors, and kings and highly placed personages played no small part in my fancies. . . . I bought myself a strict Catholic paper, that criticised very adversely the workers' movement, which was attracting notice. Its aim was to educate in a patriotic and religious direction. . . . I took the warmest interest in the events that occurred in the royal families, and I took the death of the Crown Prince of Austria so much to heart that I wept a whole day. . . . Political events [also] held me in suspense. The possibility of a war with Russia roused my patriotic enthusiasm. I saw my brother already returning from the battlefield covered with glory. . . .

When a particularly strong anti-Semitic feeling was noticeable in political life, I sympathised with it for a time. A broad sheet, "How Israel Attained Power and Sovereignty over all the Nations of the Earth," fascinated me. . . .

About this time an Anarchist group was active. Some mysterious murders which had taken place were ascribed to the Anarchists, and the police made use of them to oppress the rising workmen's movement. . . . I followed the trial of the Anarchists with passionate sympathy. I read all the speeches, and because, as always happens, Social Democrats, whom the authorities really wanted to attack, were among the accused, I learned their views. I became full of enthusiasm. Every single Social Democrat . . . seemed to me a hero. . . .

There was unrest among the workers . . . and demonstrations of protest followed. When these

1890 engraving of a meeting of workers in Berlin. *(Bildarchiv Preussischer Kulturbesitz/ Art Resource, NY)*

were repeated the military entered the "threatened" streets. . . . In the evenings I rushed in the greatest excitement from the factory to the scene of the disturbance. The military did not frighten me; I only left the place when it was "cleared."

Later on my mother and I lived with one of my brothers who had married. Friends came to him, among them some intelligent workmen. One of these workmen was particularly intelligent, and . . . could talk on many subjects. He was the first Social Democrat I knew. He brought me many books, and explained to me the difference between Anarchism and Socialism. I heard from him, also for the first time, what a republic was, and in spite of my former enthusiasm for royal dynasties, I also declared myself in favour of a republican form of government. I saw everything so near and so clearly, that I actually counted the weeks which must still elapse before the revolution of state and society would take place.

From this workman I received the first Social Democratic party organ. . . . I first learned from it to understand and judge of my own lot. I learned to see that all I had suffered was the result not of a divine ordinance, but of an unjust organization of society. . . .

In the factory I became another woman. . . . I told my [female] comrades all that I had read of the workers' movement. Formerly I had often told stories when they had begged me for them. But instead of narrating . . . the fate of some queen, I now held forth on oppression and exploitation. I told of accumu-

lated wealth in the hands of a few, and introduced as a contrast the shoemakers who had no shoes and the tailors who had no clothes. On breaks I read aloud the articles in the Social Democratic paper and explained what Socialism was as far as I understood it. . . . [While I was reading] it often happened that one of the clerks passing by shook his head and said to another clerk: "The girl speaks like a man."

Questions for Analysis

1. How did Popp describe and interpret work in the factory?

2. To what extent did her socialist interpretation of factory life fit the facts she described?

3. What were Popp's political interests before she became a socialist?

4. How and why did she become a Social Democrat?

5. Was this account likely to lead other working women to socialism? Why?

Source: Slightly adapted from A. Popp, *The Autobiography of a Working Woman,* trans. E. C. Harvey (Chicago: F. G. Browne, 1913), pp. 29, 34–35, 39, 66–69, 71, 74, 82–90.

Ottoman Sultan Abdulaziz
(r. 1861–1876), supporter of vigorous modernizing reform.
(Topkapi Saray Museum/Dagli Orti/The Art Archive)

24 AFRICA, SOUTHWEST ASIA, AND WESTERN IMPERIALISM, 1800–1914

Chapter Preview

Industrialization and the World Economy
• What were the global consequences of European industrialization between 1800 and 1914?

Western Imperialism (1880–1914)
• What were the causes and consequences of European empire building after 1880?

The Islamic Heartland Under Pressure
• How did the Ottoman Empire and Egypt try to revitalize themselves, and what were the most important results?

Sub-Saharan Africa: From the Slave Trade to European Rule
• What were the most significant changes in sub-Saharan Africa, and why did they occur?

While industrialization and nationalism were transforming urban life and Western society, Western society had a profound impact on non-Western countries and regions. An ever-growing stream of products, people, and ideas flowed out of Europe at this time. The most spectacular manifestation of this many-sided Western expansion came in the late nineteenth century when the leading European nations established or enlarged their far-flung political empires.

Western industrialization and imperialism posed a profound challenge to the many, highly diverse peoples of Africa and Asia. Economic relationships changed, as Europe consolidated its industrial lead and urged Africa and Asia to sell more commodities and raw materials. Political independence and established cultural and religious values also were threatened by Western penetration. It is little wonder, therefore, that African and Asian states and peoples often tried to repel the foreigners with military force and searched for other methods when they were defeated. Stretching over two centuries, the timing of these encounters with the West certainly contributed to the great diversity of historical experiences in Africa and Asia in the years before World War I. This chapter will consider the Islamic heartland and Africa, and Chapter 25 will turn to South Asia and East Asia.

The Western challenge in the land of Islam emerged in the late seventeenth century, when the Ottoman Empire began to suffer military reversals. The Ottomans eventually responded with a series of reforms designed to modernize the army and protect the empire, but these efforts were only partly successful. The Ottoman Empire continued to lose territory throughout the nineteenth century. Its Egyptian province became increasingly independent and launched its own campaign of westernization until it went bankrupt and was conquered by Britain. Yet both the Ottoman Empire and Egypt also made real progress and laid the foundations of modern Turkey and Egypt.

In sub-Saharan Africa the slow decline of the transatlantic slave trade in the nineteenth century accompanied a great expansion of commodity exports, a shift that marked the beginning of modern economic development in this vast and diverse region. At the same time, powerful movements of Islamic revival extended the sway of Islam in West and central Africa and made Islam a more important part of everyday life and culture. In southern Africa competing groups of white settlers pressed northward and eastward after 1800, foreshadowing European conquest and empire building in the whole continent after 1880. In short, in the nineteenth century Africa experienced greater and more far-reaching changes than ever before.

INDUSTRIALIZATION AND THE WORLD ECONOMY

What were the global consequences of European industrialization between 1800 and 1914?

The Industrial Revolution created, first in Great Britain and then in continental Europe and North America, a growing and dynamic economic system. In the course of the nineteenth century that system expanded and transformed economic relations across the face of the earth. As a result the world's total income grew as never before, international trade boomed, and millions of migrants settled in distant lands. Thus Western industrialization had profound consequences for the global economy and the world's peoples.

The Rise of Global Inequality

The Industrial Revolution in Europe marked a momentous turning point in human history. From a global perspective, the ultimate significance of the Industrial Revolution was that it allowed those regions of the world that industrialized in the nineteenth century to increase their wealth and power enormously in comparison with those that did not. Moreover, this pattern of uneven global development became institutionalized, or built into the structure of the world economy, and the **lopsided world**—a world of rich lands and poor—evolved.

lopsided world *A world of rich lands and poor lands and global inequality.*

Figure 24.1 depicts the gap between the industrializing regions (mainly Europe and North America) and the non-industrializing ones (mainly Africa, Asia, and Latin America) that opened up in the late eighteenth and the nineteenth centuries. In 1750 the average standard of living was no higher in Europe as a whole than in the rest of the world. By 1970, however, the average person in the wealthiest countries had an income fully twenty-five times as great as the income received by the average person in the poorest countries of Africa and Asia. The rise in average income and well-being, first in Great Britain and then in the other developed countries, reflected the rising level of industrialization (see pages 656–657). Thus average income per person stagnated in the Third World before 1913. Only after 1945, in the era of political independence and decolonization, did the developing countries of Africa, Asia, and Latin America as a whole make real economic progress and begin the critical process of industrialization.

The rise of these enormous income disparities, which are poignant indicators of disparities in food and clothing, health

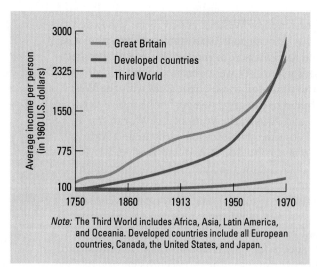

● FIGURE 24.1 **The Growth of Average Income per Person in the Third World, Developed Countries, and Great Britain, 1750–1970** (Source: P. Bairoch and M. Lévy-Leboyer, eds., *Disparities in Economic Development Since the Industrial Revolution,* published 1981, Macmillan Publishers. Reproduced with permission of Palgrave Macmillan.)

and education, life expectancy and general material well-being, has generated a great deal of debate. One school of interpretation stresses that the West used science, technology, capitalist organization, and even its critical worldview to create its wealth and greater physical well-being. Another school argues that the West used its political and economic power to steal much of its riches, continuing in the nineteenth (and twentieth) century the rapacious colonialism born of the era of European expansion.

These issues are complex, and there are few simple answers. As noted in Chapter 22, the wealth-creating potential of technological improvement and more intensive capitalist organization was indeed great. At the same time, the initial breakthroughs in the late eighteenth century rested in part on Great Britain's having already used political force to dominate a substantial part of the world economy. In the nineteenth century other industrializing countries joined with Britain to extend Western dominion over the entire world economy. Unprecedented wealth was indeed created, but the lion's share of that new wealth flowed to the West and its propertied classes and to a tiny non-Western elite of cooperative rulers, landowners, and merchants.

The World Market

World trade was a powerful stimulus to economic development in the nineteenth century. In 1913 the value of world trade was about twenty-five times what it had been in 1800, even though prices of manufactured goods and raw materials were lower in 1913 than in 1800. In a general way, the enormous increase in international commerce summed up the growth of an interlocking world economy centered in Europe.

Great Britain played a key role in using trade to tie the world together economically. In 1815 Britain already had a colonial empire, for India, Canada, Australia, and other scattered areas remained British possessions after American independence. The technological breakthroughs of the Industrial Revolution encouraged British manufacturers to seek export markets around the world. After the repeal of the Corn Laws in 1846 (see page 684), Britain also became the world's leading importer of foreign goods. Free access to Britain's market stimulated the development of mines and plantations in Africa and Asia.

The growth of trade was facilitated by the conquest of distance. The earliest railroad construction occurred in Europe and in America north of the Rio Grande; other parts of the globe saw the building of rail lines after 1860. By 1920 about a quarter of the world's railroads were in Latin America, Asia, Africa, and Australia. Wherever railroads were built, they drastically reduced transportation costs, opened new economic opportunities, and called forth new skills and attitudes.

Much of the railroad construction undertaken in Africa, Asia, and Latin America connected seaports with inland cities and regions, as opposed to linking and developing

Chronology

1780s–1860 Industrial Revolution

1808–1839 Mahmud II rules Ottoman state and enacts reforms

1809 Usuman founds Sokoto caliphate

1810–1855 Palm oil becomes "legitimate" commerce in West Africa

1830 France begins conquest of Algeria

1839–1876 Ottoman statesmen enact reforms (Tanzimat)

1863–1879 Reign of Ismail in Egypt

1871–1879 Al-Afghani preaches Islamic regeneration

1875 Ottoman state declares partial bankruptcy; European creditors take over

1876 Europeans take financial control in Egypt

1880 Western and central Sudan united under Islam

1880–1902 Europeans scramble for Africa

1880–1914 Height of Western imperialism in Asia and Africa

1884–1885 Berlin Conference

1899 Kipling, "The White Man's Burden"; Amin, *The Liberation of Women*

1899–1902 South African War

1902 Conrad, *Heart of Darkness;* Hobson, *Imperialism*

1908 Young Turks seize power in Ottoman state

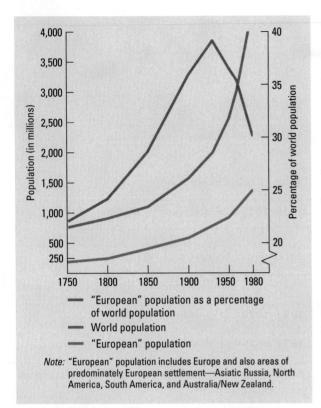

● FIGURE 24.2 **The Increase of European and World Populations, 1750–1980** (Sources: W. Woodruff, *Impact of Western Man: A Study of Europe's Role in the World Economy.* St. Martin's Press, New York, 1967, p. 103; United Nations, *Statistical Yearbook, 1982,* pp. 2–3.)

cities and regions within a given country. Thus railroads dovetailed with Western economic interests, facilitating the inflow and sale of Western manufactured goods and the export and development of local raw materials.

The power of steam also revolutionized transportation by sea. Steam power, long used to drive paddle wheelers on rivers, particularly in Russia and North America, finally began to supplant sails on the oceans of the world in the late 1860s. Lighter, stronger, cheaper steel replaced iron, which had replaced wood. Passenger and freight rates tumbled, and the shipment of low-priced raw materials from one continent to another became feasible.

The revolution in land and sea transportation helped European settlers take vast, thinly populated territories and produce agricultural products and raw materials there for sale in Europe. Improved transportation enabled Asia, Africa, and Latin America to export not only the traditional tropical products—spices, dyes, tea, sugar, coffee—but also new raw materials for industry, such as jute, rubber, cotton, and coconut oil. (See the feature "Global Trade: Indigo" on pages 720–721.)

Intercontinental trade was enormously facilitated by the Suez and Panama Canals. Of great importance, too, was large and continual investment in modern port facilities, which made loading and unloading cheaper, faster, and more dependable. Finally, transoceanic telegraph cables inaugurated rapid communications among the financial centers of the world and linked world commodity prices in a global network.

The growth of trade and the conquest of distance encouraged Europeans to make massive foreign investments beginning about 1840. Most of the capital exported did not go to European colonies or protectorates in Asia and Africa. About three-quarters of total European investment went to other European countries, the United States and Canada, Australia and New Zealand, and Latin America. Europe found its most profitable opportunities for investment in construction of the railroads, ports, and utilities that were necessary to settle and develop the lands of extensive European expansion. Much of this investment was peaceful and mutually beneficial for lenders and borrowers. The victims were Native American Indians and Australian Aborigines, who were displaced and decimated by the diseases, liquor, and weapons of an aggressively expanding Western society (see Chapter 26).

The Great Migration

A poignant human drama was interwoven with economic expansion: millions of people pulled up stakes and left their ancestral lands in one of history's greatest migrations. In the early eighteenth century the world's population entered a period of rapid growth, which continued unabated through the nineteenth and twentieth centuries, as Figure 24.2 shows. The population of Europe (including Asiatic Russia) more than doubled, from approximately 188 million in 1800 to roughly 432 million in 1900. More than 60 million people left Europe, primarily for the rapidly growing "areas of European settlement"—North and South America, Australia, New Zealand, and Siberia (see Chapter 26).

Between 1750 and 1900 the population of Asia followed the same general trend. China, by far the world's most populous country in the middle of the eighteenth century, increased from about 143 million in 1741 to a little more than 400 million in the 1840s, although total numbers grew more slowly in the turbulent late nineteenth century. Since population increased more slowly in Africa and Asia than in Europe, Europeans and peoples of predominately European origin jumped from about 22 percent of the world's total in 1850 to a high of about 38 percent in 1930.

The growing number of Europeans was a driving force behind emigration and Western expansion. The rapid increase in numbers led to relative overpopulation in area after area in Europe. Thus millions of country folk went abroad as well as to nearby cities in search of work and economic opportunity. European emigration crested in the first decade of the twentieth century, when more than five times as many men and women departed as in the 1850s.

The European migrant was most often a small peasant landowner or a village crafts-man whose traditional way of life was threatened by too little land, estate agriculture, and cheap factory-made goods. Determined to maintain or improve their precarious status, the vast majority of migrants were young and very often unmarried. Many European migrants returned home after some time abroad. One in two migrants to Argentina and probably one in three to the United States eventually returned to their native lands.

Ties of family and friendship played a crucial role in the movement of peoples. Many people from a given province or village settled together in rural enclaves or tightly knit urban neighborhoods thousands of miles away. Very often a strong individual—a businessman, a religious leader—would blaze the way and others would follow, forming a **migration chain.**

migration chain *The movement of peoples in which one strong individual would blaze the way and others would follow.*

Many young European men and women were spurred to leave by a spirit of revolt and independence. In Sweden and Norway, in Jewish Russia and Italy, these young people felt frustrated by the small privileged classes that often controlled both church and government and resisted demands for change and greater opportunity. Migration slowed when people won basic political and social reforms, such as the right to vote and social security.

A substantial number of Asians—especially Chinese, Japanese, Indians, and Filipinos—also responded to population pressure and rural hardship with temporary or permanent migration. At least 3 million Asians (in contrast to more than 60 million Europeans) moved abroad before 1920. Most went as indentured laborers to work under incredibly difficult conditions on the plantations or in the gold mines of Latin America, southern Asia, Africa, California, Hawaii, and Australia (see Chapter 25). White estate owners very often used Asians to replace or supplement blacks after the suppression of the Atlantic slave trade.

Such migration from Asia would undoubtedly have grown to much greater proportions if planters and mine owners in search of cheap labor had had their way. But usually they did not. Asians fled the plantations and gold mines as soon as possible, seeking greater opportunities in trade and towns. There they came into conflict with white settlers in areas of European settlement. These settlers demanded a halt to Asian immigration. By the 1880s Americans and Australians were building **great white walls**—discriminatory laws designed to keep Asians out.

great white walls *Discriminatory laws that appeared in the 1880s in the United States and Australia and were designed to keep Asians out.*

The general policy of "whites only" in the lands of large-scale European settlement meant that Europeans and people of European ancestry reaped the main benefits of the great migration. By 1913 people in Australia, Canada, and the United States all had higher average incomes than people in Great Britain, still Europe's wealthiest nation. This, too, was part of Western dominance in the increasingly lopsided world.

Within Asia and Africa the situation was different. Migrants from south China frequently settled in Dutch, British, and French colonies of Southeast Asia, where they established themselves as peddlers and small shopkeepers (see Chapter 25). These "overseas Chinese" gradually emerged as a new class of entrepreneurs and officeworkers. Traders from India and modern-day Lebanon performed the same function in much of sub-Saharan Africa after the European seizure in the late nineteenth century.

INDIGO

Few items shed more light on issues of production and on the prodigious growth of world trade in the nineteenth century than indigo, the oldest and most important natural colorant. The extract of leaves from a small bush that are carefully fermented in vats and processed into cakes of pigment, indigo has been highly prized since antiquity. It dyes all fabrics, does not fade with time, and yields tints ranging from light blue to the darkest purple-blue. Used primarily today as a dye for blue jeans, indigo has been used throughout history as a dye for textiles, as a pigment for painting, and for medicinal and cosmetic purposes. Global trade in the famous blue dye expanded after 1500 and was repeatedly restructured until, in the late nineteenth century, it was revolutionized by an industrializing Europe.

Indigo for local consumption could be obtained from many plants in tropical climates, but the best-known species for trade came from India. Widely grown and used in Asia, indigo trickled into Europe from western India in the High Middle Ages but was very expensive. Woad—an inferior homegrown product—remained Europe's main blue dye until the opening of a direct sea route to India by the Portuguese in 1498 reconfigured the intercontinental trade in indigo, as it did for many Asian products. Bypassing Muslim traders in the Indian Ocean and gradually overcoming the opposition of the woad interests in Europe, first Portuguese and then Dutch and English merchants and trading companies supplied European dyers and consumers with cheaper, more abundant indigo.

The Indigo Trade

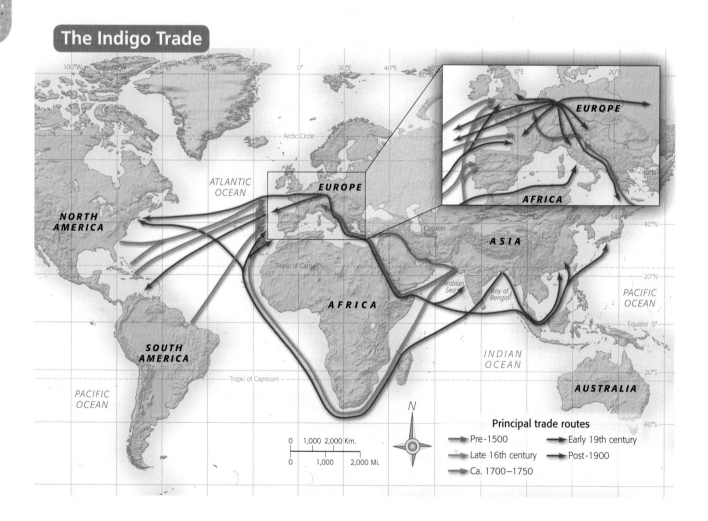

Principal trade routes

→ Pre-1500
→ Late 16th century
→ Ca. 1700–1750
→ Early 19th century
→ Post-1900

In the early seventeenth century, indigo became one of the British East India Company's chief articles of trade, and it was exported from India to Europe more than ever before. However, as European governments adopted mercantilist policies, they tried to control trade and limit the flow of gold and silver abroad for products like indigo. The result was a second transformation in the global trade in indigo.

Europeans established indigo plantations in their American colonies, and by the first half of the eighteenth century only small quantities of indigo continued to reach Europe from peasant producers in western India. Indigo plantations in Brazil, Guatemala, Haiti and the Caribbean, and South Carolina were big, capitalistic operations and frequently very profitable. They depended on slaves brought from Africa, as did the entire Atlantic economy in the eighteenth century.

In the late eighteenth century the geography of the indigo trade shifted dramatically once again: production returned to India, now largely controlled by the British. Why did this happen? Political upheaval in the revolutionary era played a key role. American independence left South Carolina outside Britain's mercantilist system; slave rebellion in Haiti in 1791 decimated some of the world's richest indigo producers; and Britain's continental blockades cut off Spain and France from their colonies. On the economy side, the takeoff in the British textile industry created surging demand for indigo. Thus in the 1780s, the British East India Company hired experienced indigo planters from the West Indies to develop indigo production in Bengal. Leasing lands from Indian *zemindars* (landlords who doubled as tax collectors), British planters coerced Bengali peasants into growing indigo, which the planters processed in their "factories." Business expanded rapidly, as planters made—and lost—fortunes in boom-and-bust cycles characteristic of commodity production in the nineteenth century.

In 1859 Bengali peasants revolted and received unexpected support from British officials advocating free-market contracts and recourse to the courts to settle disputes. As peasants pressed their case against the outraged planters, Indian professionals and intellectuals joined their cause. Winning freer and more equitable contracts, the rural-urban alliance created in the "Indigo Disturbances" marked a key step in the growth of nation-

alism in Bengal, a leading force in the subsequent drive for Indian independence.

Even as the "Indigo Disturbances" agitated Bengal, industrializing Europe discovered on its doorstep a completely new source of colorants—thick, black coal tar. This residue, a noxious byproduct from the destructive distillation of soft coal for the gas used in urban lighting and heating, was emerging as the basic material for the chemistry of carbon compounds and a new synthetic dye industry. Building on early theoretical and experimental work, British, German, and French chemists synthesized a small number of dyes between 1856 and 1869, when the first synthetic dye replaced a natural dye. Thereafter German researchers and Germany's organic chemical companies, protected by effective international patent laws after 1877, built up an interlocking global monopoly that produced more than 90 percent of the world's synthetic dyes.

Indigo was emblematic of this resounding success. Professor Adolf Bayer first synthesized indigo in 1880. But an economically viable process required many years of costly, systematic research before two leading German companies working together achieved their objective in 1897. Producers' groups in India slashed indigo prices drastically but to no avail. Indian exports of natural indigo plummeted from nineteen thousand tons in 1895 to only one thousand tons in 1913. Synthetic indigo claimed the global market, German firms earned super profits, and Indian peasants turned to different crops. Today, nearly all of the indigo produced in the world is synthetic, although limited production of natural indigo still occurs in India, as well as in parts of Africa and South America.

● **An Italian Custom in Argentina**   Italian immigrants introduced the game of *boccia* to Argentina, where it took hold and became a popular recreation for men. Dressed up in their Sunday best, these Argentinean laborers are totally focused on the game, which is something like horseshoes or shuffleboard. *(Hulton Archive/Getty Images)*

Thus in some parts of Asia and Africa the business class was both Asian and foreign, protected and tolerated by Western imperialists who found them useful.

While migration from Europe, and to a lesser extent Asia, increased in the nineteenth century, the total flow of enslaved men and women out of Africa declined very gradually after 1800. The decline began in the 1830s and continued at an accelerating pace until the 1890s, when the export of African slaves had been greatly reduced. The gradual passing of the long-standing and massive forced migration of Africans to the Americas had many far-reaching consequences for African societies, as we shall see.

WESTERN IMPERIALISM (1880–1914)

What were the causes and consequences of European empire building after 1880?

Western expansion into Asia and Africa reached its apex between about 1880 and 1914. In those years the leading European nations continued to send streams of money and manufactured goods to both continents, and they also rushed to create or enlarge vast political empires abroad. This frantic political empire building contrasted sharply with the economic penetration of non-Western territories between 1816 and 1880, which, albeit by naked military force, had left a China or a Japan "opened" but politically independent (see Chapter 25). By contrast, the empires of the late nineteenth century recalled the old European colonial empires of the seventeenth and eighteenth centuries and led contemporaries to speak of the "new imperialism."

The most spectacular manifestation of the new imperialism was the seizure of almost all of Africa, which broke sharply with previous patterns and fascinated contemporary Europeans and Americans, as we shall see later in this chapter. Although the sudden division of Africa was more striking, Europeans also extended their political control in Asia. The British expanded from their base in India, and in the 1880s the

French took Indochina (modern Vietnam, Cambodia, and Laos). India and China also experienced a profound imperialist impact (see Chapter 25).

Causes of the New Imperialism

Many factors contributed to the West's late-nineteenth-century rush for territory in Africa and Asia, and it is little wonder that controversies have raged over interpretation of the new imperialism. But despite complexity and controversy, basic causes are clearly identifiable.

Economic motives played an important role in the extension of political empires, especially the British Empire. By the late 1870s France, Germany, and the United States were industrializing rapidly behind rising tariff barriers. Great Britain was losing its industrial leadership and facing increasingly tough competition in foreign markets. In this new economic situation Britain came to value more highly its old possessions, especially its vast and highly profitable colony in India, which it had exploited most profitably for more than a century. When in the 1880s European continental powers began to grab unclaimed territories, the British followed suit immediately. They feared France and Germany would seal off their empires with high tariffs and that future economic opportunities would be lost forever.

Actually, the overall economic gains of the new imperialism proved limited before 1914. The new colonies were too poor to buy much, and they offered few immediately profitable investments. Nonetheless, colonies became important for political and diplomatic reasons. Each leading European country saw colonies as crucial to national security, military power, and international prestige.

Colonial rivalries reflected the increasing aggressiveness of European Social Darwinian theories of brutal competition among races. Thus European nations, which were seen as racially distinct parts of the dominant white race, had to seize colonies to show they were strong and virile. Moreover, the conquest of inferior peoples was just. Social Darwinism and harsh racial doctrines fostered imperialist expansion.

Ongoing industrial and technological advances, accelerating after 1880 with new industries based on scientific research (see page 702), gave Western countries unprecedented military superiority and greatly facilitated Western imperialism. Three aspects were crucial. First, the rapidly firing machine gun became an ultimate weapon in many an unequal battle. Second, newly discovered **quinine** proved effective in controlling attacks of malaria, which had previously decimated Europeans in the tropics whenever they left breezy coastal enclaves and dared to venture into mosquito-infested interiors. Third, the combination of the steamship and the international telegraph permitted Western powers to quickly concentrate their firepower in a given area when it was needed. Never before—and never again after 1914—would the technological gap between the West and non-Western regions of the world be so great.

quinine *An agent that proved effective in controlling attacks of malaria, which had previously decimated Europeans in the tropics.*

Social tensions and domestic political conflicts also contributed to overseas expansion. Conservative political leaders often manipulated colonial issues in order to divert popular attention from domestic conflicts and to create a false sense of national unity. Thus imperial propagandists relentlessly stressed that colonies benefited workers as well as capitalists, and they encouraged the masses to savor foreign triumphs and glory in the supposed increase in national prestige.

Special-interest groups in each country were powerful agents of expansion. White settlers wanted more land, and humanitarians wanted to stop the slave trade. Military men and colonial officials foresaw rapid advancement and high-paid positions in growing empires.

Imperialists did not rest the case for empire solely on naked conquest and a Darwinian racial struggle or on power politics and the need for naval bases on every ocean. Imperialists developed additional arguments to satisfy their consciences and answer their critics. A favorite idea was that Europeans and Americans could and should "civilize" supposedly primitive non-Western peoples. According to this view,

Africans and Asians would receive the benefits of modern economies, cities, advanced medicine, and higher standards of living and eventually might be ready for self-government and Western democracy.

Another argument was that imperial government protected colonized peoples from ethnic warfare and the slave trade within Africa, as well as from cruder forms of exploitation by white settlers and business people. Thus the French spoke of their sacred "civilizing mission." Similarly, Rudyard Kipling (1865–1936), who wrote extensively on Anglo-Indian life and was perhaps the most influential British writer of the 1890s, exhorted Westerners to provide humanitarian service in imperial possessions. There they should "take up the White Mans's Burden" and work for the betterment of their "new-caught sullen peoples."[1]

Imperialists claimed that peace and stability under European control would permit the spread of Christianity. In Africa Catholic and Protestant missionaries competed with Islam south of the Sahara, seeking converts and building schools. Many Africans' first real contact with Europeans and Americans was in mission schools. Some peoples, such as the Ibo in Nigeria, became highly Christianized. Such occasional successes in black Africa contrasted with the general failure of missionary efforts in the Islamic world and in much of Asia.

Western Critics of Imperialism

The expansion of empire aroused sharp, even bitter, Western critics. A forceful attack was delivered in 1902, after the unpopular South African War, by radical English economist J. A. Hobson (1858–1940) in his *Imperialism,* a work that influenced Lenin and others. Hobson contended that the rush to acquire colonies was due to the economic needs of unregulated capitalism. Moreover, Hobson argued, the quest for empire diverted popular attention away from domestic reform and the need to reduce the great gap between rich and poor at home. These and similar arguments had limited appeal because most people were sold on the idea that imperialism was economically profitable for the homeland.

Hobson and many Western critics struck home, however, with their moral condemnation of whites imperiously ruling nonwhites. Kipling and his kind were lampooned as racist bullies whose rule rested on brutality, racial contempt, and the Maxim machine gun. Polish-born novelist Joseph Conrad (1857–1924), in *Heart of Darkness* (1902), castigated the "pure selfishness" of Europeans in "civilizing" Africa. The main character in the novel, once a liberal European scholar, is corrupted by power in Africa and turns into a savage brute.

Critics charged Europeans with applying a degrading double standard and failing to live up to their own noble ideals. At home Europeans had won or were winning representative government, individual liberties, and a certain equality of opportunity. In their empires Europeans imposed military dictatorships on Africans and Asians; forced them to work involuntarily; and discriminated against them shamelessly. Only by renouncing imperialism and giving captive peoples the freedom idealized in Western society would Europeans be worthy of their traditions.

African and Asian Resistance

Primary Source:
His Story
Read a firsthand account of the hardships suffered by the Ndebele, a people of southeastern Africa, in their dealings with European colonists.

To peoples in Africa and Asia, Western expansion represented a disruptive, many-sided assault with many consequences. Everywhere it threatened traditional ruling classes, economies, and ways of life. Christian missionaries and European secular ideologies challenged established beliefs and values. African and Asian societies experienced a crisis of identity and a general pattern of reassertion, although the details of each people's story varied substantially.

● **A Missionary School**
A Swahili schoolboy leads his class-mates in a reading lesson in Dar es Salaam in German East Africa before 1914, as portraits of Emperor William II and his wife look down on the classroom. Europeans argued that they were spreading the benefits of a superior civilization with schools like this one, which is unusually solid because of its strategic location in the capital city. *(Ullstein Bilderdienst/ The Granger Collection, New York)*

Often the initial response of African and Asian rulers was to try driving the unwelcome foreigners away, as in China and Japan (see Chapter 25). Violent antiforeign reactions exploded elsewhere again and again, but the superior military technology of the industrialized West almost invariably prevailed. Beaten in battle, many Africans and Asians concentrated on preserving their cultural traditions at all costs. Others found themselves forced to reconsider their initial hostility. Some concluded that the West was indeed superior in certain ways and that it was therefore necessary to reform their societies and copy some European achievements. Thus it is possible to think of responses to the Western impact as a spectrum, with **traditionalists** at one end, westernizers or **modernizers** at the other, and many shades of opinion in between. The struggles among these groups were often intense. With time, however, the modernizers tended to gain the upper hand.

When armed resistance to European domination was thoroughly shattered by superior force, the great majority of Asians and Africans accepted imperial rule. Political participation in non-Western lands was historically limited to small elites, and the masses were used to doing what their rulers told them to do. In these circumstances Europeans governed effectively. They received considerable support from both traditionalists (local chiefs, landowners, and religious leaders) and modernizers (Western-educated professional classes and civil servants).

Nevertheless, imperial rule was in many ways an imposing edifice built on sand. Support for European rule among the conforming and accepting millions was shallow and weak. Thus the conforming masses came to follow with greater or lesser enthusiasm a few determined personalities who came to oppose the Europeans. Such leaders always arose, both when Europeans ruled directly and when they manipulated native governments, for at least two basic reasons.

First, the nonconformists—the eventual anti-imperialist leaders—developed a burning desire for human dignity. They came to feel that such dignity was incompatible

traditionalists *Those native to a colony who focused on preserving their traditional culture against imperialists at all costs.*

modernizers *Those native to a colony who believed that Western impact had affected their society in some positive ways and who wanted to reform their country in a similar manner.*

with foreign rule. Second, potential leaders found in the Western world the ideologies and justification for their protest. Thus they discovered liberalism, with its credo of civil liberty and political self-determination. They echoed the demands of anti-imperialists in Europe and America that the West live up to its own ideals.

More important, they found themselves attracted to the nineteenth-century Western ideology of nationalism, which asserted that every people—or at least every European people—had the right to control its own destiny. After 1917 anti-imperialist revolt would find another weapon in Lenin's version of Marxian socialism.

THE ISLAMIC HEARTLAND UNDER PRESSURE

How did the Ottoman Empire and Egypt try to revitalize themselves, and what were the most important results?

Stretching from West Africa into southeastern Europe and across Southwest Asia all the way to the East Indies, Islamic civilization competed successfully and continuously with western Europe for centuries. Thus from the seventh to the seventeenth centuries, Muslim forces conquered and ruled many lands, while Muslim economies generally equaled or surpassed those in Europe. Muslim societies were also proud and self-confident because they believed in the truth and the superiority of their faith.

Beginning in the late seventeenth century, the rising absolutist states of Austria and Russia began to challenge the greatest Muslim state, the vast Ottoman Empire, and gradually to reverse Ottoman rule in southeastern Europe. In the nineteenth century European industrialization and nation building further altered the long-standing balance of power, and Western expansion eventually posed a serious challenge to Muslims everywhere. In the words of a leading historian, "Muslim states and societies could no longer live in a stable and self-sufficient system of inherited culture; their need was now to generate the strength to survive in a world dominated by others."[2]

In close contact with Europe and under constant European pressure, the ruling elites both in the Ottoman Empire and in Egypt, a largely independent Ottoman province, led the way in trying to generate the strength to survive. The ongoing military crisis required, first of all, wrenching army reforms on Western lines in order to defend and preserve the state. These military reforms then snowballed into a series of innovations in education, which created modern schools and skilled specialists as well as army officers and had a powerful cultural impact on Ottoman and Egyptian elites. Western interests and governments also pushed for the adoption of the entire Western liberal creed—that is, the West demanded free trade, constitutional government, civil liberties, and equal rights for all religious groups. Western ideas challenged the superiority of Islam and undermined the traditional Muslim self-confidence.

The results of all these pressures and the momentous changes they brought were profound and paradoxical. On the one hand, the Ottoman Empire and Egypt did achieve considerable modernization on Western lines. On the other hand, these impressive accomplishments never came fast enough to offset the growing power and appetite of the West. The Islamic heartland in Southwest Asia and North Africa fell increasingly under foreign control. Only in the twentieth century did parts of the Islamic world escape Western economic and political domination.

Decline and Reform in the Ottoman Empire

Although the Ottoman Empire began to decline slowly after Suleiman the Magnificent in the sixteenth century (see pages 568–569), the relationship between the Ottomans and the Europeans in about 1750 was still one of roughly equal strength.

● **Pasha Halim Receiving Archduke Maximilian of Austria**   As this painting suggests, Ottoman leaders became well versed in European languages and culture. They also mastered the game of power politics, playing one European state off against another and securing the Ottoman Empire's survival. The black servants on the right may be slaves from the Sudan. *(Miramare Palace Trieste/Dagli Orti/ The Art Archive)*

However, in the later eighteenth century this situation began to change quickly and radically. The Ottomans fell behind western Europe in science, industrial skill, and military technology. At the same time, absolutist Russia pushed southward between 1768 and 1774. The danger that the Great Powers of Europe would gradually conquer the Ottoman Empire and divide up its vast territories was real.

Caught up in the Napoleonic wars and losing more territory to Russia, the Ottomans were forced in 1816 to grant Serbia local autonomy. In 1821 the Greeks revolted against Ottoman rule, and in 1830 they won their national independence. Facing uprisings by their Christian subjects in Europe, the Ottomans also failed to defend their Islamic provinces in North Africa. In 1830 French armies began their long and bloody conquest of the Arabic-speaking province of Algeria. By 1860, two hundred thousand French, Italian, and Spanish colonists had settled among the Muslim majority, which had been reduced to about 2.5 million by the war against the French and related famines and epidemics.

Ottoman weakness reflected the decline of the sultan's "slave army," the so-called **janissary corps**. In the sixteenth century the Ottoman sultans levied an annual slave tax of one to three thousand male children on the conquered Christian provinces in the Balkans. The boys and other slaves were raised in Turkey as Muslims, trained to

Primary Source:
Imperial Rescript
In this proclamation, Abdul Mejid announces plans to reform and modernize the Ottoman Empire, while protecting the rights of non-Muslims.

janissary corps   *The Ottoman sultan's slave army; its members soon became a corrupt and privileged hereditary caste.*

fight and administer, and joined the elite corps of the Ottoman infantry. With time, however, the janissaries became a corrupt and privileged hereditary caste. They zealously pursued their own interests and refused any military innovations that might undermine their high status.

A transformation of the army was absolutely necessary to battle the Europeans more effectively and enhance the sultanate's authority within the empire. The empire was no longer a centralized military state. Instead, local governors were becoming increasingly independent, pursuing their own interests and even seeking to establish their own governments and hereditary dynasties.

The energetic sultan Selim III (r. 1789–1807) understood these realities, but when he tried to reorganize the army, the janissaries refused to use any "Christian" equipment. In 1807 they revolted, and Selim was quickly executed in a palace revolution, one of many that plagued the Ottoman state. The reform-minded Mahmud II (r. 1808–1839) proceeded cautiously, picking loyal officers and building up his dependable artillery corps. In 1826 his council ordered the janissaries to drill in the European manner. As expected, the janissaries revolted and charged the palace, where they were mowed down by the waiting artillery corps.

The destruction and abolition of the janissaries cleared the way for building a new army, but it came too late to stop the rise of Muhammad Ali, the Ottoman governor in Egypt (see below). In 1831 his French-trained forces occupied the Ottoman province of Syria and appeared ready to depose Mahmud II. The Ottoman sultan survived, but only by begging Europe for help. Britain, Russia, and Austria responded and forced Muhammad Ali to stop his military campaign. Succeeding in reestablishing direct rule over the province of Iraq, the overconfident Ottomans were saved again in 1839 after their forces were routed trying to drive Muhammad Ali from Syria. Britain and Russia forced Muhammad Ali to return Syria to the Ottomans. European powers preferred a weak and dependent Ottoman state to a strong and revitalized Muslim entity under a dynamic leader such as Muhammad Ali.

Realizing their precarious position, liberal Ottoman statesmen launched in 1839 an era of radical reforms, which lasted with fits and starts until 1876 and culminated in a constitution and a short-lived parliament. Known as the **Tanzimat** (literally, regulations or orders), these reforms were designed to remake the empire on a western European model. The new decrees called for the equality of Muslims, Christians, and Jews before the law and in business, security of life and property, and a modernized administration and military. New commercial laws allowed free importation of foreign goods, as British advisers demanded, and permitted foreign merchants to operate freely throughout an economically dependent empire. Under heavy British pressure, slavery in the empire was drastically curtailed, though not abolished completely. Of great significance, growing numbers among the elite and the upwardly mobile embraced Western education, adopted Western manners and artistic styles, and accepted secular values to some extent.

Intended to bring revolutionary modernization such as that experienced by Russia under Peter the Great (see pages 479–480) and Japan in the Meiji era (see pages 764–766), the Tanzimat permitted partial recovery. Yet the Ottoman state and society failed to regain its earlier strength, for several reasons. First, implementation of the reforms required a new generation of well-trained and trustworthy officials, and that generation did not exist. Second, the liberal reforms failed to halt the growth of nationalism among Christian subjects in the Balkans (see Chapter 27), which resulted in crises and defeats that undermined all reform efforts. Third, the Ottoman initiatives did not curtail the appetite of Western imperialism, and European bankers gained a usurious stranglehold on Ottoman finances. In 1875 the Ottoman state had to declare partial bankruptcy and place its finances in the hands of European creditors.

Finally, the elaboration—at least on paper—of equal rights for citizens and religious communities did not create greater unity within the state. Indeed, religious disputes

Tanzimat *Radical reforms to the Ottoman Empire that were designed to remake the empire on a western European model.*

Primary Source: An Ottoman Government Decree Defines the Official Notion of the "Modern" Citizen *This document reveals a striking prejudice against communities of nomadic pastoralists, in favor of "civilized" urban folk.*

increased, worsened by the relentless interference of the Great Powers. This development embittered relations between the religious communities, distracted the government from its reform mission, and split Muslims into secularists and religious conservatives. Many conservative Muslims detested the religious reforms, which they saw as an impious departure from Islamic tradition and holy law. These Islamic conservatives became the most dependable support of Sultan Abdülhamid (r. 1876–1909), who abandoned the model of European liberalism in his long and repressive reign.

The combination of declining international power and conservative tyranny eventually led to a powerful resurgence of the modernizing impulse among idealistic Turkish exiles in Europe and young army officers in Istanbul. These fervent patriots, the so-called **Young Turks**, seized power in the revolution of 1908, and they forced the sultan to implement reforms. Failing to stop the rising tide of anti-Ottoman nationalism in the Balkans, the Young Turks helped to prepare the way for the birth of modern secular Turkey after the defeat and collapse of the Ottoman Empire in World War I (see pages 818–819).

Young Turks *Idealistic Turkish exiles in Europe and young army officers in Istanbul who seized power in the revolution of 1908 and helped pave the way for the birth of modern secular Turkey.*

Egypt: From Reform to British Occupation

The ancient land of the pharaohs had been ruled by a succession of foreigners since 525 B.C.E. and was most recently conquered by the Ottoman Turks in the early sixteenth century. In 1798 French armies under the young General Napoleon Bonaparte invaded Egypt and occupied the territory for three years as part of the war with Britain. Into the power vacuum left by the French withdrawal stepped an extraordinary Albanian-born Turkish general, **Muhammad Ali** (1769–1849).

First appointed governor of Egypt by the Turkish sultan, Muhammad Ali set out to build his own state on the strength of a large, powerful army organized along European lines. In 1820–1822 the Egyptian leader conquered much of the Sudan to secure slaves for his army, and thousands of African slaves were brought to Egypt during his reign. Because many slaves died in Egyptian captivity, Muhammad Ali turned to drafting Egyptian peasants. He also reformed the government and promoted modern industry. (See the feature "Individuals in Society: Muhammad Ali.") For a time Muhammad Ali's ambitious strategy seemed to work, but it eventually floundered when he was defeated by his Ottoman overlords and their British allies. Nevertheless, by the time of his death in 1849, Muhammad Ali had established a strong and virtually independent Egyptian state to be ruled by his family on a hereditary basis within the Turkish empire.

Muhammad Ali *The Turkish general who established a modernized and virtually independent Egyptian state.*

To pay for a modern army and industrialization, Muhammad Ali encouraged the development of commercial agriculture geared to the European market. This development had profound social implications. Egyptian peasants had been poor but largely self-sufficient, growing food on state-owned land allotted to them by tradition. Offered the possibility of profits from export agriculture, high-ranking officials and members of Muhammad Ali's family began carving large private landholdings out of the state domain, and they forced the peasants to grow cash crops for European markets. Ownership of land became very unequal. By 1913, 12,600 large estates owned 44 percent of the land and 1.4 million peasants owned only 27 percent. Estate owners "modernized" agriculture, but to the detriment of the peasants' well-being.

Muhammad Ali's policies of modernization attracted growing numbers of Europeans to the banks of the Nile. By 1863, when Muhammad Ali's grandson Ismail began his sixteen-year rule as Egypt's *khedive,* or prince, the port city of Alexandria had more than fifty thousand Europeans. Europeans served as army officers, engineers, doctors, government officials, and police officers. Others worked in trade, finance, and shipping. Above all, Europeans living in Egypt combined with landlords and officials to continue the development of commercial agriculture geared to exports. By 1900 about two hundred thousand Europeans lived in Egypt and accounted for 2 percent

● **The Opening of the Suez Canal** A long procession of eighty ships passed through the Suez Canal when it was opened in November 1869, and thousands of spectators lined the shores and joined in the celebrations. The building of the hundred-mile canal was a momentous event, cutting in half the length of the journey between Europe and Asia. *(Archives Charmet/The Bridgeman Art Library)*

of the population. As throughout the Ottoman Empire, Europeans enjoyed important commercial and legal privileges and formed an economic elite.

Ismail (r. 1863–1879) was a westernizing autocrat. Educated at France's leading military academy, he dreamed of using European technology and capital to modernize Egypt and build a vast empire in northeastern Africa. He promoted cotton production, and exports to Europe soared. Ismail also borrowed large sums and with his support the Suez Canal was completed by a French company in 1869. The canal shortened the voyage from Europe to Asia by thousands of miles. Traffic boomed. A new Cairo with long straight boulevards and modern apartment buildings grew up alongside the medieval maze of twisting lanes and beautiful historic mosques.

Major cultural and intellectual changes accompanied the political and economic ones. The Arabic of the masses, rather than the Turkish of the conquerors, became the official language, and young Egyptians educated in Europe helped spread new skills and ideas in the bureaucracy. A host of writers, intellectuals, and religious thinkers responded to the novel conditions with innovative ideas that had a powerful impact in Egypt and in other Muslim societies.

Three influential figures, who represented broad families of thought, were especially significant. The teacher and writer Jamal al-Din al-Afghani (1838/39–1897), who lived in Cairo from 1871 to 1879, preached Islamic regeneration and defense against Western/Christian aggression. Regeneration, he argued, required the purification of religious belief, the unity of all Muslim peoples, and a revolutionary overthrow of corrupt Muslim rulers and foreign exploiters. The more moderate Muhammad

Individuals IN SOCIETY

Muhammad Ali

The dynamic leader Muhammad Ali (1769–1849) stands across the history of modern Egypt like a colossus. Yet the essence of the man remains a mystery, and historians vary greatly in their interpretations of him.

Sent by the Ottomans, with Albanian troops, to oppose the French occupation of Egypt in 1799, Muhammad Ali maneuvered skillfully after the French withdrawal in 1802. In 1805 he was named *pasha,* or Ottoman governor, of Egypt. Only the Mamluks remained as rivals. Originally an elite corps of Turkish slave-soldiers, the Mamluks had become a semifeudal military ruling class living off the Egyptian peasantry. In 1811 Muhammad Ali offered to make peace, and he invited the Mamluk chiefs and their retainers to a banquet in Cairo's Citadel. As the unsuspecting guests processed through a narrow passage, his troops opened fire, slaughtering all the Mamluk leaders.

After eliminating his foes, Muhammad Ali embarked on a program of radical reforms. He reorganized agriculture and commerce, reclaiming most of the cultivated land for the state domain, which he controlled. He also established state agencies to monopolize, for his own profit, the sale of agricultural goods. Commercial agriculture geared to exports to Europe developed rapidly, especially after the successful introduction of high-quality cotton in 1821. Canals and irrigation systems along the Nile were rebuilt and expanded.

Muhammad Ali used his growing revenues to recast his army along European lines. He recruited French officers to train the soldiers. As the military grew, so did the need for hospitals, schools of medicine and languages, and secular education. Young Turks and some Egyptians were sent to Europe for advanced study. The ruler boldly financed factories to produce uniforms and weapons, and he prohibited the importation of European goods so as to protect Egypt's infant industries. In the 1830s state factories were making one-fourth of Egypt's cotton into cloth. Above all, Muhammad Ali drafted Egyptian peasants into the military for the first time, thereby expanding his army to 100,000 men. It was this force that conquered the Ottoman province of Syria, threatened the sultan in Istanbul, and triggered European intervention. Grudgingly recognized by his Ottoman overlord as Egypt's hereditary ruler in 1841, Muhammad Ali nevertheless had to accept European and Ottoman demands to give up Syria and abolish his monopolies and protective tar-

iffs. The old ruler then lost heart; his reforms languished, and his factories disappeared.

Muhammad Ali, the Albanian-born ruler of Egypt, in 1839. *(Mary Evans Picture Library)*

In the attempt to understand Muhammad Ali and his significance, many historians have concluded that he was a national hero, the "founder of modern Egypt." His ambitious state-building projects—hospitals, schools, factories, and the army—were the basis for an Egyptian reawakening and eventual independence from the Ottomans' oppressive foreign rule. Similarly, state-sponsored industrialization promised an escape from poverty and Western domination, which was foiled only by European intervention and British insistence on free trade.

A growing minority of historians question these views. They see Muhammad Ali primarily as an Ottoman adventurer. This disobedient Turkish general, they say, did not aim for national independence for Egypt, but rather "intended to carve out a small empire for himself and for his children after him."* Paradoxically, his success, which depended on heavy taxes and brutal army service, did lead to Egyptian nationalism among the Arabic-speaking masses, but that new nationalism was directed *against* Muhammad Ali and his Turkish-speaking entourage. Continuing research into this leader's life will help to resolve these conflicting interpretations.

Questions for Analysis

1. Which of Muhammad Ali's actions support the interpretation that he was the founder of modern Egypt? Which actions support the opposing view?

2. After you have studied Chapter 25, compare Muhammad Ali and the Meiji reformers in Japan. What accounts for the similarities and differences?

*K. Fahmy, *All the Pasha's Men: Mehmed Ali, His Army, and the Making of Modern Egypt* (Cambridge: Cambridge University Press, 1997), p. 310.

Abduh (1849–1905) also searched for Muslim rejuvenation and launched the modern Islamic reform movement, which became very important in the twentieth century. Abduh concluded that Muslims should return to the purity of the earliest, most essential doctrines of Islam and reject later additions that could limit Muslim creativity. This would permit a flexible, reasoned approach to change, social questions, and foreign ideas.

Finally, the writer Qasim Amin (1863–1908) represented those who found inspiration in the West in the late nineteenth century. In his influential book *The Liberation of Women* (1899), Amin argued forcefully that superior education for European women had contributed greatly to the Islamic world's falling far behind the West. The rejuvenation of Muslim societies required greater equality for women.

Egypt changed rapidly during Ismail's rule but his projects were reckless and enormously expensive. By 1876 the Egyptian government could not pay the interest on its colossal debt. Rather than let Egypt go bankrupt and repudiate its loans, France and Great Britain intervened politically to protect the European investors who held the Egyptian bonds. They forced Ismail to appoint French and British commissioners to oversee Egyptian finances so that the Egyptian debt would be paid in full. This meant that Europeans were going to determine the state budget and in effect rule Egypt.

Foreign financial control evoked a violent nationalistic reaction among Egyptian religious leaders, intellectuals, and army officers. In 1879, under the leadership of Colonel Ahmed Arabi, they formed the Egyptian Nationalist Party. Continuing diplomatic pressure, which forced Ismail to abdicate in favor of his weak son, Tewfiq (r. 1879–1892), resulted in bloody anti-European riots in Alexandria in 1882. A number of Europeans were killed, and Tewfiq and his court had to flee to British ships for safety. The British fleet then bombarded Alexandria, and a British expeditionary force decimated Arabi's forces and occupied all of Egypt.

The British said that their occupation was temporary, but British armies remained in Egypt until 1956. They maintained the façade of the khedive's government as an autonomous province of the Ottoman Empire, but the khedive was a mere puppet. The British consul, General Evelyn Baring, later Lord Cromer, ruled the country after 1883. Baring was a paternalistic reformer, and his rule did result in tax reforms and somewhat better conditions for peasants. Foreign bondholders received their interest payments, and Egyptian nationalists chaffed under foreign rule.

In Egypt the British abandoned what some scholars have called the "imperialism of free trade," which was based on economic penetration and indirect rule. They accepted a new model for European expansion in the densely populated lands of Africa and Asia. Such expansion was based on military force, political domination, and a self-justifying ideology of beneficial reform. This model was to predominate from the 1880s until 1914.

SUB-SAHARAN AFRICA: FROM THE SLAVE TRADE TO EUROPEAN RULE

What were the most significant changes in sub-Saharan Africa, and why did they occur?

From the beginning of the nineteenth century to the global depression of the 1930s, the different regions of sub-Saharan Africa experienced gradual but monumental change. The long-standing transatlantic slave trade declined and practically disappeared by the late 1860s. In the early nineteenth century Islam expanded its influence in a long belt south of the Sahara, but Africa generally remained free of European political control. After about 1880 further Islamic expansion to the south stopped, but the pace of change accelerated as France and Britain led European nations in the "scramble for Africa." Africa was divided and largely conquered by Europeans, and by 1900 the foreigners were consolidating their authoritarian empires.

African Trade and Social Change (1800–1880)

The most important development in West Africa before the European conquest was the decline of the Atlantic slave trade and the simultaneous rise of the export of palm oil and other commodities. A major break with the past, the shift in African foreign trade marked the beginning of modern economic development in sub-Saharan Africa.

Although the trade in African people was a worldwide phenomenon, the Atlantic slave trade became the most extensive and significant portion of it. The forced migration of millions of Africans—so cruel, unjust, and tragic—intensified after 1700, and especially after 1750. By the 1780s, shipments of black men and women averaged eighty thousand a year, in an attempt to satisfy the constantly rising demand for labor—and slave owner profits—in the Americas. Increasing demand resulted in rising prices for African slaves in the eighteenth century. Some African merchants and rulers who controlled exports profited, and some Africans secured foreign products that they found appealing. But the negative consequences of the expanding trade predominated in Africa, because warfare increased and enslavement spread.

Until 1700, and perhaps even 1750, almost all Europeans considered the African slave trade a legitimate business activity. After 1775 a broad campaign to abolish slavery developed in Britain. This campaign grew into one of the first peaceful mass political movements based on the mobilization of public opinion in British history. British women played a critical role in this movement, denouncing the immorality of human bondage and stressing the cruel treatment of female slaves and slave families. In 1807 Parliament declared the slave trade illegal. Britain then used its navy to seize the ships of the slave runners, liberating the captives and settling them in the British port of Freetown, in Sierra Leone.

British action had a limited impact at first. The transatlantic slave trade regained its previous massive level after peace returned to Europe in 1815, and it declined only gradually. Britain's African squadron intercepted fewer than 10 percent of all slave ships, and the demand for slaves remained high on the expanding sugar and coffee plantations of Cuba and Brazil until the 1850s and 1860s. (The United States prohibited the importation of slaves in 1808, and natural increase accounted mainly for the subsequent growth of the African American slave population there before the Civil War.) Strong incentives remained for Portuguese slave traders, as well as for those African rulers who relied on profits from the trade for power and influence.

As more nations joined Britain in outlawing the slave trade, the shipment of human cargo slackened along the West African coast. The decline began on the long stretch from Guinea and Senegal to the Gold Coast and present-day Nigeria by the 1830s and occurred thereafter in west-central Africa, in present-day Congo and Angola (see Map 24.1). At the same time the ancient but limited shipment of slaves across the Sahara and from the East African coast into the Indian Ocean and through the Red Sea expanded dramatically. Only in the 1860s did this expanding trade begin to decline rapidly. As a result of these shifting currents, exports of slaves from all of West Africa across the Atlantic declined from an estimated 5.6 million persons in the eighteenth century to 3.5 million in the nineteenth century. Yet total exports of slaves from all regions of sub-Saharan Africa declined less than half as fast in the same years, from 7.4 million to 6.1 million.[3] The abolitionist vision of "legitimate" commerce in tropical products quickly replacing illegal slave exports was not realized.

Nevertheless, beginning in West Africa, trade in tropical products did make steady progress, for several reasons. First, the oil and kernels of naturally growing palm trees already provided food for coastal populations. With Britain encouraging palm tree

● **Palm Oil for Soap and Power**   Europeans, led by the British, encouraged West Africans to stop exporting slaves and start selling palm oil from naturally growing palm trees, as seen on the left. In Europe palm oil was made into soap, which was heavily advertised and endowed with symbols and hidden messages. In this 1890s ad (*right*), the Lifebuoy soap given to British travelers becomes a lifesaving charm warding off danger in foreign lands. *(left: Corbis; right: Mary Evans Picture Library)*

palm oil   *A West African tropical product, often used to make soap; the British encouraged its cultivation as an alternative to the slave trade.*

cultivation as an alternative to the slave trade, **palm oil** sales from West Africa to Britain surged from only one thousand tons in 1810 to more than forty thousand tons in 1855. Second, the sale of palm oil admirably served the self-interest of industrializing Europe. From palm oil, manufacturers made the first good, cheap soap and mass-produced candles to light people's homes. Third, the production of peanuts for export also grew rapidly, in part because small, independent African farmers and their families could compete effectively with large-scale producers in growing peanuts.

Finally, powerful West African rulers and warlords who had benefited from the Atlantic slave trade succeeded in redirecting some of their slaves into the production of "legitimate" goods for world markets. This was possible because slavery and slave markets remained strong in sub-Saharan Africa, as local warfare and slave raiding continued to enslave large numbers of men, women, and children for many uses. Enslaved captives were sold abroad, and they became wives, concubines, and servants. They transported goods, mined gold, grew crops, and served in slave armies. For example, after the collapse of the Oyo empire, Yoruba warlords in present-day Nigeria developed palm oil plantations worked by slaves. By the 1860s and 1870s, 104 families in the city of Ibadan owned fifty thousand slaves, an average of five hundred per family.[4] As the experience of the Yoruba suggests, the slow decline of the transatlantic slave trade coincided with the most intensive use of slaves within Africa.

At the same time, a new group of African merchants—often liberated slaves from Freetown who had received some Western education—did rise to handle legitimate trade, and some grew rich. By the 1850s and 1860s legitimate African traders, flanked

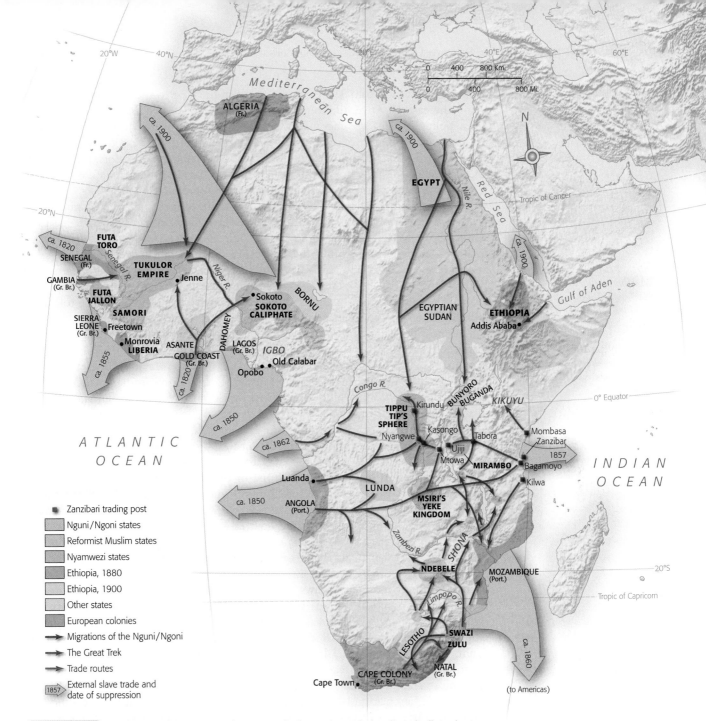

MAP 24.1 **Africa, 1800–1878** The export of African slaves declined gradually in the early nineteenth century, and by 1860 it was greatly reduced. Islamic reformers forged stronger states in West Africa, and Arab traders and Nyamwezi elites built informal empires in central Africa. In 1878 European settlement was limited to Algeria, southern Africa, and a few scattered outposts on the Atlantic coast.

by Western-educated African lawyers, teachers, and journalists, formed an emerging middle class in the coastal towns of West Africa. This tiny middle class provided new leadership that augured well for the region's future. Unfortunately for West Africans, in the 1880s and 1890s African business leadership then gave way to imperial subordination.

Islamic Revival and Expansion

In the early eighteenth century Islam had been practiced throughout the Sudanic Savanna—that vast belt of flat grasslands that stretches across Africa below the southern fringe of the Sahara from Senegal and Gambia in the west to the mountains of Ethiopia in the east—for five hundred to a thousand years, depending on the area. The cities, political rulers, and merchants in many small states were Muslim. Yet the peasant farmers and migratory cattle raisers—the vast majority of the population—generally remained true to traditional animist practices, worshiping ancestors, local shrines, and protective spirits. Many Muslim rulers shared some of these beliefs and did not try to convert their subjects in the countryside or enforce Islamic law.

Beginning in the eighteenth century and gathering strength in the early nineteenth century, a powerful Islamic revival brought reform and revolutionary change from within to the western and eastern Sudan, until this process was halted by European military conquest at the end of the nineteenth century. In essence, Muslim scholars and fervent religious leaders arose to wage successful **jihads,** or religious wars, against both animist rulers and Islamic states that they deemed corrupt. The new reformist rulers believed that African cults and religious practice could no longer be tolerated, and they often effected mass conversions of animists to Islam.

The most important of these revivalist states, the enormous **Sokoto caliphate,** illustrates the general pattern. It was founded by Usuman dan Fodio (1754–1817), an inspiring Muslim teacher who first won zealous followers among both the Fulani herders and the Hausa peasants in the Muslim state of Gobir in the northern Sudan. After his religious community was attacked by Gobir's rulers, Usuman launched the jihad of 1804, one of the most important events in nineteenth-century West Africa. Usuman claimed that the Hausa rulers of Muslim Gobir "worshiped many places of idols, and trees, and rocks, and sacrificed to them," killing and plundering their subjects without any regard for Islamic law.[5] Young religious students and discontented Fulani cattle raisers formed the backbone of the fighters, who succeeded in overthrowing the Hausa rulers and inspired more jihads in the Sudan. In 1809 Usuman founded the new Sokoto caliphate, which was ably consolidated by his son Muhammad Bello as a vast and enduring decentralized state (see Map 24.1).

The triumph of the Sokoto caliphate had profound consequences for Africa and the Sudan. First, the caliphate was based on Islamic history and law, which gave sub-Saharan Africa a sophisticated written constitution that earlier preliterate states had never achieved. This government of laws, not men, provided stability and made Sokoto one of the most prosperous regions in tropical Africa. Second, because of Sokoto and other revivalist states, Islam became much more widely and deeply rooted in sub-Saharan Africa than ever before. By 1880 the entire western and central Sudan was united in Islam. In this vast expanse Islam became an unquestioned part of everyday life and culture. Women gained greater access to education, even as veiling and seclusion became more common. Finally, Islam had always approved of slavery for non-Muslims and Muslim heretics, and "the *jihads* created a new slaving frontier on the basis of rejuvenated Islam."[6] In 1900 the Sokoto caliphate had 1 million and perhaps as many as 2.5 million slaves. Of all modern slave societies, only the American South had more, about 4 million in 1860.

Islam also expanded in East Africa, in large part because of the efforts of Sayyid Said (r. 1804–1856), the energetic imam of Oman. Reviving his family's lordship of the African island of Zanzibar and eventually moving his capital from southern Arabia to Zanzibar in 1840, Said and his Baluchi mercenaries (from present-day Pakistan) gained control of most of the Swahili-speaking East African coast. Said concentrated the shipment of slaves to the Ottoman Empire and Arabia through Zanzibar. In addition, he successfully encouraged Indian merchants to develop slave-based clove plantations in his territories. Thus from the 1820s on, Arab merchants and adventurers pressed far into the interior in search of slaves and ivory, converting and intermarrying with local Nyamwezi elites and establishing small Muslim states. The Arab immigrants brought literacy, administrative skills, and increased trade and international contact, as well as the intensification of slavery, to East Africa. In 1870, before Christian mission-

jihads *Religious wars waged by Muslim scholars and religious leaders against both animist rulers and Islamic states that they deemed corrupt.*

Sokoto caliphate *Founded in 1809 by Usuman dan Fodio, this African state was based on Islamic history and law.*

● **Celebrating the Sokoto Caliphate**   The Sokoto Caliphate still exists in modern northern Nigeria, and the Sultan of Sokoto remains an extremely influential force as the spiritual leader of Nigeria's large Muslim population. This crowd of Muslim believers is standing on a podium in 2004 to participate in bicentennial celebrations commemorating the Caliphate's foundation by Usuman dan Fodio. *(Pius Utomi Ekpei/Getty Images)*

aries and Western armies began to arrive in force, it appeared that most of the East African population would accept Islam within a generation.[7]

The Seizure of Africa (1880–1902)

Between 1880 and 1900 Britain, France, Germany, and Italy scrambled for African possessions as if their national livelihoods were at stake. By 1902 only Ethiopia in northeast Africa and Liberia on the West African coast remained independent (see Map 24.2).

In addition to the general causes underlying Europe's imperialist burst after 1880 (see pages 723–724), certain events and individuals stand out. First, as the antislavery movement succeeded in shutting down the Atlantic slave trade by the late 1860s, the persistence of slavery elsewhere attracted growing attention in Europe. Through the publications of Protestant missionaries such as David Livingstone and the fiery eye-witness accounts of the Catholic White Fathers, Europeans learned of the horrors of slave raids and the suffering of thousands of innocent victims sold within Africa and through East African ports. The public was led to believe that European rule would end this human tragedy, as well-meaning Protestants and Catholics "provided a moral justification for the conquest of Africa."[8]

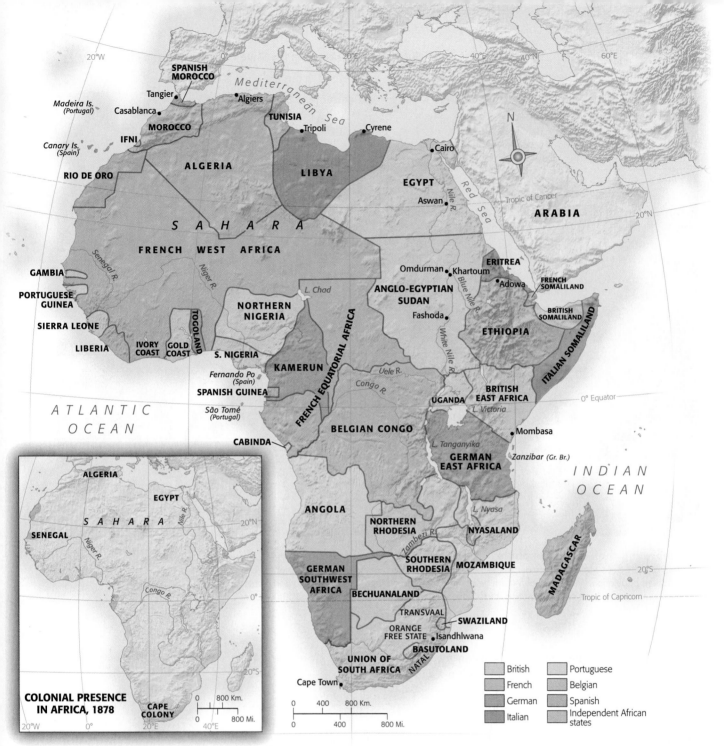

MAP 24.2 **Africa in 1878 and 1914** European nations carved up Africa after 1878 and built vast political empires. Britain and France took the most territory. Which African states remained independent?

Leopold II *The king of Belgium who colonized the Congo and sent expeditions into central Africa.*

Berlin Conference *Held in 1884 and 1885 in order to lay down some basic rules for imperialist competition in sub-Saharan Africa, it established the principle that European claims to African territory had to rest on "effective occupation" in order to be recognized by other states.*

Second, **Leopold II** of Belgium (r. 1865–1909) played a crucial role. His agents signed "treaties" with African chiefs and planted Leopold's flag along the Congo River. The French reacted by establishing a French protectorate on the north bank of the Congo River. By 1883 Europe had caught "African fever," and the race for territory was on.

To lay down some rules for this imperialist competition, Premier Jules Ferry of France and Chancellor Otto von Bismarck of Germany arranged an international conference on Africa in Berlin in 1884–1885. The **Berlin Conference,** at which no Africans were present (nor had any been invited), established the principle that European claims to African territory had to rest on "effective occupation" in order to be recognized by other states. This meant that Europeans would push relentlessly into interior regions from all sides and that no single European power would be able to claim the entire continent. The conference recognized Leopold's rule over a neutral Congo state and agreed to work to stop slavery and the slave trade in Africa.

The Berlin Conference coincided with Germany's emergence as an imperial power. In 1884 and 1885 Bismarck's Germany established protectorates over a number of small African kingdoms and societies in Togo, Cameroons, southwest Africa, and, later, East Africa (see Map 24.2). In acquiring colonies, Bismarck cooperated with France's Jules Ferry against the British. (See the feature "Listening to the Past: A French Leader Defends Imperialism" on pages 746–747.) The French expanded into West Africa and formed a protectorate on the Congo River. As for the British, they began enlarging their West African enclaves and pushed northward from the Cape Colony and westward from the East African coast.

Pushing southward from Egypt, the British were blocked in the eastern Sudan by fiercely independent Muslims, who had felt the full force of Islamic revival. In 1881 a pious local leader, Muhammad Ahmad (1844–1885), led a revolt against foreign control of Egypt. In 1885 his army massacred a British force and took the city of Khartoum, forcing the British to retreat to Cairo. Ten years later a British force returned, building a railroad to supply arms and reinforcements as it went. Finally, in 1898, these troops met their foe at Omdurman, where Sudanese Muslims armed with spears charged time and time again, only to be cut down by the recently invented machine gun. In the end eleven thousand brave but poorly armed Muslim tribesmen lay dead. Only twenty-eight Britons had been killed.

The British conquest of the Sudan exemplified the general process of empire building in Africa. The fate of the Muslim force at Omdurman was eventually inflicted on most colonized peoples who resisted European rule: they were crushed by vastly superior military force.

Southern Africa in the Nineteenth Century

The development of southern Africa diverged from the rest of sub-Saharan Africa in important ways. Whites settled in large numbers, modern capitalist industry took off, and British imperialists had to wage all-out war.

In 1652 the Dutch East India Company established a supply station at Cape Town for Dutch ships sailing between Amsterdam and Indonesia. The healthy, temperate climate and the sparse Nguni population near the Cape resulted in the colony's gradual expansion. When the British took possession in the Napoleonic wars, the Cape Colony included about twenty thousand free Dutch citizens and twenty-five thousand African slaves, with substantial mixed-race communities on the northern frontier of white settlement.

After 1815 powerful African chiefdoms, Dutch settlers—first known as Boers, and then as **Afrikaners**—and British colonial forces waged a complicated, three-cornered battle to build strong states in southern Africa. Of critical importance, the talented Zulu leader Shaka (r. 1818–1828) revolutionized African warfare between 1818 and his death in 1828, and he managed to create "the largest and most powerful African society in southern Africa in the nineteenth century."[9] Drafted by age groups and placed in highly disciplined regiments, Shaka's warriors perfected the use of a new, short stabbing spear in deadly hand-to-hand combat. Shaka's Zulu armies often destroyed their African enemies completely, sowing chaos and sending refugees fleeing in all directions. Shaka's wars also led to the consolidation of the Zulu, Swazi, and Sotho peoples into stronger states in southern Africa. By 1880 these states were largely subdued by Dutch and British invaders, but only after many hard-fought frontier wars.

Beginning in 1834, the British gradually abolished slavery in the Cape Colony and introduced colorblind legislation to protect African labor. In 1836 these measures led

Afrikaners *The descendants of the Dutch in the Cape Colony.*

● **Diamond Mining in South Africa** At first, both black and white miners could own and work claims at the diamond diggings, as this early photo suggests. However, as the industry expanded and was monopolized by European financial interests, white workers claimed the supervisory jobs and blacks were limited to dangerous low-wage labor. Mining revolutionized the South African economy. *(Royal Commonwealth Society. By permission of the Syndics of Cambridge University Library)*

about ten thousand Afrikaner cattle ranchers and farmers to make their so-called Great Trek northward into the interior (see Map 24.1). In 1845 another group of Afrikaners joined the other trekkers north of the Orange River. Over the next thirty years Afrikaner and British settlers, who often fought and usually detested each other, reached a mutually advantageous division of southern Africa. The British ruled strategically valuable coastal colonies, and the Afrikaners controlled their ranch-land republics in the interior. The Zulu, Xhosa, and other African peoples lost much of their land but remained the majority—albeit an exploited majority.

The discovery of incredibly rich deposits of diamonds in 1867 and later gold revolutionized the economy of southern Africa, making possible large-scale industrial capitalism and transforming the lives of all its peoples. Small white and black diamond diggers soon gave way to Cecil Rhodes and the powerful financiers behind his De Beers mining company, which reaped fabulous profits monopolizing the world's diamond industry. The regular, deep-level gold deposits discovered in 1886 in the Afrikaners' Transvaal republic required big foreign investment, European engineering expertise, and an enormous labor force. The "color bar" system of the diamond fields gave whites— often English-speaking immigrants—the well-paid skilled positions and put black Africans in the dangerous, low-wage jobs far below the surface. Whites lived with their families in subsidized housing. African workers lived in all-male dormitories like men in prison, closely watched by company guards. Southern Africa became the world's leading gold producer and pulled in migratory workers from all over the region.

The mining bonanza whetted the appetite of British imperialists led by the powerful Rhodes. Between 1889 and 1893 he used missionaries and a front company chartered by the British government to force African chiefs to accept British protectorates and managed to add Southern and Northern Rhodesia (modern-day Zimbabwe and Zambia) to the British Empire (see Map 24.2). Rhodes and the imperialist clique then succeeded in starting the South African War of 1899–1902 (also known as the Anglo-Boer War), Britain's greatest imperial campaign on African soil. The British needed 450,000 to crush the Afrikaners.

The long and bitter war divided whites in South Africa, but South Africa's blacks were the biggest losers. The British had promised the Afrikaners representative government in return for surrender in 1902, and they made good on their pledge. In 1910 the Cape Colony, Natal, and the two Afrikaner republics formed a new self-governing Union of South Africa. Because whites—21.5 percent of the total population in 1910—held almost all political power and because the Afrikaners outnumbered the English-speakers, following the peace settlement the Afrikaners began to regain what they had lost on the battlefield. South Africa, under a joint British-Afrikaner government within the British Empire, began the creation of a modern, segregated society that culminated in an even harsher system of racial separation, or apartheid, after World War II.

The Imperial System (1900–1930)

By 1900 most of black Africa had been conquered—or, as Europeans preferred to say, "pacified"—and a system of imperial administration was taking shape. In general, this system weakened or shattered the traditional social order and challenged accepted values.

The self-proclaimed political goal of the French and the British—the principal foreign powers—was to provide good government for their African subjects, especially after World War I. "Good government" meant, above all, law and order. It meant strong, authoritarian government, which maintained a small army and built up an African police force to put down rebellion, suppress ethnic warfare, and protect life and property. Good government required a modern bureaucracy capable of taxing and governing the population. Many African leaders and their peoples had chosen not to resist the invaders' superior force, and most others had stopped fighting after experiencing crushing military defeat. Thus the goal of law and order was widely achieved.

Colonial governments demonstrated much less interest in providing basic social services. Expenditures on education, public health, hospitals, and other social services increased after the First World War but still remained small. Europeans feared the political implications of mass education and typically relied instead on the modest efforts of state-subsidized mission schools. Moreover, they tried to make even their poorest colonies pay for themselves. Thus salaries for government workers normally absorbed nearly all tax revenues.

Economically, the imperialist goal was to draw the African interior into the world economy on terms favorable to the dominant Europeans. The key was railroads linking coastal trading centers to outposts hundreds of miles in the interior. Cheap, dependable transportation facilitated easy shipment of raw materials out and manufactured goods in. Most African railroads were built after 1900; fifty-two hundred miles were in operation by 1926, when attention turned to road building for trucks. Railroads and roads had two other important outcomes: they allowed the quick movement of troops to put down any local unrest, and they allowed many African peasants to earn wages for the first time.

● **The Governor's Arrival** This painting by an African artist depicts the landing of a high British official at a port on the East African coast. African soldiers stand at attention, ready to do the governor's bidding and maintain imperial order. *(National Museums, Tanzania)*

The focus on economic development and low-cost rule explained why colonial governments were reluctant to move decisively against slavery within Africa. Officials feared that an abrupt abolition of slavery where it existed would disrupt production and lead to costly revolts by powerful slaveholding elites, especially in Muslim areas. Thus colonial regimes settled for halfway measures designed to satisfy humanitarian groups in Europe and also make all Africans, free or slave, participate in a market economy and work for wages. Even this cautious policy was enough for many slaves to boldly free themselves by running away, and it facilitated a rapid decline of slavery within Africa. At the same time, colonial governments often imposed head taxes, payable in money or labor, to compel Africans to work for their white overlords. No aspect of imperialism was more despised by Africans than forced labor, widespread until about 1920. In some regions, particularly in West Africa, African peasants continued to respond freely to the new economic opportunities by voluntarily shifting to export crops on their own farms. Overall, the result of these developments was an increase in wage work and production geared to the world market and a decline in traditional self-sufficient farming and nomadic herding.

In sum, the imposition of bureaucratic Western rule and the gradual growth of a world-oriented cash economy between 1900 and 1930 had a revolutionary impact on large parts of Africa. The experiences of Ghana and Kenya, two very different African countries, dramatically illustrate variations on the general pattern.

Present-day Ghana (see Map 32.4 on page 1008), which takes its name from one of West Africa's famous early kingdoms, had a fairly complex economy well before British armies smashed the powerful Asante kingdom in 1873 and established the crown colony that they called the Gold Coast. Precolonial local trade was vigorous and varied, and palm oil exports were expanding. Into this sophisticated economy British colonists subsequently introduced the production of cocoa beans for the world's chocolate. Output rose spectacularly, from a few hundred tons in the 1890s to 305,000 tons in 1936. Independent peasants and energetic African business people (many of the traders were women) were mainly responsible for the spectacular success of cocoa-bean production. Creative African entrepreneurs even went so far as to build their own roads, and they sometimes reaped big profits.

The Gold Coast also showed the way politically and culturally. The westernized elite—relatively prosperous and well-educated lawyers, professionals, and journalists—and business people took full advantage of opportunities provided by the fairly en-lightened colonial regime. The black elite was the main presence in the limited local elections permitted by the British, for few permanent white settlers ventured to hot and densely populated West Africa.

Across the continent in the British East African colony of Kenya, events unfolded differently. Before the arrival of Western imperialists, East African peoples were more self-sufficient, less numerous, and less advanced commercially and politically than Afri-cans in the Gold Coast. Once the British had built their strategic railroad from the In-dian Ocean across Kenya to Uganda, foreigners from Great Britain and India moved in to exploit the situation. Indian settlers became shopkeepers, clerks, and laborers in the towns. British settlers dreamed of turning the cool, beautiful, and fertile Kenyan highlands into a "white man's country" like Southern Rhodesia or the Union of South Africa. They dismissed the local population of peasant farmers as "barbarians," fit only to toil as cheap labor on their large estates and plantations. Kenya's Africans thus expe-rienced much harsher colonial rule than did their fellow Africans in the Gold Coast.

Chapter Summary

To assess your mastery of this chapter, go to
bedfordstmartins.com/mckayworld

• *What were the global consequences of European industrialization between 1800 and 1914?*

Between 1800 and 1914 European industrialization opened up a growing gap in average income between people in the West and people in Africa, Asia, and Latin America. This new, lopsided world—a world of rich lands and poor—experienced a prodigious increase in international trade, but the lion's share of the gains from trade went to the Western nations. Millions of Europeans also moved to sparsely populated areas of European settlement, while similar migration from Asia was generally quite limited.

• *What were the causes and consequences of European empire building after 1880?*

After 1880 a handful of Western nations seized most of Africa (and parts of Asia) and rushed to build authoritarian empires. The reasons for this empire

Key Terms

lopsided world
migration chain
great white walls
quinine
traditionalists
modernizers
janissary corps
Tanzimat
Young Turks
Muhammad Ali
palm oil
jihads
Sokoto caliphate
Leopold II
Berlin Conference
Afrikaners

building included trade rivalries, competitive nationalism in Europe, and self-justifying claims of a "civilizing mission." Above all, European states had acquired unprecedented military superiority, which they used to crush resistance and impose their will.

• How did the Ottoman Empire and Egypt try to revitalize themselves, and what were the most important results?

In the Muslim heartland both the Ottoman Empire and Egypt introduced reforms to improve the military, provide technical and secular education, and expand personal liberties. In so doing, both countries prepared the way for modern nation-states in the twentieth century, but they failed to defend themselves from Western imperialism. The Ottoman Empire survived as an economic colony and groped for unity. Egypt went bankrupt and was conquered and ruled by Britain. Western domination was particularly bitter for most Muslims because they saw it profaning their religion as well as taking away their political independence.

• What were the most significant changes in sub-Saharan Africa, and why did they occur?

In sub-Saharan Africa European pressure contributed to the reorientation of the economy, which gradually turned from a focus on the Atlantic slave trade to the production of commodities for export. Islam revived and expanded until about 1870. The European conquest of Africa after 1880 led to colonial empires that improved internal security and built bureaucracies, but also treated Africans as racial inferiors. Government based on racial discrimination, which was most thoroughly developed in southern Africa, set the stage for a new anti-imperialist struggle for equality and genuine independence after the First World War.

Suggested Reading

Bagachi, Amiya Kumar. *Perilous Passage: Mankind and the Ascendancy of Capital.* 2005. A spirited radical critique of Western imperialism.

Conklin, Alice. *A Mission to Civilize: The French Republican Ideal and West Africa, 1895–1930.* 1997. An outstanding examination of French imperialism.

Cook, Scott B. *Colonial Encounters in the Age of High Imperialism.* 1996. A stimulating and very readable overview.

Curtin, P., et al. *African History: From Earliest Times to Independence,* 2d ed. 1995. An excellent discussion of Africa in the nineteenth century.

Findley, C. *The Turks in World History.* 2005. An exciting reconsideration of the Turks in long-term perspective.

Headrick, D. *Tools of Empire.* 1991. Stresses technological superiority in Western expansion.

Hourani, A. *A History of the Arab Peoples.* 1991. Brilliant on developments in the nineteenth century.

Iliffe, J. *Africans: The History of a Continent.* 1995. Outstanding and original, stressing environmental developments.

Lovejoy, P. *Transformation in Slavery: A History of Slavery in Africa,* 2d ed. 2000. A fine synthesis of current knowledge.

Mahfouz, H. *Palace of Desire.* 1991. A great novelist's portrait of an Egyptian family before 1914.

Notes

1. Rudyard Kipling, *The Five Nations* (London,1903).
2. A. Hourani, *A History of the Arab Peoples* (Cambridge, Mass.: Harvard University Press, 1991), p. 263.
3. P. Lovejoy, *Transformations in Slavery: A History of Slavery in Africa,* 2d ed. (Cambridge: Cambridge University Press, 2000), p. 142.
4. Ibid., p. 179.
5. Quoted in J. Iliffe, *Africans: The History of a Continent* (Cambridge: Cambridge University Press, 1995), p. 169.
6. Lovejoy, *Transformations in Slavery,* p. 15.
7. R. Oliver, *The African Experience* (New York: Icon Editions, 1991), pp. 164–166.
8. S. Miers and R. Roberts, eds., *The End of Slavery in Africa* (Madison: University of Wisconsin Press, 1988), p. 16.
9. R. Beck, *The History of South Africa* (Westport, Conn.: Greenwood Press, 2000), p. 63.

Listening to the PAST

A French Leader Defends Imperialism

Although Jules Ferry (1832–1893) first gained political prominence as an ardent champion of secular public education, he was most famous for his empire building. While he was French premier in 1880–1881 and again in 1883–1885, France occupied Tunisia, extended its rule in Indonesia, seized Madagascar, and penetrated the Congo. Criticized by conservatives, socialists, and some left-wing republicans for his colonial expansion, Ferry defended his policies before the French National Assembly and also elaborated a philosophy of imperialism in his writings.

In a speech to the Assembly on July 28, 1883, portions of which follow, Ferry answered his critics and summarized his three main arguments with brutal honesty. Note that Ferry adamantly insisted that imperial expansion did not weaken France in its European struggle with Germany, as some opponents charged, but rather that it increased French grandeur and power. Imperialists needed the language of patriotic nationalism to be effective.

M. Jules Ferry: Gentlemen, . . . I believe that there is some benefit in summarizing and condensing, in the form of arguments, the principles, the motives, and the various interests by which a policy of colonial expansion may be justified; it goes without saying that I will try to remain reasonable, moderate, and never lose sight of the major continental interests which are the primary concern of this country. What I wish to say, to support this proposition, is that in fact, just as in word, the policy of colonial expansion is a political and economic system; I wish to say that one can relate this system to three orders of ideas: economic ideas, ideas of civilization in its highest sense, and ideas of politics and patriotism.

In the area of economics, I will allow myself to place before you, with the support of some figures, the considerations which justify a policy of colonial expansion from the point of view of that need, felt more and more strongly by the industrial populations of Europe and particularly those of our own rich and hard working country: the need for export markets. Is this some kind of chimera? Is this a view of the future

or is it not rather a pressing need, and, we could say, the cry of our industrial population? I will formulate only in a general way what each of you, in the different parts of France, is in a position to confirm. Yes, what is lacking for our great industry, drawn irrevocably on to the path of exportation by the [free trade] treaties of 1860, what it lacks more and more is export markets. Why? Because next door to us Germany is surrounded by barriers, because beyond the ocean, the United States of America has become protectionist, protectionist in the most extreme sense. . . .

Gentlemen, there is a second point, . . . the humanitarian and civilizing side of the question. On this point the honorable M. Camille Pelletan has jeered in his own refined and clever manner; he jeers, he condemns, and he says "What is this civilization which you impose with cannonballs? What is it but another form of barbarism? Don't these populations, these inferior races, have the same rights as you? Aren't they masters of their own houses? Have they called upon you? You come to them against their will, you offer them violence, but not civilization." There, gentlemen, is the thesis; I do not hesitate to say that this is not politics, nor is it history: it is political metaphysics. *("Ah, Ah" on far left.)*

. . . Gentlemen, I must speak from a higher and more truthful plane. It must be stated openly that, in effect, superior races have rights over inferior races. *(Movement on many benches on the far left.)*

M. Jules Maigne: Oh! You dare to say this in the country which has proclaimed the rights of man!

M. de Guilloutet: This is a justification of slavery and the slave trade! . . .

M. Jules Ferry: I repeat that superior races have a right, because they have a duty. They have the duty to civilize inferior races. . . . *(Approval from the left. New interruptions from the extreme left and from the right.)*

. . . M. Pelletan . . . then touched upon a third point, more delicate, more serious, and upon which I ask your permission to express myself quite frankly. It is the political side of the question. The honorable M. Pelletan, who is a distinguished writer, always comes up with remarkably precise formulations. I will borrow

Jules Ferry, French politician and ardent imperialist. *(Corbis)*

from him the one which he applied the other day to this aspect of colonial policy.

"It is a system," he says, "which consists of seeking out compensations in the Orient with a circumspect and peaceful seclusion which is actually imposed upon us in Europe."

I would like to explain myself in regard to this. I do not like this word, "compensation," and, in effect, not here but elsewhere it has often been used in a treacherous way. If what is being said or insinuated is that any government in this country, any Republican minister could possibly believe that there are in any part of the world compensations for the disasters which we have experienced [in connection with our defeat in the Franco-Prussian War of 1870–1871], an injury is being inflicted . . . and an injury undeserved by that government. *(Applause at the center and left.)* I will ward off this injury with all the force of my patriotism! *(New applause and bravos from the same benches.)*

Gentlemen, there are certain considerations which merit the attention of all patriots. The conditions of naval warfare have been profoundly altered. ("Very true! Very true!")

At this time, as you know, a warship cannot carry more than fourteen days' worth of coal, no matter how perfectly it is organized, and a ship which is out of coal is a derelict on the surface of the sea, abandoned to the first person who comes along. Thence the necessity of having on the oceans provision stations, shelters, ports for defense and revictualling. *(Applause at the center and left. Various interruptions.)* And it is for this that we needed Tunisia, for this that we needed Saigon and the Mekong Delta, for this that we need Madagascar, that we are at Diégo-Suarez and Vohemar [two Madagascar ports] and will never leave them! *(Applause from a great number of benches.)* Gentlemen, in Europe as it is today, in this competition of so many rivals which we see growing around us, some by perfecting their military or maritime forces, others by the prodigious development of an ever growing population; in a Europe, or rather in a universe of this sort, a policy of peaceful seclusion or abstention is simply the highway to decadence! Nations are great in our times only by

means of the activities which they develop; it is not simply "by the peaceful shining forth of institutions" *(interruptions on the extreme left and right)* that they are great at this hour.

. . . [The Republican Party] has shown that it is quite aware that one cannot impose upon France a political ideal conforming to that of nations like independent Belgium and the Swiss Republic; that something else is needed for France: that she cannot be merely a free country, that she must also be a great country, exercising all of her rightful influence over the destiny of Europe, that she ought to propagate this influence throughout the world and carry everywhere that she can her language, her customs, her flag, her arms, and her genius. *(Applause at center and left.)*

Questions for Analysis

1. What was Jules Ferry's economic argument for imperial expansion? Why had colonies recently gained greater economic value?

2. How did Ferry's critics attack the morality of foreign expansion? How did Ferry try to claim the moral high ground in his response?

3. What political arguments did Ferry advance? How would you characterize his philosophy of politics and national development?

Source: Speech before the French National Assembly, July 28, 1883. Reprinted in R. A. Austen, ed., *Modern Imperialism: Western Overseas Expansion and Its Aftermath, 1776–1965* (Lexington, Mass.: D. C. Heath, 1969), pp. 70–73.

Western Warehouses and Offices in Guangzhou (Canton) Harbor, nineteenth century (detail). *(Photograph courtesy Peabody Essex Museum, Neg #M3156)*

25 ASIA IN THE ERA OF IMPERIALISM, 1800–1914

Chapter Preview

India and the British Empire in Asia
• *In what ways did India change as a consequence of British rule?*

Competition for Southeast Asia
• *Why were some Southeast Asian societies reduced to colonies and others not?*

China Under Pressure
• *Was China's decline in the nineteenth century due more to internal problems or Western imperialism?*

Japan's Rapid Transformation
• *How was Japan able to quickly master the challenges posed by the West?*

The Movement of Peoples
• *Why did people move much more in this period, and where did they go?*

During the nineteenth century, the societies of Asia underwent enormous changes—the results of population growth, social unrest, and the looming presence of Western imperialist powers. In this period half the people of the world lived in the region from India east to the Pacific Ocean, but they were very unevenly distributed. In the temperate zones of East Asia the old established monarchies of China, Japan, and Korea were all densely populated and boasted long literary traditions. India was just as densely populated but politically and culturally more diverse, with several major languages and dozens of independent rulers reigning in kingdoms large and small. What Britain and later the other Western powers initially wanted from the more developed Asian societies was to refashion trading relations to the West's benefit. At the other extreme were thinly populated and relatively primitive areas without literate cultures and sometimes even without agriculture, such as some of the islands of the Philippines and Indonesia. They could not provide manufactured goods such as porcelain or silk, but they offered opportunities for Western development, much as the Americas had earlier.

The economics of industrialization and the political rivalries among the European powers all shaped the steps taken by Western nations to gain power in Asia, and these influences changed over the course of the century. Western science and technology were making rapid advances, which gave European armies progressively greater advantages in weaponry. The Industrial Revolution made it possible for early industrializers such as Britain to produce huge surpluses of goods for which they had to find markets, shifting their interest in Asia from a place to buy goods to a place to sell goods. Britain had been able to profit from its colonization of India, and this profit both encouraged it to consolidate its rule and invited its European rivals to look for their own colonies.

The societies of Asia varied enormously at the beginning of the century, but the common encounter with the expanding West gradually gave them more in common. Often the initial response of Asian leaders was to try to drive the unwelcome foreigners away. This was seen in China, Japan, and Korea in particular. Violent antiforeign reactions exploded again and again, but the superior military technology of the industrialized West almost invariably prevailed. After suffering humiliating defeats, some Asian leaders insisted on the need to preserve their cultural traditions at all costs. Others came to the opposite conclusion that the West was indeed superior in some ways and that they would have to adopt European ideas or techniques for their own purposes. The struggles between the traditionalists and the westernizers were often intense. As nationalism took hold in the West (see Chapter 23), it found a receptive audience among the educated elites in Asia. How could the assertion that every people had the right to control its own destiny not appeal to the colonized?

By the end of the nineteenth century, most of the southern tier of Asia, from India to the Philippines, had been made colonies of Western powers. Many of these areas became major exporters of agricultural products or raw materials, including timber, rubber, tin, sugar, tea, cotton, and jute. New knowledge and new technologies spread rapidly. Railroads, telegraphs, modern sanitation, and a wider supply of inexpensive manufactured goods brought fundamental changes in everyday life. To a much greater extent than in any earlier time, Europeans were living in Asia and learning its languages and cultures, and Asians were studying Western languages or emigrating abroad. Still, cultural barriers between the colonizers and the colonized were huge. The West relied on force to conquer and rule, and it treated non-Western peoples as racial inferiors.

Not all the countries in Asia became victims of Western imperialism. Japan became the first non-Western country to use an ancient love of country to transform itself and thereby meet the many-sided challenge of Western expansion. Japan came out of the nineteenth-century crisis stronger than any other Asian nation. It became the first non-Western country to industrialize successfully and by the end of this period had become an imperialist power itself, making Korea and Taiwan its colonies.

INDIA AND THE BRITISH EMPIRE IN ASIA

In what ways did India change as a consequence of British rule?

Arriving in India on the heels of the Portuguese in the seventeenth century, the British East India Company outmaneuvered French and Dutch rivals and was there to pick up the pieces as the Mughal Empire decayed during the eighteenth century (see pages 553–554). By 1757, the company had gained control over much of India. During the nineteenth century, the British government took over, progressively unified the subcontinent, and harnessed its economy to British interests.

Communication between Britain and India became much faster, safer, and more predictable in this period. Clipper ships with their huge sails cut the voyage from Europe to India from six to three months. By the 1850s steamships were competing with clipper ships, and they made ocean travel more predictable. After the Suez Canal was opened in 1869, the voyage by steamship from England to India took only three weeks. In the 1860s cables were laid on the ocean floor, allowing telegrams to be sent from England to India. Whereas at the beginning of the nineteenth century someone in England had to wait a year or more to get an answer to a letter sent to India, by 1870 it took only a couple of months—or, if the matter was urgent, only a few hours by telegraph.

In 1818 the British East India Company controlled territory occupied by 180 million Indians—more people than lived in all of western Europe and fifty times the number of people the British had lost after the American Revolution. The British ruled with the cooperation of Indian princely allies, whom they could not afford to offend. Still, the British disbanded and disarmed local armies, introduced simpler private property laws, and enhanced the powers of local princes and religious leaders, both Hindu and Muslim. The British administrators, backed by British officers and native troops, were on the whole competent and concerned about the welfare of the Indian peasants. Slavery was outlawed and banditry suppressed. New laws designed to improve women's position in society were introduced. Sati (widow immolation) was outlawed in 1829, legal protection of widow remarriage was extended in 1856, and infanticide was banned in 1870.

The last armed resistance to British rule occurred in 1857. By that date the British military presence in India had grown to include two hundred thousand Indian sepoy troops and thirty-eight thousand British officers. The sepoys were well trained and armed with modern rifles. In 1857 groups of them, especially around Delhi, revolted in what the British called the **Great Mutiny** and the Indians called the **Great Revolt**. Their grievances were many, ranging from the use of animal grease on their rifles to the incorporation of low-caste soldiers into the army and high tax rates. The insurrection spread rapidly throughout northern and central India before it was finally crushed, primarily by native troops from other parts of India loyal to the British. Thereafter, although princely states were allowed to continue, Britain ruled India much more tightly. Moreover, the British in India were more aware that they were an occupying power and mixed less with the Indian elite.

After 1858 India was ruled by the British Parliament in London and administered by a civil service in India, the upper echelons of which were all white. In 1900 this elite consisted of fewer than thirty-five hundred top officials for a population of 300 million. In 1877 Queen Victoria adopted the title **Empress of India,** and her image became a common sight in India.

The impact of British rule on the Indian economy was multifaceted. In the early stages, the British East India Company expanded agricultural production, creating large plantations. Early crops were opium to export to China (see page 758) and tea to substitute for imports from China. India gradually replaced China as the leading exporter of tea to Europe. During the nineteenth century India also exported cotton fiber, silk, sugar, jute, coffee, and other agricultural commodities to be processed elsewhere. Clearing land for tea and coffee plantations, along with massive commercial logging operations, led to extensive deforestation.

The colonial administration invested heavily in India's infrastructure. By 1855 India's major cities had all been linked by telegraph and railroads, and postal service was being extended to local villages. By 1870 India had the fifth-largest rail network in the world—4,775 miles, carrying more than 18 million passengers a year. By 1900 the rail

Chronology

1825	Government of Japan orders foreign vessels to be turned away from Japanese ports; King Minh Mang outlaws teaching of Christianity in Vietnam
1830	Dutch institute Culture System in Indonesia
1842	Treaty of Nanjing ends Opium War
1851–1864	Taiping Rebellion in China
1853	Commodore Perry opens Japanese ports to foreign trade
1857	Great Mutiny/Great Revolt by Indian sepoys against British rule
1858	British Parliament begins to rule India
1859–1885	Vietnam becomes a colony of France
1860s	Rise of Tonghak movement in Korea
1867	Meiji Restoration in Japan
1869	Suez Canal opens
1872	Universal public schools established in Japan
1885	Foundation of Indian National Congress
1894–1895	Japan defeats China in Sino-Japanese War and gains control of Taiwan
1898	United States takes control of Philippines from Spain
1900	Boxer Rebellion in China
1904	Japan attacks Russia and starts Russo-Japanese War
1910	Korea becomes a province of Japan
1912	China's monarchy is replaced by a republic

Great Mutiny/Great Revolt *The terms used by the British and the Indians to describe the last armed resistance to British rule in India, which occurred in 1857.*

Empress of India *The title adopted by Queen Victoria in 1877 to reflect the British rule of India.*

● **British and Sikh Leaders at Lahore** The Sikh kingdom in the Punjab fell to the British in a brief war in 1845–1846. This painting depicts the British and Sikh representatives who negotiated the resulting treaty, which gave Britain control of the region. *(Courtesy of the Trustees of the British Museum)*

network had increased fivefold to 25,000 miles, and the number of passengers had increased tenfold to 188 million. By then over 370,000 Indians worked for the railroads. Irrigation also received attention, and by 1900 India had the world's most extensive irrigation system.

At the same time, Indian production of textiles suffered a huge blow. Britain imported India's raw cotton but exported machine-spun yarn and machine-woven cloth, displacing millions of Indian hand-spinners and hand-weavers. By 1900 India was buying 40 percent of Britain's cotton exports. Not until 1900 were there small steps toward industrializing India. Local Gujaratis set up textile mills in Bombay, and the Tata family started the first steel mill in Bihar in 1911. By 1914 about a million Indians worked in factories.

The standard of living of the poor did not see much improvement. Tenancy and landlessness increased with the growth in plantation agriculture. Increases in production were eaten up by increases in population, which reached approximately 300 million by 1900. There was also a negative side to improved communication. As Indians traveled more widely on the convenient trains, disease spread, especially cholera, which is transmitted by exposure to contaminated water. Pilgrims' bathing in and drinking from sacred pools and rivers worsened this problem. New sewerage and water supply systems were installed in Calcutta in the late 1860s, and the death rate there decreased, but in 1900 four out of every one thousand residents of British India still died of cholera each year.

The Indian middle class probably gained more than the poor from British rule. The British built a large educational establishment in India with instruction in English. In the words of the member of Parliament who proposed it, Thomas Macaulay, this system would form "a class of persons Indian in blood and color, but English in taste, in opinions, in morals, and in intellect."[1] Missionaries also established schools with Western curricula, and by 1870, 790,000 Indians were attending some 24,000 schools. High-caste Hindus came to form a new elite profoundly influenced by Western thought and culture.

By creating a well-educated, English-speaking Indian elite and a bureaucracy based on a modern communication system, the British laid the groundwork for a unified, powerful state. Britain placed under the same general system of law and administration the various Hindu and Muslim peoples of the subcontinent who had resisted one another for centuries. It was as if Europe, with its many states and varieties of Christianity, had been conquered and united in a single great empire. University graduates tended to look on themselves as Indians more than as residents of the separate states and kingdoms, a necessary step for the development of Indian nationalism.

In spite of these achievements, British rule rankled the educated elite. Some Indian intellectuals sought to reconcile the values of the modern West and their own traditions. Rammohun Roy (1772–1833), who had risen to the top of the native ranks in the British East India Company, founded the Hindu College in Calcutta in 1816, which offered instruction in Western languages and subjects. A few years later he founded a society to reform certain Hindu customs, especially child marriage, the caste system, and restrictions on widows. He espoused a modern Hinduism founded on the *Upanishads,* the ancient sacred texts of Hinduism.

The more that Western-style education was developed in India, the more the inequalities of the system became apparent to educated Indians. Indians were eligible to take the examinations for entry into the elite **Indian Civil Service,** but the exams were given in England, and in 1870 only 1 of the 916 members of the service was Indian. In other words, no matter how Anglicized the educated classes became, they could never become the white rulers' equals. The top jobs, the best clubs, the modern hotels, and even certain railroad compartments were sealed off to brown-skinned men and women. Most of the British elite considered the jumble of Indian peoples and castes to be racially inferior. For example, when the British Parliament in 1883 was considering a bill to allow Indian judges to try white Europeans in India, the British community rose in protest and defeated the measure. The idea of being judged by Indians was inconceivable to the Europeans, for it was clear to them that the empire in India rested squarely on racial inequality. As Lord Kitchener, one of the most distinguished British military commanders in India, stated:

It is this consciousness of the inherent superiority of the European which has won for us India. However well educated and clever a native may be, and however brave he may prove himself, I believe that no rank we can bestow on him would cause him to be considered an equal of the British officer.[2]

The peasant masses might accept such inequality as the latest version of age-old class and caste hierarchies, but the well-educated, English-speaking elite eventually could not. They had studied not only Milton and Shakespeare but also English traditions of democracy, liberty, and national pride.

In the late nineteenth century the colonial ports of Calcutta, Bombay, and Madras, now all linked by railroads, became centers of intellectual ferment. In these and other cities, newspapers in English and in regional languages gained influence. Lawyers trained in English law began agitating for Indian independence. By 1885, when educated Indians came together to found the **Indian National Congress,** demands were increasing for the equality and self-government that Britain enjoyed and had already granted white-settler colonies such as Canada and Australia (see Chapter 26). Members of the congress called for more opportunities for Indians in the Indian

Indian Civil Service *The bureaucracy that administered the government of India. Entry into its elite ranks was by examinations that Indians were eligible to take but that were offered only in England.*

Indian National Congress *A political association formed in 1885 that worked for Indian self-government.*

● **Imperial Complexities in India** Britain permitted many native princes to continue their rule if they accepted British domination. This photo shows a road-building project designed to facilitate famine relief in a southern native state. Officials of the local Muslim prince and their British "advisers" watch over workers drawn from the Hindu majority. *(Nizam's Good Works Project–Famine Relief: Road Building, Aurangabad 1895–1902, from Judith Mara Gutman,* Through Indian Eyes. *Courtesy, Private Collection)*

Civil Service and reallocation of the government budget from military expenditures to the alleviation of poverty. They advocated unity across religious and caste lines, but most members were upper-caste, Western-educated Hindus.

Defending its possessions in India became a key element of British foreign policy during the nineteenth century and led to steady expansion of the territory Britain controlled in Asia. The kingdom of Burma, to India's east, also was trying to expand, which led the British to annex Assam (located between India and Burma) in 1826, then all of Burma by 1852. Burma was then administered as a province of India. British trade between India and China went through the Strait of Malacca, making that region strategically important. Britain had taken over several Dutch territories in this region during the Napoleonic occupation of the Netherlands, including Java. After returning them to the Netherlands in 1814, Britain created its own base in the area at Singapore, later expanding into Malaya (now Malaysia) in the 1870s and 1880s. In both Burma and Malaya, Britain tried to foster economic development. Railroads were built, and trade was promoted. Burma became a major exporter of timber and rice, Malaya of tin and rubber. So many laborers were brought into Malaya for the expanding mines and plantations that its population came to be approximately one-third Malay, one-third Chinese, and one-third Indian.

COMPETITION FOR SOUTHEAST ASIA

Why were some Southeast Asian societies reduced to colonies and others not?

At the beginning of the nineteenth century, only a small part of Southeast Asia was under direct European control. Spain administered the Philippines, and the Dutch controlled Java. By the end of the century, most of the region would be in foreign hands.

The Dutch East Indies

Although Dutch forts and trading posts in the East Indies dated back to the seventeenth century, in 1816 the Dutch ruled little more than the island of Java. Thereafter they gradually brought almost all of the 3,000-mile-long archipelago under their political authority. In extending their rule, the Dutch, like the British in India, brought

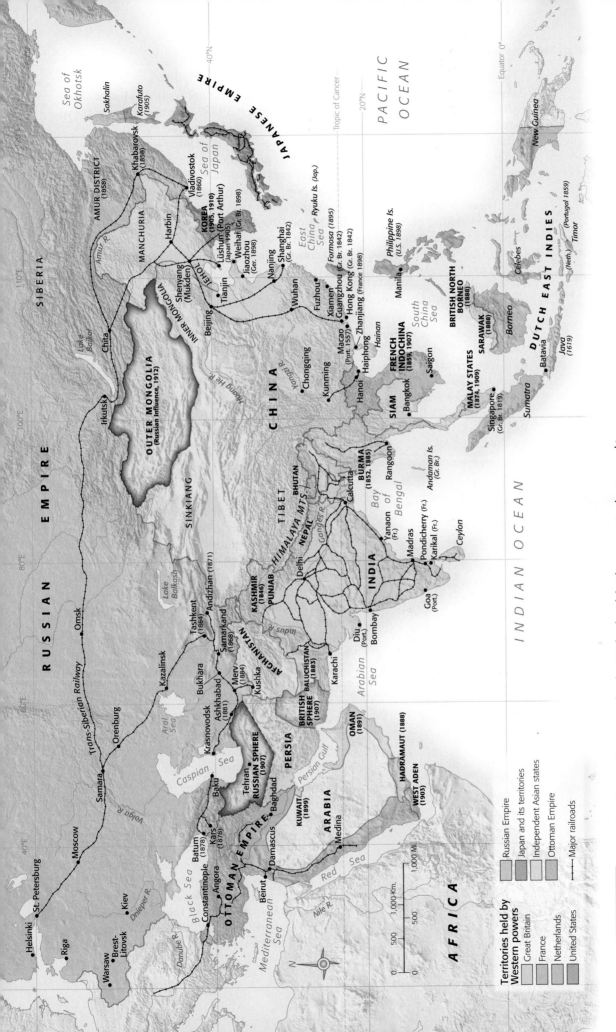

MAP 25.1 Asia in 1914 India remained under British rule, while China precariously preserved its political independence. The Dutch empire in modern-day Indonesia was old, but French control of Indochina was a product of the new imperialism.

Territories held by Western powers

Great Britain

France

Netherlands

United States

Russian Empire

Japan and its territories

Independent Asian states

Ottoman Empire

Major railroads

PACIFIC OCEAN

INDIAN OCEAN

RUSSIAN EMPIRE

SIBERIA

JAPANESE EMPIRE

CHINA

INDIA

AFRICA

OTTOMAN EMPIRE

ARABIA

PERSIA

AFGHANISTAN

DUTCH EAST INDIES

Sea of Okhotsk

Sea of Japan

East China Sea

South China Sea

Bay of Bengal

Arabian Sea

Red Sea

Black Sea

Mediterranean Sea

Caspian Sea

Aral Sea

Persian Gulf

Lake Baikal

Lake Balkash

Trans-Siberian Railway

Equator 0°

Tropic of Cancer

20°N

40°N

110°E

100°E

80°E

60°E

40°E

St. Petersburg

Helsinki

Riga

Warsaw

Brest-Litovsk

Kiev

Moscow

Samara

Orenburg

Omsk

Irkutsk

Chita

Kazalinsk

Tashkent

Andizhan (1871)

Samarkand (1868)

Bukhara

Krasnovodsk

Ashkhabad (1881)

Merv (1884)

Kushka

Baku

Batum (1878)

Kars (1878)

Tehran

RUSSIAN SPHERE (1907)

Baghdad

Damascus

Beirut

Constantinople

Angora

Medina

KUWAIT (1899)

OMAN (1891)

HADRAMAUT (1888)

WEST ADEN (1903)

BALUCHISTAN (1883)

BRITISH SPHERE (1907)

Karachi

Bombay

Diu (Port.)

Goa (Port.)

KASHMIR (1846)

PUNJAB

Delhi

NEPAL

BHUTAN

HIMALAYA MTS.

TIBET

SINKIANG

OUTER MONGOLIA (Russian influence, 1912)

INNER MONGOLIA

MANCHURIA

AMUR DISTRICT (1858)

Khabarovsk (1858)

Vladivostok (1860)

Sakhalin

Karafuto (1905)

Harbin

Shenyang (Mukden)

JEHOL

Beijing

Tianjin

KOREA (1905, 1910)

Lüshun (Port Arthur) (Japan 1905)

Weihai (Gr. Br. 1898)

Jiaozhou (Ger. 1898)

Nanjing

Shanghai

Wuhan

Chongqing

Kunming

Fuzhou

Xiamen

Guangzhou (Gr. Br. 1842)

Macao (Port. 1557)

Hong Kong (Gr. Br. 1842)

Zhanjiang (France 1898)

Haiphong

Hanoi

Hainan

Formosa (1895)

Ryuku Is. (Jap.)

Philippine Is. (U.S. 1898)

Manila

BRITISH NORTH BORNEO (1888)

SARAWAK (1888)

Borneo

Celebes

New Guinea

Timor (Portugal 1859)

(Neth.)

Java (1619)

Sumatra

Batavia

Singapore (Gr. Br. 1819)

MALAY STATES (1874, 1909)

Bangkok

SIAM

FRENCH INDOCHINA (1859, 1907)

Saigon

BURMA (1852, 1885)

Rangoon

Calcutta

Andaman Is. (Gr. Br.)

Yanaon (Fr.)

Madras

Pondicherry (Fr.)

Karikal (Fr.)

Ceylon

Amur R.

Huang He R.

Yangzi R.

Ganges R.

Indus R.

Volga R.

Dnieper R.

Danube R.

Nile R.

N

1,000 Mi.

1,000 Km.

500

500

0

0

755

diverse peoples with different languages and distinct cultural traditions into a single political entity (see Map 25.1). Thus they inadvertently created the foundations of modern-day Indonesia—the world's fourth most populous nation.

Taking over the Dutch East India Company in 1799, the Dutch government modified the company's loose control of Java and gradually built a modern bureaucratic state. Javanese resistance led to the bloody **Java War** (1825–1830). In 1830, after the war, the Dutch abolished the combination of tribute from rulers and forced labor from peasants that they had used to obtain spices, and they established instead a particularly exploitive policy called the **Culture System**. Indonesian peasants were forced to plant a fifth of their land in export crops, especially coffee and sugar, to turn over to the Dutch as their taxes. The Culture System proved highly profitable for the Dutch and brought Dutch shipping and intercontinental commerce back to life. In 1870 Dutch liberals succeeded in eliminating some of the system's most coercive elements, but the practical effects were limited because Dutch and Javanese officials still worked together to make sure the flow of goods continued.

At the end of the nineteenth century the Dutch began to encourage Western education in the East Indies. The children of local rulers and privileged elites, much like their counterparts in India, encountered new ideas in Dutch-speaking schools. They began to question the long-standing cooperation of local elites with Dutch colonialism, and they searched for a new identity. Thus anticolonial nationalism began to take shape in the East Indies in the early twentieth century, and it would blossom after World War I.

Java War *The 1825–1830 war between the Dutch government and the Javanese, fought over the extension of Dutch control of the island.*

Culture System *The Dutch policy that required Indonesian peasants to plant a fifth of their land in export crops, which were then turned over to the Dutch as taxes.*

Nguyen Dynasty *The last Vietnamese ruling house, which lasted from 1802 to 1945.*

● **The French Governor General and the Vietnamese Emperor** The twelfth emperor of the Nguyen Dynasty, Khai Dinh (1885–1925) had to find ways to get along with the French governor general (in this picture, Albert Sarraut) if he wished to preserve his dynasty. Seen here in 1917 or 1918, he had adopted Western leather shoes but otherwise tried to keep a distinct Vietnamese identity in his dress. *(Roger Viollet/Getty Images)*

Mainland Southeast Asia

Unlike India and Java, mainland Southeast Asia had escaped European rule through the eighteenth century. In 1802 the new **Nguyen Dynasty** came to power in Vietnam, putting an end to thirty years of peasant rebellion and civil war. For the first time in the country's history, a single Vietnamese monarchy ruled the entire country, and Vietnam's future appeared bright. Working through a centralizing scholar bureaucracy fashioned on the Chinese model, the dynasty energetically built irrigation canals, roads and bridges, and impressive palaces in Hue, the new capital city. In 1821 a European who had lived in India, Java, and Siam (Thailand) wrote that Hue had a "neatness, magnitude, and perfection" that made other Asian achievements look "like the works of children."[3] Yet construction placed a heavy burden on the peasants drafted to do the work, and it contributed to a resurgence of peasant uprisings.

Roman Catholic missionaries from France posed a second, more dangerous threat to Vietnam's Confucian ruling elite. The king and his advisers believed that Christianity would undermine Confucian moral values and the unity of the Vietnamese state. In 1825 King Minh Mang (r. 1820–1841) outlawed the teaching of Christianity, and soon his government began executing Catholic missionaries and Vietnamese converts. As many as thirty thousand Vietnamese Christians were executed in the 1850s. In response, in 1859–1860 a French naval force seized Saigon

José Rizal

After his death, Rizal's portrait was used to inspire patriotism. *(Cover of "The Filipino Teacher," December 1908. Museo Santisima Trinidad)*

In the mid-seventeenth century, a Chinese merchant immigrated to the Philippines and married a woman who was half Chinese, half Philippine. Because of anti-Chinese animosity, he changed his name to Mercado, Spanish for "merchant."

Mercado's direct patrilineal descendant, José Rizal (1861–1896), was born into a well-to-do family that leased a plantation from Dominican friars. Both of his parents were educated, and he was a brilliant student himself. In 1882, after completing his studies at the Jesuit-run college in Manila, he went on to Madrid to study medicine. During his ten years in Europe, not only did he earn a medical degree in Spain and a Ph.D. in Germany, but he also found time to learn several European languages and make friends with scientists, writers, and political radicals.

While in Europe, Rizal became involved with Philippine revolutionaries and contributed numerous articles to their newspaper, *La Solidaridad,* published in Barcelona. Rizal advocated making the Philippines a province of Spain, giving it representation in the Spanish parliament, replacing Spanish friars with Filipino priests, and making Filipinos and Spaniards equal before the law. He spent a year at the British Museum doing research on the early phase of the Spanish colonization of the Philippines. He also wrote two novels.

The first novel, written in Spanish, was fired by the passions of nationalism. In satirical fashion, it depicts a young Filipino of mixed blood who studies for several years in Europe before returning to the Philippines to start a modern secular school in his hometown and marry his childhood sweetheart. The church stands in the way of his efforts, and the colonial administration proves incompetent. The novel ends with the hero gunned down after the friars falsely implicate him in a revolutionary conspiracy. Rizal's own life ended up following this narrative surprisingly closely.

In 1892 Rizal left Europe, stopped briefly in Hong Kong, then returned to Manila to help his family with a lawsuit. Though he secured his relatives' release from jail, he ran into trouble himself. Because his writings were critical of the power of the church, he made many enemies, some of whom had him arrested. He was sent into exile to a Jesuit mission town on the relatively primitive island of Mindanao. There he founded a school and a hospital, and the Jesuits tried to win him back to the church. He kept busy during his four years in exile, not only teaching English, sci-

ence, and self-defense, but also maintaining his correspondence with scientists in Europe. When a nationalist secret society rose in revolt in 1896, in an effort to distance himself, he volunteered to go to Cuba to help in an outbreak of yellow fever. Although he had no connections with the secret society and was on his way across the ocean, Rizal was arrested and shipped back to Manila.

Tried for sedition by the military, Rizal was found guilty. When handed his death certificate, Rizal struck out the words "Chinese half-breed" and wrote "pure native." He was publicly executed by a firing squad in Manila at age thirty-five, making him a martyr of the nationalist cause.

Questions for Analysis

1. Did Rizal's comfortable family background contribute to his becoming a revolutionary?
2. How would Rizal's European contemporaries have reacted to his opposition to the Catholic Church?

and three surrounding provinces in southern Vietnam, making that part of Vietnam a French colony. In 1884–1885 France launched a second war against Vietnam and conquered the rest of the country. Laos and Cambodia were added to **French Indochina** in 1887. In all three countries the local rulers were left on their thrones, but France dominated and tried to promote French culture.

After the French conquest, Vietnamese patriots continued to resist with a combination of loyalty to Confucian values and intense hatred of foreign rule. After Japan's victory over Russia in 1905 (see page 767–768), a new generation of nationalists saw Japan as a model for Vietnamese revitalization and freedom. They went to Japan to study and planned for anticolonial revolution in Vietnam.

In all of Southeast Asia, only Siam succeeded in preserving its independence. Siam was sandwiched between the British in Burma (and India) and the French in Indochina. Thus geography enabled its very able King Chulalongkorn (r. 1868–1910) to balance the two competitors against each other and to escape the smothering embrace of both. Chulalongkorn had studied Greek and Latin and Western science and kept up with Western news by reading British newspapers from Hong Kong and Singapore. He outlawed slavery and implemented modernizing reforms that centralized the government so that it could more effectively control outlying provinces coveted by the imperialists. Independent Siam gradually developed a modern centralizing state similar to the states constructed by Western imperialists in their Asian possessions.

The Philippines

The United States became one of the imperialist powers in Asia when it took the Philippines from Spain in 1898.

When the Spanish established rule in the Philippines in the sixteenth century, the islands had no central government or literate culture; order was maintained by village units dominated by local chiefs. Under the Spanish, Roman Catholic churches were established, and Spanish priests able to speak the local languages became the most common intermediaries between local populations, who rarely could speak Spanish, and the new rulers. The government of Spain encouraged Spaniards to colonize the Philippines through the **encomienda system**: Spaniards who had served the Crown were rewarded with grants giving them the exclusive right to control public affairs and collect taxes in a specific locality. A local Filipino elite also developed, aided by the Spanish introduction of private ownership of land. Given the great distance between Madrid and Manila, the governor general, appointed by Spain, had almost unlimited powers over the courts and the military. Manila developed into an important entrepôt in the galleon trade between Mexico and China, and this trade also attracted a large Chinese community, which handled much of the trade within the Philippines.

Spain did not do much to promote education in the Philippines, and few Filipinos could read, write, or speak Spanish. In the late nineteenth century, however, wealthy Filipinos began to send their sons to study abroad, and a movement to press Spain for reforms emerged. When the Spanish cracked down on critics, a rebellion erupted in 1896 (see Individuals in Society: José Rizal). It was settled in 1897 with Spanish promises to reform.

In 1898, war between Spain and the United States broke out on the coast of Cuba (see page 791), and in May the American naval officer Commodore George Dewey sailed into Manila Bay and sank the Spanish fleet anchored there. Dewey called on the Philippine rebels to help defeat the Spanish forces, but when the rebels declared independence, the U.S. government refused to recognize them, despite protests by American anti-imperialists. U.S. forces fought the Philippine rebels, and by the end of the insurrection in 1902, the war had cost the lives of 5,000 Americans and about 200,000 Filipinos. In the following years, the United States introduced a form of colonial rule that included public works and economic development projects, improved education and medicine, and, in 1907, an elected legislative assembly.

French Indochina *The name given the French colonial state that ruled the region of the modern countries of Vietnam, Laos, and Cambodia.*

encomienda system *The system under which Spanish colonists were given the exclusive right to control public affairs in the Philippines and collect taxes in a specific locality.*

CHINA UNDER PRESSURE

Was China's decline in the nineteenth century due more to internal problems or Western imperialism?

In 1800 most Chinese had no reason to question the conception of China as the central kingdom: no other country had so many people, Chinese products were in great demand in foreign countries, and the borders had recently been expanded. A century later, all that had changed. In 1900 foreign troops marched into China's capital, and more and more Chinese had come to think that their government, society, and cultural values needed to be radically changed.

The Opium War

Seeing little to gain from trade with European countries, the Qing (Manchu) emperors, who had been ruling China since 1644 (see pages 585–588), permitted Europeans to trade only at the port of Guangzhou (Canton) and only through licensed Chinese merchants. Initially, the balance of trade was in China's favor, as Great Britain and the other Western nations used silver to pay for tea. By the 1820s, however, the British had found something the Chinese would buy—opium. Grown legally in British-occupied India, opium was smuggled into China, where its use and sale were illegal. Huge profits and the cravings of addicts led to rapid increases in sales, from 4,500 chests a year in 1810 to 10,000 in 1830 and to 40,000 in 1838. At this point it was China that suffered a drain of silver.

To deal with this crisis, the Chinese government dispatched Lin Zexu to Guangzhou in 1839. He dealt harshly with Chinese who purchased opium and seized the opium stores of British merchants. Lin even wrote to Queen Victoria: "Suppose there were people from another country who carried opium for sale to England and seduced your people into buying and smoking it; certainly your honorable ruler would deeply hate it and be bitterly aroused."[4] When Lin pressured the Portuguese to expel the uncooperative British from their trading post at Macao, the British settled on the barren island of Hong Kong.

Although for years the little community of foreign merchants had accepted Chinese rules, by 1839 the British, the dominant group, were ready to flex their muscles. British merchants wanted to create a market for their goods in China and get tea more cheaply by trading closer to its source in central China. They also wanted a diplomatic system more on the European model, with envoys and ambassadors, commercial treaties, and published tariffs. With the encouragement of their merchants in China, the British sent an expeditionary force from India with forty-two warships, many of them leased from the major opium trader, Jardine, Matheson, and Company.

With its control of the seas, the British easily shut down key Chinese ports and forced the Chinese to negotiate. Dissatisfied with the resulting agreement, the British sent a second, larger force, which took even more coastal cities, including Shanghai. This **Opium War** was settled at gunpoint in 1842. The resulting **Treaty of Nanjing** (Nanking) opened five ports to international trade, fixed the tariff on imported goods at 5 percent, imposed an indemnity of 21 million ounces of silver on China to cover Britain's war expenses, and ceded the island of Hong Kong to Britain. Through the clause on **extraterritoriality**, British subjects in China became answerable only to British law, even in disputes with Chinese. The treaty also had a "most-favored nation" clause, which meant that whenever one nation extracted a new privilege from China, it was extended automatically to Britain.

This treaty satisfied neither side. China continued to refuse to accept foreign diplomats at its capital in Beijing, and the expansion of trade fell far short of Western expectations. Between 1856 and 1860 Britain and France renewed hostilities with China. Seventeen thousand British and French troops occupied Beijing and set the

Primary Source: Letter to Queen Victoria, 1839
On behalf of the emperor, Lin Zexu implores Queen Victoria to halt the British opium trade in China.

Opium War *The 1839–1842 war between the British and the Chinese over limitations on trade and the importation of opium into China.*

Treaty of Nanjing *The treaty ending the Opium War; it opened five ports to international trade, fixed the tariff on imported goods, imposed an indemnity on China to cover Britain's war expenses, and ceded the island of Hong Kong to Britain, among other measures.*

extraterritoriality *The legal principle that exempts individuals from local law; it was included in the Treaty of Nanjing so that British subjects in China would be answerable only to British law.*

● **Mixed Court** In the treaty ports, beginning in 1864, disputes between Chinese and Westerners were heard by two judges, one Chinese and one representing the Western powers. These "mixed courts" applied Western law for offenses that occurred within the concessions. *(John Hillelson Agency)*

emperor's summer palace on fire. Another round of harsh treaties gave European merchants and missionaries greater privileges and forced the Chinese to open several more cities to foreign trade. Large areas in some of the treaty ports were leased in perpetuity to foreign powers; these were known as **concessions**.

concessions *Large areas of Chinese treaty ports that were leased in perpetuity to foreign powers.*

Internal Problems

China's problems in the nineteenth century, however, were not all of foreign origin. By 1850 China, for centuries the world's most populous country, had more than 400 million people. As the population grew, farm size shrank, forests were put to the plow, and surplus labor suppressed wages. When the best parcels of land were all occupied, conflicts over rights to water and tenancy increased. Hard times also led to increased female infanticide, as families felt that they could not afford to raise more than two or three children and saw sons as necessities. A shortage of marriageable women resulted, reducing the incentive for young men to stay near home and do as their elders told them. Some became bandits, others boatmen, carters, sedan-chair carriers, or, by the end of the century, rickshaw pullers.

These economic and demographic circumstances led to some of the most destructive rebellions in China's history. The worst was the **Taiping Rebellion** (1851–1864), in which some 20 million people lost their lives, making it one of the bloodiest wars in world history.

Taiping Rebellion *A massive rebellion by the believers in the religious teachings of Hong Xiuquan, begun in 1851 and not suppressed until 1864.*

This rebellion was initiated by Hong Xiuquan (1814–1864), a man from South China who had studied for the civil service examinations but never passed. His career as a religious leader began with visions of a golden-bearded old man and a middle-aged man who addressed him as younger brother and told him to annihilate devils. After reading a Christian tract given to him by a missionary, Hong interpreted his visions to mean he was Jesus' younger brother. He soon gathered followers, whom he instructed to destroy idols and ancestral temples, give up opium and alcohol, and renounce foot binding and prostitution. In 1851 he declared himself king of the Heavenly Kingdom of Great Peace (Taiping), an act of open insurrection. By 1853 the

Taipings had moved north and established their capital at the major city of Nanjing, which they held onto for a decade. From this base they set about creating a utopian society based on the equalization of landholdings and the equality of men and women. Christian missionaries quickly concluded that the Christian elements in Taiping doctrines were heretical and did not help them. To suppress the Taipings, the Manchus had to turn to Chinese scholar-officials, who raised armies on their own, revealing that the Manchus were no longer the mighty warriors they had been when they had conquered China two centuries earlier.

The Self-Strengthening Movement

After the various rebellions were suppressed, forward-looking reformers began addressing the Western threat. Under the slogan **"self-strengthening,"** they set about modernizing the military along Western lines. Arsenals and dockyards were established, and envoys were sent abroad. Recognizing that guns and ships were merely the surface manifestations of the Western powers' economic strength, some of the most progressive reformers also initiated new industries, which in the 1870s and 1880s included railway lines, steam navigation companies, coal mines, telegraph lines, and cotton spinning and weaving factories. These were the same sorts of initiatives that the British were introducing in India, but China lagged behind, especially in railroads.

These measures drew resistance from conservatives, who thought copying Western practices was compounding defeat. The highly placed Manchu official Woren objected that "from ancient down to modern times" there had never been "anyone who could use mathematics to raise a nation from a state of decline or to strengthen it in times of weakness."[5] Yet knowledge of the West gradually improved with more translations and travel in both directions. Newspapers covering world affairs began publication in Shanghai and Hong Kong. By 1880 China had embassies in London, Paris, Berlin, Madrid, Washington, Tokyo, and St. Petersburg.

Despite the enormous effort put into trying to catch up, China was humiliated yet again at the end of the nineteenth century. First came the discovery that Japan had so

"self-strengthening" *The goal of the reform movement in late-nineteenth-century China that sought to master Western technology in order to better resist Western pressure.*

● **China's First Railroad**   Soon after this railroad was constructed near Shanghai in 1876, the provincial governor bought it in order to tear it out. Many Chinese of the period saw railroads as harmful not only to the balance of nature but also to people's livelihoods, since the railroads eliminated jobs in transport like dragging boats along canals or driving pack horses. *(Private Collection)*

● **Hong Kong Tailors** In 1872 the newspaper *Shenbao* was founded in Shanghai, and in 1884 it added an eight-page weekly pictorial supplement. Influenced by the pictorial press then popular in Europe, it depicted both news and human interest stories, both Chinese and foreign. In this scene we are shown a tailor shop in Hong Kong, where Chinese tailors use sewing machines and make women's clothes in current Western styles. To Chinese readers, men making women's clothes and placing them on bamboo forms would have seemed as peculiar as the style of the dresses. *(From* Dianshizhai huabao, *a Shanghai picture magazine, 1885 or later)*

Sino-Japanese War *The 1894–1895 war between Japan and China, fought over Japanese efforts to separate Korea from Chinese influence.*

successfully modernized that it posed a threat to China (see pages 764–768). In 1894 Japanese efforts to separate Korea from Chinese influence led to the brief **Sino-Japanese War** in which China was decisively defeated, even though much of its navy had been purchased abroad at great expense. In the peace negotiations, China ceded Taiwan to Japan, agreed to a huge indemnity, and gave Japan the right to open factories in China. China's helplessness in the face of aggression led to a scramble among the European powers for concessions and protectorates in China. At the high point of this rush in 1898, it appeared that the European powers might actually divide China among themselves, the way they had recently divided Africa.

The End of Monarchy in China

China's humiliating defeat in 1895 led to a renewed drive for reform. In 1898 a group of educated young reformers gained access to the twenty-seven-year-old Qing emperor. They warned him of the fate of Poland (divided by the European powers in the eighteenth century) and regaled him with the triumphs of the Meiji reformers in Japan. They proposed redesigning China as a constitutional monarchy with modern financial and educational systems. For three months the emperor in fact issued a series of reform decrees. The Manchu establishment and the empress dowager, who had dominated the court for the past quarter century, felt threatened and not only suppressed the reform movement but imprisoned the emperor. Hope for reform from the top was dashed.

A period of violent reaction swept the country, reaching its peak in 1900 with the uprising of a secret society that foreigners dubbed the **Boxers**. The Boxers blamed China's ills on foreigners, especially the missionaries who traveled throughout China telling the Chinese that their beliefs were wrong and their customs backward. After the Boxers laid siege to the legation quarter in Beijing, a dozen nations including Japan sent twenty thousand troops to lift the siege. In the negotiations that followed, China had to accept a long list of penalties, including canceling the civil service examinations for five years (punishment for gentry collaboration) and a staggering indemnity of 450 million ounces of silver, almost twice the government's annual revenues.

After this defeat gradual reform lost its appeal. More and more Chinese were studying abroad and learning about Western political ideas, including democracy and revolution. The most famous of them was Sun Yatsen (1866–1925). Sent by his peasant family to Hawai'i, he learned English there and continued his education in Hong Kong. From 1894 on, he spent his time abroad organizing revolutionary societies and seeking financial support from overseas Chinese. He later joined forces with Chinese student revolutionaries studying in Japan, and together they attempted several times to spark rebellion. The plot that finally triggered the collapse of China's imperial system is known as the **1911 Revolution**. Army officers fearful that their connections to the revolutionaries would be exposed staged a coup and persuaded the provincial governments to secede. The powers behind the child emperor (who had ascended to the throne at the age of three in 1908) agreed to his abdication, and at the beginning of 1912 China's long history of monarchy came to an end, to be replaced by a republic modeled on Western political ideas. China had escaped direct foreign rule but would never be the same again.

Boxers *A Chinese secret society that blamed the country's ills on foreigners, especially missionaries, and rose in rebellion in 1899–1900.*

Primary Source:
The Three People's Principles and the Future of the Chinese People
Decrying the gulf between rich and poor in Europe and America, Sun Yat-Sen calls for a revolution in China that will ensure prosperity and social justice.

1911 Revolution *The uprising that brought China's monarchy to an end.*

JAPAN'S RAPID TRANSFORMATION

How was Japan able to quickly master the challenges posed by the West?

During the nineteenth century, while China's standing in the world plummeted, Japan's was rising.

European traders and missionaries first arrived in Japan in the sixteenth century, but in the early seventeenth century, in part because of the remarkable success of Catholic missionaries (see pages 602–603), the Japanese government expelled them. During the eighteenth century, Japan much more effectively than China kept foreign merchants and missionaries at bay. It limited trade to a single port (Nagasaki), where only the Dutch were allowed, and forbade Japanese to travel abroad. Because Japan's land and population were so much smaller than China's, the Western powers never expected much from Japan as a trading partner and did not press it as urgently.

The "Opening" of Japan

Wanting to play a greater role in the Pacific, the United States decided to force the Japanese to share their ports and behave as a "civilized" nation. In 1853 Commodore Matthew Perry steamed into Edo (now Tokyo) Bay and demanded diplomatic negotiations with the emperor. Some Japanese samurai urged resistance, but senior officials knew what had happened in China and how defenseless their cities would be against naval bombardment. After consulting with the daimyo (major lords), they signed a treaty with the United States that opened two ports and permitted trade.

When Japan was "opened" by **gunboat diplomacy,** it was a complex society. The emperor in Kyoto had no effective powers. For more than two hundred years real power had been in the hands of the Tokugawa shogun in Edo (see pages 591–593). The country was divided into numerous domains, each under a daimyo. Each daimyo had under him samurai, who had hereditary stipends and privileges, such as the right to wear a sword. Peasants and merchants were also legally distinct classes, and in theory social mobility from peasant to merchant or merchant to samurai was impossible. After two centuries of peace, there were many more samurai than were needed to administer or defend the country, and many lived very modestly. They were proud, however, and felt humiliated by the sudden American intrusion and the unequal treaties that the Western countries imposed. Some began agitating against the shogunate under the slogan "Revere the emperor and expel the barbarians."

When foreign diplomats and merchants began to settle in Yokohama after 1858, radical samurai reacted with a wave of antiforeign terrorism and antigovernment assassinations. The Western imperialist response was swift and unambiguous. Much as the Western powers had sent troops to Beijing a few years before, they now sent an allied fleet of American, British, Dutch, and French warships to demolish key Japanese forts, further weakening the power and prestige of the shogun's government.

The Meiji Restoration

In 1867 a coalition of reform-minded domains led a coup that ousted the Tokugawa Shogunate. The samurai who led this coup declared a return to direct rule by the emperor, not practiced in Japan for more than six hundred years. This emperor is called the Meiji emperor and this event the **Meiji Restoration,** a great turning point in Japanese history.

The domain leaders who organized the coup, called the **Meiji Oligarchs,** moved the boy emperor to Tokyo castle (previously the seat of the shogun, now the imperial palace). They used the young sovereign to win over both the lords and the commoners. During the emperor's first decade on the throne, the leaders carried him around in hundreds of grand imperial processions so that he could see his subjects and they him. The emerging press also worked to keep its readers informed of the young emperor's actions and their obligations to him. Real power, however, remained in the hands of the oligarchs.

The battle cry of the Meiji reformers had been **"strong army, rich nation."** But how were these goals to be accomplished? In an about-face that is one of history's most remarkable chapters, the determined but flexible leaders of Meiji Japan dropped their antiforeign attacks. Convinced that they could not beat the West until they mastered the secrets of its military and industrial might, they initiated a series of measures to reform Japan along modern, Western lines. One even proposed that "Japan must be reborn with America its mother and France its father."[6] In 1868 an imperial declaration promised representative government and that "knowledge shall be sought throughout the world so as to strengthen the foundations of imperial rule."[7] Within four years a delegation was traveling the world to learn what made the Western powers strong. They examined everything from the U.S. Constitution to the factories, shipyards, and railroads that made the European landscape so different from Japan's.

Japan under the shoguns had been decentralized, with most of the power over the population in the hands of the daimyos. By elevating the emperor, the oligarchs were able to centralize the government. In 1871 they abolished the domains and merged the domain armies. Following the example of the French Revolution, they dismantled the four-class legal system and declared everyone equal. This amounted to stripping the samurai (7 to 8 percent of the population) of its privileges. First the samurai's stipends were reduced; then in 1876 the stipends were replaced by one-time grants of income-bearing bonds. Most samurai had to find work or start businesses, as the value of the bonds declined with inflation. Samurai no longer were to wear their swords, long the symbols of their status. Even their monopoly on the use of force was eliminated: the new army recruited commoners along with samurai. Not surprisingly, some samurai rose to protest their loss of privileges. In one extreme case, the rebels refused to use guns in a futile effort to retain the mystique of the sword. None of these uncoordinated uprisings deflected the transition.

Several leaders of the Meiji Restoration, in France on a fact-finding mission during the Franco-Prussian War of 1870–1871, were impressed by the active participation of French citizens in the defense of Paris. This contrasted with the indifference of most Japanese peasants during the battles that led to the Meiji Restoration. For Japan to survive in the hostile international environment, they concluded, ordinary people had to be trained to fight. A conscription law, modeled on the French law, was issued in 1872. Like French law, it exempted first sons. The new War College was organized along German lines, and German instructors were recruited to teach there. Young samurai were trained to form the new professional officer corps. The success of this approach was demonstrated first in 1877, when the professionally led army of draftees crushed a major rebellion by samurai.

Many of the new institutions established in the Meiji period reached down to the local level. Universal public schools were rapidly introduced after 1872. Teachers were trained in newly established normal schools, where they learned to inculcate discipline, patriotism, and morality. Another modern institution that reached down to the local level was a national police force. In 1884 police training schools were established in every prefecture, and within a few years one- or two-man police stations were set up throughout the country. These policemen came to act as local agents of the central government. They not only dealt with crime but also enforced public health rules, conscription laws, and codes of behavior.

Those measures in time brought benefits, but at the local level they were often perceived as oppressive. Protests became very common against everything from conscription and the Western calendar to the new taxes for the compulsory schools.

In 1889 Japan became the first non-Western country to adopt the constitutional form of government. Prefectural assemblies, set up in the 1870s and 1880s, gave local elites some experience in debating political issues. The constitution, however, was handed down from above, drafted by the top political leaders and issued in the name of the emperor. A commission sent abroad to study European constitutional governments had come to the conclusion that the German constitutional monarchy would provide the best model for Japan, rather than the more democratic governments of the British, French, and Americans. The new government had a two-house parliament,

● **Japan's Modernized Army** A set of woodblock prints depicting the new sights of Tokyo included this illustration of a military parade ground. The soldiers' brightly colored Western-style uniforms undoubtedly helped make this a sight worth seeing. (Ryogoku Tsuneo Tamba Collection/Laurie Platt Winfrey, Inc.)

called the Diet. The upper house of lords was drawn largely from former lords and nobles, and the lower house was elected by a limited electorate (about 5 percent of the adult male population in 1890). Although Japan now had a government based on laws, it was authoritarian rather than democratic. The emperor was declared "sacred and inviolable," and he was sovereign. He had the right to appoint the prime minister and cabinet. He did not have to ask the Diet for funds, because wealth assigned to the imperial house was entrusted to the Imperial Household Ministry, which was outside the government's control.

Cultural change during the Meiji period was just as profound as political change. For more than a thousand years China had provided the major source of ideas and technologies introduced into Japan, ranging from the writing system to Confucianism and Buddhism, tea and silk, chopsticks and soy sauce. But in the late nineteenth century China, beset by Western pressure, had become an object lesson in the dangers of stagnation rather than a model to follow. The influential author Fukuzawa Yukichi began urging Japan to pursue **"civilization and enlightenment,"** by which he meant Western civilization. (See the feature "Listening to the Past: Escape from Asia" on pages 774–775.) Fukuzawa advocated learning Western languages and encouraged Japan to learn from the West in order to catch up with it. Soon Japanese were being told to conform to Western taste, eat meat, wear Western-style clothes, and drop customs that Westerners found odd, such as married women blackening their teeth.

Industrialization

The leaders of the Meiji Restoration, wanting to strengthen Japan's military capacity, promoted industrialization. The government paid large salaries to attract foreign experts to help with industrialization, and Japanese were encouraged to go abroad to study science and engineering.

The government played an active role in getting railroads, mines, and factories started. Japan's coal mines had produced only 390,000 tons in 1860, but by 1900 this had risen to 5 million tons. Early on the Japanese government decided to compete with China in the export of tea and silk to the West. Introducing the mechanical reeling of silk gave Japan a strong advantage, and Japan's total foreign trade increased tenfold from 1877 to 1900. The next stage was to develop heavy industry. The huge indemnity exacted from

● **Japan's First Skyscraper** Meiji Japan's fascination with things Western led to the construction of Western-style buildings. Japan's first elevator made possible this twelve-story tower built in Tokyo in 1890. Built in the entertainment district, it was filled with shops, theaters, bars, and restaurants. *(Department of Historical Documents, National Institute of Japanese Literature.)*

China in 1895 was used to establish the Yawata Iron and Steel Works. A third step would today be called import substitution. Factories such as cotton mills were set up to help cut the importation of Western consumer goods. By 1912 factory output accounted for 13 percent of the national product, even though only 3 percent of the labor force worked in factories, mostly small ones with fewer than fifty workers.

Most of the great Japanese industrial combines, known as *zaibatsu,* got their start in this period, often founded by men with government connections. Sometimes the government set up plants that they then sold to private investors at bargain prices. Successful entrepreneurs were treated as patriotic heroes.

As in Europe, the early stages of industrialization brought hardship to the countryside. Farmers often rioted as their incomes failed to keep up with prices or their tax burdens grew. In 1898 railroad workers went on strike for better working conditions and overtime pay. Still, rice production increased, death rates dropped as public health was improved, and the population grew from about 33 million in 1868 to about 45 million in 1900.

Japan as an Imperial Power

During the course of the Meiji period, Japan became an imperial power, making Taiwan and Korea into its colonies. Taiwan had been a part of China for two centuries; Korea had been an independent country with a unified government since 668. The conflicts that led to Japanese acquisition of them revolved around Korea.

The Choson Dynasty had been on the throne in Korea since 1392. Chinese influence had grown over this period as the Korean elite enthusiastically embraced Confucian teachings and studied for Chinese-style civil service examinations.

In the second half of the nineteenth century Korea found itself caught between China, Japan, and Russia, each trying to protect or extend its sphere of influence. Added to this, Westerners also began demanding that Korea be "opened." Korea's first response was to insist that its foreign relations be handled through Beijing. Matters were complicated by the rise of a religious cult in the 1860s that had strong xenophobic elements. Although the government executed the cult founder in 1864, this cult continued to gain support, especially among impoverished peasants. Thus, like China in the same period, the Korean government faced simultaneous internal and external threats.

In 1871 the U.S. minister to China took five warships to try to "open" Korea but left after exchanges of fire resulted in 250 Koreans dead without any progress in getting the Korean government to make concessions. Japan tried next and in 1876 forced the Korean government to sign an unequal treaty and open three ports to Japanese trade. On China's urging, Korea also signed treaties with the European powers in an effort to counterbalance Japan.

Over the next couple of decades reformers in China and Japan tried to encourage Korea to adopt its own "self-strengthening" movement, but Korean conservatives, including the queen (regent for the child king), did their best to undo reform efforts. In 1894, when the religious cult rose in a massive revolt, both China and Japan sent military forces, claiming to come to the Korean government's aid. They ended up fighting each other instead. With Japan's decisive victory, it gained Taiwan from China and was able to make Korea a protectorate. Japan also arranged the assassination of the Korean queen in 1895.

Just a few years later, in 1900, Japan participated with the European powers in occupying Beijing to suppress the Boxer Rebellion. In this period Japan was competing aggressively with the leading European powers for influence and territory in China, particularly in the northeast (Manchuria). There Japanese and Russian imperialism met and collided. In 1904 Japan attacked Russian forces, and after this bloody

"civilization and enlightenment" *A slogan set forth by the influential author Fukuzawa Yukichi, who urged the Japanese to abandon their ancient ways and learn the ways of the West.*

**Primary Source:
Two Proclamations of the Boxer Rebellion**
The secret society known as "The Righteous and Harmonious Fists" announces its intention to kill the "foreign devils" plaguing China.

Russo-Japanese War *The 1904–1905 war between Russia and Japan, fought over imperial influence and territory in northeast China (Manchuria).*

Russo-Japanese War Japan emerged with a valuable foothold in China—Russia's former protectorate over Port Arthur (see Map 25.1).

Japan also steadily strengthened its hold on Korea. In 1907, when the Korean king proved less than fully compliant, the Japanese forced him to abdicate in favor of his feeble-minded son. Korean resistance was suppressed in bloody fighting, and in 1910 Korea was formally annexed as a province of Japan.

Japan's victories over China and Russia changed the way European nations looked at Japan. Through negotiations Japan was able to eliminate extraterritoriality in 1899 and gain control of its own tariffs in 1911. Within Japan, the success of the military in raising Japan's international reputation added greatly to its political influence.

THE MOVEMENT OF PEOPLES

Why did people move much more in this period, and where did they go?

The nineteenth century was marked by extensive movement of people into, across, and out of Asia. In no earlier period had so many Europeans lived in Asia or so many Asians taken up residence in other countries. This vast migration both resulted from and helped accelerate the increasing integration of the world economy. Improvements in shipping and the digging of the Suez and Panama Canals made crossing the oceans faster and safer. Foreigners could survive tropical climates more easily after 1850 when the effects of malaria could be limited by taking the medicine quinine. Knowledge of foreign languages improved dramatically, and translations of works from Western to Asian languages and vice versa made the understanding of alien cultures much easier to acquire, at least for the literate.

Westerners to Asia

Imperialism brought Europeans to Asia in unprecedented numbers. By the early 1900s there were significant expatriate communities of European and American businessmen, missionaries, and colonial civil servants in many countries. The most extreme case was India. By 1863 there were already sixty-five thousand British troops in India and many more British in the civil service and commercial companies. Especially after the opening of the Suez Canal in 1869, British working in India were accompanied by their wives and children, who would return to Britain every few years on leave. By the eve of World War I, hundreds of thousands of expatriates lived in India, many since birth.

Beginning in 1809, British recruits to the British East India Company and subsequently to the Indian Civil Service were required to learn at least one Indian language fluently, but the trend, especially after the Great Revolt of 1857 (see page 751), was for the British to live separately from the Indians in their own enclaves. Houses were adapted to the local climate, with wide, well-shaded porches and large lawns. Houses and grounds were tended by Indian servants, who also minded the colonists' children, did their shopping, and handled most of their dealings with local Indians. British colonists who were curious about India and wanted to make Indian friends found social intercourse difficult, especially with Muslims and higher-caste Hindus, whose social contact with outsiders was restricted by traditional rules.

China was not under colonial occupation and so did not have so many foreign civil servants and soldiers in its cities, but it did attract more missionaries than any other Asian country. After 1860, when China agreed to allow missionaries to proselytize throughout the country, missionaries came in large numbers. Unlike the British civil servants in India, missionaries had no choice but to mix with the local population, finding the best opportunities for conversion among ordinary poor Chinese. Although the majority of missionaries devoted themselves to preaching, over the course of the nineteenth century more and more worked in medicine and education. By 1905 about three hundred fully qualified physicians were doing medical missionary work, and 250 mission hospitals and dispensaries served about 2 million patients. Missionary hospitals in Hong Kong also ran a medical school, which trained hundreds of Chinese as physicians.

Missionaries helped spread Western learning at their schools. For their elementary schools, missionaries produced textbooks in Chinese on a full range of subjects. They also translated dozens of standard works into Chinese, especially in the natural sciences, mathematics, history, and international law. By 1906 nearly sixty thousand Chinese students were attending twenty-four hundred Christian schools. Most of this activity was supported by contributions sent from America and Britain.

Missionaries in China had more success in spreading Western learning than in gaining converts. By 1900 fewer than a million Chinese were Christians. Ironically, although Western missionaries paid much less attention to Korea—the first missionary arrived there in 1884—Christianity took much stronger root there, and today about 25 percent of the Korean population is Christian. Missionaries also had some success in Vietnam, where Catholic missionaries were protected by the French government.

Asian Emigration

In the nineteenth century Asians, like Europeans, left their native countries in unprecedented numbers. As in Europe, both push and pull factors prompted people to leave home. Between 1750 and 1900 world population grew rapidly, in many places tripling. China and India were extremely densely populated countries—China with about 400 million people in the mid-nineteenth century, India with more than 200 million. Not surprisingly, these two giants were the leading exporters of people. On the pull side were the new opportunities created in part by the flow of development capital into previously underdeveloped areas. In many of the European colonies in Asia and Africa the business class came to consist of both Asian and European migrants, the Asians protected and tolerated by the Western imperialists who found them useful.

In China voluntary migration in search of opportunity had been going on for centuries. Chinese from the southern coastal regions had formed key components of the mercantile communities throughout Southeast Asia, from Siam south to Java and east to the Philippines. Chinese often assimilated in Siam and Vietnam, but they rarely did so in Muslim areas such as Java, Catholic areas such as the Philippines, and primitive tribal areas such as northern Borneo. In these places, distinct Chinese communities emerged, usually dominated by speakers of a single Chinese dialect.

With the growth in trade that accompanied the European expansion, Chinese began to settle in insular Southeast Asia in larger numbers. After Singapore was founded by the British in 1819, Chinese rapidly poured in, soon to become its dominant ethnic group. In British-controlled Malaya, some Chinese built great fortunes in the tin business, while others worked in the mines. There the Chinese community included both old overseas families long settled in the Portuguese city of Malacca, who spoke Malay, and a much larger number of more recent immigrants, most of whom spoke Cantonese. In the Spanish-controlled Philippines and Dutch-controlled Indonesia, however, the Chinese suffered repeated persecutions. Early in the nineteenth century in Borneo, the Dutch expropriated the mines that the Chinese had worked for generations. Elsewhere, however, the Dutch made use of the Chinese. In Java, for instance, Chinese merchants were used as tax collectors. Moreover, after the Dutch conquered southern Sumatra in 1864, Chinese were recruited to work in the sugar and tobacco plantations. By 1900 more than five hundred thousand Chinese were living in the Dutch East Indies.

● **Chinese Street Opera in Singapore** In Singapore there were so many Chinese people that they were able to maintain their traditional forms of entertainment, such as the opera shown here in a photograph from the 1890s. Although most of the men were still wearing the Manchu-imposed queue hairstyle, many concealed them under Western-style hats. *(Courtesy, National Museum of Singapore)*

Discovery of gold in California in 1848, Australia in 1851, and Canada in 1858 encouraged Chinese to book passage to those places (see Chapter 26). In California few arrived soon enough to strike gold, but they soon found other work. Thousands worked laying railroad tracks, and others took up mining in Wyoming and Idaho. In 1880 more than a hundred thousand Chinese men and three thousand Chinese women were living in the western United States.

Indian entrepreneurs were attracted by the burgeoning commerce of Southeast Asia, though not in quite so large numbers as Chinese. Indian migrants also moved outside Asia, especially to areas under British control. The bulk of Indian emigrants were **indentured laborers,** recruited under contract. The rise of indentured labor from Asia was a direct result of the outlawing of the African slave trade in the early nineteenth century. Sugar plantations in the Caribbean and elsewhere needed new sources of workers. In the British colonies, planters discovered that they could recruit Indian laborers to replace blacks. By 1870 more than half a million Indians had migrated to Mauritius (in the southern Indian Ocean, east of Madagascar) and to the British

indentured laborers *Laborers who in exchange for passage agreed to work for a number of years, specified in a contract.*

Caribbean, especially Trinidad. After the French abolished slavery in 1848, they recruited workers from India as well, with nearly eighty thousand Indians making the trip to the French Caribbean over the next half century. Later in the century, many Indians emigrated to British colonies in Africa, the largest numbers to South Africa. Indentured Indian laborers built the railroad in East Africa. Malaya, Singapore, and Fiji also received many emigrants from India.

Indentured laborers secured as substitutes for slaves were often treated little better than slaves, both on the ships that delivered them and on the plantations and in the mines where they worked. After abuses of this sort were exposed, the Indian government established regulations stipulating a maximum indenture period of five years, after which the migrant would be entitled to passage home. Even though government "protectors" were appointed at the ports of embarkation, exploitation of indentured workers continued largely unchecked. Few of the indentured workers were women, so the community failed to reproduce itself, and emigration had to be continued to maintain the workforce. Still, many of the migrants stayed on after their indenture.

In areas outside the British Empire, China offered the largest supply of ready labor. Starting in the 1840s, contractors arrived at Chinese ports to recruit labor for plantations and mines in Cuba, Peru, Hawai'i, Sumatra, and elsewhere. In the 1840s, for example, the Spanish government actively recruited Chinese laborers for the plantations of Cuba. They came under eight-year contracts, were paid about twenty-five cents a day, and were fed potatoes and salted beef. Between 1853 and 1873 more than 130,000 Chinese laborers went to Cuba, the majority spending their lives as virtual slaves.

Chinese laborers did not have the British government to protect them and seem to have suffered even more than Indian workers. Some of the worst abuses were in Peru, where nearly 100,000 Chinese had arrived by 1875, lured by promoters who promised them easy riches. Instead, they were set to laying railroad tracks or working on cotton plantations or in dangerous guano pits. Those who tried to flee were forced to work in chains.

India and China sent more people abroad than any other Asian countries during this period, but they were not alone. As Japan started to industrialize, its cities could not absorb all those forced off the farms, and people began emigrating in significant numbers, many to Hawai'i and later to South America. Emigration from the Philippines also was substantial, especially after it became a U.S. territory in 1898.

Asian migration to the United States, Canada, and Australia—the primary destinations of European emigrants—would undoubtedly have been greater if it had not been so vigorously resisted by the white settlers in those regions. On the West Coast of the United States, friction between Chinese and white settlers was fed by racist rhetoric that depicted Chinese as opium-smoking heathens. In 1882 Chinese were barred from becoming American citizens, and the immigration of Chinese laborers was suspended. In 1888 President Grover Cleveland declared the Chinese "impossible of assimilation with our people, and dangerous to our peace and welfare."[8]

Most of the Asian migrants discussed so far were illiterate peasants or business people, not members of the traditional educated elites. By the beginning of the twentieth century, however, another group of Asians was going abroad in significant numbers: students. Indians and others in the British colonies usually went to Britain, Vietnamese and others in the French colonies to France, and so on. Chinese eager to master modern learning most commonly went to Japan, but others went to Europe and the United States, as did Japanese students. Most of these students traveled abroad to learn about Western science, law, and government in the hope of strengthening their own countries. On their return they contributed enormously to the intellectual life of their societies, increasing understanding of the modern Western world but also becoming the most vocal advocates of overthrowing the old order and driving out the colonial masters.

Primary Source: Memorandum to Lord Selborne, High Commissioner of Transvaal

An Indian in Transvaal answers criticisms of Indian merchants made by a white merchants' group, the Anti-Asiatic Vigilance Society.

Chapter Summary

Key Terms

Great Mutiny/Great Revolt
Empress of India
Indian Civil Service
Indian National Congress
Java War
Culture System
Nguyen Dynasty
French Indochina
encomienda system
Opium War
Treaty of Nanjing
extraterritoriality
concessions
Taiping Rebellion
"self-strengthening"
Sino-Japanese War
Boxers
1911 Revolution
gunboat diplomacy
Meiji Restoration
Meiji Oligarchs
"strong army, rich nation"
"civilization and
  enlightenment"
Russo-Japanese War
indentured laborers

To assess your mastery of this chapter, go to
bedfordstmartins.com/mckayworld

• *In what ways did India change as a consequence of British rule?*

In the nineteenth century, Britain extended its rule to all of India, though often the British ruled indirectly, through local princes. Britain brought many modern advances to India, such as railroads, schools, and hospitals. Slavery was outlawed, as was widow suicide and infanticide. Resistance to British rule took several forms. In 1857 Indian soldiers in the employ of the British rose in a huge revolt, which was put down only at huge cost. Indians who received English educations turned English ideas of liberty and representative rule against the British and founded the Indian National Congress, which called for Indian independence.

• *Why were some Southeast Asian societies reduced to colonies and others not?*

By the end of the nineteenth century, most of Southeast Asia, from Burma to the Philippines, had been made colonies of Western powers, which developed them as exporters of agricultural products or raw materials including timber, rubber, tin, sugar, tea, cotton, and jute. The principal exception was Siam (Thailand), whose king was able to play the English and French off against each other and institute centralizing reforms. In the Philippines, more than three centuries of Spanish rule came to an end, but the United States took over control.

• *Was China's decline in the nineteenth century due more to internal problems or Western imperialism?*

In the nineteenth century China faced unprecedented population pressure, popular revolts, and the aggression of the Western powers. The government's efforts to suppress the opium trade led to military confrontation with Britain and numerous concessions that opened China to trade on Britain's terms. Uprisings in several parts of the country reflected worsening economic situations and proved very difficult to suppress. Further humiliations by the Western powers led to concerted efforts to modernize the military and learn other secrets of Western success, but China never quite caught up. The dynasty, humiliated by its defeat by Japan in 1895 and the occupation of Beijing by foreign powers in 1900, finally was overthrown in 1911.

• *How was Japan able to quickly master the challenges posed by the West?*

Japan was the one Asian country to quickly transform itself when confronted by the military strength of the West. It did this by overhauling its power structure. The Meiji reformers deprived the samurai of their privileges, wrote a constitution, instituted universal education, and created a modern army. At the same time they guided Japan toward rapid industrialization. By the early twentieth century Japan had become an imperialist power itself with colonies in Korea and Japan.

• *Why did people move much more in this period, and where did they go?*

The rapid pace of political and economic change in the nineteenth century led to people moving across national borders much more frequently than before. Major cities in Asia developed expatriate communities of Westerners. Asian students traveled to foreign countries, including Japan, to continue their educations. And millions more left in search of work. With the end of the African slave trade, labor recruiters from the Americas and elsewhere went to India and China to secure labor on indentured contracts. In other cases, ambitious young men who heard of gold strikes or other chances to get rich funded their own travels. As a consequence, Asian diasporas formed in many parts of the world, with the majority in Asia itself, especially Southeast Asia.

Suggested Reading

Bayly, C. A. *Indian Society and the Making of the British Empire.* 1990. A synthesis of recent research that provides a complex portrait of the interaction of Indian society and British colonial administration.

Bose, Sugata, and Ayesha Jalal. *Modern South Asia: History, Culture, Political Economy.* 1998. Incorporates recent scholarship with postcolonial perspective in a wide-ranging study.

Duus, Peter. *The Abacus and the Sword: The Japanese Penetration of Korea, 1895–1910.* 1995. Analyzes the interplay of business interests (the abacus) and military interests (the sword) in Japan's push for colonial possessions.

Fairbank, John King, and Merle Goldman. *China: A New History,* 2d ed. 2006. A treatment of China's experiences in the nineteenth century that is rich in interesting detail.

Hane, Mikiso. *Peasants, Rebels, Women and Outcastes: The Underside of Modern Japan,* 2d ed. 2003. Draws on wide-ranging sources to provide a fuller picture of Japanese history.

Irokawa, Daiichi. *The Culture of the Meiji Period.* 1988. Makes excellent use of letters, diaries, and songs to probe changes in the ways ordinary people thought during a crucial period of political change.

Masselos, Jim. *Indian Nationalism: A History,* 5th ed. 2004. A detailed account of the political movement for independence in nineteenth- and twentieth-century India.

Pruitt, Ida. *A Daughter of Han: The Autobiography of a Chinese Working Woman.* 1967. A highly revealing glimpse of Chinese society fashioned by journalist Ida Pruitt in the 1930s based on what a Chinese woman born in 1867 told Pruitt of her life.

Spence, Jonathan. *God's Chinese Son.* 1997. Tells the story of the Taipings as much as possible from their own perspective.

Steinberg, David Joel, ed. *In Search of Southeast Asia: A Modern History,* rev. ed. 1987. An impressive work on Southeast Asia by seven specialists.

Walthall, Anne. *Japan: A Cultural, Social, and Political History.* 2006. A concise overview with good coverage of local society and popular culture.

Notes

1. Quoted in S. Wolpert, *A New History of India* (New York: Oxford University Press, 1993), p. 215.

2. Quoted in K. M. Panikkar, *Asia and Western Dominance: A Survey of the Vasco da Gama Epoch of Asian History* (London: George Allen & Unwin, 1959), p. 116.

3. Quoted in D. J. Steinberg, ed., *In Search of Southeast Asia: A Modern History,* rev. ed. (Honolulu: University of Hawaii Press, 1987), p. 129.

4. Ssu-yu Teng and J. K. Fairbank, *China's Response to the West: A Documentary Survey* (New York: Atheneum, 1971), p. 26.

5. Ibid., p. 76, modified.

6. Quoted ibid., p. 289.

7. R. Tsunoda, W. T. de Bary, and D. Keene, eds., *Sources of Japanese Tradition,* vol. 2 (New York: Columbia University Press, 1964), p. 137.

8. Quoted in J. D. Spence, *The Search for Modern China* (New York: W. W. Norton, 1990), p. 215.

Listening to the
PAST

Escape from Asia

*F*ukuzawa Yukichi was one of the most prominent
*intellectuals and promoters of westernization in
Meiji Japan. His views on domestic policy were
decidedly liberal, but he took a hard-line approach to
foreign affairs. His ruthless criticism of Korea and China,
published on March 16, 1885, can be read as inviting
colonialism. In 1895, ten years after writing this call to
action, he rejoiced at Japan's victory over China in their
conflict over Korea.*

Civilization is like an epidemic of measles. The current measles in Tokyo, which has advanced eastwards
from Nagasaki in western Japan, seems to have begun
to claim more victims with the arrival of springtime.
Will we be able now to find a means of checking this
epidemic? It is obvious that we have no way to do so.
We cannot put up effective resistance, even against
an epidemic that carries with it only harm; much less
against civilization, which is always accompanied by
both harm and good, but by more good than harm.

Though our land of Japan is situated on the Eastern
edge of Asia, the spirit of its people has already shaken
off the backwardness of Asia to accept the civilization
of the West. Unfortunately, however, we have two
neighboring countries, one being called China, the
other called Korea. The people of these two countries
are no different from us Japanese people in having been brought up since olden times in the Asian
culture and customs, and yet, whether because they
are of another racial origin, or because, while similar
in culture and customs, differ from us in the main
lines of their traditional education, a comparison of
the three countries, Japan, China, and Korea, reveals
that the latter two resemble each other more closely
than they do Japan. The people of those two countries
do not know how to go about reforming and making
progress, whether individually or as a country. It is not
that they have not seen or heard of civilized things in
the present world of facile communication; yet what
their eyes and ears perceive have failed to stimulate
their minds, and their emotional attachment to ancient

manners and customs has changed little for the past
hundreds and thousands of years. In this lively theater
of civilization, where things change daily, they still
speak of education in terms of Confucianism, cite humanity, justice, civility, and wisdom as their principles
of school education, are completely obsessed only with
outward appearance, are in reality not only ignorant
of truths and principles but so extreme in their cruelty
and shamelessness that for them morality is completely
non-existent, and yet are as arrogant as if they never
gave a thought to self-examination.

In our view, these countries have no likelihood of
maintaining their independence in the current tide of
civilization's eastward advance. Let there not be the
slightest doubt that, unless they are fortunate enough
to have motivated men appear in their lands who, as
a first step to improve the condition of their countries
will plan such a great enterprise of overall reform of
their governments as our Restoration was, and succeed in altering their people's minds through political
reforms, those countries will meet their doom in but a
few years, with their territories divided among the civilized countries of the world. The reason is that China
and Korea, confronted by an epidemic of civilization
comparable to measles, are impossibly trying to ward
it off, despite its inevitability, by shutting themselves
up in a room, with the result being that they are
cutting off their supply of fresh air and asphyxiating
themselves. Though mutual help between neighboring
countries has been likened to the relationship between
the lips and the teeth, China and Korea of today cannot be of any assistance at all to our country of Japan.

Civilized western man is not without a tendency to
regard all three countries as identical because of their
geographic proximity and to apply his evaluation of
China and Korea to Japan also. For example, when
he finds that the governments of China and Korea are
old-fashioned autocracies without abiding laws, the
western man will suppose Japan too to be a lawless
country. When he finds that the gentlemen of China
and Korea are too deeply infatuated to know what

science is, the western scholar will think that Japan too is a land of Yin-Yang and the Five Elements. When the Chinese display their servility and shamelessness, they obscure the chivalrous spirit of the Japanese. When the Koreans employ cruel means of physical punishment, the Japanese too are surmised to be just as inhuman. Such examples are too numerous to count. This may be compared to the case in which most of those in a string of houses within a village or town are foolish, lawless, cruel, and inhuman; an occasional family that heeds what is just and right will be eclipsed by the other's evil and its virtue will never be noticed. It is indeed not infrequent that something similar happens in our foreign relations and indirectly interferes with them. This should be regarded a great misfortune for our country of Japan.

To plan our course now, therefore, our country cannot afford to wait for the enlightenment of our neighbors and to cooperate in building Asia up. Rather, we should leave their ranks to join the camp of the civilized countries of the West. Even when dealing with China and Korea, we need not have special scruples simply because they are our neighbors, but should behave toward them as the westerners do. One who befriends an evil person cannot avoid being involved in his notoriety. In spirit, then, we break with our evil friends of Eastern Asia.

Fukuzawa Yukichi. *(Fukuzawa Memorial Center for Modern Japanese Studies, Keio University)*

Questions for Analysis

1. What does Fukuzawa mean by "civilization"?

2. How does Fukuzawa's justification of colonialism compare to Europeans' justification of the same period?

Source: Centre for East Asian Cultural Studies, comp., *Meiji Japan Through Contemporary Sources,* Vol. 3, 1869–1894 (Tokyo: Centre for East Asian Cultural Studies, 1972), pp. 129–133, modified.

Portrait of Skikellany. The clothing worn by this important Oneida Indian of upstate New York identifies him as a member of the Northeast Woodlands Indians. *(Unknown artist, American, Portrait of a Native American Man of the Northeast Woodlands. Philadelphia Museum of Art, The Collection of Edgar William Bernice Chrysler Garbisch, 1966 [1966-219-3])*

chapter
26
NATION BUILDING IN THE WESTERN HEMISPHERE AND AUSTRALIA

Chapter Preview

Latin America (1800–1929)
• Why and how did the Spanish and Portuguese colonies of North and South America shake off European domination and develop into national states?

The United States (1789–1929)
• How does nation building in the United States look from a world history perspective?

Canada, from French Colony to Nation
• What geographical, economic, and political conditions shaped the development of Canada?

Australia, from Penal Colony to Nation
• What circumstances shaped the development of Australia?

The New Countries in Comparative Perspective
• How and why did the new countries treated in this chapter develop differently?

In the Western Hemisphere and in Australia, as in Europe, the nineteenth century was a period of nation building and industrial and commercial growth. Unlike in Europe, the century was also a time of geographic expansion and large-scale in-migration.

At the end of the eighteenth century, Canada and the countries of South America remained colonies. Their European mother countries looked on the democratic experiment of the infant United States with suspicion and scorn. The island continent of Australia, remote from Europe and economically undeveloped, served as a dumping ground for English criminals. The nineteenth century brought many challenges—including revolutions, civil wars, and foreign invasions. In some countries abolishing slavery was achieved with great difficulty. Yet by 1914 all of the countries were not only politically independent but also stronger and richer than they had been in 1800.

Many issues cross-cut all the histories of these countries in the long nineteenth century—nation building, nationalism, urbanization, racism, regional separatism, new technologies, new lands to open, new trading patterns, and new constitutional governments, to name just a few. Yet the outcomes by 1914 were strikingly different. The United States had become a major industrial power and a stable democracy with a standard of living comparable to western Europe. Canada and Australia also had stable democratic governments and high standards of living, but their economies remained predominantly agricultural. Most of the countries of Latin America suffered political instability, and their economies did not fare as well in the emerging world trade system.

LATIN AMERICA (1800–1929)

Why and how did the Spanish and Portuguese colonies of North and South America shake off European domination and develop into national states?

In 1800 the Spanish Empire in the Western Hemisphere stretched from the headwaters of the Mississippi River in present-day Minnesota to the tip of Cape Horn in the Antarctic (see Map 26.1). In addition to large regions of South America, the Spanish Empire included large parts of the present-day United States, including California. Mexico's silver mines were the richest in the world, and Mexico City had a larger population than any city in Spain. Spain believed that the great wealth of the Americas existed for its benefit, and Spanish policies fostered bitterness and the desire for independence in the colonies. Between 1806 and 1825, the Spanish colonies in Latin America were convulsed by upheavals that ultimately resulted in their separation from Spain. Until 1898 Spain did, however, retain its colonies in the Caribbean: Cuba and Puerto Rico.

Creoles *People of Spanish descent born in America.*

peninsulares *A term for natives of Spain or Portugal.*

The **Creoles**—people of Spanish descent born in America—resented the economic and political dominance of the **peninsulares,** as the colonial officials and other natives of Spain or Portugal were called. In 1800 there were about thirty thousand peninsulares and 3.5 million Creoles. Peninsulares controlled the rich export-import trade, intercolonial trade, and mining industries. The Creoles wanted to free themselves from Spain and Portugal and also to supplant the peninsulares as the ruling class. They had little interest in improving the lot of the Indians or the *mestizos* of mixed Spanish and Indian background and *mulattos* of mixed Spanish and African heritage.

Over the course of the nineteenth century, the countries of Latin America developed into national states. The predominant factors in this evolution were the heritage of colonial exploitation, a neocolonial economic structure, massive emigration from Europe and Asia, and the fusion of Amerindian, Caucasian, African, and Asian peoples.

● **Don Juan Joachin Gutierrez Altamirano Velasco, ca. 1752** In this painting by Miguel Cabrera, the pleated cuffs on Velasco's shirt, the richly embroidered and very expensive coat, the knee breeches, the tricorn hat, and the coat of arms on the wall all attest to the proud status of this member of the peninsulares, the most powerful element in colonial Mexican society. *(Miguel Cabrera, Mexican, 1695–1768, oil on canvas, 81⁵⁄₁₆ x 53½. Brooklyn Museum of Art, Museum Collection Fund, and the Dick S. Ramsay Fund 52.166.1)*

The Origins of the Revolutions

The Latin American movements for independence grew out of recent colonial grievances. By the eighteenth century, the Spanish colonies had become self-sufficient producers of foodstuffs, wine, textiles, and consumer goods. What was not produced domestically was secured through a healthy intercolonial trade. In Peru, for example, domestic agriculture supported the large mining settlements, and the colony did not have to import food. Craft workshops owned by the state or by private individuals produced consumer goods for the working class; what was not manufactured locally was bought from Mexico and transported by the Peruvian merchant marine. By 1700 Mexico and Peru were sending shrinking percentages of their revenues to Spain and retaining more for public works, defense, and administration.

Spain's humiliating defeat in the War of the Spanish Succession (1701–1713) prompted demands for sweeping reform of all of Spain's institutions, including colonial policies and practices. To improve administrative efficiency, the enlightened monarch Charles III (r. 1759–1788) carved the region of modern Colombia, Venezuela, and Ecuador out of the vast viceroyalty of Peru; it became the new viceroyalty of New Granada with its capital at Bogotá. The Crown also created the viceroyalty of Rio de la Plata (present-day Argentina) with its capital at Buenos Aires (see Map 26.1). Far more momentous was Charles III's radical overhaul of colonial trade policies to enable Spain to compete with Great Britain and Holland in the great eighteenth-century struggle for empire. The Spanish crown intended the colonies to serve as sources of raw materials and as markets for Spanish manufactured goods. Charles III's free-trade policies cut duties and restrictions drastically for Spanish merchants. In Latin America, these actions stimulated the production of crops in demand in Europe: coffee in Venezuela; sugar in the Caribbean; hides, leather, and salted beef in the Rio de la Plata viceroyalty. The volume of Spain's trade with the colonies soared, possibly as much as 700 percent between 1778 and 1788.[1]

Colonial manufacturing, which had been growing steadily, suffered severely. Colonial textiles, china, and wine, for example, could not compete with cheap Spanish products. For one thing, Latin American free laborers were paid more than European workers in the eighteenth century; this disparity helps explain the great numbers of immigrants to the colonies. Also, intercolonial transportation costs were higher than transatlantic costs. In the Rio de la Plata region, for example, heavy export taxes and light import duties shattered the wine industry. Geographical obstacles—mountains, deserts, jungles, and inadequate natural harbors—also frustrated colonial efforts to promote economic integration.

After 1789 the French Revolution and Napoleonic wars isolated Spain from Latin America. Foreign traders, especially from the United States, swarmed into Spanish-American ports. In 1796 the Madrid government lifted the restrictions against neutrals trading with the colonies, thus acknowledging Spain's inability to supply the colonies with needed goods and markets.

At the end of the eighteenth century, colonists also complained bitterly that only peninsulares were appointed to the colonies' highest judicial bodies and to other positions in the colonial governments. From 1751 to 1775, only 13 percent of appointees to the judicial bodies were Creoles.[2] According to the nineteenth-century Mexican statesman and historian Lucas Alamán (1792–1853),

This preference shown to Spaniards in political offices and ecclesiastical benefices has been the principal cause of the rivalry between the two classes; add to this the fact that Europeans possessed great wealth, which although it may have been the just reward of

Chronology

1770 Cook lands in Australia and claims land for British crown

1774 Quebec Act grants religious freedom to French Canadians

1778–1788 Height of Spain's trade with colonies

1780–1781 Tupac Amaru II leads rebellion in Peru

1786 British government establishes a penal colony at Botany Bay, Australia

1791 Constitution Act in Canada

1803 United States purchases Louisiana Territory from France

1804 Haiti achieves independence from France

1806–1825 Wars of independence in Latin America

1845 First use of term *manifest destiny* in United States; Texas and Florida admitted into United States

1861–1865 U.S. Civil War

1865–1877 U.S. Reconstruction

1867 Dominion of Canada formed

1883–1894 Mexican land laws put most land into the hands of a few individuals

1898 Spanish-American War

1901 Commonwealth of Australia formed

1904 United States takes control of Panama Canal

1914–1918 World War I

NEW
FRANCE
(Conquered by
England, 1760)

ENGLISH COLONIES
(Independence declared, 1776)

Mississippi R.

Colorado R.

40°W

40°N

ATLANTIC
OCEAN

Effective frontier
of Spanish settlement

Silver
Silver
COAHUILA

Rio Grande

FLORIDA
(Ceded to England, 1763–1783)

Gulf of Mexico

VICEROYALTY OF NEW SPAIN (1535)
BAJIO LEÓN
Guadalajara
✕ Zacatecas
✕ Guanajuato
Mexico City •
Silver
Veracruz
Cacao
Sugar
cane
Cochineal

Havana

Sugar cane
Beef
Tobacco

Sugar cane
Indigo

Sugar cane

HAITI [SAINT-DOMINGUE]
(Ceded to France, 1697)

Beef

Sugar cane
PUERTO RICO

20°N

**BRITISH
HONDURAS**
Guatemala

JAMAICA
(Conquered by England, 1655)

**SANTO
DOMINGO**

Sugar cane

Cochineal
Cacao
Indigo

Silver

Caribbean Sea

Sugar cane

Pearls

Caracas •
Cacao

Orinoco R.

Gold

Magdalena R.

• Bogotá

GUIANA

**VICEROYALTY OF
NEW GRANADA**
(Separated from
Viceroyalty of Peru,
1717, 1739)

Quito •

Equator   0°

Amazon R.

Forest
products

PACIFIC
OCEAN

**VICEROYALTY
OF PERU**
(1590s)
Lima •

Sugar cane

• Cuzco

**VICEROYALTY
OF BRAZIL**
(1720)

Sugar
cane
• Pernambuco

Sugar
cane
• Salvador

Cacao

Sugar
cane
• La Paz

Chuquisaca
(La Plata; Sucre)

✕ Potosí

Paraná R.

Diamonds
Gold

Rio de Janeiro
(Capital, 1763)

20°S

Yerba
Tobacco

São Paulo •

**VICEROYALTY OF
LA PLATA**
(Separated from
Viceroyalty of Peru,
1776)

Wheat

**AUDIENCIA
OF CHILE**
(Retained by
Viceroyalty of Peru,
1776)

Santiago •

Beef and
hides
• Montevideo

Buenos Aires •

Beef and
hides

Claimed but not
settled by Spain

A N D E S

0   500   1,000 Km.

0   500   1,000 Mi.

Spanish colonies

Viceroyalty of New Spain

Viceroyalty of New Granada

Viceroyalty of Peru and Audiencia of Chile

Viceroyalty of Rio de la Plata

Portuguese colonies

Viceroyalty of Brazil

✕ Silver mine

*Islas Malvinas
(Falkland Islands)*

Cape Horn

80°W   60°W

MAP 26.1 **Latin America Before Independence**   Consider the factors that led to the boundaries of the various Spanish and Portuguese colonies in North and South America.

effort and industry, excited the envy of Americans and was considered as so much usurpation from them; consider that for all these reasons the Spaniards had obtained a decided preponderance over those born in the country; and it will not be difficult to explain the increasing jealousy and rivalry between the two groups which culminated in hatred and enmity.[3]

Madrid's tax reforms also aggravated discontent. Like Great Britain, Spain believed its colonies should bear some of the costs of their own defense. Accordingly, Madrid raised the prices of its monopoly products, tobacco and liquor, and increased sales taxes on many items. As in the thirteen North American colonies a decade earlier, protest movements in Latin America claimed that the colonies were being unfairly taxed.

Other burdens fell on the Indians, many of whom were still subject to the *mit'a* and the *repartimiento*. The law of repartimiento required Indians to buy goods solely from local tax collectors. *Mit'a* means a turn or rotation. The practice was that every seventh household in the region between Huancavelica and Potosí in the Andes took a turn working in the silver mines, with the duration of service varying. Some historians have called this forced labor. But the Indians took their wives and other family members, who pilfered on the side, usually were not caught, and often made tidy incomes for themselves.

The racial complexion of Latin American societies is one of the most complicated in the world. Because few European women immigrated to the colonies, Spanish men formed relationships with Indian and African women. African men deprived of black women sought Indian women. The result was a population composed of every possible combination of Indian, Spanish, and African blood.

Demographers estimate that Indians still accounted for between 60 and 75 percent of the population of Latin America at the end of the colonial period, in spite of the tremendous population losses caused by the introduction of diseases in the sixteenth and seventeenth centuries. The colonies that became Peru and Bolivia had Indian majorities; the regions that became Argentina and Chile had European majorities. Indians and black slaves toiled in the silver and gold mines of Mexico, Colombia, and Peru; in the wheat fields of Chile; in the humid, mosquito-ridden cane-brakes of Mexico and the Caribbean; and in the diamond mines and coffee and sugar plantations of Brazil. Almost 40 percent of all slaves shipped from Africa went to the Caribbean, where the white elite formed a tiny minority.

Spanish theories of racial purity rejected people of mixed blood, particularly those of African descent. Peninsulares and Creoles reinforced their privileged status by showing contempt for people who were not white. Moreover, owners of mines, plantations, and factories had a vested interest in keeping blacks and Indians in servile positions. Nevertheless, nonwhites in Latin America did experience some social mobility in the colonial period, certainly more than nonwhites in North America experienced. A few mulattos rose in the army, some as high as the rank of colonel. The army and the church seem to have offered the greatest opportunities for social mobility. Many black slaves gained their freedom by fleeing to the jungles or mountains, where they established self-governing communities. Around the year 1800, Venezuela counted 2,400 fugitive slaves in a total population of 87,000.

For decades the Enlightenment ideas of Voltaire, Rousseau, and Montesquieu had been trickling into Latin America. North American ships calling at South American ports introduced the subversive writings of Thomas Paine and Thomas Jefferson. In 1794 the Colombian Antonio Nariño translated and published the French Declaration of the Rights of Man and the Citizen (Spanish authorities sentenced him to ten years in an African prison, but he lived to become the father of Colombian independence). By 1800 the Creole elite throughout Latin America was familiar with liberal Enlightenment political thought, and the Creoles wanted the "rights of man" extended to themselves.

Primary Source:
The Problems of the Indian and the Problem of the Land
Read a Marxist's analysis of the oppression of Peru's Indians, and his prescription for political change.

Resistance and Rebellion

The middle years of the eighteenth century witnessed frequent Andean Indian rebellions against the Spaniards' harsh exploitation. Five uprisings occurred in the 1740s, eleven in the 1750s, twenty in the 1760s, and twenty in the 1770s. In 1780, under the leadership of a descendant of the Inca rulers who took the name Tupac Amaru II, a massive insurrection exploded. Indian chieftains from the Cuzco region gathered a powerful force of Indians and people of mixed race. Rebellion swept across highland Peru, where many Spanish officials were executed. Before peace was restored two years later, a hundred thousand people lay dead, and vast amounts of property were destroyed. Although Spanish rule was not ended, the government abolished the repartimiento system and established assemblies in Cuzco. The revolts also raised elite fears of racial and class warfare.

As news of the rebellion of Tupac Amaru II trickled northward, it helped stimulate the Comunero Revolution in the New Granada viceroyalty (see Map 26.2). An Indian peasant army commanded by Creole captains marched on Bogotá. Dispersed by the government that made promises it did not intend to keep, the revolt in the end did little to improve the Indians' lives.

Much more than the Peruvian and Colombian revolts, the successful revolution led by Toussaint L'Ouverture (ca. 1744–1803) in Haiti aroused elite fears of black revolt and class warfare (see pages 626–627 and Map 21.1). In the seventeenth century Haiti, the western third of the island of Hispaniola, offered a haven for French and English pirates. By the end of the century Spain ceded Haiti to France and in the eighteenth century French settlers established sugar plantations there and imported African slaves to work them. Haiti soon became France's most prosperous colony and the world's chief producer of sugar and coffee.

In Haiti the French maintained a rigid social stratification of French, Creoles, freed blacks, and black slaves. When the Creoles refused the mulattos' representation in the local assemblies and in the French National Assembly of 1789, the mulattos revolted. Blacks formed guerrilla bands under the self-educated freed slave Toussaint L'Ouverture. In 1793, as part of their campaign against Napoleon, the British invaded Haiti and took all of its coastal cities. L'Ouverture, with his widespread support, soon retook the cities. In 1801 he declared himself emperor of the entire island of Hispaniola, abolished slavery, and instituted reforms. Napoleon dispatched a large army to restore French control, but the French could not take the interior. The U.S. president Thomas Jefferson, fearing that the French would use the island to invade Louisiana, aided the rebels. Weakened by yellow fever, the French withdrew. L'Ouverture negotiated peace with France, but French officials

● **Toussaint L'Ouverture, Haitian Patriot** The freed slave Toussaint L'Ouverture joined the slave rebellion in 1791 and quickly became its leader and organizing genius. A man of enormous strength and determination, L'Ouverture devoted his life to freedom for his people. He is shown here negotiating with French officials during the war with Britain. *(Getty Images)*

MAP 26.2 **Latin America in 1830** By 1830 almost all of Central America, South America, and the Caribbean islands had won independence. Note that the many nations that now make up Central America were unified when they first won independence from Mexico. Similarly, modern Venezuela, Colombia, and Ecuador were still joined in Gran Colombia.

tricked him and took him to France, where he died in prison. Still, in 1804 Haiti became the second nation (after the United States) in the Western Hemisphere to achieve independence. The revolt was also the first successful uprising of a non-European people against a colonial power, and it sent waves of fear through the upper classes in both Europe and Latin America.

Independence

In 1808 Napoleon Bonaparte deposed the Spanish king Ferdinand VII and placed his own brother on the Spanish throne (see page 635). Since everything in Spanish America was done in the name of the king, the Creoles in Latin America argued that the removal of the legitimate king shifted sovereignty to the people—that is, to themselves.

The Creoles who led the various movements for independence did not intend a radical redistribution of property or reconstruction of society. They merely rejected the authority of the Spanish crown. A distinguished scholar has described the movement for independence as

a prolonged, confused, and in many ways contradictory movement. In Mexico it began as a popular social movement and ended many years later as a conservative uprising against a liberal Spanish constitution. In Venezuela it came to be a war unto the death; in other places it was a war between a small Creole minority and the Spanish authorities. It was not an organized movement with a central revolutionary directorate. It had no Continental Congress. . . . If there was no central direction, no centrally recognized leadership, likewise there was no formally accepted political doctrine.[4]

The great hero of the movement for independence was Simón Bolívar (1783–1830), a very able general who is considered the Latin American George Washington. (See the feature "Listening to the Past: Simón Bolívar's Speculation on Latin America" on pages 812–813.) Bolívar's victories over the royalist armies won him the presidency of Gran (Greater) Colombia in 1819. He dreamed of a continental union and in 1826 summoned a conference of the American republics at Panama. The meeting achieved little. The territories of Gran Colombia splintered, and a sadly disillusioned Bolívar went into exile, saying, "America is ungovernable." Under Spain, Mexico had been united with Central America as the Viceroyalty of New Spain. In the 1830s, after independence, regional separatism resulted in its breakup into five separate countries. In South America, too, the old colonies were divided, not amalgamated. The failure of Pan-Americanism isolated individual countries, prevented collective action, and later paved the way for the political and economic intrusion of the United States and other powers.

Brazil followed a different path to independence from Portugal. When Napoleon's troops entered Portugal, the royal family fled to Brazil and made Rio de Janeiro the capital of the Portuguese Empire. The new government immediately lifted the old mercantilist restrictions and opened Brazilian ports to the ships of all friendly nations. The king returned to Portugal in 1821, leaving his son Pedro in Brazil as regent. Under popular pressure, Pedro proclaimed Brazil's independence in 1822, issued a constitution, and even led resistance against Portuguese troops. He accepted the title Emperor Pedro I (r. 1822–1834). Even though Brazil was a monarchy, Creole elites dominated society as they did elsewhere in Latin America. The reign of his successor, Pedro II (r. 1831–1889), witnessed the expansion of the coffee industry, the beginnings of the rubber industry, and massive immigration.

The Latin American wars of independence, over by 1825, differed from the American Revolution in important ways. They lasted much longer, and outside powers provided no help, leaving those involved weary and divided. Many of the peninsulares returned to Europe. Following the example of the United States, the Creole elites

Latin America, ca. 1760–1900

1764–1780	Charles III of Spain's administrative and economic reforms
1781	Comunero Revolution in New Granada
1806–1825	Latin American wars of independence against Spain
1822	Proclamation of Brazil's independence by Portugal
1825–ca. 1870	Political instability in most Latin American nations
1826	Call by Simón Bolívar for Panama conference on Latin American union
ca. 1870–1929	Latin American neocolonialism
1876–1911	Porfirio Díaz's control of Mexico
1880–1914	Massive emigration from Europe and Asia to Latin America
1888	Emancipation of slaves in Brazil; final abolition of slavery in Western Hemisphere
1898	Spanish-American War End of Spanish control over Cuba Transfer of Puerto Rico and the Philippines to the United States

wrote constitutions for their new governments, but the governments created in Latin America excluded much of the population from political participation. To a large degree the local elites took over exploiting the peasantry from the old colonial elites. Small independent farmers of the sort that became common in the United States and Canada did not gain a comparable place in Latin America. The new governments also largely confirmed the wealth and authority of the Roman Catholic Church.

The newly independent nations had difficulty achieving political stability when the wars of independence ended. The Creole leaders of the revolutions had no experience in government, and the wars left a legacy of military, not civilian, leadership. Throughout the continent, idealistic but impractical leaders proclaimed republics governed by representative assemblies. Mexico lost half its territory to the United States between 1836 and 1848, and other countries, too, had difficulty defending themselves from their neighbors.

The wars of liberation disrupted the economic life of most Latin American countries. Mexico and Venezuela in particular lost large percentages of their populations and suffered great destruction of farmland and animals. Even areas that saw relatively little violence, such as Chile and New Granada, experienced a weakening of economic life. Armies were frequently recruited by force, and when the men were demobilized, many did not return home. The consequent population dislocation hurt agriculture and mining. Guerrilla warfare disrupted trade and communications. Forced loans and the seizure of private property for military use ruined many people.

Cuba and Brazil, which had large slave populations, did not free their slaves until 1886 and 1888. Elsewhere, however, independence speeded the abolition of slavery. The destruction of agriculture in countries such as Mexico and Venezuela caused the collapse of the plantation system, and fugitive slaves could not be recaptured. Also, generals on both sides offered slaves their freedom in exchange for military service.

Although the edifice of racism persisted in the nineteenth century, Latin America offered Negroes greater economic and social mobility than did the United States. One reason for the relative racial permeability of Latin America is that the Creole elite in Latin America approved of "whitening"—that is, they viewed race mixture as a civilizing process that diminished and absorbed the dark and "barbarous" blood of

Africans and Indians. In Latin America, light-skinned colored people could rise economically and socially in a way not available to those with darker skins.

In many Latin American countries, generals ruled. In Argentina, Juan Manuel de Rosas (r. 1835–1852) assumed power amid widespread public disorder and ruled as dictator. In Mexico, liberals declared a federal republic, but incessant civil strife led to the rise of the dictator Antonio López de Santa Anna in the mid-nineteenth century. Likewise in Venezuela, strongmen, dictators, and petty aristocratic oligarchs governed from 1830 to 1892. Some countries suffered constant coups d'état; in the course of the century, Bolivia had sixty and Venezuela fifty-two.

On occasion, the ruling generals were charismatic military leaders who were able to attract mass support for their governments. Páez in Venezuela was able to present himself as a patron of the common man and maintain his popularity even though his economic policies favored the elite and he built up a personal fortune. Some, in fact, were of common origins. In Mexico, Benito Juarez, an Indian who had risen from poverty, led efforts to reduce the power of the Catholic Church and later led resistance to the "emperor" imposed by Napoleon III in 1862. He became president and served until his death in 1872.

Neocolonialism

At first, political instability discouraged foreign investment in Latin America's newly independent nations. With the general expansion of world trade after 1870 and the development of stable dictatorships, foreign investors developed Latin America as a source of raw materials and basic commodities to supply industrializing Europe and the United States. Modern business enterprises, often owned by foreign capitalists, led the way. These firms usually specialized in a single product that could be shipped through the growing international network of railroads, ports, and ocean freighters.

In Mexico, for example, North American capital supported the production of hemp, sugar, bananas, and rubber, frequently on American-owned plantations. British and American interests backed the development of tin, copper, and gold mining. By 1911 Mexico had taken third place among the world's oil producers. British financiers built Argentina's railroads, meatpacking industry, and utilities; Chile's copper and nitrate industries (nitrate is used in the production of pharmaceuticals and fertilizers); and Brazil's coffee, cotton, and sugar production. By 1904 Brazil produced 76 percent of the world's coffee.

neocolonialism *A way of referring to the political and economic systems that perpetuated Western economic domination after political independence.*

Thus, by the turn of the century, the Latin American nations were active participants in the international economic order, but foreigners controlled most of their industries and would use force to defend their economic interests. This form of economic domination is often called **neocolonialism**. The United States intervened in Latin American affairs whenever it felt its economic interests threatened. Americans secured control of the Panama Canal in 1904 on their own terms; in 1912 and 1926 U.S. Marines interfered in Nicaragua to bolster conservative governments; and the Marines who were sent to Haiti in 1915 to protect American property stayed until 1934. Another distinctive feature of neocolonialism was that each country's economy revolved around only one or two products: sugar in Cuba, nitrates and copper in Chile, meat in Argentina, coffee in Brazil. A sharp drop in the world market demand for a product could devastate the export sector and with it the nation's economic well-being. The outbreak of the First World War in 1914 drastically reduced exports of Latin American raw materials and imports of European manufactured goods, provoking a general economic crisis.

haciendas *Large landed estates.*

Many of those who worked on the plantations producing export products were Indians or mestizos. In the United States and Canada, Indians were pushed out of the way when their land was taken from them. In Latin America, many more of them were kept in place and incorporated into the social system as subordinated workers, especially on large plantations called **haciendas**.

● **Rivera: Sugar Cane**   Diego Rivera (1886–1957) used art to convey messages of social protest. Here Indians and blacks labor in the sugar-cane fields, while a white man relaxes in a hammock. (*Diego Rivera, Sugar Cane, 1931. Philadelphia Museum of Art, Gift of Mr. and Mrs. Herbert Cameron Morris [1943-46-2]*)

The late nineteenth century witnessed ever-greater concentrations of land in ever fewer hands. In places like the Valley of Mexico in southern Mexico, a few large haciendas controlled all the land. Under the dictatorship of General Porfirio Díaz, the Mexican government in 1883 passed a law allowing real estate companies (controlled by Díaz's political cronies) to survey public and "vacant" lands and to retain one-third of the land they surveyed. An 1894 law provided that land could be declared vacant if legal title to it could not be produced. Since few Indians had deeds to the land that their ancestors had worked for centuries, the door swung open to wholesale expropriation of small landowners and entire villages. Indians who dared armed resistance were crushed by government troops and carried off to virtual slave labor. Vast stretches of land came into the hands of private individuals—in one case, 12 million acres. Stripped of their lands, the Indians were an easily exploitable labor supply. Debt peonage became common: landowners paid their laborers not in cash but in vouchers redeemable only at the company store, where high prices and tricky bookkeeping kept the **peons** permanently in debt.

peons   *Low-status laborers*

Although some hacienda owners were indolent and technologically backward, scholars generally believe that most haciendas were efficient enterprises whose owners sought to maximize profits on invested capital. The Sanchez Navarro family of northwestern Mexico, for instance, engaged in a wide variety of agricultural and commercial pursuits, exploiting their lands and resources as fully as possible. With lands about the size of West Virginia, they had vast cattle ranches and sheep runs containing as many as 250,000 sheep, as well as maize, wheat, and cotton fields. Keeping their peons in debt was another way they maximized profits.

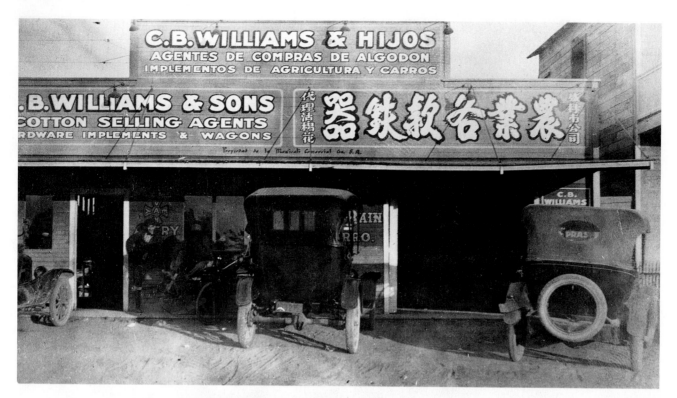

● **Business District in Mexico, 1921** Business signs in several languages—such as those here in Spanish, English, and Chinese—indicate the pluralistic, multicultural character of many Latin American cities in the early twentieth century. *(Courtesy of the photographer, C. B. Williams)*

The Impact of Immigration

In 1852 the Argentine political philosopher Juan Bautista Alberdi published *Bases and Points of Departure for Argentine Political Organization,* arguing that the development of his country—and, by extension, all of Latin America—depended on immigration. Indians and blacks, Alberdi maintained, lacked basic skills, and it would take too long to train them. Thus he pressed for massive immigration from the "advanced" countries of northern Europe and the United States. Alberdi's ideas won immediate acceptance and were even incorporated into the Argentine constitution, which declared that "the Federal government will encourage European immigration." Other Latin American countries adopted similar policies promoting immigration.

Europe had plenty of people to send. After 1880, Ireland, Great Britain, Germany, Italy, Spain, and the central European nations experienced greater population growth than their labor markets could absorb. Immigrants from Asia also flowed into South America and the Caribbean islands. For example, in the late nineteenth and early twentieth centuries, large numbers of Japanese arrived in Brazil, most settling in urban areas, especially in São Paulo. By 1920 Brazil had the largest Japanese community in the world outside of Japan. From the Middle East, Lebanese, Turks, and Syrians also entered Brazil. Between 1850 and 1880, 144,000 East Indian laborers went to Trinidad, 39,000 to Jamaica, and smaller numbers to the islands of St. Lucia, Grenada, and St. Vincent as indentured servants under five-year contracts. Perhaps one-third returned to India, but the rest stayed, saved money, and bought small businesses or land. Cuba, the largest of the Caribbean islands (about the size of Pennsylvania), had received 500,000 African slaves between 1808 and 1865. When slavery was abolished in 1886, some of the work in the sugar-cane fields was done by Chinese indentured servants, who followed the same pattern as the South Asian migrants who had gone to Trinidad. Likewise, the abolition of slavery in Mexico led to the arrival of thousands of Chinese bonded servants.

Immigration helped fuel urbanization. Buenos Aires, Rio de Janeiro, Mexico City, Montevideo, Santiago, and Havana also experienced spectacular growth. Portuguese, Italian, French, Chinese, and Japanese immigrants gave an international flavor and a more vigorous tempo to Latin American cities.

By 1914 Buenos Aires had emerged as one of the most cosmopolitan cities in the world, with a population of 3.6 million. As Argentina's political capital, the city housed all its government bureaucracies and agencies. The meatpacking, food-processing, flour-milling, and wool industries were concentrated there as well. Half of all overseas tonnage passed through the city, which was also the heart of the nation's railroad network. Elegant shops near the Plaza de Mayo catered to the expensive tastes of the elite upper classes, who constituted about 5 percent of the population. By contrast, the thousands of immigrants who toiled twelve hours a day, six days a week, on docks and construction sites and in meatpacking plants were crowded into the city's one-room tenements, furnished with a few iron cots, a table and chairs, and maybe an old trunk.

Immigrants' dreams of rapid economic success in the New World often came true. The first generation almost always did manual labor, but its sons often advanced to upper-blue-collar or white-collar jobs. The sons of successful Genoese or Neapolitan immigrants typically imitated the dress, style, and values of the Creole elite.

Immigrants brought wide-ranging skills that helped develop industry and commerce. Italian and Spanish settlers in Argentina stimulated the expansion of the cattle industry and the development of the wheat and shoe industries. In Brazil, Swiss immigrants built the cheese business, Italians gained a leading role in the coffee industry, and Japanese pioneered the development of the cotton industry. In Peru, Italians became influential in banking and the restaurant business, while the French dominated jewelry, dressmaking, and pharmaceuticals. Chinese laborers built the railroads, and in sections of large cities such as Lima, the Chinese came to dominate the ownership of shops and restaurants. European immigrants also brought anarchist and socialist ideas and became involved in union organizing.

The vast majority of migrants were unmarried males; seven out of ten people who landed in Argentina between 1857 and 1924 were single males between thirteen and forty years old. There, as in other South American countries, many of those who stayed sought out Indian or other low-status women, leading to further racial mixing.

Independence per se did little to improve the position of the poor in Latin America. Property changed hands and haciendas expanded, reflecting the concentration of wealth and greater Creole social mobility, often at the expense of the Indians. Spanish and Portuguese merchants who returned to the Iberian Peninsula were replaced by British and U.S. businessmen. Just as the United States waged wars against the Indians (see page 791–792) and pushed its frontier westward, so Brazil, Venezuela, Ecuador, Peru, and Bolivia expanded into the Amazonian frontier at the expense of indigenous peoples. Likewise, Mexico, Chile, and Argentina had their "Indian wars" and frontier expansion. Neocolonialism's modernizing influence on commerce and industry strengthened the position of the elite and allowed it to use capitalistic values and ideals as a shield against demands for fundamental socioeconomic reforms. European styles in art, clothing, housing, and literature became highly popular, particularly among members of the elite as they sought acceptance and approval by their economic masters.

Racial prejudice kept the vast bulk of the South American black population in a wretched socioeconomic position until the Second World War. European immigrants, rather than black plantation workers, gained the urban jobs. In 1893, 71.2 percent of the working population of São Paulo was foreign-born. Blacks continued to work cutting sugar cane and picking coffee.

THE UNITED STATES (1789–1929)

How does nation building in the United States look from a world history perspective?

The victory of the North American colonies and the founding of the United States seemed to validate the Enlightenment idea that a better life on earth was possible. Americans carried over into the nineteenth and twentieth centuries an unbounded optimism about the future. Although most eastern states retained a property or tax-paying qualification for the vote down to 1860, suffrage was gradually expanded to include most adult white males. The movement toward popular democracy accelerated as the young nation, confident of its "manifest destiny," pushed relentlessly across the continent. The industrializing North and the agricultural South came into conflict over extending slavery. The ensuing Civil War cost six hundred thousand American lives—more than any other war the nation has fought. The victory of the North preserved the federal system and strengthened the United States as a nation.

The years between 1865 and 1917 witnessed the building of a major industrial power. Immigrants settled much of the West, put the prairies to the plow, provided the labor to exploit the country's mineral resources, turned small provincial towns into sophisticated centers of ethnic and cultural diversity, and built the railroads that tied the country together. Most of the social and cultural changes seen in western Europe in this period (see Chapter 23)—such as improved sanitation, mass transit, faith in science, and strong identification with the nation—occurred also in the United States.

Manifest Destiny

In an 1845 issue of the *United States Magazine and Democratic Review*, editor John L. O'Sullivan boldly declared that foreign powers were trying to prevent American annexation of Texas in order to impede "the fulfillment of our manifest destiny to overspread the continent allotted by Providence for the free development of our yearly multiplying millions." O'Sullivan was articulating a sentiment prevalent in the United States since early in its history: that God had foreordained the nation to cover the entire continent. After a large-circulation newspaper picked up the phrase **manifest destiny,** it was used on the floor of Congress and soon entered the language as a catchword for and justification of expansion.

manifest destiny *Catchword for the belief that God had foreordained Americans to cover the entire continent.*

When George Washington took office in 1789, fewer than 4 million people inhabited the thirteen states on the eastern seaboard. By the time Abraham Lincoln became the sixteenth president in 1861, the United States stretched across the continent and had 31 million inhabitants.

During the colonial period, pioneers had pushed westward to the Appalachian Mountains. After independence, westward movement accelerated. The eastern states claimed all the land from the Atlantic Ocean to the Mississippi River, but two forces blocked immediate expansion. The Indians, trying to save their lands, allied with the British in Canada to prevent further American encroachment. In 1794, however, Britain agreed to evacuate border forts in the Northwest Territory, roughly the area north of the Ohio River and east of the Mississippi, and thereby end British support for the Indians. A similar treaty with Spain paved the way for southeastern expansion.

Events in Europe and the Caribbean led to a massive increase in American territory. In 1800 Spain ceded the Louisiana Territory—the land between the Mississippi River and the Rocky Mountains—to France. Three years later, Napoleon sold it to the United States for only $12 million. Spain, preoccupied with rebellions in South America, sold the Florida Territory to the U.S. government, and beginning in 1821 American settlers poured into the Mexican territory of Texas, whose soil proved excellent for the production of cotton and sugar. Southern politicians, fearing that Texas would become a refuge for fugitive slaves, pressured President John Tyler to admit Texas to the United States in 1845. The admission of Texas as the twenty-eighth state and Florida as the twenty-seventh state (also in 1845) meant the absorption of large numbers of Hispanic people into the United States. Many of them had lived in those regions since the sixteenth century, long before Anglo immigration.

The acquisition of Texas's 267,339 square miles (France, by comparison, covers 211,200 square miles) whetted American appetites for the rest of the old Spanish Empire in North America. Some expansionists even dreamed of taking Cuba and Central America.

Exploiting Mexico's political instability, President James Polk goaded Mexico into war. Mexico suffered total defeat and in the **Treaty of Guadalupe Hidalgo (1848)** surrendered its remaining claims to Texas, yielded New Mexico and California, and recognized the Rio Grande as the international border. A treaty with Great Britain in 1846 had already recognized the American settlement in the Oregon Territory. The continent had been acquired. Then, in 1898, a revolt in Cuba against an incompetent Spanish administration had consequences beyond "manifest destiny." Inflamed by press reports of Spanish atrocities, public opinion swept the United States into war. The Spanish-American War—the "splendid little war," as Secretary of State John Hay called it—lasted just ten weeks and brought U.S. control over Cuba, the Philippine Islands, and Puerto Rico. The United States had become a colonial power.

The only people who were native to this vast continent fared poorly under manifest destiny. Government officials sometimes manipulated the Indians by gathering a few chiefs, plying them with cheap whiskey, then inducing them to hand over the tribes' hunting grounds. Sometimes officials exploited rivalries among tribes or used bribes. By these methods, William Henry Harrison, superintendent of the Indians of the Northwest Territory and a future president, got some Native Americans to cede 48 million acres (see Map 26.3). He had the full backing of President Jefferson.

Treaty of Guadalupe Hidalgo (1848) *The 1848 treaty between the United States and Mexico in which Mexico ceded large tracts of land to the United States in exchange for 15 million U.S. dollars.*

MAP 26.3 **Indian Cession of Lands to the United States** Forced removal of the Creeks, Cherokees, and Chickasaws to reservations in Oklahoma led to the deaths of thousands of Native Americans on the Trail of Tears, as well as to the destruction of their cultures.

The policy of pushing the Indians westward across the Mississippi accelerated during Andrew Jackson's presidency (1829–1837). Thousands of Delawares, Shawnees, and Wyandots, tricked into moving from east of the Mississippi River to reservations west of Missouri, died of cholera and measles during the journey. The survivors found themselves hopelessly in debt for supplies and farming equipment. The state of Georgia, meanwhile, was nibbling away at Cherokee lands, which were theoretically protected by treaty with the U.S. government. Then gold was discovered on the Cherokee lands, and a gold rush took place. The Creek, Cherokee, and other tribes were rounded up, expelled, and sent beyond the western boundaries of Missouri and Arkansas.

The two decades before and after the Civil War saw a steady flow of white settlers westward to the Great Plains, where Indians hunted on horseback using rifles. The U.S. Army, in the name of protecting the migrants, fought the Indians, destroyed their lodges and horses, and slaughtered the buffalo on which they depended for food, shelter, and clothing. The federal government's policy was to confine indigenous people to reservations, where malnutrition and disease took a terrible toll.

Cultural differences aggravated conflict between white and Native Americans. Indians did not think of land in terms of private property; they believed that land, like other resources such as air and water, belonged to everyone, that individuals or groups might hold temporary stewardship over the land but that it should be respected and treasured for future generations. Americans, because they had a commander in chief (the president) who could give orders and expect them to be carried out, assumed that a respected Native American chief could make agreements binding on all tribes. But no chief could command all the Sioux, let alone all the Plains Indians. When a tribe or group of tribes opposed or disregarded a treaty made by a particular chief, the whites then claimed that the Indians as a whole had broken the treaty.

In 1868, after pursuing a policy of total war on the Plains Indians, General W. T. Sherman brokered the Treaty of Fort Laramie. This treaty promised that the United States would close western forts and grant the Sioux and Cheyenne permanent control of their ancestral lands in the Dakotas, the Black Hills, as well as the area between the Platte River and the Bighorn Mountains. A few chiefs signed; many did not. In 1874 gold was discovered in the Black Hills. Prospectors flooded into the area. By 1875 whites outnumbered Indians there. Disaster ensued. (See the feature "Individuals in Society: Crazy Horse.") During the course of the nineteenth century when the number of white residents skyrocketed from 4.3 million to 66.8 million, the number of Indians steadily declined, to a recorded 237,196 in 1900.

Black Slavery in the South

In 1619 Dutch traders brought the first black people to Virginia as prisoners as one solution to the chronic shortage of labor in North America (white indentured servants who worked for a term of years was another solution). In the early eighteenth century, as rice cultivation expanded in the Carolinas and tobacco in Virginia and Maryland, planters demanded more laborers. Between 1720 and 1770, black prisoners poured into the Southern colonies. In South Carolina, they came to outnumber whites by almost two to one. In the decades 1730 through 1760, white fears of black revolts pushed colonial legislatures to pass laws that established tight white control and blacks' legal position as slaves, enshrining the slave system in law. Racist arguments of blacks' supposed inferiority were used to justify slavery.

The American Revolution did not bring liberty to slaves. The framers of the Constitution treated private property as sacrosanct and viewed slaves as property. Antislavery sentiment was growing, however, and states from Delaware north outlawed slavery. In 1809 the United States followed Britain's lead in outlawing the importation of slaves.

For white planters and farmers, slavery proved lucrative, and ownership of slaves was a status symbol as well as a means of social control. Slavery "was at the center of

Individuals IN SOCIETY

Crazy Horse

Crazy Horse refused to be photographed, so this portrait is probably an idealization. *(Corbis)*

On June 25, 1876, in the valley of the Little Bighorn in southern Montana, Colonel George Armstrong Custer attacked an encampment of Sioux Indians. Custer had been warned that his regiment of 647 men faced a superior force of perhaps 2,500 Sioux warriors; he was specifically ordered not to attack until reinforcements arrived. Nevertheless, Custer recklessly divided his men, sending one group to scout along the left side of the valley while he led troops along the right side. In the ensuing battle Custer and his greatly outnumbered soldiers were surrounded and slaughtered by the Indians under the Sioux leader Crazy Horse (1842?–1877).

Our only verifiable evidence about Crazy Horse derives from two sources: the 1906–1907 interviews by Nebraska judge Eli Ricker of about fifty people (only ten of them Indians) and the 1930–1931 interviews by journalist Eleanor Hinman and Nebraska writer Mari Sandoz of Crazy Horse's lifelong friend, He Dog, a man then in his nineties. In both sets of interviews, most of the questions related to the last four months of Crazy Horse's life, meaning that we know nothing of his first thirty-four years. But an enormous legend has grown up around him, reflecting "a broken people's need to remember and believe in unbroken heroes . . . who remained true to the precepts of their fathers and to the ways of the culture and traditions which bred them."

The Sioux people, one of many Plains Indian tribes, scarcely knew Crazy Horse; they called him "Our Strange Man" and "Our Mystery." Short Buffalo described him as of medium build and height, with hair and complexion lighter than that of other Indians. Legend held him to be a genius at war but a lover of peace, a dreamer and a mystic who spent long periods alone on the plains. He avoided people, especially white men, and detested reservations. His people respected and loved him as much for the charity he showed the poor and oppressed as for his courage in battle.

When the Indians realized that the U.S. government intended to take back the Black Hills (see page 792), they knew that their old ways of life were ending and that they would have to yield to the white men's plans for them (life on reservations) or die opposing them. In the spring of 1876 vast numbers of Indians moved north to an encampment of the Sioux chief Sitting Bull in the region of the Little Bighorn River, creating the last great gathering of native peoples on the Great Plains. The U.S. Army followed.

Precisely what happened at Little Bighorn we will never know. With at least two thousand horses milling and charging, the battleground would have been a hell of dust and gunsmoke, making visibility very poor. Custer received wounds in the chest and head, either of which would have been fatal. But his head was not scalped nor his body mutilated. Crazy Horse survived; the huge force of Indians melted away on the plains.

Though not a traditional chief, Crazy Horse had about nine hundred followers who looked to him for protection and provision. The long winter of 1876–1877, with bitter cold and little food, wore them down. For their sake, having been promised the army's respect, his own agency, and a buffalo hunt for his people, Crazy Horse laid down his arms at Fort Robinson, Nebraska, in May 1877. He still enjoyed the respect of his people and had moral authority over them. That influence provoked jealousy among other Indians at Fort Robinson. For their part, whites feared that he would become a symbol of resistance and lead another war.

The fort's commander ordered Crazy Horse's arrest. The moment he saw, or smelled, the filthy cells where chained Indians were held, he tried to escape. In a brief melee, his Sioux enemies shouted, "Kill the son of a bitch." A white private, William Gentles, bayoneted him twice, one thrust piercing his kidneys. Crazy Horse fell to the ground, mortally wounded. Receiving no medical attention, he died that night, September 6, 1877.

Questions for Analysis

1. Being such a "loner" all his life, was Crazy Horse an "individual in society"?

2. Why would some Sioux be against Crazy Horse?

Sources: L. McMurtry, *Crazy Horse* (New York: Penguin Books, 1999); J. Keegan, *Fields of Battle: The Wars for North America* (New York: Vintage Books, 1997).

● **Slave Auction, 1850s** In a scene outside a country tavern near a river with a Mississippi-type steamer on it, an auctioneer extols a biracial girl's qualities to a group of planters *(center)*, while another dealer with a whip *(at left)* brutally separates a mother from her children. The picture was intended to send an abolitionist message. *(Carnegie Museum of Art, Pittsburgh. Gift of Mrs. W. Fitch Ingersoll)*

a well-established way of life to which [slave owners] were accustomed and attached, and the disruption or demise of which they feared above all else."[5] Since the possession of slaves brought financial profit *and* conferred social status and prestige, struggling small farmers had a material and psychological interest in maintaining black bondage. Slavery provided the means by which they might rise and the floor beneath which they could not fall.

Between 1820 and 1860, as new lands in the South and West—in Arkansas, Mississippi, Texas, and Louisiana—were put to the production of cotton and sugar, the demand for labor skyrocketed. The upper South—Maryland and Virginia—where decades of tobacco farming had reduced the fertility of the soil, supplied the slaves. Slave traders worked either independently or from firms in Charleston, Natchez, or New Orleans, the largest slave market in the United States. This period witnessed the forced migration of about 650,000 people, in many cases causing the breakup of slave families.

What impact did slavery have on the black family? A study of the entire adult slave population of North Carolina in 1860 has shown that most slave women spent their entire adult lives in settled unions with the same husband. Planters encouraged slave

MAP 26.4 **Slavery in the United States, 1861** Although many issues contributed to the tension between North and South, slavery was the fundamental, enduring force that underlay all others. Lincoln's prediction, "I believe this government cannot endure, permanently half *slave* and half free," tragically proved correct.

marriages because large slave families were in their economic interest, especially after the end of the Atlantic slave trade. As one owner put it, "marriage adds to the comfort, happiness, and health of those entering upon it, besides insuring a greater increase."[6] Evidence from all parts of the South reveals that, in spite of illiteracy, separated spouses tried to remain in touch with one another and, once slavery had been abolished, went to enormous lengths to reunite their families. Typically, a slave woman had her first child around the age of nineteen. On the Good Hope plantation in South Carolina, 80 percent of slave couples had at least four children. Almost all women had all their children by one husband, and most children grew to their teens in households with both parents present.

Freed blacks often went north in search of better opportunities. James Forten, a free black man (d. 1842) from Philadelphia, built a large sailmaking business that employed an integrated workforce. He had a reputation as a businessman of integrity and acquired considerable wealth. But most whites of the city refused to accept him as a citizen and subjected him to verbal and physical assaults.[7]

The Civil War

In the 1850s westward expansion, not moral outrage, brought the controversy over slavery to a head. As Congress created new territories, the question of whether slavery would be extended arose again and again (see Map 26.4). For years elaborate compromises were worked out, but tensions rose, and the North and South were growing increasingly different. The South was overwhelmingly agricultural on the eve of the Civil War; 90 percent of the country's industrial capacity was in the North.

Confederacy *The eleven Southern states that seceded from the United States and bonded together with a capital at Richmond, Virginia.*

Abraham Lincoln, committed to checking the spread of slavery, was elected president in 1860. To protest his victory in the presidential election of 1860, South Carolina seceded from the Union in December 1860. Ten Southern states soon followed South Carolina's example and formed the **Confederacy.** Its capital was at Richmond, Virginia.

Lincoln declared their actions illegal and to preserve the Union declared war. Only after the war had dragged on and the slaughter had become frightful on both sides, and only when it had been proved that the Southern war effort benefited considerably from slave labor, did Lincoln, reluctantly, resolve on emancipation.

The Emancipation Proclamation became effective on January 1, 1863 (two years after the abolition of serfdom in Russia; see page 694). The proclamation freed slaves only in states and areas that were in rebellion against the United States. It preserved slavery in states that were loyal to the United States or under military jurisdiction. It allowed slavery for convicted felons. The Emancipation Proclamation nevertheless spelled the doom of North American slavery. It transformed the Civil War from a political struggle to preserve the Union into a moral crusade for the liberty of Americans.

chattel slavery *Absolute legal ownership of another person, including the right to buy or sell that person.*

European and English liberals greeted the proclamation with joy. A gathering of working people in Manchester, England, wrote President Lincoln: "The erasure of that foul blot upon civilization and Christianity—**chattel slavery**—during your Presidency will cause the name of Abraham Lincoln to be honoured and revered by posterity."[8] As Lincoln acknowledged, this was a magnanimous statement, for the Civil War hurt working people in Manchester, whose factories had shut when importation of cotton from the South stopped.

The war also had important political consequences in Europe. In 1861 British and European opinion had divided along class lines. The upper classes sympathized with the American South; the commercial classes and working people sided with the North. The English people interpreted the Northern victory as a triumph of the democratic experiment over aristocratic oligarchy. Thus the United States gave a powerful stimulus to those in Britain and elsewhere who supported the cause of political democracy. When parliaments debated the extension of suffrage, the American example was frequently cited.

In April 1865, the Confederate general Robert E. Lee surrendered his army at Appomattox Court House in Virginia, ending the war. Lincoln had called for "malice toward none and charity for all" in his second inaugural address in 1864 and planned a generous policy toward the defeated South. The bullet that killed him brought on a different kind of reconstruction.

During Reconstruction (1865–1877), the vanquished South adjusted to a new social and economic order without slavery. Former slaves wanted land to farm, but, lacking cash, they soon accepted the sharecropping system: farmers paid landowners about half of a year's crops at harvest time in return for a cabin, food, mules, seed, and tools the rest of the year. Believing that education was the key to economic advancement, blacks flocked to country schools and to colleges supported by Northern religious groups. Although the Fifteenth Amendment to the U.S. Constitution forbade states to deny anyone the vote "on account of race, color, or previous condition of servitude," whites used violence, terror, and, between 1880 and 1920, so-called Jim Crow laws to prevent blacks from voting and to enforce rigid racial segregation. Lacking strong Northern support, blacks did not gain legal equality or suffrage in many parts of the old Confederacy until the 1960s. Racist assumptions and attitudes thwarted their legal, social, and economic advance.

In the construction of a black community, no institution played a larger role than the black Protestant churches. Local black churches provided hope, education, and a forum for the spread of political ideas and platforms. During Reconstruction, black preachers esteemed for their oratorical skill, organizational ability, and practical judgment held important positions in black politics. In a racist and exploitative society, the black church gave support, security, and a sense of solidarity.

Industrialization and Immigration

From the beginning, the United States attracted immigrants. Before the Civil War, the majority came from England, Ireland, and Germany. When the Irish potato crop was destroyed by a fungal disease leading to a horrific famine in 1845–1859, a million people fled overseas, the majority heading to the United States. Immigrants who arrived with nothing had to work as laborers for years, but many in time were able to acquire farms, especially if they were willing to move west as the country expanded. The Homestead Act of 1862 made land available to anyone willing to work it. From then until the end of the century, 500 million acres were put into production.

As new lands were opened, food production soared. Grain elevators, introduced in 1850, made it possible to store much more grain, which could be transported by the growing rail system as needed. The new practice of canning meant that food did not have to be eaten immediately. The development of refrigeration meant that meat could be shipped long distances. Food processing became industrial. Factories turned out crackers, cookies, and breakfast cereals.

The West also held precious metals. The discovery of gold and silver in California, Colorado, Arizona, and Montana, and on the reservations of the Sioux Indians of South Dakota (see page 792), precipitated huge gold and silver rushes. Even before 1900, miners had extracted $1.24 billion in gold and $901 million in silver from western mines. Many miners settled down to farm. By 1912 the West had been won.

Generally speaking, the settlers' lives blurred sex roles. It fell to women to make homes out of crude log cabins that had no windows or doors or out of tarpaper shacks with mud floors. Lacking cookstoves, they prepared food over open fireplaces, using all kinds of substitutes for ingredients easily available back east. Before they could wash clothes, women had to make soap out of lye and carefully saved household ashes.

Considered the carriers of "high culture," women organized whatever educational, religious, musical, and recreational activities the settlers' society possessed. Women also had to defend their homes against prairie fires and Indian attacks. These burdens were accompanied by frequent pregnancies and, often, the need to give birth without medical help or even the support of other women. The death rate for infants and young children ran as high as 30 percent in the mid-nineteenth century. Even so, these women had large families.

Influenced by ideas then circulating in England, some women began promoting the idea of rights for women. At the Seneca Falls Convention in 1848, women demanded equal political and economic rights. Others promoted women's education and opened women's colleges. It was not until 1920, however, that women in the United States got the right to vote.

England remained an important cultural influence in other spheres besides women's rights and abolition. Many books published in London were quickly reprinted in the United States once copies arrived. Popular English novelists such as Charles Dickens were popular in the United States as well. Education beyond the elementary level usually involved reading classics of English literature.

At the beginning of the nineteenth century, the place of the United States in global trade was as a producer of raw materials—cotton, tobacco, whale oil, pelts, and skins. By the end of the century the United States had become a major manufacturing power, due in part to extensive British investment in U.S. enterprises. The flow of British funds was a consequence of Britain's own industrialization, which generated enormous wealth.

Industrialization was aided by an abundance of raw materials. Huge iron ore deposits were found near the Great Lakes in 1844. Coal was widely available; oil was discovered in Pennsylvania in 1859, and oil drilling soon began. The fossil fuels coal and oil provided energy in very concentrated forms. A few pounds of coal can replace an acre of timber as a source of heat. Coal and oil are much better fuels to power steam engines and to smelt iron and other metals.

The federal government turned over vast amounts of land and mineral resources to industry for development. The railroads—the foundation of industrial expansion—received 130 million acres. By 1900 the U.S. railroad system was 193,000 miles long, connected every part of the nation, and represented 40 percent of the railroad mileage of the entire world. Immigrant workers built it.

Between 1880 and 1920, industrial production soared. By the 1890s, the United States was producing twice as much steel as Britain. New inventions such as the steam engine, the dynamo (generator), and the electric light were given industrial and agricultural applications. Large factories replaced small ones. In the automobile industry, Henry Ford of Detroit set up assembly lines. Each person working on the line performed only one task instead of assembling an entire car. In 1910 Ford sold 10,000 cars; in 1914, a year after he inaugurated the first moving assembly line, he sold 248,000 cars. The automobile increased opportunities for travel, general mobility, and change. Other new machines also had a pervasive impact. Sewing machines made cheap, varied, mass-produced clothing available to city people in department stores and to country people through mail-order catalogues.

The national economy experienced repeated cycles of boom and bust in the late nineteenth century. Serious depressions in 1873, 1884, and 1893 slashed prices and threw many people out of work. Leading industrialists responded by establishing larger corporations and consolidated companies into huge conglomerates. As a result of the merger of several small oil companies, John D. Rockefeller's Standard Oil Company controlled 84 percent of the nation's oil and most American pipelines in 1898. J. P. Morgan's United States Steel monopolized the iron and steel industries, and Swift & Co. of Chicago controlled the meat-processing industry.

Many of those who worked in the new factories were immigrants. Between 1860 and 1900, 14 million immigrants arrived in the United States, and during the peak years between 1900 and 1914, another 14 million immigrants passed through the U.S. customs inspection station at Ellis Island in New York City. Chinese, Scandinavian, and Irish immigrants laid thirty thousand miles of railroad tracks between 1867 and 1873 and another seventy-three thousand miles in the 1880s. At the Carnegie Steel Corporation, Slavs and Italians produced one-third of the world's total steel supply in 1900. Lithuanians, Poles, Croats, Scandinavians, Irish, and blacks entered the Chicago stockyards and built the meatpacking industry. Irish immigrants continued to operate the spinning frames and knitting machines of New England's textile mills. Industrial America developed on the sweat and brawn—the cheap labor—of its immigrant millions.

As in South America, immigration fed the growth of cities. In 1790 only 5.1 percent of Americans were living in centers of twenty-five hundred or more people. By 1860 this figure had risen to 19.9 percent, and by 1900 almost 40 percent were living in cities. By 1900, three of the largest cities in the world were in the United States—New York City with 3.4 million people, Chicago with 1.7 million, and Philadelphia with 1.4. In 1800, New York City had had only sixty thousand people. As in Europe (see Chapter 23), cities themselves were being transformed. By the early twentieth century, cities had electricity, sewer systems that had curbed the spread of infectious diseases, and streetcars that allowed the cities to expand, thus reducing crowding.

Still, the working conditions that these new immigrants found were often deplorable. Industrialization had created a vast class of wage workers who depended totally on their employers for work. To keep labor costs low, employers paid workers piecemeal for the number of articles they made. They hired women and children who could be paid much less than men. Some women textile workers earned as little as

THE COMING MAN—JOHN CHINAMAN.
Uncle Sam introduces Eastern Barbarism to Western Civilization.

● **Racism Rampant**
Nineteenth-century immigrants encountered terrible prejudice, as "respectable" magazines and newspapers spewed out racism, such as this cartoon from an 1869 issue of *Harper's Weekly.* The Irishman (identifiable by the shillelagh or blackthorn club, supposedly a sign of his tendency toward violence) and the Chinese man (identifiable by the pigtail, supposedly a sign of his devious obsequiousness) are both satirized as "barbarians." Well into the twentieth century, being "American" meant being of Anglo-Saxon descent. *(Harper's Weekly, August 28, 1869. Private Collection)*

$1.56 for seventy hours of work, while men received from $7 to $9 for the same work. Owners fought in legislatures and courts against the installation of costly safety devices, so working conditions in mines and mills were frightful. In 1913, even after some safety measures had been taken, twenty-five thousand people died in industrial accidents. Between 1900 and 1917, seventy-two thousand railroad worker deaths occurred. Workers responded with strikes, violence, and, gradually, unionization.

In *How the Other Half Lives* (1890), Jacob Riis, a newspaper reporter and recent immigrant from Denmark, drew national attention to what he called "the foul core of New York's slums." Riis estimated that three hundred thousand people inhabited a single square mile on New York's Lower East Side. Overcrowding, poor sanitation, and lack of health services caused frequent epidemics. The blight of slums increased crime, prostitution, alcoholism, and other drug-related addictions.

Nationalism carried different meanings in the United States than it did in Europe (see pages 679–680). It did not refer to an ancient people whose unique culture was tied to its language. Immigrants were expected to learn English and identify with their new country. As in Europe, however, much was done to promote patriotism and bring people together through flag-waving parades and other emotionally charged symbols and ceremonies. The negative side of identification with the nation was nativist sentiment—that is, intense hostility to foreign and "un-American" looks, behavior, and loyalties—among native-born Americans. Some of this antagonism sprang from deep-rooted racism. Some grew out of old Protestant suspicions of Roman Catholicism, the faith of many of the new arrivals. Long-standing anti-Semitism also played a part. A great deal of the dislike of the foreign-born sprang from fear of economic competition. To most Americans, the Chinese with their exotic looks and willingness to work for very little seemed the most dangerous. Increasingly violent agitation against Asians led to race riots in California and finally culminated in the Chinese Exclusion Act of 1882, which denied Chinese laborers entrance to the country.

In the 1890s, the nation experienced a severe economic depression. Faced with overproduction, the rich and politically powerful owners of mines, mills, and factories fought the organization of labor unions, laid off thousands of workers, slashed wages, and ruthlessly exploited their workers. Workers in turn feared that immigrant labor would drive salaries lower. The frustrations provoked during the depression boiled over into savage attacks on the foreign-born. One of the bloodiest incidents took place in western Pennsylvania in 1897, when about 150 unarmed Polish and Hungarian coal miners persuaded others to join their walkout. The mine owners convinced the local sheriff that the strike was illegal. He panicked and ordered his deputies to shoot at the strikers. Twenty-one immigrants died, and forty were wounded. The sheriff declared that the miners were only "infuriated foreigners . . . like wild beasts." Local people agreed that if the strikers had been American-born, no blood would have been shed.[9]

After the First World War, labor leaders lobbied Congress for restrictions on immigration because they feared losing the wage gains achieved during the war. In the 1920s, Congress responded with laws that set severe quotas—2 percent of resident nationals as of the 1890 census—on immigration from southern and eastern Europe. The Japanese were completely excluded (as the Chinese had been earlier). These racist laws remained on the books until 1965.

CANADA, FROM FRENCH COLONY TO NATION

What geographical, economic, and political conditions shaped the development of Canada?

In 1608 the French explorer Samuel de Champlain (1567–1635) sailed down the St. Lawrence River and established a trading post on the site of present-day Quebec. Thus began the permanent colony of New France. The fur-trading monopolies subsequently granted to Champlain by the French crown attracted settlers, and Jesuit missionaries to the Indians further increased the French population. The British, however, vigorously challenged French control of the lucrative fur trade. The mid-eighteenth-century global struggle for empire between the British and the French, known in Europe as the Seven Years' War and in North America as the French and Indian Wars, spilled into North America. In 1759, on a field next to the city of Quebec, the English defeated the French and ended the French empire in North America. By the Treaty of Paris of 1763, France ceded Canada to Great Britain.

For the French Canadians, who in 1763 numbered about ninety thousand, the British conquest was a tragedy and the central event in their history. British governors replaced the French; English-speaking merchants from Britain and the thirteen American colonies to the south took over the colony's economic affairs. The Roman Catholic Church remained and until about 1960 played a powerful role in the political and cultural, as well as the religious, life of French Canadians. Most French Canadians were farmers, though a small merchant class sold furs and imported manufactured goods.

In 1774 the British Parliament passed the Quebec Act, which granted religious freedom to French Canadians and recognized French law in civil matters, but it denied Canadians a legislative assembly, a traditional feature of British colonial government. Parliament placed power in the hands of an appointed governor and an appointed council composed of both English and French Canadians. English Canadian businessmen protested that they were being denied a basic right of Englishmen—representation.

During the American Revolution, about forty thousand Americans demonstrated their loyalty to Great Britain and its empire by moving to Canada. These "loyalists" not only altered the French-English ratio in the population but also pressed for a representative assembly. In 1791 Parliament responded with the Constitution Act, which divided the province of Quebec in two and provided for an elective assembly in each province.

MAP 26.5 **The Dominion of Canada, 1871** Shortly after the Dominion of Canada came into being in 1867 as a self-governing nation within the British Empire, new provinces were added. Vast areas of Canada were too sparsely populated to achieve provincial status. Alberta and Saskatchewan did not become part of the Dominion until 1905, Newfoundland only in 1949.

Not wanting to repeat the errors made in 1776, the British gradually extended home rule in stages between 1840 and 1867. During the American Civil War, English-American relations were severely strained, and fear of American aggression led to **confederation.** The provinces of New Brunswick and Nova Scotia joined Ontario and Quebec to form the Dominion of Canada (see Map 26.5). The Dominion Cabinet received complete jurisdiction over internal affairs, while Britain retained control over foreign policy. (In 1931 the British Statute of Westminster officially recognized Canadian autonomy in foreign affairs.)

Believing that the American constitution left the states too strong and helped to bring on the Civil War, the framers of the Canadian constitution created a powerful central government. The first prime minister, John A. Macdonald, vigorously pushed Canada's "manifest destiny" to absorb all the northern part of the continent. In 1869 his government purchased the vast Northwest Territories of the Hudson's Bay Company for $1.5 million. Fearful that the sparsely settled colony of British Columbia would join the United States, Macdonald lured British Columbia into the confederation with a subsidy to pay its debts and the promise of a transcontinental railroad. Likewise, the debt-ridden little maritime province of Prince Edward Island was drawn into confederation with a large subsidy. In five short years, between 1868 and 1873, through Macdonald's imagination and drive, Canadian sovereignty stretched from coast to coast. The completion of the Canadian Pacific Railroad in 1885 led to the formation of two new prairie provinces, Alberta and Saskatchewan, which in 1905 entered the Dominion. (Only in 1949 did the island of Newfoundland renounce colonial status and join the Dominion.)

Canada was thinly populated in the nineteenth century, and by 1900 still had only a little over 5 million people. As in the United States, the native peoples were pushed

confederation *A relatively loose form of union, leaving the separate units with substantial powers.*

● **Russian Immigrant Women in Saskatchewan** These women were Duokhobors, a religious sect that came to Canada seeking religious freedom from tsarist persecution. While most of the men took railroad jobs, the women planted the vast plains with rye, wheat, oats, and flax. Their farms and orchards flourished, and the Duokhobors played an important role in the development of western Canada. *(Saskatchewan Archives Board, photo no. R-B 1964)*

aside by Canada's development plans and their population dropped by about half during the century, to only about one hundred thousand in 1900. French Canadians remained the largest minority in the population. Distinctively different in language, law, and religion, and fiercely proud of their culture, they resisted assimilation.

Immigration picked up in the 1890s. Between 1897 and 1912, 961,000 people entered Canada from the British Isles, 594,000 from Europe, and 784,000 from the United States. Some immigrants went to work in the urban factories of Hamilton, Toronto, and Montreal. Most immigrants from continental Europe—Poles, Germans, Scandinavians, and Russians—flooded the midwestern plains and soon transformed the prairies into one of the world's greatest grain-growing regions. Between 1891 and 1914, wheat production rocketed from 2 million bushels per year to 150 million bushels. Mining also was expanded. British Columbia, Ontario, and Quebec produced large quantities of wood pulp, much of it sold to the United States. Canada's great rivers were harnessed to supply hydroelectric power for industrial and domestic use. But Canada remained a predominantly agricultural country, with less than 10 percent of its population engaged in manufacturing (and a third of them processing timber or food).

In 1914 the British government still controlled the foreign policy of all parts of the empire. When Britain declared war on Germany, Canada unhesitatingly followed.

More than six hundred thousand Canadian soldiers served with distinction in the army, some of them in the bloodiest battles in France. Canadian grain and foodstuffs supplied much of the food of the Allied troops, and Canadian metals were in demand for guns and shells. Canadian resentment, therefore, over lack of voice in the formulation of Allied war policies was understandable. In 1918 Canada demanded and received— over the initial opposition of Britain, France, and the United States—the right to participate in the Versailles Peace Conference and in the League of Nations. Since 1939 Canada has been a member of the British Commonwealth of Nations.

AUSTRALIA, FROM PENAL COLONY TO NATION

What circumstances shaped the development of Australia?

In April 1770 James Cook, the English explorer, navigator, and captain of HMS *Endeavor,* dropped anchor in a wide bay about ten miles south of the present city of Sydney on the coast of eastern Australia. Because the young botanist on board the ship, Joseph Banks, subsequently discovered thirty thousand specimens of plant life in the bay, sixteen hundred of them unknown to European science, Captain Cook called the place **Botany Bay.** Totally unimpressed by the flat landscape and its few naked inhabitants—the Aborigines, or native people—Cook sailed north along the coast (see Map 26.6). On August 21, on a rock later named Possession Island, Cook formally claimed the entire land south of where he stood for King George III, sixteen thousand miles away. Cook called the land **New South Wales.** In accepting possession, the British crown acted on the legal fiction that Australia was *Terra Nullius,* completely unoccupied, thus entirely ignoring the native people.

The world's smallest continent, Australia is about half the size of Europe and almost as large as the United States (excluding Alaska and Hawai'i). It has a temperate climate and little intense cold. Three topographical zones roughly divide the continent. The Western Plateau, a vast desert and semidesert region, covers almost twothirds of the continent. The Central Eastern Lowlands extend from the Gulf of Carpentaria in the north to western Victoria in the south. The Eastern Highlands are a complex belt of tablelands.

When Cook arrived in Australia, about three hundred thousand Aborigines lived there. A peaceful and nomadic people who had emigrated from southern Asia millennia earlier, the Aborigines lived entirely by food gathering, fishing, and hunting. They had no agriculture. Although they used spears and bows and arrows in hunting, they never practiced warfare as it was understood by more technologically advanced peoples such as the Aztecs of Mexico or the Mandinke of West Africa. When white settlers arrived, they occupied the Aborigine lands unopposed. Like the Indians of Central and South America, the Aborigines fell victim to the white peoples' diseases and to a spiritual malaise caused by the breakdown of their tribal life. Today only about fortyfive thousand pureblood Aborigines survive.

The victory of the thirteen North American colonies in 1783 inadvertently contributed to the establishment of a colony in Australia five years later. Crime in England was increasing in the 1770s and 1780s, and the transportation of felons "beyond the seas" seemed the answer to the problem of overcrowded prisons. Before 1775 the British government had shipped about one thousand convicts annually to Georgia. After that became impossible, the prisons were so full that old transport ships in southern naval ports were being used to house criminals, and pressure on the government to do something was intense. Finally, in August 1786, the British Cabinet

Botany Bay   *A bay on the coast of eastern Australia in which numerous specimens of plant life were discovered. It later became home to a penal colony.*

New South Wales   *The name given to Australia by James Cook, the English explorer; today it is the name of the most populous of the six states of Australia.*

approved the establishment of a penal colony at Botany Bay to serve as "a remedy for the evils likely to result from the late alarming and numerous increase of felons in this country, and more particularly in the metropolis (London)."[10] The name "Botany Bay" became a byword for the forced and permanent exile of criminals. In May 1787, a fleet of eleven ships packed with one thousand felons and their jailers sailed for Australia. After an eight-month voyage, it landed in Sydney Cove on January 28, 1788.

Mere survival in an alien world was the first challenge. Because the land at Botany Bay proved completely unsuited for agriculture and lacked decent water, the first governor, Arthur Phillip, moved the colony ten miles north to Port Jackson, later called Sydney. Announcing that those who did not work would not eat, Phillip set the prisoners to planting seeds. Coming from the slums of London, the convicts knew nothing of agriculture, and some were too ill or old to work. Moreover, the colony lacked draft animals and plows. For years the colony of New South Wales tottered on the brink of starvation.

Up until the penal colony system was abolished in 1869, a total of 161,000 convicts were transported to Australia. Transportation rested on two premises: that criminals should be punished and that they should not be a financial burden on the state. Convicts became free when their sentences expired or were remitted. Few returned to England.

For the first thirty years, men far outnumbered women. Because the British government refused to allow wives to accompany their convict-husbands, prostitution flourished. Many women convicts, if not professional prostitutes when they left England, became such during the long voyage south.

● **Governor Arthur's Proclamation** To communicate to Aborigines the idea of equal justice for all, the governor of Van Dieman's land (modern Tasmania) in 1830 had picture boards displayed. This one shows an Aborigine being hung for killing a settler with a spear, and a settler being hung for shooting an aborigine with a rifle. *(Mitchell Library, State Library of New South Wales)*

Army officers, government officials, and free immigrants chose favorite convicts as mistresses.

Officers and jailers, though descended from the middle and lower middle classes, tried to establish a colonial gentry and to impose the rigid class distinctions that they had known in England. Known as **exclusionists,** this self-appointed colonial gentry tried to exclude from polite society all freed or emancipated persons, called **emancipists.** Deep and bitter class feeling took root.

Governor Phillip and his successors urged the Colonial Office to send free settlers to Australia, not just prisoners. After the end of the Napoleonic wars in 1815, a steady stream of people relocated. The end of the European wars also released capital for potential investment. But investment in what? What commodity could be developed and exported to England?

exclusionists *The officers and jailers who tried to establish a colonial gentry and impose rigid class distinctions from England.*

emancipists *The lower strata of the Australian social order in the mid-nineteenth century, made up of former convicts.*

Immigrants explored several possibilities. In the last decade of the eighteenth century, for example, sealing seemed a good prospect. Sealing merchants hired Aborigine women to swim out to the seal rocks, lie down among the seals until their suspicions were dulled, and then at a signal rise up and club the seals to death. In 1815 a single ship carried sixty thousand sealskins to London (a normal cargo contained at least ten thousand skins). Such destruction rapidly depleted the seals.

Credit for the development of the product that was to be Australia's staple commodity for export—wool—goes to John Macarthur (1767–1834). Granted a large tract of Crown lands and assigned thirty convicts to work for him, Macarthur conducted experiments in the production of fine merino wool. In 1800 he sent sample fleeces to England to determine their quality. He also worked to attract the financial support of British manufacturers.

The report of J. T. Bigge, an able lawyer sent out in 1819 to evaluate the colony, proved decisive. Persuaded by large landowners like Macarthur, Bigge reported that wool was the country's future staple. He recommended that convicts be removed from the temptations of towns and seaports and dispersed to work on the estates of men of capital. He also urged that British duties on colonial wool be suspended. The

MAP 26.6 **Australia** Because of the vast deserts in western Australia, cities and industries developed mainly in the east. Australia's early geographical and cultural isolation bred a sense of inferiority. Air travel, the communications revolution, and the massive importation of Japanese products and American popular culture have changed that.

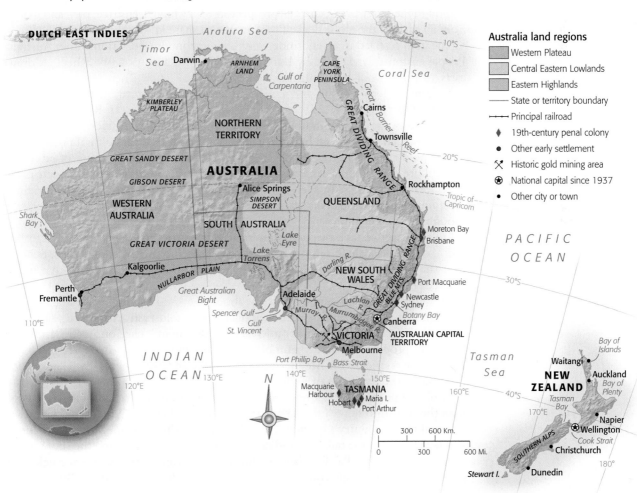

Colonial Office accepted this advice, and the pastoral economy of Australia, as the continent was beginning to be called, began.

Australia's temperate though capricious climate is ideally suited to sheep farming. Moreover, wool production requires much land and little labor—precisely the situation in Australia. In 1830 the sheep population reached a half million. After 1820 the commercial importance of Australia exceeded its significance as a penal colony, and wool exports steadily increased, from 75,400 pounds in 1821, to 2 million pounds in 1830, to 24 million pounds in 1845.

Settlers also experimented with wheat farming. Soil deficiencies and the dry climate slowed early production, but farmers eventually developed a successful white-grained winter variety. By 1900 wheat proved Australia's second most valuable crop.

Population shortage remained a problem through the nineteenth century. In the quest for British immigrants, Australia could not compete with North America. The twelve-thousand-mile journey to Australia cost between £20 and £25 and could take five weary months. By contrast, the trip to Canada or the United States cost only £5 and lasted just ten weeks. To reduce the financial disincentives, immigrants were offered free passage by the government. Still, over 2.5 million British immigrants went to North America and only 223,000 to Australia.

Population in the early nineteenth century concentrated on the eastern coast of the continent. The growth of sheep farming led to the opening of the interior. The Ripon Land Regulation Act of 1831, which provided land grants, attracted free settlers. By 1850 Australia had five hundred thousand inhabitants. The discovery of gold in Victoria in 1851 quadrupled that number in a few years. Gold fever convulsed Australia. Although the government charged prospectors a very high license fee, men and women from all parts of the globe flocked to Australia to share in the fabulous wealth.

The gold rush led to an enormous improvement in transportation within Australia. People customarily traveled by horseback or on foot and used two-wheel ox-drawn carts to bring wool from inland ranches to coastal cities. Then two newly arrived Americans, Freeman Cobb and James Rutherford, built sturdy four-wheel coaches capable of carrying heavy cargo and of negotiating the bush tracks. Railroad construction began in the 1870s, and by 1890, nine thousand miles of track were laid. Railroad construction, financed by British investors, stimulated agricultural production.

The gold rush also provided the financial means for the promotion of education and culture. Public libraries, museums, art galleries, and universities opened in the thirty years after 1851. In keeping with the overwhelmingly British ethnic origin of most immigrants to Australia, these institutions dispensed a distinctly British culture, though a remote and provincial version.

On the negative side, the large numbers of Asians in the goldfields—in Victoria in 1857, one adult male in seven was Chinese—sparked bitter racial prejudice. Scholars date the "white Australia policy" to the hostility, resentment, and fear that whites showed the Chinese.

Although Americans numbered only about five thousand in Victoria and Asians forty thousand, Americans, with their California gold-rush experience, aggressive ways, and "democratic" frontier outlook, exercised an influence on Australian society far out of proportion to their numbers. On the Fourth of July in 1852, 1854, and 1857 (anniversaries of the American Declaration of Independence), anti-Chinese riots occurred in the goldfields of Victoria.

"Colored peoples" (as all nonwhites were called in Australia) adapted more easily than the British to the warm climate and worked for lower wages. Thus they proved essential to the country's economic development in the nineteenth century. Chinese and Japanese built the railroads and ran the market gardens near, and the shops in, the towns. Filipinos and Pacific Islanders did the hard work in the sugar-cane fields. Afghanis and their camels controlled the carrying trade in some areas. But fear that

● **The Life of Emigration** Some of the advertising designed to attract people to move to Australia was aimed at children. This wooden box contains a 38-piece wooden puzzle of scenes of the life of a family moving from Britain to Australia, from their departure to clearing ground and sheering sheep. It dates to about 1840. *(Photograph courtesy of the State Library of South Australia, SA Memory Website)*

colored labor would lower living standards and undermine Australia's distinctly British culture triumphed. The Commonwealth Immigration Restriction Act of 1901 closed immigration to Asians and established the "white Australia policy," which remained on the books until the 1970s.

In 1850 the British Parliament had passed the Australian Colonies Government Act, which allowed the four most populous colonies—New South Wales, Tasmania, Victoria, and South Australia—to establish colonial legislatures, determine the franchise, and frame their own constitutions. By 1859 all but one colony was self-governing. The provincial parliament of South Australia was probably the most democratic in the world, since it was elected by universal manhood suffrage and by secret ballot. Other colonies soon adopted the secret ballot. In 1902 Australia became one of the first countries in the world to give women the vote.

The Commonwealth of Australia came into existence on January 1, 1901. From the British model, Australia adopted the parliamentary form of government in which a cabinet is responsible to the House of Commons. From the American system, Australia took the concept of decentralized government, whereby the states and the federal government share power.

Deep loyalty to the mother country led Australia to send 329,000 men and vast economic aid to Britain in the First World War. The issue of conscription, however, bitterly divided the country, partly along religious lines. About one-fourth of Australia's population was (and is) Irish and Roman Catholic. Although the Catholic population, like the dominant Anglican one, split over conscription, the powerful, influential, and long-lived Catholic archbishop of Melbourne, Daniel Mannix (1864–1963), publicly supported Irish nationalism and denounced the English and the European war. Twice submitted to public referendum, conscription twice failed.

Australia's staggering 213,850 casualties in World War I exerted a traumatic effect on Australian life and society. With the young men died the illusion that remote Australia could escape the problems and sins of the Old World. But the experience of the Great War forged a sense of national identity among the states of Australia.

At the Paris Peace Conference in 1919, Australian delegates succeeded in excluding recognition of the principle of racial equality in the League of Nations Covenant. Australians did not want Asian immigrants. The treaties that followed the war allowed Australia a mandate over German New Guinea and the equatorial island of Nauru. Nauru had vast quantities of phosphates that Australian wheat fields needed as fertilizer. The former penal colony had become a colonial power.

• • • • • • • • • • • • • • •

THE NEW COUNTRIES IN COMPARATIVE PERSPECTIVE

How and why did the new countries treated in this chapter develop differently?

Looked at from the perspective of world history, there was much that the new countries of the Western Hemisphere and Australia had in common. All of them began as European colonies. All had indigenous populations who suffered from the arrival of Europeans. For all of them the nineteenth century was a period of nation building, and all had achieved self-rule by the end of the century. In all of them, the languages of the colonial powers—English, French, Spanish, and Portuguese—became the languages of government after independence. All provided European financiers with investment opportunities, not only in the expansion of agricultural enterprises, but also in mines, transportation, and manufacturing. By the end of the nineteenth century, all of the countries had become connected to the rest of the world through global trade. Another global current they all felt was nationalism, which in these countries meant mass identification with the country rather than identification with an ancient people and its language. All at one time or another allowed or encouraged immigration, and many had also imported slaves from Africa. Discrimination on the basis of ethnic origin and race was pervasive in all of them.

Despite so many similarities, the countries covered in this chapter were already very different by 1914. By then the United States had become one of the half-dozen richest and most powerful countries in the world. That could not be said of any of the others. The United States had built a strong industrial base; the economies of most of the other countries were still predominantly agricultural. The three English-speaking countries had established strong democratic traditions; most of the countries of Latin America were controlled by narrow elites or military strongmen, with much of the population excluded from the political process. Of the countries of Latin America, only Argentina, with its temperate climate, fertile prairies, and large influx of European immigrants approached the prosperity of the United States, Canada, or Australia.

What accounts for these differences in outcomes? That the three countries that began as British colonies ended up as stable democracies strongly suggests that their common origins mattered. Even though they obtained independence in different ways, the British tradition of representative government shaped the political culture of each of the new states. By the time they achieved independence, their citizens were already accustomed to elections and local self-government. That was not true of any of the former Spanish or Portuguese colonies.

The United States also benefited from its size. That a single country was formed by the original thirteen colonies in North America and preserved through the Civil War, gave the United States the advantages of substantial size from the beginning. In addition it had room to expand west into territory with many advantages—temperate climate, navigable rivers, and abundant arable land and mineral resources. The expansion of the United States was made possible by the willingness of France and Spain to sell it large territories in the early years and its own willingness to aggressively pursue expansion at the expense of the Indians and Mexico. As a consequence of its original size and subsequent expansion, the United States became the largest of the new countries in population. The only country that had more land was Canada, and much of Canada's land was too far north to be of high value. If Simón Bolívar had succeeded in forming a union of the Spanish-speaking countries of South America, it might have shared some of the advantages of size that the United States had

Certainly it was important that the United States did not long remain a supplier for Europe of raw materials and basic commodities, but was quick to industrialize. Why did the United States industrialize in the nineteenth century at a much more rapid rate than any of the other countries of the Western Hemisphere? Many reasons can be suggested. It had ample resources such as iron, coal, petroleum, and fertile land. Its political policies helped. The government put few obstacles in the way of those who built the great enterprises. Through much of the nineteenth century, the United States placed high tariffs on imports in order to discourage importing European goods and to foster its own industries. It had no difficulty attracting both capital and immigrants from abroad. The United States developed a social structure that rewarded self-made men and encouraged innovation. At the beginning of the nineteenth century, the most crucial advances in industrial technology were made in Europe, but by the beginning of the next century, they were just as likely to come from the United States. It was the United States that introduced streetcars and Henry Ford who developed the assembly line.

Once the United States became an industrialized country, its economic advantages accelerated, as its citizens had more money to buy the products of its industries, its capitalists had more income to invest, educational levels rose as the advantages of learning became clearer, it attracted more immigrants, and so on. Countries further behind could not easily catch up. Another way to put this is that the United States escaped the neocolonial situation. Because its economy diversified early, when world trade quickened after 1870, the United States was in just as advantageous a position as Britain, France, and Germany.

Chapter Summary

Key Terms

Creoles
peninsulares
neocolonialism
haciendas
peons
manifest destiny
Treaty of Guadalupe
  Hidalgo (1848)
Confederacy
chattel slavery
confederation
Botany Bay
New South Wales
exclusionists
emancipists

To assess your mastery of this chapter, go to
bedfordstmartins.com/mckayworld

• *Why and how did the Spanish and Portuguese colonies of North and South America shake off European domination and develop into national states?*

In Latin America dissatisfaction with Spanish colonial rule grew over the course of the eighteenth century, both on the part of the Indians and mestizos and on the part of the Creoles of European ancestry who resented the privileges granted those from Spain. The wars of independence that lasted from 1805 to 1825 ended colonial status but also led to fragmentation into more than a dozen separate countries. Frequently, military dictators gained political power. Many Indians and mestizos worked on haciendas, often constrained by debt peonage. Many of the large plantations produced basic commodities for the international market, dominated by foreign powers.

• *How does nation building in the United States look from a world history perspective?*

The United States was the first of the European colonies in the New World to gain its independence, and it remained a step ahead during the nineteenth century both in attracting immigrants and in industrializing. The North's victory in the bloody Civil War, fought over the issues of slavery and union, assured the permanence of the Union, but racial equality remains the American dilemma. Domestic matters preoccupied the country through most of the nineteenth century, as it subdued the continent, linked it with railroads, and built gigantic steel, oil, textile, food-processing, and automobile industries. Nationalist sentiment grew, and after 1898, the United States became a colonial power and a major player in international affairs.

• *What geographical, economic, and political conditions shaped the development of Canada?*

The development of Canada was shaped by the emergence of the United States to its south, not only because many loyalists fled to Canada after the American Revolution, but also because Britain did not want to repeat its experience with its earlier American colonies. Adopting the British model of cabinet government and utilizing rich natural resources, the provinces of Canada formed a strong federation with close economic ties to the United States. French separatism, centered in Quebec, remains the Canadian dilemma.

• *What circumstances shaped the development of Australia?*

Australia is much farther from Britain than North America is, and it was colonized later. The first European settlers were forcibly transported to Australia as convicts, but by the mid-nineteenth century Australia was attracting large numbers of Irish and English immigrants and smaller numbers from other countries. As in the United States and Canada, the discovery of gold quickened the pace of immigration. Because of Australia's dry climate, farming concentrated on sheep raising and wheat. After 1850 Australia was largely self-governing and in 1901 drafted a constitution that utilized political features of both the British and the American political systems.

• How and why did the new countries treated in this chapter develop differently?

Of all the new countries of the Western Hemisphere and Australia, only one had become a great power by 1914—the United States. Like the other countries that had begun as British colonies, it developed a stable democracy based on representative government and an expanding electorate. Political stability aided its rapid industrialization, which was also fostered by its rich endowment of natural resources and its ability to attract capital and immigrants. By the beginning of the twentieth century, many of the countries of Latin America, by contrast, seemed trapped in neocolonial systems that kept much of their population poor.

Suggested Reading

Bayly, C. A. *The Birth of the Modern World.* 2003. Useful for viewing the countries of the Western Hemisphere in the context of global developments.

Berlin, Ira. *Many Thousands Gone: The First Two Centuries of Slavery in North America.* 1998. An excellent study that shows how varied slavery was in different times and places.

Burkholder, Mark A., and Lyman Johnson. *Colonial Latin America,* 6th ed. 2007. A broad, comprehensive survey of Latin American history in the colonial period.

Foner, Eric. *Reconstruction: America's Unfinished Revolution, 1863–1877.* 1988. A lucidly written social history that gives attention to the role of former slaves in remaking their world.

Howe, Irving. *World of Our Fathers.* 1976. Brilliant account of the lives of Jews and other immigrants in American cities.

Hughes, Robert. *The Fatal Shore.* 1987. Beautifully written account of the origins of Australia as a penal colony, drawing on diaries and letters.

Morton, Desmond. *A Short History of Canada,* 6th ed. 2006. Well-written popular history.

Rodriguez O., J. E. *The Independence of Spanish America.* 1998. An up-to-date treatment focusing on nation building.

Stampp, K. M. *America in 1857: A Nation on the Brink.* 1990. The best comprehensive treatment of the pre–Civil War years.

Terrill, Ross. *The Australians.* 1987. Offers an attractive appreciation of the Australian people and the society they made, from the first settlers to the present.

White, Richard. *"It's Your Misfortune and None of My Own": A History of the American West.* 1991. Includes environmental, urban, ethnic, and women's history, as well as the more familiar story.

Notes

1. See B. Keen and M. Wasserman, *A Short History of Latin America* (Boston: Houghton Mifflin, 1980), pp. 109–115.

2. M. Burkholder and D. S. Chandler, *From Impotence to Authority: The Spanish Crown and the American Audiencias, 1687–1808* (Columbia: University of Missouri Press, 1977), p. 145.

3. Quoted in J. Lynch, *The Spanish-American Revolutions, 1808–1826* (New York: Norton, 1973), p. 18.

4. F. Tannenbaum, *Ten Keys to Latin America* (New York: Random House, 1962), pp. 69–71.

5. See P. J. Parish, *Slavery: History and Historians* (New York: Harper & Row, 1989), pp. 45–46.

6. H. G. Gutman, *The Black Family in Slavery and Freedom, 1750–1925* (New York: Random House, 1977).

7. See J. Winch, *A Gentleman of Color: The Life of James Forten* (New York: Oxford University Press, 2002), passim.

8. Quoted in S. E. Morison, *The Oxford History of the American People* (New York: Oxford University Press, 1965), p. 654.

9. Quoted in J. Higham, *Strangers in the Land: Patterns of American Nativism, 1860–1925* (New York: Atheneum, 1971), pp. 89–90.

10. Quoted in R. Hughes, *The Fatal Shore* (New York: Knopf, 1987), p. 66.

Listening to the PAST

Simón Bolívar's Speculation on Latin America

Descended from a wealthy Venezuelan family, Simón Bolívar (1783–1830) was educated privately by tutors, who instilled in him the liberal and republican ideals of the French Enlightenment. He traveled to Europe and in 1805, while in Rome, dedicated himself to liberating his country from Spanish rule. Returning to Venezuela, Bolívar worked as a diplomat, a statesman, and, above all, the general who defeated the Spaniards and liberated northern regions of the continent. When he entered Caracas, the citizens called him "the Liberator," and the name stuck.

Almost two generations earlier, on July 4, 1776, the Second Continental Congress had adopted the Declaration of Independence, justifying the thirteen colonies' independence and appealing for European support with a long diatribe against King George III's supposedly tyrannical acts. It was a document of propaganda. In 1815 Simón Bolívar addressed a letter to the governor of Jamaica responding to the latter's request for Bolívar's views on prospects for Latin American liberation and the establishment of one unified nation. Bolívar's "Letter from Jamaica" expresses Latin American ideals and came to serve purposes comparable to those served by the Declaration of Independence.

Kingston, Jamaica, September 6, 1815.

My dear Sir:

. . . With what a feeling of gratitude I read that passage in your letter in which you say to me: "I hope that the success which then followed Spanish arms may now turn in favor of their adversaries, the badly oppressed people of South America." I take this hope as a prediction. . . . The hatred that the Peninsula [Spain and Portugal] has inspired in us is greater than the ocean between us. . . .

Europe could do Spain a service by dissuading her from her rash obstinacy, thereby at least sparing her the costs she is incurring and the blood she is expending. And if she will fix her attention on her own precincts she can build her prosperity and power upon more solid foundations than doubtful conquests, precarious commerce, and forceful exactions from remote and powerful peoples. Europe herself, as a matter of common sense policy, should have prepared and executed the project of American independence, not alone because the world balance of power so necessitated, but also because this is the legitimate and certain means through which Europe can acquire overseas commercial establishments. . . .

It is even more difficult to foresee the future fate of the New World, to set down its political principles, or to prophesy what manner of government it will adopt. . . . We are a young people. We inhabit a world apart, separated by broad seas. We are young in the ways of almost all the arts and sciences, although, in a certain manner, we are old in the ways of civilized society. . . . We are, moreover, neither Indian nor European, but a species midway between the legitimate proprietors of this country and the Spanish usurpers. In short, though Americans by birth we derive our rights from Europe, and we have to assert these rights against the rights of the natives, and at the same time we must defend ourselves against the invaders. This places us in a most extraordinary and involved situation. Notwithstanding that it is a type of divination to predict the result of the political course which America is pursuing, I shall venture some conjectures which, of course, are colored by my enthusiasm and dictated by rational desires rather than by reasoned calculations. . . .

We have been harassed by a conduct which has not only deprived us of our rights but has kept us in a sort of permanent infancy with regard to public affairs. If we could at least have managed our domestic affairs and our internal administration, we could have acquainted ourselves with the processes and mechanics of public affairs. We should also have enjoyed a personal consideration, thereby commanding a certain unconscious respect from the people, which is so necessary to preserve amidst revolutions. That is why I say we have even been deprived of an active tyranny, since we have not been permitted to exercise its functions.

The Liberator: Simón Bolívar. *(akg-images)*

Americans today, and perhaps to a greater extent than ever before, who live within the Spanish system occupy a position in society no better than that of serfs destined for labor, or at best they have no more status than that of mere consumers. Yet even this status is surrounded with galling restrictions, such as being forbidden to grow European crops, or to store products which are royal monopolies, or to establish factories of a type the Peninsula itself does not possess. To this add the exclusive trading privileges, even in articles of prime necessity, and the barriers between American provinces, designed to prevent all exchange of trade, traffic, and understanding. In short, do you wish to know what our future held?—simply the cultivation of the fields of indigo, grain, coffee, sugar cane, cacao, and cotton; cattle raising on the broad plains; hunting wild game in the jungles; digging in the earth to mine its gold—but even these limitations could never satisfy the greed of Spain. . . .

More than anyone, I desire to see America fashioned into the greatest nation in the world, greatest not so much by virtue of her area and wealth as by her freedom and glory. Although I seek perfection for the government of my country, I cannot persuade myself that the New World can, at the moment, be organized as a great republic. Since it is impossible, I dare not desire it; yet much less do I desire to have all America a monarchy because this plan is not only impracticable but also impossible. Wrongs now existing could not be righted, and our emancipation would be fruitless. The American states need the care of paternal governments to heal the sores and wounds of despotism and war. . . .

From the foregoing, we can draw these conclusions: The American provinces are fighting for their freedom, and they will ultimately succeed. Some provinces as a matter of course will form federal and some central republics; the larger areas will inevitably establish monarchies, some of which will fare so badly that they will disintegrate in either present or future revolutions. To consolidate a great monarchy will be no easy task, but it will be utterly impossible to consolidate a great republic.

It is a grandiose idea to think of consolidating the New World into a single nation, united by pacts into a single bond. It is reasoned that, as these parts have a common origin, language, customs, and religion, they ought to have a single government to permit the newly formed states to unite in a confederation. But this is not possible. . . . Would to God that some day we may have the good fortune to convene . . . an august assembly of representatives of republics, kingdoms, and empires to deliberate upon the high interests of peace and war with the nations of the other three-quarters of the globe. This type of organization may come to pass in some happier period of our regeneration. But any other plan . . . would be meaningless.

When success is not assured, when the state is weak, and when results are distantly seen, all men hesitate; opinion is divided, passions rage, and the enemy fans these passions in order to win an easy victory because of them. As soon as we are strong and under the guidance of a liberal nation which will lend us her protection, we will achieve accord in cultivating the virtues and talents that lead to glory. Then will we march majestically toward that great prosperity for which South America is destined.

Questions for Analysis

1. Compare the arguments in the Declaration of Independence (see page 614) and the "Letter from Jamaica."

2. For Bolívar, what are the prospects for Latin American unity as one nation?

Source: A. J. Andrea and J. H. Overfield, eds., *The Human Record,* vol. 2, rev. ed. (Boston: Houghton Mifflin, 1994).

In the Trenches. French soldiers in a trench man a machine gun, the weapon that killed so many, in this chilling work by Christopher Nevinson. *(Art Resource, NY/© Tate, London, 2008)*

27

THE GREAT BREAK: WAR AND REVOLUTION

In the summer of 1914 the nations of Europe went willingly to war. They believed they had no other choice. Moreover, both peoples and governments confidently expected a short war leading to a decisive victory. Such a war, they believed, would "clear the air," and then European society could go on as before. They were wrong. The First World War was long, indecisive, and tremendously destructive. It quickly degenerated into a senseless military stalemate lasting four years. To the shell-shocked generation of survivors, it became simply the Great War.

THE FIRST WORLD WAR

How did Europe's system of alliances contribute to the outbreak of World War I?

The First World War clearly marked a great break in the course of world history. The war accelerated the growth of nationalism in Asia (see Chapter 28), and it consolidated America's position as a global power. Yet the war's greatest impact was on Europe. A noted British political scientist contends that even in victorious Great Britain, the First World War was *the* great turning point in government and society, "as in everything else in modern British history. . . . There's a much greater difference between the Britain of 1914 and, say, 1920, than between the Britain of 1920 and today."[1] This strong statement was as true for all Europe as for Britain.

The Bismarckian System of Alliances

France's defeat in 1871 (see page 692) and the founding of the German Empire opened a new era in international relations. In just ten years, from 1862 to 1871, Bismarck had made Prussia-Germany—traditionally the weakest of the Great Powers—the most powerful nation in Europe. Yet, Bismarck declared Germany a "satisfied" power, having no territorial ambitions within Europe and desiring only peace.

But how to preserve the peace? Bismarck needed first to keep an embittered France diplomatically isolated and without military allies. His second concern was the threat to peace posed by Austria-Hungary and Russia. These two enormous multinational empires had many conflicting interests, particularly in the Balkans, where the Ottoman Empire was losing its grip. To avoid Germany's being dragged into a great war between the two rival empires, Bismarck devised an alliance system to restrain both Russia and Austria-Hungary, to prevent conflict between them, and to isolate a hostile France.

Three Emperors' League *A conservative alliance that linked the monarchs of Austria-Hungary, Germany, and Russia against radical movements.*

First, Bismarck created the **Three Emperors' League** in 1873 to link the conservative monarchs of Austria-Hungary, Germany, and Russia. In 1877 and 1878, when Russia's victories over the Ottoman Empire threatened the balance of Austrian and Russian interests in the Balkans and the balance of British and Russian interests in the Middle East, Bismarck played sincere peacemaker at the Congress of Berlin in 1878 (see page 817). But his balancing efforts infuriated Russian nationalists, leading Bismarck to conclude a defensive military alliance with Austria against Russia in 1879. Motivated by tensions with France, Italy joined Germany and Austria to form the Triple Alliance in 1882.

Bismarck's foreign policy accomplishments after 1871 were impressive. He maintained good relations with Britain and Italy while encouraging France in Africa but keeping France isolated in Europe. In 1887 Bismarck brokered the Russian-German Reinsurance Treaty, by which both states promised neutrality if the other was attacked. For almost a generation he maintained German leadership in international affairs, working successfully for peace by managing conflicts and by restraining Austria-Hungary and Russia with defensive alliances.

The Rival Blocs

In 1890 the young, impetuous German emperor William II forced Bismarck to resign. William then adamantly refused to renew the Russian-German Reinsurance Treaty. This prompted long-isolated republican France to court absolutist Russia, offering loans, arms, and friendship. In 1894 France and Russia became military allies, pledging to remain so as long as the Triple Alliance of Austria, Germany, and Italy existed. Continental Europe was now dangerously divided into two rival blocs.

Great Britain's foreign policy became increasingly crucial. Long content with "splendid isolation" and no permanent alliances, Britain after 1891 found itself the only uncommitted Great Power. Alliance with France or Russia seemed highly unlikely. With a vast and rapidly expanding empire, Britain was often in serious conflict with these countries around the world.

Britain also squabbled with Germany, but many Germans and some Britons felt that a "natural alliance" united the advanced, racially related Germanic and Anglo-Saxon peoples. However, the generally good relations that had prevailed between Prussia and Great Britain since the mid-eighteenth century, and certainly under Bismarck, gave way after 1890 to a bitter Anglo-German rivalry.

There were several reasons for this tragic development. Commercial rivalry between Germany and Great Britain in world markets, William II's tactless public statements, and Germany's pursuit of world power all unsettled the British. Above all, Germany's decision in 1900 to expand greatly its battle fleet challenged Britain's long-standing naval supremacy. This decision coincided with the hard-fought South African War (1899–1902) between the British and the Afrikaner republics of South Africa, which convinced British leaders that Britain was overextended around the world. The South African War also revealed widespread anti-British feeling across Europe. Thus British leaders prudently set about shoring up their exposed position with alliances and agreements.

Britain began by improving its often-strained relations with the United States and then concluded a formal alliance with Japan in 1902. Next, Britain responded favorably to the advances of France's skillful foreign minister Théophile Delcassé, who offered to accept British rule in Egypt if the British supported French plans to dominate Morocco. The resulting Anglo-French Entente of 1904 settled all outstanding colonial disputes between Britain and France.

Frustrated by Britain's turn toward France in 1904, Germany's leaders decided to test the entente's strength and foolishly insisted in 1905 on an international conference on the whole Moroccan question. Germany's crude bullying forced France and Britain closer together, and Germany left the resulting Algeciras Conference of 1906 empty-handed and isolated (except for Austria-Hungary).

The Moroccan crisis and the Algeciras Conference led to something of a diplomatic revolution. Britain, France, Russia, and even the United States began to view Germany as a potential threat that might seek to dominate all Europe. At the same time, German leaders began to suspect sinister plots to "encircle" Germany and block its development as a world power. In 1907 Russia, battered by its disastrous war with Japan and the 1905 revolution, agreed to settle its quarrels with Great Britain in Persia and Central Asia with a special Anglo-Russian Agreement. Germany's blustering paranoia only increased after this agreement, as did Britain's thinly disguised hostility.

Germany's decision to add an enormously expensive fleet of big-gun battleships to its already expanding navy also heightened tensions after 1907. German nationalists saw a large navy as the legitimate mark of a great world power. But British leaders such as David Lloyd George considered it a detestable military challenge that forced them to spend the "People's Budget" (see page 706) on battleships rather than social welfare. In 1909 the *London Daily Mail* hysterically informed its readers that "Germany is deliberately preparing to destroy the British Empire."[2] By then Britain was psychologically, if not officially, in the Franco-Russian camp. Europe's leading nations were divided into two hostile blocs, both ill-prepared to deal with upheaval on Europe's southeastern frontier.

The Outbreak of War

In the early twentieth century, a Balkans war was as inevitable as anything can be in human history. The reason was simple: nationalism was destroying the Ottoman Empire in Europe and threatening to break up the Austro-Hungarian Empire. Greece had long before led the struggle for national liberation, winning its independence in 1830. In 1875 widespread nationalist rebellion in the Ottoman Empire resulted in Turkish repression, Russian intervention, and Great Power tensions. With Bismarck's help, delegates at the 1878 Congress of Berlin worked out the partial division of Turkish possessions in Europe. Austria-Hungary obtained the right to "occupy and administer" Bosnia and Herzegovina. Serbia and Romania won independence, and a part of Bulgaria won local autonomy. But the Ottoman Empire retained important Balkan holdings (see Map 27.1).

By 1903 Balkan nationalism was asserting itself once again. Serbia led the way, becoming openly hostile toward both Austria-Hungary and the Ottoman Empire. The Slavic Serbs looked to Slavic Russia for support of their national aspirations. To block

Chronology

1879–1918 Alliance between Austria and Germany (the "Central Powers")

1891–1917 Alliance between Russia and France

1912 First Balkan War

1914 Assassination of Archduke Francis Ferdinand; formation of Triple Entente (Great Britain, France, Russia); Ottoman Empire joins Central Powers

1914–1918 World War I

1916 Britain crushes Irish Easter Rebellion; Auxiliary Service Law requires German males aged seventeen to sixty to work for war effort; Rasputin murdered

1916–1918 Growth of antiwar sentiment throughout Europe

1917 United States declares war on Germany; Bolshevik Revolution in Russia

1919 Treaty of Versailles

● **German Warships Under Full Steam** As suggested by these impressive ships engaged in battle exercises in 1907, Germany did succeed in building a large modern navy. But Britain was equally determined to maintain its naval superiority, and the spiraling arms race helped poison relations between the two countries. *(Archives Charmet/The Bridgeman Art Library)*

Serbian expansion and to take advantage of Russia's weakness after the 1905 revolution, Austria in 1908 formally annexed Bosnia and Herzegovina, with their large Serbian, Croatian, and Muslim populations. Serbia erupted in rage but could do nothing without Russian support.

Then two nationalist wars, the First and Second Balkan Wars in 1912 and 1913, finally destroyed the centuries-long Ottoman presence in Europe (see Map 27.2). This sudden but long-awaited event elated the Balkan nationalists and dismayed Austria-Hungary's multinational leaders. The former hoped and the latter feared that Austria might be next to be broken apart.

Within this tense context Archduke Francis Ferdinand, heir to the Austrian and Hungarian thrones, and his wife, Sophie, were assassinated by ultranationalist Serbian revolutionaries on June 28, 1914, during a state visit to the Bosnian capital of Sarajevo. Austria-Hungary's leaders held Serbia responsible and presented Serbia with an unconditional ultimatum on July 23. The Serbs had just forty-eight hours to agree to demands that amounted to Austrian control of the Serbian state. When Serbia replied moderately but evasively, Austria began to mobilize and then declared war on Serbia on July 28. Austria-Hungary had deliberately chosen war in a last-ditch attempt to stem the rising tide of hostile nationalism within its borders and to save its empire. The "Third Balkan War" had begun.

Of prime importance in Austria-Hungary's fateful decision was Germany's unconditional support. Emperor William II and his chancellor, Theobald von Bethmann-Hollweg, gave Austria-Hungary a "blank check," although realizing that war between Austria and Russia was the likely result. A resurgent Russia could not simply stand by and watch the Serbs be crushed. Yet Bethmann-Hollweg apparently hoped that while

Russia (and therefore France) would go to war, Great Britain would remain neutral, unwilling to fight for "Russian aggression" in the distant Balkans.

Military plans and timetables, rather than diplomacy, soon began to dictate policy, however. On July 28, as Austrian armies bombarded Belgrade, Tsar Nicholas II ordered a partial mobilization against Austria-Hungary, but almost immediately found this was impossible. The Russian general staff had assumed a war with both Austria and Germany: Russia could not mobilize against one without mobilizing against the other. Therefore, on July 29 Russia ordered full mobilization and in effect declared general war.

Germany faced the same conundrum. The German general staff had only prepared for a two-front war: first knocking out France with a lightning attack through neutral Belgium before turning on Russia. So on August 2, 1914, General Helmuth von Moltke demanded that Belgium permit German armies to pass through its territory. Belgium, whose neutrality had been solemnly guaranteed in 1839 by all the great states including Prussia, refused. Germany attacked. Thus, Germany's response to a war in the Balkans was an all-out invasion of France by way of neutral Belgium on August 3. Great Britain reacted by joining France and declaring war on Germany the following day. The First World War had begun.

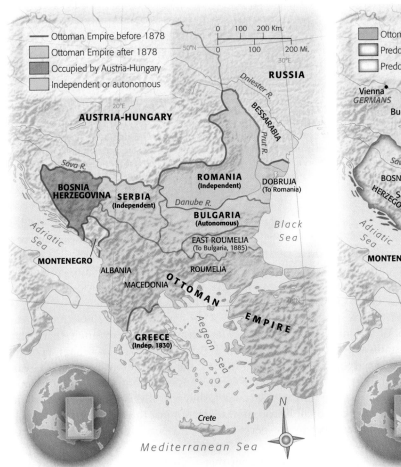

MAP 27.1 **The Balkans After the Congress of Berlin, 1878** The Ottoman Empire suffered large territorial losses but remained a power in the Balkans.

MAP 27.2 **The Balkans in 1914** Ethnic boundaries did not follow political boundaries, and Serbian national aspirations threatened Austria-Hungary.

● **Nationalist Opposition in the Balkans** This band of well-armed and determined guerrillas from northern Albania was typical of groups fighting against Ottoman rule in the Balkans. Balkan nationalists succeeded in driving the Ottoman Turks out of most of Europe, but their victory increased tensions with Austria-Hungary and among the Great Powers. *(Roger-Viollet/Getty Images)*

In reflecting on the Great War's origins, it seems clear that Austria-Hungary deliberately started a conflict. The Third Balkans War was Austria-Hungary's desperate response to the revolutionary drive of Serbian nationalists to unify all Serbs in a single state. Moreover, in spite of Russian intervention, Germany was clearly most responsible for turning a third war in the Balkans into the Great War by its attack on Belgium and France. Why Germany was so aggressive in 1914 is less certain.

Diplomatic historians stress that after Bismarck's resignation in 1890 German leaders lost control of the international system. The Germans felt increasingly that their new country's status as a world power was declining, while the status of Britain, France, Russia, and the United States was growing. Indeed, the **Triple Entente** powers—Great Britain, France, and Russia—were checking Germany's vague but real aspirations and working to strangle Austria-Hungary, Germany's only real ally. Germany's aggression in 1914 reflected the failure of all European leaders, not just those in Germany, to incorporate Bismarck's mighty empire permanently and peacefully into the international system.

A more controversial interpretation argues that while Germany industrialized and urbanized rapidly after 1870 and had a popularly elected parliament, political power remained concentrated in the hands of the monarchy, army, and nobility. Frightened by the socialist movement and a wave of strikes in 1914, the German ruling class was

Triple Entente *The alliance of Great Britain, France, and Russia in the First World War.*

determined to hold on to power and willing to gamble on a diplomatic victory or even war as the means of rallying the masses to its side and preserving the existing system.

Above all, the triumph of nationalism was a crucial underlying precondition of the Great War. Nationalism was at the heart of the Balkan wars, and it drove the spiraling arms race. In each country the great majority of the population rallied to defend their nation and enthusiastically embraced war in August 1914. Patriotic nationalism brought unity in the short run.

In all of this, Europe's governing classes fatally underestimated the risk of war to themselves in 1914. They had forgotten that great wars and great social revolutions very often go hand in hand. Metternich's alliance of conservative forces in support of international peace and the social status quo had become a distant memory.

Stalemate and Slaughter

When the Germans invaded Belgium in August 1914, everyone believed the war would be short: "The boys will be home by Christmas." The Belgian army heroically defended its homeland, however, and then fell back to join a rapidly landed British army corps near the Franco-Belgian border. Instead of quickly capturing Paris in a vast encircling movement, dead-tired German soldiers by the end of August were advancing along an enormous front in the scorching summer heat. On September 6 the French attacked a gap in the German line at the Battle of the Marne. For three days France threw everything into the attack. At one point the French government desperately requisitioned all the taxis of Paris to rush reserves to the troops at the front. Finally, the Germans fell back. Paris and France had been miraculously saved (see Map 27.3).

The two stalled armies now began to dig trenches to protect themselves from machine-gun fire. Eventually an unbroken line of parallel trenches stretched over four hundred miles from the Belgian ports to the Swiss frontier. By November 1914 the defenders on both sides had dug in behind rows of trenches, mines, and barbed wire, and the slaughter on the western front had begun in earnest. For days and even weeks ceaseless shelling by heavy artillery supposedly "softened up" the enemy in a given area (and also signaled the coming attack). Then young draftees and their junior officers went "over the top" of the trenches in frontal attacks on the enemy's line.

The human cost was staggering; territorial gains were minuscule. The massive French and British offensives during 1915 never gained more than three miles of blood-soaked earth from the enemy. In the Battle of the Somme in the summer of 1916, the British and French gained an insignificant 125 square miles at the cost of 600,000 dead or wounded, and the Germans lost 500,000 men. In that same year the unsuccessful German campaign against Verdun cost 700,000 lives on both sides. British poet Siegfried Sassoon (1886–1967) wrote of the Somme offensive, "I am staring at a sunlit picture of Hell."

The year 1917 was equally terrible. The hero of Erich Remarque's great novel *All Quiet on the Western Front* (1929) describes a typical attack:

● **"Never Forget!"**   This 1915 French poster with its passionate headline dramatizes Germany's brutal invasion of Belgium in 1914. Neutral Belgium is personified as a traumatized mother, assaulted and ravished by savage outlaws. The "rape of Belgium" featured prominently—and effectively—in anti-German propaganda. *(Mary Evans Picture Library)*

MAP 27.3 The First World War in Europe The trench war on the western front was concentrated in Belgium and northern France, while the war in the east encompassed an enormous territory.

Main map labels

ATLANTIC OCEAN

GREAT BRITAIN
London

IRELAND

North Sea

NORWAY

SWEDEN

FINLAND
Helsinki

Petrograd (St. Petersburg)

Moscow

Treaty of Brest-Litovsk, March 1918

R U S S I A

Kiev

UKRAINE

Armistice line, December 1917

ESTONIA
LATVIA
Riga
COURLAND
LITHUANIA
Wilno (Vilnius)
BELARUS

Baltic Sea

Farthest Russian advance, 1914

Masurian Lakes 1914
Tannenberg 1914
E. PRUSSIA
Warsaw
KINGDOM OF POLAND (Russia)
Brest-Litovsk
Vistula R.

British blockade line

Jutland 1916
DENMARK
Kiel
Elbe R.

NETHERLANDS

GERMANY
Berlin

GALICIA
Dniester R.
MAY 1915

LUXEMBOURG
ALSACE-LORRAINE
Rhine R.

BELGIUM
Louvain
Western front

Paris
Seine R.
FRANCE
Bordeaux
Loire R.
Garonne R.
Ebro R.
SPAIN

SWITZERLAND

AUSTRIA-HUNGARY
Vienna
Budapest

TRANSYLVANIA

ROMANIA
Bucharest

Caporetto 1917
AUG. 1917
MAR. 1918
Italian front
Po R.
ITALY
Rome
Elba
Corsica
Sardinia
Balearic Is.
Rhône R.

SERBIA
Sarajevo
MONTENEGRO
Adriatic Sea
ALBANIA
Balkan front

BULGARIA
1917–1918
1916
1915
GREECE

Black Sea

Constantinople
O T T O M A N   E M P I R E
Dardanelles
Gallipoli 1915

Crete

Cyprus

Mediterranean Sea

Malta
Sicily
TUNISIA (France)
Tunis

0   200   400 Km.
0   200   400 Mi.

N

Legend (main map)

- Triple Entente and its Allies
- Central Powers
- Neutral nations
- Greatest extent of territory gained by Germany–Austria
- Battle line

Inset map

NETHERLANDS
Antwerp
Brussels
Ghent
Ostend
FLANDERS
Calais
Dover
English Channel

BELGIUM
Liège
Schelde R.
Meuse R.

LUXEMBOURG
ARDENNES
Sedan
ARGONNE FOREST
St. Quentin
Somme
Somme R.
Arras
Amiens
Compiègne
Belleau Wood
Reims
Château-Thierry
Marne II
Marne I
Châlons-sur-Marne
Paris
Seine R.
Aisne R.
Marne R.

FRANCE

Verdun
St. Mihiel
Nancy
LORRAINE
Moselle R.
Saar R.

GERMANY
Cologne
Coblenz
Rhine R.
Ruhr R.

ALSACE
Strasbourg
Epinal
Mulhouse
Basel

Legend (inset map)

- Germany, 1914
- German offensive, 1915
- Greatest extent of territory gained by Germany, Sept. 1914
- Front at beginning of 1915
- German offensive, Summer 1918
- Armistice line, November 1918
- Major battle

0   25   50 Km.
0   25   50 Mi.

We see men living with their skulls blown open; we see soldiers run with their two feet cut off. . . . Still the little piece of convulsed earth in which we lie is held. We have yielded no more than a few hundred yards of it as a prize to the enemy. But on every yard there lies a dead man.

Such was war on the western front.

Trench warfare shattered an entire generation of young men. Millions who could have provided political creativity and leadership after the war were forever missing. Millions were killed, and millions more who lived through the holocaust were maimed, shell-shocked, embittered, and profoundly disillusioned. The young soldiers went to war believing in the world of their leaders and elders—the pre-1914 world of order, progress, and patriotism. Then, in Remarque's words, the "first bombardment showed us our mistake, and under it the world as they had taught it to us broke in pieces."

trench warfare *Fighting behind rows of trenches, mines, and barbed wire; the cost in lives was staggering and the gains in territory minimal.*

The Widening War

On the eastern front slaughter did not degenerate into suicidal trench warfare. With the outbreak of war, the "Russian steamroller" immediately moved into eastern Germany but suffered appalling losses against the Germans under General Paul von Hindenburg and General Erich Ludendorff at the Battle of Tannenberg and the Battle of the Masurian Lakes in August and September 1914. Russia never threatened Germany again (see Map 27.3). On the Austrian front enormous armies seesawed back and forth. But with the help of German forces, the Austrians reversed the Russian advances of 1914 and forced the Russians to retreat deep into their own territory in the 1915 eastern campaign. A staggering 2.5 million Russians were killed, wounded, or taken prisoner that year.

These changing tides of victory and hopes of territorial gains brought neutral countries into the war. Italy, a member of the Triple Alliance since 1882, had declared its neutrality in 1914 on the grounds that Austria had launched a war of aggression. Then, in May 1915, Italy joined the Triple Entente of Great Britain, France, and Russia in return for promises of Austrian territory. In October 1914 the Ottoman Empire joined with Austria and Germany, by then known as the Central Powers. The following September Bulgaria followed the Ottoman Empire's lead in order to settle old scores with Serbia (see Map 27.3).

The entry of the Ottoman Turks carried the war into the Middle East, a momentous development. In 1915 British forces tried to take the Dardanelles and Constantinople from Turkey but were badly defeated. The British were more successful at inciting the Arabs to revolt against their Turkish overlords. An enigmatic British colonel, soon known to millions as Lawrence of Arabia, helped lead the Arab revolt in early 1917. In 1918 British armies totally smashed the old Ottoman state, drawing primarily on imperial forces from Egypt, India, Australia, and New Zealand. Thus war brought revolutionary change to the Middle East (see pages 848–857).

War also spread to some parts of Africa and East Asia. Instead of revolting as the Germans hoped, French and British colonial subjects supported their foreign masters, providing critical supplies and fighting in Europe and in the Ottoman Empire. They also helped local British and French commanders seize Germany's colonies around the globe. More than a million Africans served in the various armies of the warring powers, with more than double that number serving as porters to carry equipment. The opportunity to fight against and kill Europeans, and the spectacle of Europeans fighting each other to protect their nations' freedom and their individual rights, had a profound impact on these soldiers. African American soldiers serving in France also gained a new sense of dignity and self-worth from their experiences in the war. The Japanese, allied in Asia with the British since 1902, similarly used the war to grab German outposts in the Pacific Ocean and on the Chinese mainland, infuriating Chinese patriots and heightening long-standing tensions between China and Japan.

Another crucial development in the expanding conflict came in April 1917 when the United States declared war on Germany. American intervention grew out of the war at sea, sympathy for the Triple Entente, and the increasing desperation of total war. At the beginning of the war Britain and France had established a total naval blockade to strangle the Central Powers. No neutral ship was permitted to sail to Germany with any cargo. The blockade annoyed Americans, but effective propaganda about German atrocities in occupied Belgium as well as lush profits from selling war supplies to Britain and France blunted American indignation.

Moreover, in early 1915 Germany launched a counter-blockade using the murderously effective submarine, a new weapon that sank ships without the traditional niceties of fair warning under international law. In May a German submarine sank the British passenger liner **Lusitania,** which was also carrying arms and munitions. More than a thousand people, including 139 Americans, died. President Woodrow Wilson protested vigorously. Germany was forced to restrict its submarine warfare for almost two years, or face almost certain war with the United States.

Early in 1917 the German military command—confident that improved submarines could starve Britain into submission before the United States could come to its

Lusitania *The name of the British passenger liner sunk by a German submarine that claimed more than a thousand lives.*

● **The Tragic Absurdity of Trench Warfare** As soldiers charged across a scarred battlefield and overran an enemy trench, the dead defender on the right would fire no more. But this was only another futile charge that would yield much blood and little land. A whole generation was being decimated by the slaughter. *(By courtesy of the Trustees of the Imperial War Museum)*

● **Otto Dix: War (detail)** Returning to Germany after the war, Dix was haunted by the horrors he had seen. This vivid expressionist masterpiece, part of a triptych painted in 1929–1932, probes the tormented memory of endless days in muddy trenches and dugouts, living with rats and lice and the constant danger of exploding shells, snipers, and all-out attack. Many who escaped death or dismemberment were mentally wounded forever by their experiences. *(Staatliche Kunstsammlungen Dresden. © 2002 Artists Rights Society [ARS], New York/ VG Bild-Kunst, Bonn)*

rescue—resumed unrestricted submarine warfare. Like the invasion of Belgium, this was a reckless gamble. "German submarine warfare against commerce," President Wilson told a sympathetic Congress and people, "is a warfare against mankind." Thus the last uncommitted great nation, as fresh and enthusiastic as Europe had been in 1914, entered the world war in April 1917. The United States eventually tipped the balance in favor of the Triple Entente and its allies.

THE HOME FRONT

How did total war impact the home fronts of the major European combatants?

Before looking at the Great War's final year, let us turn our attention to the people on the home front. War's impact on them was no less massive than on the men crouched in the trenches.

Mobilizing for Total War

In August 1914 most Europeans greeted the outbreak of hostilities enthusiastically, believing their own nation was in the right and defending itself from aggression. Except for a few extreme left-wingers, even socialists supported the war. Everywhere the support of the patriotic masses and working class contributed to national unity and an energetic war effort.

● **Hair for the War Effort**   Blockaded and cut off from overseas supplies, Germany mobilized effectively to find substitutes at home. This poster calls on German women—especially young women with long flowing tresses—to donate their hair, which was used to make rope. Children were organized by their teachers into garbage brigades to collect every scrap of useful material. *(akg-images)*

total war   *In each country during the First World War, a government of national unity that began to plan and control economic and social life in order to make the greatest possible military effort.*

War Raw Materials Board   *Masterminded by Walter Rathenau, this was set up by the German government to ration and distribute raw materials.*

Auxiliary Service Law   *A German law requiring all males between the ages of seventeen and sixty to work only at jobs considered critical to the war effort.*

By mid-October generals and politicians began to realize that, with no end in sight, more than patriotism would be needed to win the war. Every country experienced a relentless, desperate demand for men and weapons. In each country change had to come, and fast, to keep the war machine from sputtering to a stop.

The change came through national unity governments that began to plan and control economic and social life in order to wage **total war**. Governments imposed rationing, price and wage controls, and even restrictions on workers' freedom of movement. These total war economies involved entire populations, blurring the old distinction between soldiers on the battlefield and civilians at home. Based on tremendously productive industrial economies, total war yielded an effective—and therefore destructive—war effort on all sides. (See the feature "Listening to the Past: The Experience of War" on pages 842–843.)

However awful the war was, the ability of central governments to manage and control highly complicated economies increased and strengthened their powers, often along socialist lines. With the First World War socialism for the first time became a realistic economic blueprint rather than a utopian dream. Germany went furthest in developing a planned economy to wage total war.

As soon as war began, the Jewish industrialist Walter Rathenau convinced the German government to set up the **War Raw Materials Board** to ration and distribute raw materials. Under Rathenau's direction every useful material from foreign oil to barnyard manure was inventoried and rationed. Moreover, the board launched successful attempts to produce substitutes, such as synthetic rubber and synthetic nitrates, needed to make explosives and essential to the blockaded German war machine. An aggressive recycling campaign augmented these efforts. Food was also rationed, with men and women doing hard manual work receiving extra rations. During the war's final two years only children and expectant mothers received milk rations. Many people were living on less than a thousand calories a day. At the same time, Germany's failure to tax the war profits of private firms heavily enough contributed to massive deficit financing, inflation, the growth of a black market, and the eventual re-emergence of class conflict.

Following the terrible Battles of Verdun and the Somme in 1916, military leaders Hindenburg and Ludendorff became Germany's real rulers. They decreed the ultimate mobilization for total war: all agriculture, industry, and labor must be "used exclusively for the conduct of War."[3] In December 1916 military leaders rammed through the Reichstag the **Auxiliary Service Law**, which required all males between seventeen and sixty to work only at jobs considered critical to the war effort. Many more women also followed those already working into war factories, mines, and steel mills. Thus in Germany total war led to history's first "totalitarian" society.

Great Britain mobilized for total war less rapidly and less completely than Germany, for it could import materials from its empire and from the United States. In June 1915, however, a serious shortage of shells led to the establishment of the Ministry of Munitions under David Lloyd George. The ministry organized private industry to

● **Waging Total War** A British war plant strains to meet the insatiable demand for trench-smashing heavy artillery shells. Quite typically, many of these defense workers are women. *(By courtesy of the Trustees of the Imperial War Museum)*

produce for the war, controlled profits, allocated labor, fixed wage rates, and settled labor disputes. By December 1916 the British economy was largely planned and regulated directly by the state.

The Social Impact

The social impact of total war was no less profound than the economic impact, though again there were important national variations. The military's insatiable needs created a tremendous demand for workers. This situation—seldom, if ever, seen before 1914, when unemployment and poverty had been facts of urban life—brought about momentous changes.

One such change was greater power and prestige for labor unions. Having proved their loyalty in August 1914, labor unions cooperated with war governments on work rules, wages, and production schedules in return for real participation in important decisions. This entry of labor leaders into policymaking councils paralleled the entry of socialist leaders into the war governments.

Women's roles also changed dramatically. In every country large numbers of women, displaying a growing sense of independence, left home and domestic service to work in industry, transportation, and offices. Moreover, women became highly visible—not only as munitions workers but as bank tellers, mail carriers, even police officers. Women also served as nurses and doctors at the front. (See the feature "Individuals in Society: Vera Brittain.") In general, the war greatly expanded the range of women's activities and changed attitudes toward women. As a direct result of women's many-sided war effort, Britain, Germany, and Austria granted women the right to vote immediately after the war.

War promoted social equality, blurring class distinctions and lessening the gap between rich and poor. Greater equality was reflected in full employment, rationing according to physical needs, and a sharing of hardships. Society became more uniform and more egalitarian, in spite of some war profiteering.

Death itself had no respect for traditional social distinctions. It savagely decimated both the young aristocratic officers who led the charge and the mass of drafted peasants and unskilled workers who followed. Death, however, often spared the aristocrats of labor—the skilled workers and foremen. Their lives were too valuable to squander at the front, for they were needed to train the newly recruited women and older unskilled men laboring valiantly in war plants at home.

Growing Political Tensions

> **Primary Source:**
> **Mud and Khaki, Memoirs of an Incomplete Soldier**
> *Read from the memoirs of a British soldier, and imagine the horrors of trench warfare and poison gas in World War I.*

During the war's first two years most soldiers and civilians supported their governments. Even in Austria-Hungary—the most vulnerable of the belligerents with its competing nationalities—loyalty to the state and monarchy remained astonishingly strong through 1916. Belief in a just cause, patriotic nationalism, the planned economy, and a sharing of burdens united peoples behind their various national leaders.

Each government employed rigorous censorship to control public opinion, and each used propaganda to maintain popular support. German propaganda pictured black soldiers from France's African empire raping German women. The French and British ceaselessly recounted and exaggerated German atrocities in Belgium and elsewhere. Patriotic posters and slogans, slanted news, and biased editorials inflamed national hatreds and helped sustain superhuman efforts.

By spring 1916, however, people were beginning to crack under the strain of total war. In April 1916 Irish nationalists in Dublin tried to take advantage of this situation and rose up against British rule in an Easter Rebellion. The rebels were crushed after a week of bitter fighting and their leaders executed. Strikes and protest marches over inadequate food flared up on every home front. Soldiers' morale began to decline. Italian troops mutinied. Numerous French units refused to fight for a time after the disastrous French offensive of May 1917. War-weariness and defeatism also swept France's civilian population before Georges Clemenceau emerged as a ruthless and effective wartime leader in November 1917. Clemenceau (1841–1929) established a virtual dictatorship, pouncing on strikers and jailing without trial anyone who dared to suggest a compromise peace with Germany.

The Central Powers experienced the most strain. In October 1916 a young socialist crying "Down with Absolutism! We want peace!" assassinated Austria's chief minister.[4] When the feeble old Emperor Francis Joseph died the following month a unifying symbol disappeared. Conflicts among nationalities grew, and both Czech and Yugoslav leaders demanded autonomous democratic states for their peoples. The strain of total war and of the Auxiliary Service Law was also evident in Germany. By 1917 national political unity was collapsing and prewar social conflicts re-emerging. Some socialists in the Reichstag voted against war credits, and in July 1917 a coalition of socialists and Catholics passed a resolution calling for a compromise "peace without annexations or reparations." Conservatives and military leaders found such a peace unthinkable. Thus militaristic Germany, like its ally Austria-Hungary (and its enemy France), began to crack in 1917. But it was Russia that collapsed first and saved the Central Powers—for a time.

Vera Brittain

Vera Brittain, marked forever by her wartime experiences. (Vera Brittain Archive, William Ready Division of Archives and Research Collections, McMaster University Library)

Although the Great War upended millions of lives, it struck Europe's young people with the greatest force. For Vera Brittain (1893–1970), as for so many in her generation, the war became life's defining experience, which she captured forever in her famous autobiography, *Testament of Youth* (1933).

Brittain grew up in a wealthy business family in northern England, bristling at small-town conventions and discrimination against women. Very close to her brother Edward, two years her junior, Brittain read voraciously and dreamed of being a successful writer. Finishing boarding school and beating down her father's objections, she prepared for Oxford's rigorous entry exams and won a scholarship to its women's college. Brittain also fell in love with Roland Leighton, an equally brilliant student from a literary family and her brother's best friend. All three, along with two more close friends, Victor Richardson and Geoffrey Thurlow, confidently prepared to enter Oxford in late 1914.

When war suddenly approached in July 1914, Brittain shared with millions of Europeans a thrilling surge of patriotic support for her government, a pro-war enthusiasm she later played down in her published writings. She wrote in her diary that her "great fear" was that England would declare its neutrality and commit the "grossest treachery" toward France.* She seconded Roland's decision to enlist, agreeing with her sweetheart's glamorous view of war as "very ennobling and very beautiful." Later, exchanging anxious letters in 1915 with Roland in France, Vera began to see the conflict in personal, human terms. She wondered if any victory or defeat could be worth Roland's life.

Struggling to quell her doubts, Brittain redoubled her commitment to England's cause and volunteered as an army nurse. For the next three years she served with distinction in military hospitals in London, Malta, and northern France, repeatedly torn between the vision of noble sacrifice and the reality of human tragedy. She lost her sexual inhibitions caring for mangled male bodies, and she longed to consummate her love with Roland. Awaiting his return on leave on Christmas Day in 1915, she was greeted instead with a telegram: Roland had been killed two days before.

Roland's death was the first of the devastating blows that eventually overwhelmed Brittain's idealistic patriotism. In 1917, first Geoffrey and then Victor died from gruesome wounds. In early 1918, as the last great German offensive covered the floors of her war-zone hospital with maimed and dying German prisoners, the bone-weary Vera felt a common humanity and saw only more victims. A few weeks later brother Edward—her last hope—died in action. When the war ended, she was, she said, a "complete automaton," with "my deepest emotions paralyzed if not dead."

Returning to Oxford and finishing her studies, Brittain gradually recovered. She formed a deep, restorative friendship with another talented woman writer, Winifred Holtby, published novels and articles, and became a leader in the feminist campaign for gender equality. She also married and had children. But her wartime memories were always there. Finally, Brittain succeeded in coming to grips with them in *Testament of Youth,* her powerful antiwar autobiography. The unflinching narrative spoke to the experiences of an entire generation and became a runaway bestseller. Above all, perhaps, Brittain captured the ambivalent, contradictory character of the war, when millions of young people found excitement, courage, and common purpose but succeeded only in destroying their lives with their superhuman efforts and futile sacrifices. Becoming ever more committed to pacifism, Brittain opposed England's entry into World War II.

Questions for Analysis

1. What were Brittain's initial feelings toward the war? How did they change as the conflict continued? Why did they change?

2. Why did Brittain volunteer as a nurse, as many women did? How might wartime nursing have influenced women of her generation?

3. In portraying the ambivalent, contradictory character of World War I for Europe's youth, was Brittain describing the contradictory character of all modern warfare?

*Quoted in the excellent study by P. Berry and M. Bostridge, *Vera Brittain: A Life* (London: Virago Press, 2001), p. 59; additional quotes are from pp. 80 and 136. This work is highly recommended.

THE RUSSIAN REVOLUTION

How and why did the war lead to the Russian Revolution?

The 1917 Russian Revolution, directly related to the Great War, had a significance far beyond the wartime agonies of a single European nation. The Russian Revolution opened a new era, with a radically new prototype of state and society.

The Fall of Imperial Russia

Like their allies and their enemies, Russians embraced war with patriotic enthusiasm in 1914. At the Winter Palace, while kneeling throngs sang "God Save the Tsar," Tsar Nicholas II (r. 1894–1917) vowed never to make peace as long as the enemy stood on Russian soil. For a moment Russia was united. But soon the war began to take its toll.

Unprecedented artillery barrages quickly exhausted Russia's supplies of shells and ammunition, and better-equipped German armies inflicted terrible losses—one and a half million casualties and nearly another million captured in 1915 alone. In that year substantial numbers of Russian soldiers were sent to the front without rifles; they were told to find their arms among the dead. Nevertheless, Russia's battered peasant army continued to fight courageously. The Duma, (the lower house of the Russian parliament) and local governments led the effort toward full mobilization, setting up special committees to coordinate defense, industry, transportation, and agriculture. Although these efforts improved the military situation some, there were many failures, and Russia mobilized less effectively for total war than did the other warring nations.

The great problem was leadership. Under the constitution resulting from the 1905 revolution (see pages 694–695), the tsar retained complete control over the bureaucracy and the army. A kindly, slightly stupid man, Nicholas failed to form a close partnership with his citizens in order to fight the war more effectively. He relied instead on the old bureaucratic apparatus, distrusting the moderate Duma, rejecting popular involvement, and resisting calls to share power. As a result, the Duma, the educated middle classes, and the masses became increasingly critical of the tsar's leadership. In response, Nicholas announced in September 1915 that he was traveling to the front to lead Russia's armies.

His departure was a fatal turning point, as the hysterical German-born empress, Tsarina Alexandra, now took control of the government. She tried to rule absolutely in her husband's absence with an uneducated Siberian preacher, appropriately nicknamed "Rasputin" (Russian for the "Degenerate"), as her most trusted adviser. Rasputin gained her trust by miraculously stopping the bleeding, perhaps through hypnosis, of her hemophiliac son Alexis, Alexandra's fifth child and heir to the throne. In this atmosphere of unreality the government slid steadily toward revolution.

In a desperate attempt to right the situation, three members of the high aristocracy murdered Rasputin in December 1916, sending the empress into semipermanent shock. In the meantime, food shortages worsened and morale declined. On March 8 a women's bread march in Petrograd (formerly St. Petersburg) started riots, which spread throughout the city. The tsar ordered troops to restore order, but discipline broke down, and the soldiers joined the revolutionary crowd. The Duma declared a provisional government on March 12, 1917. Three days later Nicholas abdicated.

The Provisional Government

The March revolution was joyfully accepted throughout the country. After generations of arbitrary authoritarianism, the provisional government quickly established equality before the law; freedom of religion, speech, and assembly; the right of unions to organize and strike; and other classic liberal measures. But both moderate socialist and liberal leaders of the provisional government rejected social revolution. The government formed in May 1917, which included the socialist Alexander Kerensky, refused to confiscate large landholdings and give them to peasants, fearing that such drastic action in the countryside would only complete the disintegration of Russia's peasant army. For the patriotic Kerensky, who became prime minister in July, as for other moderate socialists, the continuation of war was still the all-important national duty. There would be plenty of time for land reform later; for now all the government's efforts were directed toward a last offensive in July. Meanwhile human suffering and warweariness grew, sapping the provisional government's limited strength.

From its first day the provisional government had to share power with a formidable rival—the **Petrograd Soviet** (or council) of Workers' and Soldiers' Deputies. Modeled on the revolutionary soviets of 1905, the Petrograd Soviet was a huge, fluctuating mass meeting of two thousand to three thousand workers, soldiers, and socialist intellectuals. This counter- or half-government issued its own radical orders, further weakening the provisional government. Most famous of these was **Army Order No. 1** (March 1917), which stripped officers of their authority and gave power to elected committees of common soldiers.

Army Order No. 1 led to a total collapse of army discipline and the summary execution of many an officer. Meanwhile, masses of peasant soldiers began "voting with their feet," to use Lenin's graphic phrase. They returned to their villages to get a share of the land, which peasants were simply seizing from landowners in a great agrarian upheaval. Liberty was turning into anarchy in the summer of 1917, offering an unparalleled opportunity for the most radical and most talented of Russia's many socialist leaders, Vladimir Ilyich Lenin (1870–1924).

Lenin and the Bolshevik Revolution

Lenin's whole life had been dedicated to the revolutionary cause. Born into the middle class, Lenin became an implacable enemy of imperial Russia when his older brother was executed for plotting to kill the tsar in 1887. As a law student Lenin began searching for a revolutionary faith and found it in Marxian socialism. Exiled to Siberia for three years because of socialist agitation, Lenin studied Marxian doctrines with religious ferocity. After his release he lived for seventeen years in western Europe and developed his own revolutionary interpretations of Marxian thought.

Three interrelated ideas were central for Lenin. First, turning to the early firebreathing Marx of 1848 and *The Communist Manifesto* for inspiration, Lenin stressed that only violent revolution could destroy capitalism. Lenin's second, more original idea was that a socialist revolution was possible even in a country like Russia, where capitalism was not fully developed. There the industrial working class was small, but the poor peasants were also potential revolutionaries.

● **"The Russian Ruling House"** This wartime cartoon captures the ominous, spellbinding power of Rasputin over Tsar Nicholas II and his wife, Alexandra. Rasputin's manipulations disgusted Russian public opinion and contributed to the monarchy's collapse. *(Stock Montage)*

Petrograd Soviet
A counter-government that was a huge, fluctuating mass meeting of two to three thousand workers, soldiers, and socialist intellectuals.

Army Order No. 1 *A radical order of the Petrograd Soviet that stripped officers of their authority and placed power in the hands of elected committees of common soldiers.*

● **Lenin Rallies Worker and Soldier Delegates**   At a midnight meeting of the Petrograd Soviet, the Bolsheviks rise up and seize power on November 6, 1917. This painting from the 1940s idealizes Lenin, but his great talents as a revolutionary leader are undeniable. In this re-creation Stalin, who actually played only a small role in the uprising, is standing behind Lenin, already his trusty right-hand man. *(Sovfoto)*

Bolsheviks   *The "majority group"; this was Lenin's camp of the Russian party of Marxian socialism.*

Lenin believed that at a given moment revolution was determined more by human leadership than by vast historical laws. Thus was born his third basic idea: the necessity of a highly disciplined workers' party, strictly controlled by a dedicated elite, a vanguard, of intellectuals and full-time revolutionaries like Lenin himself. This elite would not stop until revolution brought it to power.

Lenin's theories and methods did not go unchallenged by other Russian Marxists. At a Social Democratic Labor Party congress in London in 1903, Lenin demanded a small, disciplined, elitist party; his opponents wanted a more democratic party with mass membership. The Russian party of Marxian socialism was divided then into two rival factions. Lenin's camp was called **Bolsheviks,** or "majority group"; his opponents were *Mensheviks,* or "minority group." Lenin's majority did not last, but he kept the Bolshevik name and developed the party he wanted anyhow: tough, disciplined, revolutionary.

Lenin, from neutral Switzerland, saw the war as a product of imperialistic rivalries and as a marvelous opportunity for class war and socialist upheaval. After the March revolution the German government provided safe passage for Lenin, his wife, and about twenty trusted colleagues across Germany and back into Russia in April 1917. The Germans hoped that Lenin would undermine Russia's sagging war effort. They were not disappointed.

Arriving triumphantly at Petrograd's Finland Station on April 3, Lenin attacked at once. To the great astonishment of the local Bolsheviks, he rejected all cooperation with the "bourgeois" provisional government of the liberals and moderate socialists. His slogans were radical in the extreme: "All power to the soviets"; "All land to the peasants"; "Stop the war now." Never a slave to Marxian determinism, Lenin was a superb tactician and realized his moment had come.

Throughout the summer the Bolsheviks markedly increased their popular support, while Prime Minister Kerensky's unwavering support for the war lost him all credit with the army, the only force that might have saved him and democratic government in Russia. In October the Bolsheviks gained a fragile majority in the Petrograd Soviet. It was Lenin's supporter Leon Trotsky (1879–1940), an independent radical Marxist, who brilliantly executed the Bolshevik seizure of power. On the night of November 6, militant Trotsky followers from the Petrograd Soviet joined with trusty Bolshevik soldiers to seize government buildings and arrest provisional government members. At the congress of soviets a Bolshevik majority—roughly 390 of 650 turbulent delegates—then declared that all power had passed to the soviets and named Lenin head of the new government.

The Bolsheviks came to power for three key reasons. First, by late 1917 democracy had given way to anarchy, leaving a power vacuum. Second, in Lenin and Trotsky the Bolsheviks had an utterly determined and truly superior leadership. Third, in 1917

The Russian Revolution

1914	Russia enthusiastically enters the First World War.
1915	Russia suffers one and a half million casualties. Progressive bloc calls for a new government responsible to the Duma rather than to the tsar. Tsar Nicholas adjourns the Duma and departs for the front; Alexandra and Rasputin exert a strong influence on the government.
December 1916	Rasputin is murdered.
March 8, 1917	Bread riots take place in Petrograd (St. Petersburg).
March 12, 1917	Duma declares a provisional government.
March 15, 1917	Tsar Nicholas abdicates without protest.
April 3, 1917	Lenin returns from exile and denounces the provisional government.
May 1917	Reorganized provisional government, including Kerensky, continues the war. Petrograd Soviet issues Army Order No. 1, granting military power to committees of common soldiers.
Summer 1917	Agrarian upheavals: peasants seize estates; peasant soldiers desert the army to participate.
October 1917	Bolsheviks gain a majority in the Petrograd Soviet.
November 6, 1917	Bolsheviks seize power; Lenin heads the new "provisional workers' and peasants' government."
November 1917	Lenin accepts peasant seizure of land and worker control of factories; all banks are nationalized.
January 1918	Lenin permanently disbands the Constituent Assembly.
February 1918	Lenin convinces the Bolshevik Central Committee to accept a humiliating peace with Germany in order to safeguard the revolution.
March 1918	Treaty of Brest-Litovsk: Russia loses one-third of its population. Trotsky as war commissar begins to rebuild the Russian army.
Summer 1918	White armies oppose the Bolshevik Revolution.
1918–1922	Great civil war takes place.
1919	White armies are on the offensive but divided politically; they receive little benefit from Allied intervention.
1922	Lenin and the Red Army are victorious.

the Bolsheviks appealed to many soldiers and urban workers, people who were exhausted by war and eager for socialism.

Dictatorship and Civil War

History is full of short-lived coups and unsuccessful revolutions. The truly monumental accomplishment of Lenin, Trotsky, and the rest of the Bolsheviks was not taking power but keeping it and conquering the chaos they had helped create. How was this done?

Lenin had the genius to profit from developments over which he and the Bolsheviks had no control. Since summer 1917 an unstoppable peasant revolution had been sweeping across Russia as peasants seized and divided among themselves the estates of the landlords and the church. Thus Lenin's first law, which supposedly gave land to

● "You! Have You Volunteered?" A Red Army soldier makes a compelling direct appeal to the ordinary citizen and demands all-out support for the Bolshevik cause in this 1920 poster by Dmitri Moor, a popular Soviet artist. Lenin recognized the importance of visual propaganda in a vast country with limited literacy, and mass-produced posters like this one were everywhere during the civil war of 1918–1922. *(Stephen White, University of Glasgow)*

Constituent Assembly *A freely elected assembly promised by the Bolsheviks that was permanently disbanded after one day on Lenin's orders after Bolshevik delegates won fewer than one-fourth of the seats.*

war communism *The application of the total-war concept to a civil conflict; the Bolsheviks seized grain from peasants, introduced rationing, nationalized all banks and industry, and required everyone to work.*

the peasants, actually merely approved what peasants were already doing. Lenin then met urban workers' greatest demand with a decree in November 1917 giving direct control of individual factories to local workers' committees.

Lenin also acknowledged that Russia had lost the war with Germany and that the only realistic position was peace at any price. That price was very high. Germany demanded in December 1917 that the Soviet government give up all its western territories. These areas were inhabited by Poles, Finns, Lithuanians, and other non-Russians. The Bolsheviks surrendered a third of old Russia's population in the Treaty of Brest-Litovsk in March 1918. With peace, however, Lenin had escaped the certain disaster of continued war and could pursue his goal of absolute political power for the Bolsheviks—now renamed Communists—within Russia.

In November 1917 the Bolsheviks had cleverly proclaimed their regime only a "provisional workers' and peasants' government," promising that a freely elected **Constituent Assembly** would draw up a new constitution. But after Bolshevik delegates won fewer than one-fourth of the seats, the Constituent Assembly met for only one day, on January 18, 1918. Bolshevik soldiers acting under Lenin's orders then permanently disbanded it.

The destruction of the democratically elected Constituent Assembly revealed the Bolsheviks' true intentions, and people who had risen up for self-rule in November realized they were again getting dictatorship from the capital. For the next three years "Long live the [democratic] soviets; down with the Bolsheviks" was a popular slogan. Officers of the old army organized the so-called White opposition to the Bolsheviks in southern Russia, Ukraine, Siberia, and west of Petrograd. The Whites came from many social groups united only by their hatred of the Bolsheviks—the Reds. By the end of 1918 White armies were on the attack. In October 1919 it appeared they might triumph as they closed in on Lenin's government from three sides. Yet they did not. Intense fighting continued through 1920, and the tide turned. Although some White forces held out until 1923, the Red Army captured Vladivostok in October 1922 and that effectively marked the end of the civil war. Lenin had won.

Lenin and the Bolsheviks won for several reasons. Strategically, they controlled the center, while the Whites were always on the fringes and disunited. Moreover, the poorly defined political program of the Whites was vaguely conservative, and it did not unite all the foes of the Bolsheviks under a progressive, democratic banner. Most important, the Communists quickly developed a better army, an army for which the divided Whites were no match.

The Bolsheviks also mobilized the home front. Establishing **war communism**—the application of the total-war concept to a civil conflict—they seized grain from peasants, introduced rationing, nationalized all banks and industry, and required everyone to work. Although these measures contributed to a breakdown of normal economic activity, they also served to maintain labor discipline and to keep the Red Army supplied.

"Revolutionary terror" also contributed to the Communist victory. The old tsarist secret police was reestablished as the **Cheka,** which hunted down and executed thousands of real or supposed foes, such as the tsar and his family and other "class enemies." The terror caused by the secret police became a tool of the government. The Cheka sowed fear, and fear silenced opposition.

Finally, foreign military intervention in the civil war ended up helping the Communists. The Allies (the Americans, British, and Japanese) sent troops to Archangel and Vladivostok to prevent war materiel that they had sent to the provisional government from being captured by the Germans. After the Soviet government nationalized all foreign-owned factories without compensation and refused to pay all of Russia's foreign debts, Western governments, particularly France, began to support White armies. While these small and halfhearted efforts did little to help the Whites' cause, they did permit the Communists to appeal to the patriotic nationalism of ethnic Russians.

Together, the Russian Revolution and the Bolshevik triumph were one reason why the First World War was such a major turning point in modern history. A radically new government, based on socialism and one-party dictatorship, came to power in a great European state, maintained power, and eagerly encouraged worldwide revolution. Although Russia was undoubtedly headed for some kind of political crisis before 1914, it is hard to imagine the triumph of the most radical proponents of change and reform except in a situation of total collapse. That was precisely what happened to Russia in the First World War.

Cheka *The re-established tsarist secret police, which hunted down and executed thousands of real or suspected foes, sowing fear and silencing opposition.*

THE PEACE SETTLEMENT

Why is the peace settlement following World War I considered by most historians to have been a terrible failure?

Victory over revolutionary Russia temporarily boosted sagging German morale. In spring 1918 the Germans launched their last major attack against France. It failed. With breathtaking rapidity, the United States, Great Britain, and France then decisively defeated Germany militarily. Austria-Hungary and the Ottoman Empire broke apart and ceased to exist. The guns of world war finally fell silent. Then, as civil war spread in Russia and as chaos engulfed much of eastern Europe, the victorious Western Allies came together in Paris to establish a lasting peace.

Expectations were high; optimism almost unlimited. Laboring intensively, the allies soon worked out terms for peace with Germany and for the creation of the peacekeeping **League of Nations.** The 1919 peace settlement, however, turned out to be a failure and only sowed the seeds of another war. Surely this was the ultimate tragedy of the Great War that cost $332 billion and left 10 million people dead and another 20 million wounded. How did this tragedy happen? Why was the peace settlement unsuccessful?

League of Nations *A permanent international organization established during the peace conference in Paris in January 1919; it was designed to protect member states from aggression and avert future wars.*

The End of the War

After the March 1917 Russian Revolution, there were major strikes in Germany. To quell these demonstrations and counter a growing peace movement, the German military established a virtual dictatorship and exploited the collapse of Russian armies in the harsh Treaty of Brest-Litovsk. With victory in the east quieting German moderates, General Ludendorff and company fell on France once more in the great spring offensive of 1918. For a time German armies pushed forward, coming within thirty-five miles of Paris, but they never broke through. They were decisively stopped in July at the second Battle of the Marne, where 140,000 fresh American soldiers saw action.

Adding 2 million men in arms to the war effort by August, the late but massive American intervention decisively tipped the scales in favor of Allied victory.

By September British, French, and American armies were advancing steadily on all fronts. On October 4 the emperor formed a new, more liberal German government to sue for peace. As negotiations over an armistice dragged on, an angry and frustrated German people finally rose up. On November 3 sailors in Kiel mutinied, and throughout northern Germany soldiers and workers established revolutionary councils on the Russian soviet model. Austria-Hungary surrendered to the Allies the same day. With army discipline collapsing, the German emperor abdicated and fled to Holland. Socialist leaders in Berlin proclaimed a German republic on November 9 and simultaneously agreed to tough Allied terms of surrender. The armistice went into effect at 11 A.M. on November 11, 1918. The war was over.

The German Revolution of November 1918 resembled the Russian Revolution of March 1917. In both countries a popular uprising toppled an authoritarian monarchy, and moderate socialists took control of the government. But when Germany's radical socialists tried to seize power, the moderate socialists called on the army to crush the attempted coup. Thus Germany had a political revolution, but without a communist second installment. It was Russia without Lenin's Bolshevik triumph.

Military defeat brought political revolution to Austria-Hungary, as it had to Germany, Russia, and the Ottoman Empire (see pages 848–854). In Austria-Hungary the revolution was primarily nationalistic and republican in character. Independent Austrian, Hungarian, and Czechoslovak republics were proclaimed. A greatly expanded Serbian monarchy united the South Slavs and took the name Yugoslavia. The prospect of firmly establishing the new national states overrode class considerations for most people in east-central Europe.

The Treaty of Versailles

The peace conference opened in the Versailles Palace near Paris in January 1919 with seventy delegates representing twenty-seven victorious nations. There were great expectations. A young British diplomat later wrote that the victors "believed in nationalism, we believed in the self-determination of peoples." Indeed, "we were journeying to Paris . . . to found a new order in Europe. We were preparing not Peace only, but Eternal Peace."[5] This general optimism and idealism had been greatly strengthened by President Wilson's January 1918 peace proposal, the Fourteen Points, which stressed national self-determination and the rights of small countries.

The real powers at the conference were the United States, Great Britain, and France. Germany was not allowed to participate, and Russia was locked in civil war and did not attend. Italy was considered one of the Big Four, but its role was quite limited. Almost immediately the three Allies began to quarrel. President Wilson insisted that the first order of business be the creation of the League of Nations, for he passionately believed that only a permanent international organization could protect member states from aggression and avert future wars. Wilson had his way, although Lloyd George of Great Britain and especially Clemenceau of France were unenthusiastic. They were primarily concerned with punishing Germany.

Playing on British nationalism, Lloyd George had already won a smashing electoral victory in December on the popular platform of making Germany pay for the war. Although personally inclined to make a somewhat moderate peace with Germany, Lloyd George was a captive of demands for a total victory worthy of the sacrifices of total war against a totally depraved enemy. As Rudyard Kipling summed up the general British feeling at war's end, the Germans were "a people with the heart of beasts."[6]

France's Georges Clemenceau, like most French people, also wanted old-fashioned revenge. In addition, he wanted lasting security for France, which, he believed, required the creation of a buffer state between France and Germany, the permanent demilitarization of Germany, and vast German reparations. Otherwise, he feared, Germany would sooner or later attack France again. Moreover, France had no English Channel (or Atlantic Ocean) as a reassuring barrier against German aggression. Wilson, supported by Lloyd George, would hear none of this. Clemenceau's demands seemed vindictive, violating morality and the principle of national self-determination. By April the conference was deadlocked on the German question, and Wilson packed his bags to go home.

In the end, Clemenceau agreed to a compromise. He gave up the French demand for a Rhineland buffer state in return for a formal defensive alliance with the United States and Great Britain. Both Wilson and Lloyd George also promised their countries would come to France's aid if attacked. Thus Clemenceau appeared to win his goal of French security, as Wilson had won his of a permanent international organization.

The terms of the **Treaty of Versailles** between the Allies and Germany were not unreasonable as a first step toward re-establishing international order. Germany's colonies were given to France, Britain, and Japan as League of Nations mandates. Germany's territorial losses within Europe were minor, thanks to Wilson. Alsace-Lorraine was returned to France. Parts of Germany inhabited primarily by Poles were ceded to the new Polish state, in keeping with the principle of national self-determination. The treaty limited Germany's army to one hundred thousand men and allowed no new military fortifications in the Rhineland (see Map 27.4).

● **The Allied Leaders at Versailles** The old tiger, Clemenceau of France, gestures with his walking stick to the scholarly Woodrow Wilson, as the strong-willed Lloyd George strides forward on the left. The negotiations at Versailles were difficult and often bitter, but the Allies reached a compromise agreement and imposed it on Germany. *(Corbis)*

More harshly, the Allies declared that Germany (with Austria) was responsible for the war and had therefore to pay reparations equal to all civilian damages caused by the war. These much-criticized "war-guilt" and "reparations" clauses expressed inescapable popular demands for German blood. The actual reparations figure was not set, however, and there was the clear possibility it might be set at a reasonable level in the future when tempers had cooled.

When presented with the treaty, the German government protested vigorously, but there was no alternative. On June 28, 1919, German representatives of the ruling moderate Social Democrats and Catholic parties signed the treaty in the Hall of Mirrors at Versailles.

The Allies concluded separate peace treaties with the other defeated powers—Austria, Hungary, Bulgaria, and Turkey. For the most part these treaties merely ratified the existing situation in east-central Europe following the breakup of the Austro-Hungarian Empire (see Map 27.4). Like Austria, Hungary was a particularly big loser, as its "captive" nationalities (and some interspersed Hungarians) were ceded to Romania, Czechoslovakia, Poland, and Yugoslavia. Italy acquired some Austrian territory. The Ottoman Empire was broken up. France received Lebanon and Syria. Britain took Iraq and Palestine, which was to include a Jewish national homeland first

Treaty of Versailles *The World War I treaty that declared Germany responsible for the war; it limited Germany's army to one hundred thousand men and forced Germany to pay reparations equal to all civilian damages caused by the war.*

Primary Source: The Zionist Organization's Memorandum to the Peace Conference in Versailles *See how the Zionist Organization promoted the idea of a Jewish state in Palestine to the Allies meeting in Versailles.*

MAP 27.4 **Territorial Changes in Europe After World War I** The Great War brought tremendous changes to eastern Europe. Empires were shattered, and new nations were established. A dangerous power vacuum was created between Germany and Soviet Russia.

promised by Britain in 1917. Officially League of Nations mandates, these Allied acquisitions were one of the most imperialistic elements of the peace settlement. Another was mandating Germany's holdings in China to Japan (see page 862). The age of Western, and Eastern, imperialism lived on.

American Rejection of the Versailles Treaty

The 1919 peace settlement was not perfect, but for war-shattered Europe it was an acceptable beginning. The organizing framework was national self-determination, which had played such a critical role in starting the war. Germany was punished but not dismembered. A new world organization complemented a traditional defensive alliance of victorious powers. The serious remaining problems could be worked out in the future. Moreover, Allied leaders wanted a quick settlement for another reason: they detested Lenin and feared his Bolshevik Revolution might spread. The best answer to Lenin's unending calls for worldwide upheaval, they realized, was peace and tranquility for war-weary peoples.

There were, however, two great interrelated obstacles to such peace: Germany and the United States. Plagued by communist uprisings, reactionary plots, and popular disillusionment with losing the war, Germany's moderate socialists and their liberal and Catholic supporters faced an enormous challenge. They needed time (and luck) if they were to establish firmly a peaceful and democratic republic. Progress in this direction required understanding yet firm treatment of Germany by the victorious Western Allies.

In the United States, there was a quick reversion to prewar preferences for isolationism and no entangling alliances, which caused the U.S. Senate and, to a lesser extent, the American people to reject Wilson's handiwork. Republican senators led by Henry Cabot Lodge refused to ratify the Treaty of Versailles without changes in the articles creating the League of Nations. The key issue was the League's power—more apparent than real—to require member states to take collective action against aggression. Opponents believed this requirement gave away Congress's constitutional right to declare war. In failing health, Wilson rejected all attempts at compromise, and thereby ensured the treaty would never be ratified by the United States in any form and the United States would never join the League of Nations. Moreover, the Senate refused to ratify Wilson's defensive alliance with France and Great Britain. America turned its back on Europe.

The Wilson-Lodge fiasco and return to isolationism represented a tragic and cowardly renunciation of America's responsibility. Using America's action as an excuse, Great Britain, too, refused to ratify its defensive alliance with France. Betrayed by its allies, France would very shortly take actions against Germany that fed the fires of German resentment and seriously undermined democratic forces in the new German republic. The great hopes of early 1919 had turned to ashes by year's end. The Western alliance had collapsed, and a grandiose plan for permanent peace had given way to a fragile truce. For this and for what came later, the United States must share a large part of the blame.

Chapter Summary

To assess your mastery of this chapter, go to
bedfordstmartins.com/mckayworld

• *How did Europe's system of alliances contribute to the outbreak of World War I?*

Following the Franco-Prussian War of 1870–1871, the German Chancellor Otto van Bismarck sought to maintain peace in Europe by negotiating a series of alliances among the various nations. When Kaiser William II became German emperor in 1888, however, he forced Bismarck to resign, refused to renew the Russian-German Reinsurance Treaty, and raised tensions across Europe. He caused France and Russia to join together against the Triple Alliance of Germany, Austria, and Italy, and he also alienated Great Britain, which later joined France and Russia in an alliance known as the Triple Entente. Commercial rivalry between Great Britain and Germany and Germany's challenge to Great Britain's long-standing naval supremacy also drove the two great powers further apart. Europe's leaders allowed extreme nationalism and militarism to dictate

Key Terms

Three Emperors' League
Triple Entente
trench warfare
Lusitania
total war
War Raw Materials Board
Auxiliary Service Law
Petrograd Soviet
Army Order No. 1
Bolsheviks
Constituent Assembly
war communism
Cheka
League of Nations
Treaty of Versailles

political decisions and foreign policy. Austria's attack on Serbia in July 1914 seemed to set the two great alliances in motion, like giant machines, blindly fulfilling their security obligations to their allies and moving inexorably to war.

• How did total war impact the home fronts of the major European combatants?

The Great War as a total war caused an administrative revolution that continues to influence European governments today. This revolution, born of the need to mobilize entire societies and economies for total war, greatly increased government power in the West. After the guns grew still, government planning of highly complicated economies and wholesale involvement in daily social life did not disappear. Liberal market capitalism and a well-integrated world economy were among the many casualties of the administrative revolution, and greater social equality, particularly for women and workers, was everywhere one of its results. Thus even in European countries where a communist takeover never came close to occurring, society still experienced a great revolution, and socialism became a realistic economic blueprint that many countries adopted.

• How and why did the war lead to the Russian Revolution?

After three years of horrible slaughter on the eastern front, the Russian people were tired of the autocratic rule of Tsar Nicholas II and wanted change. In March 1917 the Tsar abdicated, and the reins of government were taken over by a provisional government controlled by moderate social democrats under the leadership of Alexander Kerensky. Kerensky refused to pull Russia out of the war, however, and the massive waste of Russian lives continued until army discipline completely collapsed in resistance to the war. This opened the way for a second Russian revolution, this time led by Vladimir Lenin and his communist Bolshevik party, in November 1917. The Bolsheviks established a radical regime, smashed existing capitalist institutions, and stayed in power with a new kind of authoritarian rule. Whether the new Russian regime was truly Marxian or socialist was questionable, but it indisputably posed a powerful, ongoing revolutionary challenge to Europe and its colonial empires.

• Why is the peace settlement following World War I considered by most historians to have been a terrible failure?

Finally, the "war to end war" brought not peace but only a fragile truce. Over President Woodrow Wilson's protests, France and Great Britain viewed the Versailles Treaty as an opportunity to take revenge on Germany for the war and to ruin it. The treaty denied Germany an empire by taking away its colonies; militarily the treaty forced Germany to destroy its army and navy; and economically the victors demanded exorbitant war reparations. The Allies also took control of key Germany industries and raw material producing regions. And the Germans were humiliated by a key article in the treaty that forced them to take full responsibility for causing the war. While the Allies failed to maintain their wartime solidarity, Germany remained unrepentant and soon had more grievances to nurse. The vengeful treaty allowed Adolf Hitler to rally the German people around him, to promise to restore Germany to its former greatness, and to lead them into World War II with visions of national (and Germanic) glory.

Suggested Reading

Ecksteins, Modris. *Rites of Spring: The Great War and the Birth of the Modern Age.* 1989. An imaginative cultural investigation that has won critical acclaim.

Ellis, John. *Eye-Deep in Hell.* 1976. A vivid account of trench warfare.

Fromkin, David. *Europe's Last Summer: Who Started the Great War?* 2004. Well-argued, compulsively readable discussion of responsibility for the war by a master historian.

Fussell, Paul. *The Great War and Modern Memory.* 1975. Probes all the powerful literature inspired by the war.

Gilbert, Martin. *The First World War: A Complete History.* 1994. Comprehensive in one volume by a major military historian.

Gorham, Deborah. *Vera Brittain: A Feminist Life.* 1996. A major study of Brittain's life.

Hobsbawm, Eric. *The Age of Extremes: A History of the World, 1914–1991.* 1996. Offers a provocative interpretation of the "short twentieth century," with a good description of war and revolution.

Macmillan, Margaret. *Paris, 1919: Six Months That Changed the World.* 2001. A masterful account of the negotiations and the issues at the Versailles Peace Conference.

Massie, Raymond. *Nicholas and Alexandra.* 1971. A moving popular biography of Russia's last royal family and the terrible health problem of the heir to the throne.

Ousby, Ian. *The Road to Verdun: World War I's Most Momentous Battle and the Folly of Nationalism.* 2002. A moving reconsideration of the famous siege.

Pasternak, Boris. *Doctor Zhivago.* 1958. A justly celebrated, great historical novel of the Russian Revolution era, including the civil war that followed, by a Nobel Prize–winning author.

Read, Christopher. *From Tsar to Soviets: The Russian People and Their Revolution, 1917–1921.* 1996. A social history of the revolution focusing on ordinary Russian men and women.

Reed, John. *Ten Days That Shook the World.* 1919. The classic eyewitness account of the Russian Revolution by a young, pro-Bolshevik American.

Strachan, Hew. *The First World War.* 2004. Thorough one-volume history by one of the premier Great War historians.

Tuchman, Barbara. *The Guns of August.* 1962. A marvelous account of the dramatic first month of the war and the beginning of the military stalemate.

Volkogonov, Dmitri. *Lenin: A New Biography.* 1994. A lively study with some new revelations by a well-known postcommunist Russian historian.

Wade, Rex. *The Russian Revolution, 1917.* 2000. Comprehensive and accessible history of the revolution.

Wall, Richard, and Jay Winter, eds. *The Upheaval of War: Family, Work, and Welfare in Europe, 1914–1918.* 1988. An excellent collection of essays that probes the enormous consequences of the war for people and society.

Notes

1. M. Beloff, quoted in *U.S. News & World Report,* March 8, 1976, p. 53.
2. Quoted in J. Remak, *The Origins of World War I* (New York: Holt, Rinehart & Winston, 1967), p. 84.
3. Quoted in F. P. Chambers, *The War Behind the War, 1914–1918* (London: Faber & Faber, 1939), p. 168.
4. Quoted in R. O. Paxton, *Europe in the Twentieth Century* (New York: Harcourt Brace Jovanovich, 1975), p. 109.
5. H. Nicolson, *Peacemaking 1919* (New York: Grosset & Dunlap Universal Library, 1965), pp. 8, 31–32.
6. Quoted ibid., p. 24.

Listening to the
PAST

The Experience of War

World War I was a total war: it enlisted the efforts of men, women, adults, and children, both at home and on the battlefield. It was a terrifying and painful experience for all those involved. To be sure, it was not the romantic endeavor it was purported to be. The documents below offer two different wartime experiences. The first excerpt is from a letter written by a German soldier fighting in the trenches. The second is from the diary of a Viennese woman. As you read both passages, think about the different ways war and its consequences were made real for these two people.

A German Soldier Writes from the Trenches, March 1915

Souchez, March 11th, 1915
"So fare you well, for we must now be parting," so run the first lines of a soldier-song which we often sang through the streets of the capital. These words are truer than ever now, and these lines are to bid farewell to you, to all my nearest and dearest, to all who wish me well or ill, and to all that I value and prize.

Our regiment has been transferred to this dangerous spot, Souchez. No end of blood has already flowed down this hill. A week ago the 142nd attacked and took four trenches from the French. It is to hold these trenches that we have been brought here. There is something uncanny about this hill-position. Already, times without number, other battalions of our regiment have been ordered here in support, and each time the company came back with a loss of twenty, thirty or more men. In the days when we had to stick it out here before, we had 22 killed and 27 wounded. Shells roar, bullets whistle; no dugouts, or very bad ones; mud, clay, filth, shell-holes so deep that one could bathe in them.

This letter has been interrupted no end of times. Shells began to pitch close to us—great English 12-inch ones—and we had to take refuge in a cellar. One such shell struck the next house and buried four men, who were got out from the ruins horribly mutilated. I saw them and it was ghastly!

Everybody must be prepared now for death in some form or other. Two cemeteries have been made up here, the losses have been so great. I ought not to write that to you, but I do so all the same, because the newspapers have probably given you quite a different impression. They tell only of our gains and say nothing about the blood that has been shed, of the cries of agony that never cease. The newspaper doesn't give any description either of *how* the "heroes" are laid to rest, though it talks about "heroes' graves" and writes poems and such-like about them. Certainly in Lens I have attended funeral-parades where a number of dead were buried in one large grave with pomp and circumstance. But up here it is pitiful the way one throws the dead bodies out of the trench and lets them lie there, or scatters dirt over the remains of those which have been torn to pieces by shells.

I look upon death and call upon life. I have not accomplished much in my short life, which has been chiefly occupied with study. I have commended my soul to the Lord God. It bears His seal and is altogether His. Now I am free to dare anything. My future life belongs to God, my present one to the Fatherland, and I myself still possess happiness and strength.

A Viennese Woman Remembers Home Front Life

Ten dekagrammes [3½ ounces] of horse-flesh per head are to be given out to-day for the week. The cavalry horses held in reserve by the military authorities are being slaughtered for lack of fodder, and the people of Vienna are for a change to get a few mouthfuls of meat of which they have so long been deprived. Horse-flesh! I should like to know whether my instinctive repugnance to horse-flesh as food is personal, or whether my dislike is shared by many other housewives. My loathing of it is based, I believe, not on a physical but on a psychological prejudice.

I overcame my repugnance, rebuked myself for being sentimental, and left the house. A soft, steady rain was falling, from which I tried to protect myself with galoshes, waterproof, and umbrella. As I left the house before seven o'clock and the meat distribution

A ration coupon used in the city of Eisenberg showing Germans waiting in line for their meager rations. *(akg-images)*

did not begin until nine o'clock, I hoped to get well to the front of the queue.

No sooner had I reached the neighbourhood of the big market hall than I was instructed by the police to take a certain direction. I estimated the crowd waiting here for a meagre midday meal at two thousand at least. Hundreds of women had spent the night here in order to be among the first and make sure of getting their bit of meat. Many had brought with them improvised seats—a little box or a bucket turned upside down. No one seemed to mind the rain, although many were already wet through. They passed the time chattering, and the theme was the familiar one: What have you had to eat? What are you going to eat? One could scent an atmosphere of mistrust in these conversations: they were all careful not to say too much or to betray anything that might get them into trouble.

At length the sale began. Slowly, infinitely slowly, we moved forward. The most determined, who had spent the night outside the gates of the hall, displayed their booty to the waiting crowd: a ragged, quite freshly slaughtered piece of meat with the characteristic yellow fat. [Others] alarmed those standing at the back by telling them that there was only a very small supply of meat and that not half the people waiting would get a share of it. The crowd became very uneasy and impatient, and before the police on guard could prevent it, those standing in front organized an attack on the hall which the salesmen inside were powerless to repel. Everyone seized whatever he could lay his hands on, and in a few moments all the eatables had vanished. In the confusion stands were overturned, and the police forced back the aggressors and closed the gates. The crowds waiting outside, many of whom had been there all night and were soaked through, angrily demanded their due, whereupon the mounted police made a little charge, provoking a wild panic and much screaming and cursing. At length I reached home, depressed and disgusted, with a broken umbrella and only one galosh.

We housewives have during the last four years grown accustomed to standing in queues; we have also grown accustomed to being obliged to go home with empty hands and still emptier stomachs. Only very rarely do those who are sent away disappointed give cause for police intervention. On the other hand, it happens more and more frequently that one of the pale, tired women who have been waiting for hours collapses from exhaustion. The turbulent scenes which occurred to-day inside and outside the large market hall seemed to me perfectly natural. In my dejected mood the patient apathy with which we housewives endure seemed to me blameworthy and incomprehensible.

Questions for Analysis

1. How does the soldier see the war he is in? Is it a grand patriotic effort? Or is it a story of senseless bloodshed and loss of life?

2. How did the soldiers cope with the reality of war in the trenches?

3. How does the experience of the Viennese woman differ from the soldier's?

4. Were the women who pillaged the food hall "blameworthy" or "incomprehensible," as the Viennese woman put it?

Sources: Alfons Ankenbrand, in *German Students' War Letters,* ed. A. F. Wedd (London: Methuen, 1929), pp. 72–73; *Blockade: The Diary of an Austrian Middle-Class Woman, 1914–1924,* trans. Winifred Ray (New York: Ray Long & Richard Smith, 1932), pp. 63–68.

Victory at Smyrna. Turks celebrate victory over Greek forces at Smyrna in October 1922. This was one of the final battles in the Turkish War for Independence that led to establishing the Republic of Turkey in 1923.
(Price/Getty Images)

28 NATIONALISM IN ASIA, 1914–1939

Chapter Preview

The First World War and Western Imperialism

• How did modern nationalism—the dominant force in most of the world in the twentieth century—develop in Asia between the First and Second World Wars?

The Middle East

• How did the collapse of the Ottoman Empire in World War I shape the history of the Middle East for the rest of the century?

Toward Self-Rule in India

• What role did Gandhi and his campaign of militant nonviolence play in leading India to independence from the British?

Turmoil in East Asia

• Why did some of the Asian nationalist movements come into brutal conflict?

From Asia's perspective the First World War was largely a European civil war that shattered Western imperialism's united front and convulsed prewar relationships throughout Asia. Most crucially, the war speeded the development of modern nationalism in Asia. Before 1914 the nationalist gospel of anti-imperialist political freedom and racial equality had already won converts among Asia's westernized, educated elites. In the 1920s and 1930s it increasingly won the allegiance of the masses. As in nineteenth-century Europe, nationalism in Asia between 1914 and 1939 became a mass movement with potentially awesome power.

There were at least three reasons for the upsurge of nationalism in Asia. First and foremost, nationalism provided the most effective means of organizing the anti-imperialist resistance both to direct foreign rule and to indirect Western domination. Second, nationalism called for fundamental changes and challenged old political and social practices and beliefs. Thus modernizers used it to contest the influence and power of conservative traditionalists. Third, nationalism offered a vision of a free and prosperous future, and provided an ideology to ennoble the sacrifices the struggle would require.

Nationalism also had a dark side. As in Europe (see page 679), Asian nationalists developed a strong sense of "we" and "they." "They" were often the enemy—the oppressor. European imperialists were just such a "they," and nationalist feeling generated the power to destroy European empires and challenge foreign economic domination. But, as in Europe, Asian nationalism also stimulated bitter conflicts and wars between peoples, in two different ways.

First, it stimulated conflicts between relatively homogeneous peoples in large states, rallying, for example, Chinese against Japanese and vice versa. Second, nationalism often heightened tensions between ethnic (or religious) groups within states, especially states with diverse populations, like British India and the Ottoman Empire. Such states had been formed by authoritarian rulers and their armies and bureaucracies, very much like the Austro-Hungarian and Russian empires before 1914. When their rigid rule declined or snapped, the different nationalistic peoples might easily quarrel, seeking to divide the existing state or to dominate the enemy "they" within its borders.

The modern nationalism movement has never been monolithic. In Asia especially, where the new and often narrow ideology of nationalism was grafted onto old, rich, and complex civilizations, the range of historical experience has been enormous. Between the outbreak of the First and Second World Wars each Asian country developed a distinctive national movement rooted in its own unique culture and history. Each nation's people created their own national reawakening, which renovated thought and culture as well as politics and economics.

THE FIRST WORLD WAR AND WESTERN IMPERIALISM

How did modern nationalism—the dominant force in most of the world in the twentieth century—develop in Asia between the First and Second World Wars?

Every Asian national movement sought genuine freedom from foreign imperialism. The First World War profoundly affected these aspirations by altering relations between Asia and Europe. In the words of a distinguished Indian historian, "the Great War of 1914–1918 was from the Asian point of view a civil war within the European community of nations."[1] For four years Asians watched Kipling's haughty bearers of "the White Man's Burden" (see page 724) vilifying and destroying each other. Japan's defeat of imperial Russia in 1904 (see page 768) had shown that an Asian power could beat a European Great Power; now for the first time Asians saw the entire West as divided and vulnerable.

In China and Japan few people particularly cared who won the distant war in Europe. In British India and French Indochina enthusiasm was also limited, but the war's impact was unavoidably greater. Total war required that the British and the French draft their colonial subjects into the conflict, uprooting hundreds of thousands of Asians to fight the Germans and the Ottoman Turks. This too had major consequences. An Indian or Vietnamese soldier who fought in France and came in contact there with democratic and republican ideas was less likely to accept foreign rule when he returned home.

The British and the French also made rash promises to gain the support of colonial peoples during the war. British leaders promised Europe's Jewish nationalists a homeland in Palestine, while promising Arab nationalists independence from the Ottoman Empire. In India the British were forced in 1917 to announce a new policy of self-governing institutions in order to counteract Indian popular unrest fanned by wartime inflation and heavy taxation. After the war the nationalist genie the colonial powers had called on refused to slip meekly back into the bottle.

President Wilson's war aims also raised the hopes of peoples under imperial rule. In January 1918 Wilson proposed his Fourteen Points (see page 836), whose key idea was national self-determination for the peoples of Europe and the Ottoman Empire. Wilson also recommended that in all colonial questions "the interests of native populations be given equal weight with the desires of European governments," and he seemed to call for national self-rule. This subversive message had enormous appeal for educated Asians, fueling their hopes of freedom.

Military service and Wilsonian self-determination also fired the hopes of some Africans and some visionary African American supporters of African freedom. The First World War, however, had less impact on European imperialism in sub-Saharan Africa than in Asia and the Arab world. For sub-Saharan Africa, the Great Depression and the Second World War were much more influential in the growth of nationalist movements (see pages 1000–1004).

After winning the war, the Allies tried to re-establish or increase their political and economic domination in Asia and Africa. Although fatally weakened, Western imperialism remained very much alive in 1918, partly because President Wilson was no revolutionary. At the Versailles Peace Conference he compromised on colonial questions in order to achieve some of his European goals and the creation of the League of Nations. Also, Allied statesmen and ordinary French and British citizens quite rightly believed their colonial empires had contributed to their ultimate victory over the Central Powers. They would not give up such valuable possessions voluntarily. If pressed, Europeans said their administration was preparing colonial subjects for eventual self-rule, but only in the distant future.

The compromise at Versailles between Wilson's vague, moralistic idealism and the European preoccupation with "good administration" was a system of League of Nations mandates over Germany's former colonies and the old Ottoman Empire. Article 22 of the League of Nations Covenant, which was part of the Treaty of Versailles, assigned territories "inhabited by peoples incapable of governing themselves" to various "developed nations." "The well-being and development of such peoples" was declared "a sacred trust of civilization." The **Permanent Mandates Commission**, whose members came from European countries with colonies, was created to oversee the developed nations' fulfillment of their international responsibility. Thus the League elaborated a new principle—development toward the eventual goal of self-government—but left its implementation to the colonial powers themselves.

The mandates system demonstrated that Europe was determined to maintain its imperial power and influence, leaving patriots throughout Asia bitterly disappointed after the First World War. They saw France, Great Britain, and other nations—industrialized Japan was the only Asian state to obtain mandates—grabbing Germany's colonies as spoils of war and extending the existing system of colonial rule in Muslim North Africa into the territories of the old Ottoman Empire. Yet Asian patriots did not give up. They preached national self-determination and struggled to build mass movements capable of achieving freedom and independence.

In this struggle Asian nationalists were encouraged by Soviet communism. After seizing power in 1917, Lenin declared that the Asian inhabitants of the new Soviet Union were complete equals of the Russians with a right to their own development. (In actuality this equality hardly existed, but the propaganda was effective nonetheless.) The Communists also denounced European and American imperialism and

Chronology

1914–1918 World War I

1915 Japan seizes German holdings in China and expands into southern Manchuria

1916 Sykes-Picot Agreement divides Ottoman Empire between Britain and France

1916–1917 Arab revolt against Turkish rule grows

1917 Balfour Declaration establishes Jewish homeland in Palestine

1919 Amritsar Massacre in India; May Fourth Movement in China; Treaty of Versailles

1920 Faisal proclaimed king of Syria but quickly deposed by French, who establish their mandate in Syria

1920s New Culture Movement challenges traditional Chinese values

1920s–1930s Large numbers of Jews immigrate to Palestine; Hebrew becomes common language there

1923 Sun Yatsen allies Nationalist Party with Chinese Communists; Kita Ikki advocates ultranationalism in Japan

1923–1938 Mustafa Kemal imposes Western reforms to modernize and secularize Turkey

1925–1941 Reign of Reza Shah Pahlavi in Iran

1927 Jiang Jieshi, leader of Nationalist Party, purges his Communist allies

1930 Gandhi leads Indians on march to the sea to protest the British salt tax

1931 Japan occupies Manchuria

1932 Iraq gains independence in return for military alliance with Great Britain

1934 Mao leads Chinese Communists on Long March; Philippines gain self-governing commonwealth status from United States

1935 Turkish National Assembly introduces family names on European model; Mustafa Kemal granted the surname Atatürk

1937 Japanese militarists launch general attack on China; Rape of Nanjing

Permanent Mandates Commission *A commission created by the League of Nations to oversee the developed nations' fulfillment of their international responsibility.*

pledged to support revolutionary movements in all colonial countries, even when they were primarily movements of national independence led by "middle-class" intellectuals instead of by revolutionary workers. Foreign political and economic exploitation was the immediate enemy, they said, and socialist revolution could wait until Western imperialism had been defeated. The example, ideology, and support of Soviet communism exerted a powerful influence in the 1920s and 1930s, particularly in China and French Indochina.

Nationalism's appeal in Asia was not confined to territories under direct European rule. The extraordinary growth of international trade after 1850 had drawn millions of Asian peasants and shopkeepers into the Western-dominated world economy, disrupting local markets and often creating hostility toward European businessmen. Moreover, Europe and the United States had forced even the most solid Asian states, China and Japan, to accept unequal treaties and humiliating limitations on their sovereignty. Thus the nationalist promise of genuine economic independence and true political equality with the West appealed as powerfully in old but weak states like China as in colonial territories like British India.

Finally, as in Russia after the Crimean War or in Japan after the Meiji Restoration, the nationalist creed after World War I went hand in hand with acceptance of modernization by the educated elites. Modernization promised changes that would enable old societies to compete effectively with the world's leading nations.

THE MIDDLE EAST

How did the collapse of the Ottoman Empire in World War I shape the history of the Middle East for the rest of the century?

The most flagrant attempt to expand Western imperialism occurred in the Middle East, or, more accurately, Southwest Asia—the vast expanse that stretches eastward from the Suez Canal and Turkey's Mediterranean shores across the Tigris-Euphrates Valley and the Iranian Plateau to the Arabian Sea and the Indus Valley. There the

● **Prince Faisal and His British Allies** On board a British warship on route to the Versailles Peace Conference in 1919, Prince Faisal is flanked on his right by the British officer T. E. Lawrence—popularly known as Lawrence of Arabia because of his daring campaign against the Turks. Faisal failed to win political independence for the Arabs, as the British backed away from the vague pro-Arab promises they had made during the war. *(Rowley Atterbury)*

British and the French successfully encouraged an Arab revolt in 1916 and destroyed the Ottoman Empire. Europeans then sought to replace Turks as principal rulers throughout the region, even in Turkey itself. Turkish, Arab, and Iranian nationalists, as well as Jewish nationalists arriving from Europe, reacted violently. They struggled to win dignity and nationhood, and as the Europeans were forced to make concessions, they sometimes came into sharp conflict with each other, most notably in Palestine.

The First World War and the Arab Revolt

Long subject to European pressure, the Ottoman Empire failed to reform and modernize in the late nineteenth century (see pages 726–729). Declining international stature and domestic tyranny led to revolutionary activity among idealistic exiles and young army officers who wanted to seize power and save the Ottoman state. These patriots, the so-called **Young Turks,** succeeded in the 1908 revolution, and subsequently they were determined to hold together the remnants of the vast multiethnic empire. Defeated by Bulgaria, Serbia, and Greece in the Balkan War of 1912, and stripped of practically all territory in Europe, the Young Turks redoubled their efforts in Southwest Asia. The most important of their possessions were Syria—consisting of modern-day Lebanon, Syria, Israel, and Jordan—and Iraq. The Ottoman Turks also claimed the Arabian peninsula but exercised only loose control there.

For centuries the largely Arabic populations of Syria and Iraq had been tied to their Ottoman rulers by their common faith in Islam (though there were Christian Arabs as well). Yet beneath the surface, ethnic and linguistic tensions simmered between Turks and Arabs, who were as different as Chinese and Japanese.

Young Turk actions after 1908 made the embryonic "Arab movement" a reality. The majority of Young Turks promoted a narrow Turkish nationalism. They further centralized the Ottoman Empire and extended the sway of the Turkish language, culture, and race. In 1909 the Turkish government brutally slaughtered thousands of Armenian Christians, a prelude to the wholesale massacre of more than a million Armenians during the First World War. Meanwhile, Arab discontent grew.

In late 1914 the Turks willingly joined forces with Germany and Austria-Hungary. The Young Turks were pro-German because the Germans had helped reform the Ottoman armies before the war and had built important railroads, like the one to Baghdad. Alliance with Germany permitted the Turks to renounce the limitations on Ottoman sovereignty that the Europeans had imposed in the nineteenth century and also to settle old scores with Russia, the Turks' historic enemy.

The Young Turks' fatal alliance with the Central Powers pulled the entire Middle East into the European civil war and made it truly a global conflict. While Russia attacked the Ottomans in the Caucasus, the British protected their rule in Egypt and the Suez Canal, the lifeline to India. Thus Arab leaders opposed to Ottoman rule suddenly found an unexpected ally in Great Britain. The foremost Arab leader was Hussein ibn-Ali (1856–1931), a direct descendant of the prophet Muhammad. As the **sharif,** or chief magistrate, of Mecca, the Muslim world's holiest city, Hussein governed much of the Ottoman Empire's territory along the Red Sea, an area known as the Hejaz (see Map 28.1). Basically anti-Turkish, Hussein refused the Turkish sultan's call for a holy war against the Triple Entente. His refusal pleased the British, who feared a Muslim revolt in India.

In 1915 Hussein won vague British commitments for an independent Arab kingdom. When the British attempt to take the Dardanelles and capture Constantinople in 1915 failed miserably, Britain (and Russia) badly needed a new ally on the Ottoman front. In 1916 Hussein revolted against the Turks, proclaiming himself king of the Arabs. Hussein joined forces with the British under T. E. Lawrence, who in 1917 led Arab tribesmen and Indian soldiers in a highly successful guerrilla war against the Turks on the Arabian peninsula. In September 1918 British armies and their Arab allies rolled into Syria and occupied Damascus.

Young Turks *Idealistic Turkish exiles in Europe and young army officers in Istanbul who seized power in the revolution of 1908 and helped pave the way for the birth of modern secular Turkey.*

**Primary Source:
Letter from Turkey,
Summer 1915**
Read an eyewitness account of the Armenian genocide, by a U.S. missionary from Massachusetts.

sharif *A term for the chief magistrate of Mecca.*

BULGARIA

Black Sea 30°E 40°E SOVIET UNION 50°E

Istanbul
(Constantinople)

Batum

Ceded by Soviet
Union in 1921.

Kars

Baku

Caspian Sea

GREECE

Izmir
(Smyrna)

Ankara

TURKEY

Tabriz

PERSIA
(IRAN)

Tehran

Tigris R.

Euphrates R.

Aleppo

SYRIA

Baghdad

Mediterranean Sea

Crete

Dodecanese
(It.)

Cyprus
(Gr. Br.)

LEBANON

Beirut

Damascus

IRAQ

Kut el
Amara

PALESTINE

Jerusalem

Amman

Basra

TRANSJORDAN

KUWAIT

Cairo

*Suez
Canal*

NEUTRAL ZONE

NEUTRAL
ZONE

Persian Gulf

BAHRAIN

EGYPT

HEJAZ
(Independent 1916;
to Nejd 1925)

Boundary undefined

QATAR

TRUCIAL
OMAN

OMAN

Gulf of Oman

Medina

Riyadh

Boundary undefined

Nile R.

Red Sea

NEJD
(SAUDI ARABIA)

20°N

Mecca

ANGLO-EGYPTIAN
SUDAN

ASIR
(Independent 1917;
to Nejd 1920)

Arabian Sea

ERITREA

YEMEN
(Independent
1918)

Boundary undefined

HADHRAMAUT

ADEN

Socotra
(Gr. Br.)

FRENCH
SOMALILAND

Gulf of Aden

Blue Nile R.

ABYSSINIA

BRITISH
SOMALILAND

ITALIAN
SOMALILAND

10°N

0   150   300 Km.

0   150   300 Mi.

Ottoman Empire in 1914

British protectorate in 1914

Area controlled under mandates
from the League of Nations, 1920

British Mandate

French Mandate

International boundaries,
1923

MAP 28.1 **The Partition of the Ottoman Empire, 1914–1923** The decline of the mighty Ottoman Empire began in 1699, when the Habsburgs conquered Hungary, and it accelerated after 1805, when Egypt became virtually independent. By 1914 the Ottoman Turks had been pushed out of the Balkans, and their Arab provinces were on the edge of revolt. That revolt erupted in the First World War and contributed greatly to the Ottomans' defeat. When the Allies then attempted to implement their plans, including independence for the Armenian people, Mustafa Kemal arose to forge in battle the modern Turkish state.

In the Ottoman province of Iraq, Britain occupied Basra in 1914 and captured Baghdad in 1917. Arabs rejoiced, and many patriots expected a large, unified Arab state to rise from the dust of the Ottoman collapse. Within two years, however, Arab nationalists felt bitterly betrayed by Great Britain and its allies, and this bitterness left a legacy of distrust and hatred toward the West.

Arab bitterness was partly directed at secret wartime treaties between Britain and France to divide and rule the old Ottoman Empire. In the 1916 **Sykes-Picot Agreement,** Britain and France secretly agreed that France would receive modern-day Lebanon, Syria, and much of southern Turkey, and Britain would receive Palestine, Jordan, and Iraq. The Sykes-Picot Agreement contradicted British (and later Wilsonian) promises concerning Arab independence after the war, and left Arab nationalists feeling cheated and betrayed.

A related source of Arab bitterness was Britain's wartime commitment to a Jewish homeland in Palestine. The **Balfour Declaration** of November 1917, made by the British foreign secretary Arthur Balfour, declared that

His Majesty's Government views with favor the establishment in Palestine of a National Home for the Jewish People, and will use their best endeavors to facilitate the achievement

Sykes-Picot Agreement *The 1916 secret agreement between Britain and France that divided up the Arab lands of Lebanon, Syria, southern Turkey, Palestine, Jordan, and Iraq.*

Balfour Declaration *A 1917 statement by British foreign secretary Arthur Balfour that supported the idea of a Jewish homeland in Palestine.*

● **The Armenian Atrocities**   When in 1915 some Armenians welcomed Russian armies as liberators after years of persecution, the Ottoman government ordered a genocidal mass deportation of its Armenian citizens from their homeland in the empire's eastern provinces. This photo, taken in Kharpert in 1915 by a German businessman from his hotel window, shows Turkish guards marching Armenian men off to a prison, where they will be tortured to death. A million Armenians died from murder, starvation, and disease during World War I. *(Armenian Library and Museum of America Archives)*

of this object, it being clearly understood that nothing shall be done which may prejudice the civil and religious rights of existing non-Jewish communities in Palestine, or the rights and political status enjoyed by Jews in any other country.

As careful reading reveals, the Balfour Declaration made contradictory promises to European Jews and Middle Eastern Arabs.

Some British Cabinet members apparently believed the Balfour Declaration would appeal to German, Austrian, and American Jews and thus help the British war effort. Others sincerely supported the Zionist vision of a Jewish homeland, but also believed that this homeland would then be grateful to Britain and help maintain British control of the Suez Canal.

In 1914 Jews were about 11 percent of the predominantly Arab population in the Ottoman territory that became, under British control, Palestine. The "National Home for the Jewish People" mentioned in the Balfour Declaration implied to the Arabs— and to the Zionist Jews as well—some kind of Jewish state that would be incompatible with majority rule. Moreover, a state founded on religious and ethnic exclusivity was out of keeping with both Islamic and Ottoman tradition, which had historically been more tolerant of religious diversity and minorities than had the Christian monarchs or nation-states in Europe.

Despite strong French objections, Hussein's son Faisal (1885–1933) attended the Versailles Peace Conference, but his efforts to secure Arab independence came to nothing. President Wilson wanted to give the Arab case serious consideration, but the British and the French were determined to rule Syria, Iraq, and Palestine as League of Nations mandates, and accept only the independence of Hussein's kingdom of Hejaz. In response, Arab nationalists met in Damascus as the General Syrian Congress in 1919 and unsuccessfully called again for political independence. (See the feature "Listening to the Past: Arab Political Aspirations in 1919" on pages 874–875.) Brushing aside Arab opposition, the British mandate in Palestine formally incorporated the Balfour Declaration and its commitment to a Jewish national home. In March 1920 Faisal's followers met as the Syrian National Congress and proclaimed Syria independent, with Faisal as king. A similar congress declared Iraq an independent kingdom.

Western reaction to events in Syria and Iraq was swift and decisive. A French army stationed in Lebanon attacked Syria, taking Damascus in July 1920. Faisal fled, and the French took over. Meanwhile, the British put down an uprising in Iraq with bloody fighting and established effective control there. Western imperialism appeared to have replaced Turkish rule in the Middle East (see Map 28.1).

The Turkish Revolution

In November 1918 the Allied fleet entered Constantinople, the Ottoman capital. A young English official wrote that he found the Ottoman Empire "utterly smashed." The Turks were "worn out," and without bitterness they awaited the construction of a "new system."[2] The Allies' new system was blatant imperialism, which proved harsher for the defeated Turks than for the "liberated" Arabs. A treaty forced on the helpless sultan dismembered Turkey and reduced it to a puppet state. Great Britain and France occupied parts of Turkey, and Italy and Greece claimed shares as well. There was a sizable Greek minority in western Turkey, and Greek nationalists cherished the "Great Idea" of a modern Greek empire modeled on long-dead Christian Byzantium. In 1919 Greek armies carried by British ships landed on the Turkish coast at Smyrna, met little resistance from the exhausted Turkish troops, and advanced into the interior. Turkey seemed finished.

But Turkey produced a great leader and revived to become an inspiration to the entire Middle East. Mustafa Kemal (1881–1938), the father of modern Turkey, was a military man, and sympathetic to the Young Turk movement. Kemal had distinguished himself in the Great War by directing the successful defense of the Dardanelles against

British attack. After the armistice, Mustafa Kemal watched with anguish the Allies' aggression and the sultan's cowardice. In early 1919 he began working to unify Turkish resistance.

The sultan, bowing to Allied pressure, initially denounced Kemal, but the cause of national liberation proved more powerful. The catalyst was the Greek invasion and attempted annexation of much of western Turkey. A young Turkish woman described feelings she shared with countless others:

After I learned about the details of the Smyrna occupation by Greek armies, I hardly opened my mouth on any subject except when it concerned the sacred struggle. . . . I suddenly ceased to exist as an individual. I worked, wrote and lived as a unit of that magnificent national madness.[3]

Refusing to acknowledge the Allied dismemberment of their country, the Turks battled on through 1920 despite staggering defeats. The next year the Greeks advanced almost to Ankara, the nationalist stronghold in central Turkey. There Mustafa Kemal's forces took the offensive and won a great victory. The Greeks and their British allies sued for peace. The resulting **Treaty of Lausanne** (1923) solemnly abolished the hated capitulations, which gave Europeans special privileges in the Ottoman Empire (see page 563), and recognized a truly independent Turkey. Turkey lost only its former Arab provinces.

Mustafa Kemal believed Turkey should modernize and secularize along Western lines. His first moves were political. Drawing on his prestige as a war hero, Kemal called on the National Assembly to depose the sultan and establish a republic. He had himself elected president and moved the capital from cosmopolitan Constantinople (now Istanbul) to Ankara in the Turkish heartland. Kemal savagely crushed the demands for independence of ethnic minorities like the Armenians and the Kurds, but he realistically abandoned all thought of winning back lost Arab territories. He then created a one-party system—partly inspired by the Bolshevik example—in order to work his will.

Kemal's most radical changes pertained to religion and culture. For centuries most believers' intellectual and social activities had been regulated by Islamic religious authorities. Profoundly influenced by the example of western Europe, Mustafa Kemal set out, like the philosophes of the Enlightenment, to limit religious influence in daily affairs. But, like Russia's Peter the Great, he employed dictatorial measures rather than reason to reach his goal. Kemal simply decreed a revolutionary separation of church and state. Secular law codes inspired by European models replaced religious courts. State schools replaced religious schools and taught such secular subjects as science, mathematics, and social sciences.

Mustafa Kemal also struck down many entrenched patterns of behavior. Women, traditionally secluded and inferior to males in Islamic society, received the right to vote. Civil law on a European model, rather than the Islamic code, now governed marriage. Women could seek divorces, and no man could have more than one wife at a time. Men were forbidden to wear the tall red fez of the Ottoman era as headgear; government employees were ordered to wear business suits and felt hats, erasing the visible differences between Muslims and "infidel"

Treaty of Lausanne   *The 1923 treaty that ended the Turkish war and recognized the territorial integrity of a truly independent Turkey.*

● **Mustafa Kemal**   Surnamed Atatürk, meaning "father of the Turks," Mustafa Kemal and his supporters imposed revolutionary changes aimed at modernizing and westernizing Turkish society and the new Turkish government. Dancing here with his adopted daughter at her high-society wedding, Atatürk often appeared in public in elegant European dress—a vivid symbol for the Turkish people of his radical break with traditional Islamic teaching and custom. *(Hulton Archive/Getty Images)*

Europeans. The old Arabic script was replaced with a new Turkish alphabet based on Roman letters, which facilitated massive government efforts to spread literacy after 1928. Finally, in 1935, family names on the European model were introduced. The National Assembly granted Mustafa Kemal the surname **Atatürk,** which means "father of the Turks."

By his death in 1938, Atatürk and his supporters had consolidated their revolution. Government-sponsored industrialization was fostering urban growth and new attitudes, encouraging Turks to embrace business and science. Poverty persisted in rural areas, as did some religious discontent among devout Muslims. But like the Japanese after the Meiji Restoration, the Turkish people had rallied around the nationalist banner to repulse European imperialism and were building a modern secular nation-state.

Iran and Afghanistan

In Persia (renamed Iran in 1935), strong-arm efforts to build a unified modern nation ultimately proved less successful than in Turkey. In the late nineteenth century Iran had also been subject to extreme foreign pressure, which stimulated efforts to reform the government as a means of reviving Islamic civilization. In 1906 a nationalistic coalition of merchants, religious leaders, and intellectuals revolted. The despotic shah was forced to grant a constitution and establish a national assembly, the **Majlis.** Nationalist hopes ran high.

Yet the 1906 Iranian revolution was doomed to failure, largely because of European imperialism. Without consulting Iran, Britain and Russia in 1907 simply divided the country into spheres of influence. Britain's sphere ran along the Persian Gulf; the Russian sphere encompassed the whole northern half of Iran (see Map 28.1). Thereafter Russia intervened constantly. It blocked reforms, occupied cities, and completely dominated the country by 1912. When Russian power collapsed in the Bolshevik Revolution, British armies rushed into the power vacuum. By bribing corrupt Iranians, Great Britain in 1919 negotiated a treaty allowing the installation of British "advisers" in every government department.

The Majlis refused to ratify the treaty, and the blatant attempt to make Iran a British satellite aroused the national spirit. In 1921 reaction against the British brought to power a military dictator, Reza Shah Pahlavi (1877–1944), who proclaimed himself shah in 1925 and ruled until 1941.

Inspired by Turkey's Mustafa Kemal, the patriotic, religiously indifferent Reza Shah had three basic goals: to build a modern nation, to free Iran from foreign domination, and to rule with an iron fist. The challenge was enormous. Iran was a vast, undeveloped country of deserts, mountain barriers, and rudimentary communications. The rural population was mostly poor and illiterate, and among the Persian majority were sizable ethnic minorities with their own aspirations. Furthermore, Iran's powerful religious leaders hated Western (Christian) domination but were no less opposed to a more secular, less Islamic society.

To realize his vision of a strong Iran, the energetic shah created a modern army, built railroads, and encouraged commerce. He won control over ethnic minorities such as the Kurds in the north and Arab tribesmen on the Iraqi border. He reduced the privileges granted to foreigners and raised taxes on the powerful Anglo-Persian Oil Company, which had been founded in 1909 to exploit the first great oil strike in the Middle East. Yet Reza Shah was less successful than Atatürk.

Because the European-educated elite in Iran was smaller than the comparable group in Turkey, the idea of re-creating Persian greatness on the basis of a secularized society attracted relatively few determined supporters. Many powerful religious leaders turned against Reza Shah, and he became increasingly brutal, greedy, and tyrannical, murdering his enemies and lining his pockets. His support of Hitler's Nazi Germany also exposed Iran's tenuous and fragile independence to the impact of European conflicts.

Atatürk *The name bestowed on the Turkish president Mustafa Kemal; it means "father of the Turks."*

Majlis *The national assembly established by the despotic shah of Iran in 1906.*

Primary Source:
The Link Between the Education of Girls and the Advancement of Iranian Society, 1907, 1909
Two articles argue that, if Iran is to become truly "civilized," it must recognize the virtues of educating women.

Afghanistan, meanwhile, was nominally independent in the nineteenth century, but
the British imposed political restrictions and constantly meddled in the country's affairs. In 1919 the violently anti-British amir Amanullah (1892–1960) declared a holy
war on the British government in India and won complete independence for the first
time. Amanullah then decreed revolutionary reforms designed to hurl his primitive
country into the twentieth century. The result was tribal and religious revolt, civil war,
and retreat from reform. Islam remained both religion and law. A powerful but primitive patriotism enabled Afghanistan to win political independence from the West, but
not to build a modern society.

The Arab States and Palestine

French and British mandates established at gunpoint forced Arab nationalists to seek
independence by gradual means after 1920. Arab nationalists were indirectly aided by
Western taxpayers, who wanted cheap—that is, peaceful—empires. As a result, Arabs
won considerable control over local affairs in the mandated states, except Palestine,
though the mandates remained European satellites in international and economic
affairs.

In Iraq, the wily British chose Faisal, whom the French had deposed in Syria, as
king. Faisal obligingly gave British advisers broad behind-the-scenes control. The
king also accepted British ownership of Iraq's oil fields, consequently giving the West
a stranglehold on the Iraqi economy. Given the severe limitations imposed on him,
Faisal (r. 1921–1933) proved to be an able ruler, gaining the support of his people
and encouraging moderate reforms. In 1932 he secured Iraqi independence at the
price of a restrictive long-term military alliance with Great Britain.

Egypt had been occupied by Great Britain since 1882 (see page 732) and a British
protectorate since 1914. Following intense nationalist agitation after the Great War,
Great Britain in 1922 proclaimed Egypt formally independent but continued to occupy the country militarily and control its politics. In 1936, the British agreed to restrict their troops to their bases in the Suez Canal Zone.

The French were less compromising in Syria. They practiced a policy of divide-and-rule, carving out a second mandate in Lebanon and generally playing off ethnic and religious minorities against each other. Lebanon eventually became a republic, dominated by a very slender Christian majority and under French protection. Arab nationalists in Syria finally won promises of Syrian independence in 1936 in return for a treaty of friendship with France.

In short, the Arab states gradually freed themselves from Western political mandates but not from the Western military threat or from pervasive Western influence. Of great importance, large Arab landowners and urban merchants increased their wealth and political power after 1918, and they often supported the Western hegemony, from which they benefited greatly. Western control of the newly discovered Arab oil fields helped to convince radical nationalists that economic independence and genuine freedom had not yet been achieved.

Relations between the Arabs and the West were complicated by the tense situation in the British mandate of Palestine, and that situation deteriorated in the interwar years. Both Arabs and Jews denounced the British, who tried unsuccessfully to compromise with both sides. Arab nationalist anger, however, was aimed primarily at Jewish settlers. The key issue was Jewish migration from Europe to Palestine.

Zionism *The movement toward Jewish political nationhood started by Theodor Herzl.*

A small Jewish community had survived in Palestine ever since the dispersal of the Jews in Roman times. But Jewish nationalism, known as **Zionism,** took shape in Europe in the late nineteenth century under the leadership of Theodor Herzl (see page 707). Herzl believed that only a Jewish state could guarantee Jews dignity and security. The Zionist movement encouraged the world's Jews to settle in Palestine, but until 1921 the great majority of Jewish emigrants preferred the United States.

After 1921 the situation changed radically. An isolationist United States drastically limited immigration from eastern Europe, where war and revolution had kindled anti-Semitism. Moreover, the British began honoring the Balfour Declaration despite Arab protests. Thus Jewish immigration to Palestine from turbulent Europe grew rapidly. In the 1930s German and Polish persecution created a mass of Jewish refugees. By 1939 the Jewish population of Palestine had increased almost fivefold since 1914 and accounted for about 30 percent of all inhabitants.

Jewish settlers in Palestine faced formidable difficulties. Although much of the land purchased by the Jewish National Fund was productive, the sellers of such land were often wealthy absentee Arab landowners who cared little for their Arab tenants' welfare. When the new Jewish owners subsequently replaced those age-old Arab tenants with Jewish settlers, Arab farmers and intellectuals burned with a sense of injustice. Moreover, most Jewish immigrants came from urban backgrounds and preferred to establish new cities like Tel Aviv or to live in existing towns, where they competed with the Arabs. The land issue combined with economic and cultural friction to harden Arab protest into hatred. Anti-Jewish riots and even massacres ensued.

The British gradually responded to Arab pressure and tried to slow Jewish immigration. This effort satisfied neither Jews nor Arabs, and by 1938 the two communities were engaged in an undeclared civil war. On the eve of the Second World War, the frustrated British proposed an independent Palestine with the number of Jews permanently limited to only about one-third of the total population. Zionists felt themselves in grave danger.

kibbutz *A Jewish collective farm on which each member shared equally in the work, rewards, and defense of the farm.*

In the face of adversity Jewish settlers from many different countries gradually succeeded in forging a cohesive community. Hebrew, for centuries used only in religious worship, was revived as a living language to bind the Jews in Palestine together. Despite its slow beginnings, rural development achieved often remarkable results. The key unit of agricultural organization was the **kibbutz,** a collective farm on which each member shared equally in the work, rewards, and defense of the farm. An egalitarian socialist ideology also characterized industry, which grew rapidly. By 1939 a new but old nation was emerging in the Middle East.

Reuven Rubin: First Fruits (or First Pioneers) (1923) Whereas Jerusalem was the center of Jewish religious culture and conservative art in the 1920s, the new coastal city of Tel Aviv sprang up secular, and it gloried in avant-garde modern art (see pages 884–886). In this painting Rubin, a leader of Tel Aviv's modernist school, depicts Jewish pioneers in a stark, two-dimensional landscape and conveys an exotic "Garden of Eden" flavor. Arriving from Romania, Rubin was bowled over by Palestine. "The world about me became clear and pure: life was formless, blurred, primitive." *(Reuven Rubin, First Fruits, 1922, Coll. Rubin Museum, Tel-Aviv, Israel)*

TOWARD SELF-RULE IN INDIA

What role did Gandhi and his campaign of militant nonviolence play in leading India to independence from the British?

The national movement in British India grew out of two interconnected cultures, Hindu and Muslim, which came to see themselves as fundamentally different in rising to challenge British rule. Nowhere has modern nationalism's power both to unify and to divide been more strikingly demonstrated than in India.

Promises and Repression (1914–1919)

Indian nationalism had emerged in the late nineteenth century (see page 753), and when the First World War began, the British feared revolt. Instead, Indians supported the war effort. About 1.2 million Indian soldiers and laborers voluntarily served in Europe, Africa, and the Middle East. The British government in India and the native Indian princes sent large supplies of food, money, and ammunition. In return, the British opened more good government jobs to Indians and made other minor concessions.

As the war in distant Europe ground on, however, inflation, high taxes, food shortages, and a terrible influenza epidemic created widespread suffering and discontent. The prewar nationalist movement revived, stronger than ever, and moderates and radicals in the Indian National Congress joined forces. Moreover, in 1916 Hindu leaders in the Congress Party hammered out an alliance—the **Lucknow Pact**—with India's Muslim League. The League was founded in 1906 to uphold Muslim

Lucknow Pact *A 1916 alliance between Hindus leading the Indian National Congress and the Muslim League.*

Jallianwala Bagh Massacre This is a highly dramatized painting of the massacre in the Jallian-wala Bagh (Garden) in Amritsar on April 13, 1919. Having banned gatherings of five persons or more, General Dyer ordered the fifty British Indian Army troops under his command to open fire on unarmed men, women, and children who had gathered on a Sunday to celebrate the Sikh festival of *Baisakhi*. The soldiers fired 1,650 rounds of ammunition (until they ran out of bullets), killing nearly 400 and wounding some 1,100 others. The terror-stricken people had no means of escape for the Indian troops blocked the only exit from the Bagh. *(Courtesy, Indialog Publications Pvt. Ltd., Delhi. Photo: Amrit and Rabindra Dingh, Fine Arts, U.K.)*

> **Primary Source:**
> **An Indian Nationalist Condemns the British Empire**
> *In this excerpt from a speech, an Indian nationalist and feminist accuses the British Empire of betraying its ideals and losing its soul.*

interests, as, under British rule, the once-dominant Muslim minority had fallen behind the Hindu majority. The Lucknow Pact forged a powerful united front of Hindus and Muslims and called for putting India on equal footing with self-governing British dominions like Canada, Australia, and New Zealand.

The British response was contradictory. On the one hand, the secretary of state for India made the unprecedented announcement in August 1917 that British policy in India called for the "gradual development of self-governing institutions and the progressive realization of responsible government." In late 1919 the British established a dual administration: part Indian and elected, part British and authoritarian. Such uncontroversial activities as agriculture and health were transferred from British to Indian officials who were accountable to elected provincial assemblies. More sensitive matters like taxes, police, and the courts remained solely in British hands.

Old-fashioned authoritarian rule seriously undermined the positive impact of this reform. Despite the unanimous opposition of the elected Indian members, the British in 1919 rammed the repressive Rowlatt Acts through India's Imperial Legislative Council. These acts indefinitely extended wartime "emergency measures" designed to curb unrest and root out "conspiracy." The result was a wave of rioting across India.

Under these tense conditions a crowd of some ten thousand gathered to celebrate a Sikh religious festival in an enclosed square in the Sikh holy city of Amritsar in the northern Punjab province. Unknown to the crowd, the local English commander, General Reginald Dyer, had banned all public meetings that very day. Dyer marched his native Gurkha troops into the square and, without warning, ordered them to fire into the unarmed mass at point-blank range until the ammunition ran out. Offical British records of the Amritsar Massacre list 379 killed and 1,137 wounded, but these figures remain hotly contested for being too low. India stood on the verge of more violence and repression and, sooner or later, terrorism and guerrilla war. That India took a different path to national liberation was due largely to Mohandas "Mahatma" Gandhi (1869–1948), the most influential Indian of modern times.

The Roots of Militant Nonviolence

By the time of Gandhi's birth in 1869, the Indian subcontinent was firmly controlled by the British. Part of the country was ruled directly by British (and subordinate Indian) officials, answerable to the British Parliament in London. In each of the so-called protected states, the native prince—usually known as the *maharaja*—remained the titular ruler, although he was bound to the British by unequal treaties and had to accept the "advice" of the British resident assigned to his court.

Gandhi grew up in one of the small protected states north of Bombay. Gandhi's father was the well-to-do head of a large extended family. Gandhi's mother was devoted but undogmatic in religious matters, and she exercised a strong influence on her son.

After his father's death, Gandhi went to study law in England. After passing the English bar and returning to India, he decided in 1893 to try a case for some wealthy Indian merchants in South Africa. It was a momentous decision.

In South Africa, Gandhi took up the plight of the expatriate Indian community. White plantation owners there imported poor Indians as indentured laborers on five-year renewable contracts. When some Indians completed their terms and remained in South Africa as free persons and economic competitors, the Dutch and British settlers passed brutally discriminatory laws. Poor Indians had to work on plantations or return to India; rich Indians lost the vote. Gandhi undertook his countrymen's legal defense, and in 1896 a white mob almost lynched the "coolie lawyer."

Meanwhile, Gandhi was searching for a spiritual theory of social action. He studied Hindu and Christian teachings, and gradually developed a weapon for the weak that he called **Satyagraha**. Gandhi conceived of Satyagraha, loosely translated as "Soul Force," as a means of striving for truth and social justice through love, suffering, and conversion of the oppressor. Its tactic is active nonviolent resistance.

As the undisputed leader of South Africa's Indians before the First World War, Gandhi put his philosophy into action. When South Africa's white government severely restricted Asian immigration and internal freedom of movement, Gandhi organized a nonviolent mass resistance campaign. Thousands of Indian men and women marched in peaceful protest and withstood beatings, arrest, and imprisonment.

In 1914, South Africa's exasperated whites agreed to many of the Indians' demands. They passed a law abolishing discriminatory taxes on Indian traders, recognizing the legality of non-Christian marriages, and permitting the continued immigration of free Indians. Satyagraha—militant nonviolence in pursuit of social justice—proved itself a powerful force in Gandhi's hands.

Gandhi Leads the Way

In 1915 Gandhi returned to India. His reputation had preceded him: the masses hailed him as a *Mahatma,* or "Great Soul"—a Hindu title of veneration for a man of great knowledge and humanity. Drawing on his South African experience, Gandhi in 1920 launched a national campaign of nonviolent resistance to British rule. Denouncing British injustice, he urged his countrymen to boycott British goods, jobs, and honors. He told peasants not to pay taxes or buy English cloth or the heavily taxed liquor. Gandhi electrified the people, initiating a revolution in Indian politics.

The nationalist movement had previously touched only the tiny, prosperous, Western-educated elite. Now both the illiterate masses of village India and the educated classes

Satyagraha *Loosely translated as "Soul Force," which Gandhi believed was the means of striving for truth and social justice through love, suffering, and conversion of the oppressor.*

● **Gandhi Arrives in Delhi, October 1939** A small frail man, Gandhi possessed enormous courage and determination. His campaign of nonviolent resistance to British rule inspired the Indian masses and mobilized a nation. Here he arrives for talks with the British viceroy after the outbreak of World War II. *(Corbis)*

heard Gandhi's call for militant nonviolent resistance. It particularly appealed to the masses of Hindus who were not members of the warrior caste or the so-called military races and who were traditionally passive and nonviolent. The British had regarded ordinary Hindus as cowards. Gandhi told them that they could be courageous and even morally superior:

What do you think? Wherein is courage required—in blowing others to pieces from behind a cannon, or with a smiling face to approach a cannon and be blown to pieces? Who is the true warrior—he who keeps death always as a bosom-friend, or he who controls the death of others? Believe me that a man devoid of courage and manhood can never be a passive resister.[4]

Gandhi made Congress into a mass political party, welcoming members from every ethnic group and cooperating closely with the Muslim minority.

In 1922 some Indian resisters turned to violence, murdering twenty-two policemen. Savage riots broke out, and Gandhi abruptly called off his campaign. Arrested for fomenting rebellion, Gandhi told the British judge that he had committed "a Himalayan blunder to believe that India had accepted nonviolence." Released from prison after two years, Gandhi set up a commune, established a national newspaper, and set out to reform Indian society and improve the lot of the poor. He welcomed the outcaste untouchables, worked to help child widows, and promoted native cottage industry production. For Gandhi moral improvement, social progress, and the national movement went hand in hand. Above all, Gandhi nurtured national identity, self-respect, and courage in India's people.

The 1920–1922 resistance campaign left the British severely shaken, but the commission formed in 1927 to consider further steps toward self-rule included no Indian members. Indian resentment was intense. In 1929 the radical nationalists, led by the able and aristocratic Jawaharlal Nehru (1889–1964), pushed through the National Congress a resolution calling for virtual independence within a year. The British stiffened, and Indian radicals talked of a bloody showdown.

Into this tense situation Gandhi masterfully reasserted his leadership, taking a hard line toward the British, but insisting on nonviolent methods. He organized a massive resistance campaign against the hated salt tax, which affected every Indian family. Gandhi himself led fifty thousand people in a spectacular march to the sea where he made salt in defiance of the law. A later demonstration at the British-run Dhrasana salt works resulted in many of the 2,500 nonviolent marchers being beaten senseless by policemen in a brutal and well-publicized encounter. Over the next months the British arrested Gandhi and sixty thousand other protesters for making and distributing salt. In 1931 the frustrated and unnerved British released Gandhi from jail and sat down to negotiate with him, as an equal, over Indian self-rule. Negotiations resulted in a new constitution in 1935, which greatly strengthened India's parliamentary representative institutions. It was practically a blueprint for independence, which came quickly after World War II.

Despite his best efforts, Gandhi failed to heal a widening split between Hindus and Muslims. Indian nationalism, based largely on Hindu symbols and customs, increasingly disturbed the Muslim minority. Tempers mounted and both sides committed atrocities. By the late 1930s Muslim League leaders were calling for the creation of a Muslim nation in British India, a "Pakistan" or "land of the pure." As in Palestine, the rise of conflicting nationalisms in India would lead to tragedy (see pages 990–994).

TURMOIL IN EAST ASIA

Why did some of the Asian nationalist movements come into brutal conflict?

Because of the efforts of the Meiji reformers, nationalism and modernization were well developed in Japan by 1914. Japan competed politically and economically with the world's leading nations, building its own empire and proclaiming its special mission in Asia. China lagged far behind, but after 1912 the pace of nationalist development there began to quicken.

In the 1920s the Chinese nationalist movement managed to win a large measure of political independence from the imperialist West and promoted extensive modernization. These achievements were soon undermined, however, by internal conflict and war with an expanding Japan. Nationalism also flourished elsewhere in Asia, scoring a major victory in the Philippine Islands.

The Rise of Nationalist China

The 1911 Revolution, which overthrew the Qing Dynasty (see page 763), opened an era of unprecedented change for Chinese society. Before the revolution many progressive Chinese realized that fundamental technological and political reforms were necessary to save the Chinese state, but most hoped to preserve the traditional core of Chinese civilization and culture. The fall of the ancient dynastic system shattered such hopes. If the emperor himself was no longer sacred, what was?

The central figure in the revolution was a crafty old military man, Yuan Shigai (Yüan Shih-k'ai). Called out of retirement to save the dynasty, Yuan (1859–1916) betrayed the Manchus and convinced the revolutionaries that he could unite the country peacefully and prevent foreign intervention. Once elected president of the republic, however, Yuan concentrated on building his own power. In 1913 he used military force to dissolve China's parliament and ruled as a dictator. China's first modern revolution had failed.

The extent of the failure became apparent only after Yuan's death in 1916. The central government in Beijing almost disintegrated. For more than a decade power resided in a multitude of local military leaders, the so-called warlords. Their wars, taxes, and corruption created terrible suffering.

● **Students Demonstrating in Tiananmen Square, Beijing, Summer 1919** The news that the Versailles Peace Conference left China's Shandong Peninsula in Japanese hands brought an explosion of student protest on May 4, 1919. Student demonstrations in the capital's historic Tiananmen Square continued through June, as the May Fourth Movement against foreign domination took root and grew. *(Photo from Kautz Family YMCA Archives. Reproduced with permission.)*

Foreign imperialism intensified the agony of warlordism. Although China declared its neutrality in 1914, Japan used the Great War as an opportunity to seize Germany's holdings on the Shandong (Shantung) Peninsula and in 1915 forced China to accept Japanese control of Shandong and southern Manchuria (see Map 28.2). Japan's expansion angered China's growing middle class and enraged China's young patriots. On May 4, 1919, five thousand students in Beijing exploded against the decision of the Versailles Peace Conference to leave the Shandong Peninsula in Japanese hands. This famous incident launched the **May Fourth Movement**, which opposed both foreign domination and warlord government.

The May Fourth Movement and the anti-imperialism of Bolshevik Russia renewed Chinese nationalist hopes. In 1923 Sun Yatsen (1866–1925) decided to ally his Nationalist Party, or Guomindang (Kuomintang), with the Communist Third International and the newly formed Chinese Communist Party. The result was the first of many so-called national liberation fronts, in keeping with Lenin's blueprint for temporarily uniting all anticonservative, anti-imperialist forces in a common revolutionary struggle.

Sun, however, was no Communist. In his *Three Principles of the People,* elaborating on the official Nationalist Party ideology—nationalism, democracy, and people's livelihood—nationalism remained of prime importance:

Compared to the other peoples of the world we have the greatest population and our civilization is four thousand years old; we should be advancing in the front rank with the nations of Europe and America. But the Chinese people have only family and clan solidarity, they do not have national spirit. . . . If we do not earnestly espouse nationalism and weld together our four hundred million people into a strong nation, there is a danger of China's

May Fourth Movement *A nationalist movement against foreign imperialists; it began as a student protest against the decision of the Versailles Peace Conference to leave the Shandong Peninsula in the hands of Japan.*

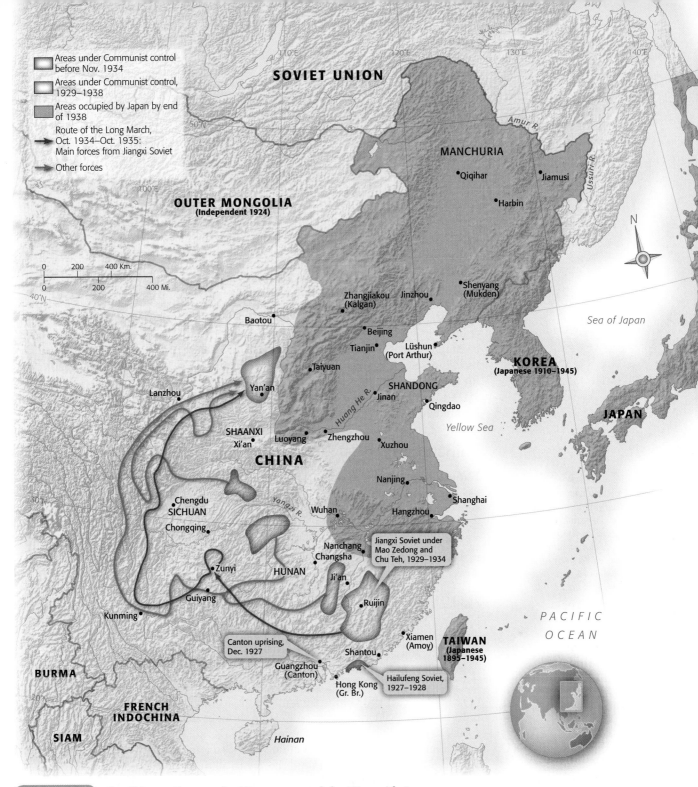

Legend:
- Areas under Communist control before Nov. 1934
- Areas under Communist control, 1929–1938
- Areas occupied by Japan by end of 1938
- Route of the Long March, Oct. 1934–Oct. 1935: Main forces from Jiangxi Soviet
- Other forces

SOVIET UNION

MANCHURIA

Qiqihar

Jiamusi

Harbin

Amur R.

Ussuri R.

OUTER MONGOLIA
(Independent 1924)

0   200   400 Km.
0   200   400 Mi.

Baotou

Zhangjiakou (Kalgan)

Jinzhou

Shenyang (Mukden)

Sea of Japan

Beijing

Tianjin

Lüshun (Port Arthur)

KOREA
(Japanese 1910–1945)

JAPAN

Taiyuan

SHANDONG

Jinan

Qingdao

Yellow Sea

Lanzhou

Yan'an

Huang He R.

SHAANXI

Xi'an

Luoyang

Zhengzhou

Xuzhou

CHINA

Nanjing

Shanghai

Chengdu

SICHUAN

Yangzi R.

Wuhan

Hangzhou

Chongqing

Jiangxi Soviet under Mao Zedong and Chu Teh, 1929–1934

Zunyi

Nanchang

Changsha

Ji'an

HUNAN

Guiyang

Ruijin

PACIFIC OCEAN

Kunming

Canton uprising, Dec. 1927

Xiamen (Amoy)

TAIWAN
(Japanese 1895–1945)

Shantou

BURMA

Guangzhou (Canton)

Hong Kong (Gr. Br.)

Hailufeng Soviet, 1927–1928

FRENCH INDOCHINA

SIAM

Hainan

N

MAP 28.2 **The Chinese Communist Movement and the War with Japan, 1927–1938** After urban uprisings ordered by Stalin failed in 1927, Mao Zedong succeeded in forming a self-governing Communist soviet in mountainous southern China. Relentless Nationalist attacks between 1930 and 1934 finally forced the Long March to Yenan, where the Communists were well positioned for guerrilla war against the Japanese.

being lost and our people being destroyed. If we wish to avert this catastrophe, we must espouse nationalism and bring this national spirit to the salvation of the country.[5]

Democracy, in contrast, had a less exalted meaning. Sun equated it with firm rule by the Nationalists, who would improve people's lives through land reform and welfare measures.

Sun planned to use the Nationalist Party's revolutionary army to crush the warlords and reunite China under a strong central government. When Sun unexpectedly died in 1925, Jiang Jieshi (Chiang Kai-shek), the young Japanese-educated director of the party's army training school, took his place. In 1926 and 1927 Jiang (1887–1975) led Nationalist armies in a successful attack on warlord governments in central and northern China. In 1928 the Nationalists established a new capital at Nanjing (Nanking). Foreign states recognized the Nanjing government, and superficial observers believed China to be truly reunified.

In fact, national unification was only skin-deep. China remained a vast agricultural country plagued by foreign concessions, regional differences, and a lack of modern communications. Moreover, the uneasy alliance between the Nationalist Party and the Chinese Communist Party had turned into a bitter, deadly rivalry. Justifiably fearful of Communist subversion of the Nationalist government, Jiang decided in April 1927 to liquidate his left-wing "allies" in a bloody purge. Chinese Communists went into hiding and vowed revenge.

China's Intellectual Revolution

Nationalism was the most powerful idea in China between 1911 and 1929, but it was only one aspect of a complex intellectual revolution, generally known as the **New Culture Movement,** that hammered at traditional Chinese thought and custom, advocated cultural renaissance, and pushed China into the modern world.

The New Culture Movement was founded by young Western-oriented intellectuals in Beijing during the May Fourth era. These intellectuals fiercely attacked China's ancient Confucian ethics, which subordinated subjects to rulers, sons to fathers, and wives to husbands. As modernists, they provocatively advocated new and anti-Confucian virtues: individualism, democratic equality, and the critical scientific method. They also promoted the use of simple, understandable written language as a means to clear thinking and mass education. China, they said, needed a whole new culture, a radically different worldview.

Many intellectuals thought the radical worldview China needed was Marxian socialism. It too was Western in origin, "scientific" in approach, and materialist in its denial of religious belief and Confucian family ethics. But while liberalism and individualism reflected the bewildering range of Western thought since the Enlightenment, Marxian socialism offered the certainty of a single all-encompassing creed. As one young Communist intellectual exclaimed, "I am now able to impose order on all the ideas which I could not reconcile; I have found the key to all the problems which appeared to me self-contradictory and insoluble."[6]

Though undeniably Western, Marxism provided a means of criticizing Western dominance, thereby salving Chinese pride. Chinese Communists could blame China's pitiful weakness on rapacious foreign capitalistic imperialism. Thus Marxism, as modified by Lenin and applied by the Bolsheviks in the Soviet Union, appeared as a means of catching up with the hated but envied West. For Chinese believers, it promised salvation soon.

Chinese Communists could and did interpret Marxism-Leninism to appeal to the masses—the peasants. Mao Zedong (Mao Tse-tung) in particular quickly recognized the impoverished Chinese peasantry's enormous revolutionary potential. A member of a prosperous, hard-working peasant family, Mao (1893–1976) converted to Marx-

New Culture Movement *An intellectual revolution, sometimes called the Chinese Renaissance, that attacked traditional Chinese, particularly Confucian, culture and promoted Western ideas of science, democracy, and individualism, from around 1916 to 1923.*

Primary Source:
Our Attitude Toward Modern Civilization of the West
A Chinese professor rejects the idea that Eastern civilization is more "spiritual" than the "materialistic" West.

● **Mao Zedong** Adapting Marxian theory to Chinese reality, Mao concentrated on the revolutionary potential of the peasantry. In this propagandistic painting, typical of Chinese art after the Communist takeover in 1949, the young Mao speaks to a group of worshipful peasant soldiers on the Long March, while Lenin and Marx look down with approval. *(Library of Congress)*

ian socialism in 1918. He began his revolutionary career as an urban labor organizer. In 1925 protest strikes by Chinese textile workers against their Japanese employers unexpectedly spread from the big coastal cities to rural China, prompting Mao to reconsider the peasants. Investigating the rapid growth of radical peasant associations in Hunan province, Mao argued passionately in a 1927 report that

the force of the peasantry is like that of the raging winds and driving rain. It is rapidly increasing in violence. No force can stand in its way. The peasantry will tear apart all nets which bind it and hasten along the road to liberation. They will bury beneath them all forces of imperialism, militarism, corrupt officialdom, village bosses and evil gentry.[7]

Mao's first experiment in peasant revolt—the Autumn Harvest Uprising of September 1927—was not successful, but Mao learned quickly. He advocated equal distribution of land and broke up his forces into small guerrilla groups. After 1928 he and his supporters built up a self-governing Communist soviet, centered at Ruijin (Juichin) in southeastern China, and dug in against Nationalist attacks.

China's intellectual revolution also stimulated profound changes in popular culture and family life. After the 1911 Revolution Chinese women enjoyed increasingly greater freedom and equality. Foot binding was outlawed and attacked as cruel and uncivilized. Arranged marriages and polygamy declined. Women gradually gained unprecedented educational and economic opportunities. Thus rising nationalism and the intellectual revolution interacted with monumental changes in Chinese family life. (See the feature "Individuals in Society: Ning Lao, a Chinese Working Woman.")

From Liberalism to Ultranationalism in Japan

The efforts of the Meiji reformers (see page 764) to build a powerful nationalistic state and resist Western imperialism were spectacularly successful and deeply impressed Japan's fellow Asians. The Japanese, alone among Asia's peoples, had mastered modern industrial technology by 1910 and fought victorious wars against both China and Russia. The First World War brought more triumphs. In 1915 Japan easily seized Germany's Asian holdings and held on to most of them as League of Nations mandates. The Japanese economy expanded enormously. Profits soared as Japan won new markets that wartime Europe could no longer supply.

In the early 1920s Japan seemed to make further progress on all fronts. Most Japanese nationalists believed that Japan had a semidivine mission to enlighten and protect Asia, but some were convinced that they could achieve their goal peacefully. In 1922 Japan signed a naval arms limitation treaty with the Western powers and returned some of its control over the Shandong Peninsula to China. These conciliatory moves reduced tensions in East Asia. At home Japan seemed headed toward genuine democracy. The electorate expanded twelvefold between 1918 and 1925 as all males over

● **Japanese Suffragists** In the 1920s Japanese women pressed for political emancipation in demonstrations like this one, but they did not receive the right to vote until 1946. Like these suffragists, some young women adopted Western fashions. Most workers in modern Japanese textile factories were also women. *(Time Life Pictures/Getty Images)*

Ning Lao, a Chinese Working Woman

The tough and resilient Ning Lao (*right*) with Ida Pruitt. *(Reproduced with permission of Eileen Hsu-Belzer)*

The voice of the poor and uneducated is often muffled in history. Thus *A Daughter of Han,* a rare autobiography of an illiterate working woman as told to an American friend, offers unforgettable insights into the evolution of ordinary Chinese life and family relations.

Ning Lao was born in 1867 to poor parents in the northern city of Penglai on the Shandong Peninsula. Her foot binding was delayed to age nine, "since I loved so much to run and play." When the bandages were finally drawn tight, "my feet hurt so much that for two years I had to crawl on my knees."* Her arranged marriage at age fourteen was a disaster. She found that her husband was a drug addict ("in those days everyone took opium to some extent") who sold everything to pay for his habit. Yet "there was no freedom then for women," and "it was no light thing for a woman to leave her house" and husband. Thus Ning Lao endured her situation until her husband sold their four-year-old daughter to buy opium. Taking her remaining baby daughter, she fled.

Taking off her foot bandages, Ning Lao became a beggar. Her feet began to spread, quite improperly, but she walked without pain. And the beggar's life was "not the hardest one," she thought, for a beggar woman could go where she pleased. To care better for her child, Ning Lao became a servant and a cook in prosperous households. Some of her mistresses were concubines (secondary wives taken by rich men in middle age), and she concluded that concubinage resulted in nothing but quarrels and heartache. Hot tempered and quick to take offense and leave an employer, the hard-working woman always found a new job quickly. In time she became a peddler of luxury goods to wealthy women confined to their homes.

The two unshakable values that buoyed Ning Lao were a tough, fatalistic acceptance of life—"Only fortune that comes of itself will come. There is no use to seek for it"—and devotion to her family. She eventually returned to her husband, who had mellowed, seldom took opium, and was "good" in those years. "But I did not miss him when he died. I had

*Ida Pruitt, *A Daughter of Han: The Autobiography of a Chinese Working Woman* (New Haven, Conn.: Yale University Press, 1945), p. 22. Other quotations are from pages 83, 62, 71, 182, 166, 235, and 246.

my newborn son and I was happy. My house was established. . . . Truly all my life I spent thinking of my family." Her lifelong devotion was reciprocated by her son and granddaughter, who cared for her well in her old age.

Ning Lao's remarkable life story encompasses both old and new Chinese attitudes toward family life. Her son moved to the capital city of Beijing, worked in an office, and had only one wife. Her granddaughter, Su Teh, studied in missionary schools and became a college teacher and a determined foe of arranged marriages. She personified the trend toward greater freedom for Chinese women.

Generational differences also highlighted changing political attitudes. When the Japanese invaded China and occupied Beijing in 1937, Ning Lao thought that "perhaps the Mandate of Heaven had passed to the Japanese . . . and we should listen to them as our new masters." Her nationalistic granddaughter disagreed. She urged resistance and the creation of a new China, where the people governed themselves. Leaving to join the guerrillas in 1938, Su Teh gave her savings to her family and promised to continue to help them. One must be good to one's family, she said, but one must also work for the country.

Questions for Analysis

1. Compare the lives of Ning Lao and her granddaughter. In what ways were they different and similar?

2. In a broader historical perspective, what do you find most significant about Ning Lao's account of her life? Why?

twenty-five won the vote. Two-party competition was intense. Japanese living standards were the highest in Asia. Literacy was universal.

Japan's remarkable rise, however, was accompanied by serious problems. Japan had a rapidly growing population, but scarce natural resources. As early as the 1920s Japan was exporting manufactured goods in order to pay for imports of food and essential raw materials. Deeply enmeshed in world trade, Japan was vulnerable to every boom and bust. These economic realities broadened support for Japan's colonial empire. Before World War I, Japanese leaders saw colonial expansion primarily in terms of international prestige and national defense. They believed that control of Taiwan, Korea, and Manchuria provided an essential "outer ring of defense" to protect the home islands from Russian attack and Anglo-American imperialism. Now, in the 1920s, Japan's colonies also seemed essential for markets, raw materials, and economic growth.

Japan's rapid industrial development also created an imbalanced "dualistic" economy. The modern sector consisted of a handful of giant conglomerate firms, the **zaibatsu,** or "financial combines." Zaibatsu firms like Mitsubishi employed thousands of workers and owned banks, mines, steel mills, cotton factories, shipyards, and trading companies, all of them closely interrelated. Zaibatsu firms wielded enormous economic power and dominated the other sector of the economy, an unorganized multitude of peasant farmers and craftsmen. The result was financial oligarchy, corruption of government officials, and a weak middle class.

Behind the façade of party politics, the old and new elites—the emperor, high government officials, big businessmen, and military leaders—were jockeying savagely for the real power. Cohesive leadership, which had played such an important role in Japan's modernization by the Meiji reformers, had ceased to exist. By far the most serious challenge to peaceful progress, however, was fanatical nationalism. As in Europe, ultranationalism first emerged in Japan in the late nineteenth century but did not flower fully until the First World War and the 1930s.

Though often vague, Japan's ultranationalists shared several fundamental beliefs. They were violently anti-Western. They rejected democracy, big business, and Marxian socialism, which they blamed for destroying the older, superior Japanese practices they wanted to restore. Reviving old myths, they stressed the emperor's godlike qualities and the samurai warrior's code of honor and obedience. Despising party politics, they assassinated moderate leaders and plotted armed uprisings to achieve their goals. Above all else, the ultranationalists preached foreign expansion. Like Western imperialists shouldering "the White Man's Burden," Japanese ultranationalists thought their mission was a noble one. "Asia for the Asians" was their anti-Western rallying cry. As the famous ultranationalist Kita Ikki wrote in 1923, "Our seven hundred million brothers in China and India have no other path to independence than that offered by our guidance and protection."[8]

The ultranationalists were noisy and violent in the 1920s, but it took the Great Depression of the 1930s to tip the scales decisively in their favor. The worldwide depression, which had dire consequences for many countries (see Chapter 29), hit Japan like a tidal wave in 1930. Exports and wages collapsed; unemployment and raw suffering soared. Starving peasants ate the bark off trees and sold their daughters to brothels. The ultranationalists blamed the system, and people listened.

Japan Against China

Among those who listened with particular care were young Japanese army officers in Manchuria, the underpopulated, resource-rich province of northeastern China controlled by the Japanese army since its victory over Russia in 1905. Many junior Japanese officers in Manchuria came from the peasantry and were distressed by the stories

zaibatsu *Giant conglomerate firms in Japan.*

● **Japanese Atrocities in China**   In December 1937, after the fall of the Chinese capital Nanjing, Japanese soldiers went on a horrifying rampage. These Japanese recruits are using Chinese prisoners of war as live targets in a murderous bayonet drill. Other Chinese prisoners were buried alive by their Japanese captors. *(Hulton Archive/Getty Images)*

of rural suffering they heard from home. They also knew the Japanese army's budget and prestige had declined in the prosperous 1920s.

The rise of Chinese nationalism worried the young officers most. This new political force, embodied in the Guomindang unification of China, challenged Japanese control over Manchuria. In response, junior Japanese officers in Manchuria, in cooperation with top generals in Tokyo, secretly manufactured an excuse for aggression in late 1931. They blew up some Japanese-owned railroad tracks near the city of Shenyang (Mukden) and then with reinforcements rushed in from Korea quickly occupied all of Manchuria in "self-defense."

In 1932 Japan proclaimed Manchuria an independent state and installed a member of the old Qing Dynasty as puppet emperor. When the League of Nations condemned its aggression in Manchuria, Japan resigned in protest. Japanese aggression in Manchuria showed that the army, though reporting directly to the Japanese emperor, was clearly an independent force subject to no outside control.

The Japanese puppet state named Manchukuo in northeast China became the model for the subsequent conquest and occupation of China and then Southeast Asia. Throughout the 1930s, the Japanese worked to integrate Manchuria (and Korea and

Taiwan) into a large, self-sufficient economic bloc that provided resources, markets, and investment opportunities safe from Western power in East Asia. While exporting raw materials, state-sponsored Japanese companies in Manchuria also built steel mills and heavy industry to supply vital military goods. At home, newspapers and newsreels glorified Japan's efforts and mobilized public support for colonial empire.

For China the Japanese conquest of Manchuria was disastrous. Japanese aggression in Manchuria drew attention away from modernizing efforts. The Nationalist government promoted a massive boycott of Japanese goods but lost interest in social reform. Above all, the Nationalist government after 1931 completely neglected land reform and the Chinese peasants' grinding poverty.

As in many poor agricultural societies throughout history, Chinese peasants paid roughly half of their crops to their landlords as rent. Land ownership was very unequal. One study estimated that a mere 4 percent of families, usually absentee landlords living in cities, owned fully half the land. Poor peasants and farm laborers—70 percent of the rural population—owned only one-sixth of the land. As a result, peasants were heavily in debt and chronically underfed. A contemporaneous Chinese economist spelled out the revolutionary implications: "It seems clear that the land problem in China today is as acute as that of eighteenth-century France or nineteenth-century Russia." Mao Zedong certainly agreed.

Having abandoned land reform, partly because they themselves were often landowners, the Nationalists under Jiang Jieshi devoted their energies between 1930 and 1934 to great campaigns of encirclement and extermination against the Communists' rural power base in southeastern China. In 1934 they closed in for the kill, but, in one of the most incredible sagas of modern times, the main Communist army broke out, beat off attacks, and retreated 6,000 miles in twelve months to a remote region on the northwestern border (see Map 28.2). Of the estimated 100,000 men and women who began the **Long March,** only 8,000 to 10,000 reached the final destination. There Mao built up his forces once again, established a new territorial base, and won local peasant support by undertaking land reform.

Long March *The 6,000-mile retreat of the Communist army to a remote region on the northwestern border of China, during which tens of thousands lost their lives.*

In Japan politics became increasingly chaotic. In 1937 the Japanese military and the ultranationalists were in command. Unable to force China to cede more territory in northern China, they used a minor incident near Beijing as a pretext for a general attack. This marked the beginning of World War II in Asia, although Japan issued no declaration of war. The Nationalist government, which had just formed a united front with the Communists, fought hard, but Japanese troops quickly took Beijing and northern China. Taking the great port of Shanghai after ferocious combat, the Japanese launched an immediate attack up the Yangzi River (see Map 28.2).

Foretelling the horrors of World War II, the Japanese air force bombed Chinese cities and civilian populations with unrelenting fury. Nanjing, the capital, fell in December 1937. Entering the city, Japanese soldiers went berserk and committed dreadful atrocities over seven weeks. Tens of thousands of Chinese were killed, and many thousands of women were raped. The "Rape of Nanjing" combined with other Japanese atrocities to outrage world opinion. The Western Powers denounced Japanese aggression but, with tensions rising in Europe, took no action.

By late 1938 Japanese armies occupied sizable portions of coastal China (see Map 28.2). But the Nationalists and the Communists had retreated to the interior, and both refused to accept defeat. In 1939, as Europe edged toward another great war, the undeclared war between China and Japan bogged down in a savage stalemate. The bloody undeclared war provided a spectacular example of conflicting nationalisms.

Southeast Asia

The tide of nationalism was also rising in Southeast Asia. Like their counterparts in India, China, and Japan, nationalists in French Indochina, the Dutch East Indies, and the Philippines urgently wanted genuine political independence and freedom from foreign rule. In both French Indochina and the Dutch East Indies, they ran up against an imperialist stone wall. The obstacle to Filipino independence came from America and Japan.

In the words of one historian, "Indochina was governed by Frenchmen for Frenchmen, and the great liberal slogans of liberty, equality, and fraternity were not considered to be export goods for overseas dominions."[9] This uncompromising attitude stimulated the growth of an equally stubborn communist opposition under Ho Chi Minh, which despite ruthless repression emerged as the dominant anti-French force.

In the East Indies—modern Indonesia—the Dutch made some concessions after the First World War, establishing a people's council with very limited lawmaking power. But in the 1930s the Dutch cracked down hard, jailing all the important nationalist leaders. Like the French, the Dutch were determined to hold on.

In the Philippines, however, a well-established nationalist movement achieved greater success. As in colonial Latin America, the Spanish in the Philippines had been indefatigable missionaries. By the late nineteenth century the Filipino population was 80 percent Catholic. Filipinos shared a common cultural heritage and a common racial origin. Education, especially for girls, was quite advanced for Southeast Asia, and already in 1843 a higher percentage of people could read in the Philippines than in Spain itself. Economic development helped to create a westernized elite, which turned first to reform and then to revolution in the 1890s. As in Egypt and Turkey, long-standing intimate contact with Western civilization created a strong nationalist movement at an early date.

Filipino nationalists were bitterly disillusioned when the United States, having taken the Philippines from Spain in the Spanish-American War of 1898, ruthlessly beat down a patriotic revolt and denied the universal Filipino desire for independence. The Americans claimed the Philippines were not ready and might be seized by Germany or Britain. As the imperialist power in the Philippines, the United States encouraged education and promoted capitalistic economic development. As in British India, an elected legislature was given some real powers. In 1919 President Wilson even promised eventual independence, though subsequent Republican administrations saw it as a distant goal.

As in India and French Indochina, demands for independence grew. One important contributing factor was American racial attitudes. Americans treated Filipinos as inferiors and introduced segregationist practices borrowed from the American South. American racism made passionate nationalists of many Filipinos. However, it was the Great Depression that had the most radical impact on the Philippines.

As the United States collapsed economically, the Philippines suddenly appeared to be a liability rather than an asset. American farm groups lobbied for protection from cheap Filipino sugar. To protect American jobs, labor unions demanded an end to Filipino immigration. In 1934 Congress made the Philippines a self-governing commonwealth and scheduled independence for 1944. Sugar imports were reduced, and immigration limited to only fifty Filipinos per year.

Like Britain and France in the Middle East, the United States was determined to hold on to its big military bases in the Philippines as it permitted increased local self-government and promised eventual political independence. Some Filipino nationalists denounced the continued presence of U.S. fleets and armies. Others were less certain that the American presence was the immediate problem. Japan was fighting in China and expanding economically into the Philippines and throughout Southeast Asia. By 1939 a new threat to Filipino independence appeared to come from Asia itself.

Chapter Summary

Key Terms

Permanent Mandates
 Commission
Young Turks
sharif
Sykes-Picot Agreement
Balfour Declaration
Treaty of Lausanne
Atatürk
Majlis
Zionism
kibbutz
Lucknow Pact
Satyagraha
May Fourth Movement
New Culture Movement
zaibatsu
Long March

To assess your mastery of this chapter, go to
bedfordstmartins.com/mckayworld

• *How did modern nationalism—the dominant force in most of the world in the twentieth century—develop in Asia between the First and Second World Wars?*

The Asian nationalist revolt against the West began before the First World War. But only after 1914 did Asian nationalist movements broaden their bases sufficiently to challenge Western domination effectively. These mass movements sought human dignity as well as political freedom. Generally speaking, Asian nationalists favored modernization and adopted Western techniques and ideas even as they rejected Western rule. Everywhere Asian nationalists had to fight long and hard, though their struggle gained momentum from growing popular support and the encouragement of the Soviet Union.

• *How did the collapse of the Ottoman Empire in World War I shape the history of the Middle East for the rest of the century?*

The collapse of the Ottoman Empire in World War I left a power vacuum that both Western imperialists and Turkish, Arab, Persian, and Jewish and other nationalists sought to fill. The Turks, who had ruled the old Ottoman Empire, created the modern secular state of Turkey under the leadership of Mustafa Kemal. He brutally crushed the budding nationalism of the Kurds and Armenians. A nationalist movement in Iran, led by the military dictator Reza Shah Pahlavi, gained independence from British control, as did Afghanistan under the anti-British amir Amanullah. The British made promises to both the Palestinians and Jewish Zionists regarding independent homelands in Palestine, creating an impasse that has yet to be settled. France and England had divided areas of the Middle East between them during the war, and then claimed jurisdiction over them as League of Nations mandates. The British and French maintained various degrees of control over the Arab states of Iraq, Syria, Lebanon, Egypt, and Arabia after the war but lost much of their influence over the next two decades as Arab nationalists pushed for complete independence.

• *What role did Gandhi and his campaign of militant nonviolence play in leading India to independence from the British?*

In facing the might of the British Empire Gandhi knew that the Indian people were not capable of fighting a military campaign against the British without suffering hundreds of thousands, perhaps millions, of deaths. But he realized that a few thousand British could do nothing if 350 million Indians refused to cooperate or obey British laws. By employing active, nonviolent resistance, which he called Satyagraha, Gandhi and his millions of Hindu and Muslim followers were able to bring British colonial rule in India to a standstill, leading to Indian independence in 1947. Regrettably, however, Gandhi was not able to control the extreme religious nationalism of the Muslims and Hindus following independence. After bloody massacres on both sides, Muslim Pakistan and Bangladesh split off from predominantly Hindu India (see Chapter 32).

• **Why did some of the Asian nationalist movements come into brutal conflict?**

Asia's nationalist movements arose out of separate historical experiences and distinct cultures. Variations on the common theme of nationalism were evident in China, Japan, and the Philippines. This diversity helps explain why Asian peoples became defensive in their relations with one another while rising against Western rule. Like earlier nationalists in Europe, Asian nationalists developed a strong sense of "we" and "they"; "they" included other Asians as well as Europeans. Nationalism meant freedom, modernization, and cultural renaissance, but it nonetheless proved to be a mixed blessing.

Suggested Reading

Chang, Jung, and Jon Halliday. *Mao: The Unknown Story.* 2006. New, and very controversial, biography of the Chinese leader.

Chow, Tse-tung. *The May Fourth Movement: Intellectual Revolution in Modern China.* 1960. The classic study of the Chinese intellectual revolution that began in 1919.

Erikson, Eric. *Gandhi's Truth: On the Origins of Militant Nonviolence.* 1969. A classic study of Gandhi's life and the origins of Satyagraha.

Fromkin, David. *A Peace to End All Peace: The Fall of the Ottoman Empire and the Creation of the Modern Middle East.* 2001. A very thorough but very readable introduction to the Middle East in the early twentieth century.

Hourani, Albert, and Malise Ruthven. *History of the Arab Peoples.* 2003. One of the best single volume histories of the Arab peoples.

Hsü, Immanuel C.Y. *The Rise of Modern China,* 6th ed. 1999. Sixth edition of a classic history of modern China.

Irokawa, Daikichi. *The Age of Hirohito: In Search of Modern Japan.* 1995. An excellent brief account by a leading Japanese historian.

Lacqueur, Walter. *A History of Zionism. From the French Revolution to the Establishment of the State of Israel.* 1972. Good general history of Zionism and the founding of Israel.

Mango, Andrew. *Atatürk.* 2000. Rich, well-researched biography of this complex Turkish leader.

Myers, Ramon H., and M. Peattie, eds. *The Japanese Colonial Expansion, 1895–1945.* 1984. Broad collection of essays covering all of Japan's colonial empire, both formal and informal.

Osborne, Milton. *Southeast Asia: An Introductory History,* 9th ed. 2005. Ninth edition of the classic introduction to the region's history.

Owen, Norman, David Chandler, and William R. Roff. *The Emergence of Southeast Asia: A New History.* 2004. New history looking at both individual countries and social and economic themes, including gender and ecology.

Reischauer, Edwin O. *Japan: The Story of Nation,* 4th ed. 1991. The classic history in its fourth edition by America's leading historian on Japan.

Spence, Jonathan. *The Search for Modern China.* 1990. Important study of modern China by a leading Chinese scholar.

Wolpert, Stanley. *India.* 2005. An excellent introduction to India's history.

Young, Louise. *Japan's Total Empire: Manchuria and the Culture of Wartime Imperialism.* 1998. A fascinating pioneering work on Japanese imperialism.

Notes

1. K. M. Panikkar, *Asia and Western Dominance: A Survey of the Vasco da Gama Epoch of Asian History* (London: George Allen & Unwin, 1959), p. 197.

2. H. Armstrong, *Turkey in Travail: The Birth of a New Nation* (London: John Lane, 1925), p. 75.

3. Quoted in Lord Kinross, *Atatürk: A Biography of Mustafa Kemal, Father of Modern Turkey* (New York: Morrow, 1965), p. 181.

4. Quoted in E. Erikson, *Gandhi's Truth: On the Origins of Militant Nonviolence* (New York: W. W. Norton, 1969), p. 225.

5. Quoted in W. T. deBary, W. Chan, and B. Watson, *Sources of Chinese Tradition* (New York: Columbia University Press, 1964), pp. 768–769.

6. Quoted in J. F. Fairbank, E. O. Reischauer, and A. M. Craig, *East Asia: Tradition and Transformation* (Boston: Houghton Mifflin, 1973), p. 774.

7. Quoted in B. I. Schwartz, *Chinese Communism and the Rise of Mao* (Cambridge, Mass.: Harvard University Press, 1951), p. 74.

8. Quoted in W. T. deBary, R. Tsunoda, and D. Keene, *Sources of Japanese Tradition,* vol. 2 (New York: Columbia University Press, 1958), p. 269.

9. Quoted in W. Bingham, H. Conroy, and F. Iklé, *A History of Asia,* vol. 2, 2d ed. (Boston: Allyn and Bacon, 1974), p. 480.

Listening to the PAST

Arab Political Aspirations in 1919

Great Britain and France had agreed to divide up the Arab lands, and the British also had made conflicting promises to Arab and Jewish nationalists. However, President Wilson insisted at Versailles that the right of self-determination should be applied to the conquered Ottoman territories, and he sent an American commission of inquiry to Syria, even though the British and French refused to participate. The commission canvassed political views throughout greater Syria, and its long report with many documents reflected public opinion in the region in 1919.

To present their view to the Americans, Arab nationalists from present-day Syria, Lebanon, Israel, and Jordan came together in Damascus as the General Syrian Congress, and they passed the following resolution on July 2, 1919. In addition to the Arab call for political independence, the delegates addressed the possibility of French rule under a League of Nations mandate and the establishment of a Jewish national home.

We the undersigned members of the General Syrian Congress, meeting in Damascus on Wednesday, July 2nd, 1919, . . . provided with credentials and authorizations by the inhabitants of our various districts, Moslems, Christians, and Jews, have agreed upon the following statement of the desires of the people of the country who have elected us to present them to the American Section of the International Commission; the fifth article was passed by a very large majority; all the other articles were accepted unanimously.

1. We ask absolutely complete political independence for Syria within these boundaries. [Describes the area including the present-day states of Syria, Lebanon, Israel, and Jordan.]

2. We ask that the Government of this Syrian country should be a democratic civil constitutional Monarchy on broad decentralization principles, safeguarding the rights of minorities, and that the King be the Emir Faisal, who carried on a glorious struggle in the cause of our liberation and merited our full confidence and entire reliance.

3. Considering the fact that the Arabs inhabiting the Syrian area are not naturally less gifted than other more advanced races and that they are by no means

less developed than the Bulgarians, Serbians, Greeks, and Roumanians at the beginning of their independence, we protest against Article 22 of the Covenant of the League of Nations, placing us among the nations in their middle stage of development which stand in need of a mandatory power.

4. In the event of the rejection by the Peace Conference of this just protest for certain considerations that we may not understand, we, relying on the declarations of President Wilson that his object in waging war was to put an end to the ambition of conquest and colonization, can only regard the mandate mentioned in the Covenant of the League of Nations as equivalent to the rendering of economical and technical assistance that does not prejudice our complete independence. And desiring that our country should not fall a prey to colonization and believing that the American Nation is farthest from any thought of colonization and has no political ambition in our country, we will seek the technical and economical assistance from the United States of America, provided that such assistance does not exceed 20 years.

5. In the event of America not finding herself in a position to accept our desire for assistance, we will seek this assistance from Great Britain, also provided that such assistance does not infringe the complete independence and unity of our country and that the duration of such assistance does not exceed that mentioned in the previous article.

6. We do not acknowledge any right claimed by the French Government in any part whatever of our Syrian country and refuse that she should assist us or have a hand in our country under any circumstances and in any place.

7. We oppose the pretensions of the Zionists to create a Jewish commonwealth in the southern part of Syria, known as Palestine, and oppose Zionist migration to any part of our country; for we do not acknowledge their title but consider them a grave peril to our people from the national, economical, and political points of view. Our Jewish compatriots shall enjoy our common rights and assume the common responsibilities.

Palestinian Arabs protest against large-scale Jewish migration into Palestine. *(Roger-Viollet/Getty Images)*

8. We ask that there should be no separation of the southern part of Syria, known as Palestine, nor of the littoral western zone, which includes Lebanon, from the Syrian country. We desire that the unity of the country should be guaranteed against partition under whatever circumstances.

9. We ask complete independence for emancipated Mesopotamia [today's Iraq] and that there should be no economical barriers between the two countries.

10. The fundamental principles laid down by President Wilson in condemnation of secret treaties impel us to protest most emphatically against any treaty that stipulates the partition of our Syria country and against any private engagement aiming at the establishment of Zionism in the southern part of Syria; therefore we ask the complete annulment of these conventions and agreements.

The noble principles enunciated by President Wilson strengthen our confidence that our desires emanating from the depths of our hearts, shall be the decisive factor in determining our future; and that President Wilson and the free American people will be our supporters for the realization of our hopes, thereby proving their sincerity and noble sympathy with the aspiration of the weaker nations in general and our Arab people in particular.

We also have the fullest confidence that the Peace Conference will realize that we would not have risen against the Turks, with whom we had participated in all civil, political, and representative privileges, but for their violation of our national rights, and so will grant us our desires in full in order that our political rights may not be less after the war than they were before, since we have shed so much blood in the cause of our liberty and independence.

We request to be allowed to send a delegation to represent us at the Peace Conference to defend our rights and secure the realization of our aspirations.

Questions for Analysis

1. What kind of state did the delegates want?

2. How did the delegates want to modify an unwanted League of Nations mandate to make it less objectionable?

3. Did the delegates view their "Jewish compatriots" and the Zionists in different ways? Why?

Source: "Resolution of the General Syrian Congress at Damascus, 2 July 1919," from the *King-Crane Commission Report,* in *Foreign Relations of the United States: Paris Peace Conference, 1919,* 12: 780–781.

Outside and Inside. This detail of George Grosz's *Draussen und Drinnen* (Outside and Inside) captures the uncertainty and anxiety of the 1920s. *(Estate of George Grosz/ Licensed by VAGA, New York, NY. Photo: akg-images)*

29 THE AGE OF ANXIETY IN THE WEST

Allied diplomats meeting in Paris in early 1919 had optimistic plans for building a lasting peace. Most held high hopes for happier times and looked forward to life returning to normal after the terrible trauma of total war—life in the familiar prewar terms of peace, prosperity, and progress. These hopes were in vain. The Great Break—the First World War and the Russian Revolution—had mangled too many things beyond repair. Thus in the 1920s and 1930s, as Asians developed renewed self-confidence and forged powerful nationalist movements directed against Western domination (see Chapter 28), many in the West felt themselves increasingly adrift in a strange, uncertain, and uncontrollable world. They saw themselves living in an age of anxiety, an age of continual crisis (which would last until the early 1950s). In almost every area of human experience, they went searching for ways to put meaning back into life.

UNCERTAINTY IN MODERN THOUGHT

What was the nature of the uncertainty in modern thought in Europe at the beginning of the twentieth century, and what did the doubts and searching mean for Western thought, art, and culture?

A complex revolution in thought and ideas was under way in Western society before the First World War, but relatively few people were aware of it. After the war new and upsetting ideas began to spread through the entire population. Western society began to question and even abandon many cherished values and beliefs that had guided it since the eighteenth-century Enlightenment and the nineteenth-century triumph of industrial development, scientific advances, and evolutionary thought.

● **Kollwitz: The Grieving Parents** After the renowned German artist Kathe Kollwitz learned in October 1914 that her son Peter had died in battle, the heartbroken mother conceived of a sculpture to honor his memory. Yet her efforts were repeatedly overwhelmed by sorrow. Only in 1931 could she complete this graveside memorial in a military cemetery, a telling indication of the war's ongoing devastation for millions. The grieving father and mother are finally reunited with their son, and they beg forgiveness for the mad war their generation inflicted on its children. *(John Parker, Photographer/© Artists Rights society (ARS), New York/VG Bild-Kunst, Bonn)*

Before 1914 most people in the West still believed in progress, reason, and individual rights. Progress was a daily reality, apparent in the rising standard of living, the taming of the city, and the steady increase in popular education. Such developments also encouraged the comforting belief in the logical universe of Newtonian physics and faith that a rational human mind could understand that universe through intellectual investigation. There were also laws of society, like the laws of science, which rational human beings could discover and then wisely act on. At the same time, individual rights were actually increasing. Well-established rights were gradually spreading to women and workers, and new "social rights," such as old-age pensions, were emerging. In short, before World War I most Europeans and North Americans had a moderately optimistic view of the world, and with good reason.

Nevertheless, since the 1880s a small band of serious thinkers and creative writers had been attacking these optimistic ideas. These critics rejected the general faith in progress and the power of the rational human mind. Their numbers expanded after the experience of history's most destructive war—a war that suggested to many that human beings were a pack of violent, irrational animals quite capable of tearing the individual and his or her rights to shreds. Disorientation and pessimism were particularly acute in the 1930s, when harsh dictatorships and the Great Depression transformed old certainties into bitter illusions.

In the early 1920s no one expressed this state of uncertainty better than French poet and critic Paul Valéry (1871–1945): "We think of what has disappeared, and we are almost destroyed by what has been destroyed; we do not know what will be born, and we fear the future, not without reason."[1] Above all, Valéry saw the "cruelly injured mind" besieged by doubts and suffering from anxieties. New ideas and discoveries in philosophy, physics, psychology, and literature contributed to this general intellectual crisis of the twentieth century.

Modern Philosophy

Among those thinkers in the late nineteenth century who challenged the belief in progress and the general faith in the rational human mind, German philosopher Friedrich Nietzsche (1844–1900) was particularly influential. A Lutheran minister's son, Nietzsche utterly rejected Christianity. In 1872 he argued that ever since classical Athens, the West had overemphasized rationality and stifled the passion and animal instinct that drive human activity and true creativity. Nietzsche questioned all values. He claimed that Christianity embodied a "slave morality" that glorified weakness, envy, and mediocrity. In Nietzsche's most famous line, a wise fool proclaims that "God is dead," murdered by lackadaisical modern Christians who no longer truly believe in Him. Nietzsche regarded the pillars of conventional morality—reason, democracy, progress, respectability—as outworn social and psychological constructs that suffocated self-realization and excellence. Little read during his lifetime, Nietzsche attracted growing attention in the early twentieth century, and his influence remains enormous to this day.

French philosophy professor Henri Bergson (1859–1941) also expressed growing dissatisfaction with established ideas before 1914. Bergson argued that immediate experience and intuition were as important as rational and scientific thinking for understanding reality. Rejecting democracy, French socialist Georges Sorel (1847–1922) frankly characterized Marxian socialism as an inspiring but unprovable religion rather than a rational scientific truth. Socialism would come to power, he believed, through a great, violent strike of all working people, which would miraculously shatter capitalist society.

The First World War accelerated the revolt against established certainties in philosophy, but that revolt went in two very different directions. In English-speaking countries, logical empiricism (or logical positivism) gained acceptance in university circles. In continental Europe the primary development in philosophy was existentialism.

Logical empiricism was truly revolutionary. It rejected most concerns of traditional philosophy, from God's existence to the meaning of happiness, as nonsense. Austrian philosopher Ludwig Wittgenstein (1889–1951), who spent much of his life at Cambridge, is primarily responsible for this postulation.

Wittgenstein argued in his pugnacious *Tractatus Logico-Philosophicus* (*Essay on Logical Philosophy*) in 1922 that philosophy is only the logical clarification of thoughts. It therefore becomes the study of language, which expresses thoughts. In Wittgenstein's opinion the great philosophical issues of the ages—God, freedom, morality, and so on—are quite literally senseless, for statements about them can be neither tested by scientific experiments nor demonstrated by the logic of mathematics. Logical empiricism drastically reduced the scope of philosophical inquiry. Anxious people could find few, if any, answers in this direction.

Some looked to **existentialism** for answers. Highly diverse and even contradictory, existential thinkers were loosely united in a courageous search for moral values in a world of terror and uncertainty. Theirs were the age of anxiety's true voices.

Most existential thinkers in the twentieth century were atheists. Often inspired by Nietzsche, they did not believe a Supreme Being had established humanity's fundamental nature and given life its meaning. In the words of the famous French existentialist Jean-Paul Sartre (1905–1980), human beings simply exist: "They turn up, appear on the scene." Only then do they seek to define themselves. Honest human beings are terribly alone, hounded by despair and the meaningless of life, for there is no God to help them. The crisis of the existential thinker epitomized the modern intellectual crisis—the shattering of traditional beliefs in God, reason, and progress.

Existentialists did recognize that human beings, unless they kill themselves, must act. Indeed, in Sartre's words, "man is condemned to be free." There is therefore the possibility—indeed, the necessity—of giving life meaning through actions, of defining

Chronology

1919 Treaty of Versailles; Keynes, *Economic Consequences of the Peace;* Rutherford splits the atom; Freudian psychology gains popular attention; Gropius founds the Bauhaus

1920s Existentialism gains prominence

1920s–1930s Dadaism and surreal artistic movements

1922 Wittgenstein writes on logical empiricism; Woolf, *Jacob's Room;* Joyce, *Ulysses;* Eliot, *The Waste Land*

1923 French and Belgian armies occupy the Ruhr

1924 Dawes Plan

1925 Hitler, *Mein Kampf*

1926 Germany joins League of Nations

1928 Kellogg-Briand Pact

1929 Faulkner, *The Sound and the Fury*

1929–1939 Great Depression

1932 Franklin Roosevelt elected U.S. president

1934 Riefenstahl, *The Triumph of the Will,* documentary film on Nazi rally

1935 Creation of Works Progress Administration as part of New Deal

1936–1937 Popular Front government in France

logical empiricism *A revolt against established certainties in philosophy that rejected most of the concerns of traditional philosophy, from the existence of God to the meaning of happiness, as nonsense and hot air.*

existentialism *A highly diverse and even contradictory system of thought that was loosely united in a courageous search for moral values in a world of terror and uncertainty.*

oneself through choices. To do so, individuals must become "engaged," choose their own actions courageously and consistently and be fully aware of their responsibility for their own behavior.

Existentialism came of age in France during and immediately after World War II. With Hitler's barbarous wartime regime, people had to choose whether to join the resistance or abet the murderous Nazis. Sartre himself was active in the resistance; he and his colleagues offered a powerful answer to the profound moral issues of the day.

The Revival of Christianity

The loss of faith in human reason and in continual progress also led to a renewed interest in Christianity. Christianity and religion in general had been on the defensive in intellectual circles since the Enlightenment. In the years before 1914 some theologians, especially Protestant ones, interpreted Christian doctrine and the Bible so they did not seem to contradict science, evolution, and common sense. Christ became primarily the greatest moral teacher, and his divine "supernatural" aspects were strenuously played down.

Especially after World War I, several thinkers and theologians began to revitalize Christian fundamentals. Sometimes described as Christian existentialists because they shared the loneliness and despair of atheistic existentialists, they stressed human beings' sinful nature, the need for faith, and the mystery of God's forgiveness. The revival of fundamental Christian belief was fed by rediscovery of the work of nineteenth-century Danish religious philosopher Søren Kierkegaard (1813–1855). Rejecting formalistic religion, Kierkegaard resolved his personal anguish over his imperfect nature by making a total religious commitment to a remote and majestic God.

Similarly, Swiss Protestant theologian Karl Barth (1886–1968) maintained that religious truth is made known to human beings only through God's grace. As sinful creatures whose reason and will are hopelessly flawed, people must accept God's Word and the supernatural revelation of Jesus Christ with awe, trust, and obedience. Lowly mortals should not expect to "reason out" God and his ways.

After 1914 religion became much more relevant and meaningful than it had been before the Great War, and many illustrious individuals turned to religion between about 1920 and 1950. Though often of a despairing, existential variety, religion was one meaningful answer to terror and anxiety. In the words of a famous Roman Catholic convert, English novelist Graham Greene, "One began to believe in heaven because one believed in hell."[2]

The New Physics

By the late nineteenth century science was one of the main pillars supporting Western society's optimistic and rationalistic worldview. Darwin's concept of evolution had been accepted and assimilated in most intellectual circles. Progressive minds believed science was based on hard facts and controlled experiments, producing an unerring and almost completed picture of reality. Unchanging natural laws seemed to determine physical processes and permit useful solutions to more and more problems. All this was comforting, especially to people no longer committed to traditional religious beliefs. And all this was challenged by the new physics.

An important first step toward the new physics was the discovery at the end of the nineteenth century that atoms were not like hard, permanent little billiard balls. They were actually composed of many far-smaller, fast-moving particles, such as electrons and protons. Polish-born physicist Marie Curie (1867–1934) and her French husband Pierre (1859–1906) discovered that radium constantly emits subatomic particles and thus does not have a constant atomic weight. German physicist Max Planck (1858–1947) showed in 1900 that subatomic energy is emitted in uneven little spurts, which Planck called "quanta," and not in a steady stream, as previously believed.

Planck's discovery called into question the old sharp distinction between matter and energy and challenged the old view of atoms as the stable, basic building blocks of nature.

In 1905 German-born Jewish genius Albert Einstein (1879–1955) further undermined Newtonian physics. His famous theory of special relativity postulated that time and space are relative to the observer's viewpoint and that only the speed of light is constant for all frames of reference in the universe. To make his revolutionary and paradoxical idea somewhat comprehensible to the nonmathematical layperson, Einstein used analogies involving moving trains. For example, if a woman in the middle of a moving car gets up and walks forward to the door, she has moved a half car length relative to the train. But relative to an observer on the embankment, she has moved farther. The closed framework of Newtonian physics was quite limited in comparison with the framework of Einsteinian physics, which unified an apparently infinite universe with the incredibly small, fast-moving subatomic world. Moreover, Einstein's theory stated that matter and energy are interchangeable and that even a particle of matter contains enormous levels of potential energy.

The 1920s opened the "heroic age of physics," in the apt words of one of its leading pioneers, Ernest Rutherford (1871–1937). Breakthrough followed breakthrough. In 1919 Rutherford first split the atom. By 1944 seven subatomic particles had been identified, of which the most important was the **neutron**. The neutron's capacity to pass through other atoms allowed for even more intense experimental bombardment of matter, leading to chain reactions of unbelievable force. This was the road to the atomic bomb.

● **Unlocking the Power of the Atom** Many of the fanciful visions of science fiction came true in the twentieth century, although not exactly as first imagined. This 1927 cartoon satirizes a professor who has split the atom and unwittingly destroyed his building and neighborhood in the process. In the Second World War professors harnessed the atom in bombs and decimated faraway cities and their inhabitants. *(Mary Evans Picture Library)*

Although few nonscientists understood this revolution in physics, its implications as presented by newspapers and popular writers were disturbing to millions of men and women in the 1920s and 1930s. The new universe was strange and troubling, seemingly lacking any absolute objective reality. Everything was "relative"—that is, dependent on the observer's frame of reference. Moreover, science appeared distant from human experience and human problems. When, for example, Planck was asked what science could contribute to resolving conflicts of values, he responded simply, "Science is not qualified to speak to this question."

neutron *The most important of the subatomic particles because its capacity to pass through other atoms allowed for intense experimental bombardment of matter, leading to chain reactions of unbelievable force.*

Freudian Psychology

With physics presenting an uncertain universe so unrelated to ordinary human experience, questions about the human mind's power and potential assumed special significance. The findings and speculations of psychologist Sigmund Freud (1856–1939) were particularly disturbing.

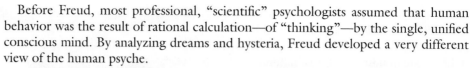

Before Freud, most professional, "scientific" psychologists assumed that human behavior was the result of rational calculation—of "thinking"—by the single, unified conscious mind. By analyzing dreams and hysteria, Freud developed a very different view of the human psyche.

According to Freud, human behavior is basically irrational. The key to understanding the mind is the primitive, irrational unconscious, which he called the **id**. The unconscious is driven by sexual, aggressive, and pleasure-seeking desires and is locked in constant battle with the mind's two other parts: the rationalizing conscious (the **ego**), which mediates what a person *can* do, and ingrained moral values (the **superego**), which specify what a person *should* do. Human behavior is a product of a fragile compromise between instinctual drives and the controls of rational thinking and moral values. Since the instinctual drives are extremely powerful, the ever-present danger for individuals and whole societies is that unacknowledged drives will overwhelm the control mechanisms in a violent, distorted way. Yet Freud also agreed with Nietzsche that the mechanisms of rational thinking and traditional moral values can be too strong. They can repress sexual desires too effectively, crippling individuals and entire peoples with guilt and neurotic fears.

Freudian psychology and clinical psychiatry had gained international scholarly attention by 1910, but only after 1918 did they receive popular attention. Many interpreted Freud as saying the first requirement for mental health is an uninhibited sex life. This popular interpretation reflected and encouraged growing sexual experimentation, particularly among middle-class women. For more serious students, Freudian psychology drastically undermined the old easy optimism about the rational and progressive nature of the human mind.

id *Freudian term for the primitive, irrational unconscious.*

ego *Freudian term for the rationalizing conscious that mediates what a person can do.*

superego *Freudian term for the ingrained moral values, which specify what a person should do.*

Twentieth-Century Literature

Literature also reflected the general intellectual climate of pessimism, relativism, and alienation. The great nineteenth-century novelists had typically written as all-knowing narrators, describing realistic characters in an understandable, if sometimes harsh, society. In the twentieth century most major writers adopted the limited, often confused viewpoint of a single individual. Like Freud, these novelists focused on the complexity and irrationality of the human mind, where feelings, memories, and desires are forever scrambled. For example, the great French novelist Marcel Proust (1871–1922), in his semi-autobiographical *Remembrance of Things Past* (1913–1927), tried to discover the innermost meaning of his childhood memories as he withdrew from the present to dwell on the past.

Serious novelists also used the **stream-of-consciousness technique** to explore the psyche. In *Jacob's Room* (1922) Virginia Woolf (1882–1941) created a novel made up of a series of internal monologues. William Faulkner (1897–1962), perhaps America's greatest twentieth-century novelist, used the same technique in *The Sound and the Fury* (1929), much of whose intense drama is confusedly seen through an idiot's eyes. The most famous stream-of-consciousness novel is *Ulysses,* which Irish novelist James Joyce (1882–1941) published in 1922. Into an account of an ordinary day in the life of an ordinary man, Joyce weaves an extended ironic parallel between his hero's aimless wanderings through Dublin's streets and pubs and the adventures of Homer's hero Ulysses on his way home from Troy. Abandoning conventional grammar and blending foreign words, puns, bits of knowledge, and scraps of

● **Virginia Woolf** Her novels captured sensations like impressionist paintings, and her home attracted a circle of artists and writers known as the Bloomsbury Group. Many of Woolf's essays dealt with women's issues and urged greater opportunity for women's creativity. *(Gisèle Freund/Photo Researchers, Inc.)*

memory together in bewildering confusion, the language of *Ulysses* is intended to mirror modern life itself: a gigantic riddle waiting to be unraveled.

Creative writers rejected the idea of progress. Some even described "anti-utopias," nightmare visions of things to come. In 1918 Oswald Spengler (1880–1936) published *The Decline of the West,* in which he argued that every culture experiences a life cycle of growth and decline. Western civilization, in Spengler's opinion, was in its old age, and death was approaching in the form of conquest by the yellow race. T. S. Eliot (1888–1965) depicts a world of growing desolation in his famous poem *The Waste Land* (1922). Franz Kafka's (1883–1924) novels *The Trial* (1925) and *The Castle* (1926) portray helpless individuals crushed by inexplicably hostile forces.

Englishman George Orwell (1903–1950) had witnessed the nightmarish reality of the Nazi state and its Stalinist counterpart by 1949 when he wrote perhaps the ultimate in anti-utopian literature: *1984.* In a future world, Big Brother—the dictator—and his totalitarian state use a new kind of language, sophisticated technology, and psychological terror to strip a weak individual of his last shred of human dignity. The supremely self-confident chief of the Thought Police tells the tortured and broken Winston Smith, "If you want a picture of the future, imagine a boot stamping on a human face—forever."[3] A phenomenal bestseller, *1984* spoke to millions of people in the age of anxiety.

> **stream-of-consciousness technique** *A literary technique in which James Joyce and others used interior monologue to explore the human psyche.*

MODERN ART AND MUSIC

What new forms did art and music take during the age of anxiety?

Throughout the twentieth and early twenty-first centuries, there has been considerable unity in the arts. The "modernism" of the immediate prewar years and the 1920s is still strikingly modern. Like scientists, creative artists rejected old forms and old values. Modernism in art and music has meant constant experimentation and a search for new kinds of expression. And though many people find the varied modern visions of the arts strange, disturbing, and even ugly, the twentieth century will probably stand as one of history's great artistic eras.

Architecture and Design

Modernism in the arts was loosely unified by a revolution in architecture. This revolution intended to transform the physical framework of urban society according to a new principle: **functionalism.** Buildings, like industrial products, should be useful and "functional"—that is, they should serve the purpose for which they were made. Franco-Swiss genius Le Corbusier (1887–1965) insisted that "a house is a machine for living in."[4]

The United States, with its rapid urban growth and lack of rigid building traditions, pioneered in the new architecture. In the 1890s the Chicago school of architects, led by Louis H. Sullivan (1856–1924), used cheap steel, reinforced concrete, and electric elevators to build skyscrapers and office buildings lacking almost any exterior ornamentation.

In Europe architectural leadership centered in German-speaking countries until Hitler took power in 1933. In 1911 twenty-eight-year-old Walter Gropius (1883–1969) broke sharply with the past in his design of the Fagus shoe factory at Alfeld, Germany—a clean, light, elegant building of glass and iron. After the First World War Gropius merged the schools of fine and applied arts at Weimar into a single interdisciplinary school, the Bauhaus. Throughout the 1920s the Bauhaus, with its stress on functionalism and good design for everyday life, attracted enthusiastic students from all over the world. It had a great and continuing impact.

> **functionalism** *The principle that buildings, like industrial products, should serve the purpose for which they were made as well as possible.*

Modern Painting and Music

Modern painting grew out of a revolt against French impressionism. The *impressionism* of such French painters as Claude Monet (1840–1926), Pierre Auguste Renoir (1841–1919), and Camille Pissarro (1830–1903) was, in part, a kind of "superrealism." Leaving exact copying of objects to photography, these artists sought to capture the momentary overall feeling, or impression, of light falling on a real-life scene before their eyes. By 1890, when impressionism was finally established, a few artists known as *postimpressionists,* or sometimes as *expressionists,* were already striking out in new directions. After 1905 art increasingly took on a nonrepresentational, abstract character, a development that reached its high point after World War II.

Though individualistic in their styles, postimpressionists were united in their desire to know and depict unseen, inner worlds of emotion and imagination. In *The Starry Night* (1889), for example, the great Dutch expressionist Vincent van Gogh (1853–1890) painted the moving vision of his mind's eye. Paul Gauguin (1848–1903), the French stockbroker-turned-painter, pioneered in expressionist techniques, though he used them to infuse his work with tranquility and mysticism. In 1891 Gauguin fled to the South Pacific, where he found inspiration in Polynesian forms, colors, and legends and painted his greatest works. Gauguin believed the picture's form and design were important in themselves and the painter need not try to represent objects on canvas as the eye actually saw them.

Fascination with form, as opposed to light, was characteristic of postimpressionism and expressionism. Paul Cézanne (1839–1906), who profoundly influenced twentieth-

● **Van Gogh: The Starry Night** Van Gogh absorbed impressionism in Paris, but under the burning sun of southern France he went beyond the portrayal of external reality. In *The Starry Night* (1889) flaming cypress trees, exploding stars, and a comet-like Milky Way swirl together in one great cosmic rhythm. Painting an inner world of intense emotion and wild imagination, van Gogh contributed greatly to the rise of expressionism in modern art. *(Digital image © The Museum of Modern Art/Licensed by Scala/Art Resource, NY)*

century painting, was particularly committed to form and ordered design. He told a young painter, "You must see in nature the cylinder, the sphere, and the cone."[5] As Cézanne's later work became increasingly abstract and nonrepresentational, it also moved away from the traditional three-dimensional perspective toward the two-dimensional plane, which has characterized much of modern art.

In 1907 a young Spaniard in Paris, Pablo Picasso (1881–1973), founded another movement—*cubism*. In his first great cubist work, *Les Demoiselles d'Avignon* (1907), Picasso sought to create a new visual reality and provoked a revolutionary upheaval in art. Since the Renaissance, artists had represented objects from a single viewpoint and created unified human forms. Yet Picasso's female figures appear broken into large, flat planes with heads that are twisted, fractured dislocations (see the illustration on the next page). The faces of three figures resemble large wooden African masks, as the artist reinforced his radical new view of reality with a strikingly non-Western depiction of the human form. Cubism concentrated on a complex geometry of zigzagging lines and sharply angled, overlapping planes, but the distorted subjects generally remained at least vaguely recognizable.

The influence of Polynesian art on Gauguin and of carved African masks on Picasso reflected the growing importance of non-Western artistic traditions in Europe in the late nineteenth and early twentieth centuries. Japanese woodcuts had fascinated the great early impressionist Edouard Manet (1832–1883), for example, and he incorporated certain Japanese techniques into his painting. The work of many other European artists revealed comparable non-Western inspiration.

About 1910 came the ultimate stage in the development of abstract, nonrepresentational art. Artists such as the Russian-born Wassily Kandinsky (1866–1944) turned away from nature completely. "The observer," said Kandinsky, "must learn to look at [my] pictures . . . as form and color combinations . . . as a representation of mood and not as a representation of *objects*."[6]

In the 1920s and 1930s prewar artistic movements were extended and consolidated. The most notable new developments were *dadaism* and *surrealism*. Dadaism attacked all accepted standards of art and behavior, delighting in outrageous conduct. After 1924 many dadaists were attracted to surrealism, which became very influential in art in the late 1920s and 1930s. Surrealists, such as Salvador Dali (1904–1989), painted fantastic worlds of wild dreams and complex symbols, where watches melted and giant metronomes beat time in precisely drawn but impossible alien landscapes.

Refusing to depict ordinary visual reality, surrealist painters made powerful statements about the age of anxiety. Picasso's twenty-six-foot-long mural *Guernica* was inspired by the fascist bombing of the ancient Spanish town of Guernica during the Spanish civil war. Using only the mournful colors of black, white, and gray, the painting combines the free distortion of expressionism, cubism's overlapping planes, and the surrealist fascination with grotesque subject matter. Picasso hoped it would be an unforgettable attack on "brutality and darkness."

Developments in modern music were strikingly parallel to those in painting. Composers, too, were attracted by the emotional intensity of expressionism. The pulsating, dissonant rhythms and the dancers' earthy representation of lovemaking in the ballet *The Rite of Spring* by composer Igor Stravinsky (1882–1971) practically caused a riot when first performed in Paris in 1913 by Sergei Diaghilev's famous Russian dance company.

After the experience of the First World War, when irrationality and violence seemed to pervade the human psyche, expressionism in opera and ballet flourished. Some composers turned their backs on long-established musical conventions. As abstract painters arranged lines and color but did not draw identifiable objects, so modern composers arranged sounds without creating recognizable harmonies. Accustomed to the harmonies of classical and romantic music, audiences generally resisted modern atonal music.

● **Picasso: Les Demoiselles d'Avignon** Originating in memories of a brothel scene in Barcelona, this is one of the twentieth century's most influential paintings. Picasso abandoned unified perspective and depicted instead fragmented figures and distorted forms in his search for the magical violence of a pictorial breakthrough. The three faces on either side were inspired by African masks. *(Digital image © The Museum of Modern Art/Licensed by Scala/Art Resource, NY/© Estate of Pablo Picasso/ Artists Rights Society [ARS], New York)*

MOVIES AND RADIO

How did the movies and the radio affect society when they first appeared?

Until after World War II at the earliest, the revolutionary changes in art and music appealed mainly to a minority of "highbrows" and not to the general public. That public was primarily and enthusiastically wrapped up in movies, radio, and advertising. Standardized commercial entertainment replaced the long-declining traditional arts and amusements of people in villages and small towns.

Moving pictures were first shown as a popular novelty in naughty peepshows— "What the Butler Saw"—and penny arcades in the 1890s, especially in Paris. The first movie houses, dating from an experiment in Los Angeles in 1902, showed short silent action films such as the eight-minute *Great Train Robbery* of 1903. On the eve of the First World War, full-length feature films such as the Italian *Quo Vadis* and the American *Birth of a Nation,* coupled with improvements in picture quality, suggested the screen's vast possibilities.

During the First World War the United States became the dominant force in the rapidly expanding silent-film industry, and Charlie Chaplin (1889–1978), a funny little Englishman working in Hollywood, was unquestionably the king of the "silver

Primary Source:

U.S. Senate Speech, June 29, 1922

Find out why a U.S. Senator called for a national board of film censorship.

screen." In his enormously popular role as a lonely tramp, complete with baggy trousers, battered derby, and an awkward, shuffling walk, Chaplin symbolized the "gay spirit of laughter in a cruel, crazy world."[7] Chaplin also demonstrated that in the hands of a genius the new medium could combine mass entertainment and artistic accomplishment.

The early 1920s were also the great age of German films. Protected and developed during the war, the large German studios excelled in bizarre expressionist dramas, beginning with *The Cabinet of Dr. Caligari* in 1919. Unfortunately, their period of creativity was short-lived. By 1926 American money was drawing the leading German talents to Hollywood and consolidating America's international domination. European producers remained at a great disadvantage until "talkies" permitted a revival of national film industries in the 1930s, particularly in France.

Whether foreign or domestic, motion pictures became the main entertainment of the masses until after the Second World War. Motion pictures, featuring glittering stars such as Ginger Rogers and Fred Astaire, and fanciful cartoons of Mickey Mouse, offered ordinary people a temporary escape from the hard realities of international tensions, uncertainty, unemployment, and personal frustrations. Escapist entertainment was especially appealing during the Great Depression.

Radio became possible with the transatlantic "wireless" communication of Guglielmo Marconi (1874–1937) in 1901 and the development of the vacuum tube in 1904, which permitted the transmission of speech and music. Only in 1920, however, were the first major public broadcasts made in Great Britain and the United States. Singing from London in English, Italian, and French, "the world's very best, the soprano Nellie Melba,"[8] was heard simultaneously all over Europe on June 16, 1920. This historic event captured the public's imagination, and radio's meteoric career was launched.

Every major country quickly established national broadcasting networks. In the United States these were privately owned and financed by advertising. In Great Britain Parliament set up an independent public corporation, the British Broadcasting Corporation (BBC), supported by licensing fees. Elsewhere in Europe the typical pattern was direct government control. Radio quickly became popular and influential. By the late 1930s more than three-fourths of the households in both democratic Great Britain and dictatorial Germany had at least one cheap, mass-produced radio.

Radio was particularly well suited for political propaganda. Dictators such as Mussolini and Hitler controlled the airwaves and could reach enormous national audiences with their frequent, dramatic speeches. In democratic countries politicians such as President Franklin Roosevelt and Prime Minister Stanley Baldwin effectively used informal "fireside chats" to bolster their support.

Motion pictures also became powerful tools of indoctrination, especially in countries with dictatorial regimes. Lenin encouraged the development of Soviet film making and beginning in the mid-1920s a series of epic films, the most famous of which were directed by Sergei Eisenstein (1898–1948), brilliantly dramatized the communist view of Russian history.

● **The Great Dictator** In 1940 the renowned actor and director Charlie Chaplin abandoned the little tramp to satirize the "great dictator," Adolf Hitler. Chaplin had strong political views and made a number of films with political themes as the escapist fare of the Great Depression gave way to the reality of the Second World War. *(The Museum of Modern Art/Still Film Archives)*

In Germany Hitler turned to a young and immensely talented woman film maker, Leni Riefenstahl (1902–2003), for a masterpiece of documentary propaganda, *The Triumph of the Will.* Based on the Nazi Party rally at Nuremberg in 1934, her film was a brilliant and all-too-powerful depiction of Germany's "Nazi rebirth." Mass culture's new media were potentially dangerous instruments of political manipulation.

THE SEARCH FOR PEACE AND POLITICAL STABILITY

How did leaders deal with the political dimensions of uncertainty and try to re-establish real peace and prosperity between 1919 and 1939?

As established patterns of thought and culture were challenged and mangled by the ferocious impact of World War I, so also was the political fabric stretched and torn by the consequences of the great conflict. The Versailles settlement had established a shaky truce, not a solid peace.

The pursuit of real and lasting peace proved difficult for many reasons. Germany hated the Treaty of Versailles. France was fearful and isolated. Britain was undependable, and the United States had turned its back on European problems. Eastern Europe was in ferment, and no one could predict the future of communist Russia. In addition, the international economic situation was poor and greatly complicated by war debts and disrupted patterns of trade. Yet for a time, from 1925 to late 1929, it appeared that peace and stability were within reach.

Germany and the Western Powers

Germany held the key to lasting peace, yet all Germans believed the Treaty of Versailles represented a harsh, dictated peace and should be revised or repudiated as soon as possible. The treaty had neither broken nor reduced Germany, potentially still the strongest country in Europe. Thus the treaty had fallen between two stools: too harsh for a peace of reconciliation, too soft for a peace of conquest.

Moreover, France and Great Britain disagreed over Germany. By the end of 1919 France wanted to stress the harsh elements in the Treaty of Versailles. The war on the western front had been fought mainly on French soil, and the expected costs of reconstruction, as well as of repaying war debts to the United States, were staggering. Thus French politicians believed that massive reparations from Germany were a vital economic necessity. America's failure to ratify the treaty left many French leaders believing that strict implementation of all the treaty's provisions was France's last best hope. Large reparation payments could hold Germany down indefinitely, and France would realize its goal of security.

The British soon felt differently. Prewar Germany had been Great Britain's second-best market in the entire world, and after the war a healthy, prosperous Germany appeared to be essential to the British economy. Indeed, many English people agreed with the analysis of the young English economist John Maynard Keynes (1883–1946). In his famous *Economic Consequences of the Peace* (1919) Keynes argued that astronomical reparations and harsh economic measures would impoverish Germany and increase economic hardship in all countries. Only a complete revision of the foolish treaty could save Germany—and Europe. Keynes's attack stirred deep guilt feelings about Germany in the English-speaking world, feelings that often paralyzed English and American leaders in their relations with German leaders between the First and Second World Wars.

The British were suspicious of France's army—the largest in Europe—and the British and French were also at odds over their League of Nations mandates in the Middle

Primary Source: An Economist Analyzes the Versailles Treaty and Finds It Lacking
Read how an American economist condemned the Allies for ignoring, in the provisions of the Versailles Treaty, "the economic rehabilitation of Europe."

East (see page 847). While France and Britain drifted in different directions, the Allied reparations commission completed its work. In April 1921 it announced that Germany had to pay the enormous sum of 132 billion gold marks ($33 billion) in annual installments of 2.5 billion gold marks. Facing possible occupation of more of its territory, the young German republic—known as the Weimar Republic—made its first payment in 1921. Then in 1922, wracked by rapid inflation and political assassinations and motivated by hostility and arrogance as well, the Weimar Republic announced its inability to pay more and proposed a reparations moratorium for three years.

The British were willing to accept a moratorium, but the French were not. Led by their prime minister, Raymond Poincaré (1860–1934), they decided they had to either call Germany's bluff or see the entire peace settlement dissolve to France's great disadvantage. So, despite strong British protests, in January 1923 armies of France and its ally Belgium occupied the Ruhr district, industrial Germany's heartland, creating the most serious international crisis of the 1920s.

Strengthened by a wave of patriotism, the German government ordered the people of the Ruhr to stop working and to nonviolently resist the French occupation. The coal mines and steel mills of the Ruhr grew silent, leaving 10 percent of Germany's total population in need of relief. The French responded by sealing off not only the Ruhr but also the entire Rhineland from the rest of Germany, letting in only enough food to prevent starvation.

By summer 1923 France and Germany were engaged in a great test of wills. French armies could not collect reparations from striking workers at gunpoint. But French occupation was paralyzing Germany and its economy and had turned rapid German inflation into runaway inflation. Needing to support the striking Ruhr workers and their employers, the German government began to print money to pay its bills. Prices soared. German money rapidly lost all value, and so did anything else with a stated fixed value.

● **"Hands Off the Ruhr"** The French occupation of the Ruhr to collect reparations payments raised a storm of patriotic protest in Germany. This anti-French poster of 1923 turns Marianne, the personification of French republican virtue, into a vicious harpy. *(International Instituut voor Sociale Geschiedenis)*

Runaway inflation brought about a social revolution. Many retired and middle-class people saw their savings wiped out. Catastrophic inflation cruelly mocked the old middle-class virtues of thrift, caution, and self-reliance. Many Germans felt betrayed. They hated and blamed the Western governments, their own government, big business, the Jews, the workers, and the communists for their misfortune. The crisis left them psychologically prepared to follow radical leaders.

In August 1923, as the mark fell and political unrest grew throughout Germany, Gustav Stresemann (1878–1929) became German chancellor. Stresemann adopted a compromising attitude. He called off the peaceful resistance campaign in the Ruhr and in October agreed in principle to pay reparations but asked for a re-examination of Germany's ability to pay. Poincaré accepted. His hard line was becoming increasingly unpopular with French citizens, and was hated in Britain and the United States. (See the feature "Individuals in Society: Gustav Stresemann.")

More generally, in both Germany and France power was finally passing to the moderates, who realized that continued confrontation was a destructive, no-win situation. Thus after five years of hostility and tension, Germany and France decided to try compromise and cooperation. The British, and even the Americans, were willing to help. The first step was a reasonable compromise on the reparations question.

Hope in Foreign Affairs (1924–1929)

The reparations commission appointed an international committee of financial experts headed by American banker Charles G. Dawes to re-examine reparations. The resulting **Dawes Plan** (1924) was accepted by France, Germany, and Britain. Germany's yearly reparations were reduced and depended on the level of German economic prosperity. Germany would also receive large loans from the United States to promote German recovery. In short, Germany would get private loans from the United States and pay reparations to France and Britain, thus enabling those countries to repay the large sums they owed the United States.

This circular flow of international payments was complicated and risky, but for a while it worked. Germany experienced a spectacular economic recovery. By 1929 its wealth and income were 50 percent greater than in 1913. With prosperity and large, continual inflows of American capital, Germany easily paid about $1.3 billion in reparations in 1927 and 1928, enabling France and Britain to pay the United States. Thus, America belatedly played a part in the general economic settlement that facilitated the worldwide recovery of the late 1920s.

This economic settlement was matched by a political settlement in 1925 among European leaders meeting in Locarno, Switzerland. Germany and France solemnly pledged to accept their common border, and both Britain and Italy agreed to fight either France or Germany if one invaded the other. Stresemann also agreed to settle boundary disputes with Poland and Czechoslovakia by peaceful means, and France promised those countries military aid if Germany attacked them. For years a "spirit of Locarno" gave Europeans a sense of growing security and stability in international affairs.

Other developments also strengthened hopes. In 1926 Germany joined the League of Nations, where Stresemann continued his "peace offensive." In 1928 fifteen countries signed the Kellogg-Briand Pact, initiated by French prime minister Aristide Briand and U.S. secretary of state Frank B. Kellogg. This multinational pact "condemned and renounced war as an instrument of national policy." The signing states agreed to settle international disputes peacefully. The pact fostered the cautious optimism of the late 1920s and also encouraged the hope that the United States would accept its international responsibilities.

Domestic politics also offered reason to hope. During the Ruhr occupation and the great inflation, Germany's republican government appeared ready to collapse. In 1923 communists momentarily entered provincial governments, and in November an obscure nobody named Adolf Hitler proclaimed a "national socialist revolution" in a Munich beer hall. Hitler's plot to seize government control was poorly organized, however, and easily crushed. Hitler was sentenced to prison, where he outlined his theories and program in his book **Mein Kampf** (*My Struggle*, 1925). Throughout the 1920s, Hitler's National Socialist Party attracted support only from a few fanatical anti-Semites, ultranationalists, and disgruntled former servicemen.

The moderate businessmen who tended to dominate the various German coalition governments believed that economic prosperity demanded good relations with the Western Powers, and they supported parliamentary government at home. Elections were held regularly, and as the economy boomed, republican democracy appeared to have growing support among a majority of Germans.

Dawes Plan *The product of the reparations commission, accepted by Germany, France, and Britain, that reduced Germany's yearly reparations, made payment dependent on German economic prosperity, and granted Germany large loans from the United States to promote recovery.*

Mein Kampf *A book written by Adolf Hitler in which he outlines his theories and program for a "national socialist revolution."*

Gustav Stresemann

Foreign Minister Gustav Stresemann of Germany (*right*) leaves a meeting with Aristide Briand, his French counterpart. *(Corbis)*

The German foreign minister Gustav Stresemann (1878–1929) is a controversial historical figure. Hailed by many as a hero of peace, he was denounced as a traitor by radical German nationalists and then by Hitler's Nazis. After World War II, revisionist historians stressed Stresemann's persistent nationalism and cast doubt on his peaceful intentions. Weimar Germany's most renowned leader is a fascinating example of the restless quest for convincing historical interpretation.

Stresemann's origins were modest. His parents were Berlin innkeepers and retailers of bottled beer, and only Gustav of their five children was able to attend high school. Attracted first to literature and history, Stresemann later turned to economics, earned a doctoral degree, and quickly reached the top as a manager and director of German trade associations. A highly intelligent extrovert with a knack for negotiation, Stresemann entered the Reichstag in 1907 as a business-oriented liberal and nationalist. When World War I erupted, he believed, like most Germans, that Germany had acted defensively and was not at fault. He emerged as a strident nationalist and urged German annexation of conquered foreign territories. Germany's collapse in defeat and revolution devastated Stresemann. He seemed a prime candidate for the hateful extremism of the far right.

Yet although Stresemann opposed the Treaty of Versailles as an unjust and unrealistic imposition, he turned back toward the center. He accepted the new Weimar Republic and played a growing role in the Reichstag as the leader of his own small probusiness party. His hour came in the Ruhr crisis, when French and Belgian troops occupied the district. Named chancellor in August 1923, he called off passive resistance and began talks with the French. His government also quelled communist uprisings; put down rebellions in Bavaria, including Hitler's attempted coup; and ended runaway inflation with a new currency. Stresemann fought to preserve German unity, and he succeeded.

Voted out as chancellor in November 1923, Stresemann remained as foreign minister in every government until his death in 1929. Proclaiming a policy of peace and agreeing to pay reparations, he achieved his greatest triumph in the Locarno agreements of 1925 (see page 890). But the interlocking guarantees of existing French and German borders (and the related agreements to resolve peacefully all disputes with Poland and Czechoslovakia) did not lead the French to make any further concessions that might have disarmed Stresemann's extremist foes. Working himself to death, he made little additional progress in achieving international reconciliation and sovereign equality for Germany.

Stresemann was no fuzzy pacifist. Historians debunking his "legend" are right in seeing an enduring love of nation in his defense of German interests. But Stresemann, like his French counterpart Aristide Briand, was a statesman of goodwill who wanted peace through mutually advantageous compromise. A realist trained by business and politics in the art of the possible, Stresemann also reasoned that Germany had to be a satisfied and equal partner if peace was to be secure. His unwillingness to guarantee Germany's eastern borders (see Map 27.4 on page 838), which is often criticized, reflects his conviction that keeping some Germans under Polish and Czechoslovak rule created a ticking time bomb in Europe. Stresemann was no less convinced that war on Poland would almost certainly recreate the Allied coalition that had crushed Germany in 1918.* His insistence on the necessity of peace in the east as well as the west was prophetic. Hitler's 1939 invasion of Poland resulted in an even mightier coalition that almost annihilated Germany in 1945.

Questions for Analysis

1. What did Gustav Stresemann do to promote reconciliation in Europe? How did his policy toward France differ from that toward Poland and Czechoslovakia?

2. What is your interpretation of Stresemann? Does he arouse your sympathy or your suspicion and hostility? Why?

*Robert Grathwol, "Stresemann: Reflections on His Foreign Policy," *Journal of Modern History* 45 (March 1973): 52–70.

● **An American in Paris** The young Josephine Baker suddenly became a star in 1925 when she brought an exotic African eroticism to French music halls. American blacks and Africans had a powerful impact in Europe in the 1920s and 1930s. *(Hulton Archive/Getty Images)*

There were, however, sharp political divisions in the country. Many unrepentant nationalists and monarchists populated the right and the army. Members of Germany's Communist Party received directions from Moscow, and they endlessly accused the Social Democrats of betraying the revolution. The working classes were divided politically, but most supported the socialist, but nonrevolutionary, Social Democrats.

The situation in France had numerous similarities to that in Germany. Communists and socialists battled for the workers' support. After 1924 the democratically elected government rested mainly in the hands of moderate coalitions, and business interests were well represented. France's great accomplishment was rapid rebuilding of its war-torn northern region, and good times prevailed until 1930.

France attracted artists and writers from all over the world in the 1920s. Much of the intellectual and artistic ferment of the times flourished in Paris. As writer Gertrude Stein (1874–1946), a leader of the large colony of American expatriates living in Paris, later recalled, "Paris was where the twentieth century was."[9]

Britain, too, faced challenges after 1920. The wartime trend toward greater social equality continued, however, helping maintain social harmony. The great problem was unemployment, which throughout the 1920s hovered around 12 percent. The state provided unemployment benefits and supplemented those payments with subsidized housing, medical aid, and increased old-age pensions. These and other measures kept living standards from seriously declining, defused class tensions, and pointed the way toward the welfare state Britain established after World War II.

Relative social harmony was accompanied by the Labour Party's rise as a determined champion of the working classes and of greater social equality. Committed to moderate, "revisionist" socialism, the Labour Party under Ramsay MacDonald (1866–1937) governed the country in 1924 and 1929. Yet Labour moved toward socialism gradually and democratically, so that the middle classes were not overly frightened as the working classes won new benefits.

The Conservatives under Stanley Baldwin (1867–1947) showed the same compromising spirit on social issues, and Britain experienced only limited social unrest in the 1920s and 1930s. In 1922 Britain granted southern, Catholic Ireland full autonomy after a bitter guerrilla war, thereby removing another source of prewar friction. Thus developments in both international relations and domestic politics gave the leading democracies cause for cautious optimism in the late 1920s.

• • • • • • • • • • • •

THE GREAT DEPRESSION (1929–1939)

Why did democratic leaders fail to effectively address problems created by the depression?

Like the Great War, the Great Depression must be spelled with capital letters. Economic depressions occurred regularly throughout the nineteenth century, but this depression was exceptionally long and severe. It struck the entire world with evergreater intensity from 1929 to 1933, and recovery was uneven and slow. Only with the Second World War did the depression disappear in much of the world.

Everywhere the social and political consequences of prolonged economic collapse were enormous. Economic depression was a major factor in Japan's fatal turn from peaceful trade and foreign investment in the 1920s to aggressive empire building and militarism in the 1930s (see pages 868–870). Elsewhere in Asia, agricultural depression devastated millions of peasants and small farmers. The price of rice—Asia's staff of life and main cash crop—fell by two-thirds between 1929 and 1932. With debts to local moneylenders fixed in value and taxes to colonial governments hardly ever reduced, peasants in the 1930s struggled under crushing debt and suffered severely.

In Latin America and Africa agricultural producers also suffered greatly from the collapse in prices, while urban workers faced pay cuts and high unemployment. Several Latin American countries tried to turn away from export economies based on agriculture and instead promoted state-sponsored industrialization and national self-sufficiency. In West Africa anticolonial nationalism attracted widespread support for the first time in the 1930s, setting the stage for strong independence movements after World War II. Chapter 32 examines the powerful, many-sided impact of the Great Depression in Latin America and Africa.

In Europe and the United States the depression shattered the fragile optimism of political leaders in the late 1920s. Mass unemployment made insecurity a reality for millions of ordinary people. In desperation, people looked for leaders who would "do something." They willingly supported radical attempts to deal with the crisis by both democratic leaders and dictators.

The Economic Crisis

Though economic activity was already declining moderately in many countries by early 1929, the U.S. stock market crash in October of that year really started the Great Depression. The American stock market boom, which had seen stock prices double between early 1928 and September 1929, was built on borrowed money. Wealthy investors, speculators, and people of modest means had bought stocks by paying only a small fraction of the total purchase price and borrowing the remainder from their stockbrokers. Such buying "on margin" was extremely dangerous. When prices started falling, the hard-pressed margin buyers started selling to pay their debts. The result was a financial panic. Countless investors and speculators were wiped out in a matter of days or weeks.

The financial panic in the United States triggered a worldwide financial crisis, and that crisis resulted in a drastic decline in production in country after country. Throughout the 1920s American bankers and investors had lent large sums to many countries, and as panic broke, New York bankers began recalling their short-term loans. Frightened Europeans began to withdraw their savings from banks, leading to general financial chaos. The recall of American loans also accelerated the collapse in world prices, as business people dumped goods in a frantic attempt to get cash to pay what they owed.

The financial chaos led to a general crisis of production. Between 1929 and 1933 world output of goods fell by an estimated 38 percent. As this happened, each country turned inward and tried to go it alone. Country after country followed the example of the United States, which raised protective tariffs to their highest levels ever in 1930 and tried to seal off shrinking national markets for American producers only.

Although opinions differ, two factors probably best explain the relentless slide to the bottom from 1929 to early 1933. First, the international economy lacked a leadership able to maintain stability when the crisis came. The seriously weakened British, the world economy's traditional leaders, "couldn't and the United States wouldn't" stabilize the international economic system in 1929.[10] Instead, the United States cut back its international lending and erected high tariffs.

The second factor was national economic policy. In almost every country, governments cut their budgets and reduced spending when they should have run large deficits in an effort to stimulate their economies. After World War II such a "counter-cyclical policy," advocated by John Maynard Keynes, became a well-established weapon against depression. But in the 1930s orthodox economists generally regarded Keynes's prescription with horror.

Mass Unemployment

The need for large-scale government spending was tied to mass unemployment. As the financial crisis led to production cuts, workers lost their jobs and had little money to buy goods. This led to still more production cuts and still more unemployment, until millions were out of work. In Britain unemployment had averaged 12 percent in the 1920s; between 1930 and 1935 it averaged more than 18 percent. In Japan 3 million people were out of work. Far worse was the case of the United States. In the 1920s unemployment there had averaged only 5 percent; in 1932 it soared to about 33 percent of the entire labor force: 14 million people were out of work. Only by pumping new money into the economy could the government increase demand and break the vicious cycle of decline.

Along with economic effects, mass unemployment posed a great social problem. Poverty increased dramatically, although in most industrialized countries unemployed workers generally received some kind of meager unemployment benefits or public aid that prevented starvation. (See the feature "Listening to the Past: Life on the Dole in Great Britain" on pages 900–901.) Millions of people lost their spirit, condemned to an apparently hopeless search for work or to idle boredom. Homes and ways of life were disrupted in millions of personal tragedies. In 1932 workers in Manchester, England, appealed to their city officials—a typical appeal echoed throughout the Western world:

We tell you that thousands of people . . . are in desperate straits. We tell you that men, women, and children are going hungry. . . . We tell you that great numbers are being rendered distraught through the stress and worry of trying to exist without work. . . .

If you do not do this—if you do not provide useful work for the unemployed—what, we ask, is your alternative? Do not imagine that this colossal tragedy of unemployment is going on endlessly without some fateful catastrophe. Hungry men are angry men.[11]

Only strong government action could deal with mass unemployment, a social powder keg preparing to explode.

The New Deal in the United States

Of all the major industrial countries, only Germany was harder hit by the Great Depression, or reacted more radically to it, than the United States. Depression was so traumatic in the United States because the 1920s had been a period of complacent prosperity. The Great Depression and the response to it marked a major turning point in American history.

President Herbert Hoover (1874–1964) and his administration initially reacted to the stock market crash and economic decline with dogged optimism and limited action. But when the full force of the financial crisis struck Europe in the summer of 1931 and boomeranged back to the United States, people's worst fears became reality. Banks failed; unemployment soared. In 1932 industrial production fell to about 50 percent of its 1929 level. In these tragic circumstances Franklin Delano Roosevelt (1882–1945), an inspiring wheelchair-bound aristocrat previously crippled by polio, won a landslide electoral victory in 1932 with grand but vague promises of a "**New Deal** for the forgotten man."

Roosevelt's basic goal was to preserve capitalism by reforming it. Rejecting socialism and government ownership of industry, Roosevelt undertook capitalist reform through forceful government intervention in the economy. In this choice Roosevelt was flexible, pragmatic, and willing to experiment. Roosevelt and his "brain trust" of advisers adopted policies echoing the American experience in World War I, when the American economy had been thoroughly planned and regulated.

New Deal *Franklin Delano Roosevelt's plan to reform capitalism through forceful government intervention in the economy.*

● **Isaac Soyer: Employment Agency (1937)** The frustration and agony of looking for work against long odds are painfully evident in this American masterpiece. The time-killing, pensive resignation, and dejection seen in the four figures are only aspects of the larger problem. One of three talented brothers born in Russia and trained as artists in New York, Isaac Soyer worked in the tradition of American realism and concentrated on people and the influence of their environment. *(Oil on canvas, 34¼ x 45 in. Whitney Museum of American Art, New York, Purchase 37.44)*

Innovative programs promoted agricultural recovery, a top priority. As in Asia, Africa, and Latin America, American farmers were hard hit by the Great Depression. Roosevelt's decision to leave the gold standard and devalue the dollar was designed to raise American prices and save farmers. The Agricultural Adjustment Act (1933) aimed at raising prices and farm income by limiting production. For a while, these measures worked.

Roosevelt then attacked the key problem of mass unemployment. New agencies were created to undertake a vast range of public works projects so that the federal government could employ directly as many people as financially possible. The most famous of these was the **Works Progress Administration (WPA)**, set up in 1935. One-fifth of the entire labor force worked for the WPA at some point in the 1930s, constructing public buildings, bridges, and highways. The WPA was enormously popular, and the prospect of a government job helped check the threat of social revolution in the United States.

Such relief programs were part of the New Deal's fundamental commitment to use the federal government to provide for the welfare of all Americans. This commitment marked a profound shift from the traditional stress on family support and community responsibility. Embraced by a large majority in the 1930s, this shift proved to be one of the New Deal's most enduring legacies.

Other social measures aimed in the same direction. Following the path blazed by Germany's Bismarck in the 1880s (see page 704), the U.S. government in 1935 established a national social security system, with old-age pensions and unemployment benefits, to protect workers against some of life's uncertainties. The National Labor Relations Act of 1935 gave union organizers the green light by declaring collective bargaining to be U.S. policy. Union membership more than doubled, from 4 million in 1935 to 9 million in 1940. In general, between 1935 and 1938 government rulings and social reforms chipped away at the privileges of the wealthy and tried to help ordinary people.

Yet despite undeniable accomplishments in social reform, the New Deal was only partly successful as a response to the Great Depression. At the height of the recovery in May 1937, 7 million workers were still unemployed, in contrast to a high of 15 million in 1933. The economic situation then worsened seriously in the recession of 1937 and 1938, and unemployment was still a staggering 10 million when war broke out in Europe in September 1939. The New Deal brought fundamental reform, but it never did pull the United States out of the depression.

The Scandinavian Response to the Depression

Of all the Western democracies, the Scandinavian countries under socialist leadership responded most successfully to the challenge of the Great Depression. After the First World War the socialists became the largest political party in Sweden and then in Norway. In the 1920s they passed important social reform legislation for both peasants and workers, gained practical administrative experience, and developed a unique kind of socialism. Flexible and nonrevolutionary, Scandinavian socialism grew out of a strong tradition of cooperative community action. Even before 1900, Scandinavian agricultural cooperatives had shown how individual peasant families could join together for everyone's benefit. Labor leaders and capitalists were also inclined to work together.

When the economic crisis struck in 1929, socialist governments in Scandinavia built on this pattern of cooperative social action. Sweden pioneered the use of large-scale deficits to finance public works and thereby maintain production and employment. Scandinavian governments also increased social welfare benefits, from old-age pensions and unemployment insurance to subsidized housing and maternity allowances. All this spending required a large bureaucracy and high taxes, first on the rich and then on practically everyone. Yet both private and cooperative enterprise thrived, as

Works Progress Administration (WPA) *The most famous of Roosevelt's New Deal programs, it employed one-fifth of the entire labor force at some point in the 1930s, constructing public buildings, bridges, and highways.*

did democracy. Some observers saw Scandinavia's welfare socialism as an appealing "middle way" between sick capitalism and cruel communism or fascism.

Recovery and Reform in Britain and France

In Britain MacDonald's Labour government and then, after 1931, the Conservative-dominated coalition government followed orthodox economic theory. The budget was balanced, but unemployed workers received barely enough welfare to live. Despite government lethargy, the economy recovered considerably after 1932. By 1937 total production was about 20 percent higher than in 1929. In fact, for Britain the years after 1932 were actually somewhat better than the 1920s had been, quite the opposite of the situation in the United States and France.

This recovery reflected the gradual reorientation of the British economy. After abandoning the gold standard in 1931 and establishing protective tariffs in 1932, Britain concentrated increasingly on the national, rather than the international, market. The Industrial Revolution's old export industries, such as textiles and coal, continued to decline, but new industries, such as automobiles and electrical appliances, grew in response to British home demand. These developments encouraged Britain to look inward and avoid unpleasant foreign questions.

Because France was relatively less industrialized and more isolated from the world economy, the Great Depression came there late. But once the depression hit France, it stayed and stayed. Decline was steady until 1935, and a short-lived recovery never brought production or employment back up to predepression levels. Economic stagnation both reflected and heightened an ongoing crisis of political instability. As before 1914, the French parliament consisted of many political parties that could never cooperate for very long. In 1933, for example, five coalition cabinets formed and fell in rapid succession.

The French lost the underlying unity that had made government instability bearable before 1914. Fascist-type organizations agitated against parliamentary democracy and looked to Mussolini's Italy and Hitler's Germany for inspiration. In February 1934 French fascists rioted and threatened to overturn the republic. At the same time, the Communist Party and many workers looked to Stalin's Russia for guidance. Moderate republicanism's vital center was sapped from both sides.

Frightened by the fascists' growing strength at home and abroad, French Communists, Socialists, and Radicals formed an alliance—the **Popular Front**—for the May 1936 national elections. Their clear victory reflected the trend toward polarization. The number of Communists in parliament jumped dramatically, and the Socialists, led by Léon Blum, became the strongest party in France. The really quite moderate Radicals slipped badly, and the conservatives lost ground to the semifascists.

In the next few months Blum's Popular Front government made the first and only real attempt to deal with France's social and economic problems during the 1930s. Inspired by Roosevelt's New Deal, the Popular Front encouraged the union movement and launched a far-reaching program of social reform, complete with paid vacations and a forty-hour workweek. Popular with workers and the lower middle class, these measures were quickly sabotaged by rapid inflation and cries of revolution from fascists and frightened conservatives. Wealthy people sneaked their money out of the country, labor unrest grew, and France entered a severe financial crisis. Blum was forced to announce a "breathing spell" in social reform.

The Spanish civil war also fanned the fires of political dissension. Communists demanded that France support the Spanish republicans, while many French conservatives would gladly have joined Hitler and Mussolini in aiding the Spanish fascists. Extremism grew, and France itself verged on civil war. Blum was forced to resign in June 1937, and the Popular Front quickly collapsed. An anxious and divided France drifted aimlessly once again, preoccupied by Hitler and German rearmament.

Popular Front *A New Deal–inspired party in France led by Léon Blum that encouraged the union movement and launched a far-reaching program of social reform, complete with paid vacations and a forty-hour workweek.*

Chapter Summary

To assess your mastery of this chapter, go to
bedfordstmartins.com/mckayworld

Key Terms

logical empiricism
existentialism
neutron
id
ego
superego
stream-of-consciousness
  technique
functionalism
Dawes Plan
Mein Kampf
New Deal
Works Progress
  Administration (WPA)
Popular Front

• **What was the nature of the uncertainty in modern thought in Europe at the beginning of the twentieth century, and what did the doubts and searching mean for Western thought, art, and culture?**

After the First World War, Western society entered a complex and difficult era—truly an age of anxiety. Intellectual life underwent a crisis marked by pessimism, uncertainty, and fascination with irrational forces. Scientists continued to make previously unimaginable discoveries. Einstein's theory of relativity and Marie Curie's work with protons and electrons are but two of the discoveries that totally changed our understanding of the universe. Sigmund Freud revolutionized the field of psychology with his methods of psychoanalysis and his studies of human behavior.

• **What new forms did art and music take during the age of anxiety?**

Ceaseless experimentation and rejection of old forms characterized art and music. Architects abandoned the excessive ornamentation of the past and turned to functionalism. This new principle dictated that buildings be designed to be functional and useful. The Bauhaus movement in Germany drew students from all over the world to study functionalism in fine and applied arts. Art seemed to be in a constant state of change, with the Spanish artist Pablo Picasso making a revolutionary break with the past when he introduced the style of art known as cubism. This was followed by abstract art, as exemplified by such artists as Wassily Kandinsky. Musical compositions, such as the works of Igor Stravinsky, were strikingly parallel to the expressionist developments in art.

• **How did the movies and the radio affect society when they first appeared?**

Motion pictures and radio provided a new, standardized entertainment for the masses. Intellectual and artistic developments that before 1914 had been confined to small avant-garde groups gained wider currency, as did the insecure state of mind they expressed. The first movie stars, such as Charlie Chaplin, became familiar household names. Radio and movies allowed political leaders such as Adolf Hitler and Franklin Roosevelt to reach mass audiences instantly for the first time. These new wonders of modern mass communication became political propaganda tools, for bad or for good.

• **How did leaders deal with the political dimensions of uncertainty and try to re-establish real peace and prosperity between 1919 and 1939?**

The death and destruction caused by World War I led to political and economic disruption across Europe in the years following the war. In the 1920s moderate political leaders replaced the World War I generation and groped to create an enduring peace and rebuild prewar prosperity. The Dawes Plan was one example of how Europe and America worked to create financial stability in Europe. For a brief period late in the decade they seemed to have succeeded.

• *Why did democratic leaders fail to effectively address problems created by the depression?*

The Great Depression shattered the fragile stability briefly achieved after World War I. Uncertainty returned with redoubled force in the 1930s. The international economy collapsed, and unemployment affected millions worldwide. The democracies turned inward as they sought to cope with massive domestic problems and widespread disillusionment. Generally speaking, they were not very successful. The old liberal ideals of individual rights and responsibilities, elected government, and economic freedom, even when they managed to survive, seemed ineffective and outmoded to many. In many countries these ideals were abandoned completely.

Suggested Reading

Andelman, David A. *A Shattered Peace: Versailles 1919 and the Price We Pay Today.* 2007. Clearly written history of the Versailles peace conference and how it has shaped world history to the present day.

Arnason, Harvey H., and Peter Kalb. *History of Modern Art.* 2003. Classic history of modern art, including painting, sculpture, architecture, and photography.

Burrow, J. W. *The Crisis of Reason: European Thought, 1848–1914.* 2000. Elegantly explores transformations in European thought in the decades before the Great War.

Camus, Albert. *The Stranger,* 1942, and *The Plague,* 1947. The greatest existential novelist at his unforgettable best in these two novels.

Cantor, Norman, and Mindy Cantor. *The American Century: Varieties of Culture in Modern Times.* 1998. Pugnacious and stimulating survey.

Gay, Peter. *Modernism: The Lure of Heresy.* 2007. A personal perspective on twentieth-century high culture by a leading intellectual and cultural historian.

Issacson, Walter. *Einstein: His Life and Universe.* 2007. New, well-received introduction to Einstein's life and work.

Jacobson, Jon. *Locarno Diplomacy: Germany and the West, 1925–1929.* 1972. Superb study of Stresemann and enduring tensions after the Locarno breakthrough.

Judt, Tony. *The Burden of Responsibility: Blum, Camus, Aron, and the French Twentieth Century.* 1998. Probes the moral and intellectual issues of the modern age.

Kindleberger, Charles P. *The World in Depression, 1929–1939.* 1986. Perhaps the best analytical account of the global origins, events, and aftermath of the Great Depression.

Martin, Benjamin. *France and the Après Guerre: Illusions and Disillusionments.* 1999. Solid work with masterful portraits of key figures.

Mazower, Mark. *Dark Continent: Europe's Twentieth Century.* 2000. Provocative history of the forces of communism, fascism, and liberal democracy at war.

Orwell, George, *The Road to Wigan Pier.* 1937. A nonfiction study of poverty among the English working class by one of the century's greatest novelists.

Smith, Bernard. *Modernism's History: A Study in Twentieth-Century Thought and Ideas.* 1998. Admirably straightforward with a global perspective.

Solomon, Robert C. *Existentialism.* 2004. Accessible and comprehensive introduction to existentialist thought.

Weitz, Eric D. *Weimar Germany: Promise and Tragedy.* 2007. Intellectually stimulating introduction to the Weimar world.

Winders, James A. *European Culture Since 1848: From Modernism to Postmodern and Beyond.* 1998. Lively and accessible mosaic of cultural and intellectual history.

Winter, Jay. *Sites of Memory, Sites of Meaning: The Great War in European Cultural History.* 1995. Excellent study of the war's influence on literature, art, and society.

Wolfe, Tom. *From Bauhaus to My House.* 1981. Lively critique of modern architecture.

Notes

1. P. Valéry, *Variety,* trans. M. Cowley (New York: Harcourt Brace, 1927), pp. 27–28.

2. G. Greene, *Another Mexico* (New York: Viking Press, 1939), p. 3.

3. G. Orwell, *1984* (New York: New American Library, 1950), p. 220.

4. C. E. Jeanneret-Gris (Le Corbusier), *Towards a New Architecture* (London: J. Rodker, 1931), p. 15.

5. Quoted in A. H. Barr, Jr., *What Is Modern Painting?* 9th ed. (New York: Museum of Modern Art, 1966), p. 27.

6. Quoted ibid., p. 25.

7. R. Graves and A. Hodge, *The Long Week End: A Social History of Great Britain, 1918–1939* (New York: Macmillan, 1941), p. 131.

8. Quoted in A. Briggs, *The Birth of Broadcasting,* vol. 1 (London: Oxford University Press, 1961), p. 47.

9. Quoted in R. J. Sontag, *A Broken World, 1919–1939* (New York: Harper & Row, 1971), p. 129.

10. C. P. Kindleberger, *The World in Depression, 1929–1939* (Berkeley: University of California Press, 1973), p. 292.

11. Quoted in S. B. Clough et al., eds., *Economic History of Europe: Twentieth Century* (New York: Harper & Row, 1968), pp. 243–245.

Listening to the PAST

Life on the Dole in Great Britain

Periodic surges in unemployment were an old story in capitalist economies, but the long-term joblessness of millions in the Great Depression was something new and unexpected. In Britain especially, where the depression followed a weak postwar recovery, large numbers suffered involuntary idleness for years at a time. Whole families lived "on the dole," the weekly welfare benefits paid by the government.

One of the most insightful accounts of unemployed workers was written by the British journalist and novelist George Orwell (1903–1950), who studied the conditions in northern England and wrote The Road to Wigan Pier *(1937), excerpted here. An independent socialist who distrusted rigid Marxism, Orwell believed that socialism could triumph in Britain if it came to mean "justice and liberty" for a commonsense majority. Orwell's disillusionment with authoritarian socialism and communism pervades his most famous work,* 1984 *(1949).*

When you see the unemployment figures quoted at two millions, it is fatally easy to take this as meaning that two million people are out of work and the rest of the population is comparatively comfortable. . . . [Adding in the destitute,] you might take the number of underfed people in England (for *everyone* on the dole or thereabouts is underfed) as being, at the very most, five millions.

This is an enormous under-estimate, because, in the first place, the only people shown on unemployment figures are those actually drawing the dole—that is, in general, heads of families. An unemployed man's dependants do not figure on the list unless they too are drawing a separate allowance. . . . In addition there are great numbers of people who are in work but who, from a financial point of view, might equally be unemployed, because they are not drawing anything that can be described as a living wage. Allow for these and their dependants, throw in as before the old-age pensioners, the destitute and other nondescripts, and you get an *underfed* population of well over ten millions. . . .

Take the figures for Wigan, which is typical enough of the industrial and mining districts. . . . The total popula-

tion of Wigan is a little under 87,000; so that at any moment more than one person in three out of the whole population—not merely the registered workers—is either drawing or living on the dole. . . .

Nevertheless, in spite of the frightful extent of unemployment, it is a fact that poverty—extreme poverty—is less in evidence in the industrial North than it is in London. Everything is poorer and shabbier, there are fewer motor-cars and fewer well-dressed people; but also there are fewer people who are obviously destitute. . . . In the industrial towns the old communal way of life has not yet broken up, tradition is still strong and almost everyone has a family—potentially, therefore, a home. In a town of 50,000 or 100,000 inhabitants there is no casual and as it were unaccounted-for population; nobody sleeping in the streets, for instance. Moreover, there is just this to be said for the unemployment regulations, that they do not discourage people from marrying. A man and wife on twenty-three shillings a week are not far from the starvation line, but they can make a home of sorts; they are vastly better off than a single man on fifteen shillings. . . .

But there is no doubt about the deadening, debilitating effect of unemployment upon everybody, married or single, and upon men more than upon women. . . . Everyone who saw Greenwood's play *Love on the Dole* must remember that dreadful moment when the poor, good, stupid working man beats on the table and cries out, "O God, send me some work!" This was not dramatic exaggeration, it was a touch from life. That cry must have been uttered, in almost those words, in tens of thousands, perhaps hundreds of thousands of English homes, during the past fifteen years.

But, I think not again—or at least, not so often. . . . When people live on the dole for years at a time they grow used to it, and drawing the dole, though it remains unpleasant, ceases to be shameful. Thus the old, independent, workhouse-fearing tradition is undermined. . . .

So you have whole populations settling down, as it were, to a lifetime of the P.A.C. . . . Take, for instance, the fact that the working class think nothing of getting

This poster was used in the election campaign of 1931, when unemployment rose to a new record high. *(Conservative Research Department/The Bridgeman Art Library)*

married on the dole. . . . Life is still fairly normal, more normal than one really has the right to expect. Families are impoverished, but the family-system has not broken up. The people are in effect living a reduced version of their former lives. Instead of raging against their destiny they have made things tolerable by lowering their standards.

But they don't necessarily lower their standards by cutting out luxuries and concentrating on necessities; more often it is the other way about—the more natural way, if you come to think of it. Hence the fact that in a decade of unparalleled depression, the consumption of all cheap luxuries has increased. The two things that have probably made the greatest difference of all are the movies and the mass-production of cheap smart clothes since the war. The youth who leaves school at fourteen and gets a blind-alley job is out of work at twenty, probably for life; but for two pounds ten on the hire-purchase system he can buy himself a suit which, for a little while and at a little distance, looks as though it had been tailored in Saville Row. The girl can look like a fashion plate at an even lower price. . . . You can stand on the street corner, indulging in a private daydream of yourself as Clark Gable or Greta Garbo, which compensates you for a great deal. . . .

Trade since the war has had to adjust itself to meet the demands of underpaid, underfed people, with the result that a luxury is nowadays almost always cheaper than a necessity. One pair of plain solid shoes costs as much as two ultra-smart pairs. . . . And above all there is gambling, the cheapest of all luxuries. Even people on the verge of starvation can buy a few days' hope ("Something to live for," as they call it) by having a penny on a sweepstake. . . . Twenty million people are underfed but literally everyone in England has access to a radio. What we have lost in food we have gained in electricity. Whole sections of the working class who have been plundered of all they really need are being compensated, in part, by cheap luxuries which mitigate the surface of life.

Do you consider all this desirable? No, I don't. But it may be that the psychological adjustment which the

working class are visibly making is the best they could make in the circumstances. They have neither turned revolutionary nor lost their self-respect; merely they have kept their tempers and settled down to make the best of things on a fish-and-chip standard. The alternative would be God knows what continued agonies of despair; or it might be attempted insurrections which, in a strongly governed country like England, could only lead to futile massacres and a régime of savage repression.

Questions for Analysis

1. According to Orwell, "extreme poverty" was less visible in the northern industrial towns than in London. Were family relations important in this regard?

2. What were the consequences of long-term unemployment for English workers? Were some of the consequences surprising?

3. From Orwell's description, did radical revolution seem likely in England in the depression?

Source: Excerpts from Chapter V in *The Road to Wigan Pier* by George Orwell, copyright © 1958 and renewed 1986 by the Estate of Sonia B. Orwell. Reprinted by permission of Houghton Mifflin Harcourt Publishing Company.

A Crowd of Enthusiastic Hitler Supporters, in a photograph by Hugo Jaeger. *(Time Life Pictures/Getty Images)*

chapter

30 DICTATORSHIPS AND THE SECOND WORLD WAR

The era of anxiety and economic depression was also a time of growing strength for political dictatorship. Popularly elected governments and basic civil liberties declined drastically. In Europe on the eve of the Second World War, liberal democratic governments were surviving only in Great Britain, France, the Low Countries, the Scandinavian nations, and neutral Switzerland. Dictatorship seemed the wave of the future worldwide. Thus the intellectual and economic crisis discussed in Chapter 29 and the decline in liberal political institutions and the rise of dictatorships discussed in this chapter were interrelated elements of a global crisis.

The mid-twentieth-century era of dictatorship is a highly disturbing chapter in the history of civilization. The key development was not only the resurgence of authoritarian rule but also the rise of a particularly ruthless and dynamic tyranny that reached its full realization in the Soviet Union and Nazi Germany in the 1930s. Stalin and Hitler mobilized their peoples for enormous undertakings and ruled with unprecedented severity. Hitler's mobilization was ultimately directed toward racial aggression and territorial expansion, and his sudden attack on Poland in 1939 started World War II. Hitler's successes then encouraged the Japanese to expand their stalemated Chinese campaign into a vast Pacific war by attacking Pearl Harbor and advancing into South Asia.

Nazi and Japanese armies were defeated by a great coalition, and today we want to believe that the era of totalitarian dictatorship was a terrible accident, that Stalin's slave labor camps and Hitler's gas chambers "can't happen again." But the cruel truth is that horrible atrocities continue to plague the world in our time. The Khmer Rouge inflicted genocide on its people in Kampuchea, and civil war led to ethnically motivated atrocities in Bosnia, Rwanda, Burundi, and Sudan, recalling the horrors of the Second World War. And there are other examples. A deeper understanding of these brutal dictatorships will help us guard against their recurrence.

AUTHORITARIAN STATES

What was the nature of twentieth-century dictatorships and authoritarian rule?

Both conservative and radical dictatorships arose in the 1920s and the 1930s. Although they sometimes overlapped in character and practice, they were in essence profoundly different. Conservative authoritarian regimes were an old story in world history. Radical, totalitarian dictatorships were a new and frightening development.

Conservative Authoritarianism

The traditional form of antidemocratic government in world history was conservative authoritarianism. Like Russia's tsars and China's emperors, the leaders of such governments tried to prevent major changes that would undermine the existing social order. To do so, they relied on obedient bureaucracies, vigilant police departments, and trustworthy armies. They forbade popular participation in government or else severely limited it to natural allies such as landlords, bureaucrats, and high church officials. They persecuted liberals, democrats, and socialists as subversive radicals, often consigning them to jail, exile, or death.

Yet old-fashioned authoritarian governments were limited in their power and in their objectives. They had neither the ability nor the desire to control many aspects of their subjects' lives. Preoccupied with the goal of mere survival, these governments largely limited their demands to taxes, army recruits, and passive acceptance. As long as the people did not try to change the system, they often had considerable personal independence.

After the First World War, this kind of authoritarian government revived, especially in Latin America and in the less-developed eastern part of Europe. In eastern Europe parliamentary regimes founded on the wreckage of empires in 1918 fell one by one. By early 1938 only Czechoslovakia remained true to liberal political ideals. Conservative dictators also took over in Spain and Portugal.

There were several reasons for this development. These lands lacked strong traditions of self-government, with its necessary restraint and compromise. Moreover, many of these new states, such as Yugoslavia, were torn by ethnic conflicts that threatened their very existence. Dictatorship appealed to nationalists and military leaders as a way to repress such tensions and preserve national unity. Large landowners and the church were still powerful forces in these predominantly agrarian areas, and they often looked to dictators to save them from progressive land reform or communist agrarian upheaval. Finally, the Great Depression delivered the final blow to fragile democracies in Austria, Bulgaria, Romania, Greece, Estonia, and Latvia.

Although some of the conservative authoritarian regimes adopted certain Hitlerian and fascist characteristics in the 1930s, their general aims were limited. They were concerned more with maintaining the status quo than with mobilizing the masses or forcing society into rapid change or war. This tradition continued into the late twentieth century, especially in some of the Latin American military dictatorships.

Radical Totalitarian Dictatorships

By the mid-1930s a new kind of radical dictatorship had emerged in the Soviet Union, Germany, and, to a lesser extent, Italy. Scholars generally agree that these radical dictatorships violently rejected liberal values and exercised unprecedented control over the masses. Further interpretation of these regimes, however, has caused heated controversy and debate.

One extremely useful approach relates the radical dictatorships to the rise of modern totalitarianism. The concept of **totalitarianism** emerged in the 1920s and 1930s.

totalitarianism *A dictatorship that exercises unprecedented control over the masses and seeks to mobilize them for action.*

In 1924 Benito Mussolini spoke of the "fierce totalitarian will" of his movement in Italy. In the 1930s observers linked Italian and especially German fascism with Soviet communism in "a 'new kind of state' that could be called totalitarian." "All doubts" about the totalitarian nature of both dictatorships "were swept away for most Americans,"[1] following the Hitler-Stalin alliance in 1939.

Some scholars argue that modern totalitarian dictatorship burst on the scene with the revolutionary total war effort of 1914–1918. The war called forth a tendency to subordinate all institutions and all classes to the state in order to achieve one supreme objective: victory. As the French thinker Elie Halévy put it in 1936 in his influential *The Era of Tyrannies,* the varieties of modern totalitarian tyranny—fascism, Nazism, and communism—could be thought of as "feuding brothers" with a common father: the nature of modern war.[2]

Halévy and others believed Lenin and the Bolsheviks carried the crucial experience of World War I further during the Russian civil war. Lenin showed how a dedicated minority could achieve victory over a less determined majority and subordinate institutions and human rights to the needs of a single group—the Communist Party—and its leader. Lenin's model of single-party dictatorship inspired imitators, including Adolf Hitler. The modern totalitarian state reached maturity in the 1930s in the Stalinist U.S.S.R. and Nazi Germany.

Scholars have also argued that the totalitarian state used modern technology and communications to exercise complete political power, and then complete control over the economic, social, intellectual, and cultural aspects of people's lives as well. Deviation from the norm, even in art or family behavior, could become a crime.

This vision of total state represented a radical revolt against liberalism. Classical liberalism (see page 679) sought to limit state power and protect individual rights. Moreover, liberals stood for rationality, peaceful progress, economic freedom, and a strong middle class. All of that disgusted totalitarians. They believed in willpower, preached conflict, and worshiped violence. The individual was infinitely less valuable than the state.

Unlike old-fashioned authoritarianism, modern totalitarianism was based not on an elite but on people who had already become engaged in the political process, most notably through commitment to nationalism and socialism. Thus totalitarian societies were fully mobilized societies moving toward some goal and possessing boundless dynamism. As soon as one goal was achieved, another arose at the leader's command. As a result totalitarianism was a *permanent* revolution, an *unfinished* revolution, in which rapid, profound change imposed from on high went on forever.

There were major differences between Stalin's communist U.S.S.R. and Hitler's Nazi Germany. Soviet communism, growing out of Marxian socialism, seized all private property (except personal property) for the state and crushed the middle classes.

Chronology

1921	New Economic Policy in Soviet Union
1922	Mussolini seizes power in Italy
1924–1929	Buildup of Nazi Party in Germany
1927	Stalin comes to power in Soviet Union
1928	Stalin's first five-year plan
1929	Start of collectivization in Soviet Union; Lateran Agreement
1929–1939	Great Depression
1932–1933	Famine in Ukraine
1933	Hitler appointed chancellor in Germany; Nazis begin to control intellectual life and blacklist authors
1934	Sergei Kirov, Stalin's number-two man, is murdered
1935	Mussolini invades Ethiopia
1936	Start of great purges under Stalin
1939	Germany occupies Czech lands; Germany invades Poland; Britain and France declare war on Germany
1940	Japan signs formal alliance with Germany and Italy
1941	SS stops Jewish emigration from Europe; Germany invades Soviet Union; bombing of Pearl Harbor; United States enters war
1941–1945	Six million Jews killed in death camps
1944	Allied invasion at Normandy
1945	Atomic bombs dropped on Japan; end of war

● **Nazi Mass Rally, 1936** This picture captures the essence of the totalitarian interpretation of dynamic modern dictatorship. The uniformed members of the Nazi Party have willingly merged themselves into a single force and await the command of the godlike leader. *(AP/Wide World Photos)*

Nazi Germany, growing out of extreme nationalism and racism, criticized big landowners and industrialists, but both private property and the middle classes survived. This difference in property and class relations led some scholars to speak of "totalitarianism of the left"—Stalinist Russia—and "totalitarianism of the right"—Nazi Germany.

A second group of observers in the 1930s approached radical dictatorships outside the Soviet Union through the concept of **fascism**. These writers severely criticized fascism, linking it to decaying capitalism and domestic class conflict. Mussolini and Hitler, however, proudly used the term to describe their movements' supposedly "total" and revolutionary character. Orthodox Marxists argued that powerful capitalists used fascist ideology to create a mass movement capable of destroying the revolutionary working class and thus protect their enormous profits.

fascism *A movement characterized by extreme, often expansionist nationalism, an antisocialism aimed at destroying working-class movements, alliances with powerful capitalists and landowners, a dynamic and violent leader, and glorification of war and the military.*

Comparative studies of European fascist movements show that they shared many characteristics, including extreme nationalism, an antisocialism aimed at destroying working-class movements, alliances with powerful capitalists and landowners, a dynamic and violent leader, and glorification of war and the military. These studies also highlight how fascist movements generally failed to gain political power.

In recent years, many historians have tended to adopt a third approach, emphasizing the uniqueness of developments in each country. This is especially true for Hitler's Germany, where some elements of the totalitarian interpretation have been nuanced and revised. A similar revaluation of Stalin's U.S.S.R. is in progress now that communism's collapse has opened the former Soviet Union's archives to new research.

In summary, despite conflicting interpretations the concept of totalitarianism remains a valuable tool for historical understanding. It correctly highlights that both Hitler's Germany and Stalin's Soviet Union made an unprecedented "total claim" on the beliefs and behaviors of their respective citizens.[3] As for fascism, antidemocratic, antisocialist fascist movements sprang up all over Europe, but only in Italy and Germany (and some would say Spain) were they able to take power. Finally, it is important to remember that the problem of Europe's radical dictatorships is complex, with few easy answers.

STALIN'S SOVIET UNION

How were the five-year plans part of the totalitarian order in the Soviet Union?

Lenin's harshest critics claim that he established the basic outlines of a modern totalitarian dictatorship after the Bolshevik Revolution and during the Russian civil war. If this is so, then Joseph Stalin (1879–1953) certainly finished the job. A master of political infighting, Stalin cautiously consolidated his power and eliminated his enemies in the mid-1920s. Then in 1928, as the ruling Communist Party's undisputed leader, he launched the first **five-year plan**—the "revolution from above," as he so aptly termed it.

Extremely ambitious, the five-year plans marked the beginning of a renewed attempt to mobilize and transform Soviet society along socialist lines. The means Stalin and the small Communist Party elite chose in order to do so were constant propaganda, enormous sacrifice, and unlimited violence and state control. Thus many historians argue that the Soviet Union in the 1930s became a dynamic, modern totalitarian state.

five-year plan *Launched by Stalin and termed "revolution from above," its ultimate goal was to generate new attitudes, new loyalties, and a new socialist humanity.*

From Lenin to Stalin

By spring 1921 Lenin and the Bolsheviks had won the civil war, but they ruled a shattered and devastated land. Many farms were in ruins, and food supplies were exhausted. Drought and war in southern Russia combined to produce the worst famine in generations. Industrial production also broke down completely. The Bolsheviks had destroyed the economy as well as their foes.

In the face of economic disintegration, riots by peasants and workers, and an open rebellion by previously pro-Bolshevik sailors at Kronstadt, Lenin changed course. In March 1921 he announced the **New Economic Policy (NEP)**, which re-established limited economic freedom in an attempt to rebuild agriculture and industry. Peasant producers could sell their surpluses in free markets, as could private traders and small handicraft manufacturers. Heavy industry, railroads, and banks, however, remained wholly nationalized.

New Economic Policy (NEP) *Lenin's policy of re-establishing limited economic freedom in an attempt to rebuild agriculture and industry in the face of economic disintegration.*

The NEP was shrewd and successful both politically and economically. Politically, it was a necessary but temporary compromise with the Soviet Union's overwhelming peasant majority, which Lenin realized was the only force capable of overturning his government. Economically, the NEP brought rapid recovery. In 1926 industrial output surpassed the level of 1913, and Soviet peasants were producing almost as much grain as before the war.

As the economy recovered, an intense power struggle began in the Communist Party's inner circles, for Lenin left no chosen successor when he died in 1924. The principal contenders were the stolid Stalin and the flamboyant Trotsky.

Joseph Dzhugashvili—later known as Stalin—was a shoemaker's son. He studied for the priesthood but was expelled from his theological seminary. By 1903 he was a Bolshevik revolutionary in southern Russia. Stalin was a good organizer but had no experience outside Russia. Trotsky, an inspiring leader who had planned the 1917 takeover (see page 832) and created the victorious Red Army, appeared to have all the advantages. Yet it was Stalin who succeeded Lenin, because he gained the all-important support of the party, the only genuine source of power in the one-party state. Rising to general secretary of the party's Central Committee just before Lenin's first stroke in 1922, Stalin used his office to win friends and allies with jobs and promises.

With cunning skill Stalin gradually achieved absolute power between 1922 and 1927. Stalin used the moderates to crush Trotsky, then he turned against the moderates and destroyed them as well. Stalin's final triumph came at the party congress of December 1927, which condemned all "deviation from the general party line"

● **Kazimir Malevich: Suprematism, ca. 1917** Russian artists occupied a prominent position in the international avant-garde in the early twentieth century, and the Ukrainian-born Malevich is widely recognized as a leading figure in the development of modern abstract art. Malevich originated the theory of suprematism, whereby he abandoned images from nature and painted pure forms that were beautiful in themselves, as in this outstanding example. When the Bolsheviks condemned abstraction and demanded "socialist realism," Malevich returned to more recognizable forms and taught design. *(Erich Lessing/Art Resource, NY)*

formulated by Stalin. He then launched his revolution from above—the real revolution for millions of ordinary citizens.

The Five-Year Plans

The 1927 party congress marked the end of the NEP and the beginning of the era of socialist five-year plans. The first five-year plan had staggering economic objectives. In just five years, total industrial output was to increase by 250 percent and agricultural production by 150 percent, and one-fifth of the peasants were to give up their private plots and join socialist collective farms. By 1930 economic and social change was sweeping the country.

Stalin unleashed his "second revolution" for a variety of interrelated reasons. First, like Lenin, Stalin and his militant supporters were deeply committed to socialism as they understood it. Second, there was the old problem of catching up with the advanced and presumably hostile Western capitalist nations. "We are fifty or a hundred years behind the advanced countries," Stalin said in 1931, "We must make good this distance in ten years. Either we do it, or we shall go under."[4]

Domestically, there was the peasant problem. For centuries peasants had wanted to own the land, and finally they had it. Sooner or later, the communists reasoned, the peasants would become conservative little capitalists and threaten the regime. Therefore, Stalin decided on a preventive war against the peasantry in order to bring it under the state's absolute control.

That war was **collectivization**—the forcible consolidation of individual peasant farms into large, state-controlled enterprises. Beginning in 1929 peasants were ordered to give up their land and animals and become members of collective farms. As for the **kulaks,** the better-off peasants, Stalin instructed party workers to "liquidate them as a class." Stripped of land and livestock, the kulaks were generally not even permitted to join the collective farms. Many starved or were deported to forced-labor camps for "re-education."

Since almost all peasants were in fact poor, the term *kulak* soon meant any peasant who opposed the new system. Whole villages were often attacked. One conscience-stricken colonel in the secret police confessed to a foreign journalist,

I am an old Bolshevik. I worked in the underground against the Tsar and then I fought in the Civil War. Did I do all that in order that I should now surround villages with machine guns and order my men to fire indiscriminately into crowds of peasants? Oh, no, no![5]

Forced collectivization led to disaster. Many peasants slaughtered their animals and burned their crops in sullen, hopeless protest. Between 1929 and 1933 the number of horses, cattle, sheep, and goats in the Soviet Union fell by at least half. Nor were the state-controlled collective farms more productive. Grain output barely increased between 1928 and 1938. Collectivized agriculture made no substantial financial contribution to Soviet industrial development during the first five-year plan.

The disaster's human dimension was absolutely staggering. Stalin himself confided to Winston Churchill at Yalta in 1945 that 10 million people had died in the course of collectivization. In Ukraine the drive against peasants snowballed into a general assault on Ukrainians as reactionary nationalists and enemies of socialism. The result was a terrible man-made famine in Ukraine in 1932 and 1933, which probably claimed 6 million lives.

Collectivization was a cruel but real victory for communist ideologues. By 1938, 93 percent of peasant families had been herded onto collective farms. Regimented as state employees and dependent on the state-owned tractor stations, the collectivized peasants were no longer even a potential political threat to the regime.

The industrial side of the five-year plans was more successful—indeed, quite spectacular. Soviet industry produced about four times as much in 1937 as in 1928. No other major country had ever achieved such rapid industrial growth. Heavy industry led the way; consumer industry grew quite slowly. Urban development accelerated, and more than 25 million people migrated to cities during the 1930s.

The sudden creation of dozens of new factories (and the increasingly voracious military) demanded tremendous resources purchased at enormous sacrifice. The money was collected from the people by means of heavy, hidden sales taxes. Firm labor discipline and foreign engineers also made important contributions to rapid industrialization. Trade unions lost most of their power, and individuals could not move without police permission. When factory managers needed more hands they were sent millions of "unneeded" peasants from collective farms over the years.

Foreign engineers were hired to plan and construct many of the new factories. Highly skilled American engineers, hungry for work in the depression years, were particularly important until newly trained Soviet experts began to replace them after 1932. Siberia's new gigantic steel mills were modeled on America's best. Thus Stalin's planners harnessed even the skill and technology of capitalist countries to promote the surge of socialist industry.

Life and Culture in Soviet Society

Stalin's five-year plans aimed also to create a new kind of society and human personality. The utopian vision of a new humanity floundered, but Stalin did build a new society whose broad outlines existed into the mid-1980s.

collectivization *The forcible consolidation of individual peasant farms into large, state-controlled enterprises.*

kulaks *Better-off peasants who were stripped of land and livestock under Stalin. They generally were not permitted to join the collective farms, and many of them starved or were deported to forced-labor camps for "re-education."*

● **"Let's All Get to Work, Comrades!"** Art in the Stalinist era generally followed the official doctrine of socialist realism, representing objects in a literal style and celebrating Soviet achievements. Characteristically, this poster glorifies the working class, women's equality (in hard labor at least), mammoth factories, and the Communist Party (represented by the hammer and sickle by the woman's foot). Assailed by propaganda, Soviet citizens often found refuge in personal relations and deep friendships. *(From Art of the October Revolution, Mikhail Guerman [Aurora Publishers, Leningrad]. Reproduced by permission)*

Primary Source:
Letters to Izvestiya on the Abortion Issue, May–June 1936
Find out what some citizens of the Soviet Union thought about a proposed ban on abortion.

Life was hard in Stalin's Soviet Union. Because consumption was reduced to pay for investment, there was no improvement in the average standard of living. The masses lived primarily on black bread and wore old, shabby clothing. Stores experienced constant shortages, although very heavily taxed vodka was always readily available. Housing shortages were a particularly serious problem. A relatively lucky family received one room for all its members and shared both a kitchen and a toilet with others on the floor. Less fortunate people built scrap-lumber shacks in shantytowns.

Despite the hardships, idealism and ideology had real appeal for many communists, who saw themselves heroically building the world's first socialist society while capitalism crumbled and fascism rose in the West. This optimistic belief in the Soviet Union's future also attracted many disillusioned Westerners to communism in the 1930s.

On a more practical level Soviet workers did receive some important social benefits, such as old-age pensions, free medical services, free education, and child day-care centers. Unemployment was almost unknown. Finally, there was the possibility of personal advancement.

The keys to improving one's position were specialized skills and technical education. Rapid industrialization required massive numbers of trained experts, such as skilled workers, engineers, and plant managers. Thus the Stalinist state broke with the egalitarian policies of the 1920s and provided tremendous incentives to those who could serve its needs. A growing technical and managerial elite joined with the political and artistic elites in a new upper class, whose members were rich, powerful, and insecure. Thus millions struggled for an education.

Soviet society's radical transformation profoundly affected women's lives. Marxists traditionally believed that both capitalism and middle-class husbands exploited women. The Russian Revolution of 1917 immediately proclaimed complete equality of rights for women. In the 1920s divorce and abortion were made easily available, and women were urged to work outside the home and liberate themselves sexually. After Stalin came to power, sexual and familial liberation was played down, and the most lasting changes for women involved work and education.

While many peasant women continued to work on farms, millions of women now toiled in factories and heavy construction. The more determined women entered the ranks of the better-paid specialists in industry and science. Medicine practically became a woman's profession. By 1950, 75 percent of all doctors in the Soviet Union were women. The massive mobilization of women was a striking characteristic of the Soviet state.

Culture lost its autonomy in the 1930s and became thoroughly politicized through constant propaganda and indoctrination. Party activists lectured workers in factories and peasants on collective farms, while newspapers, films, and radio broadcasts endlessly recounted socialist achievements and capitalist plots. Writers and artists who could effectively combine genuine creativity and political propaganda became the darlings of the regime.

Mussolini and Fascism in Italy   **911**

Stalinist Terror and the Great Purges

In the mid-1930s the great offensive to build socialism and a new socialist personality culminated in ruthless police terror and a massive purging of the Communist Party. In late 1934 Stalin's number-two man, Sergei Kirov, was suddenly and mysteriously murdered. Although Stalin himself probably ordered Kirov's murder, he used the incident to launch a reign of terror.

In August 1936 sixteen prominent Old Bolsheviks confessed to all manner of plots against Stalin in spectacular public show trials in Moscow. Then in 1937 the secret police arrested a mass of lesser party officials and newer members, also torturing them and extracting more confessions for more show trials. In addition to the party faithful, union officials, managers, intellectuals, army officers, and countless ordinary citizens were struck down. In all at least 8 million people were probably arrested, and millions of these were executed or never returned from prisons and forced-labor camps.

Stalin recruited 1.5 million new members to take the place of those purged. Thus more than half of all Communist Party members in 1941 had joined since the purges. "These new men were 'thirty-something' products of the Second Revolution of the 1930s, Stalin's upwardly mobile yuppies, so to speak."[6] This new generation of Stalin-formed Communists served the leader effectively until his death in 1953, and then governed the Soviet Union until the early 1980s.

Stalin's mass purges remain baffling, for almost all historians believe that those purged posed no threat and confessed to crimes they had not committed. Revisionist historians have challenged the long-standing interpretation that blames the great purges on Stalin's cruelty or madness. They argue that Stalin's fears were exaggerated but genuine and were shared by many in the party and in the general population who were bombarded daily with ideology and political slogans. Investigations and trials snowballed into a mass hysteria, a new witch-hunt.[7] In short, a popular but deluded Stalin found large numbers of willing collaborators for crime as well as for achievement.

● ● ● ● ● ● ● ● ● ● ● ● ● ● ● ● ●

MUSSOLINI AND FASCISM IN ITALY

How was Italian fascism a halfway house between conservative authoritarianism and modern totalitarianism?

Mussolini's movement and his seizure of power in 1922 were important steps in the rise of dictatorships between the two world wars. Like all the future dictators, the young Mussolini hated liberalism and wanted to destroy it in Italy. He and his supporters were the first to call themselves "fascists"—revolutionaries determined to create a certain kind of totalitarian state. Few scholars today would argue that Mussolini succeeded. His dictatorship was brutal and theatrical, but it remained a halfway house between conservative authoritarianism and modern totalitarianism.

The Seizure of Power

In the early twentieth century Italy was a liberal state with civil rights and a constitutional monarchy. On the eve of the First World War the parliamentary regime finally granted universal male suffrage. But there were serious problems. Poverty was widespread, and many peasants were more attached to their villages and local interests than to the national state. Moreover, the papacy, many devout Catholics, conservatives, and landowners remained strongly opposed to the middle-class lawyers and politicians who ran the country largely for their own benefit. Church-state relations were often tense. Class differences were also extreme, and by 1912 the Socialist Party's radical wing led the powerful revolutionary socialist movement.[8]

● **Hitler and Mussolini in Italy, May 1938** At first Mussolini distrusted Hitler, but Mussolini's conquest of Ethiopia in 1936 and Hitler's occupation of the Rhineland brought the two dictators together in a close alliance. State visits by Mussolini to Berlin in 1937 and by Hitler to Rome in 1938 included gigantic military reviews, which were filmed to impress the whole world. Uniformed Italian fascists accompany this motorcade. *(Time Life Pictures/Getty Images)*

The war worsened the political situation. Having fought on the Allied side almost exclusively for purposes of territorial expansion, the parliamentary government bitterly disappointed Italian nationalists with Italy's modest gains at Versailles. Workers and peasants also felt cheated: to win their support during the war, the government had promised social and land reform, which it did not deliver after the war.

The Russian Revolution inspired and energized Italy's revolutionary socialist movement, and radical workers and peasants began occupying factories and seizing land in 1920. These actions scared and mobilized the property-owning classes. Thus by 1921 revolutionary socialists, antiliberal conservatives, and frightened property owners were all opposed—though for different reasons—to the liberal parliamentary government.

Into these crosscurrents of unrest and fear stepped the blustering, bullying Benito Mussolini (1883–1945). Son of a village schoolteacher and a poor blacksmith, Mussolini began his political career as a Socialist Party leader and radical newspaper editor before World War I. Expelled from the Italian Socialist Party for supporting the war and wounded in 1917, Mussolini returned home and began organizing bitter war veterans into a band of fascists— from the Italian word for "a union of forces."

At first Mussolini's program was a radical combination of nationalist and socialist demands, including territorial expansion, workers' benefits, and land reform for peasants. It competed directly with the well-organized Socialist Party and failed to get off the ground. When Mussolini saw that his violent verbal assaults on rival Socialists won him growing support from conservatives and the frightened middle classes, he shifted gears in 1920. In thought and action Mussolini was a striking example of the turbulent uncertainty of the age of anxiety.

Black Shirts *A private army under Mussolini that destroyed Socialist newspapers, union halls, and Socialist Party headquarters, eventually pushing Socialists out of the city governments of northern Italy.*

Mussolini and his private army of **Black Shirts** began to grow violent, attacking Socialist organizers and meetings. Few people were killed, but Socialist newspapers, union halls, and local Socialist Party headquarters were destroyed. A skillful politician, Mussolini allowed his followers to convince themselves that they were not just opposing the "Reds" but were also making a real revolution of their own, helping the little people against the established interests.

With the government breaking down in 1922, largely because of the chaos created by his direct-action bands, Mussolini stepped forward as the savior of order and property, demanding the existing government's resignation and his own appointment by the king. In October 1922 a large group of fascists marched on Rome to threaten the king and force him to call on Mussolini. The threat worked. Victor Emmanuel III (r. 1900–1946), who had no love for the old liberal politicians, asked Mussolini to form a new cabinet. Thus, after widespread violence and a threat of armed uprising, Mussolini seized power "legally." The king and parliament immediately granted Mussolini dictatorial authority for one year.

The Regime in Action

Mussolini became dictator on the strength of Italians' rejection of parliamentary government coupled with fears of Soviet-style revolution. In 1924 he declared his desire to "make the nation Fascist," and imposed a series of repressive measures. Press freedom was abolished, elections were fixed, and the government ruled by decree. Mussolini arrested his political opponents, disbanded all independent labor unions, and put dedicated Fascists in control of Italy's schools. He created a fascist youth movement, fascist labor unions, and many other fascist organizations. He trumpeted his goal in a famous slogan of 1926: "Everything in the state, nothing outside the state, nothing against the state." By year's end Italy was a one-party dictatorship under Mussolini's unquestioned leadership.

Mussolini, however, did not complete the establishment of a modern totalitarian state. His Fascist Party never destroyed the old power structure. Interested primarily in personal power, Mussolini was content to compromise with the old conservative classes that controlled the army, the economy, and the state. He never tried to purge these classes or even move very vigorously against them. He controlled labor but left big business to regulate itself, profitably and securely. There was no land reform.

Mussolini also drew increasing support from the Catholic Church. In the **Lateran Agreement** of 1929, he recognized the Vatican as a tiny independent state and agreed to give the church heavy financial support. The pope urged Italians to support Mussolini's government.

Nothing better illustrates Mussolini's unwillingness to harness everyone and everything for dynamic action than his treatment of women. He abolished divorce and told women to stay at home and produce children. In 1938 women were limited by law to a maximum of 10 percent of the better-paying jobs in industry and government. Italian women appear not to have changed their attitudes or behavior in any important way under fascist rule.

Mussolini's government passed no racial laws until 1938 and did not persecute Jews savagely until late in the Second World War, when Italy was under Nazi control. Nor did Mussolini establish a truly ruthless police state. Only twenty-three political prisoners were condemned to death between 1926 and 1944. In spite of much pompous posing by the chauvinist leader, Mussolini's fascist Italy, though repressive and undemocratic, was never really totalitarian.

Lateran Agreement *A 1929 agreement that recognized the Vatican as a tiny independent state, with Mussolini agreeing to give the church heavy financial support. In turn, the pope expressed his satisfaction and urged Italians to support Mussolini's government.*

HITLER AND NAZISM IN GERMANY

Why were Hitler and his Nazi regime initially so popular?

The most frightening dictatorship developed in Nazi Germany. A product of Hitler's evil genius, as well as of Germany's social and political situation and the general attack on liberalism and rationality in the age of anxiety, the Nazi movement shared some of the characteristics of Mussolini's Italian model and fascism. But Nazism asserted an unlimited claim over German society and proclaimed the ultimate power of its endlessly aggressive leader—Adolf Hitler. Nazism's aspirations were truly totalitarian.

The Roots of Nazism

Nazism grew out of many complex developments, of which the most influential were extreme nationalism and racism. These two ideas captured the mind of the young Hitler, and it was he who dominated Nazism for as long as it lasted.

Nazism *A movement born of extreme nationalism and racism and dominated by Adolf Hitler for as long as it lasted.*

Born the fourth child of a successful Austrian customs official and an indulgent mother, Adolf Hitler (1889–1945) spent his childhood in small towns in Austria. He did poorly in high school and dropped out at age sixteen. He then headed to Vienna, where he found most of the perverted beliefs that guided his life.

In Vienna Hitler soaked up extreme German nationalism, which was particularly strong there. Austro-German nationalists believed Germans to be a superior people and central Europe's natural rulers. They often advocated union with Germany and violent expulsion of "inferior" peoples as the means of maintaining German domination of the Austro-Hungarian Empire. Hitler was deeply impressed by Vienna's mayor, Karl Lueger (1844–1910). With the help of the Catholic trade unions, Lueger had won the support of Vienna's lower classes, and he showed Hitler the enormous potential of anticapitalist and antiliberal propaganda.

From Lueger and others Hitler eagerly absorbed virulent anti-Semitism, racism, and hatred of Slavs. He developed an unshakable belief in the crudest, most exaggerated distortions of the Darwinian theory of survival, the superiority of Germanic races, and the inevitability of racial conflict. Anti-Semitism and racism became Hitler's most passionate convictions, his explanation for everything. The Jews, he claimed, directed an international conspiracy of finance capitalism and Marxian socialism against German culture, German unity, and the German race. Hitler's belief was totally irrational, but he never doubted it.

Hitler greeted the outbreak of the Great War as a salvation. The struggle and discipline of war gave his life meaning, and when Germany was suddenly defeated in 1918, Hitler's world was shattered. Convinced that Jews and Marxists had "stabbed Germany in the back," he vowed to fight on.

In late 1919 Hitler joined a tiny extremist group in Munich called the German Workers' Party, which promised a uniquely German "national socialism" that would abolish the injustices of capitalism and create a mighty "people's community." By 1921 Hitler had gained absolute control of this small but growing party. Already a master of mass propaganda and political showmanship, his most effective tool was the mass rally, where he often worked his audience into a frenzy with wild attacks on the Versailles treaty, the Jews, war profiteers, and Germany's Weimar Republic.

In late 1923 the Weimar Republic seemed on the verge of collapse, and Hitler, inspired by Mussolini's recent easy victory, attempted an armed uprising in Munich. Despite the failure of the poorly organized plot and Hitler's arrest, Nazism had been born.

Hitler's Road to Power

At his trial Hitler violently denounced the Weimar Republic, and he gained enormous publicity and attention. Moreover, he learned from his unsuccessful revolt. Hitler concluded that he had to undermine, rather than overthrow, the government and come to power legally through electoral competition. He also used his brief prison term to dictate *Mein Kampf*. There he expounded on his basic themes: "race," with a stress on anti-Semitism; "living space," with a sweeping vision of war and conquered territory; and the leader-dictator, called the **Führer,** with unlimited, arbitrary power.

Führer *"Leader-dictator" with unlimited, arbitrary power; this title was bestowed upon Adolf Hitler.*

In the years of prosperity and relative stability between 1924 and 1929, Hitler concentrated on building his National Socialist German Workers' Party, or Nazi Party. The Nazis remained a small splinter group, however, until the 1929 Great Depression shattered economic prosperity and presented Hitler with a fabulous opportunity. By the end of 1932 an incredible 43 percent of the labor force was unemployed. Industrial production fell by one-half between 1929 and 1932. No factor contributed more to Hitler's success than the economic crisis. Hitler began promising German voters economic as well as political and international salvation.

Hitler rejected free-market capitalism and advocated government programs to bring recovery. He pitched his speeches especially to middle- and lower-middle-class groups and to skilled workers striving for middle-class status. As the economy collapsed, great numbers of these people "voted their pocketbooks"[9] and deserted the conservative and moderate parties for the Nazis. In the 1930 election the Nazis won 6.5 million votes and 107 seats, and in July 1932 the Nazis gained 14.5 million votes—38 percent of the total—and became the largest party in the Reichstag.

Hitler and the Nazis also appealed strongly to German youth. Indeed, in some ways the Nazi movement was a mass movement of young Germans. Hitler himself was only forty in 1929, and he and most of his top aides were much younger than other leading German politicians. "National Socialism is the organized will of the youth," proclaimed the official Nazi slogan. In 1931 almost 40 percent of Nazi Party members were under thirty, compared with 20 percent of Social Democrats. National recovery, exciting and rapid change, and personal advancement made Nazism appealing to millions of German youths.

Hitler also came to power because normal democratic government broke down. Germany's economic collapse in the Great Depression convinced many voters that the country's republican leaders were stupid and corrupt, thereby adding to Hitler's appeal. Disunity on the left was another nail in the republic's coffin. The Communists refused to cooperate with the Social Democrats, even though the two parties together outnumbered the Nazis in the Reichstag, even after the 1932 elections. German Communists (and the still complacent Stalin) believed that Hitler's fascism represented the last agonies of monopoly capitalism and that a communist revolution would soon follow his taking power.

Finally, Hitler excelled in dirty backroom politics. In 1932 he succeeded in gaining support from key people in the army and big business who thought they could use him to their own advantage. Many conservative and nationalistic politicians thought similarly. Thus in January 1933 Hindenburg legally appointed Hitler, leader of Germany's largest party, chancellor of Germany.

The Nazi State and Society

Hitler quickly and skillfully established an unshakable dictatorship. When the Reichstag building was partly destroyed by fire, Hitler blamed the Communist Party, and he convinced President Hindenburg to sign dictatorial emergency acts that practically abolished freedom of speech and assembly and most personal liberties. He also called for new elections.

When the Nazis won only 44 percent of the votes, Hitler immediately outlawed the Communist Party and arrested its parliamentary representatives. Then on March 23, 1933, the Nazis forced through the Reichstag the so-called **Enabling Act,** which gave Hitler absolute dictatorial power for four years. Hitler and the Nazis took over the government bureaucracy intact, installing many Nazis in top positions.

Hitler next outlawed strikes and abolished independent labor unions, which were replaced by the Nazi Labor Front. Professional people—doctors and lawyers, teachers and engineers—also saw their previously independent organizations swallowed up in Nazi associations. Publishing houses and universities were put under Nazi control, and passionate students and pitiful professors burned forbidden books in public squares. Modern art and architecture were ruthlessly prohibited. Life became violently anti-intellectual. As the cynical Joseph Goebbels, later Nazi minister of propaganda, put it, "When I hear the word 'culture' I reach for my gun."[10] By 1934 a brutal dictatorship characterized by frightening dynamism and total obedience to Hitler was already largely in place.

In June 1934 Hitler ordered his elite personal guard—the SS—to arrest and shoot without trial roughly a thousand long-time Nazi storm troops. Shortly thereafter army leaders surrendered their independence and swore a binding oath of "unquestioning obedience . . . to the Leader of the German State and People, Adolf Hitler." The SS grew rapidly. Under its methodical, inhuman leader, Heinrich Himmler

Enabling Act *The act pushed through the Reichstag by the Nazis that gave Hitler absolute dictatorial power for four years.*

Ganz Deutschland
hört den Führer

mit dem Volksempfänger

● **Reaching a National Audience** This poster ad promotes the VE-301 receiver, "the world's cheapest radio," and claims that "All Germany listens to the Führer on the people's receiver." Constantly broadcasting official views and attitudes, the state-controlled media also put the Nazis' favorite entertainment—gigantic mass meetings that climaxed with Hitler's violent theatrical speeches—on an invisible stage for millions. (*Bundesarchiv Koblenz Plak 003-022-025*)

Primary Source:

Speech to the National Socialist Women's Association, September 1935

Learn what the Nazis believed were the proper roles for women in society—from the woman appointed to disseminate their beliefs.

(1900–1945), the SS joined with the political police, the Gestapo, to expand its network of special courts and concentration camps. Nobody was safe.

From the beginning Jews were a special object of Nazi persecution. By late 1934 most Jewish lawyers, doctors, professors, civil servants, and musicians had lost their jobs and the right to practice their professions. In 1935 the infamous Nuremberg Laws classified as Jewish anyone having one or more Jewish grandparents and deprived Jews of all rights of citizenship. By 1938 roughly one-quarter of Germany's half million Jews had emigrated, sacrificing almost all their property in order to leave Germany.

In late 1938 the attack on the Jews accelerated. A well-organized wave of violence destroyed homes, synagogues, and businesses, after which German Jews were rounded up and made to pay for the damage. It became very difficult for Jews to leave Germany. Some Germans privately opposed these outrages, but most went along or looked the other way. Although this lack of response reflected the individual's helplessness in a totalitarian state, it was more certainly a sign of the strong popular support Hitler's government enjoyed.

Hitler's Popularity

Hitler had promised the masses economic recovery—"work and bread"—and he delivered, launching a large public works program to pull Germany out of the depression. Work began on superhighways, offices, gigantic sports stadiums, and public housing. In 1935 Germany turned decisively toward rearmament. Unemployment dropped steadily, and by 1938 everyone had work. The average standard of living increased moderately. Business profits rose sharply. For millions of people economic recovery was tangible evidence that Nazi promises were more than show and propaganda.

For the masses of ordinary German citizens who were not Jews, Slavs, Gypsies, Jehovah's Witnesses, communists, or homosexuals, Hitler's government meant greater equality and more opportunities. In 1933 class barriers in Germany were generally high. Hitler's rule introduced changes that lowered these barriers. For example, stiff educational requirements favoring the well-to-do were relaxed. The new Nazi elite included many young and poorly educated dropouts, rootless lower-middle-class people like Hitler who rose to the top with breathtaking speed. More generally, the Nazis tolerated privilege and wealth only as long as they served party needs.

Yet few historians today believe that Hitler and the Nazis brought about a real social revolution, as an earlier generation of scholars often argued. The well-educated classes held on to most of their advantages, and only a modest social leveling occurred in the Nazi years. Significantly, the Nazis shared with the Italian fascists the stereotypical view of women as housewives and mothers. Only under the relentless pressure of war did they reluctantly mobilize large numbers of German women for office and factory work.

Not all Germans supported Hitler, however, and a number of German groups actively resisted him after 1933. Tens of thousands of political enemies were imprisoned, and thousands were executed. In the first years of Hitler's rule, the principal resisters were trade union communists and socialists. The expansion of the SS system of terror after 1935 smashed most of these leftists. Catholic and Protestant churches produced a second group of opponents. Their efforts were directed primarily at preserving genuine religious life, however, not at overthrowing Hitler. Finally in 1938 (and again from 1942 to 1944) some high-ranking army officers, who feared the consequences of Hitler's reckless aggression, plotted, unsuccessfully, against him.

Aggression and Appeasement (1933–1939)

Although economic recovery and somewhat greater opportunity for social advancement won Hitler support, the guiding and unique concepts of Nazism remained space and race—the territorial expansion of the superior German race. As we shall see, German expansion was facilitated by the uncertain, divided, pacific Western democracies, which tried to buy off Hitler to avoid war.

Hitler realized that his aggressive policies had to be carefully camouflaged at first, for the Treaty of Versailles limited Germany's army to only a hundred thousand men. As Hitler told some army commanders in February 1933, the early stages of his policy of "conquest of new living space in the East and its ruthless Germanization" had serious dangers. If France had real leaders, Hitler said, it would "not give us time but attack us, presumably with its eastern satellites."[11] Thus while Hitler loudly proclaimed his peaceful intentions, Germany's withdrawal from the League of Nations in October 1933 indicated its determination to rearm. When in March 1935 Hitler established a general military draft and declared the "unequal" Versailles treaty disarmament clauses null and void, some European leaders appeared to understand the danger and warned him against future aggressive actions.

But the emerging united front against Hitler quickly collapsed. Britain adopted a policy of appeasement, granting Hitler everything he could reasonably want (and more) in order to avoid war. The last chance to stop the Nazis came in March 1936 when Hitler suddenly marched his armies into the demilitarized Rhineland, brazenly violating the Treaties of Versailles and Locarno. An uncertain France would not move without British support, however, and Britain refused to act (see Map 30.1).

British appeasement, which practically dictated French policy, lasted far into 1939. It was motivated by British feelings of guilt toward Germany and the pacifism of a population still horrified by the memory of the Great War. As in Germany, many powerful British conservatives underestimated Hitler. They also believed that Soviet communism was the real danger and that Hitler could be used to stop it. Such strong anticommunist feelings made an alliance between the Western Powers and Stalin unlikely.

As Britain and France opted for appeasement and the Soviet Union watched all developments suspiciously, Hitler found powerful allies. In 1935 the bombastic Mussolini attacked the independent African kingdom of Ethiopia. The Western Powers and the League of Nations piously condemned Italian aggression, but Hitler supported Italy energetically. In 1936 Italy and Germany signed an agreement on close cooperation, the so-called Rome-Berlin Axis. Japan, which wanted support for its occupation of Manchuria, soon joined the Axis alliance.

At the same time, Germany and Italy intervened in the Spanish civil war (1936–1939). Their support eventually

Primary Source:

The Centerpiece of Nazi Racial Legislation: The Nuremberg Laws
These laws defined who was a Jew, forbade marriage between Germans and Jews, and paved the way for the Holocaust.

● **Hitler's Success with Aggression** This biting criticism of appeasing leaders by the cartoonist David Low appeared shortly after Hitler remilitarized the Rhineland. Appeasement also appealed to millions of ordinary citizens in Britain and France who wanted to avoid another great war at any cost. *(Solo Syndication/Associated Newspapers)*

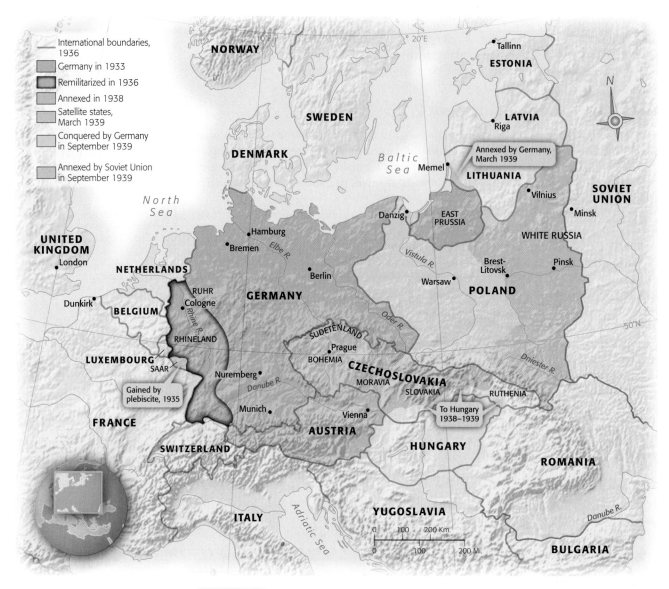

Legend:
- International boundaries, 1936
- Germany in 1933
- Remilitarized in 1936
- Annexed in 1938
- Satellite states, March 1939
- Conquered by Germany in September 1939
- Annexed by Soviet Union in September 1939

MAP 30.1 **The Growth of Nazi Germany, 1933–1939** Until March 1939, Hitler brought ethnic Germans into the Nazi state; then he turned on the Slavic peoples, whom he had always hated. He stripped Czechoslovakia of its independence and prepared for an attack on Poland in September 1939.

helped General Francisco Franco's fascist movement defeat republican Spain. Spain's only official aid came from the Soviet Union, for public opinion in Britain and especially in France was hopelessly divided on the Spanish question.

In late 1937 Hitler moved forward with his plans to crush Austria and Czechoslovakia as the first step in his long-contemplated drive to the east for living space. By threatening Austria with invasion, Hitler forced the Austrian chancellor in March 1938 to put local Nazis in control of the government. The next day German armies moved in unopposed, and Austria became two provinces of Greater Germany (see Map 30.1).

Simultaneously, Hitler began demanding that the pro-Nazi, German-speaking minority of western Czechoslovakia—the Sudetenland—be turned over to Germany. Democratic Czechoslovakia, however, was prepared to defend itself. Moreover, France had been Czechoslovakia's ally since 1924, and if France fought, the Soviet Union was pledged to help. War appeared inevitable, but appeasement triumphed again. In September 1938 Prime Minister Chamberlain flew to Germany three times in fourteen days. In these negotiations, to which the Soviet Union was deliberately not invited, Chamberlain and the French agreed with Hitler that the Sudetenland should be ceded to Germany immediately. Returning to London from the Munich Conference, Chamberlain told cheering crowds that he had secured "peace with honor . . . peace for our time." Sold out by the Western Powers, Czechoslovakia gave in.

Hitler's armies occupied the remainder of Czechoslovakia in March 1939. The effect on Western public opinion was electrifying. For the first time, there was no possible rationale of self-determination for Nazi aggression, because Hitler was treating the Czechs and Slovaks as captive peoples. When Hitler used the question of German minorities in Danzig as a pretext to confront Poland, a suddenly militant Chamberlain declared that Britain and France would fight if Hitler attacked his eastern neighbor. Hitler did not take these warnings seriously and decided to press on.

In an about-face that stunned the world, Hitler offered and Stalin signed a ten-year Nazi-Soviet nonaggression pact in August 1939. Each dictator promised to remain neutral if the other became involved in war. An attached secret protocol ruthlessly divided eastern Europe into German and Soviet zones "in the event of a political territorial reorganization." The British and French felt betrayed for they, too, had been negotiating with Stalin. But Stalin had remained distrustful of Western intentions, and Hitler had offered territorial gain.

For Hitler, everything was set. He told his generals on the day of the nonaggression pact, "My only fear is that at the last moment some dirty dog will come up with a mediation plan." On September 1, 1939, German armies and warplanes smashed into Poland from three sides. Two days later Britain and France, finally true to their word, declared war on Germany. The Second World War had begun.

THE SECOND WORLD WAR

How did Hitler's actions lead to another world war?

War broke out in both western and eastern Europe because Hitler's ambitions were essentially unlimited. On both war fronts Nazi soldiers scored enormous successes until late 1942, establishing a horrifyingly vast empire of death and destruction. Hitler's victories increased tensions in Asia between Japan and the United States and prompted Japan to attack the United States and overrun much of Southeast Asia. Yet reckless German and Japanese aggression also raised a mighty coalition determined to smash the aggressors. Led by Britain, the United States, and the Soviet Union, the Grand Alliance—to use Winston Churchill's favorite term—functioned quite effectively in military terms. Thus the Nazi and Japanese empires proved short-lived.

Hitler's Empire in Europe (1939–1942)

Using planes, tanks, and trucks in the first example of a **blitzkrieg,** or "lightning war," Hitler's armies crushed Poland in four weeks. The Soviet Union quickly took its part of the booty—the eastern half of Poland and the Baltic states of Lithuania, Estonia, and Latvia. In the west French and British armies dug in; they expected another war of attrition and economic blockade. But in spring 1940 the lightning war struck again. After occupying Denmark, Norway, and Holland, German motorized columns broke through southern Belgium and into France.

blitzkrieg *"Lightning war" using planes, tanks, and trucks, the first example of which Hitler used to crush Poland in four weeks.*

Events Leading to World War II

1919	Treaty of Versailles is signed; J. M. Keynes publishes *Economic Consequences of the Peace.*
1919–1920	U.S. Senate rejects the Treaty of Versailles.
1921	Germany is billed $33 billion in reparations.
1922	Mussolini seizes power in Italy; Germany proposes a moratorium on reparations.
January 1923	France and Belgium occupy the Ruhr; Germany orders passive resistance to the occupation.
October 1923	Stresemann agrees to reparations based on Germany's ability to pay.
1924	Dawes Plan: German reparations are reduced and put on a sliding scale; large U.S. loans to Germany are recommended to promote German recovery; Adolf Hitler dictates *Mein Kampf.*
1924–1929	Spectacular German economic recovery occurs; circular flow of international funds enables sizable reparations payments.
1925	Treaties of Locarno promote European security and stability.
1926	Germany joins the League of Nations.
1928	Kellogg-Briand Pact renounces war as an instrument of international affairs.
1929	U.S. stock market crashes.
1929–1939	Great Depression rages.
1931	Japan invades Manchuria.
1932	Nazis become the largest party in the Reichstag.
January 1933	Hitler is appointed chancellor of Germany.
March 1933	Reichstag passes the Enabling Act, granting Hitler absolute dictatorial power.
October 1933	Germany withdraws from the League of Nations.
1935	Nuremberg Laws deprive Jews of all rights of citizenship.
March 1935	Hitler announces German rearmament.
June 1935	Anglo-German naval agreement is signed.
October 1935	Mussolini invades Ethiopia and receives Hitler's support.
March 1936	German armies move unopposed into the demilitarized Rhineland.
July 1936	Civil war breaks out in Spain.
1937	Japan invades China; Rome-Berlin Axis in effect.
March 1938	Germany annexes Austria.
September 1938	Munich Conference: Britain and France agree to German seizure of the Sudetenland from Czechoslovakia.
March 1939	Germany occupies the rest of Czechoslovakia; appeasement ends in Britain.
August 1939	Nazi-Soviet nonaggression pact is signed.
September 1, 1939	Germany invades Poland.
September 3, 1939	Britain and France declare war on Germany.

As Hitler's armies poured into France, aging marshal Henri-Philippe Pétain formed a new French government—the so-called Vichy government—and accepted defeat. By July 1940 Hitler ruled practically all of western continental Europe; Italy was an ally, the Soviet Union a friendly neutral (see Map 30.2). Only Britain, led by the uncompromising Winston Churchill (1874–1965), remained unconquered.

To mount an amphibious invasion of Britain, Germany first needed to gain control of the air. In the Battle of Britain, up to a thousand German planes attacked British airfields and key factories in a single day, dueling with British defenders high in the skies. In September Hitler angrily began indiscriminately bombing British cities in an attempt to break British morale. British aircraft factories increased production, and the heavily bombed people of London defiantly dug in. In September and October 1940 Britain was beating Germany three to one in the air war. There was no possibility of an immediate German invasion of Britain.

Hitler now allowed his lifetime obsession with a vast eastern European empire for the "master race" to dictate policy. In June 1941 German armies suddenly attacked the Soviet Union along a vast front. By October Leningrad was practically surrounded, Moscow was besieged, and most of Ukraine had been conquered. But the Soviets did not collapse, and when a severe winter struck German armies outfitted in summer uniforms, the invaders were stopped.

Stalled in Russia, Hitler had come to rule an enormous European empire stretching from the outskirts of Moscow to the English Channel. He and the top Nazi leadership began building their **New Order.** In doing so, they showed what Nazi victory would have meant.

Hitler's New Order was based firmly on the guiding principle of Nazi totalitarianism: racial imperialism. Within this New Order the Nordic peoples—the Dutch, Norwegians, and Danes—received preferential treatment, for they were racially related to the Germans. The French, an "inferior" Latin people, occupied the middle position.

New Order *Hitler's program, based on the guiding principle of racial imperialism that gave preferential treatment to the Nordic peoples.*

● **London, 1940** Hitler believed that his relentless terror bombing of London—the "blitz"—could break the will of the British people. He was wrong. The blitz caused enormous destruction, but Londoners went about their business with courage and calm determination, as this unforgettable image of a milkman in the rubble suggests. *(Hulton-Deutsch Collection/Corbis)*

Slavs in the conquered eastern territories were treated with harsh hatred as "subhumans." Hitler envisioned a vast eastern colonial empire where Poles, Ukrainians, and Russians would be enslaved and forced to die out, while Germanic peasants resettled the resulting abandoned lands. Hitler needed countless helpers, however, and these accomplices came forth. Himmler and the elite SS corps shared Hitler's ideology of barbarous racial imperialism. Supported (or condoned) by military commanders and German policemen in the occupied territories, the SS corps pressed relentlessly to implement the program of destruction and to create a "mass settlement space" for Germans. Many Poles, captured communists, Gypsies, and Jehovah's Witnesses were murdered in cold blood.

MAP 30.2 **World War II in Europe** The map shows the extent of Hitler's empire at its height, before the Battle of Stalingrad in late 1942 and the subsequent advances of the Allies until Germany surrendered on May 7, 1945.

Finally, the Nazi state condemned all European Jews to extermination in the **Holocaust.** After the fall of Warsaw the Nazis began deporting all German Jews to occupied Poland, and in 1941 expulsion spiraled into extermination on the Russian front. Himmler's SS killing squads and regular army units forced Soviet Jews to dig giant pits, which became mass graves as the victims were lined up on the edge and cut down by machine guns. Then in late 1941 Hitler and the Nazi leadership, in some still-debated combination, ordered the SS to stop all Jewish emigration from Europe and speeded up planning for mass murder. All over the Nazi empire Jews were systematically arrested, packed like cattle onto freight trains, and dispatched to extermination camps.

Arriving at their destination, small numbers of Jews were sent to nearby slave labor camps, where they were starved and systematically worked to death. (See the feature "Individuals in Society: Primo Levi.") But most victims were taken by force or deception to "shower rooms," which were actually gas chambers. For fifteen to twenty minutes came the terrible screams and gasping sobs of men, women, and children choking to death on poison gas. Then, only silence. Special camp workers quickly yanked the victims' gold teeth from their jaws, and the bodies were then cremated, or sometimes boiled for oil to make soap. The extermination of European Jews was the ultimate monstrosity of Nazi racism and racial imperialism. By 1945, 6 million Jews had been murdered.

Who was responsible for this terrible crime? An older generation of historians usually laid most of the guilt on Hitler and the Nazi leadership. Ordinary Germans had little knowledge of the extermination camps, it was argued, and those who cooperated had no alternative given the brutality of Nazi terror and totalitarian control. But in recent years many studies have revealed a much broader participation of German people in the Holocaust and popular indifference (or worse) to the Jews' fate.

In most occupied countries, local non-German officials also cooperated in the arrest and deportation of Jews. As in Germany, only a few exceptional bystanders did not turn a blind eye. Thus some scholars have concluded that the key for most Germans (and most people in occupied countries) was that they felt no personal responsibility for Jews and therefore were not prepared to help them. This meant that many individuals, conditioned by Nazi racist propaganda but also influenced by peer pressure and brutalizing wartime violence, were psychologically prepared to perpetrate ever-greater crimes, from mistreatment to arrest to mass murder.

Holocaust *The attempted extermination of all European Jews by the Nazi state.*

> **Primary Source:**
> **Memoirs**
> *Read what the man responsible for administering and overseeing the Holocaust thought and felt about his "work."*

● **Prelude to Murder** This photo captures the terrible inhumanity of Nazi racism. Frightened and bewildered families from the soon-to-be-destroyed Warsaw Ghetto are being forced out of their homes by German soldiers for deportation to concentration camps. There they face murder in the gas chambers. *(Hulton Archive/Getty Images)*

Japan's Asian Empire

By late 1938, 1.5 million Japanese troops were bogged down in China, holding a great swath of territory but unable to defeat the Nationalists and the Communists (see pages 868–870). Nor had Japan succeeded in building a large, self-sufficient Asian economic zone, for it still depended on oil and scrap metal from the Netherlands East Indies and the United States. Thus Japanese leaders followed events in Europe closely, looking for alliances and actions that might improve their position in Asia. At home they gave free rein to the anti-Western ultranationalism that had risen in the 1920s and 1930s (see pages 866, 868): proclaiming Japan's liberating mission in Asia; glorifying the warrior virtues of honor and sacrifice; and demanding absolute devotion to the semidivine emperor. (See the feature "Listening to the Past: Radical Nationalism for Japanese Students" on pages 934–935).

The outbreak of war in Europe in 1939 and Hitler's early victories opened up opportunities for the Japanese in Asia. In China the Japanese redoubled their brutal efforts to crush peasant support for the Nationalists and the Communists. Implementing a brutal "three-alls" policy—"kill all, burn all, destroy all"—Japanese troops massacred whole villages, torched buildings, slaughtered farm animals, and committed shocking atrocities. In March 1940 the Japanese set up a Chinese puppet government in Nanjing, but the fighting—and the atrocities—continued until the war ended.

In Southeast Asia European empires appeared vulnerable. In September 1940 Japan signed a formal alliance with Germany and Italy and forced the French to accept Japanese domination of northern French Indochina. The United States had repeatedly condemned Japanese aggression in China. Now the United States also opposed Japanese expansion, because it feared that embattled Britain would collapse if it lost the support of its Asian colonies. Applying economic sanctions in October 1940, the United States stopped scrap iron sales to Japan and later froze all Japanese assets in the United States.

Japan's invasion of southern Indochina in July 1941 further worsened relations with the United States. President Franklin Roosevelt demanded that Japan withdraw from China, keeping only Manchuria. Japan refused. The United States responded by cutting off U.S. oil sales to Japan and thereby reducing Japan's oil supplies by 90 percent. Japanese leaders now increasingly believed that war with the United States was inevitable, for Japan's battle fleet would run out of fuel in eighteen months and its industry would be crippled. After much debate Japanese leaders decided to launch a surprise attack on the United States. They hoped to cripple their Pacific rival, gain time to build a defensible Asian empire, and eventually win an ill-defined compromise peace.

The Japanese attack on the U.S. naval base at Pearl Harbor in the Hawaiian Islands was a complete surprise but a limited success. On December 7, 1941, the Japanese sank or crippled every American battleship, but by chance all the American aircraft carriers were at sea and escaped unharmed. This enabled rapid American recovery, because aircraft carriers dominated the Pacific war. More important, most Americans felt superior to the Japanese, and they were humiliated by this unexpected defeat. Pearl Harbor overwhelmed American isolationism and brought Americans together in a spirit of anger and revenge.

Hitler immediately declared war on the United States. Simultaneously, Japanese armies successfully attacked European and American colonies in Southeast Asia. Japanese armies were small (because most soldiers remained in China), but they were well trained, well led, and highly motivated. They defeated larger Dutch and British armies to seize the Netherlands East Indies and its rich oil fields, and the British colonies of Hong Kong, Malaya, and Singapore. After American forces surrendered the Philippines in May 1942, Japan held a vast empire in Southeast Asia and the western Pacific (see Map 30.3).

Individuals IN SOCIETY

Primo Levi

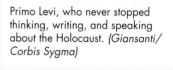

Primo Levi, who never stopped thinking, writing, and speaking about the Holocaust. *(Giansanti/ Corbis Sygma)*

Most Jews deported to Auschwitz were murdered as soon as they arrived, but the Nazis made some prisoners into slave laborers and a few of these survived. Primo Levi (1919–1987), an Italian Jew, became one of the most influential witnesses to the Holocaust and its death camps.

Like much of Italy's small Jewish community, Levi's family belonged to the urban professional classes. The young Primo graduated in 1941 from the University of Turin with highest honors in chemistry. But since 1938, when Italy introduced racial laws, he had faced growing discrimination, and two years after graduation he joined the antifascist resistance movement. Quickly captured, he was deported to Auschwitz with 650 Italian Jews in February 1944. Stone-faced SS men picked only ninety-six men and twenty-nine women to work in their respective labor camps. Primo was one of them.

Nothing prepared Levi for what he encountered. The Jewish prisoners were kicked, punched, stripped, branded with tattoos, crammed into huts, and worked unmercifully. Hoping for some sign of prisoner solidarity in this terrible environment, Levi found only a desperate struggle of each against all and enormous status differences among prisoners. Many stunned and bewildered newcomers, beaten and demoralized by their bosses—the most privileged prisoners—simply collapsed and died. Others struggled to secure their own privileges, however small, because food rations and working conditions were so abominable that ordinary Jewish prisoners perished in two to three months.

Sensitive and noncombative, Levi found himself sinking into oblivion. But instead of joining the mass of the "drowned," he became one of the "saved"—a complicated surprise with moral implications that he would ponder all his life. As Levi explained in *Survival in Auschwitz* (1947), the usual road to salvation in the camps was some kind of collaboration with German power.* Savage German criminals were released from prison to become brutal camp guards; non-Jewish political prisoners competed for jobs entitling them to better conditions; and, especially troubling for Levi, a small number of Jewish men plotted and struggled

for the power of life and death over other Jewish prisoners. Though not one of these Jewish bosses, Levi believed that he himself, like almost all survivors, had entered the "gray zone" of moral compromise. Only a very few superior individuals, "the stuff of saints and martyrs," survived the death camps without shifting their moral stance.

For Levi, compromise and salvation came from his profession. Interviewed by a German technocrat for the camp's synthetic rubber program, Levi performed brilliantly in scientific German and savored his triumph as a Jew over Nazi racism. Work in the warm camp laboratory offered Levi opportunities to pilfer equipment that could then be traded for food and necessities with other prisoners. Levi also gained critical support from three saintly prisoners who refused to do wicked and hateful acts. And he counted "luck" as essential for his survival: in the camp infirmary with scarlet fever in February 1945 as advancing Russian armies prepared to liberate the camp, Levi was not evacuated by the Nazis and shot to death like most Jewish prisoners.

After the war Primo Levi was forever haunted by the nightmare that the Holocaust would be ignored or forgotten. Always ashamed that so many people whom he considered better than himself had perished, he wrote and lectured tirelessly to preserve the memory of Jewish victims and guilty Nazis. Wanting the world to understand the Jewish genocide in all its complexity so that never again would people tolerate such atrocities, he grappled tirelessly with his vision of individual choice and moral compromise in a hell designed to make the victims collaborate and persecute each other.

Questions for Analysis

1. Describe Levi's experience at Auschwitz. How did camp prisoners treat each other? Why?

2. What does Levi mean by the "gray zone"? How is this concept central to his thinking?

3. Will a vivid historical memory of the Holocaust help prevent future genocide?

---

*Primo Levi, *Survival in Auschwitz: The Nazi Assault on Humanity,* rev. ed. 1958 (London: Collier Books, 1961), pp. 79–84, and *The Drowned and the Saved* (New York: Summit Books, 1988). These powerful testimonies are highly recommended.

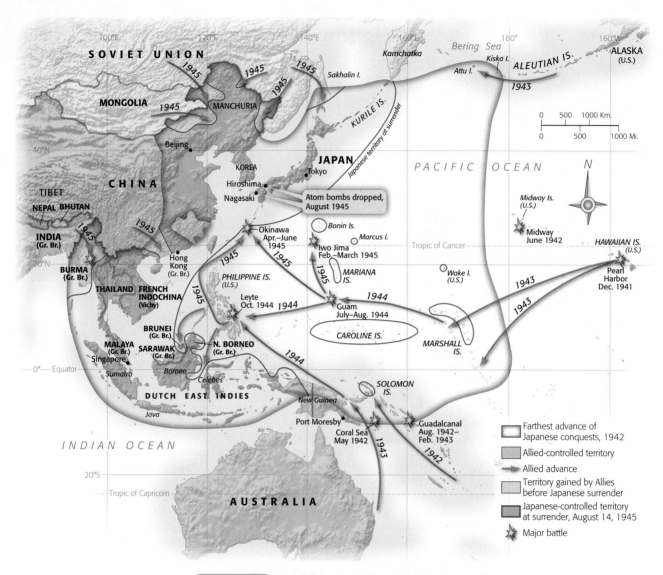

MAP 30.3 **World War II in the Pacific** Japanese forces overran an enormous amount of territory in 1942, which the Allies slowly recaptured in a long, bitter struggle. As this map shows, Japan still held a large Asian empire in August 1945, when the unprecedented devastation of atomic warfare suddenly forced it to surrender.

The Japanese claimed they were freeing Asians from Western imperialism, and they called their empire the Greater East Asian Co-prosperity Sphere. Some, perhaps many, Japanese army officers and officials sincerely believed that they were creating a mutually advantageous union for Asia's long-term development. Initially they tapped currents of nationalist sentiment, and most local populations were glad to see the Western Powers go. But Asian faith in "co-prosperity" and support for Japan steadily declined as the war went on. Why was this so?

A key factor was that although the Japanese set up anticolonial governments and promised genuine independence, real power always rested with Japanese military commanders and their superiors in Tokyo. The "independent" governments established in the Philippines, French Indochina, Burma, and the Netherlands East Indies were basically shams. Moreover, the Japanese never treated local populations as equals.

● **The War in the Philippines** U.S. and Philippine forces held out on the Bataan peninsula until April 1942, when seventy-six thousand soldiers surrendered to the Japanese military. Most of the prisoners were sick, wounded, or suffering from malnutrition, and the Japanese systematically executed many of them. Other prisoners, such as those pictured here, were marched to exhaustion without water in the blazing sun on the infamous Bataan Death March, and many were bayoneted or beaten to death. (Bettmann/Corbis)

As Japanese living standards plummeted and heavy industry sputtered, the Japanese occupiers exploited local peoples for Japan's wartime needs. They cut wages, imposed supply quotas on raw materials, and drafted local people for military and labor service. Ships left for Japan laden with rice, oil, and raw materials, but they returned empty, if they returned at all.

The Japanese often exhibited great cruelty toward prisoners of war and civilians, as they had toward the Chinese since 1937. After the fall of Hong Kong in December 1941, for example, wounded prisoners there were murdered and burned, and there was a mass rape of nurses. Elsewhere Korean, Dutch, and Indonesian women were forced into sexual bondage, providing sex for Japanese soldiers as "comfort women." Recurring cruel behavior also aroused local populations against the invaders.

The Grand Alliance

While the Nazis and the Japanese built their savage empires, the Allies faced the hard fact that chance, rather than choice, had brought them together. Stalin had been cooperating fully with Hitler between August 1939 and June 1941, and only the Japanese attack on Pearl Harbor in December 1941 had overwhelmed powerful isolationism in the United States.

As a first step toward building an unshakable alliance, U.S. president Franklin D. Roosevelt accepted the policy of **"Europe first"** as proposed by Winston Churchill (Chamberlain's successor as British prime minister). Only after Hitler was defeated would the United States turn toward the Pacific for an all-out attack on Japan, the lesser threat. The Americans and the British also put immediate military needs first, consistently postponing tough political questions relating to the eventual peace settlement that might have split the alliance.

To further encourage mutual trust, the Allies adopted the principle of the "unconditional surrender" of Germany and Japan. This policy cemented the Grand Alliance because it denied Germany and Japan any hope of dividing their foes.

"Europe first" *The military strategy, set forth by Churchill and adopted by Roosevelt, that called for the defeat of Hitler in Europe before the United States launched an all-out strike against Japan in the Pacific.*

The Grand Alliance's military resources were awesome. The United States possessed a unique capacity to wage global war with its mighty industry, large population, and national unity. These were all harnessed in 1942 to gear up rapidly for all-out war. In 1943 America out produced not only Germany, Italy, and Japan but also all of the rest of the world combined.[12]

Britain continued to make a great contribution as well. The British economy was totally and effectively mobilized, and the sharing of burdens through rationing and heavy taxes on war profits maintained social harmony. Britain, the impregnable floating fortress, became a gigantic frontline staging area for the decisive blow to the heart of Germany.

As for the Soviet Union, so great was its strength that it might well have defeated Germany without Western help. In the face of the German advance, whole factories and populations were successfully evacuated to eastern Russia and Siberia. There war production was reorganized and expanded, and the Red Army was increasingly well supplied and well led. Above all, Stalin drew on the massive support and heroic determination of the Soviet people, especially those in the central Russian heartland. Broad-based Russian nationalism, as opposed to narrow communist ideology, became the powerful unifying force in what the Soviet people appropriately called the "Great Patriotic War of the Fatherland."

Finally, the United States, Britain, and the Soviet Union had the resources of much of the world at their command. They were also aided by a growing resistance movement against the Nazis throughout Europe, even in Germany. After the Soviet Union was invaded in June 1941, communists throughout Europe took the lead in the underground resistance, joined by a growing number of patriots, Christians, and agents sent by governments-in-exile in London.

The War in Europe (1942–1945)

Barely halted at the gates of Moscow and Leningrad in 1941, the Germans renewed their offensive against the Soviet Union in 1942 and attacked the southern city of Stalingrad in July. In November 1942 Soviet armies counterattacked, quickly surrounding the entire German Sixth Army of 300,000 men. By late January 1943 only 123,000 soldiers were left to surrender. Hitler, who had refused to allow a retreat, suffered a catastrophic defeat. In summer 1943 the larger, better-equipped Soviet armies took the offensive and began moving forward (see Map 30.2).

Not yet prepared to attack Germany directly through France, the Western Allies saw heavy fighting in North Africa (see Map 30.2). In summer 1942 British forces finally defeated combined German and Italian armies at the Battle of El Alamein, only seventy miles from Alexandria. Almost immediately thereafter an Anglo-American force landed in Morocco and Algeria. These French possessions, which were under the control of Pétain's Vichy French government, quickly went over to the Allied side.

Having driven the Axis powers from North Africa by spring 1943, Allied forces invaded Italy. War-weary Italians deposed Mussolini, and the new Italian government publicly accepted unconditional surrender in September 1943. Italy, it seemed, was liberated. But then German commandos in a daring raid rescued Mussolini and put him at the head of a puppet government. German armies seized Rome and all of northern Italy. Fighting continued in Italy.

Indeed, bitter fighting continued in Europe for almost two years. Germany, less fully mobilized for war than Britain in 1941, applied itself to total war in 1942 and enlisted millions of German women and millions of prisoners of war and slave laborers from all across occupied Europe in that effort. Between early 1942 and July 1944 German war production actually tripled in spite of heavy bombing by the British and American air forces. Terrorized at home and frightened by the prospect of unconditional surrender, the Germans fought on with suicidal stoicism.

On June 6, 1944, American and British forces under General Dwight Eisenhower landed on the beaches of Normandy, France, in history's greatest naval invasion. In a hundred dramatic days more than 2 million men and almost a half million vehicles pushed inland and broke through German lines. Rejecting proposals to strike straight at Berlin in a massive attack, Eisenhower moved forward cautiously on a broad front. Not until March 1945 did American troops cross the Rhine and enter Germany.

The Soviets, who had been advancing steadily since July 1943, reached the outskirts of Warsaw by August 1944. On April 26, 1945 the Red Army met American forces on the Elbe River. The Allies had closed their vise on Nazi Germany and overrun Europe. As Soviet forces fought their way into Berlin, Hitler committed suicide in his bunker, and on May 7 the remaining German commanders capitulated.

The War in the Pacific (1942–1945)

While gigantic armies clashed on land in Europe, the greatest naval battles in history decided the fate of warring nations in Asia. In April 1942 the Japanese devised a complicated battle plan to take Port Moresby in New Guinea and also destroy U.S. aircraft carriers in an attack on Midway Island (see Map 30.3). Having broken the secret Japanese code, the Americans skillfully deployed the small number of ships at their disposal and won decisive naval victories. First, in the Battle of the Coral Sea in May 1942, an American carrier force halted the Japanese advance on Port Moresby and relieved Australia from the threat of invasion. Then, in the Battle of Midway in June 1942, American carrier-based pilots sank all four of the attacking Japanese aircraft carriers and established overall naval equality with Japan in the Pacific.

● **"Follow Me!"**   This painting by Charles McBarron, Jr., shows the action at Red Beach on October 20, 1944, in the Battle of Leyte Gulf in the Philippine Islands. It captures the danger and courage of U.S. troops, which had to storm well-fortified Japanese positions again and again in their long island-hopping campaign. The officer exhorts his men, and death is all around. *(The Granger Collection, New York)*

Badly hampered in the ground war by the Europe first policy, the United States gradually won control of the sea and air as it geared up massive production of aircraft carriers, submarines, and fighter planes. By 1943 the United States was producing one hundred thousand aircraft a year, almost twice as many as Japan produced in the entire war. By 1944 hundreds of American submarines were hunting in "wolf packs," decimating shipping and destroying economic links in Japan's far-flung, overextended empire. In July 1943 the Americans and their Australian allies opened an "island-hopping" campaign toward Japan. Pounding Japanese forces on a given island with saturation bombing, American army and marine units would then hit the beaches with rifles and flamethrowers and secure victory in hand-to-hand combat.

The Pacific war was brutal—a "war without mercy," in the words of a leading American scholar—and atrocities were committed on both sides.[13] Aware of Japanese atrocities in China and the Philippines, the U.S. Marines and Army troops seldom took Japanese prisoners after the Battle of Guadalcanal in August 1942, killing even those rare Japanese soldiers who offered to surrender. American forces moving across the central and western Pacific in 1943 and 1944 faced unyielding resistance and this resistance hardened American hearts as American casualties kept rising. A product of spiraling violence, mutual hatred, and dehumanizing racial stereotypes, the war without mercy intensified as it moved toward Japan.

In June 1944 giant U.S. bombers began a relentless bombing campaign of the Japanese home islands. In October 1944 American forces under General Douglas MacArthur landed on Leyte Island in the Philippines. The Japanese believed they could destroy MacArthur's troops and transport ships before the main American fleet arrived. The result was the four-day Battle of Leyte Gulf, the greatest battle in naval history, with 282 ships involved. The Japanese lost 13 large warships, including

Primary Source:
The Decision to Use the Atomic Bomb
Learn why President Truman was advised to drop atomic bombs on Japan—from the chairman of the committee that gave him that advice.

4 aircraft carriers, while the Americans lost only 3 small ships in their great triumph. The Japanese navy was practically finished.

In spite of massive defeats, Japanese troops continued to fight with enormous courage and determination. Indeed, the bloodiest battles of the Pacific war took place on Iwo Jima in February 1945 and on Okinawa in June 1945. MacArthur and his commanders believed the conquest of Japan might cost a million American casualties and possibly 10 million to 20 million Japanese lives. In fact, Japan was almost helpless, its industry and dense, fragile wooden cities largely destroyed by incendiary bombing and uncontrollable hurricanes of fire. Yet the Japanese seemed determined to fight on, if only with bamboo spears, ever ready to die for a hopeless cause.

On August 6 and 9, 1945, the United States dropped atomic bombs on Hiroshima and Nagasaki in Japan. Mass bombing of cities and civilians, one of the terrible new practices of World War II, had led to the final nightmare—unprecedented human destruction in a single blinding flash. On August 14, 1945, the Japanese announced their surrender. The Second World War, which had claimed the lives of more than 50 million soldiers and civilians, was over.

● **A Hiroshima Survivor Remembers**   Yasuko Yamagata was seventeen when she saw the brilliant blue-white "lightning flash" that became a fiery orange ball consuming everything that would burn. Thirty years later Yamagata painted this scene, her most unforgettable memory of the atomic attack. An incinerated woman, poised as if running with her baby clutched to her breast, lies near a water tank piled high with charred corpses. *(Courtsey, Hiroshima Peace Memorial Museum)*

Chapter Summary

To assess your mastery of this chapter, go to
bedfordstmartins.com/mckayworld

● *What was the nature of twentieth-century dictatorships and authoritarian rule?*

The Second World War marked the climax of the tremendous practical and spiritual maladies of the age of anxiety, which led in many lands to the rise of dictatorships. Many of these dictatorships were variations on conservative authoritarianism, but there was also a fateful innovation—a new kind of radical dictatorship that was exceptionally dynamic and theoretically unlimited in its actions. The totalitarian regimes formed in the 1920s and 1930s—specifically in Hitler's Germany and Stalin's Russia, and to a lesser extent in Mussolini's Italy, Franco's Spain, Hirohito's Japan, and Salazar's Portugal—were violent, dynamic, and profoundly antiliberal. They all, to a greater or lesser extent, asserted a total claim on the lives of their citizens, posed ambitious goals, and demanded popular support. Stalin's Russia and Hitler's Germany in particular

Key Terms

totalitarianism
fascism
five-year plan
New Economic Policy (NEP)
collectivization
kulaks
Black Shirts
Lateran Agreement
Nazism
Führer
Enabling Act
blitzkrieg
New Order
Holocaust
"Europe first"

exuded tremendous dynamism and awesome power. That dynamism, however, was channeled in quite different directions. Stalin and the Communist Party aimed at building their kind of socialism and the new socialist personality at home. Hitler and the Nazi elite aimed at unlimited territorial and racial aggression on behalf of a "master race"; domestic recovery was only a means to that end.

• *How were the five-year plans part of the totalitarian order in the Soviet Union?*

The five-year plans initiated in the Soviet Union in 1928 were a critical part of Stalin's efforts to totally control the Russian economy and society. Meant to introduce a "revolution from above," the plans were extremely ambitious efforts to modernize and industrialize the U.S.S.R. along socialist lines and to create a new socialist humanity. They set staggering industrial and agricultural objectives and replaced private lands with (often forced) collectivization. Labor unions were severely weakened, and foreign experts from Europe and America were brought in to lend their skill and expertise to the building of new factories and machinery in order to catch up with the more advanced capitalist nations of the West.

• *How was Italian fascism a halfway house between conservative authoritarianism and modern totalitarianism?*

In Italy Mussolini's hatred of liberalism led him to set up the first fascist government. Although brutal in its methods, it was never truly a totalitarian state on the order of Hitler's Germany or Stalin's Soviet Union. Mussolini did create a one-party dictatorship by abolishing press freedoms, disbanding independent trade unions, rigging elections, and ruling by decree. Mussolini allowed the old conservative classes to retain control of the economy, army, and the state bureaucracy. He gained the support of the Roman Catholic Church by recognizing the Vatican as a tiny independent state in 1929. Racial laws were never a very significant aspect of Mussolini's rule, as they were for Hitler, and Jews were not severely persecuted until Italy came under Nazi control toward the end of World War II. Thus, though repressive and undemocratic, fascist Italy was never really a totalitarian state.

• *Why were Hitler and his Nazi regime initially so popular?*

Hitler created a model totalitarian state in Germany, initially with the support of most of the German people. Hitler began by drawing on the anger and sense of betrayal many Germans felt after losing the Great War, and the humiliation of the terms of the Versailles Treaty. The war was followed by a period of astronomical inflation and unemployment. He added to the economic and patriotic discontent by drawing on the racist sentiments about "inferior" peoples, such as the Jews and the Slavs, which had deep roots in German history and culture. He convinced many Germans that Jews and Marxists had caused Germany to lose the war, and that a worldwide Jewish conspiracy continued to harm German culture, German unity, and the German race. Hitler was also a master of mass propaganda and political showmanship and effectively used the new propaganda tools of the movies and the radio to reach mass audiences. When the Great Depression struck, Hitler appealed to people's economic welfare, and made great promises that caused voters to desert the old leaders and turn to this dynamic new voice. Finally, Hitler was successful in gaining the support of Germany's young people by directly answering their needs and concerns, by appointing young party members to positions of power, and by emphasizing rapid change, national recovery, and personal advancement.

• How did Hitler's actions lead to another world war?

Hitler and his Nazi followers' genocidal racism and unlimited aggression made war inevitable, first with the western European democracies, then with hated eastern neighbors, and finally with the United States. Plunging Europe into the ultimate nightmare, unlimited aggression unwittingly forged a mighty coalition that smashed the racist Nazi empire and its leader. In the words of the ancient Greeks, he whom the gods would destroy, they first make mad.

Suggested Reading

Applebaum, Anne. *Gulag.* 2004. An excellent survey of Stalin's labor-death camps.

Arendt, Hannah. *The Origins of Totalitarianism.* 1951. Controversial, classic philosophical-historical study.

Brendon, Piers. *The Dark Valley. A Panorama of the 1930s.* Masterful, sweeping account of this tumultuous decade.

Brooker, Paul. *Twentieth Century Dictatorships: The Ideological One-Party State.* 1995. Comparative analysis.

Fitzpatrick, Sheila. *Everyday Stalinism: Ordinary Life in Extraordinary Times.* 1999. Social and cultural history.

Gilbert, Martin. *The Second World War: A Complete History,* rev. ed. 2004. Massively detailed global survey.

Glantz, David M. *When Titans Clashed: How the Red Army Stopped Hitler.* 1995. Authoritative account of the Eastern Front in World War II.

Hasegawa, Tsuyoshi. *Racing the Enemy: Stalin, Truman and the Surrender of Japan.* 2005. Masterful diplomatic history with controversial new account of the end of the war.

Hillberg, Raul. *The Destruction of the European Jews, 1933–1945,* rev. ed. 3 vols. 1985. A monumental classic.

Hsiung, James C., and Seven Levine, eds. *China's Bitter Victory: The War with Japan, 1937–1945.* 1992. Investigates various aspects of the long struggle.

Keegan, John. *The Second World War.* 1990. Broad survey by a distinguished military historian.

Kershaw, Ian. *The Nazi Dictatorship, Problems and Perspectives of Interpretation,* 2nd ed. 1989. Interpretive, historiographical.

Levi, Primo. *Survival at Auschwitz.* 1947. First published in English as *If This Is a Man;* memoir and meditation on the meaning of survival.

Lewin, Moshe. *The Making of the Soviet System.* 1985. Social history, especially agrarian.

Marrus, Michael. *The Holocaust in History.* 1987. Classic interpretive survey.

Weinberg, Gerhard. *World at Arms: A Global History of World War II.* 1994. Global survey with political-diplomatic emphasis.

Wright, Gordon. *The Ordeal of Total War,* rev. ed. 1997. Explores scientific, psychological, and economic dimensions of the war.

Notes

1. A. Gleason, *Totalitarianism: The Inner History of the Cold War* (New York: Oxford University Press, 1995), p. 50.

2. E. Halévy, *The Era of Tyrannies* (Garden City, N.Y.: Doubleday, 1965), pp. 265–316, esp. p. 300.

3. I. Kershaw, *The Nazi Dictatorship: Problems and Perspectives of Interpretation,* 2d ed. (London: Edward Arnold, 1989), p. 34.

4. Quoted in A. G. Mazour, *Soviet Economic Development: Operation Outstrip, 1921–1965* (Princeton, N.J.: Van Nostrand, 1967), p. 130.

5. Quoted in I. Deutscher, *Stalin: A Political Biography,* 2d ed. (New York: Oxford University Press, 1967), p. 325.

6. M. Malia, *The Soviet Tragedy: A History of Socialism in Russia* (New York: Free Press, 1994), p. 248.

7. R. Thurston, *Life and Terror in Stalin's Russia, 1934–1941* (New Haven, Conn.: Yale University Press, 1996), esp. pp. 16–106; and Malia, *The Soviet Tragedy,* pp. 227–270.

8. R. Vivarelli, "Interpretations on the Origins of Fascism," *Journal of Modern History* 63 (March 1991): 41.

9. W. Brustein, *The Logic of Evil: The Social Origins of the Nazi Party, 1925–1933* (New Haven, Conn.: Yale University Press, 1996), pp. 52, 182.

10. Quoted in R. Stromberg, *An Intellectual History of Modern Europe* (New York: Appleton-Century-Crofts, 1966), p. 393.

11. Quoted in K. D. Bracher, *The German Dictatorship: The Origins, Structure and Effects of National Socialism* (New York: Praeger, 1970), p. 289.

12. H. Willmott, *The Great Crusade: A New Complete History of the Second World War* (New York: Free Press, 1989), p. 255.

13. J. Dower, *War Without Mercy: Race and Power in the Pacific War* (New York: Pantheon, 1986).

Listening to the
PAST

Radical Nationalism for Japanese Students

In August 1941, only four months before Japan's coordinated attack on Pearl Harbor and colonial empires in Southeast Asia, Japan's Ministry of Education issued "The Way of Subjects." Required reading for high school and university students, this twenty-page pamphlet summed up the basic tenets of Japanese ultranationalism, which had become dominant in the 1930s.

As this selection suggests, ultranationalism in Japan combined a sense of mission with intense group solidarity and unquestioning devotion to a semidivine emperor. Thus Japanese expansion into Manchuria and the war in China were part of Japan's sacred calling to protect the throne and to free Asia from Western exploitation and misrule. Of course, an unknown percentage of students (and adults) did not believe that the myths of Japan's state religion were literally true. Nevertheless, they were profoundly influenced by extremist nationalism: Japanese soldiers' determination to fight to the death was a prime indicator of that influence.

The way of the subjects of the Emperor issues from the policy of the Emperor and is to guard and maintain the Imperial Throne coexistent with the Heavens and the Earth. This is not an abstract principle but a way of daily practices based on history. The life and activities of the nation are all attuned to the task of strengthening the foundation of the Empire. . . .

Modern history, in a nutshell, has been marked by the formation of unified nations in Europe and their contests for supremacy in the acquisition of colonies. . . . Their march into all parts of the world paved the way for their subsequent world domination politically, economically, and culturally and led them to believe that they alone were justified in their outrageous behavior. . . .

The thoughts that have formed the foundation of Western civilization since the early modern period are individualism, liberalism, materialism, and so on. These thoughts regard the strong preying on the weak as reasonable, unstintedly promote the pursuit of luxury and pleasure, encourage materialism, and stimulate competition for acquiring colonies and

securing trade, thereby leading the world to a veritable hell of fighting and bloodshed [in the First World War]. . . . [Thereafter] a vigorous movement was started by Britain, France, and the United States to maintain the status quo by any means. Simultaneously, a movement aiming at social revolution through class conflict on the basis of thoroughgoing materialism like Communism also vigorously developed. On the other hand, Nazism and Fascism arose with great force. The basic principles of the totalitarianism in Germany and Italy are to remove the evils of individualism and liberalism.

That these [totalitarian] principles show great similarity to Eastern culture and spirit is a noteworthy fact that suggests the future of Western civilization and the creation of a new culture. Thus, the orientation of world history has made the collapse of the old world order a certainty. Japan has hereby initiated the construction of a new world order based on moral principles.

The Manchurian Affair [the Japanese invasion of Manchuria in 1931] was a violent outburst of Japanese national life long suppressed. Taking advantage of this, Japan in the glare of all the Powers made a step toward the creation of a world based on moral principles and the construction of a new order. This was a manifestation of the spirit, profound and lofty, embodied in the founding of Empire, and an unavoidable action for its national life and world mission. . . .

The general tendency of world domination by Europe and America has begun to show signs of a change since the Russo-Japanese War of 1904–05. Japan's victory attracted the attention of the entire world, and this caused a reawakening of Asiatic countries, which had been forced to lie prostrate under British and American influence, with the result that an independence movement was started.

Hopes to be free of the shackles and bondage of Europe and America were ablaze among the nations of India, Turkey, Arabia, Thailand, Vietnam, and others. This also inspired a new national movement in China. Amid this stormy atmosphere of Asia's reawakening,

Japan has come to be keenly conscious of the fact that the stabilization of East Asia is her mission, and that the emancipation of East Asian nations rests solely on her efforts. . . .

Japan has a political mission to help various regions in the Greater East Asian Co-prosperity Sphere [the Japanese term for Japan's Asian empire], which are reduced to a state of quasi-colony by Europe and America, and rescue them from their control. Economically, this country will have to eradicate the evils of their exploitation and then set up an economic structure for coexistence and co-prosperity. Culturally, Japan must strive to fashion East Asian nations to abandon their following of European and American culture and to develop Eastern culture for the purpose of contributing to the creation of a just world. The East has been left to destruction for the past several hundred years. Its rehabilitation is not an easy task. It is natural that unusual difficulties attend the establishment of a new order and the creation of a new culture. Overcoming these difficulties will do much to help in establishing a world dominated by morality, in which all nations can co-operate and all people can secure their proper positions. . . .

In Japan, the Emperors of a line unbroken for ages eternal govern and reign over it, as the Heavens and the Earth endure, since the Imperial Foundress, Amaterasu-o-Mikami, . . . caused Her grandson Ninigi-no-Mikoto to descend on the eight great countries and She commanded him, saying: "This country, fruitful and abounding in rice, is the land over which Our descendants shall rule. Go you, therefore, down and reign over it. Under you and your offspring it shall prosper as long as the Heavens and the Earth endure." . . .

The Imperial Family is [therefore] the fountain source of the Japanese nation, and national and private lives issue from this. In the past, foreign nationals came to this country only to enjoy the benevolent rule of the Imperial Family, and became Japanese subjects spiritually and by blood. The Imperial virtues are so great and boundless that all are assimilated into one.

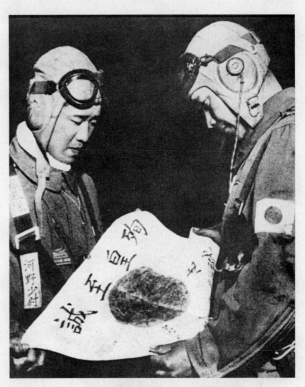

Kamikaze pilots ponder the message on the flag that they will take on their suicide mission: "All for the Emperor, we are happy to die for him." (Archives Mondadori, Milan)

Here is the reason for the present glorious state, in which the Emperor and his subjects are harmonized into one great unit. That the myriad subjects with one mind are glad to be unified in their devotion to the Throne is the substance of the Imperial subjects.

The way of the subjects is to be loyal to the Emperor in disregard of self. . . . To serve the Emperor is its key point. Our lives will become sincere and true when they are offered to the Emperor and the state. . . . All must be unified under the Emperor. Herein lies the significance of national life in Japan.

Questions for Analysis

1. How does "The Way of Subjects" interpret modern history? In what ways do Western thought and action threaten Japan?

2. What is Japan's mission in Asia?

3. What is the basis of Japanese sovereignty? What is the individual's proper role in society?

Source: "The Way of Subjects," in *Tokyo Record,* copyright 1943 by Otto D. Tolischus and renewed 1970 by Naya G. Tolischus. Reprinted by permission of Houghton Mifflin Harcourt Publishing Company.

Duck and Cover. These American schoolchildren in the 1950s practice the "duck and cover" drill in the event of a nuclear attack from the Soviet Union. *(Bettmann/Corbis)*

31 GLOBAL RECOVERY AND DIVISION BETWEEN SUPERPOWERS

After the defeat of the Axis powers in Europe and of Japan in Asia, recovery began around the world from this most devastating war. Hopes of world peace quickly faded, however, when differences in Allied economic and political ideologies set aside during wartime came to the fore. A three-part global division soon developed. The democratic and capitalist "First World"—the United States and its allies, including Japan—confronted the Marxist communist "Second World"—the Soviet Union and its allies. The "Third World," the often newly independent and so-called nonaligned nations of Latin America, Africa, and Asia, were forced to negotiate with the other two. This chapter discusses the First and Second Worlds and the cold war they fought for forty years.

After World War II, a battered western Europe once again had to dig itself out from under rubble. Having avoided wartime destruction and occupation, the United States, Canada, Australia, and New Zealand quickly converted their economies to peacetime production. After seven years of Allied occupation, Japan began the economic recovery and social transformation that by the 1960s made it one of the world's leading economic powers. Having experienced massive death and destruction in two world wars, the Soviet Union sought to protect itself from future attacks from the west by occupying eastern Europe and establishing communist dictatorships there. Although the U.S.S.R. became more humane and less totalitarian after Stalin's death in 1953, his successors continued to rule eastern European countries as though they were imperial colonies.

In the early 1970s the global economic boom of the early cold war years—the 1950s and 1960s—finally came to an end. Domestic political stability and social harmony evaporated, and several countries experienced major crises. Serious economic difficulties returned with distressing regularity to Europe, Asia, and the Americas in the 1980s and 1990s. These difficulties encompassed much of the globe, a trend that accelerated the knitting together of peoples and regions.

The spectacular collapse of communism in eastern Europe in 1989 and the end of the cold war reinforced global integration. The result was monumental change, especially in postcommunist eastern Europe. A similar though less dramatic transformation also occurred in the nations of western Europe as they moved toward greater unity within the European Union.

THE DIVISION OF EUROPE

What were the causes of the cold war?

In 1945 triumphant American and Russian soldiers embraced along the Elbe River in the heart of vanquished Germany. At home the soldiers' loved ones erupted in joyous celebration. Yet victory was flawed. The Allies could not cooperate politically in peacemaking. The United States and the Soviet Union soon found themselves at loggerheads. By the end of 1947 Europe was rigidly divided, West versus East, in a cold war eventually waged around the world.

The Origins of the Cold War

Almost as soon as the unifying threat of Nazi Germany disappeared, the Soviet Union and the United States began to quarrel. Hostility between the Eastern and Western superpowers was the sad but logical outgrowth of military developments, wartime agreements, and long-standing political and ideological differences dating back to World War I.

In the early phases of the Second World War, the Americans and the British made military victory their highest priority. They consistently avoided discussion of Stalin's war aims and the shape of the eventual peace settlement, fearing that hard bargaining

● **The Big Three** In 1945 a triumphant Winston Churchill, an ailing Franklin Roosevelt, and a determined Joseph Stalin met at Yalta in southern Russia to plan for peace. Cooperation soon gave way to bitter hostility. *(F.D.R. Library)*

might encourage Stalin to make a separate peace with Hitler. They focused instead on the policy of unconditional surrender to solidify the alliance.

By late 1943 decisions that would affect the shape of the postwar world could no longer be postponed. Stalin, Roosevelt, and Churchill met in Teheran, Iran, in November 1943, and there the **Big Three** reaffirmed their determination to crush Germany and searched for the appropriate military strategy. Churchill argued that American and British forces should attack Germany's "soft underbelly" through the Balkans. Roosevelt, however, agreed with Stalin that a joint American-British frontal assault through France would be better. Soviet, rather than American and British armies, would then liberate eastern Europe.

The Big Three met again in February 1945 at Yalta on the Black Sea in southern Russia. By then, the Red Army had occupied most of eastern Europe and advancing Soviet armies were within a hundred miles of Berlin. American and British forces had yet to cross the Rhine into Germany. Moreover, the United States was far from defeating Japan. In short, the Soviet Union's position was strong and America's weak. The increasingly sick and apprehensive Roosevelt could do little but double his bet on Stalin's peaceful intentions. At Yalta the Big Three agreed that Germany would be divided into zones of occupation and would pay the Soviet Union heavy reparations. At American insistence Stalin agreed to declare war on Japan after Germany's defeat. As for Poland and eastern Europe—"that Pandora's Box of infinite troubles," according to American secretary of state Cordell Hull—the Big Three reached an ambiguous compromise: eastern European governments were to be freely elected but pro-Russian.

Almost immediately this compromise broke down. Even before the Yalta Conference, communists arriving home with the Red Army controlled Bulgaria and Poland. Elsewhere in eastern Europe pro-Soviet "coalition" governments of several parties were formed, but key ministerial posts were reserved for Moscow-trained communists.

At the postwar Potsdam Conference in July 1945, long-avoided differences over eastern Europe were finally debated. When the compromising Roosevelt died in April, the more assertive Harry Truman became U.S. president, and he now demanded immediate free elections throughout eastern Europe. Stalin refused point-blank. "A freely elected government in any of these East European countries would be anti-Soviet," he admitted simply, "and that we cannot allow."[1]

Here, then, is the key to the much-debated origins of the cold war. American ideals, pumped up by the crusade against Hitler, and American politics, heavily influenced by millions of U.S. voters of eastern European heritage, demanded free elections in Soviet-occupied eastern Europe. Stalin, who had lived through two enormously destructive German invasions, wanted absolute military security from Germany and its

Chronology

1945–1952	Allied occupation of Japan
1945–early 1960s	Decolonization of Asia and Africa
1947	Truman Doctrine; Marshall Plan
1949	Formation of NATO
1950–1970	Enormous growth rate in Japanese economy
1953–1964	De-Stalinization of Soviet Union
1957	Formation of Common Market
1961	Building of Berlin Wall
1962	Solzhenitsyn, *One Day in the Life of Ivan Denisovich;* Cuban missile crisis
1964	Civil Rights Act in United States
1964–1973	Principal years of U.S. involvement in Vietnam War
1973	OPEC oil embargo
1985	Glasnost leads to greater freedom of speech and expression in the Soviet Union
November 1989	Collapse of Berlin Wall
1989–1991	Fall of communism in Soviet Union and eastern Europe
1990–1992	Collapse of Japanese stock market
1991–2000	Resurgence of nationalism and ethnic conflict in eastern Europe
1993	Formation of European Union
May–June 2005	France and Holland vote against ratification of the European Union constitution

Big Three *Stalin, Roosevelt, and Churchill.*

potential eastern European allies once and for all. He believed only communist states could be truly dependable allies. By the middle of 1945 the United States had no way to determine political developments in eastern Europe short of war, and war was out of the question. Stalin would have his way.

West Versus East

America's response to Stalin's exaggerated conception of security was to "get tough." In May 1945 Truman abruptly cut off all aid to Russia. In October he declared that America would never recognize any government established by force against the free will of its people. His declaration, however, applied only to Europe and to countries threatened by communism, not to British and French colonies in Asia and Africa, for example, or to Latin American right-wing dictatorships. In March 1946 former British prime minister Churchill ominously informed an American audience that an "iron curtain" had fallen across the European continent, dividing Germany and all of Europe into two antagonistic camps. Yet the United States also responded to the popular desire to "bring the boys home" and demobilized with great speed. America had 12 million men in uniform when the war against Japan ended in September 1945; by 1947 there were only 1.5 million, in contrast to 6 million in the Soviet Union. Some historians have argued that American leaders believed the atomic bomb gave the United States all the power it needed and that "getting tough" really meant "talking tough."

Stalin's agents quickly renewed the "ideological struggle against capitalist imperialism." France's and Italy's large, well-organized Communist parties challenged their own governments with violent criticisms and large strikes. The Soviet Union also put pressure on Iran, Turkey, and Greece, and a bitter civil war raged in China. By spring 1947 many Americans believed Stalin was determined to export communism throughout Europe and around the world.

Truman Doctrine *The U.S. plan to contain communism to areas already occupied by the Red Army.*

The United States responded with the **Truman Doctrine,** which aimed at "containing" communism. Truman told Congress in March 1947, "I believe it must be the policy of the United States to support free people who are resisting attempted subjugation by armed minorities or by outside pressure." Truman asked Congress for military aid for Greece and Turkey. Then, in June, Secretary of State George C. Marshall offered Europe economic aid—the **Marshall Plan**—to help it rebuild. Stalin refused Marshall Plan assistance for all of eastern Europe, where he had established Soviet-style, one-party communist dictatorships.

Marshall Plan *The plan of economic aid to Europe to help it rebuild, which Stalin refused for all of eastern Europe.*

On July 24, 1948, Stalin blocked all highway traffic through the Soviet zone of Germany to Berlin. The Western allies responded by flying hundreds of planes over the Soviet roadblocks to supply provisions to the West Berliners. After 324 days the Soviets backed down: containment seemed to work. In 1949, therefore, the United States formed an anti-Soviet military alliance of Western governments: the North Atlantic Treaty Organization (NATO). Stalin countered by tightening his hold on his satellites, later united in the Warsaw Pact. Europe was divided into two hostile blocs.

As tensions rose in Europe, the cold war spread to Asia. In 1945 as the defeated Japanese surrendered, Korea, like Germany, was divided into Soviet and American zones of occupation, which became in 1948 a communist North Korea and an anti-communist South Korea. In late 1949 the Communists triumphed in China (see page 983), frightening and angering many Americans, who saw new evidence of a powerful worldwide communist conspiracy. When the Russian-backed communist forces of North Korea invaded South Korea in spring 1950, President Truman acted swiftly. American-led United Nations forces under U.S. general Douglas MacArthur intervened.

The Korean War was bitterly fought and extremely bloody. Initially, the well-equipped North Koreans almost conquered the entire peninsula, but the South

Koreans and the Americans rallied and drove their foes north to the Chinese border. At that point China intervened, and its armies pushed the South Koreans and Americans back south. The war then seesawed back and forth near where it had begun. President Truman rejected General MacArthur's call to attack China and fired him. In 1953 a fragile truce was finally negotiated, and the fighting stopped. Thus the United States extended its policy of containing communism to Asia but drew back from invading communist China and possible nuclear war.

RENAISSANCE AND CRISIS IN WESTERN EUROPE

How and why, despite the cold war, did western Europe recover so successfully from the ravages of war and Nazism?

As the cold war divided Europe into two blocs, the future appeared bleak on both sides of the iron curtain. Yet western Europe recovered to enjoy unprecedented economic prosperity and peaceful social transformation. Then, in the early 1970s, the cycle turned abruptly. A downturn in the world economy hit western Europe hard with serious social and psychological consequences.

The Postwar Challenge

After the war economic conditions in western Europe were terrible. Runaway inflation and black markets testified to severe shortages and hardships. Many questioned whether Europe would ever recover.

Suffering was most intense in defeated Germany. The major territorial change of the war had moved the Soviet Union's border far to the west. Poland was in turn compensated for this loss to the Soviets with land taken from Germany (see Map 31.1). To solidify these boundary changes, 13 million people were driven from their homes throughout eastern Europe and forced to resettle in a greatly reduced Germany. By spring 1947 refugee-clogged, hungry, prostrate Germany verged on total collapse and threatened to drag down the rest of Europe.

Yet western Europe began to recover. New groups and leaders with new ideas came forward. Progressive Catholics and their Christian Democrat political parties were particularly influential. In Italy antifascist Alcide De Gasperi and in Germany anti-Nazi Konrad Adenauer took power, steadfastly rejecting totalitarianism and narrow nationalism and placing their faith in democracy and cooperation. Socialists and communists active in the resistance against Hitler emerged from the war with increased power and prestige, especially in France and Italy. In the immediate postwar years welfare measures such as family allowances, health insurance, and increased public housing were enacted throughout much of continental Europe. Social reform complemented political transformation, creating solid foundations for a great European renaissance.

There were many reasons for this amazing recovery. The United States speeded the process by providing western Europe with massive economic aid through the Marshall Plan and with ongoing military protection through NATO, which featured American troops stationed permanently in Europe, and the American nuclear umbrella. As Marshall Plan aid poured in, western Europe's battered economies began to turn the corner in 1948, and Europe entered a period of unprecedented economic progress lasting into the late 1960s.

Western European governments also adopted a variety of imaginative and successful economic and social strategies. Postwar West Germany adopted a free-market economy while maintaining the extensive social welfare network inherited from the

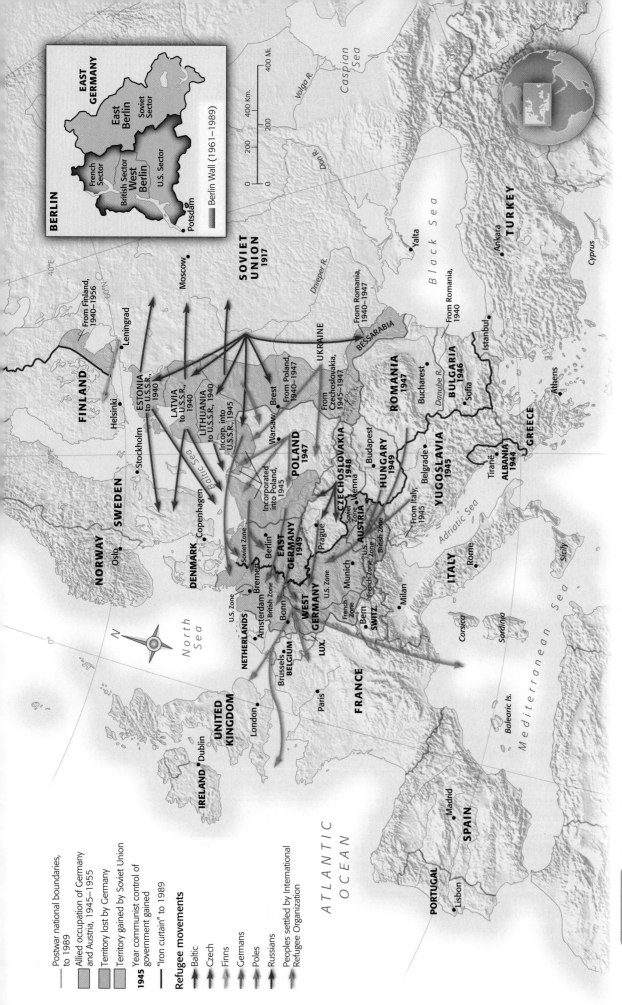

MAP 31.1 **The Results of World War II in Europe** Millions of refugees fled westward because of war and territorial changes. The Soviet Union and Poland took land from Germany, which the Allies partitioned into occupation zones. Those zones subsequently formed the basis of the East and West German states as the iron curtain fell to divide both Germany and Europe. Austria was detached from Germany, but the Soviets subsequently permitted Austria to reunify as a neutral state.

BERLIN

EAST GERMANY

Soviet Sector

East Berlin

French Sector

British Sector

West Berlin

U.S. Sector

Potsdam

Berlin Wall (1961–1989)

400 Mi.
400 Km.
200
200
0
0

Postwar national boundaries, to 1989

Allied occupation of Germany and Austria, 1945–1955

Territory lost by Germany

Territory gained by Soviet Union

1945 Year communist control of government gained

"Iron curtain" to 1989

Refugee movements

Baltic

Czech

Finns

Germans

Poles

Russians

Peoples settled by International Refugee Organization

N

North Sea

ATLANTIC OCEAN

IRELAND • Dublin

UNITED KINGDOM

London •

• Paris

FRANCE

SPAIN

Madrid •

PORTUGAL

Lisbon •

Balearic Is.

Corsica

Sardinia

Mediterranean Sea

Sicily

ITALY

Rome •

Milan •

SWITZ.

Bern •

French Zone

LUX.

BELGIUM

Brussels •

NETHERLANDS

Amsterdam •

British Zone

U.S. Zone

Bonn •

WEST GERMANY

Bremen •

U.S. Zone

French Zone

Munich •

U.S. Zone

AUSTRIA

Vienna •

Soviet Zone

British Zone

From Italy, 1945

Adriatic Sea

YUGOSLAVIA 1945

Belgrade •

Tiranë •

ALBANIA 1944

GREECE

Athens •

NORWAY

Oslo •

SWEDEN

Stockholm •

DENMARK

Copenhagen •

Soviet Zone

Berlin

EAST GERMANY 1949

Prague •

CZECHOSLOVAKIA 1948

Budapest •

HUNGARY 1949

ROMANIA 1947

Bucharest •

Danube R.

BULGARIA 1946

Sofia •

Black Sea

TURKEY

Ankara •

Istanbul •

Cyprus

Helsinki •

FINLAND

From Finland, 1940–1956

Leningrad •

ESTONIA to U.S.S.R., 1940

LATVIA to U.S.S.R., 1940

LITHUANIA to U.S.S.R., 1940

Incorp. into U.S.S.R., 1945

Baltic Sea

Incorporated into Poland, 1945

Warsaw •

POLAND 1947

Brest •

From Poland, 1940–1947

UKRAINE

From Czechoslovakia, 1945–1947

BESSARABIA

From Romania, 1940–1947

From Romania, 1940

Yalta •

SOVIET UNION 1917

Moscow •

Dnieper R.

Don R.

Volga R.

Caspian Sea

20°E

40°E

0°

60°N

● **Affair of the Scarves**   Muslim women protest France's September 2004 ban on the wearing of all "conspicuous" religious apparel by the country's 12 million schoolchildren, including Jewish skullcaps, Sikh turbans, large Christian crosses, and Islamic veils and scarves. The ban is meant to enforce France's tradition, going back to the French Revolution, of a strict separation between church and state. *(AP Photo/ Wide World Photos)*

Hitler era. The French established a new kind of planning commission that set ambitious but flexible goals for the French economy, using the nationalized banks to funnel money into key industries. France achieved the most rapid economic development in its long history.

European workers also deserve some credit for the economic turnaround. They worked hard for low wages in hopes of a better future. Moreover, during the Great Depression, few Europeans had been able to afford many of the new consumer products. Thus in 1945 the electric refrigerator, the washing machine, and the automobile were rare luxuries, and there was great potential demand, which manufacturers moved to satisfy.

Migrant laborers from the Mediterranean basin (southern Italy, North Africa, Turkey, Greece, and Yugoslavia) also played a key role in Europe's postwar recovery. They accepted the most menial and least desirable jobs for the lowest pay. Europeans assumed that rising birthrates among the majority population would eventually fill the labor shortages, so at first they labeled the migrants "guest workers" to signal their temporary status. By the 1980s, however, as millions more migrants arrived from Europe's former colonies and settled in every European nation, it was clear their presence would be permanent. Their full integration into the economic, political, and social life of these countries has been incomplete, creating a backlash against them by the majority populations and a simmering anger within the immigrant communities. Immigrants resent what seems a second-class citizenship, poor working conditions and wages, a perceived lack of respect for ethnic and religious traditions, and alleged mistreatment by police.

Finally, western European nations abandoned protectionism and gradually created a large, unified market. This historic action, which certainly stimulated the economy, was part of a larger search for European unity.

"Building Europe" and Decolonization

Western Europe's political recovery in the generation after 1945 was unprecedented. Republics were re-established in France, West Germany, and Italy. Constitutional monarchs were restored in Belgium, the Netherlands, and Norway. Democratic governments took root again and thrived in an atmosphere of civil liberties and individual freedom.

A similarly extraordinary achievement was the march toward a united Europe. Many Europeans believed that only unity could forestall future European conflict and that only a new "European nation" could reassert western Europe's influence in world affairs dominated by the United States and the Soviet Union.

The experience of close cooperation among European states for Marshall Plan aid led European federalists to turn toward economics as a way of attaining genuine unity. On May 9, 1950 (now "Europe Day"), French foreign minister Robert Schuman proposed an international organization to control and integrate all European steel and coal production. France, West Germany, Italy, Belgium, the Netherlands, and Luxembourg joined together in 1952. In 1957 the six nations of the Coal and Steel Community signed the Treaty of Rome, creating the European Economic Community, generally known as the **Common Market**. The treaty's primary goal was a gradual reduction of all tariffs among the six in order to create a single market almost as large as that of the United States.

Common Market *The European Economic Community created in 1957.*

The Common Market was a great success, encouraging hopes of rapid progress toward political as well as economic union in western Europe. In the 1960s, however, a resurgence of more traditional nationalism in France led by Charles de Gaulle, French president from 1958 to 1969, frustrated these hopes. Viewing the United States as the main threat to genuine French (and European) independence, he withdrew all French military forces from the "American-controlled" NATO command as France developed its own nuclear weapons. Within the Common Market de Gaulle refused to permit majority rule. Thus throughout the 1960s the Common Market thrived economically but remained a union of sovereign states.

As Europe moved toward greater economic unity in the postwar era, its centuries-long overseas expansion was dramatically reversed. Between 1945 and the early 1960s almost every colonial territory gained formal independence. This rolling back of Western expansion—or **decolonization**—marks one of world history's great turning points. The basic cause of imperial collapse was the rising demand by Asian and African peoples for national self-determination and racial equality (see Chapter 32). Yet decolonization also involved the imperial powers, and considering the process from their perspective helps explain why independence came so quickly and why a kind of neocolonialism subsequently evolved in some former colonies.

European empires had been sustained by an enormous imbalance of power between the rulers and the ruled. By 1945 that imbalance had almost vanished. Moreover, most

● **African Independence** Britain's Queen Elizabeth II pays an official visit in 1961 to Ghana, the former Gold Coast colony. Accompanying the queen at the colorful welcoming ceremony is Ghana's popular Kwame Nkrumah, who was educated in black colleges in the United States and led Ghana's breakthrough to independence in 1957. *(Bettmann/Corbis)*

Europeans viewed their empires after 1945 very differently than they had before 1914. Empires had rested on self-confidence and self-righteousness; Europeans had believed their superiority to be not only technical and military but also spiritual and moral. The horrors of the Second World War destroyed such complacent arrogance and gave imperialism's opponents much greater influence in Europe. After 1945 many Europeans were willing to let go of their colonies more or less voluntarily and to concentrate on rebuilding at home.

European political and business leaders still wanted some ties with the former colonies, however. As a result, western European countries actually managed to increase their economic and cultural ties with their former African colonies in the 1960s and 1970s. This situation led many Third World leaders and scholars to charge that western Europe (and the United States) had imposed a system of **neocolonialism** designed to perpetuate Western economic domination and undermine political independence, just as the United States had subordinated the new nations of Latin America in the nineteenth century (see Chapter 26).

decolonization *The reversal of Europe's overseas expansion caused by the rising demand of Asian and African peoples for national self-determination, racial equality, and personal dignity.*

neocolonialism *A system designed to perpetuate Western economic domination and undermine the promise of political independence.*

The Changing Class Structure

A more mobile and more democratic European society developed after World War II as old class barriers relaxed and class distinctions became fuzzier. Most noticeably, the structure of the middle class changed. In the nineteenth and early twentieth centuries the model for the middle class had been the independent, self-employed property owner who ran a business or practiced a liberal profession such as law or medicine. After 1945 a new breed of managers and experts required by large corporations and government agencies replaced traditional property owners as leaders of the middle class. They tried to give their children the all-important advanced education, but only rarely could they pass on the positions they had attained. Thus the new middle class, based largely on specialized skills and high levels of education, was more open, democratic, and insecure than the old propertied middle class.

The structure of the lower classes also became more flexible and open. There was a mass exodus from farms and the countryside. Meanwhile, the industrial working class ceased to expand, but job opportunities for white-collar and service employees grew rapidly. Such employees bore a greater resemblance to the new middle class of salaried specialists than to industrial workers, who themselves were also better educated and more specialized.

European governments also reduced class tensions with a series of social reforms. Many of these reforms—such as increased unemployment benefits and more extensive old-age pensions—simply strengthened social security measures first pioneered in Bismarck's Germany. Other programs were new, such as state-run, comprehensive national health systems. Most countries introduced family allowances—direct government grants to parents to help them raise their children—that helped many poor families make ends meet. Maternity grants and inexpensive public housing for low-income families and individuals were also common. These and other social reforms provided a humane floor of well-being and promoted greater equality.

Economic and Social Dislocation (1970–1990)

For twenty years after 1945 most Europeans were preoccupied with economic progress and consumerism. In the late 1960s a new era of uncertainty and crisis dawned as radical European college students joined a global wave of demonstrations and protests by young people challenging authority, questioning tradition, and voicing their opposition to consumerism, politics, racism, sexism, and war. The year 1968 marked the high point of this loud, sometimes violent, but brief movement for political and social change. An economic crisis in the 1970s, however, brought more serious challenges for the average person.

The crisis had two main causes. First, the postwar international monetary system was based on the U.S. dollar. In 1971 its value fell sharply, and inflation accelerated worldwide. Fixed rates of exchange were abandoned, and uncertainty replaced predictability in international trade and finance.

Even more damaging was the dramatic reversal in the price and availability of energy. Cheap oil fueled the postwar boom. (See the feature "Global Trade: Oil" on pages 948–949.) In 1971 the Arab-led Organization of Petroleum Exporting Countries—OPEC—decided to reverse the decline in the crude oil price by presenting a united front against the oil companies. After the Arab-Israeli war in October 1973, OPEC placed an embargo on oil exports, and crude oil prices quadrupled in a year. The rapid price rise was economically destructive, but the world's big powers did nothing. The Soviet Union, itself an oil exporter, benefited directly; the United States was immobilized by the Watergate crisis in politics (see page 961). Thus governments, companies, and individuals could only deal piecemeal with the so-called oil shock—which was really an earthquake.

Following the upheaval in the international monetary system, the revolution in energy prices plunged the world into its worst economic decline since the 1930s. Unemployment rose; productivity and living standards declined. By 1976 a modest recovery was in progress, but when Iranian oil production collapsed during Iran's fundamentalist Islamic revolution (see page 999), crude oil prices doubled again in 1979. In summer 1985, unemployment rates in western Europe rose to their highest levels since the Great Depression. Global recovery was painfully slow until late 1993.

Western Europe's welfare system, fashioned in the postwar era, prevented mass suffering through extended benefits for the unemployed, free medical care, and special allowances for the needy. But increased government spending was not matched by higher taxes, causing a rapid growth of budget deficits, national debts, and inflation. By the late 1970s a powerful reaction against government's ever-increasing role had set in. Growing voter dissatisfaction helped bring Conservative Margaret Thatcher (b. 1925) to power in Britain in 1979. Prime Minister Thatcher slowed government spending and privatized industry by selling off state-owned companies to private investors. Of great social significance, her government encouraged low- and moderate-income renters in state-owned housing projects to buy their apartments at rock-bottom prices. This step created a whole new class of property owners, thereby eroding the

OPEC *An Arab-led organization of countries that export oil that helps set policies and prices on its trade.*

● **Sharjah Archaeological Museum, United Arab Emirates** Like other major cities in the oil-rich United Arab Emirates such as Dubai and Abu Dhabi, Sharjah possesses some of the most interesting and beautiful modern architecture in the world. The Archaeological Museum shown here is located in a complex of buildings devoted to the sciences, arts, history, and Islam near the Cultural (or Qur'an) Roundabout. *(Courtesy, Fotogalerie SAE)*

electoral base of Britain's socialist Labour Party. Other Western governments introduced austerity measures to slow the seemingly inexorable growth of public spending and the welfare state.

Individuals felt the impact of austerity at an early date. Indeed, the very real threat of unemployment—or "underemployment" in a dead-end job—seemed to shape the outlook of a whole generation. Students in the 1980s were serious, practical, and often conservative. As one young woman at a French university told a reporter in 1985, "Jobs are the big worry now, so everyone wants to learn something practical."[2] In France as elsewhere, the shift away from the romantic visions and political activism of the late 1960s was remarkable.

Harder times also meant that more women entered or remained in the workforce after they married. Although attitudes related to personal fulfillment were one reason for the continuing increase—especially for well-educated upper-middle-class women—many wives in poor and middle-class families worked outside the home because of economic necessity. As in preindustrial Europe, the wives' earnings provided the margin of survival for millions of hard-pressed families.

• • • • • • • • • • • • • • • • • • •

THE SOVIET UNION AND EASTERN EUROPE (1945–1991)

Why did a reform movement eventually triumph in eastern Europe in 1989 and bring an end to the cold war?

While western Europe surged ahead economically after World War II, postwar economic recovery in eastern Europe proceeded along Soviet lines, and changes in the Soviet Union strongly influenced political and social developments. That trend remained true more than forty years later, when radical reform in the Soviet Union opened the door to popular revolution in the eastern European satellites—and ultimately to the collapse of the Soviet Union itself.

Stalin's Last Years

Americans were not the only ones who felt betrayed by Stalin's postwar actions. The "Great Patriotic War of the Fatherland" had fostered Russian nationalism and a relaxation of totalitarian terror. Having made a heroic war effort, the vast majority of the Soviet people hoped in 1945 that a grateful party and government would grant greater freedom and democracy. Such hopes were soon crushed.

Even before war's end, Stalin was moving his country back toward rigid dictatorship. As early as 1944 Communist Party members received a new motivating slogan: "The war on Fascism ends, the war on capitalism begins."[3] Stalin's new Western foe provided him with an excuse for re-establishing a harsh dictatorship. He purged thousands of returning soldiers and ordinary civilians in 1945 and 1946, and he revived the terrible forced-labor camps of the 1930s. Culture and art were purged in violent campaigns that reimposed rigid anti-Western ideological conformity. Orthodox Christianity again came under attack and anti-religion policies were reimplemented. In 1949 Stalin launched a savage verbal attack on Soviet Jews, accusing them of being pro-Western and antisocialist.

In the political realm Stalin reasserted the Communist Party's complete control of the government and his absolute mastery of the party. Five-year plans were reintroduced to cope with the enormous task of economic reconstruction. Once again heavy and military industry were given top priority, and consumer goods, housing, and collectivized agriculture were neglected. Everyday life was very hard. In short, it was the 1930s all over again in the Soviet Union, although police terror was less intense.

GLOBAL TRADE

OIL

Crude oil is a liquid hydrocarbon that is located in certain rocks below the earth's crust. Although it is found throughout the world, the Persian Gulf and Caspian Sea areas contain about three-quarters of the world's proven reserves. The uses of crude oil are limited, but it may be refined into valuable products such as kerosene, gasoline, and fuel oil.

Oil has been used throughout history, although it did not become a worldwide commodity until the nineteenth century. In antiquity, the Sumerians and Babylonians mixed evaporated oil from tar pits with sand to make asphalt for waterproofing ships and paving roads. Islamic societies in the Middle East used small quantities of oil for lighting, although cooking fires were probably the main source of light.

In Europe, lamp oil—from animal fats and plants—was a luxury. The nineteenth century brought revolutionary changes in lighting—the "industrialization of light." By the 1840s manufacturers in coal-rich Europe were distilling coal into crude oil and gas, which were sold for lighting. North America followed suit. Thus when E. L. Drake drilled the first successful oil well in Pennsylvania in 1859, a growing demand for lamp oil already existed. The production of kerosene, easily distilled from the light oils of Pennsylvania, took off as American consumers accepted the bright, clean-burning, and relatively inexpensive oil for use in their lamps.

The modern oil industry operated on a global scale from the beginning. After the late 1860s the United States exported two-thirds of its kerosene, first in wooden barrels, then in large tin cans, and finally in tankers for bulk distribution. The leading producer was John D. Rockefeller's Standard Oil, which held a monopoly on kerosene until the U.S. government broke the corporation into separate companies in 1911. Most kerosene went to Europe at first, but other markets grew rapidly.

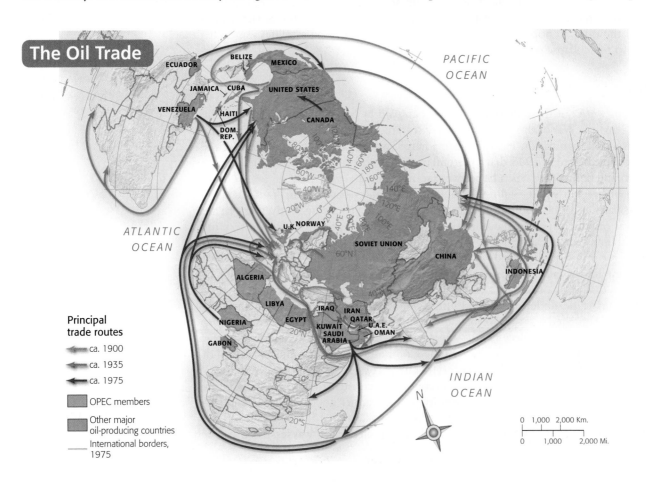

The Oil Trade

Principal trade routes
- ca. 1900
- ca. 1935
- ca. 1975

OPEC members

Other major oil-producing countries

International borders, 1975

"FIRST WE'LL VACATION AT THE SHORE, THEN WE'LL GO TO THE MOUNTAINS, THEN UP TO THE LAKE....."

In the 1870s the Baku region on the Caspian Sea, home of an ancient artisan oil industry, introduced drilling, brought in fabulous gushers, and created a Russian refining industry. Russian capitalists fought well-publicized "oil wars" with Standard Oil for world kerosene markets.

International differences were significant. In the United States and western Europe kerosene appealed especially to farmers and urban working people, who had previously lacked decent lighting. The affluent urban classes generally continued to use coal-distilled gas until the 1880s, when electricity from central power stations began to replace gas in elegant neighborhoods. In China peasants rejected bulk distribution and insisted on kerosene in tin cans, recycling them into valuable all-purpose containers. Russia pioneered in using oil as fuel, as the refining of heavy Baku crude yielded abundant thick "leftovers"—an excellent power source for riverboats, railroads, and factories.

During the twentieth century oil became a major fuel source as kerosene production declined. Until 1941 the explosive growth of automobiles in the United States was easily outpaced by the development of domestic oil fields, enabling the United States to sell one-third of all the oil consumed beyond its borders. In oil-poor Europe (Russia excepted), fuel oil loomed large as a strategic material. After 1919 the British government took control of the two oil companies in Iran and Iraq to guarantee supplies for Britain's military and industrial needs. Germany distilled coal into synthetic gasoline, and Hitler relentlessly pushed production of this very expensive alternative to free his war machine from dependence on foreign oil.

The international oil trade shifted dramatically after 1945. The United States, previously producing half the world's oil, became the world's largest importer. The Middle East, producing very modestly in the 1920s and 1930s, became the world's leading exporter. At the same time, western Europe and Japan shifted from coal to oil to drive their factories and fuel their automobiles. Nevertheless, the American and British oil companies in the Middle East expanded output so rapidly—sixteen times between 1948 and 1972—that the inflation-adjusted price for Middle Eastern oil actually fell substantially in these years.

Increasingly dissatisfied with their share of the profits, the main exporting countries—Iran, Iraq, Kuwait, Saudi Arabia, and Venezuela—organized OPEC (Organization of Petroleum Exporting Countries) in 1960 to gain control of their oil resources. In 1973, during the Arab-Israeli war, OPEC engineered a fourfold price increase with enormous global consequences. The exporting states also nationalized their oil industries, reducing foreign companies to simple buyers and transporters. The oil exporters used their financial windfalls to improve health and living standards somewhat, but vast sums went for lavish spending by the elite and for overly ambitious development projects. Above all, money went for expensive military hardware from the industrialized countries, which increased tensions and prolonged the terrible war between Iraq and Iran in the 1980s (see page 999).

A price collapse followed the upward price revolution of the 1970s. In the 1980s and early 1990s conservation, greater efficiency, recession, environmental concerns, and significant new oil discoveries outside the Middle East eliminated much of the inflation-adjusted price increases of the 1970s. By 2002 some argued that oil was really "just another commodity." The outbreak of the Iraq War in 2003, however—followed by natural disasters such as Hurricane Katrina; instability in Nigeria, Venezuela, and other major oil-producing countries; and skyrocketing demand for oil from China and India—sent oil to nearly $150 per barrel by July 2008, creating another global energy crisis.

Stalin then exported the Stalinist system to eastern Europe. Rigid ideological indoctrination, attacks on religion, and a lack of civil liberties were soon facts of life in the region's one-party states. Industry was nationalized and the middle class stripped of its possessions. Only Yugoslavia's Josip Tito (1892–1980), the popular resistance leader and Communist Party chief, could resist Soviet domination successfully, because there was no Russian army in Yugoslavia.

Limited De-Stalinization and Stagnation

In 1953 the aging Stalin died. Even as his heirs struggled for power, they realized that reforms were necessary because of the widespread fear and hatred induced by Stalin's political terrorism. They curbed secret police powers and gradually closed many forced-labor camps. Change was also necessary for economic reasons. Agriculture was in bad shape, and shortages of consumer goods were discouraging hard work and initiative. Moreover, Stalin's belligerent foreign policy had led directly to a strong Western alliance, isolating the Soviet Union.

The Communist Party leadership was badly split on just how much change to permit. Conservatives wanted few changes. Reformers, led by Nikita Khrushchev (1894–1971), argued for major innovations and won. Khrushchev launched an all-out attack on Stalin and his crimes. At a Twentieth Party Congress closed session in 1956, he described in gory detail to startled delegates how Stalin had tortured and murdered thousands of loyal Communists, bungled the country's defense by trusting Hitler, and "supported the glorification of his own person." Khrushchev's "secret speech" strengthened the reform movement.

de-Stalinization *The liberalization of the post-Stalin Soviet Union, led by reformer Nikita Khrushchev.*

The liberalization of the Soviet Union—labeled **de-Stalinization** in the West—was genuine. The Communist Party jealously maintained its monopoly on political power, but Khrushchev shook up the party and brought in new members. Some resources were shifted from heavy industry and the military toward consumer goods and agriculture, and controls over workers were relaxed. The Soviet Union's very low standard of living finally began to improve and continued to rise substantially throughout the booming 1960s.

De-Stalinization created great ferment among writers and intellectuals who hungered for cultural freedom. The writer Aleksandr Solzhenitsyn (b. 1918) created a sensation when his *One Day in the Life of Ivan Denisovich* was published in the Soviet Union in 1962. Solzhenitsyn's novel portrays life in a Stalinist concentration camp in grim detail and is a damning indictment of the Stalinist past.

Khrushchev also de-Stalinized Soviet foreign policy. "Peaceful coexistence" with capitalism was possible, he argued, and great wars were not inevitable. Between 1955 and 1957 cold war tensions relaxed.

De-Stalinization stimulated rebelliousness in the eastern European satellites, where communist reformers and the masses sought greater liberty and national independence. Poland won greater autonomy in 1956 when extensive rioting brought in a new government. Hungary experienced a real and tragic revolution. Led by students and workers—the classic urban revolutionaries—the people of Budapest installed a liberal communist reformer as their new chief in October 1956. After the new government promised free elections and renounced Hungary's military alliance with Moscow, Russian leaders ordered an invasion and crushed the revolution. When the United States did not come to their aid, Hungarians and most eastern Europeans concluded that their only hope was to strive for small domestic gains while following Russia obediently in foreign affairs.

By late 1962 there was strong opposition in Soviet party circles to Khrushchev's policies. De-Stalinization posed a dangerous threat to Stalin's still living and still powerful former henchmen, to party authority, and to the whole system. What is more, Khrushchev's policy toward the West was erratic and ultimately unsuccessful. When

● **Czechs Protest Soviet Invasion in 1968**   A young Czech girl shouts "Ivan go home" at Russian soldiers sitting on tanks in Prague during the Soviet invasion of Czechoslovakia in August 1968. *(Bettmann/Corbis)*

Khrushchev ordered missiles with nuclear warheads installed in Fidel Castro's communist Cuba in 1962, U.S. president John F. Kennedy countered with a naval blockade of Cuba. After a tense diplomatic crisis Khrushchev agreed to remove the missiles, and looked like a bumbling buffoon. Within two years of the Cuban missile crisis he was gone in a bloodless palace revolution.

After Leonid Brezhnev (1906–1982) and his supporters took over in 1964, they talked quietly of Stalin's "good points," stopped further liberalization, and launched a massive arms buildup, determined never to suffer Khrushchev's humiliation in the face of American nuclear superiority.

In the wake of Khrushchev's reforms, the 1960s brought modest liberalization and more consumer goods to eastern Europe, as well as somewhat greater national autonomy. In January 1968 reform elements in the Czechoslovakian Communist Party gained a majority and replaced a long-time Stalinist leader with Alexander Dubček (1921–1992), whose new government launched dramatic reforms. The determination of the Czech reformers to build what they called "socialism with a human face" frightened hard-line Communists. Thus in August 1968, five hundred thousand Russian and eastern European troops occupied Czechoslovakia, and the Czech experiment in humanizing communism came to an end. Shortly afterward, Brezhnev declared the so-called **Brezhnev Doctrine,** according to which the Soviet Union and its allies could intervene in any socialist country whenever they saw the need.

The aftermath of intervention in Czechoslovakia also brought a certain re-Stalinization of the U.S.S.R. Free expression and open protest disappeared. Dissidents were blacklisted or quietly imprisoned in jails or mental institutions. Unlike in the Stalinist era, though, dictatorship was collective rather than personal, and coercion replaced uncontrolled terror. This compromise seemed to suit the leaders and a majority of the people, and the Soviet Union appeared stable in the 1970s and early 1980s.

Brezhnev Doctrine   *The doctrine created after the Soviet invasion of Czechoslovakia in 1968, according to which the Soviet Union and its allies had the right to intervene in any socialist country whenever they saw the need.*

A rising standard of living for ordinary people contributed to stability, although the economic crisis of the 1970s greatly slowed the rate of improvement, and long lines and shortages persisted. The exclusive privileges enjoyed by the Communist Party elite also reinforced the system. Ambitious individuals had tremendous incentive to do as the state wished in order to gain access to special, well-stocked stores, attend superior schools, and travel abroad.

Another source of stability was the enduring nationalism of ordinary Russians. Party leaders successfully identified themselves with Russian patriotism, stressing their role in saving the motherland during the Second World War and protecting it now from foreign foes, including eastern European "counter-revolutionaries." Moreover, the politically dominant Great Russians, only half of the total Soviet population, held the top positions in the Soviet Union's non-Russian republics.

Beneath this stability, however, the Soviet Union was experiencing a social revolution. Three aspects of this revolution were particularly significant. First, the urban population continued its rapid growth in the 1960s and 1970s. In 1985 two-thirds of all Soviet citizens lived in cities, and one-fourth lived in big cities. This expanding urban population abandoned its old peasant ways, exchanging them for more education, better job skills, and greater sophistication. Second, the number of highly trained scientists, managers, and specialists expanded prodigiously, jumping fourfold between 1960 and 1985. Third, the education that created expertise also helped foster the growth of Soviet public opinion. Educated people read, discussed, and formed definite ideas about social questions from environmental pollution to urban transportation. They increasingly saw themselves as worthy of having a voice in society's decisions, even its political decisions. These changes set the stage for the dramatic reforms of the Gorbachev era.

The Gorbachev Era

The Soviet Union's Communist Party elite seemed safe in the early 1980s from any challenge from below. The party's long-established system of centralized control reached down to factories, neighborhoods, and villages. The party hierarchy continued to manipulate every aspect of national life. Organized opposition was impossible, and average people simply left politics to the bosses.

The country had serious problems, however. The massive state and party bureaucracy discouraged personal initiative and promoted economic inefficiency and apathy among the masses and the rapidly growing class of well-educated urban experts. Therefore, when Brezhnev died in 1982, efforts were made to improve economic performance and to combat worker absenteeism and high-level corruption. These efforts set the stage for the emergence in 1985 of Mikhail Gorbachev (b. 1931), the most vigorous Soviet leader since Stalin.

Smart, charming, and tough, Gorbachev believed in communism, but realized it was failing. Gorbachev also realized full well that success at home required better relations with the West, for the wasteful arms race had had a disastrous impact on Soviet Union living standards. Gorbachev attempted to save the Soviet system by reforming it. He elaborated a series of reform policies he labeled democratic socialism, or "socialism with a democratic face," which were designed to revive and even remake the vast Soviet Union.

The first set of reforms was intended to transform and restructure the economy. This economic restructuring, or **perestroika,** permitted freer prices, more independence for state enterprises, and the setting up of some profit-seeking private cooperatives. The reforms were rather timid, however, and when the economy stalled, Gorbachev's popular support gradually eroded.

Gorbachev's bold and far-reaching campaign of openness, or **glasnost,** was much more successful. Where censorship, dull uniformity, and outright lies had long char-

perestroika *The economic "restructuring" reform implemented by Gorbachev that permitted an easing of government price controls on some goods, more independence for state enterprises, and the setting up of profit-seeking private cooperatives to provide personal services for consumers.*

glasnost *"Openness," part of Gorbachev's campaign to "tell it like it is," marked a break from the past; long-banned writers sold millions of copies of their works, and denunciations of Stalin and his terror were standard public discourse.*

acterized public discourse, the new frankness led rather quickly to something approaching free speech and free expression, a veritable cultural revolution.

Democratization was the third of Gorbachev's reforms, and it led to the first free elections in the Soviet Union since 1917. Gorbachev and the party remained in control, but a minority of critical independents was elected in April 1989 to a revitalized Congress of People's Deputies, and many top-ranking Communists were defeated.

Democratization also encouraged demands for greater autonomy by non-Russian minorities, especially in the Baltic region and in the Caucasus. These demands certainly went beyond what Gorbachev had envisaged. But whereas China's Communist Party leaders brutally massacred similar pro-democracy demonstrators in Beijing (Peking) in June 1989 (see page 986), Gorbachev drew back from repression. Thus nationalist demands continued to grow.

Finally, the Soviet leader brought "new political thinking" to foreign affairs. He withdrew Soviet troops from Afghanistan and sought to reduce East-West tensions. Of enormous historical importance, Gorbachev repudiated the Brezhnev Doctrine, pledging to respect the political choices of eastern Europe's peoples. By 1989 it seemed the tragic Soviet occupation of eastern Europe might gradually wither away.

Primary Source:
The Last Heir of Lenin Explains His Reform Plans: Perestroika and Glasnost
Read President Gorbachev's analysis of the Soviet Union's decline, and his prescriptions for reform.

The Revolutions of 1989

Instead of gradually changing, history accelerated. In 1989 a series of largely peaceful revolutions swept across eastern Europe. These revolutions overturned existing communist regimes and led to the formation of governments dedicated to democratic elections, human rights, and national rejuvenation. Eastern Europe changed dramatically almost overnight.

The Poles led the way. Poland had been an unruly satellite from the beginning. After widespread riots in 1956, Polish communists dropped their efforts to impose Soviet-style collectivization on the peasants and to break the Roman Catholic Church. Faced with an independent agriculture and a vigorous church, the communists failed to monopolize society. They also failed to manage the economy effectively and instead sent it into a nosedive by the mid-1970s. Then the "Polish miracle" occurred: Cardinal Karol Wojtyla, archbishop of Cracow, was elected pope, and in June 1979 he returned to his native land to preach the love of Christ and country and the "inalienable rights of man." Pope John Paul II electrified the Polish nation, and the economic crisis became a spiritual crisis as well.

In August 1980 scattered strikes snowballed into a working-class revolt. Led by a feisty electrician and devout Catholic named Lech Walesa, the workers organized an independent trade union they called **Solidarity**. In response, Communist Party leader General Wojciech Jaruzelski proclaimed martial law in December 1981 and arrested Solidarity's leaders. (See the feature "Listening to the Past: A Solidarity Leader Speaks from Prison" on pages 974–975.) Though outlawed and driven underground, Solidarity maintained its organization and strong popular support. By 1988 widespread labor unrest and raging inflation had brought Poland to the brink of economic collapse. Solidarity pressured Poland's frustrated Communist Party leaders into legalizing Solidarity and allowing free elections in June 1989 for some seats in the Polish parliament. Solidarity won every contested seat. A month later the editor of Solidarity's weekly newspaper was sworn in as the first noncommunist leader in eastern Europe in a generation. Soon Poland was not alone in its revolution.

In Czechoslovakia communism died in ten days in December 1989 during the so-called **Velvet Revolution** that peacefully ousted Communist leaders. It grew out of massive street protests led by students and intellectuals, and led to Václav Havel's election as president in 1989. (See the feature "Individuals in Society: Václav Havel.")

In Romania revolution was violent and bloody. There the iron-fisted communist dictator Nicolae Ceauşescu, alone among eastern European bosses, ordered his

Solidarity *Led by Lech Walesa, this group of Polish workers organized a free and democratic trade union that quickly became the union of a nation.*

Velvet Revolution *The moment when communism died in 1989 with an ousting of Communist bosses in only ten days; it grew out of popular demonstrations led by students, intellectuals, and a dissident playwright.*

● **Fall of the Berlin Wall** A man stands atop the partially destroyed Berlin Wall flashing the V for victory sign as he and thousands of other Berliners celebrate the opening of the Berlin Wall in November 1989. Within a year the wall was torn down, communism collapsed, and the cold war ended. *(AP Photo/Wide World Photos)*

ruthless security forces to slaughter thousands, thereby sparking an armed uprising. After Ceauşescu's forces were defeated, the tyrant and his wife were captured and executed by a military court.

In Hungary growing popular resistance forced the Communist Party to renounce one-party rule and schedule free elections for early 1990. Hungarians gleefully tore down the barbed-wire "iron curtain" that separated Hungary and Austria (see Map 31.1) and opened their border to refugees from East Germany.

As thousands of dissatisfied East Germans passed through Czechoslovakia and Hungary on their way to thriving West Germany, a protest movement arose in East Germany. Desperately hoping to stabilize the situation, East Germany's Communist Party leaders opened the Berlin Wall in November 1989, then were swept aside. In general elections in March 1990 a conservative-liberal "Alliance for Germany" won and quickly negotiated an economic union with West Germany.

Three factors contributed to this rapid reunification. First, the opening of the Berlin Wall was critically important. In the first week alone almost 9 million East Germans—roughly half the country's population—poured across the border into West Germany. Although almost all returned home, the joy of warm welcomes from long-lost friends and family aroused long-dormant hopes of unity among ordinary citizens. Second, West German chancellor Helmut Kohl moved skillfully to reassure American, Soviet, and European leaders they need not fear a reunified Germany. At the same time, he promised the ordinary people of bankrupt East Germany an immediate economic bonanza—a one-for-one exchange of all East German marks held in savings accounts and pensions into much more valuable West German marks. Finally, Kohl and Gorbachev signed a historic agreement in July 1990 in which United Germany solemnly affirmed its peaceful intentions and pledged never to develop nuclear, biological, or chemical weapons. On October 3, 1990, East and West Germany merged, forming a single nation under West Germany's constitution and laws.

Cold War Finale and Soviet Disintegration

Germany's peaceful reunification accelerated the pace of agreements to reduce armaments and liquidate the cold war. In November 1990 delegates from twenty-two European countries joined those from the United States and the Soviet Union in Paris and agreed to a scaling down of all their armed forces. The **Paris Accord** was for all practical purposes a general peace treaty, bringing an end to World War II and the cold war.

Peace in Europe encouraged the United States and the Soviet Union to scrap a significant portion of their nuclear arsenals. In September 1991 President George H. W. Bush unilaterally declared another major cut in American nuclear weapons. He also canceled the around-the-clock alert status for American bombers outfitted with atomic bombs. Gorbachev quickly followed suit. For the first time in four decades Soviet and American nuclear weapons were no longer standing ready to destroy capitalism, communism, and life itself.

Paris Accord *A general peace treaty that brought an end to World War II and the cold war that followed; it called for a scaling down of all armed forces and the acceptance of all existing borders as legal and valid.*

Individuals IN SOCIETY

Václav Havel

On the night of November 24, 1989, the revolution in Czechoslovakia reached its climax. Three hundred thousand people had poured into Prague's historic Wenceslas Square to continue the massive protests that had erupted a week earlier after the police savagely beat student demonstrators. Now all eyes were focused on a high balcony. There an elderly man with a gentle smile and a middle-aged intellectual wearing jeans and sport jacket stood arm in arm and acknowledged the cheers of the crowd. "Dubček-Havel," the people roared. "Dubček-Havel!" Alexander Dubček, who represented the failed promise of reform communism in the 1960s (see page 951), was symbolically passing the torch to Václav Havel, who embodied the uncompromising opposition to communism that was sweeping the country. That very evening, the hard-line Communist government resigned, and soon Havel was the unanimous choice to head a new democratic Czechoslovakia. Who was this man to whom the nation turned in 1989?

Born in 1936 into a prosperous, cultured, upper-middle-class family, the young Havel was denied admission to the university because of his class origins. Loving literature and philosophy, he gravitated to the theater, became a stagehand, and emerged in the 1960s as a leading playwright. His plays were set in vague settings, developed existential themes, and poked fun at the absurdities of life and the pretensions of communism. In his private life, Havel thrived on good talk, Prague's lively bar scene, and officially forbidden rock 'n' roll.

In 1968 the Soviets rolled into Czechoslovakia, and Havel watched in horror as a tank commander opened fire on a crowd of peaceful protesters in a small town. "That week," he recorded, "was an experience I shall never forget."* The free-spirited artist threw himself into the intellectual opposition to communism and became its leading figure for the next twenty years. The costs of defiance were enormous. Purged and blacklisted, Havel lifted barrels in a brewery and wrote bitter satires that could not be staged. In 1977 he and a few other dissidents publicly protested Czechoslovakian violations of the Helsinki Accord on human rights, and in 1989 this Charter '77 group became the inspiration for Civic Forum, the democratic coalition that toppled communism. Havel spent five years in prison and was constantly harassed by the police.

Václav Havel, playwright, dissident leader, and the first postcommunist president of the Czech Republic. (Chris Niedenthal/stockphoto.com)

Havel's thoughts and actions focused on truth, decency, and moral regeneration. In 1975, in a famous open letter to Czechoslovakia's Communist boss, Havel wrote that the people were indeed quiet, but only because they were "driven by fear. . . . Everyone has something to lose and so everyone has reason to be afraid." Havel saw lies, hypocrisy, and apathy undermining and poisoning all human relations in his country: "Order has been established—at the price of a paralysis of the spirit, a deadening of the heart, and a spiritual and moral crisis in society."[†]

Yet Havel saw a way out of the Communist quagmire. He argued that a profound but peaceful revolution in human values was possible. Such a revolution could lead to the moral reconstruction of Czech and Slovak society, where, in his words, "values like trust, openness, responsibility, solidarity and love" might again flourish and nurture the human spirit. Havel was a voice of hope and humanity who inspired his compatriots with a lofty vision of a moral postcommunist society. As president of his country (1989–2003), Havel continued to speak eloquently on the great questions of our time.

Questions for Analysis

1. Why did Havel oppose Communist rule? How did his goals differ from those of Dubček and other advocates of reform communism?

2. Havel has been called a "moralist in politics." Is this a good description of him? Why? Can you think of a better one?

*Quoted in M. Simmons, *The Reluctant President: A Political Life of Václav Havel* (London: Methuen, 1991), p. 91.

[†]Quoted ibid., p. 110.

The great question then became whether the Soviet Union would also experience a popular anticommunist revolution. In February 1990 the Communist Party suffered stunning defeats in local elections throughout the country. Democrats and anticommunists won clear majorities in the Russian Federation's major cities. Separating himself further from Communist Party hardliners, a hard-pressed Gorbachev asked Soviet citizens to ratify a new constitution, which formally abolished the Communist Party's monopoly of political power and expanded the power of the Congress of People's Deputies. Gorbachev then convinced a majority of deputies to elect him president of the Soviet Union.

Gorbachev's eroding power and unwillingness to risk a popular election for the presidency strengthened his rival, Boris Yeltsin (b. 1931). A radical reform communist, Yeltsin became the most prominent figure in the democratic movement in the Russian Federation. In May 1990, as leader of the Russian parliament, Yeltsin boldly announced that Russia would declare its independence from the multiethnic Soviet Union. This move broadened the base of the anticommunist movement by skillfully joining the patriotism of ordinary Russians with the democratic aspirations of big-city intellectuals.

In August 1991 Gorbachev survived an attempted coup by Communist Party hardliners who wanted to preserve Communist Party power and the multinational Soviet Union; they succeeded only in destroying both. An anticommunist revolution swept the Russian Federation as the Communist Party was outlawed and its property confiscated. Yeltsin and his liberal allies declared Russia independent and withdrew from the Soviet Union. All the other Soviet republics followed suit; the Soviet Union—and Gorbachev's job as its president—ceased to exist on December 25, 1991 (see Map 31.2).

● **Celebrating Victory, August 1991** A Russian soldier flashes the victory sign in front of the Russian parliament, as the last-gasp coup attempt of Communist hardliners is defeated by Boris Yeltsin and an enthusiastic public. The soldier has cut the hammer and sickle out of the Soviet flag, consigning those famous symbols of proletarian revolution to what Trotsky once called the "garbage can of history." *(Filip Horvat/Corbis Saba)*

MAP 31.2 **Russia and the Successor States** After the attempt in August 1991 to depose Gorbachev failed, an anticommunist revolution swept the Soviet Union. Led by Russia and Boris Yeltsin, the republics that formed the Soviet Union declared their sovereignty and independence. Eleven of the fifteen republics then formed a loose confederation called the Commonwealth of Independent States, but the integrated economy of the Soviet Union dissolved into separate national economies, each with its own goals and policies.

THE UNITED STATES: CONFRONTATION AND TRANSFORMATION

What cold war tradeoffs between anticommunism and anticolonialism did the United States make?

After World War II, superpower status forced the United States to play a leading role on the world stage in the second half of the twentieth century. America had no other option, however, as long as another superpower held political and economic ideologies diametrically opposed to democracy and capitalism. Confrontation with the Soviet Union dominated U.S. foreign policy throughout the cold war. The Soviet Union's collapse in 1991 left Americans grappling with questions about the United States' new position in the world as the only superpower.

After 1945, members of America's World War II generation had babies, built houses, bought cars, and created the largest economy in the world. They also started to face up to the contradictions inherent in the promotion of democracy abroad and the denial of civil rights at home, and in calling for self-determination in eastern Europe while fighting what many considered a colonial war in Vietnam. As America tried to contain communism around the globe, it underwent an internal transformation that gave African Americans, women, and other minorities the social, political, and economic rights promised in the U.S. Constitution, and America's young gained a new voice in society and politics.

America's Economic Boom and Civil Rights Revolution

The Second World War ended the Great Depression in the United States, bringing about a great economic boom. Unemployment practically vanished, and Americans' well-being increased dramatically. As in western Europe, the U.S. economy advanced fairly steadily for a generation.

Prosperity helps explain why postwar domestic politics consisted largely of modest adjustments to the status quo until the 1960s. Truman's upset victory in 1948 demonstrated that Americans had no interest in undoing Roosevelt's social and economic reforms. In 1952 American voters turned to General Dwight D. Eisenhower (1890–1969), a national hero and self-described moderate. In 1960 young John F. Kennedy (1917–1963) captured the popular imagination. He revitalized the old Roosevelt coalition and modestly expanded existing liberal legislation before being struck down by an assassin's bullet in 1963.

Belatedly and reluctantly, complacent postwar America did experience a genuine social revolution: after a long struggle African Americans (and their white supporters) threw off a deeply entrenched system of segregation and discrimination. This civil rights movement advanced on several fronts. Eloquent lawyers from the National Association for the Advancement of Colored People (NAACP) challenged school segregation in the courts. In 1954 they won a landmark decision in the Supreme Court, which ruled in *Brown v. Board of Education* that "separate educational facilities are inherently unequal." Blacks also effectively challenged institutionalized inequality by using Gandhian methods of nonviolent, peaceful resistance (see page 860), such as bus boycotts, sit-ins, and demonstrations. In describing his principles for change, the civil rights leader Martin Luther King, Jr. (1929–1968), said that "Christ furnished the spirit and motivation, while Gandhi furnished the method." He told the white power structure, "We will not hate you, but we will not obey your evil laws."[4]

Civil Rights Act   *A 1964 act that prohibited discrimination in public services and on the job.*

● **The March on Washington, August 1963**   The march marked a dramatic climax in the civil rights struggle. More than two hundred thousand people gathered at the Lincoln Memorial to hear the young Martin Luther King, Jr., deliver his greatest address, the "I have a dream" speech. *(Time Life Pictures/ Getty Images)*

With African American support in key Northern states, Democrat Lyndon Johnson (1908–1973) won the 1964 presidential election in a liberal landslide. He repaid liberals' support by getting enacted the 1964 **Civil Rights Act**, which prohibited discrimination in public services and on the job, and the 1965 Voting Rights Act, which firmly guaranteed all blacks the right to vote. By the 1970s substantial numbers of blacks held public office throughout the Southern states, proof of major changes in American race relations.

In the mid-1960s Americans also generally supported President Johnson's "unconditional war on poverty" and the new social legislation behind it. Congress and the administration created a host of antipoverty projects, such as medical care for the poor and aged, free preschools for poor children, and community-action programs. Thus the United States promoted the kind of fundamental social reform that western Europe had embraced immediately after the Second World War. It became more of a welfare state as government spending for social benefits rose dramatically, approaching European levels for some programs.

Youth and the Counterculture

Economic prosperity and a more democratic class structure had a powerful impact on youth throughout North America and western Europe. The "baby boomers" born after World War II developed a distinctive and very international youth culture. This youth culture became increasingly oppositional in the 1960s, interacting with leftist thought to create a counterculture that rebelled against parents, authority figures, and the status quo.

Young people in the United States took the lead. American college students in the 1950s were docile and were often dismissed as the "Silent Generation," but some young people did revolt against the conformity of middle-class suburbs. The "beat" movement of the late 1950s expanded on the theme of revolt, and this subculture quickly spread to major American and western European cities.

Rock music helped tie this international subculture together. Rock grew out of the black music culture of rhythm and blues, which was flavored with country and western music to make it more accessible to white teenagers. Artists Elvis Presley and the Beatles became enormously popular, while suggesting personal and sexual freedom many older people found disturbing. Bob Dylan, a young folksinger turned rock poet, captured the radical aspirations of some youth when he sang that "the times they are a'changing."

Several factors contributed to the emergence of the international youth culture in the 1960s. First, mass communications and youth travel linked countries and continents together. Second, the postwar baby boom meant that young people formed an unusually large part of the population and therefore exercised exceptional influence on society as a whole. Third, postwar prosperity and greater equality gave young people more purchasing power than ever before. This enabled them to set their own trends and fads in everything from music to fashion to chemical stimulants to sexual behavior. Finally, prosperity meant that good jobs were readily available.

The youth culture practically fused with the counterculture in opposition to the established order in the late 1960s. Student protesters embraced romanticism and revolutionary idealism, dreaming of complete freedom and simpler, purer societies. The materialistic West was hopelessly rotten, but better societies were being built in the newly independent countries of Asia and Africa, or so many young radicals believed. Thus the Vietnam War took on special significance. Many politically active students in the United States and Europe believed America was fighting an immoral and imperialistic war against a small and heroic people who wanted only national unity and human dignity. Worldwide student opposition increased as the Vietnam War intensified.

> **Primary Source:**
> **Feminist Manifestoes from the Late 1960s**
> *Learn why feminists in the United States opposed all forms of patriarch, and protested institutions like the Miss America Pageant.*

The United States in World Affairs (1964–1991)

American involvement in Vietnam was a product of the cold war and the ideology of containment (see page 940). After France's defeat in Indochina in 1954 (see page 989), the Eisenhower administration refused to sign the Geneva Accords, which temporarily divided the country into two zones pending national unification by means of free elections. President Eisenhower then acquiesced in the anticommunist South Vietnamese government's refusal to accept the verdict of elections and provided military aid to help that government resist communist North Vietnam. President Kennedy increased the number of American "military advisers" to sixteen thousand.

In 1964 and 1965 President Johnson greatly expanded America's role in the Vietnam conflict, declaring "I am not going to lose Vietnam. I am not going to be the President who saw Southeast Asia go the way China went."[5] American strategy was to "escalate" the war sufficiently to break the will of the North Vietnamese and their

● **Anti– and Pro–Vietnam War Protesters Clash** America became a divided country as the Vietnam War dragged on and American casualties mounted. In May 1970 New York City hardhat construction workers and other prowar sympathizers break up an antiwar demonstration by several hundred young protesters on Wall Street. *(Bettmann/Corbis)*

southern allies without resorting to "overkill," which might risk war with the entire Communist bloc. Thus South Vietnam received massive military aid; American forces in the South grew to a half million men; and the United States bombed North Vietnam with ever-greater intensity. But there was no invasion of the North or naval blockade. In the end the American strategy of gradual escalation backfired. It was the Americans who grew weary and the American leadership that cracked.

The undeclared war in Vietnam, visible every night on American television, eventually divided the nation. At first, support was strong. The politicians, the media, and the population as a whole saw the war as part of a legitimate defense against communist totalitarianism in all poor countries. But an antiwar movement quickly emerged on college campuses, partly because of the military draft. In October 1965 student protesters joined forces with old-line socialists, New Left intellectuals, and pacifists in antiwar demonstrations in fifty American cities. By 1967 a growing number of critics denounced the war as a criminal intrusion into a complex and distant civil war.

Criticism reached a crescendo after the Vietcong Tet Offensive against major South Vietnamese cities in January 1968. The attack was a military failure, but it resulted in heavy losses on both sides, and it belied Washington's claims that victory in South Vietnam was in sight. In March 1968 President Johnson announced he would not stand for re-election, and in October he called for negotiations with North Vietnam.

Elected by a razor-slim margin in 1968, Richard Nixon (1913–1994) sought to disengage America gradually from Vietnam and the accompanying national crisis. He intensified the continuous bombardment of the enemy while simultaneously pursuing peace talks with the North Vietnamese. He also began a slow process of withdrawal from Vietnam in a process called "Vietnamization," cutting American forces there from 550,000 to 24,000 in four years. Moreover, he launched a flank attack in diplomacy. He journeyed to China in 1972 and reached a spectacular if limited reconciliation with the People's Republic of China.

Re-elected in 1972, Nixon and Secretary of State Henry Kissinger finally reached a peace agreement with North Vietnam in 1973, which allowed the remaining American forces to complete their withdrawal. Fighting declined markedly in South Vietnam. The storm of crisis in the United States seemed to have passed.

On the contrary, the country reaped the **Watergate** whirlwind. Nixon had authorized special units to conduct domestic spying activities that went beyond the law. One such group broke into Democratic Party headquarters in Washington's Watergate building in June 1972 and was promptly arrested. Facing the threat of impeachment for trying to cover up the affair, a beleaguered Nixon resigned in disgrace in 1974.

Watergate *The scandal in which Nixon's assistants broke into Democratic Party headquarters in July 1972.*

The renewed political crisis flowing from the Watergate affair had profound consequences. First, Watergate resulted in a major power shift away from the presidency and toward Congress, especially in foreign affairs. Therefore, as an emboldened North Vietnam launched a general invasion against South Vietnamese armies in early 1974, Congress refused to permit any American military response. After more than thirty-five years of battle, the Vietnamese communists unified their country in 1975 as a harsh dictatorial state—a second consequence of the U.S. crisis. Third, South Vietnam's fall shook America's postwar confidence and left Americans divided and uncertain about America's proper role in world affairs.

One alternative to containing communism was **détente,** or progressive relaxation of cold war tensions. Détente reached its high point in 1975 when all European nations (except isolationist Albania), the United States, and Canada signed the Helsinki Accord. These nations agreed that Europe's existing political frontiers could not be changed by force, and they solemnly guaranteed the human rights and political freedoms of their citizens. Optimistic hopes for détente faded quickly, however, when Brezhnev's Soviet Union ignored the human rights provisions of the Helsinki Accord and in December 1979 invaded Afghanistan to save an unpopular Marxist regime. Thus, once again, many alarmed Americans looked to NATO to thwart communist expansion. Jimmy Carter (b. 1924), elected president in 1976, pushed the Western alliance to apply economic sanctions to the Soviet Union, but among the European allies only Great Britain supported Carter's plan. Some observers felt the alliance had lost its cohesiveness.

détente *The progressive piecemeal relaxation of cold war tensions.*

Yet the Western alliance endured. The U.S. military buildup launched by Jimmy Carter was greatly accelerated by Ronald Reagan (1911–2004). The Reagan administration concentrated especially on nuclear arms and an expanded navy as keys to American power in the renewed crusade against the Soviet Union—which the president anathematized as the "evil empire."

Reagan found invaluable conservative allies in Britain's strong-willed Margaret Thatcher (see page 946) and in West Germany's distinctly pro-American Helmut Kohl (see page 954). Together they also gave indirect support to ongoing efforts to liberalize communist eastern Europe and probably helped convince Mikhail Gorbachev that endless cold war conflict was foolish and dangerous. With the Soviet Union's collapse, the United States emerged as the world's lone superpower.

In 1991 the United States used its military superiority on a grand scale in a quick war in southwestern Asia after Iraq's strongman, Saddam Hussein (1937–2006), invaded Kuwait in August 1990 (see page 999). Reacting vigorously, the United States called on the United Nations to turn back Iraqi aggression. With United Nations General Assembly and Security Council consent, a U.S.-led military coalition smashed Iraqi forces in a lightning-quick desert campaign when a defiant Hussein refused to withdraw from Kuwait.

The Gulf War demonstrated the awesome power of the rebuilt and revitalized U.S. military. In the flush of victory President Bush spoke of a "new world order," apparently meaning the United States and a cooperative United Nations working together to impose peace and security throughout the world.

JAPAN'S RESURGENCE AS A FIRST WORLD POWER

How did Japan recover so quickly after its total defeat in World War II to become an economic superpower?

In 1945 Japan and China, East Asia's two great powers, lay exhausted and devastated. Japanese aggression had sown extreme misery in China and reaped an atomic whirlwind at Hiroshima and Nagasaki. The future looked bleak. Yet both nations recovered even more spectacularly than western Europe. In the course of recovery the two countries went their separate ways. Japan under American occupation turned from military expansion to democracy. It experienced extraordinarily successful economic development until the 1990s and in the process joined the ranks of First World nations both politically and economically. China under Mao Zedong (Mao Tse-tung) transformed itself into a strong, one-party Communist state. Although Mao initially sought a working relationship with Stalin and the Soviet Union, he soon led China off on its own as a nonaligned nation. Not until the late 1970s did the reborn giants begin moving closer together, as China retreated from Maoist communism and moved toward capitalism. China is discussed in Chapter 32.

● **Ancient Shinto Practices in Modern Japan**   Ancient religious practices and modern technology come together as Shinto priests perform a ceremony of purification in front of a reactor pressure chamber in Japan. *(Yoshitaka Nakatani/PLUS ONE, Inc., Tokyo)*

Japan's American Revolution

When American occupation forces landed in the Tokyo-Yokohama area after Japan's surrender in August 1945, they found only smokestacks and giant steel safes standing amid miles of rubble in what had been the heart of industrial Japan. Japan lay helpless before its conqueror.

Japan, like Nazi Germany, was formally occupied by all the Allies, but real power resided in American hands. General Douglas MacArthur (1880–1964), the five-star hero of the Pacific, exercised almost absolute authority. MacArthur and the Americans had a revolutionary plan for defeated Japan, introducing fundamental reforms designed to make Japan a free, democratic society along American lines. The exhausted, demoralized Japanese, who had feared a worse fate, accepted passively. Long-suppressed liberal leaders emerged to offer crucial support and help carry the reforms forward.

Japan's sweeping American revolution began with demilitarization and a systematic purge. A special international tribunal tried and convicted as war criminals twenty-five top government leaders and army officers. Other courts sentenced hundreds to death and sent thousands to prison. Over 220,000 politicians, businessmen, and army officers were declared ineligible for office.

The American-dictated, British-style constitution of 1946 allowed the emperor to remain the "symbol of the State." Real power, however, resided in the Japanese Diet, whose members were popularly elected by all adults. A bill of rights granted basic civil liberties and freed all political prisoners, including communists. Article 9 of the new constitution also abolished all Japanese armed forces and declared that Japan forever renounced war. Japan's resurrected liberals enthusiastically supported this American move to destroy militarism.

The American occupation left Japan's powerful bureaucracy largely intact and used it to implement the fundamental social and economic reforms that were rammed through the Japanese Diet. Many had a New Deal flavor. The occupation promoted the Japanese labor movement and introduced American-style antitrust laws. The American reformers proudly "emancipated" Japanese women, granting them equality before the law. The occupation also imposed revolutionary land reform. This reform strengthened the small, independent peasant, who became a staunch defender of postwar democracy.

America's efforts to remake Japan in its own image were powerful but short-lived. By 1948, as China went communist, American leaders began to see Japan as a potential ally, not as an object of social reform. The American command began purging leftists and rehabilitating prewar nationalists. The occupation ended in 1952. Under the treaty terms Japan regained independence, and the United States retained its vast military complex in Japan. Japan became America's chief Asian ally in the fight against communism. With American encouragement Japan also developed an effective "Defense Force." A sophisticated modern army in everything but name, it was never deployed in a conflict area until a tiny contingent was sent to Iraq in 2004.

"Japan, Inc."

Japan's economic recovery, like Germany's, proceeded painfully slowly immediately after the war. During the Korean War, however, the economy took off and grew with spectacular speed for a whole generation. Japan served as a base for American military operations during the Korean War, and billions of dollars in military contracts and aid poured into the Japanese economy. Between 1950 and 1970 the real growth rate of Japan's economy—adjusted for inflation—averaged a breathtaking 10 percent a year. Already by the 1960s Japan had the third-largest economy in the world. Even after the shock of much higher energy prices in 1973, the petroleum-poor Japanese did considerably better than most other peoples. In 1975 Japan joined France, West Germany, Italy, Great Britain, and the United States to form the G6, the world's six leading industrialized nations. In 1986 Japan's average per capita income exceeded that in the United States for the first time.

Japan's emergence as an economic superpower fascinated outsiders. Many Asians and Africans looked to Japan for the secrets of successful modernization, but some of Japan's Asian neighbors again feared Japanese exploitation. And in the 1970s and 1980s some Americans and Europeans bitterly accused **"Japan, Inc."** of an unfair alliance between government and business and urged their own governments to retaliate.

Japan's remarkable economic surge had deep roots in Japanese history, culture, and national character. When Commodore Perry arrived in the mid-nineteenth century, Japanese agriculture, education, and material well-being were advanced even by European standards. Moreover, a culturally homogeneous Japanese society put group needs before individual needs. The Meiji reformers who redefined Japan's primary task as catching up with the West, had the support of a sophisticated and disciplined people (see pages 764–766). By 1952, this tight-knit, group-centered society had reassessed its future and worked out a new national consensus. Japan's new task was to build its economy and compete efficiently in world markets. Improved living standards emerged as a related goal after the initial successes of the 1950s.

In a system of managed capitalism, the government decided which industries were important, then made loans and encouraged mergers to create powerful firms in those industries. Antitrust regulations introduced by the Americans were quickly scrapped, and the home market was protected from foreign competition by various measures. Big business was valued and respected in postwar Japan because it served the national goal and mirrored Japanese society. Workers were hired for life immediately after they

"Japan, Inc." *A nickname developed in the 1980s to describe the intricate relationship of the business world of Japan and its government. Many European nations believed that this collusion gave the Japanese an unfair trading advantage and urged their own governments to retaliate.*

● **Searching for Work** Japanese young people, who once could expect many first job offers after leaving school, have suffered severely from the recession that began in 2001. These job seekers, like many others, have headed to Young Hellowork in Tokyo, the nation's first employment center designed specifically for young men and women. *(Kazuhiro Nogi/AFP/Corbis)*

finished school, and employees' social lives revolved around the company. (Discrimination against women remained severe: their wages and job security were strikingly inferior to men's.) Most unions became moderate, agreeable company unions. The social and economic distance between salaried managers and workers was slight and often breached. *Efficiency, quality,* and *quantity* were the watchwords.

Japan in the Post–Cold War World

The 1990s brought a sharp reversal in Japan's economic performance and a decade of frustration. Financial problems were critical. Driven to great heights by excessive optimism, the Japanese stock market dropped by 65 percent from 1990 to 1992. The bursting of the speculative bubble crippled Japanese banks, stymied economic growth, and led to record postwar unemployment of 4.5 percent in 1998. Unemployment remained around that number through 2007. Japan also faced increasingly tough competition from its industrializing neighbors in Asia (see Chapter 32), especially in the important American market. In the early twentieth-first century the economy has fluctuated between recovery and recession, with economic growth occurring from 2005 through 2007, and then declining again in 2008.

Postwar Japanese society, with its stress on discipline and cooperation as opposed to individualism and competition, has generally proved well adapted to meet the challenges of modern industrial urban society. For example, Japan, almost alone among industrial nations, has experienced a marked decrease in crime over the past generation. Similarly, since the 1970s the Japanese have addressed such previously neglected problems as serious industrial pollution and limited energy resources. Unemployment rates, though high by Japanese standards, remain below those for most other industrialized countries, which have averaged around 5 to 7 percent in the 2000s. Long-term problems that have to be addressed include a massive government debt, a declining population, the aging of the population, and dependence on foreign sources for energy, forest products, and minerals needed for modern industry.

THE POST–COLD WAR ERA IN EUROPE (1991 TO THE PRESENT)

What have been the consequences of the collapse of the Soviet Union and the end of communism there and in eastern Europe for Europe as a whole?

The end of the cold war and the Soviet Union's collapse ended the division of Europe into two opposing camps. Thus, although Europe in the 1990s was a collage of diverse peoples with their own politics, cultures, and histories, the entire continent now shared a commitment to capitalism and democracy (see Map 31.3).

Common Patterns and Problems

In economic affairs European leaders embraced, or at least accepted, a large part of the neoliberal, free-market vision of capitalist development. This vision differed markedly from western Europe's still-dominant welfare capitalism.

Two factors were particularly important in explaining the shift to tough-minded capitalism. First, Europeans were following practices and ideologies revived and enshrined in the 1980s by Ronald Reagan in the United States and Margaret Thatcher in Great Britain. Western Europeans especially took free-market prescriptions more seriously during the presidency of Bill Clinton (1993–2001) because U.S. prestige and power were so high after the cold war ended and because the U.S. economy outperformed its western European counterparts. Second, market deregulation and the privatization of state-controlled enterprises in different European countries were integral parts of the momentous trend toward a wide-open, wheeler-dealer global economy. The rules of this global economy, laid down by powerful Western governments, multinational corporations, and big banks and international financial organizations such as the International Monetary Fund (IMF), called for the free movement of capital and goods and services, low inflation, and limited government deficits. Accepting these rules and attempting to follow them was the price of participating in the global economy.

The freer global economy had powerful social consequences. Millions of ordinary citizens in western Europe were wary of global capitalism and freer markets as they challenged hard-won social achievements. As in the United States and Great Britain in the 1980s, many Europeans generally opposed the unemployment that accompanied corporate downsizing, the efforts to reduce the power of labor unions, and, above all, government plans to reduce social benefits. The reaction was particularly intense in France and Germany, where unions remained strong and socialists championed a minimum of change in social policies.

In the 1990s political developments across Europe were also loosely unified by common patterns and problems. Most obviously, the demise of European communism brought the apparent triumph of liberal democracy everywhere. All countries embraced genuine electoral competition, with elected presidents and legislatures, and they guaranteed basic civil liberties. For the first time since before the French Revolution almost all of Europe followed the same general political model, although the variations were endless.

Recasting Eastern Europe and Russia Without Communism

With Soviet-style communism in ruins, eastern Europeans experienced continued rapid change. In Russia politics and economics were closely intertwined as President Boris Yeltsin sought to create conditions that would prevent a return to communism and right the faltering economy. Following the example of some postcommunist governments in eastern Europe, Yeltsin opted in January 1992 for breakneck liberalization.

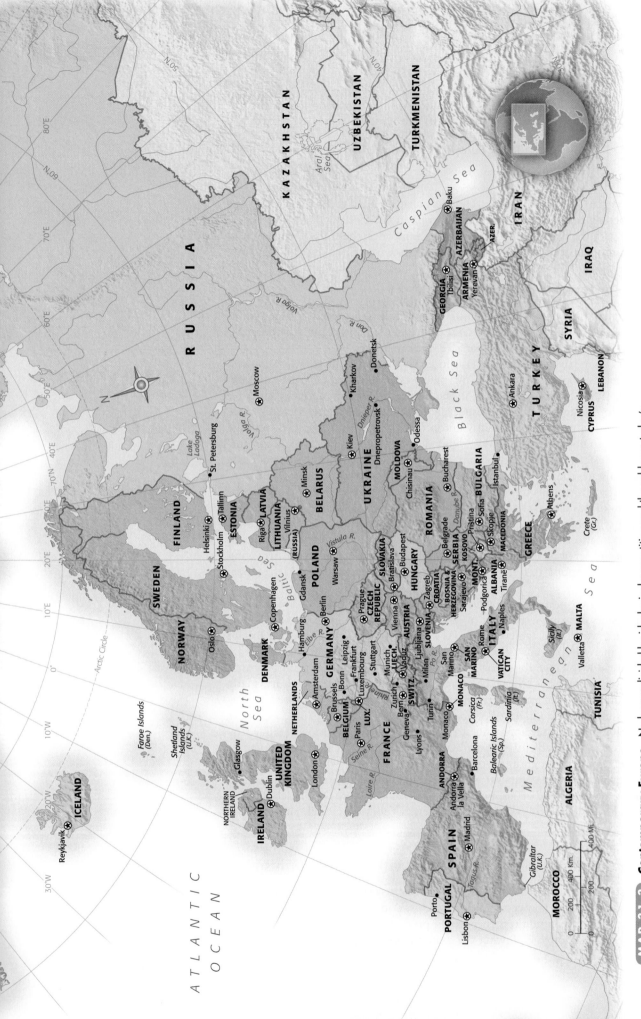

MAP 31·3 Contemporary Europe No longer divided by ideological competition and the cold war, today's Europe features a large number of independent states. Several of these states were previously part of the Soviet Union and Yugoslavia, both of which broke into many different countries. Czechoslovakia also divided on ethnic lines, while a reunited Germany emerged, once again, as the dominant nation in central Europe.

This shock therapy freed prices on 90 percent of all Russian goods, with the exception of bread, vodka, oil, and public transportation. The government also launched a rapid privatization of industry and turned thousands of factories and mines over to new private companies. However, control of the privatized companies usually remained in their old bosses' hands.

Yeltsin and his advisers believed shock therapy would revive production and bring prosperity after a brief period of hardship. The results were quite different. Prices soared and production fell sharply. The expected months of hardship stretched into years. By 1996 the Russian economy produced at least one-third and possibly one-half less than in 1991. From 1992 to 2001 the Russian economy fell by almost 30 percent—roughly equivalent to the United States during the Great Depression. In 2005 Russia's GDP (gross domestic product) was still lower than in 1991, but it has been growing sharply, averaging around 6.5 to 7 percent from 2003 through 2007.

Rapid economic liberalization worked poorly in Russia for several reasons. With privatization, powerful state industrial monopolies simply became powerful private monopolies, which cut production and raised prices to limit losses and maximize profits. Powerful managers forced Yeltsin's government to hand out enormous subsidies and credits to reinforce the positions of big firms or avoid bankruptcies. The managerial elite also combined with criminal elements to intimidate would-be rivals, preventing the formation of new firms. In addition, many Russians—told for decades that all capitalists were "speculators" and "exploiters"—were not interested in starting new businesses.

Runaway inflation and poorly executed privatization brought a profound social revolution to Russia. A new capitalist elite acquired great wealth and power. Managers, former officials, and financiers who came out of the privatization process with large shares of the old state monopolies stood at the top of Russian society.

At the other extreme the vast majority saw their savings become practically worthless. Pensions lost much of their value, and people sold personal goods to survive. The quality of public services and health care declined precipitously—so far that the average Russian male's life expectancy dropped from sixty-nine years in 1991 to fifty-nine years in 2007. In 2003 Russia's per capita income was lower than at any time since 1978, meaning essentially that there had been no economic progress for twenty-five years.

Political problems remained as well. Either the tsar or the Communist Party had dominated Russian politics for four hundred years. Newly formed political parties were naturally weak and inexperienced. Russia also had no law or court system that could deal with crime and corruption. Yet all politicians looked to the ballot box for legitimacy, as the election of President Vladimir Putin, Yeltsin's handpicked successor, clearly indicated in 2000. Putin's stress on public order and economic reform was popular.

During his seven and a half years in office, however, Putin became progressively more authoritarian, harking back even to the days of Communist Party rule. Under Putin, significant restrictions were placed on media freedoms, regional elections were abolished, and the distinction between judicial and executive authority collapsed. Putin consolidated the power and authority of the state around himself and his closest advisers, closing off the development of democratic pluralism and an independent legal system in Russia. Putin also supported renationalization of some industries and more state regulation of energy policy and economic planning in general. As Marshall Goldman observed, Putin's "increased involvement in economic matters is worrisome. It means that, under Putin, Russia is reversing some of the most important economic and political reforms it adopted after freeing itself from the yoke of communism."[6]

Putin's illiberal tendencies were also evident in his brutal military campaign against the separatist movement in Chechnya, a tiny republic of 1 million Muslims in southern Russia (see Map 31.2). Putin used the excuse of the global war on terror to try to destroy all Chechen opposition to Russian domination. An estimated two hundred thousand Chechen civilians have died in the war, many more have become refugees, and the country's infrastructure has been destroyed. Chechen resistance to Russian domination continues.

Putin's increasingly authoritarian rule drew criticism from many quarters, both within and outside Russia. He came under increasing pressure from the European Union countries and even from the United States to back away from some of his most undemocratic positions. Though economically now only a middle-tier country, Russia still retains the world's second-largest nuclear arsenal. That requires the rest of the world to acknowledge and negotiate with Russia.

Developments in eastern Europe shared important similarities with those in Russia, as many problems were the same. First, the postcommunist states worked to replace state planning and socialism with market mechanisms and private property. Second, Western-style electoral politics took hold, and as in Russia these politics were marked by intense battles between presidents and parliaments and by weak political parties. Third, ordinary citizens and the elderly were the big losers, while the young and former Communist Party members were the big winners. Regional inequalities persisted. Capital cities such as Warsaw, Prague, and Budapest concentrated wealth, power, and opportunity while provincial centers stagnated and industrial areas declined.

The postcommunist era saw more than a difficult transition to market economies and freely elected governments in eastern Europe, however. Eastern Europeans had never fully accepted communism, which the opposition of 1989 linked to Russian imperialism and the loss of national independence. The joyous crowds that toppled communist regimes believed they were liberating the nation as well as the individual. Thus as communism died, nationalism was reborn, as had occurred when authoritarian multinational empires had broken apart after World War I.

● **Putin and Democracy** After the Soviet Union's collapse in 1991, Russia's new leaders instituted a number of democratic reforms. After taking office in 2000, however, Russian President Vladimir Putin, who worked as a KGB agent during the Soviet era, was accused of rolling back many of these measures, including weakening the power of the Russian parliament, curbing the freedom of the media, restricting individual freedoms, using the war on terrorism to attack opponents, and centralizing and concentrating power in the president's office. It remains to be seen whether Dmitry Medvedev, who succeeded Putin as president in May 2008, will continue Putin's policies. Medvedev appointed Putin as prime minister of Russia the day after his inauguration. *(Robert Ariail/© The State/distributed by Newspaper Enterprise Association, Inc.)*

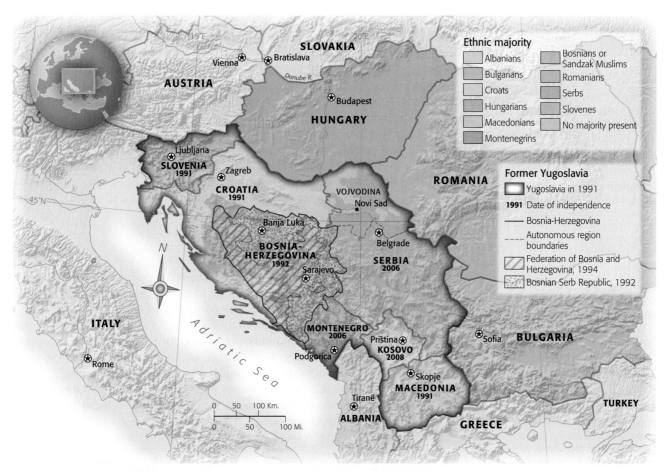

MAP 31.4 **The Breakup of Yugoslavia** Yugoslavia had the most ethnically diverse population in eastern Europe. The Republic of Croatia had substantial Serbian and Muslim minorities. Bosnia-Herzegovina had large Muslim, Serbian, and Croatian populations, none of which had a majority. In June 1991 Serbia's brutal effort to seize territory and unite all Serbs in a single state brought a tragic civil war to the region. Six new states have now emerged from parts of the old Yugoslavia—Serbia (2006), Montenegro (2006), Bosnia-Herzegovina (1992), Croatia (1991), Macedonia (1991), and Slovenia (1991). In February 2008 Kosovo declared its independence from Serbia but ethnic conflict between the majority Albanian population and the Serbian minority (who oppose independence) continues.

The response to this opportunity was varied. Poland, the Czech Republic, and Hungary were the most successful in making the transition. They managed to control national and ethnic tensions that might have destroyed their postcommunist reconstruction. The popular goal of "rejoining the West" also was a powerful force for moderation in these countries. They hoped to find security in NATO membership, which came in 1997, and prosperity by joining western Europe's economic union (see pages 970–971).

The great postcommunist tragedy was Yugoslavia, which under Josip Tito had been a federation of republics and regions. After Tito's death in 1980, power passed increasingly to the sister republics. This decentralization encouraged a revival of regional and ethnic conflicts, made worse by charges of ethnically inspired massacres during World War II and by a dramatic economic decline in the mid-1980s.

The revolutions of 1989 accelerated the breakup of Yugoslavia. When Serbian president Slobodan Milosevic attempted to grab land from other republics and unite all Serbs in a "greater Serbia," a civil war broke out that eventually involved Kosovo, Slovenia, Croatia, and Bosnia-Herzegovina (see Map 31.4). The civil war unleashed ruthless brutality, with murder, rape, the destruction of villages, the herding of refugees into concentration camps, and charges of "ethnic cleansing"—genocide—against opposing ethnic groups.

Serbian aggression appalled the Western nations. From March to June 1999 the Western powers, led by the United States, carried out heavy bombing attacks on the Serbian capital, Belgrade, on Serbian strategic sites, and on Serbian military forces. They were demanding that Milosevic withdraw Serbian armies. The impoverished Serbs eventually voted the still-defiant Milosevic out of office in September 2000, and in July 2001 a new pro-Western Serbian government turned him over to a war crimes tribunal in the Netherlands to stand trial for crimes against humanity. The civil wars in the former Yugoslavia were a monument to human cruelty. But ongoing efforts to preserve peace, repatriate refugees, and try war criminals also testified to the regenerative power of liberal values and human rights.

European Union (EU) *The new name given to the European Community in 1993.*

Unity and Identity in Western Europe

The movement toward western European unity received a powerful second wind in the 1990s. French president François Mitterrand and German chancellor Helmut Kohl took the lead in pushing for the monetary union of European Community members, and the Maastricht Agreement of 1992 created a single EU currency, the euro. In 1993 the European Community proudly rechristened itself the **European Union (EU).** Financial markets began using the euro on January 1, 1999, and the euro replaced national currencies in twelve EU countries in January 2002.

Western European elites and opinion makers generally supported this step toward economic union. They saw monetary union as a means of coping with Europe's ongoing economic problems, imposing financial discipline, cutting costs, and reducing high unemployment. These elites also saw monetary union as a historic, irreversible step toward basic political unity.

Not all Europeans supported economic union, however. Many people resented the unending flow of rules handed down by the EU's growing bureaucracy, which sought to standardize everything from cheeses to day care. Moreover, many people feared that more power in the hands of distant bureaucrats would undermine popular sovereignty and democratic control. Above all, ordinary citizens feared that the new Europe was being created at their expense. Joining the monetary union required governments to meet stringent fiscal standards and impose budget cuts and financial austerity. The resulting reductions in health care and social benefits hit ordinary citizens and did nothing to reduce western Europe's high unemployment rate.

The movement toward union also raised profound questions about the meaning of European unity and identity. Would the EU remain an exclusive Western club, or would it expand to include the postcommunist nations of eastern Europe? If some of them were included, how could Muslim Turkey's long-standing application for membership be ignored? Conversely, how could a union of twenty-five to thirty countries have any real unity?

Western Europeans proceeded cautiously at first in considering new requests for EU mem-

● **Srebrenica** When Bosnia officially declared its independence in 1992, a brutal three-year civil war broke out between Bosniaks and Croats on the one hand and Bosnian Serbs on the other. Supported by Serbia, Bosnian Serb militias practiced ethnic cleansing in those areas under their control. In July 1995 Bosnia Serb militiamen slaughtered more than 8,000 Muslim men and boys in the town of Srebrenica, Bosnia. Here a Bosnian woman weeps over the coffins of 335 newly discovered bodies found in a mass grave in 2004. *(AFP/Getty Images)*

bership. Sweden, Finland, and Austria, with strong capitalist economies, were admitted. The highly successful introduction of the euro in January 2002, however, encouraged the EU to accelerate plans for an ambitious enlargement to the east. On May 1, 2004, ten new members joined the EU: Cyprus, the Czech Republic, Slovakia, Slovenia, Latvia, Lithuania, Estonia, Hungary, Malta, and Poland. The additions brought the EU's population to 450 million, making it the world's largest trading bloc. Future candidates for membership include countries in the Balkans, former members of the old Soviet Union, and Turkey.

A proposed EU constitution binding EU member states even closer together was scheduled to go into effect in 2007. First, however, it needed approval by voters in all twenty-five countries. In late May and early June 2005 voters in two EU founding member states, France and Holland, voted overwhelmingly against the constitution and threw the entire process into confusion. Dutch officials cancelled a September 2007 referendum to approve a nearly identical reform treaty, intended to replace the original constitution treaty, when it became clear Dutch voters would reject it. An Irish "no" vote in June 2008 on the Libson Treaty, the most recent attempt at a European constitution, halted the process again. A united Europe under a common constitution remains a dream for the foreseeable future.

Chapter Summary

To assess your mastery of this chapter, go to **bedfordstmartins.com/mckayworld**

• What were the causes of the cold war?

Ideological, political, and security differences going back to the years following the Great War began pulling the United States and the Soviet Union apart before World War II ended. A critical difference was over the future of eastern Europe after the war. Stalin refused, in his meetings with Churchill, Roosevelt, and Truman, to consider free elections in eastern Europe that might put in place anti-Soviet governments. The Western allies, and especially the United States, pushed hard for free elections, but there was little they could do to stop the Soviet occupying forces from installing pro-Soviet communist leaders in these countries. Forty years of political and military standoffs followed.

• How and why, despite the cold war, did western Europe recover so successfully from the ravages of war and Nazism?

In western Europe the massive aid provided by the Marshall Plan gave a quick jump-start to recovery. These countries focused all their resources on economic recovery and growth. Keynesian economic policies that encouraged governments to increase spending, even while incurring large deficits, were adopted by most western European countries. Workers, including many migrant laborers from the Mediterranean basin, advanced the economic turnaround by working hard for low wages. Pent-up demand for basic consumer products, like automobiles, refrigerators, and washing machines, encouraged full-blown economic production. Efforts to unite western Europe into a single large market helped as well to stimulate European economies.

Key Terms

Big Three
Truman Doctrine
Marshall Plan
Common Market
decolonization
neocolonialism
OPEC
de-Stalinization
Brezhnev Doctrine
perestroika
glasnost
Solidarity
Velvet Revolution
Paris Accord
Civil Rights Act
Watergate
détente
"Japan, Inc."
European Union (EU)

• *Why did a reform movement eventually triumph in eastern Europe in 1989 and bring an end to the cold war?*

The communist system in eastern Europe and the U.S.S.R. was tightened up in the Brezhnev years (1964–1982). Then, in the 1980s, public opposition to Soviet domination spread throughout the Soviet-bloc countries, eventually leading to the revolutions of 1989 and to free elections, the restoration of civil liberties, and the institution of capitalist economies in eastern Europe.

• *What cold war tradeoffs between anticommunism and anticolonialism did the United States make?*

At the beginning of the cold war the United States was faced with a difficult dilemma: to support anticolonial movements around the world, or to stand by France and Great Britain, its two major allies in World War II and potentially in the cold war, but also the two largest colonial powers. American leaders generally viewed the Soviet Unions and the spread of communism as the greatest dangers they faced, and therefore turned their back on Third World liberation movements in order to gain the support of Great Britain and France in the cold war. This stance had its most tragic consequences when the United States went to the aid of France in its efforts to hold onto its colony of Vietnam.

• *How did Japan recover so quickly after its total defeat in World War II to become an economic superpower?*

Before World War II Japan was one of the world's leading industrial nations. By the end of the war Japan lay exhausted and devastated, facing what seemed a bleak future. Allied occupation forces, however, under the direction of General Douglas MacArthur, set about helping Japan rebuild economically and develop a stable democratic government. Social and economic reforms were pushed through a new, and popularly elected, Diet (Japanese parliament). Article 9 of the new Japanese constitution abolished the military and renounced war. Eager to have a stable capitalist ally against communism in Asia, the United States guaranteed Japanese security with its own forces. America also poured billions of dollars into the Japanese economy, particularly during the Korean War when Japan served as a military operations base for American forces. Japan's economic growth skyrocketed in the 1950s and 1960s, surpassing even western Europe's success in postwar recovery.

• *What have been the consequences of the collapse of the Soviet Union and the end of communism there and in eastern Europe for Europe as a whole?*

The collapse of the Soviet Union and of communism there and across eastern Europe left little option for these countries but to adopt liberal democracy and free market capitalism. Europe was no longer divided, and differences in political organization, human rights, and economic philosophy became less pronounced in the 1990s than at any time since 1914. Eastern Europe especially struggled to rejoin the West and replace the bankrupt communist order with efficient capitalist democracies. Results varied greatly, and ordinary citizens often experienced real hardships. But in the early twenty-first century there appeared to be few attractive alternatives to global liberalism, and no effort was made to restore economic planning or one-party rule. This outcome suggests that the anticommunist revolutions of 1989 marked a major turning point in world history.

Suggested Reading

Ash, Timothy Garton. *The Polish Revolution: Solidarity,* 3d ed. 2002. A definitive account of the role of the Solidarity movement in the Polish revolution and its subsequent fate.

Dobbs, Michael. *Down with Big Brother: The Fall of the Soviet Empire.* 1997. A superb account by a journalist who covered eastern Europe.

Eksteins, Modris. *Walking Since Daybreak: A Story of Eastern Europe, World War II, and the Heart of Our Century.* 1999. A powerful, partly autobiographical account that is highly recommended.

Gaddis, John Lewis. *The Cold War. A New History.* 2005. A concise, authoritative, and accessible account of the cold war by one of its leading historians.

Grass, Günter. *The Tin Drum.* 1963. Nobel prize winner explores the spiritual dimension of West German recovery in his world-famous novel.

Halberstam, David. *The Coldest Winter. America and the Korean War.* 2007. One of America's finest journalist-historian's last, and perhaps best, history.

Hughes, H. Stuart. *Sophisticated Rebels: The Political Culture of European Dissent, 1968–1987.* 1988. Provocatively analyzes the culture and politics of protest in Europe.

Kagan, Robert. *Of Paradise and Power: America and Europe in the New World Order.* 2004. Controversial but brilliant analysis of the post–cold war world.

Karnow, Stanley. *Vietnam. A History,* 2d ed. 1997. One of the best and most comprehensive accounts of all sides in the war.

Kingston, Jeffrey. *Japan's Quiet Transformation: Social Change and Civil Society in the 21st Century. Politics, Economics and Society.* 2004. Leading scholar considers Japan's economic problems in the 1990s and their effects on Japanese politics and society.

Lampe, J. *Yugoslavia as History: Twice There Was a Country,* 2d ed. 2000. Considers judiciously and insightfully the history and violent collapse of Yugoslavia.

Laqueur, Walter. *Europe in Our Time: A History, 1945–1992.* 1992. Excellent, comprehensive study of postwar Europe, with extensive bibliography.

Sheehan, Neil. *A Bright and Shining Lie: John Paul Vann and America in Vietnam.* 1988. Classic account of the Vietnam War built around a biography of one of its harshest critics, Lieutenant Colonel Vann.

Urwin, Derek W. *The Community of Europe. A History of European Integration since 1945,* 2d ed. 1995. Eloquent history of all aspects of European attempts at economic and political union since 1945.

Wapshott, Nicholas. *Ronald Reagan and Margaret Thatcher: A Political Marriage.* 2007. Particularly good analysis of their policies of economic conservatism and anticommunism in the 1980s.

Notes

1. Quoted in N. Graebner, *Cold War Diplomacy, 1945–1960* (Princeton, N.J.: Van Nostrand, 1962), p. 17.
2. *Wall Street Journal,* June 25, 1985, p. 1.
3. Quoted in D. Treadgold, *Twentieth Century Russia,* 5th ed. (Boston: Houghton Mifflin, 1981), p. 442.
4. Regarding Gandhi's methods: see M. L. King, Jr., *Stride Toward Freedom: The Montgomery Story* (New York: Perennial Library, 1964), p. 67. Regarding evil laws: quoted in S. E. Morison et al., *A Concise History of the American Republic* (New York: Oxford University Press, 1977), p. 697.
5. Quoted in Morison, *Concise History,* p. 735.
6. M. Goldman, "Putin and the Oligarchs," *Foreign Affairs* 83 (November/December 2004): 44.

Listening to the
PAST

A Solidarity Leader Speaks from Prison

Solidarity built a broad-based alliance of intellectuals, workers, and the Catholic Church. That alliance was one reason that Solidarity became such a powerful movement in Poland. Another reason was Solidarity's commitment to social and political change through nonviolent action. That commitment enabled Solidarity to avoid a bloodbath in 1981 and thus maintain its structure after martial law was declared, although at the time foreign observers often criticized Lech Walesa's leadership for being too cautious and unrealistic.

Adam Michnik was one of Walesa's closest coworkers. Whereas Walesa was a skilled electrician and a devout Catholic, Michnik was an intellectual and disillusioned Communist. Their faith in nonviolence and in gradual change bound them together. Trained as a historian but banned from teaching because of his leadership in student strikes in 1968, Michnik earned his living as a factory worker. In 1977 he joined with others to found the Committee for the Defense of Workers (KOR), which supported workers fired for striking. In December 1981, Michnik was arrested with the rest of Solidarity's leadership. While in prison until July 1994, he wrote his influential Letters from Prison, *from which this essay is taken.*

Why did Solidarity renounce violence? This question returned time and again in my conversations with foreign observers. I would like to answer it now. People who claim that the use of force in the struggle for freedom is necessary must first prove that in a given situation it will be effective and that force, when it is used, will not transform the idea of liberty into its opposite.

No one in Poland is able to prove today that violence will help us to dislodge Soviet troops from Poland and to remove the communists from power. The U.S.S.R. has such enormous military power that confrontation is simply unthinkable. In other words, we have no guns. Napoleon, upon hearing a similar reply, gave up asking further questions. However, Napoleon was above all interested in military victories and not building democratic, pluralistic societies. We, by contrast, cannot leave it at that.

In our reasoning, pragmatism is inseparably intertwined with idealism. Taught by history, we suspect that by using force to storm the existing Bastilles we shall unwittingly build new ones. It is true that social change is almost always accompanied by force. But it is not true that social change is merely a result of the violent collision of various forces. Above all, social changes follow from a confrontation of different moralities and visions of social order. Before the violence of rulers clashes with the violence of their subjects, values and systems of ethics clash inside human minds. Only when the old ideas of the rulers lose this moral duel will the subjects reach for force—sometimes. This is what happened in the French Revolution and the Russian Revolution—two examples cited in every debate as proof that revolutionary violence is preceded by a moral breakdown of the old regime. But both examples lose their meaning when they are reduced to such compact notions, in which the Encyclopedists are paired with the destruction of the Bastille, and the success of radical ideologies in Russia is paired with the storming of the Winter Palace. An authentic event is reduced to a sterile scheme.

In order to understand the significance of these revolutions, one must remember Jacobin and Bolshevik terror, the guillotines of the sans-culottes, and the guns of the commissars. Without reflection on the mechanisms in victorious revolutions that gave birth to terror, it is impossible to even pose the fundamental dilemma facing contemporary freedom movements. Historical awareness of the possible consequences of revolutionary violence must be etched into any program of struggle for freedom. The experience of being corrupted by terror must be imprinted upon the consciousness of everyone who belongs to a freedom movement. [Or], as Simone Weil wrote, freedom will again become a refugee from the camp of the victors. . . .

Solidarity's program and ethos are inextricably tied to this strategy. Revolutionary terror has always been justified by a vision of an ideal society. In the name of this vision, Jacobin guillotines and Bolshevik execution squads carried out their unceasing, gruesome work.

Solidarity activist Adam Michnik in 1984, appearing under police guard in the military court that sentenced him to prison. *(Wide World Photos)*

The road to God's Kingdom on Earth led through rivers of blood.

Solidarity has never had a vision of an ideal society. It wants to live and let live. Its ideals are closer to the American Revolution than to the French. . . . The ethics of Solidarity, with its consistent rejection of the use of force, has a lot in common with the idea of nonviolence as espoused by Gandhi and Martin Luther King, Jr. But it is not an ethic representative of pacifist movements.

Pacifism as a mass movement aims to avoid suffering; pacifists often say that no cause is worth suffering or dying for. The ethics of Solidarity are based on an opposite premise: that there are causes worth suffering and dying for. Gandhi and King died for the same cause as the miners in Wujek who rejected the belief that it is better to remain a willing slave than to become a victim of murder [and who were shot down by police for striking against the imposition of martial law in 1981]. . . .

But ethics cannot substitute for a political program. We must therefore think about the future of Polish-Russian relations. Our thinking about this key question must be open; it should consider many different possibilities. . . .

The Soviet state has a new leader; he is a symbol of transition from one generation to the next within the Soviet elite. This change may offer an opportunity, since Mikhail Gorbachev has not yet become a prisoner of his own decisions. No one can rule out the possibility that an impulse for reform will spring from the top of the hierarchy of power. This is exactly what happened in the time of Alexander II and, a hundred years later, under Khrushchev. Reform is always possible, even in the face of resistance by the old apparatus. . . .

So what can now happen [in Poland]?

The "fundamentalists" say, no compromises. Talking about compromise, dialogue, or understanding demobilizes public opinion, pulls the wool over the eyes of the public, spreads illusions. Walesa's declarations about readiness for dialogue were often severely criticized from this point of view. I do not share the fundamentalist point of view. . . . The logic of fundamentalism precludes any attempt to find compromise, even in the future. It harbors not only the belief that

communists are ineducable but also a certainty that they are unable to behave rationally, even in critical situations—that, in other words, they are condemned to suicidal obstinacy.

This is not so obvious to me. Historical experience shows that communists were sometimes forced by circumstances to behave rationally and to agree to compromises. Thus the strategy of understanding must not be cast aside. We should not assume that a bloody confrontation is inevitable and, consequently, rule out the possibility of evolutionary, bloodless change. This should be avoided all the more inasmuch as democracy is rarely born from bloody upheavals. We should be clear in our minds about this: The continuing conflict may transform itself into either a dialogue or an explosion. The TKK [the underground Temporary Coordinating Committee of outlawed Solidarity] and [Lech] Walesa are doing everything in their power to make dialogue possible. Their chances of success will be greater if the level of self-organization of independent Polish society increases. For street lynchings, angry crowds are enough; compromise demands an organized society.

Questions for Analysis

1. Are Michnik's arguments for opposing the government with nonviolent actions convincing?

2. How did Michnik's study of history influence his thinking? What lessons did he learn?

3. Analyze Michnik's attitudes toward the Soviet Union and Poland's Communist leadership. What policies did he advocate? Why?

Source: Adam Michnik, *Letters from Prison and Other Essays,* trans. Maya Latynski (Berkeley and Los Angeles: University of California Press, 1985), pp. 86–89, 92, 95, by permission of the University of California Press. Copyright © 1985 by The Regents of the University of California.

African Market. This bustling market in Monrovia, Liberia, reflects the vibrant diversity of modern Africa. *(Tim Hetherington/ Panos Pictures)*

32 LATIN AMERICA, ASIA, AND AFRICA IN THE CONTEMPORARY WORLD

Historians often describe the cold war era as "bipolar," consisting of (1) the United States and its allies in the West and East and (2) the Soviet Union and its allies in the West and East. Of course, the world was not truly bipolar. Two-thirds of the world's people were certainly influenced by the two superpowers' actions and were often willing or unwilling participants in their global power struggle. Just as often, they simply watched anxiously from the sidelines, hoping the two giants would not destroy them and the planet with nuclear weapons. While the United States and the Soviet Union faced each other in a deadly confrontation, people in the so-called Third World went about their daily lives.

The term *Third World* has its origins in the 1950s, when many thinkers, journalists, and politicians viewed Africa, Asia, and Latin America as a single entity, different from both the capitalist, industrialized "First World" and the communist, industrialized "Second World." Or, in contemporary scholarly jargon, they imagined and "constructed" Africa, Asia, and Latin America as a unit for effective analysis and action. Despite differences in history and culture, African, Asian, and Latin American countries—for a generation—did share many characteristics linking them together that encouraged a common consciousness and ideology.

First, nearly all African, Asian, and Latin American countries had experienced political or economic domination, nationalist reaction, and a struggle for genuine independence. Precisely because of their shared sense of past injustice and continued exploitation, many influential Latin Americans identified with the Third World, despite their countries' greater affluence.

Second, Asian, African, and most Latin American countries had—many still do—predominately agricultural economies, earning the majority of their revenues from one or two cash crops whose production was frequently controlled and exploited by First World countries or by multinational agribusinesses. In the second half of the twentieth century they became united by their growing awareness of their common poverty and dependency on First World markets to set prices and buy their raw materials.

Third, in the 1950s and 1960s a majority of people in most poor countries lived in the countryside and depended on agriculture for a living. By contrast, most First World people lived in cities and depended mainly on industry and urban services for employment. Not everyone in the Third World was poor; a small elite were quite wealthy. But the average standard of living was low, and massive poverty was ever present.

Finally, Third World peoples were united in their opposition to political and economic oppression in all its forms, particularly colonialism, neocolonialism, and racism. Their leaders believed genuine independence and social justice were the real challenges before them, and they worked in the United Nations for a restructuring of the world economic system (see page 1023).

LATIN AMERICA: MOVING TOWARD DEMOCRACY

How was Latin America similar to, and different from, the other Third World nations?

After the Second World War Latin America experienced a many-faceted recovery, somewhat similar to that of Europe, though beginning earlier. After a generation, Latin America also experienced its own period of turbulence and crisis. Many Latin American countries responded by establishing authoritarian military regimes until, in the late 1980s, Latin America copied eastern Europe by electing civilian governments and embracing economic liberalism for the first time since the 1920s.

Economic Nationalism in Latin America

The growth of economic nationalism was a common development throughout Latin America in much of the twentieth century. Just as Spanish and Portuguese colonies won political independence in the early nineteenth century, much of recent history has witnessed a quest for genuine economic independence. To understand the rise of economic nationalism, one must remember that Latin American countries developed as producers of foodstuffs and raw materials exported to Europe and the United States in return for manufactured goods and capital investment. This exchange brought considerable economic development but exacted a heavy price: neocolonialism (see pages 786–787). Latin America became dependent on foreign markets, products, and investments. Industry did not develop, and large landowners profited the most from economic development, using their advantage to enhance their social and political power.

The Great Depression made matters worse. Prices and exports of Latin American commodities collapsed as Europe and the United States drastically reduced their purchases and raised tariffs to protect domestic products. With their foreign sales plummeting, Latin American countries could not buy the industrial goods they needed from abroad. The global depression provoked a profound shift toward economic nationalism after 1930, as popularly based governments worked to reduce foreign influence and gain control of their own economies and natural resources. These efforts were fairly successful. By the late 1940s factories in Argentina, Brazil, and Chile could generally satisfy domestic consumer demand for the products of light industry. In the 1950s some countries began moving into heavy industry. Economic nationalism and the rise of industry are particularly striking in the two largest and most influential countries, Mexico and Brazil, which account for half of Latin America's population.

Primary Source:
Speech to the Nation
In this excerpt from a radio address given in 1938, President Lázaro Cárdenas announces his decision to nationalize the Mexican oil industry.

The Mexican Revolution of 1910 overthrew the elitist, upper-class rule of the tyrant Porfirio Díaz, culminating in 1917 in a new constitution. This radical nationalistic document called for universal suffrage, massive land reform, benefits for labor, and strict control of foreign capital. Progress was modest until 1934, when a charismatic young Indian from a poor family, Lázaro Cárdenas, became president and dramatically revived the languishing revolution. Under Cárdenas many large estates were divided among small farmers or were returned undivided to Indian communities. Meanwhile, state-supported Mexican businessmen built many small factories to meet domestic needs. In 1938 Cárdenas nationalized the petroleum industry. Also, the 1930s saw the flowering of a distinctive Mexican culture that proudly embraced the long-despised Indian past.

In the 1940s and 1950s more moderate Mexican presidents used the state's power to promote industrialization, and the Mexican economy grew rapidly until the late 1960s. The upper and middle classes reaped the lion's share of the benefits.

Brazilian politics was dominated by the coffee barons and by regional rivalries after the fall of Brazil's monarchy in 1889. Regional rivalries and deteriorating economic conditions allowed a military revolt led by Getúlio Vargas to seize control of the federal government in 1930. Vargas established a mild dictatorship that lasted until 1945. His rule was generally popular, combining effective economic nationalism and moderate social reform.

Modernization continued for the next fifteen years, and Brazil's economy boomed. Economic nationalism was especially vigorous under the flamboyant President Juscelino Kubitschek. Between 1956 and 1960 the government borrowed heavily from international bankers to promote industry and build the new capital of Brasília in the midst of a wilderness. Kubitschek's slogan was "Fifty Years' Progress in Five." By the late 1950s economic and social progress seemed to be bringing less violent, more democratic politics to Latin America. These expectations were shaken by the Cuban Revolution.

Authoritarianism and Democracy in Latin America

Achieving nominal independence in 1898 as a result of the Spanish-American War, Cuba was practically an American protectorate until the 1930s. Cuba's political institutions were weak and its politicians corrupt. Yet Cuba was one of Latin America's most prosperous countries by the 1950s, although enormous differences remained between rich and poor.

Fidel Castro (b. 1927) and his guerrilla forces overthrew the Cuban government in late 1958. Castro had promised a "real" revolution, and it soon became clear that

Chronology

1946–1964 Decolonization in Africa and Asia

1947 Separation of India and Pakistan

1948 End of British mandate in Palestine; Jews proclaim state of Israel

1949–1954 Mass arrests, forced-labor camps, and Communist propaganda in China

1949–present Harsh restrictions against religion and speech in China

1956 Nasser nationalizes Suez Canal Company

1964–1973 Vietnam War

1965 Cultural Revolution in China; intellectuals are exiled and art is destroyed

1967 Six-Day War in Israel

1975–present Slower population growth in Asia and Latin America

Late 1970s–present Revival of Islamic fundamentalism

1978 Islamic revolution in Iran

1980–1988 Iran-Iraq War

1989 Chinese military puts down student revolt in Tiananmen Square

1991 Congress Party in India embraces Western capitalist reforms; Gulf War

1994 Nelson Mandela becomes president of South Africa

1995 Assassination of Israeli prime minister Yitzhak Rabin

2004 Death of PLO leader Yasir Arafat

2008 Retirement of Cuban president Fidel Castro after 49 years as ruler

● **Brasília: Metropolitan Cathedral** The Metropolitan Cathedral at night in Brazil's capital city, Brasília. The cathedral was inaugurated in 1970, ten years after the inauguration of the planned city that replaced Rio de Janeiro as Brazil's capital. *(Augusto C. B. Real)*

"real" meant "communist." Middle-class Cubans began fleeing to Miami. Cuban relations with the Eisenhower administration deteriorated rapidly. In April 1961 the U.S. president, John Kennedy, tried to use Cuban exiles to topple Castro, but Kennedy abandoned the exiles as soon as they landed ashore at the Bay of Pigs.

After routing the Bay of Pigs forces, Castro moved to build an authoritarian communist society: an alliance with the Soviet bloc; a Communist Party dictatorship; state ownership; a Castro cult; prisons and emigration to silence opposition; and the exportation of communist revolutions throughout Latin America. Fearing Castro would succeed, the United States in 1961 funded the new hemispheric Alliance for Progress, intended to promote long-term economic development and social reform.

U.S. aid contributed modestly to continued Latin American economic development in the 1960s, but democratic social reforms—the other half of the Alliance for Progress formula—stalled. Conflict between leftist movements and ruling elites grew, won most often by the elites and their military allies, but at the cost of imposing a new kind of conservative authoritarianism. By the late 1970s only Costa Rica, Venezuela, Colombia, and Mexico retained some measure of democratic government. Brazil, Argentina, and Chile represented the general trend.

In Brazil, intense political competition in the early 1960s prompted President João Goulart to swing to the left to gain fresh support. When Goulart appeared ready to use force to break up landed estates and extend the vote to Brazil's many illiterates, army leaders staged a coup in 1964. Industrialization and urbanization went forward under right-wing military rule, but social inequalities increased.

In Argentina the military ousted the dictatorial populist and economic nationalist Juan Perón in 1955 and restored elected democratic government. Then, worried by a Peronist revival and following the Brazilian example, the army took control in 1966 and again in 1976 after a brief civilian interlude. Repression escalated following each military takeover. Though culturally and economically advanced, Argentina became a brutal military dictatorship.

Events in Chile were truly tragic, given its long tradition of democracy and moderate reform. When Salvador Allende, a doctor and the Marxist head of a coalition of communists, socialists, and radicals, won a plurality in 1970, he was duly elected president by the Chilean Congress. Allende completed the nationalization of the American-owned copper companies and proceeded to socialize private industry, accelerate the breakup of landed estates, and radicalize the poor. Marxism in action evoked a powerful backlash. In 1973, with widespread conservative support and U.S. backing, the traditionally impartial army struck in a well-organized coup. Allende died, probably murdered, and thousands of his supporters were arrested, or worse. As in Argentina, the military imposed a harsh despotism.

The military governments that revived antidemocratic authoritarianism in Latin America blocked not only Marxist and socialist programs but most liberal and moderate reforms as well. The new authoritarians were, however, determined modernizers, deeply committed to nationalism, industrialization, technology, and some modest social progress. They even promised free elections in the future.

That time came in the 1980s, when another democratic wave gained momentum throughout Latin America. In Argentina the military government of General Leopoldo Galtieri gradually lost almost all popular support because of its "dirty war" against its own citizens, in which thousands arbitrarily accused of opposing the regime were imprisoned, tortured, and murdered. In 1982, in a desperate gamble to rally the people, Argentina's military rulers seized the Falkland (or Malvinas) Islands (see Map 26.2 on page 783) from Great Britain. The British rout of Argentina's poorly led

● **Justice for the Victims of Chile's General Pinochet** With their faces covered with death masks, demonstrators outside Britain's High Court in 2000 hold up crosses carrying pictures of the "Disappeared"—the thousands kidnapped and allegedly murdered between 1973 and 1988 under the military dictatorship of General Pinochet. The High Court ruled against extraditing Pinochet to Spain to stand trial, but he was finally charged with torture and murder when he returned to Chile. *(Dan Chung/Reuters New-Media Inc./Corbis)*

troops forced the humiliated generals to schedule national elections. The democratically elected government prosecuted the former military rulers for their crimes and laid solid foundations for liberty and political democracy.

The Brazilian military was relatively successful in its industrialization effort, but proved unable (or unwilling) to improve the social and economic position of the masses. In 1985, after twenty-one years of rule, the military leaders allowed civilian politicians to have a try. Chile also turned from right-wing military dictatorship to elected government. Thus by the late 1980s, 94 percent of Latin Americans lived under regimes that guaranteed elections and civil liberties.

The most dramatic developments in Central America occurred in Nicaragua. In 1979 the Sandinistas, a broad coalition of liberals, socialists, and Marxist revolutionaries, drove long-time dictator Anastasio Somoza from power. The new leaders wanted genuine political and economic independence from the United States, as well as thoroughgoing land reform, some nationalized industry, and friendly ties with communist countries. These policies infuriated the Reagan administration, which sought to overthrow the Sandinista government by creating a counterrevolutionary mercenary army, the Contras, and supplying it with military aid funded illegally through military weapons sales to Iran. After years of civil war, the Nicaraguan economy collapsed, and the Sandinista government's popularity eventually declined. The Sandinistas surrendered power when they were defeated in free elections by a coalition of opposition parties.

The Reagan administration also helped engineer a 1986 coup in Haiti, where "Papa Doc" Duvalier, followed by his son, "Baby Doc," had for decades ruled in one of the most repressive dictatorships in the Americas, with U.S. support. Although "Baby Doc" was forced into exile, the country experienced a period of violence and disorder until semi-fair elections were held in 1994 with the help of U.S. military intervention. More than thirteen years later, however, Haiti remained not only the Western Hemisphere's poorest country but also in political turmoil with no improvement in sight.

Latin America in the 1990s

In the 1990s Latin America's popularly elected governments relaxed economic relations with other countries, moving decisively from tariff protection and economic nationalism toward free markets and international trade. In so doing, they revitalized their economies and registered solid gains. In 1994 Mexico joined with the United States and Canada in the North American Free Trade Agreement (NAFTA). Hoping to copy the success of the European Union, twelve South American countries (Brazil, Argentina, Paraguay, Uruguay, Venezuela, Bolivia, Colombia, Ecuador, Peru, Guyana, Suriname, and Chile) met in Cuzco, Peru, in December 2004 and signed the Cuzco Declaration, announcing the formation of the Union of South American Nations. The Constitutive Treaty formally establishing the union was signed on May 23, 2008, in Brasília, Brazil. The union will provide a free-trade zone for its members and compete economically with the United States and the European Community.

• • • • • • • • • • • • • • • •

THE RESURGENCE OF EAST ASIA

How did the defeat of Japan lead to East Asian resurgence after World War II?

Except for Japan, most Asian countries recovered slowly after World War II. In the early 1950s the two Koreas and China were at war in the Korean peninsula, and the Vietnamese were fighting among themselves and against the French. The Nationalist Chinese in Taiwan were adjusting to life in exile from the mainland. Hong Kong, Singapore, Indonesia, South Korea, and the Philippines were recovering from years of colonial rule and Japanese occupation. Over the next forty years, China and the "Asian Tigers" developed some of the largest and fastest-growing economies in the world, but liberal democracy remained elusive.

The Communist Victory in China

Communism triumphed in China for many reasons. As a noted historian forcefully argued, however, "Japanese aggression was . . . the most important single factor in Mao's rise to power."[1] Half of Japan's overseas armies were pinned down in China in 1945, in a long war that exhausted the established government and its supporters. Jiang Jieshi's Nationalists had mobilized 14 million men, and a staggering 3 million Chinese soldiers had been killed or wounded. The war created massive Chinese deficits and runaway inflation, hurting morale and ruining lives. Mao and the Communists had avoided pitched battles and concentrated on winning peasant support and forming a broad anti-Japanese coalition. By reducing rents, promising land redistribution, enticing intellectuals, and spreading propaganda, Mao and the Communists emerged in peasant eyes as the true patriots, the genuine nationalists.

When Japan suddenly collapsed in August 1945, Communists and Nationalists both rushed to seize evacuated territory. Heavy fighting broke out in Manchuria, and civil war began in earnest in April 1946. By 1948 the demoralized Nationalist forces were disintegrating before the better-led, more determined Communists. The following year Jiang Jieshi and 2 million mainland Chinese fled to Taiwan, and in October 1949 Mao Zedong proclaimed the People's Republic of China.

Within three years the Communists consolidated their rule. The Communist government seized the holdings of landlords and rich peasants—10 percent of the farm population had owned between 70 and 80 percent of the land—and distributed it to 300 million poor peasants and landless laborers. This revolutionary land reform was extremely popular. Meanwhile, as Mao admitted in 1957, eight hundred thousand "class enemies" were summarily liquidated between 1949 and 1954; the true figure is probably much higher. All visible opposition from the old ruling groups was destroyed.

Finally, Mao and the Communists reunited China's 550 million inhabitants in a strong centralized state. Claiming a new Mandate of Heaven, they set out to prove that China was once again a great power. This was the real significance of China's participation in the Korean War. From 1950 to 1953, the Chinese army's ability to fight the American "imperialists" to a bloody standstill on the Korean peninsula mobilized the masses and increased Chinese self-confidence.

Mao's China

Wanting to assert Chinese power and prestige in world affairs, Mao and the party looked to the Soviet Union for inspiration in the early 1950s. Along with the gradual collectivization of agriculture, China adopted a typical Soviet-style five-year plan to develop large factories and heavy industry rapidly. Russian specialists built many Chinese plants. Soviet economic aid was also considerable. The first five-year plan was successful, as undeniable economic growth followed the Communists' social revolution.

In the cultural and intellectual realms, too, the Chinese followed the Soviet example. Basic civil and political rights, which the Nationalists had seriously curtailed, were now simply abolished. Temples and churches were closed, and press freedom died. Soviet-style puritanism took hold, as the Communists quickly eradicated prostitution and drug abuse, which they had long regarded as humiliating marks of exploitation and national decline. They enthusiastically promoted Soviet-Marxian ideas concerning women and the family. Full equality, work outside the home, and state-supported child care became primary goals.

Great Leap Forward *Mao Zedong's acceleration of development in which industrial growth was to be based on small-scale backyard workshops run by peasants living in gigantic self-contained communes.*

By the mid-1950s China seemed to be firmly set on the Marxist-Leninist course of development, but in 1958 it began to go its own way. Mao proclaimed a spectacular acceleration of development, a **Great Leap Forward** in which soaring industrial growth would be based on small-scale backyard workshops run by peasants living in gigantic self-contained communes. The creation of a new socialist personality that rejected individualism and traditional Confucian family values, such as filial piety and acceptance of parental authority, was a second goal.

The intended great leap produced an economic disaster, for frantic efforts with primitive technology often resulted only in chaos. In the countryside land went untilled as peasants turned to industrial production. As many as 20 million to 30 million people died in famines that swept the country in 1960–1961, one of the greatest human disasters in world history. When Soviet premier Nikita Khrushchev criticized Chinese policy in 1960, Mao condemned him and his Russian colleagues as detestable "modern revisionists." The Russians abruptly cut off economic and military aid, splitting the communist world apart.

Mao lost influence in the party after the Great Leap Forward fiasco and the Sino-Soviet split, but in 1965 the old revolutionary staged a dramatic comeback. Fearing that China was becoming bureaucratic, capitalistic, and "revisionist" like the Soviet Union, Mao launched the **Great Proletarian Cultural Revolution.** He sought to purge the party and to recapture the revolutionary fervor of his guerrilla struggle (see pages 864–865). The army and the nation's young people, especially students, responded enthusiastically, organizing themselves into radical cadres called **Red Guards.** The young people denounced their teachers and practiced rebellion in the name of revolution. One Red Guard manifesto exulted that "Revolution is rebellion, and rebellion is the soul of Mao Tse-tung's thought."[2]

Great Proletarian Cultural Revolution *A movement launched by Mao Zedong that attempted to purge the party of time-serving bureaucrats and recapture the revolutionary fervor of his guerrilla struggle.*

Red Guards *Radical cadres formed by young people who would attack anyone identified as an enemy of either the Communist Party or Chairman Mao.*

The Red Guards sought to erase all traces of "feudal" and "bourgeois" culture and thought. Ancient monuments and countless works of art, antiques, and books were destroyed. Party officials, professors, and intellectuals were exiled to remote villages to purify themselves with heavy labor. Universities were shut down for years. Thousands of people died, many of them executed, and millions more were sent to rural forced-labor camps. The Red Guards attracted enormous worldwide attention and served as an extreme model for the student rebellions in the West in the late 1960s (see page 959).

The Limits of Reform

Mao and the Red Guards succeeded in mobilizing the masses, shaking up the party, and creating greater social equality. But the Cultural Revolution also created growing chaos and a general crisis of confidence, especially in the cities. Persecuted intellectuals, technicians, and purged party officials launched a counterattack on the radicals and regained much of their influence by 1969. Thus China shifted to the right at the same time that Europe and the United States did. This shift in China opened the door to a limited but lasting reconciliation between China and the United States in 1972.

The moderates were led by Deng Xiaoping (1904–1997), a long-time member of the Communist elite who had been branded a dangerous capitalist agent during the Cultural Revolution. After Mao's death in 1976, Deng and his supporters initiated a series of new policies, embodied in the ongoing campaign of the "Four Modernizations"—agriculture, industry, science and technology, and national defense.

China's 800 million peasants experienced the greatest and most beneficial change from this modernization campaign, what Deng proudly called China's "second revolution." At first glance this may seem surprising. Peasant support had played a major role in the 1949 Communist victory. After 1949 land reform and rationing undoubtedly improved the diet of poor peasants. Subsequently, literacy campaigns taught rural people how to read, and "barefoot doctors"—local peasants trained to do simple

● **Shaming of Enemies During the Cultural Revolution**   During the Chinese Cultural Revolution in the 1960s, young Chinese militants and Red Guards attacked people identified as enemies of the Communist Party and Chairman Mao. Many of these "enemies" were intellectuals such as teachers and artists, but they could be neighbors and even parents who were considered bourgeoisie. Here a victim is paraded through the streets wearing a dunce cap with his crimes written on it. *(Wide World Photos)*

diagnosis and treatment—brought modern medicine to the countryside. But rigid collectivized agriculture failed to provide either the peasants or the country with adequate food. Levels of agricultural production and per capita food consumption were only slightly higher in the mid-1970s than in 1937, before the war with Japan.

Determined to modernize the economy, Deng looked to the peasants as natural allies. China's peasants were allowed to farm the land in small family units rather than in large collectives and to produce what they could produce best and "dare to be rich." Peasants responded enthusiastically, increasing food production by more than 50 percent between 1978 and 1984.

The successful use of free markets and family responsibility in agriculture encouraged further economic experimentation. Foreign capitalists were allowed to open factories in southern China, and they successfully exported Chinese products around the world. Chinese private enterprise was also permitted in cities, where snack shops, beauty parlors, and a host of small businesses sprang up. China's Communist Party leaders also drew on the business talent of wealthy "overseas" Chinese in Hong Kong and Taiwan who knew the world market, needed new sources of cheap labor, and played a key role in the emerging Greater China. The Chinese economy grew rapidly between 1978 and 1987, and per capita income doubled in these years.

Change, however, was also circumscribed. Most large-scale industry remained state owned, and cultural change proceeded slowly. Above all, the Communist Party zealously preserved its monopoly of political power. When the worldwide movement for greater democracy and political freedom in the late 1980s also took root in China, the government responded by banning all demonstrations and slowing the trend toward a freer economy. Inflation then soared to more than 30 percent a year. The economic

● **Chinese Students in 1989** These exuberant demonstrators in Tiananmen Square personify the idealism and optimism of China's prodemocracy movement. After some hesitation the Communist government crushed the student leaders and their supporters with tanks and executions, reaffirming its harsh, authoritarian character. (*Erika Lansner/stockphoto.com*)

Tiananmen Square *The site of a Chinese student revolt in 1989 at which Communists imposed martial law and arrested, injured, or killed hundreds of students.*

reversal, the continued lack of political freedom, and the conviction that Chinese society was becoming more corrupt led China's idealistic university students to spearhead demonstrations in April 1989.

The students evoked tremendous popular support, and more than a million people streamed into Beijing's central **Tiananmen Square** on May 17 supporting their demands. The government then declared martial law and ordered the army to clear the students. Masses of courageous Chinese citizens blocked the soldiers' entry into the city for two weeks, but in the early hours of June 4, 1989, tanks rolled into Tiananmen Square. At least 700 students died as a wave of repression, arrests, and executions descended on China. China's Communist leaders claimed they had saved the country from plots to destroy socialism and national unity.

In the months after Tiananmen Square communism fell in eastern Europe, the Soviet Union broke apart, and China's rulers felt vindicated. They believed their strong action had preserved Communist power, prevented chaos, and demonstrated the limits of permissible reform. After some hesitation Deng, and his successor Jiang Zemin, reaffirmed economic liberalization. Private enterprise and foreign investment boomed in the 1990s. Consumerism was encouraged, and the living standard rose. But critics of Communist rule were jailed, and every effort was made to ensure the People's Army would again crush the people if ordered. Thus China coupled growing economic freedom with continued political repression, embracing only one half of the trend toward global liberalization and rejecting the other.

These policies continued into the twenty-first century. In 2001, after long negotiations, China joined the World Trade Organization, giving it all the privileges and obligations of participation in the liberal global economy. Politically communist, China now has a full-blown capitalist economy. From 1978, when Deng Xiaoping took over and launched economic reforms, through 2008, the Chinese economy has grown at an average annual rate of over 9 percent; foreign trade at an average of 16 percent. Average per capita income in China has doubled every ten years.

But China continues to have a miserable human rights record. In 2002 Hu Jintao succeeded the aging Jiang Zemin, and introduced modest legal reforms. He remains clearly committed, however, to maintaining a strong authoritarian state. As China prepared to host the 2008 Summer Olympic Games, there was some hope that, as promised, China's Communist leaders would make significant human rights, labor rights, and press freedom reforms before the games began. In spring 2008, however, the Chinese harshly crushed demonstrations in Tibet (see the feature "Individuals in Society: The Dalai Lama" on page 1061), which sparked worldwide protest, including disruption of the Olympic torch global relay. As the Olympic Games opened in August 2008, the Chinese, with only perfunctory pressure from world leaders, had made no effort to institute democratic reforms.

The Asian "Economic Tigers"

China's exploding economy has replicated the rapid industrial progress that characterized first Japan and then Asia's "Economic Tigers" (or "Four Dragons")—Taiwan, Hong Kong, Singapore, and South Korea.

Both South Korea and Taiwan were typical underdeveloped countries in the early postwar years—poor, small, agricultural, densely populated, and lacking in natural resources. They also had suffered from Japanese imperialism and from destructive civil wars with communist foes. Yet they managed to make good. How was this possible?

First, economic development became a national mission in South Korea and Taiwan. Radical land reform expropriated large landowners and drew the mass of small farmers into a competitive market economy. Probusiness governments cooperated with capitalists, opposed strikes, and did nothing to improve the long hours and low wages of self-sacrificing workers. These governments protected their own farmers and industrialists from foreign competition while also securing almost free access to the large American market. Second, both countries succeeded in preserving many cultural fundamentals even as they accepted and mastered Western technology. Third, tough nationalist leaders—Park Chung Hee in South Korea and Jiang Jieshi in Taiwan—maintained political stability at the expense of genuine political democracy.

After a military coup overthrew Park in 1980, South Korea suffered under an even more authoritarian regime through the 1980s until democracy was restored at the end of the decade. South Korea's economy, however, continued to grow and expand. By the late 1990s South Korea had one of the largest economies in the world and is a world leader in shipbuilding and high-technology products. Its GDP is about twenty times larger than North Korea's.

In 1949 after Jiang Jieshi had fled to Taiwan with his Nationalist (Kuomintang) troops and around 2 million refugees, he re-established the Republic of China (ROC) in exile. Over the next fifty years, Taiwan created one of the world's most highly industrialized capitalist economies, becoming a world leader in high-technology and electronic manufacturing and design.

● **Lights in the Night in the Eastern Hemisphere**   This NASA photo uniquely illustrates differences in wealth between the North and South. Human-made lights shine brightly from developed countries and heavily populated cities. Africa's continent-wide economic poverty is clearly evident, while North Korea sits in stark dark contrast to the blaze of light from South Korea and the other "Asian Tigers." *(Image by Craig Mayhew and Robert Simmons, NASA GSFC)*

A large threatening cloud hangs over the island, however. As one of the United Nations' founding members in 1945, Jiang's ROC government held one of the Security Council's five permanent seats. In 1971 the United Nations expelled the ROC, and its Security Council seat was given to the People's Republic of (mainland) China. This action left Taiwan in political limbo: should it remain the ROC or become an independent Republic of Taiwan? Meanwhile, mainland China claims authority over Taiwan, considers it part of "One China," and has threatened to attack if Taiwan declares its formal independence. Pro-independence candidate Chen Shui-bian defeated the Kuomintang candidate in 2000 to become the first non-Kuomintang president in Taiwan's postwar history. Though he adopted a somewhat more moderate stance, he still supported independence and remained defiant toward the mainland. On January 12, 2008, however, the Taiwanese people gave the Kuomintang Party (KMT) a landslide victory in parliamentary elections, and Chen immediately resigned as chairperson of his Democratic Progressive Party. The KMT won 81 of 113 seats in parliament. In March 2008 the KMT leader, Ma Ying-jeou, won the presidential elections with 58 percent of the vote. He has dropped talk of Taiwanese independence and is seeking closer relations with the mainland. Thus, the tension surrounding the standoff between China and Taiwan, potentially one of most explosive situations in the world, may have eased.

In 1965 the largely Chinese city of Singapore was pushed out of the Malayan-dominated Federation of Malaysia. The independent city-state of Singapore prospered on the hard work and inventiveness of its largely Chinese population. Singapore's government promoted education, private enterprise, high technology, and affordable housing for all citizens. Since the mid-1990s Singapore has enjoyed one of the highest per capita incomes in the world. The government, dominated by the People's Action Party since independence, forcefully promotes conservative family values and strict social discipline.

The British first occupied Hong Kong in 1841. Primarily a center of oceanic trade in the nineteenth century, Hong Kong turned to finance, such as banking and insurance, and to manufacturing in the twentieth. On July 1, 1997, the United Kingdom returned Hong Kong to Chinese control. Under the agreement Hong Kong became the Hong Kong Special Administrative Region (SAR) of China, and China promised that, under its "one country, two systems" formula, China's socialist economic system would not be imposed on Hong Kong. Hong Kong remains one of the most vibrant global economies. It is the world's tenth-largest trading entity and eleventh-largest banking center, and it continues to have one of the world's highest per capita GDPs.

Since recovering from a series of economic crises in the late 1990s, a vibrant, independent East Asia has emerged as an economic powerhouse, an event of enormous significance in long-term historical perspective.

Political and Economic Progress in Southeast Asia

While the Philippines and Indonesia gained independence quickly after 1945, the attainment of stable political democracy proved a more difficult goal. As ethnic conflicts and cold war battles divided their countries, Filipino and Indonesian leaders frequently turned to authoritarian rule and military power in an effort to impose order and unity. By the early twenty-first century both the Philippines and Indonesia were moving toward more stable governments and growing economies.

During the Second World War the Philippine Islands suffered greatly under Japanese occupation. After the war the United States retained its large military bases (they were finally closed in 1992) but granted the Philippines independence in 1946. The Philippines pursued American-style two-party competition until 1965 when President Ferdinand Marcos (1917–1989) subverted the constitution and ruled as dictator. In 1986 a widespread popular rebellion forced him into exile and Corazón Aquino became president. Aquino and the presidents who have followed her have made some progress in improving the economy. Many Filipinos work abroad. Their remittances back home, plus rapid growth in exports to China and strong sales of semiconductor electronics, helped the Philippine economy grow at over 7 percent in 2007. Despite the growing economy, communist insurgents and Muslim separatists continue to threaten the Philippines' political stability.

The Netherlands East Indies emerged in 1949 as independent Indonesia under the nationalist leader Achmed Sukarno (1901–1970). Like the Philippines, the populous new nation encompassed a variety of peoples, islands, and religions (85 percent of the population practices Islam; see Map 32.2 on page 995). A military coup led by General Suharto forced Sukarno out in 1965. Suharto's authoritarian rule concentrated mainly on economic development. Blessed with large oil revenues, Indonesia achieved solid economic growth for a generation. Increasingly tied to the world economy, Indonesia in 1997 was suddenly devastated by financial crisis. Suharto was forced to resign in 1998.

After Suharto's fall, freely elected governments attacked corruption and reversed the economic decline. In 2000 Indonesia gave East Timor political independence. In 2004 in the first direct presidential elections ever held, the Indonesians elected Susilo Bambang Yudhoyono as president. Despite years of natural disasters—a 2004 Indian Ocean tsunami, earthquakes, severe floods, and outbreaks of the bird flu (avian influenza)—and militant Islamic terrorist acts, the economy grew at over 6 percent in 2007, its fastest pace in eleven years.

The Reunification of Vietnam

French Indochina experienced the bitterest struggle for independence in Southeast Asia. The French tried to reimpose imperial rule there after the communist and nationalist guerrilla leader Ho Chi Minh (1890–1969) declared an independent republic in 1945, but they were decisively defeated in the 1954 Battle of Dien Bien Phu. At the subsequent international peace conference, French Indochina gained independence. Laos and Cambodia became separate states, and Vietnam was "temporarily" divided into two hostile sections at the seventeenth parallel pending elections to select a single unified government within two years.

● **Capitalism in Today's Vietnam** Swarms of "angry bees" in the street of Hanoi, Vietnam, where there are an estimated four million people and two million bikes. Motorbikes make up 90 percent of all the vehicles on the road in this rapidly modernizing country, and their numbers will only increase as Vietnam adopts market capitalism and its citizens have more disposable income. An accident death rate of over one thousand per month caused the government to mandate safety helmets as of 2008. (Maxim Marmur/Getty Images)

The elections were never held, and a civil war soon broke out between the two Vietnamese governments, one communist and the other anticommunist. The United States invested tremendous military effort but fought its Vietnam War (1964–1973) as a deeply divided country (see pages 959–961). The tough, dedicated communists eventually proved victorious in 1975 and created a unified Marxist nation. In 1986 Vietnamese communists began to turn from central planning toward freer markets and private initiative with mixed results. The Vietnamese economy has grown 7 to 8 percent per year since 1990, but these numbers are deceiving because inflation and unemployment are also very high. Vietnam remains one of the poorest countries in the region. Still, Communist officials are committed to a market economy, and Vietnam became the World Trade Organization's 150th member on January 11, 2007. Vietnam's Communist leaders, however, continue to zealously guard their monopoly of political power.

NEW NATIONS AND OLD RIVALRIES IN SOUTH ASIA

How did Hindus and Muslims adjust to the end of British colonial rule?

The South Asian subcontinent has transformed itself no less spectacularly than China, Japan, and the "Asian Tigers." India's national independence movements triumphed decisively over weakened and demoralized British imperialism after the Second World War. The newly independent nations of India, Pakistan, and Bangladesh exhibited many variations on the dominant themes of national renaissance and modernization, especially as the struggle for political independence receded into the past. Ethnic and religious rivalries greatly complicated the process of renewal and development.

The End of British India

After the First World War, Mahatma Gandhi and the Indian Congress Party developed the philosophy of Satyagraha (militant nonviolence) to oppose British rule of India and to lessen oppression of the Indian poor by the Indian rich (see pages 857–861). Gradually and grudgingly, Britain's rulers introduced reforms culminating in limited self-government in 1937.

The Second World War accelerated the drive toward independence. In 1942 Gandhi called on the British to "Quit India" and threatened another civil disobedience campaign. He and the other Congress leaders were quickly arrested and jailed for most of the war. Thus, India's wartime support for hard-pressed Britain was substantial but not always enthusiastic. Meanwhile, the Congress Party's prime political rival skillfully seized the opportunity to increase its influence.

Muslim League *The rival to the Indian Congress, it argued for separate homelands for Muslims and Indians.*

That rival was the **Muslim League,** led by the English-educated lawyer Muhammad Ali Jinnah (1876–1948). Jinnah feared Hindu domination of an independent Indian state led by the Congress Party. Asserting in nationalist terms the right of Muslim areas to separate from the Hindu majority, Jinnah described the Muslims of India as "a nation with our distinct culture and civilization, . . . our own distinctive outlook on life and of life."[3] In March 1940 Jinnah called on the British government to grant the Muslim and Hindu peoples separate homelands by dividing India into autonomous national states. Gandhi regarded Jinnah's two-nation theory as simply untrue and as promising the victory of hate over love.

Britain's Labour government agreed to speedy independence for India after 1945, but conflicting Hindu and Muslim nationalisms and religious hatred led to murderous clashes between the two communities in 1946. When it became clear that Jinnah

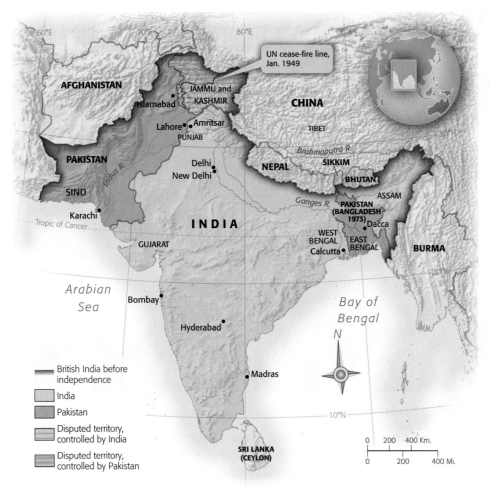

MAP 32.1 **The Partition of British India, 1947** Violence and fighting were most intense where there were large Hindu and Muslim minorities—in Kashmir, the Punjab, and Bengal. The tragic result of partition, which occurred repeatedly throughout the world in the twentieth century, was a forced exchange of populations and greater homogeneity on both sides of the border.

and the Muslim League would accept nothing less than an independent Pakistan, India's last viceroy—war hero Lord Louis Mountbatten (1900–1979)—proposed partition. Both sides accepted. At midnight on August 14, 1947, one-fifth of humanity gained political independence (see Map 32.1).

Yet independence through partition brought tragedy. In the weeks following independence communal strife exploded into an orgy of massacres and mass expulsions. Perhaps a hundred thousand Hindus and Muslims were slaughtered, and an estimated 5 million made refugees. Congress Party leaders were completely powerless to stop the wave of violence. "What is there to celebrate?" exclaimed Gandhi in reference to independence, "I see nothing but rivers of blood."[4] In January 1948, Gandhi himself was gunned down by a Hindu fanatic.

After the ordeal of independence, relations between India and Pakistan—both members of the British Commonwealth—remained tense. Fighting over the disputed area of Kashmir continued until 1949 and broke out again in 1965–1966, 1971, and 1999 (see Map 32.1).

Pakistan and Bangladesh

Pakistan's western and eastern provinces were separated by more than a thousand miles of Indian territory, as well as by language, ethnic background, and social custom. They shared only the Muslim faith. The Bengalis of East Pakistan constituted a

● **Bhutto's Assassination** Pakistani presidential candidate Benazir Bhutto stands up in her campaign van just moments before she was assassinated on December 27, 2007. In the initial confusion it was reported that an assassin fired at her with a pistol and then threw a bomb. Scotland Yard investigators later determined that she died when the force of the bomb explosion slammed her head into part of the open hatch. *(AP Images)*

majority of Pakistan's population as a whole but were neglected by the central government, which remained in the hands of West Pakistan's elite after Jinnah's death. In essence, East Pakistan remained a colony of West Pakistan.

Tensions came to a head in the late 1960s. Bengali leaders calling for virtual independence were charged with treason, and martial law was proclaimed in East Pakistan. In 1971 the Bengalis revolted. Despite savage repression the Bengalis won their independence as the new nation of Bangladesh in 1973. Bangladesh is the world's eighth most populous country, and also one of its poorest.

Emerging as completely separate states after 1973, Pakistan and Bangladesh both moved erratically from semi-authoritarian one-party rule toward competitive parliamentary systems with open elections. In the process each also experienced a series of military takeovers, restorations of civilian authority, political assassinations, and charges of official corruption. Each achieved some economic improvement but little social progress, especially for women.

India Since Independence

Jawaharlal Nehru (1889–1964) and the Congress Party ruled India for a generation after independence and introduced major social reforms. Hindu women and even young girls were granted legal equality, including the right to vote, to seek divorce, and to marry outside their castes. The constitution abolished the untouchable caste. In practice less discriminatory attitudes toward women and untouchables evolved slowly—especially in the villages, where 85 percent of the people lived.

The Congress Party leadership tried with modest success to develop the country economically by means of democratic socialism. But population growth of about 2.4 percent per year ate up much of the increase in output. Intense poverty remained the lot of most people and encouraged widespread corruption within the bureaucracy. The Congress Party maintained a moralizing neutrality in the cold war and sought to group India and other newly independent states in Asia and Africa into a "third force" of "nonaligned" nations. This effort culminated in the Afro-Asian Conference in Bandung, Indonesia, in 1955.

Nehru's daughter, Indira Gandhi (1917–1984), became prime minister in 1966. Mrs. Gandhi (whose deceased husband was no relation to Mahatma Gandhi) dominated Indian political life for a generation. In 1975 Mrs. Gandhi subverted parliamentary democracy and proclaimed a state of emergency. Attacking dishonest officials, black-marketeers, and tax evaders, she also threw the weight of the government behind a heavy-handed campaign of mass sterilization to reduce population growth. More than 7 million men were sterilized in 1976.

Many believed that Mrs. Gandhi's emergency measures marked the end of the parliamentary democracy and Western liberties introduced in the last phase of British rule. But Mrs. Gandhi—true to the British tradition—called for free elections. She suffered a spectacular electoral defeat, largely because of the vastly unpopular sterilization campaign and her subversion of democracy. Her successors, however, fell to fighting among themselves, and in 1980 Mrs. Gandhi won an equally stunning electoral victory. Her defeat and re-election undoubtedly strengthened India's democratic tradition.

Separatist ethnic nationalism plagued Mrs. Gandhi's last years in office. Democratic India remained a patchwork of religions, languages, and peoples, always threatening to further divide the country along ethnic or religious lines. Most notable among these were the 15 million Sikhs of the Punjab in northern India (see Map 32.1), who have their own religion—a blend of Islam and Hinduism—and a distinctive culture. Most Sikhs wanted greater autonomy for the Punjab, and by 1984 some Sikh radicals were fighting for independence. Mrs. Gandhi cracked down hard, and she was assassinated by Sikhs in retaliation. Violence followed as Hindu mobs slaughtered over a thousand Sikhs throughout India.

Elected prime minister in 1984 by a landslide sympathy vote, one of Mrs. Gandhi's sons, Rajiv Gandhi (1944–1991), showed considerable skill at effecting a limited reconciliation with a majority of the Sikh population. Under his leadership the Congress Party also moved away from the socialism of his mother and grandfather. In 1991 the Congress Party wholeheartedly embraced market reforms, capitalist development, and Western technology and investment. These reforms were successful, and since the 1990s India's economy has experienced explosive growth.

Holding power almost continuously from 1947, the Congress Party was challenged increasingly by Hindu nationalists in the 1990s. These nationalists argued forcefully that India was based, above all, on Hindu culture and religious tradition and that these values had been badly compromised by the Western secularism of Congress Party leaders and by the historical influence of India's Muslims. Campaigning also for a strong Indian military, the Hindu nationalist party finally gained power in 1998. The new government immediately exploded nuclear devices, asserting its vision of a militant Hindu nationalism. In 2004 a center-left coalition, the United Progressive Alliance (UPA), dominated by the Congress Party, regained control of the government.

Pakistan also exploded a nuclear weapon in 1998, and relations between Pakistan and India continued to worsen. In December 2001, the two nuclear powers had massive armies facing each other, poised for war, until intense diplomatic pressure forced them to step back from the abyss. In April 2005 both sides agreed to open business and trade relations and to work to negotiate a peaceful solution to the Kashmir dispute. Since then, although Islamic and Hindu chauvinism remain strong, this agreement has reduced the immense hostility that existed between the two countries.

● **Indira Gandhi's Funeral**   Covered with beautiful flower wreaths and carried to her funeral pyre by devoted friends, the body of the assassinated leader was then cremated in a solemn public ceremony according to Hindu religion and custom. Although the strong-willed Gandhi flirted with dictatorship, she nurtured and strengthened modern India's vibrant democratic tradition. *(David Turnley/Corbis)*

THE ISLAMIC HEARTLAND

What was the dual nature of nationalism in the Islamic heartland?

Throughout the vast *Ummah* ("world of Islam"; see Map 32.2), nationalism remained the primary political force after 1945. Anti-Western and anticommunist in most instances, Muslim nationalism generally combined a strong secular state with deep devotion to Islam. Cold war conflicts and enormous oil resources enhanced the region's global standing.

Nationalism in the Arab countries of North Africa and Southwest Asia wore two faces. The idealistic side focused on the Pan-Arab dream of uniting all Arabs in a single nation that would be strong enough to resist the West, defeat the new state of Israel, and achieve genuine independence. Despite political and economic alliances like the Arab League, this vision floundered on intense regional, ideological, and personal rivalries. Thus a more practical Arab nationalism focused largely on nation building within former League of Nations mandates and European colonies.

Subsequent one-party dictatorships, corruption, and continued daily hardship, however, caused some Islamic preachers and devoted laypeople in the late 1970s to charge that the model of modernizing, Western-inspired nationalism, had failed. These critics, labeled fundamentalists in the West, urged a return to strict Islamic principles and traditional morality. They evoked a sympathetic response among many educated Muslims as well as among villagers and city dwellers, and in Iran they gained power.

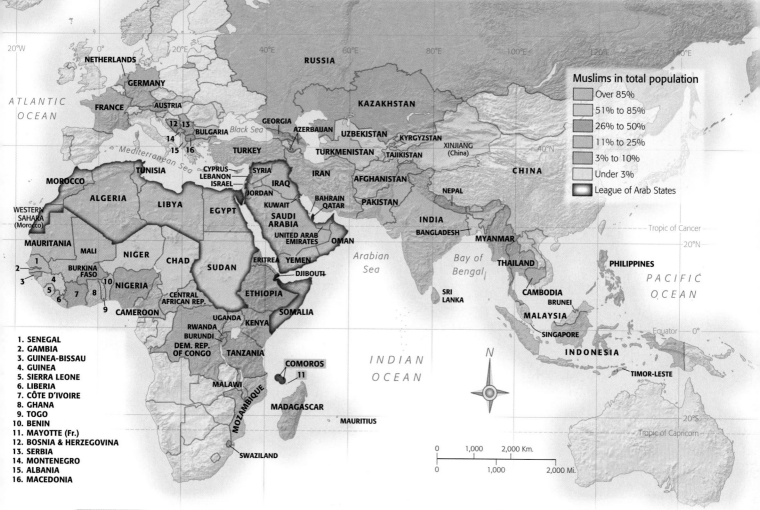

Muslims in total population
- Over 85%
- 51% to 85%
- 26% to 50%
- 11% to 25%
- 3% to 10%
- Under 3%
- League of Arab States

1. SENEGAL
2. GAMBIA
3. GUINEA-BISSAU
4. GUINEA
5. SIERRA LEONE
6. LIBERIA
7. CÔTE D'IVOIRE
8. GHANA
9. TOGO
10. BENIN
11. MAYOTTE (Fr.)
12. BOSNIA & HERZEGOVINA
13. SERBIA
14. MONTENEGRO
15. ALBANIA
16. MACEDONIA

MAP 32.2 **Modern Islam, 2007** Although the Islamic heartland remains the Middle East and North Africa, Islam is growing steadily in Africa south of the Sahara and is the faith of heavily populated Indonesia. (*Source: Data from* CIA World Factbook, *2007*)

The Arab-Israeli Conflict

Before the Second World War, Arab nationalists were loosely united in their opposition to the colonial powers and to Jewish migration to Palestine. The British had granted independence to Egypt and Iraq before the war, and the French followed suit with Syria and Lebanon in 1945. Attention then focused even more sharply on British-mandated Palestine. The situation was volatile. Jewish settlement in Palestine was strenuously opposed by the Palestinian Arabs and the seven independent states of the newly founded Arab League (Egypt, Iraq, Jordan, Lebanon, Saudi Arabia, Syria, and Yemen). Murder and terrorism flourished, nurtured by bitterly conflicting Arab and Jewish nationalisms.

The British announced in 1947 their intention to withdraw from Palestine in 1948. The insoluble problem was dumped in the United Nations' lap. In November 1947 the United Nations General Assembly passed a plan to partition Palestine into two separate states—one Arab and one Jewish (see Map 32.3). The Jews accepted, but the Arabs rejected, partition of Palestine.

By early 1948 an undeclared civil war was raging in Palestine. When the British mandate officially ended on May 14, 1948, the Jews proclaimed the state of Israel. Arab countries immediately attacked the new Jewish state, but the Israelis drove off the invaders and conquered more territory. Roughly nine hundred thousand Arab refugees fled or were expelled from old Palestine. This war left an enormous legacy of Arab bitterness toward Israel and its political allies, Great Britain and the United

Primary Source:
Arab and Israeli Soccer Players Discuss Ethnic Relations in Israel, 2000
Learn how Arabs and Jews get along in the world of professional soccer in Israel.

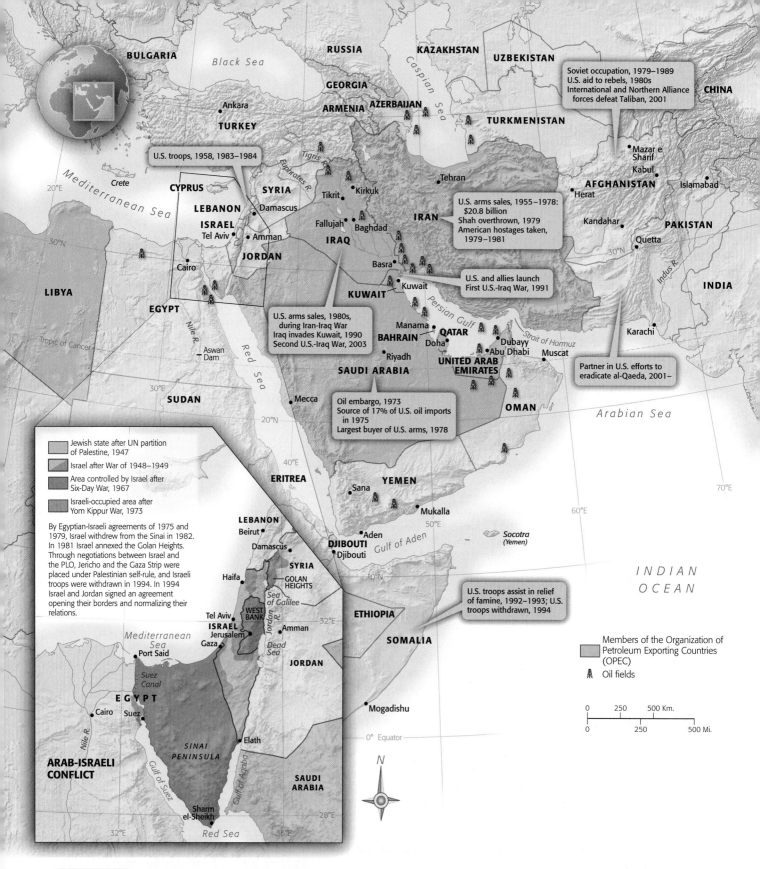

MAP 32.3 **Palestine, Israel, and the Middle East**

Since the British mandate expired on May 14, 1948, there have been five major wars and innumerable armed clashes in what was formerly Palestine. After winning the War of Independence in 1948, Israel achieved spectacular victories in 1967 in the Six-Day War, occupying the Sinai Peninsula, the Golan Heights, and the West Bank. The Yom Kippur War of 1973 eventually led to the Israeli evacuation of the Sinai and peace with Egypt. In 1993 Israel and the Palestine Liberation Organization agreed in principle to self-rule for Palestinian Arabs in the West Bank in five years, and in 1994 the Gaza Strip and Jericho were placed under the administration of the Palestinian Authority. Negotiations in Washington in 2000 failed to reach a final peace agreement, and armed conflict began again. The Israeli army reoccupied much of the West Bank, and the peace process collapsed. The election of Mahmoud Abbas as PLO leader following the death of Yasir Arafat in 2004 resulted in resumed negotiations and some concessions by both sides. These included, in July and August 2005, the removal of all Jewish settlers from the Gaza Strip.

States. It also led in 1964 to the creation of the **Palestine Liberation Organization (PLO)**, a loose union of Palestinian refugee groups opposed to Israel.

The Development of Egypt

In Egypt the humiliation of Arab defeat triggered a nationalist revolution. A young army colonel named Gamal Abdel Nasser (1918–1970) drove out the corrupt and pro-Western king Farouk in 1952. Nasser enjoyed powerful influence in the Middle East and throughout Asia and Africa.

Nasser preached the gospel of neutralism in the Cold War, but accepted Soviet aid to demonstrate Egypt's independence of the West. Relations with Israel and the West worsened, and in 1956 Nasser nationalized the European-owned Suez Canal Company, Europe's last vestige of power in the Middle East. Outraged, the British and French joined forces with the Israelis and successfully invaded Egypt. The Americans, however, unexpectedly sided with the Soviets and forced the British, French, and Israelis to withdraw from Egypt. Nasser's great victory encouraged anti-Western radicalism, hopes of Pan-Arab political unity, and a vague "Arab socialism." Yet the Arab world remained deeply divided except in their bitter opposition to Israel and support for the right of Palestinian refugees to return to their homeland.

In late 1977 Egypt's president Anwar Sadat made a pathbreaking official visit to Israel, which led to direct negotiations between Israel and Egypt, effectively mediated by U.S. president Jimmy Carter, and a historic though limited peace settlement. Each country gained: Egypt got back the Sinai Peninsula, which Israel had taken in the 1967 Six-Day War (see Map 32.3), and Israel obtained peace and normal relations with Egypt. Israel also kept the Gaza Strip, taken from Egypt in 1967 and home to about 1 million Palestinians. Some Arab leaders denounced Sadat's initiative as treason.

After Sadat's assassination by Islamic radicals in 1981, Egypt's relations with Israel deteriorated badly. Yet Egypt and Israel maintained their fragile peace, and Sadat's successor as president, Hosni Mubarak (r. 1981 to present), concentrated on curbing fundamentalism and promoting economic development.

Israel and the Palestinians

In 1988 young Palestinians in the occupied territories began a prolonged campaign of rock throwing and civil disobedience against Israeli soldiers. Inspired increasingly by Islamic fundamentalists, the Palestinian uprising eventually posed a serious challenge not only to Israel but also to the secular Palestinian liberation movement, long led from abroad by Yasir Arafat (1929–2004). The result was an unexpected and mutually beneficial agreement in 1993 between Israel and the PLO. Israel agreed to recognize Arafat's organization and start a "peace process" that granted Palestinian self-rule in Gaza and Jericho and called for self-rule throughout the West Bank in five years. In return, Arafat renounced terrorism and abandoned the long-standing demand that Israel must withdraw from all land occupied in the 1967 war.

The 1993 agreement and the peace process were hotly debated in an increasingly divided Israel. In 1995 a right-wing Jewish extremist assassinated Prime Minister Yitzhak Rabin (r. 1992–1995). In 1996 a coalition of opposition parties won a slender majority, charging the Palestinian leadership with condoning anti-Jewish terrorism. The new Israeli government limited Palestinian self-rule where it existed and expanded Jewish settlements in the West Bank. On the Palestinian side, dissatisfaction with the peace process grew. Between 1993 and 2000 the number of Jewish settlers in the West Bank doubled to two hundred thousand and Palestinian per capita income declined by 20 to 25 percent. In addition, many Palestinians viewed Arafat's administration as corrupt and self-serving.

Palestine Liberation Organization (PLO) *Created in 1964, a loose union of Palestinian refugee groups opposed to Israel and working toward Palestinian home rule.*

● **Israel's Wall of Separation** A Palestinian man waves as he walks across the hills near Jerusalem, where Israel's wall of separation divides Israeli and Palestinian territory. Israelis argue that the wall, made of concrete and covered with razor wire, protects them from Palestinian militants and suicide bombers. Increasingly it is described by Palestinians and others as a Berlin Wall–like structure, a symbol of Israelis forcing a separation, an Israeli version of apartheid, between the two peoples. *(AP Photo/ Wide World Photos)*

Nevertheless, in early 2000 Arafat, Israeli prime minister Ehud Barak, and U.S. president Bill Clinton met in Washington to negotiate a final peace agreement. The key Israeli proposal, however, did not offer what the Palestinians wanted—a sovereign and independent state—and they rejected it. The failed negotiations unleashed an explosion of tit-for-tat violence beginning in September 2000 in Israel and in the West Bank and Gaza Strip. In 2003 the Israelis began building a "fence" around the West Bank, which has met opposition from Israelis and Palestinians alike.

The death of Yasir Arafat, the PLO's long-time leader, in November 2004 marked a major turning point in the Israeli-Palestinian dispute. Mahmoud Abbas, Arafat's successor, is viewed as moderate and pragmatic. After taking office in January 2005, he immediately called for a peaceful solution to the conflict. Peace talks between the two sides have made very little progress, however, and in some ways matters have become worse. In January 2006 the militant Palestinian Islamist political party Hamas won elections in the Gaza Strip, seizing control from Abbas and the PLO. (See the Epilogue.) While Hamas remains isolated in Gaza, Abbas and the Israelis have been negotiating over the West Bank, with some renewed U.S. involvement by President George W. Bush and Secretary of State Condoleezza Rice in 2007–2008.

Nationalism, Fundamentalism, and Competition

The recent history of the non-Arab states of Turkey and Iran and of the Arab state of Iraq (see Map 32.2) testifies to the diversity of national development in the Muslim world. It also dramatically illustrates the intense competition between rival states and the growing strength of Islamic revival.

Turkey remained basically true to Atatürk's vision of a thoroughly modernized, secularized, Europeanized state (see pages 852–854). Islam continued to exert less influence in daily life and thought as Turkey joined NATO in 1952 and eventually sought full membership in the European Union (EU). Turkey, however, was not one of the ten eastern European countries admitted to the EU in 2004. Many Europeans questioned Turkey's dedication to the protection of human rights and feared that Turkish membership in the EU would result in a large inflow of unwanted Muslim immigrants. Turkey's long-running dispute with the Cyprian Greeks over Cyprus (which became an EU member in 2004) and continued refusal to take responsibility for its role in the Armenian genocide during World War I have further clouded its chances for membership.

After 1945 Iran tried again to follow Turkey's example, as it had before 1939 (see page 854). Once again its success was limited. The new shah—Muhammad Reza Pahlavi (r. 1941–1979), the son of Reza Shah Pahlavi—angered Iranian nationalists by courting Western powers and Western oil companies. In 1953, the freely elected prime minister Muhammad Mossaddeq tried to nationalize the British-owned Anglo-Iranian Oil Company, and the shah was forced to flee to Europe. But Mossaddeq's victory was short-lived. Loyal army officers, with the help of the American CIA, quickly restored the shah to his throne.

The shah set out to build a powerful modern nation to ensure his rule. Iran's gigantic oil revenues provided the necessary cash. The shah undermined the power bases of the traditional politicians—large landowners and religious leaders—by means of land reform, secular education, and increased power for the central government. Modernization surged forward, but at the price of ancient values, widespread corruption, and harsh dictatorship. The result was a violent reaction against modernization and secular values: an Islamic revolution in 1979 aimed at infusing strict Islamic principles into all aspects of personal and public life. Led by the Islamic cleric Ayatollah Ruholla Khomeini, the fundamentalists deposed the shah and tried to build their vision of a true Islamic state.

Iran's Islamic republic frightened its neighbors. Iraq, especially, feared that Iran—a nation of Shi'ite Muslims—would succeed in getting Iraq's Shi'ite majority to revolt against its Sunni leaders. Thus in September 1980 Iraq's strongman, Saddam Hussein (1937–2006), launched a surprise attack. With their enormous oil revenues and military machines, Iranians and Iraqis—Persians and Arabs—clashed in a savage eight-year conflict that killed hundreds of thousands of soldiers before finally grinding to a halt in 1988.

Emerging from the eight-year war with a big, tough army equipped by Western countries and the Soviet bloc, Hussein now eyed Kuwait's great oil wealth. In August 1990 he ordered his forces to overrun his tiny southern neighbor and proclaimed its annexation to Iraq. To Saddam's surprise, his aggression brought a vigorous international response and touched off the Gulf War. In early 1991 his troops were chased out of Kuwait by an American-led, United Nations–sanctioned military coalition, which included some Arab forces from Egypt, Syria, and Saudi Arabia.

Iraq and Iran went in different directions in the 1990s. The United Nations Security Council imposed stringent economic sanctions on Iraq as soon as it invaded Kuwait, and these sanctions remained after the Gulf War to force Iraq to destroy its weapons of mass destruction. United Nations inspectors destroyed many such weapons, but the United States charged Iraq with deceit and ongoing weapons development. An American-led invasion of Iraq in 2003 overthrew Saddam Hussein's regime (see pages 1025–1026).

As secular Iraq spiraled downward toward collapse and foreign occupation, Iran appeared to back away from fundamentalism. Following the constitution established by the Ayatollah Khomeini, executive power in Iran was divided between a Supreme Leader and twelve-member Guardian Council selected by high Islamic clerics, and a president and parliament elected by universal male and female suffrage. After 1990 the Supreme Leader remained a very conservative religious leader, but a growing reform movement pressed for a relaxation of strict Islamic decrees and elected a moderate, Mohammad Khatami, as president in 1997 and again in 2001. The Supreme

Leader, controlling the army and the courts, vetoed many of Khatami's reform measures and jailed some of the religious leadership's most vocal opponents.

Khatami had to step down in 2005, and elections were held in June. Dubious election returns gave the presidency to an ultraconservative Islamic hardliner, Mahmoud Ahmadinejad. His populist speeches and actions have made him quite popular among some elements of Iranian society. His calls for Israel's destruction; support of extremist groups in Iraq, Gaza, and Lebanon; and refusal to suspend Iran's nuclear program, however, have caused much anxiety and anger in the West. Despite this setback, many Iranians believe moderate, secular reform is inevitable, for, as one Iranian journalist observed, "Fundamentalism is good for protest, good for revolution, and good for war, but not so good for development. No country can organize its society on fundamentalism."[5]

Algeria and Civil War

The important North African country of Algeria also illustrated the development of nationalism and then fundamentalism. Nationalism in the French colony of Algeria was emboldened by Nasser's great triumph in Egypt and by France's defeat in Indochina. But Algeria's large European population—known as the *pieds noirs* ("black feet") because its members wore black shoes instead of sandals—was determined to keep Algeria part of France, and the Algerian war for independence was long, bitter, and bloody. Finally, in 1962, Algeria became an independent Arab state. The European population quickly fled.

The victorious anticolonial movement, known as the **National Liberation Front** (FLN), used revenues from Algeria's nationalized oil fields to promote state-owned industries, urban growth, and technical education. But the FLN also imposed a one-party state, crushing dissent. In the 1980s many dissatisfied Algerians looked to Islam for moral and social revival, and in the early 1990s the Islamic opposition swept municipal and national elections. The FLN called out the army, claiming the fundamentalists would "hijack" democracy and create an Islamic dictatorship. Military rule then led to growing violence and armed struggle between the government and the fundamentalist opposition that has lasted into the 2000s. Algeria's ruthless civil war placed in bold relief the cultural and ideological divisions simmering just below the surface in the Muslim world.

● **Iranian Elections, June 2005** This Iranian woman displays her support for the relatively moderate former Iranian president, Akbar Hashemi Rafsanjani, during an election rally in June 2005. To the surprise, shock, and dismay of Iranian moderates and many in the West, the ultraconservative mayor of Teheran, Mahmoud Ahmadinejad, won a landslide victory. With his election all the governing organs of the Iranian government were in the hands of ultraconservative Islamic hardliners. (*AP Photo/Wide World Photos*)

IMPERIALISM AND NATIONALISM IN SUB-SAHARAN AFRICA

How did Kwame Nkrumah represent the new leaders of independent Africa?

National Liberation Front *The name of the victorious anticolonial movement in Algeria.*

Most of sub-Saharan Africa won political independence fairly rapidly after World War II. Only Portugal's colonies and white-dominated southern Africa remained beyond the reach of African nationalists by 1964. The rise of independent states in sub-Saharan Africa resulted directly from both a reaction against Western imperialism and the growth of African nationalism.

The Growth of African Nationalism

Western intrusion was the critical factor in the development of African nationalism, as it had been in Asia and the Middle East. But two things were different about Africa. First, because the imperial system and Western education did not solidify in Africa until after 1900 (see pages 741–743), national movements began to come of age only in the 1920s and reached maturity after 1945. Second, Africa's multiplicity of ethnic groups, coupled with imperial boundaries that often bore no resemblance to existing ethnic boundaries, greatly complicated the development of political—as distinct from cultural—nationalism. Was a modern national state to be based on ethnic or clan loyalties (as it had been in France and Germany)? Was it to be a continent-wide union of all African peoples? Or would the multiethnic territories arbitrarily carved out by competing European empires become the new African nations? Only after 1945 did a tentative answer emerge.

A few educated West Africans in British colonies had articulated a kind of black nationalism before 1914. But the first real impetus came from the United States and the British West Indies. The most renowned participant in this "black nationalism" was W. E. B. Du Bois (1868–1963). The first black to receive a Ph.D. from Harvard, this brilliant writer and historian organized Pan-African congresses in Paris during the Versailles Peace Conference and in Brussels in 1921. **Pan-Africanists** sought black solidarity and, eventually, a vast self-governing union of all African peoples. The flamboyant Jamaican-born Marcus Garvey (1887–1940) was the most influential Pan-Africanist voice in Africa. Young, educated Africans rallied to his call of "Africa for the Africans" and European expulsion from Africa.

Pan-Africanists *People, such as Marcus Garvey, who promoted solidarity among all blacks and the eventual self-governing union of all African peoples.*

In the 1920s many educated French and British Africans experienced a strong surge of pride and cultural nationalism. African intellectuals in Europe formulated and articulated the rich idea of *négritude,* or blackness: racial pride, self-confidence, and joy in black creativity and the black spirit. This westernized African elite pressed for more equal access to government jobs, modest steps toward self-government, and an end to humiliating discrimination. They claimed the right to speak for ordinary Africans and denounced the government-supported chiefs as "Uncle Toms," yet their demands remained moderate.

The Great Depression was the decisive turning point in the development of African nationalism. For the first time unemployment was widespread among educated Africans. African peasants and small business people who had been drawn into world trade, and who sometimes profited from booms, also felt the agony of the decade-long bust, as did urban workers. In some areas the result was unprecedented mass protest. The Gold Coast **cocoa holdups** of 1930–1931 and 1937–1938 are the most famous examples.

cocoa holdups *A mass protest in the 1930s by Gold Coast producers of cocoa, who refused to sell their beans to British firms and instead sold them directly to European and American chocolate manufacturers.*

Cocoa completely dominated the Gold Coast's economy. As prices plummeted after 1929, cocoa farmers refused to sell their beans to the large British firms that fixed prices and monopolized the export trade. Instead, the farmers organized cooperatives to cut back production and sell their crops directly to European and American chocolate manufacturers. The cocoa holdups succeeded in mobilizing much of the population against the foreign companies and demonstrated the power of mass organization and mass protest. Mass movements for national independence would not be far behind.

Achieving Independence with New Leaders

The repercussions of the Second World War in black Africa greatly accelerated the changes begun in the 1930s. Many African soldiers who served in India were powerfully impressed by Indian nationalism. As mines and plantations strained to meet wartime demands, towns mushroomed into cities where tin-can housing, inflation, and shortages of consumer goods created discontent and hardship.

Nationalism in Black Africa

1919	Du Bois organizes first Pan-African congress.
1920s	Cultural nationalism grows among Africa's educated elites.
1929	Great Depression brings economic hardship and discontent.
1930–1931	Farmers in the Gold Coast organize first cocoa holdups.
1939–1945	World War II accelerates political and economic change.
1951	Nkrumah and Convention People's Party win national elections in Ghana.
1957	Nkrumah leads Ghana—former Gold Coast—to independence.
1958	De Gaulle offers commonwealth status to France's African territories; Guinea alone chooses independence.
1960	Nigeria becomes an independent state.
1966	Ghana's Nkrumah deposed in military coup.
1967	Ibos secede from Nigeria to form state of Biafra.
1979	Nigeria's military rulers permit elected civilian government.
1980	Blacks rule Zimbabwe—formerly Southern Rhodesia—after long civil war with white settlers.
1984	South Africa's whites maintain racial segregation and discrimination.
1989–1990	South African government begins process of reform; black leader Nelson Mandela freed from prison.
1994	Mandela elected president of South Africa.

Western imperialist attitudes also changed. Both the British and the French acknowledged the need for rapid social and economic improvement in their colonies; both began sending money and aid on a large scale for the first time. The principle of self-government was written into the United Nations charter and was supported by Great Britain's postwar Labour government. Thus the key question for African colonies became their rate of progress toward self-government. The British and the French were in no rush. But a new breed of African leader was emerging. Impatient and insistent, these modern African nationalists were remarkably successful: by 1964 almost all of western, eastern, and central Africa had achieved statehood, usually without much bloodshed.

These new postwar African leaders formed an elite by virtue of advanced European or American education, and they were profoundly influenced by Western thought. But compared with the interwar generation of educated Africans, they were more radical and humbler in social origin. Among them were former schoolteachers, union leaders, government clerks, and unemployed students, as well as lawyers and prize-winning poets.

Postwar African leaders accepted prevailing colonial boundaries to avoid border disputes and achieve freedom as soon as possible. Sensing a loss of power, traditional rulers sometimes became the new leaders' worst political enemies. Skillfully, the new leaders channeled postwar hope and discontent into support for mass political organizations. Eventually they came to power by winning the general elections that the colonial governments belatedly called to choose their successors.

Ghana Shows the Way

Perhaps the most charismatic of this generation of African leaders was Kwame Nkrumah (1909–1972). Nkrumah spent ten years studying in the United States, where he was deeply influenced by European socialists and Marcus Garvey. Nkrumah returned to the Gold Coast immediately after the Second World War and entered politics. Under his leadership the Gold Coast—which he rechristened "Ghana"—became the first independent African state to emerge from colonialism.

Nkrumah came to power by building a radical mass party appealing particularly to modern elements—former servicemen, market women, union members, urban toughs, and cocoa farmers. He and his party injected the joy and enthusiasm of religious revivals into their rallies and propaganda: "Self-Government Now" was their credo, secular salvation the promise.

Rejecting halfway measures—"We prefer self-government with danger to servitude in tranquility"—Nkrumah and his Convention People's Party staged strikes and riots. Arrested, the "Deliverer of Ghana" campaigned from jail and saw his party win a smashing victory in the 1951 national elections. Called from prison to head the transitional government, Nkrumah and his nationalist party defeated both westernized moderates and more traditional political rivals in free elections. By 1957 Nkrumah had achieved worldwide fame and influence as Ghana became independent.

> **Primary Source:**
> **Parable of the Eagle, Limbo, Prayer for Peace, Vultures**
> *The literature of four African writers expresses the traumatic effects of colonialism.*

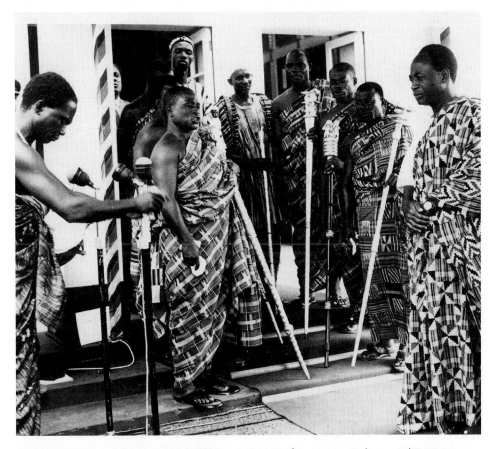

● **The Opening of Parliament in Ghana**   As part of an ancient ritual, two medicine men pour out sacred oil and call on the gods to bless the work of the Second Parliament and President Kwame Nkrumah, standing on the right. The combination of time-honored customs and modern political institutions was characteristic of African states after they secured independence. *(Wide World Photos)*

After Ghana's breakthrough, independence for other African colonies followed rapidly. As in Algeria, the main problem in some colonies was the permanent white settlers, as distinguished from the colonial officials. Wherever white settlers were numerous, as in Kenya, they sought to preserve their privileged position. But only in Southern Rhodesia and South Africa were whites numerous enough to prevail for long. Southern Rhodesian whites declared independence illegally in 1965 and held out until 1980, when black nationalists won a long liberation struggle and renamed the country Zimbabwe. Majority rule in South Africa took even longer.

French-Speaking Regions

Primary Source:
Comments on Algeria, April 11, 1961
Read excerpts of a press conference held by Charles de Gaulle, in which he declares France's willingness to accept Algerian independence.

Decolonization took a somewhat different course in French-speaking Africa. France tried hard to hold on to Indochina and Algeria after 1945. Thus although France upped its aid to its African colonies, independence remained a dirty word until Charles de Gaulle came to power in 1958. Seeking to head off radical nationalists and receiving the crucial support of moderate black leaders, de Gaulle chose a divide-and-rule strategy. He divided the French West Africa and French Equatorial Africa federations into thirteen separate governments, thus creating a "French commonwealth." Plebiscites were called in each territory to ratify the new arrangement. An affirmative vote meant continued ties with France; a negative vote signified immediate independence and a complete break with France.

De Gaulle's gamble was shrewd. The educated black elite—as personified by the influential poet-politician Léopold Sédar Senghor, who now led Senegal's government—loved France and dreaded a sudden divorce. (See the feature "Individuals in Society: Léopold Sédar Senghor, Poet and Statesman.") They also wanted French aid to continue. France, in keeping with its ideology of assimilation, had given the vote to its educated colonial elite after the Second World War, and about forty Africans held French parliamentary seats after 1946. For both cultural and practical reasons, therefore, French Africa's leaders tended to be moderate and in no rush for independence.

In Guinea, however, a young nationalist named Sekou Touré (1922–1984) led his people in overwhelming rejection of the new constitution in 1958. Inspired by Ghana's Nkrumah, Touré laid it out to de Gaulle face-to-face: "We have to tell you bluntly, Mr. President, what the demands of the people are. . . . We have one prime and essential need: our dignity. But there is no dignity without freedom. . . . We prefer freedom in poverty to opulence in slavery."[6]

The Belgians, long-time practitioners of paternalism coupled with harsh, selfish rule in their enormous Congo colony, had always discouraged the development of an educated elite. In 1959, therefore, when after wild riots they suddenly decided to grant independence, the fabric of government simply broke down. Independence was soon followed by violent ethnic conflict, civil war, and foreign intervention. The Belgian Congo was the great exception to black Africa's generally peaceful and successful transition to independence between 1957 and 1964.

• • • • • • • • • • • • • • • • •

SUB-SAHARAN AFRICA SINCE 1960

What are some of the common features of independent Africa since 1960?

The facility with which most of black Africa achieved independence stimulated buoyant optimism in the early 1960s. But within a generation democratic government and civil liberties gave way to one-party rule or military dictatorship and widespread corruption.

The rise of authoritarian government in Africa after independence must be viewed in historical perspective. Representative institutions on the eve of independence were

Léopold Sédar Senghor, Poet and Statesman

President Léopold Sédar Senghor in 1965. *(Hulton Archive/Getty Images)*

Of all the modern leaders in French-speaking Africa, Léopold Sédar Senghor (1906–2001) was the most famous and the most intriguing. His early years in a dusty village in southern Senegal were happy and varied. Later, in cold and lonely Paris, he would feast on memories of this "kingdom of childhood." Senghor's father, a successful peanut merchant, lived in the port city of Joal and had two dozen children and several wives. His last wife, Senghor's mother, remained in her village, where her extended family taught the boy the legends and mysteries of his people. In a famous poem, Senghor later wrote that his mother's brother, Uncle Waly the shepherd, could hear "what is beyond hearing," and that he lovingly explained to the wondering child "the signs that the Ancestors give in the calm seas of the constellations."*

Islam is Senegal's majority religion and the Wolof its dominant ethnic group. But Senghor's family was staunchly Christian and of the Serer people, and when he was seven, his practical father sent him to a French mission school near Joal. Learning French and Wolof, Senghor made rapid progress. When he was seventeen, his teachers sent him on to the colonial capital of Dakar, where he became the top student in the predominately white lycée. In 1928 he received a rare scholarship for advanced study in Paris. Working hard in elite schools and settling on a university career, Senghor became the first African to win the equivalent of a Ph.D. He then took a position as a classics teacher in a lycée near Paris. It was an extraordinary achievement.

Senghor's chance to pursue advanced education reflected French colonial policy in Africa. The French believed that most Africans deserved only a little practical schooling, but they also wanted to create a tiny elite of "black Frenchmen." This elite would link the French rulers and the African masses, who would need permanent French guidance. In the 1930s the brilliant Senghor seemed a model of elitist assimilation.

In fact, however, Senghor was experiencing a severe identity crisis. Who was he? How could he reconcile his complex African heritage with his French education and culture? Making close friends with other black intellectuals in Paris and strongly influenced by African

American music and literature, Senghor concluded that he would never be a "black Frenchman," for in European eyes the most accomplished African always remained exotic and inferior. He then found a new identity in racial pride and the idea of *négritude,* or blackness (see page 1001). Yet Senghor did not repudiate Europe. Instead, he reconciled his identity crisis—his being torn "between the call of the Ancestors and the call of Europe"—by striving to hold his "two sides" in equilibrium and "peaceful accord." He advocated "cross-fertilization" for Africa and Europe, which, he believed, would benefit both continents.†

Serving in the French army in World War II and turning to politics after 1945, Senghor was elected Senegal's deputy to the French National Assembly. Idolized in Senegal, he joined with other African deputies to press for greater autonomy, as well as for harmony between France and Africa. He led Senegal into Charles de Gaulle's "French commonwealth" in 1958 and then on to independence in 1960. All the major political parties in Senegal were merged to form a one-party government, with Senghor as president. Wisely avoiding dictatorship, ethnic conflict, and military rule, he led Senegal until 1980, when he retired voluntarily. Lionized in France as a great poet and statesman, Senghor was increasingly criticized by some young Senegalese, who grumbled that the aging leader had become too cooperative with France—a real "black Frenchman."

Questions for Analysis

1. What cultural and intellectual forces influenced Senghor's development? Why did he have difficulty reconciling these influences?

2. How did Senghor fit into the whole process of decolonization and African independence?

*Quoted in J. Vaillant, *Black, French, and African: A Life of Léopold Sédar Senghor* (Cambridge, Mass.: Harvard University Press, 1990), p. 18.

†Ibid., p. 146.

an imperial afterthought, and the new African countries faced tremendous challenges. Above all, ethnic divisions threatened civil conflicts that could tear the fragile states apart. Yet this did not happen. Strong leaders used nationalism, first harnessed to throw off foreign rule, to build one-party regimes and promote unity. Unfortunately, nation building by idealistic authoritarians often deteriorated into brutal dictatorships, frequent military coups, and civil strife. Then, in the early 1990s, a powerful reaction to this decline, inspired by the eastern European revolutions, resulted in a surge of democratic protest, which achieved major political gains and rekindled in part the optimism of the independence era.

Striving for National Unity

Africa's imperial legacy is more negative than positive. Although some countries left generally better legacies than others—Britain's was better than Belgium's or Portugal's, for example—overall the "civilizing mission" did more harm than good. On something of a positive note, the forty or so states (see Map 32.4 on page 1008) inherited varying degrees of functioning bureaucracies, some elected political leaders, and some modern infrastructure—transportation, schools, hospitals, and the like. And every country inherited the cornerstone of imperial power—a tough, well-equipped army to maintain order. But other features of the imperialist legacy served to torment independent Africa.

The disruption of traditional life had caused real suffering and resulted in unobtainable post-independence expectations. The prevailing export economies were weak, lopsided, and concentrated in foreign hands. Technical, managerial, and medical skills were in acutely short supply. Above all, the legacy of political boundaries imposed by foreigners without regard to ethnic and cultural groupings weighed heavily on post-independence Africa. Nearly every new state encompassed a variety of peoples who might easily develop conflicting national aspirations.

Great Britain and France had granted their African colonies democratic government as they prepared to depart. Yet belated Western-style democracy served the new multiethnic states poorly. After freedom from imperialism no longer provided a unifying common objective, political parties often coalesced along regional and ethnic lines. Many African leaders concluded that democracy threatened to destroy the existing states and prevent social and economic progress. Thus these leaders maintained the authoritarian tradition they inherited from the imperialists, and free elections often gave way to dictators and one-party rule.

After Ghana won its independence, for instance, Nkrumah jailed without trial his main opponents—chiefs, lawyers, and intellectuals—and outlawed opposition parties. Nkrumah worked to build a "revolutionary" one-party state and a socialist economy. By the mid-1960s his grandiose economic projects had almost bankrupted Ghana, and in 1966 the army suddenly seized power while he was visiting China.

The French-speaking countries also shifted toward one-party government to promote state unity and develop distinctive characteristics that could serve as the basis for statewide nationalism. Mali followed Guinea into Marxist radicalism. Senegal and the Ivory Coast stressed moderation and close economic and cultural ties with France.

Like Nkrumah, many of the initial leaders at the helm of one-party states were eventually overthrown by military leaders. The rise of would-be Napoleons was lamented by many Western liberals and African intellectuals, who often failed to note that military rule was also widespread in Latin America, Asia, and the Near East in the 1970s and 1980s.

As elsewhere, military rule in Africa was authoritarian and undemocratic. In Uganda, for instance, the brutal Idi Amin (1925?–2003) seized power in 1971, packed the army with his ethnic supporters, and terrorized the population for a decade. Yet military regimes generally did manage to hold their countries together, and many, like their Latin American counterparts (see pages 979–982), were committed to social and economic modernization. Drawing on an educated and motivated elite, they sometimes accomplished much. As economic and social conditions stagnated and often declined in African countries from the mid-1970s to the early 1990s, however, army leaders and dictators became more and more greedy and dishonest. By the late 1980s military rulers and one-party authoritarian regimes were coming under increasing pressure to hand over power to more democratic forces.

Nigeria, Africa's Giant

Nigeria's history illustrates just how difficult genuine nation building could be after independence was achieved. "Nigeria" was a name coined by the British to designate their nineteenth-century conquests in the Niger River basin, which encompassed many ancient kingdoms and hundreds of ethnic groups. Also, for administrative convenience, the British consolidated the northern Muslim territories and the southern Christian or animist areas. Despite this diverse population, by 1945 Nigeria had spawned a powerful independence movement, and independence was achieved in 1960 (see Map 32.4).

The key constitutional question was the relationship between the central government and the various regions. Ultimately Nigeria adopted a federal system, whereby the national government at Lagos shared power with three regional or state governments in

● **Nigerian Presidential and Parliamentary Elections, April 2003**   In April 2003, Nigeria held its first presidential and parliamentary elections since the end of military rule in 1999. Over 60 million voters turned out across the country to choose for candidates from thirty political parties. Here federal police watch as election officials begin counting the ballots after sorting them by party. *(Corbis)*

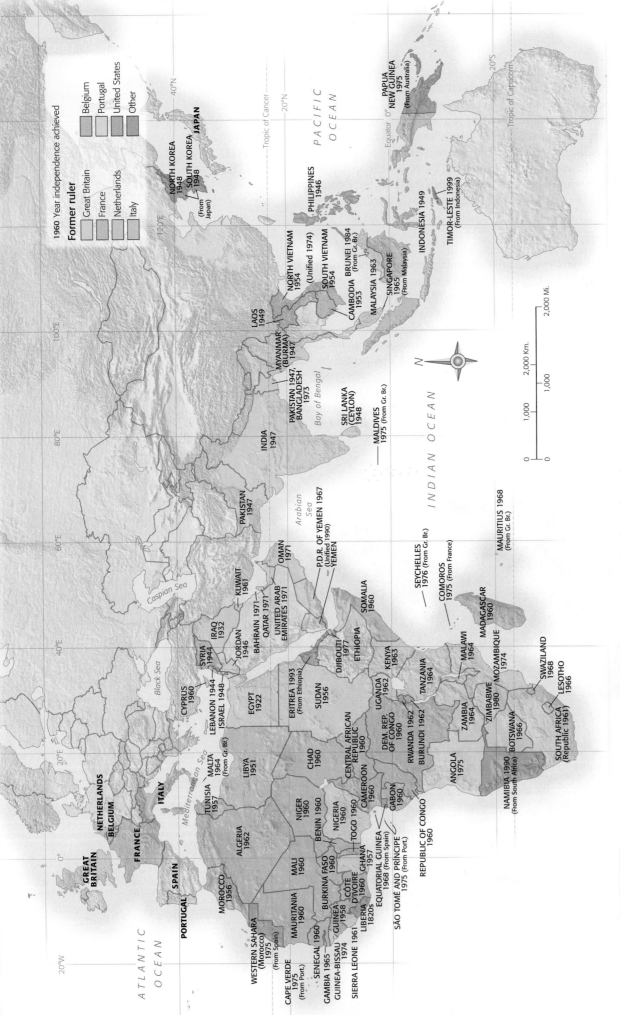

MAP 32.4 **The New States in Africa and Asia** Divided primarily along religious lines into two states, British India led the way to political independence in 1947. Most African territories achieved statehood by the mid-1960s, as European empires passed away, unlamented.

Former ruler

1960 Year independence achieved

- Great Britain
- France
- Netherlands
- Italy
- Belgium
- Portugal
- United States
- Other

the north, west, and east. Each region had a dominant ethnic group and a corresponding political party. The parties were expected to cooperate in the national parliament, and the rights of minorities were protected by law.

After independence Nigerians' bright hopes gradually dimmed because of growing ethnic rivalries. In 1967 these intense rivalries erupted into a civil war. The crisis began in 1964 when some young military officers, many of whom were Ibos from the southeast, seized the government and executed its leaders.

At first the young officers were popular, but the Muslim northerners had long distrusted the hard-working, clannish, non-Muslim Ibos. When the Ibo-led military council proclaimed a centralized dictatorship, wild mobs in northern cities massacred thousands of Ibos. When a group of northern officers then seized the national government in a countercoup, the traumatized Ibos revolted and proclaimed the independent state of Biafra in 1967.

The Biafran war lasted three years. The Ibos fought with heroic determination, believing that political independence was their only refuge from genocide. Heavily outnumbered, the Ibos were gradually surrounded. Perhaps millions starved to death as Biafra became a symbol of monumental human tragedy.

Having preserved the state in the 1960s, Nigeria's military rulers focused on building a nation in the 1970s. Although the federal government held the real power, the country was divided into nineteen small, manageable units to handle local and cultural matters. The defeated Ibos were pardoned, and Iboland was rebuilt with federal oil revenues.

Except for a couple of brief periods of civilian rule, combinations of Hausa-Fulani Muslim army officers ruled until 1998, when the brutal military dictator General Sani Abacha suddenly died and gave Nigeria renewed hope for unity and democracy. In 1999 Nigerians voted in free elections and re-established civilian rule; the April 2003 elections marked the first civilian transfer of power in Nigeria's history.

Nigeria is the world's eleventh-largest oil producer and a member of OPEC. Oil provides about 20 percent of Nigeria's GDP, 95 percent of its foreign exchange earnings, and about 65 percent of its budgetary revenues. Nigeria still needs to diversify its economy, however, if it is to overcome massive poverty and become economically stable. Nigeria's leaders must also calm the religious strife that continues to divide the country. Since 2000, riots between Muslims and non-Muslims have left thousands dead in the predominately Muslim northern Nigerian states, where there is a movement to implement shari'a (Islamic law) as the law of the state.

The Struggle in Southern Africa

After the great rush toward political independence in the early 1960s, decolonization stalled. Southern Africa remained under white minority rule, largely because of the numerical strength and determination of its white settlers.

In Portuguese Angola and Mozambique, the white population actually increased from 70,000 to 380,000 between 1940 and the mid-1960s, as white settlers using forced native labor established large coffee farms. As economic exploitation grew, so did resentment. Nationalist liberation movements arose to wage unrelenting guerrilla warfare. After a coup overturned the long-established dictatorship in Portugal, African liberation forces seized control in Angola and Mozambique in 1975. Shortly thereafter a coalition of nationalist groups also won in Zimbabwe after a long struggle.

The battle in South Africa threatened to be still worse. The racial conflict in the white-ruled Republic of South Africa could be traced back in part to the outcome of the South African War (see page 816). After the British finally conquered the inland Afrikaner republics, they agreed to grant all of South Africa self-government—South

Africa became basically a self-governing British dominion, like Canada and Australia—as soon as possible. English and moderate Afrikaners ruled jointly and could also decide which nonwhites, if any, should vote.

In 1913 the new South African legislature passed the **Native Land Act,** which limited black ownership of land to native reserves encompassing a mere one-seventh of the country. Poor, overpopulated, and too small to feed themselves, the rural native reserves served as a pool of cheap, temporary black labor for white farms, gold mines, and urban factories. Legally, the black worker was only a temporary migrant who could be returned at will by the employer or the government. The native reserves system, combining racial segregation and indirect forced labor, formed the foundation of white supremacy in South Africa.

Some extreme Afrikaner nationalists, however, refused to accept defeat and any British political presence. They elaborated an even more potently racist Afrikaner nationalist platform of white supremacy and racial segregation that between 1910 and 1948 gradually won them political power from their English-speaking settler rivals. After their decisive 1948 electoral victory, Afrikaner nationalists spoke increasingly for a large majority of South African whites.

Once in control, successive Afrikaner governments wove the somewhat haphazard early racist measures into an authoritarian fabric of racial discrimination and inequality. This system was officially known as **apartheid,** meaning "apartness" or "separation." The population was divided into four legally unequal racial groups: whites, blacks, Asians, and racially mixed "coloureds." Although Afrikaner propagandists claimed that apartheid served the interests of all racial groups by preserving separate cultures and racial purity, most observers saw it as a way of maintaining the lavish privileges of the white minority, which accounted for only one-sixth of the total population.

After 1940, South Africa became the most highly industrialized country in Africa. Rapid urbanization followed, changing the face of the country, but good jobs in the cities were reserved for whites. Whites lived in luxurious modern central cities. Blacks, as temporary migrants, were restricted to outlying black townships plagued by poverty, crime, and white policemen.

South Africa's harsh white supremacy elicited many black nationalist protests from the 1920s onward. By the 1950s blacks—and their coloured, white, and Asian allies—were staging large-scale peaceful protests. A turning point came in 1960, when police at Sharpeville fired into a crowd of demonstrators and killed sixty-nine blacks. The main black nationalist organization—the **African National Congress (ANC)**—was then outlawed but sent some of its leaders abroad to establish new headquarters. Other members, led by a young black lawyer named Nelson Mandela (b. 1918), stayed in South Africa to set up an underground army to oppose the government. Captured after seventeen months, Mandela was tried for treason and sentenced to life imprisonment. (See the feature "Listening to the Past: The Struggle for Freedom in South Africa" on pages 1018–1019.)

By the late 1970s the white government had apparently destroyed the moderate black opposition within South Africa. Operating out of the sympathetic black states of Zimbabwe and Mozambique to the north, the militant ANC turned increasingly to armed struggle. South Africa struck back hard and forced its neighbors to curtail the ANC's guerrilla activities. Fortified by these successes, South Africa's white leaders launched in 1984 a program of cosmetic "reforms." For the first time, the 3 million coloureds and the 1 million South Africans of Asian descent were granted limited parliamentary representation. But no provision was made for any representation of the country's 22 million blacks, and laws controlling black movement and settlement were maintained.

The government's self-serving reforms provoked black indignation and triggered a massive reaction. In the segregated townships young black militants took to the

---

Native Land Act   *A 1913 South African law that limited black ownership of land to native reserves encompassing only one-seventh of the country.*

apartheid   *The system of racial segregation and discrimination that was supported by the Afrikaner government.*

African National Congress (ANC)   *The main black nationalist organization in South Africa; it was led by Nelson Mandela.*

Primary Source:
The Rivonia Trial Speech to the Court
Read how Nelson Mandela defended himself against charges of treason before an all-white South African court in 1964.

● **Men of Destiny** Nelson Mandela shakes hands with Frederik de Klerk following a televised presidential debate in the 1994 electoral campaign. Mandela won and replaced de Klerk as president of South Africa after 350 years of white supremacy. De Klerk became vice president. Both leaders vowed to build a multiracial democratic society. *(Mark Peters/Sipa Press)*

streets, attacking in particular black civil servants and policemen as agents of white oppression. Heavily armed white security forces clashed repeatedly with black protesters, who turned funerals for fallen comrades into mass demonstrations. Between 1985 and 1989 five thousand died and fifty thousand were jailed without charges because of the political unrest.

By 1989 the white government and the black opposition had reached an impasse. Black protesters had been bloodied but not beaten, and their freedom movement had gathered worldwide support. The U.S. Congress had applied strong sanctions against South Africa in October 1986, and the Common Market had followed. The white government still held power, but harsh repression of black resistance had failed.

The political stalemate ended in September 1989 with the election of a new state president, Frederik W. de Klerk, an Afrikaner lawyer and politician. A late-blooming reformer, de Klerk cautiously opened a dialogue with ANC leaders. Negotiating with Nelson Mandela, whose reputation had soared during his long years in prison, de Klerk lifted the state of emergency, legalized the ANC, and freed Mandela in February 1990. Mandela then courageously suspended the ANC's armed struggle and met with de Klerk for serious talks on South Africa's political future. They reached an agreement calling for universal suffrage, which meant black majority rule. They also guaranteed the civil and economic rights of minorities, including job security for white government workers.

Elected South Africa's first black president by an overwhelming majority in May 1994, Mandela told his jubilant supporters of his "deep pride and joy—pride in the ordinary, humble people of this country. . . . And joy that we can loudly proclaim from the roof tops—free at last!"[7] Heading the new "government of national unity," which included de Klerk as vice president, Mandela and the South African people set about building a democratic, multiracial nation. The new constitution guaranteed all political parties some legislative seats until 1998.

In an imaginative attempt to heal the wounds of apartheid, the new black majority government established the Truth and Reconciliation Commission. This commission let black victims speak out and share their suffering, and it also offered white perpetrators amnesty from prosecution in return for fully confessing their crimes. Mandela's ministers repudiated their earlier socialist beliefs and accepted global capitalism as the only way to develop the economy and reduce widespread black poverty.

In 1999 Thabo Mbeki succeeded Mandela as South Africa's president. The magnitude of the problems facing Mandela and Mbeki in availability of health care, housing, electricity, water, and the other amenities necessary for a decent standard of living in the twenty-first century were truly daunting, but significant progress has been made. Much still needs to be done, and all under the heavy burden of the worst AIDS crisis in the world (see pages 1055–1056). Still, South Africa at independence had a better education system, a more viable infrastructure, and a more diversified economy than any other African country. Many people across southern Africa, and even farther north, are looking to South Africa to be the economic engine that drives the continent.

Political Reform in Africa Since 1990

Democracy's triumph in South Africa was part of a broad trend toward elected civilian government that swept through sub-Saharan Africa after 1990. Political protesters rose up and forced one-party authoritarian regimes to grant liberalizing reforms and call national conferences, which often led to competitive elections and new constitutions. These changes occurred in almost all African countries; in the words of two leading scholars, "they amounted to the most far-reaching shifts in African political life since the political independence of thirty years earlier."[8]

Many factors contributed to this historic watershed. The anticommunist revolutions of 1989 in eastern Europe were extremely important. They showed Africans that even the most well-entrenched one-party regimes could be opposed, punished for prolonged misrule, and replaced with electoral competition and even democracy. The decline of military rule in Latin America and the emerging global trend toward political and economic liberalism worked in the same direction.

The end of the cold war also transformed Africa's relations with Russia and the United States. Both superpowers had viewed Africa as an important cold war battleground, and both had given large-scale military and financial aid to their allies, as well as to "uncommitted" African leaders who often played one side against the other. Communism's collapse in Europe brought an abrupt end to communist aid to Russia's African clients, leaving them weakened and much more willing to compromise with opposition movements.

American involvement in Africa also declined. During the cold war U.S. leaders had generally supported "pro-Western" African dictators, no matter how corrupt or repressive. This interventionist policy gave way to a less intense (and much cheaper) interest in free elections and civil rights in the 1990s. A striking example of this evolution was steadfast U.S. support for the "anticommunist" General Mobutu Sese Seko after he seized power in 1965 in Zaire (the former Belgian Congo, renamed the Democratic Republic of the Congo in 1997). Mobutu looted and impoverished his country for decades before the United States cut off aid in the early 1990s, thereby helping an opposition group topple the dying tyrant in 1997.

If events outside Africa established conditions favoring political reform, Africans themselves were the principal actors in the shift toward democracy. They demanded reform because long years of mismanagement and repression had delegitimized one-party rule.

Above all, the strength of the democratic opposition rested on a growing class of educated urban Africans, for post-independence governments had enthusiastically expanded opportunities in education, especially higher education. In the typical West African state of Cameroon, the number of students graduating from the French-speaking national university jumped from a minuscule 213 in 1961 to 10,000 in 1982 and 41,000 in 1992.[9] The growing middle class of educated professionals—generally pragmatic, moderate, and open to new ideas—chafed at the ostentatious privilege of tiny closed elites and pressed for political reforms that would democratize social and economic opportunities. Thus after 1990 sub-Saharan Africa participated fully in the global trend toward greater democracy and human rights.

The world's media have generally focused on the African governments and economies that failed in the years since 1990. Eight years into the twenty-first century, however, many African countries continue to make significant progress in the consolidation of democracy and human rights. Even some of the countries that experienced horrible civil war and nearly complete disintegration in the 1990s and early 2000s—such as Sierra Leone, Liberia, Angola, the Central African Republic, and Guinea-Bissau—have begun to pull back from the abyss. Ivory Coast experienced years of civil war after its first-ever military coup in 1999. Rebels continue to control the country's northern half, but they and the government met and signed the Ouagadougou Agreement in March 2007, committing themselves to disarmament and reunification and the holding of elections sometime in 2008.

Democracy, however, is still a long struggle away in many African countries. All of North Africa remains under the control of one-party, authoritarian rulers, and Eritrea, Ethiopia, Equatorial Guinea, Zimbabwe, Swaziland, Cameroon, and Gambia have increasingly brutal dictatorships. Sudan's authoritarian Islamic rulers ended their long civil war with the Christians and animists in the south, only to have pro-government Arab militias attack Muslim ethnic Africans in the western Darfur region. The genocidal attacks have caused tens of thousands of deaths and an estimated 2 million refugees. Congo-Kinshasa, Rwanda, Burundi, and Somalia remain perilously close to the abyss of unimaginable violence they experienced in the 1990s. In Kenya, riots following the bitterly contested and questionable re-election of Mwai Kibaki as president on December 27, 2007, resulted in over 250 deaths in the first week after the election. Often considered one of Africa's most stable nations, Kenya unexpectedly erupted into chaos, with interethnic violence forcing hundreds of thousands to flee their homes.

Many of the most stable, democratic countries are in southern Africa: Botswana, South Africa, Zambia, and Namibia have all made the transition from colonialism to democracy. With a few stops and starts, Malawi, Nigeria, Niger, and Madagascar are also making good progress. Much of the political progress is closely linked to economic progress. As Zimbabwe's authoritarian regime under Robert Mugabe has created a corrupt, immoral, human rights nightmare, it has also suffered total economic collapse. More politically stable countries such as Ghana have seen their economies grow and foreign investments increase. Countries in western and central Africa may soon undergo revolutionary political and economic change as a result of the oil and natural gas boom in those regions. Chad, Mauritania, Angola, Nigeria, Gabon, São Tomé and Príncipe, Congo Brazzaville, and Equatorial Guinea could all benefit from complete economic turnarounds, and others will follow.

• • • • • • • • • • • • • • • • • • • •

INTERPRETING THE EXPERIENCES OF THE EMERGING WORLD

How do the writings of Chinua Achebe represent the common experiences of peoples in the emerging world?

Having come of age during and after the struggle for political emancipation, numerous intellectuals embraced the vision of Third World solidarity, and some argued that genuine independence and freedom from outside control required a total break with the former colonial powers and a total rejection of Western values. This was the mes-

● **Nigeria's Conscience** Chinua Achebe's powerful novels focus on complex and believable individuals caught up in the unfolding drama of colonialism, independence, and nation building in Africa. Achebe is an intensely serious writer, a man who speaks for his people and believes in the high moral calling of literature and art. *(Photo, Chido Nangwu)*

sage of Frantz Fanon (1925–1961) in his powerful study of colonial peoples, *The Wretched of the Earth* (1961).

According to Fanon, a French-trained black psychiatrist from the Caribbean island of Martinique, decolonization is always a violent and totally consuming process whereby one "species" of men, the colonizers, is completely replaced by an absolutely different species—the colonized, the wretched of the earth. During decolonization the colonized masses mock colonial values, "insult them, and vomit them up" in a psychic purge.

Fanon believed that throughout Africa and Asia the former imperialists and their local collaborators—the "white men with black faces"—remained the enemy:

During the colonial period the people are called upon to fight against oppression; after national liberation, they are called upon to fight against poverty, illiteracy, and underdevelopment. The struggle, they say, goes on.

. . . We are not blinded by the moral reparation of national independence; nor are we fed by it. The wealth of the imperial countries is our wealth too. . . . Europe is literally the creation of the Third World. The wealth which smothers her is that which was stolen from the underdeveloped peoples.[10]

Fanon's passionate, angry work became a sacred text for radicals attacking imperialism and struggling for liberation.

As countries gained independence and self-rule, some writers looked beyond wholesale rejection of the industrialized powers. They too were "anti-imperialist," but often also activists and cultural nationalists who applied their talents to celebrating the rich histories and cultures of their peoples. Many did not hesitate to criticize their own leaders or fight against oppression and corruption.

The Nigerian writer Chinua Achebe (b. 1930) rendered these themes with acute insight and vivid specificity in his short, moving novels. Achebe sought to restore his people's self-confidence by reinterpreting the past. For Achebe the "writer in a new nation" had first to embrace the "fundamental theme":

This theme—quite simply—is that the African people did not hear of culture for the first time from Europeans; that their societies were not mindless but frequently had a philosophy of great depth and volume and beauty; that they had poetry and above all, they had dignity. It is this dignity that many African peoples all but lost in the colonial period, and it is this that they must now regain. The worst thing that can happen to any people is the loss of their dignity and self-respect. The writer's duty is to help them regain it by showing what happened to them, what they lost.[11]

In *Things Fall Apart* (1958) Achebe achieved his goal by vividly bringing to life the men and women of an Ibo village at the beginning of the twentieth century, with all their virtues and frailties. Woven into the story are the proverbs and wisdom of a sophisticated people and the beauty of a vanishing world. In later novels Achebe portrays the post-independence disillusionment of many writers and intellectuals, which reflected trends in many developing nations in the 1960s and 1970s: the rulers seemed increasingly corrupted by Western luxury and estranged from the rural masses.

From the 1970s onward Achebe was active in the struggle for democratic government in Nigeria. In his novel *Anthills of the Savannah* (1989), he calls upon Africa to stand on its own two feet, take responsibility, and realize that widespread corruption is frustrating hopes of progress and genuine independence. Yet in his recent essays and speeches he also returns to his earlier theme of the West's enduring low opinion of Africa—ever the "dark continent," the savage, non-Western "other world."

The Nobel Prize–winning novelist V. S. Naipaul, born in Trinidad in 1932 of Indian parents, also castigated governments in the developing countries for corruption, ineptitude, and self-deception. Another of Naipaul's recurring themes is the poignant loneliness and homelessness of people uprooted by colonialism and Western expansion.

Chapter Summary

To assess your mastery of this chapter, go to
bedfordstmartins.com/mckayworld

• *How was Latin America similar to, and different from, the other Third World nations?*

Nearly all the countries of Central and South America had gained their independence by the mid-1800s. This was just the time when Europe initiated a second great period of colonization that resulted in the colonization of much of Africa, Asia, and the Middle East. Despite their independence, many Latin Americans still believed the West was economically exploiting their countries through a form of neocolonialism. Politically throughout most of the twentieth century, Latin American countries were ruled by conservative, authoritarian leaders, some of them harsh and cruel dictators supported by the West. Thus many Latin Americans felt closer ties to the colonized peoples of Asia and Africa than they did to Western colonizers. In the 1980s much of Latin America turned toward free elections, civil liberties, and freer markets, abandoning the long-standing commitment to economic nationalism.

• *How did the defeat of Japan lead to East Asian resurgence after World War II?*

When World War II ended with the Japanese defeat, long suppressed nationalist movements pushed for political independence across East Asia. Mao Zedong's Communist forces took over in China, and the pro-Western Nationalist leader Jiang Jieshi was defeated. Meanwhile, thirty-five years of Japanese occupation of the Korean peninsula ended only to have the country divided, with the northern half controlled by a communist government installed by Stalin. The North became one of the harshest dictatorships and poorest countries in the world, while the South became one of the "Asian tigers," a modern, industrial powerhouse with one of the highest standards of living in the world. The other Asian tigers—Taiwan, Hong Kong, and Singapore—also left the war and colonial rule behind them to develop vibrant global economies. Vietnam had to fight a long war of independence against the French and then the Americans before beginning an economic recovery.

Key Terms

Great Leap Forward
Great Proletarian Cultural Revolution
Red Guards
Tiananmen Square
Muslim League
Palestine Liberation Organization (PLO)
National Liberation Front
Pan-Africanists
cocoa holdups
Native Land Act
apartheid
African National Congress (ANC)

• How did Hindus and Muslims adjust to the end of British colonial rule?

The Hindu and Muslim populations of India threw off British colonial rule only to go to war among themselves. Mahatma Gandhi was unable to convince the two groups to remain united in an independent India, and the Muslims broke away to create two new countries, Bangladesh and Pakistan. Pakistan and India have remained at odds ever since, often violently, because of religious hatred and territorial disputes in the Kashmir region of northwest India.

• What was the dual nature of nationalism in the Islamic heartland?

The Muslim world was also rejuvenated after 1945, most notably under Nasser in Egypt. Nasser was respected throughout the Arab world for having stood up to the West and was a symbol of the pan-Arab, anti-Western movement. Pan-Arabism, the uniting of all Arabs into a single nation, was a dream of many Arabs, but regional, ideological, and personal rivalries made such unification impossible. Nationalism thus took a more traditional turn as individual states developed out of territories that had been League of Nations mandates and European colonies. Common to all these states was a deep devotion to Islam.

• How did Kwame Nkrumah represent the new leaders of independent Africa?

In black Africa a generation of nationalist leaders successfully guided colonial territories to self-rule by the middle of the 1960s. The father of independent Africa was Kwame Nkrumah, a Ghanaian who, like many African nationalists, had spent many years studying in the West. He returned to Ghana after World War II and led an independence movement against British rule. Again, like many other nationalist leaders, Nkrumah was arrested by the British after leading mass strikes and demonstrations and was elected while in jail to lead a transitional government. In 1957 Ghana became the first sub-Saharan country to gain independence from colonial rule.

• What are some of the common features of independent Africa since 1960?

By the mid-1960s nearly all African countries had won independence. The two largest colonial powers, Britain and France, had tried, although belatedly, to set up democratic governments in their former colonies. The new leaders of these countries, however, soon turned their backs on democracy and resorted to authoritarian, one-party rule. Opposition parties were outlawed, and political opponents were jailed, sent into exile, or killed. Many of these early dictators were overthrown by military juntas, as happened, for example, in Ghana and Nigeria. Despite the high expectations all Africans held after throwing off colonial rule, most have lived, and continue to live, under harsh and corrupt authoritarian governments.

• How do the writings of Chinua Achebe represent the common experiences of peoples in the emerging world?

There are many artists in the emerging world who have eloquently described the common experiences of peoples living under colonial rule and then in newly independent nations. One of the most famous of these artists is Chinua Achebe, a Nigerian writer whose novels have been translated into many languages because of their universal appeal. One of Achebe's primary themes is that Africans had their own cultures, philosophies, poetry, and dignity before the Europeans arrived and tried to force their own values on the peoples they colonized. This theme he fully developed in his first and most widely read novel, *Things Fall Apart.* In later novels Achebe described the disillusionment felt by many Africans (and peoples of Asia and Latin America as well) with the corruption and authoritarian rule of post-independence governments.

Suggested Reading

Beck, Roger B. *The History of South Africa.* 2000. Introduction to South African history with emphasis on the twentieth century.

Chang, Jung, and Jon Halliday. *Mao: The Unknown Story.* 2005. Controversial new biography of the Chinese communist leader.

Church, Peter. *A Short History of South-East Asia.* 4th ed. 2005. A concise but comprehensive survey of the region's history.

Collins, Robert O., and James M. Burns. *A History of Sub-Saharan Africa.* 2007. Clearly written introduction to the continent's history.

Davidson, Basil. *The Black Man's Burden: Africa and the Curse of the Nation State.* 1993. A thought-provoking reconsideration by a noted historian.

Du Bois, W. E. B. *The World and Africa.* 1947. A classic text by the distinguished American black thinker.

Jayakar, Pupul. *Indira Gandhi: An Intimate Biography.* 1993. Very readable narrative of the powerful and controversial Indian prime minister.

Guha, Ramachandra. *India After Gandhi: The History of the World's Largest Democracy.* 2007. In-depth study of the last sixty years of Indian history and development.

Kenyatta, Jomo. *Facing Mount Kenya.* 1953. Powerful commentary and autobiography by one of Africa's foremost revolutionary and political leaders.

Lowenthal, Abraham F., and Gregory F. Treverton, eds. *Latin America in a New World.* 1994. Analyzes the move toward regional cooperation and market economies.

Meredith, Robyn. *The Elephant and the Dragon: The Rise of India and China and What It Means for All of Us.* 2005. Useful and accessible introduction to these two economic giants.

Mahbubani, Kishore. *The New Asian Hemisphere: The Irresistible Shift of Global Power to the East.* 2008. A history and analysis of the rise of Asia in world politics and economics by one of Asia's leading intellectuals.

Nehru, Jawaharlal. *An Autobiography.* 1962. Classic personal account of India's history in the first half of twentieth century by its first president.

Osborne, Milton. *Southeast Asia: An Introductory History.* 9th rev. ed. 2005. Classic introduction to the region.

Wasserstrom, Jeffrey N., ed. *Twentieth Century China: New Approaches.* 2002. Collection of essays on cultural and national developments using recently released archives.

Notes

1. S. Schram, *Mao Tse-tung* (New York: Simon and Schuster, 1966), p. 151.
2. Quoted in P. B. Ebrey, ed., *Chinese Civilization and Society: A Source Book* (New York: Free Press, 1981), p. 393.
3. Quoted in W. Bingham, H. Conroy, and F. Iklé, *A History of Asia,* vol. 2, 2d ed. (Boston: Allyn and Bacon, 1974), p. 459.
4. Quoted in K. Bhata, *The Ordeal of Nationhood: A Social Study of India Since Independence, 1947–1970* (New York: Atheneum, 1971), p. 9.
5. Quoted in B. Baktiari and H. Vaziri, "Iran's Liberal Revolution?" *Current History,* January 2002, p. 21.
6. Quoted in R. Hallett, *Africa Since 1875: A Modern History* (Ann Arbor: University of Michigan Press, 1974), pp. 378–379.
7. *Chicago Tribune,* May 3, 1994, section 1, p. 5.
8. M. Bratton and N. van de Walle, *Democratic Experiments in Africa: Regime Transitions in Comparative Perspectives* (Cambridge: Cambridge University Press, 1997), p. 3.
9. D. Birmingham and P. Martin, eds., *History of Central Africa: The Contemporary Years Since 1960* (London: Routledge, 1998), p. 59.
10. F. Fanon, *The Wretched of the Earth* (New York: Grove Press, 1968), pp. 43, 93–94, 97, 102.
11. C. Achebe, *Morning Yet on Creation Day* (London: Heinemann, 1975), p. 81.

Listening to the PAST

The Struggle for Freedom in South Africa

Many African territories won political freedom in the mid-1960s, but in South Africa the struggle was long and extremely difficult. Only in 1990 did the white government release Nelson Mandela from prison and begin negotiations with the famous black leader and the African National Congress (ANC). Only in 1994 did Mandela and the ANC finally come to power and establish a new system based on majority rule and racial equality.

Born in 1918 into the royal family of the Transkei, Nelson Mandela received an education befitting the son of a chief. But he ran away to escape an arranged marriage, experienced the harsh realities of black life in Johannesburg, studied law, and became an attorney. A born leader with a natural air of authority, Mandela was drawn to politics and the ANC. In the 1950s the white government responded to the growing popularity of Mandela and the ANC with tear gas and repression.

In 1960 the ANC called a general strike to protest the shooting of peaceful protesters at Sharpeville. Acts of sabotage then shook South Africa, and Mandela led the underground opposition. Betrayed by an informer, he was convicted of treason in 1964 and sentenced to life imprisonment. Mandela defended all of the accused in the 1964 treason trial. The following selection is taken from Mandela's opening statement.

At the outset, I want to say that the suggestion made by the State in its opening that the struggle in South Africa is under the influence of foreigners or communists is wholly incorrect. I have done whatever I did, both as an individual and as a leader of my people, because of my experience in South Africa and my own proudly felt African background, and not because of what any outsider might have said.

In my youth in the Transkei I listened to the elders of my tribe telling stories of the old days. Amongst the tales they related to me were those of wars fought by our ancestors in defence of the fatherland. . . . I hoped then that life might offer me the opportunity to serve my people and make my own humble contribution to their freedom struggle. . . .

It is true that there has often been close cooperation between the ANC [African National Congress] and the Communist Party. But cooperation is merely proof of a common goal—in this case the removal of White supremacy—and is not proof of a complete community of interests. . . . What is more, for many decades communists were the only political group in South Africa who were prepared to treat Africans as human beings and their equals; who were prepared to eat with us, talk with us, live with us, and work with us. . . . Because of this, there are many Africans who today tend to equate freedom with communism. . . .

I turn now to my own position. I have denied that I am a communist. . . . [But] I am attracted by the idea of a classless society, an attraction which springs in part from Marxist reading and, in part, from my admiration of the structure and organization of early African societies in this country. The land, then the main means of production, belonged to the tribe. There were no rich or poor and there was no exploitation. . . .

[Unlike communists] I am an admirer of the parliamentary system of the West. . . . [Thus] I have been influenced in my thinking by both West and East. . . . [I believe] I should be absolutely impartial and objective. I should tie myself to no particular system of society other than of socialism. I must leave myself free to borrow the best from the West and from the East. . . .

Our fight is against real, and not imaginary, hardships or, to use the language of the State Prosecutor, "so-called hardships." . . . Basically, we fight against two features which are the hallmarks of African life in South Africa and which are entrenched by legislation which we seek to have repealed. These features are poverty and lack of human dignity, and we do not need communists or so-called "agitators" to teach us about these things.

South Africa is the richest country in Africa, and could be one of the richest countries in the world. But it is a land of extremes and remarkable contrasts. The Whites enjoy what may well be the highest standard of living in the world, while Africans live in poverty and

Nelson Mandela at the time of his imprisonment in 1964. (Mohamed Lounes/Gamma)

misery. . . . Poverty goes hand in hand with malnutrition and disease. . . .

The lack of human dignity experienced by Africans is the direct result of the policy of White supremacy. White supremacy implies Black inferiority. Legislation designed to preserve White supremacy entrenches this notion. . . . Because of this sort of attitude, Whites tend to regard Africans as a separate breed. They do not look upon them as people with families of their own; they do not realize that they have emotions. . . .

Africans want to be paid a living wage. Africans want to perform work which they are capable of doing, and not work which the Government declares them to be capable of. . . . Africans want a just share in the whole of South Africa; they want security and a stake in society.

Above all, we want equal political rights, because without them our disabilities will be permanent. I know this sounds revolutionary to the Whites in this country, because the majority of voters will be Africans. This makes the White man fear democracy.

But this fear cannot be allowed to stand in the way of the only solution which will guarantee racial harmony and freedom for all. It is not true that the enfranchisement of all will result in racial domination. Political division, based on color, is entirely artificial and, when it disappears, so will the domination of one color group by another. The ANC has spent half a century fighting against racialism. When it triumphs it will not change that policy.

This then is what the ANC is fighting. Their struggle is a truly national one. It is a struggle of the African people, inspired by their own suffering and their own experience. It is a struggle for the right to live.

During my lifetime I have dedicated myself to this struggle of the African people. I have fought against White domination, and I have fought against Black domination. I have cherished the ideal of a democratic and free society in which all persons live together in harmony and with equal opportunities. It is an ideal which I hope to live for and to achieve. But if need be, it is an ideal for which I am prepared to die.

Questions for Analysis

1. How does Nelson Mandela respond to the charge that he and the ANC are controlled by communists?

2. What factors influenced Mandela's thinking? In what ways has he been influenced by "both East and West" and by his African background?

3. According to Mandela, what is wrong with South Africa? What needs to be done?

4. What are Mandela's goals for South Africa? Are his goals realistic, idealistic, or both?

Source: Slightly adapted from Nelson Mandela, *No Easy Walk to Freedom: Articles, Speeches and Trial Addresses* (London: Heinemann, 1973), pp. 163, 179–185, 187–189. Reprinted by permission of Heinemann Publishers (Oxford) Ltd.

Forum on Cultures. The May 2004 opening ceremony of the five-month Forum on Cultures in Barcelona, Spain, which addressed issues of peace, cultural diversity, and sustainable development on earth. *(AP Photo/Wide World Photos)*

33 A NEW ERA IN WORLD HISTORY

Communism's collapse in Europe in 1991 opened a new era in world history—one that arrived with promises of peace, democracy, and economic prosperity. Millions of people still living under repressive, authoritarian, corrupt regimes were inspired to start pressing their governments for political and human rights. Certainly for most Europeans the end of the cold war has had positive consequences. For many people in Africa, Asia, and Latin America, however, the results have been mixed. What is more, the post-1991 optimism soon faded as new tensions, conflicts, and divisions arose.

In the first part of this chapter we look at the global political and economic systems, formal and informal, with which we enter the twenty-first century. These are the broad systems under which the peoples of the world live and work. The latter part of the chapter takes a closer look at the global issues directly affecting ordinary people's lives. We live in a global age. Economic cycles, international treaties and agreements, multinational organizations, and global threats connect the world's citizens in complex networks. Every day around the world billions of individuals are confronted with similarly complex global issues that impact each of them in an immediate and personal way. As we bring our history of the world's societies to a close, let us look at our interconnected planet once again, this time focusing on ordinary people and the global changes and challenges they face.

Because people living in developing nations make up at least two-thirds of the earth's population, many of the people discussed here live in the so-called Third World, where the changes and challenges of the new millennium are perhaps greatest. We should not forget, though, that there really is no "Third World." There is only a set of conditions—such as poverty, disease, hunger, and unemployment—that are at their worst in the poorest or developing countries but exist in all countries.

GLOBAL UNITY OR CONTINUED DIVISION?

What is the global political situation in the early twenty-first century, and how do competing nation-states address common problems?

The end of the cold war superpower confrontation brought dramatic changes to the global political situation. Yet nation-states, the traditional building blocks of global politics, continued to exist. An astonishing aspect of recent scientific and technological achievements is the lack of any corresponding change in the way the human race governs—or fails to govern—itself. Sovereign nation-states continue to reign supreme, reinforced by enormous military power. The embryonic growth of an effective global political organization, of a government that could protect nations from themselves, appears permanently arrested, although efforts to control weapons of mass destruction, global warming, and other universal threats have sometimes led to global agreements. The tension generated by powerful, independent nation-states in a fragile and interdependent world remains one of the most striking and dangerous characteristics of our small planet.

Nation-States and the United Nations

The rise of the nation-state and the global triumph of nationalism have been grand themes of modern world history. The independent territorial nation-state—sometimes containing separatist ethnic groups striving for nationhood in their own right—remains the fundamental political organization in the early twenty-first century. Yet surely from a global perspective the nation-state as the basic building block of political organization can no longer be taken so easily for granted.

Has the nation-state system, with its apparently inevitable conflicts, become a threat to life on the planet? Some historians have thought so. In *Mankind and Mother Earth* (1976), the renowned British historian Arnold Toynbee (1889–1975) expressed the post-1914 disillusionment of many European and American intellectuals. Borrowing a term from the ancient Greeks, he explained that the spread of the western European political idea of the national state, first to eastern Europe and then to Asia and Africa, had created a fatal discrepancy:

the discrepancy between the political partition of the Oikoumené [the habitat of the human race] into local sovereign states and the global unification of the Oikoumené on technological and economic planes. This misfit is the crux of mankind's present plight. Some form of global government is now needed for keeping the peace . . . and for reestablishing the balance between Man and the rest of the biosphere.[1]

Some members of Toynbee's generation gave this question of world government serious consideration and came up with the League of Nations. Although the League had only a short life, the idea of a global authority transcending sovereign states remained alive. The World War II generation revived the idea and founded the **United Nations** in San Francisco in 1945. President Franklin D. Roosevelt and Democrats in the Wilsonian tradition pushed its creation, believing America's failure to join the League of Nations had contributed to the tragic breakdown of "collective security" in the 1930s.

The United Nations' main purpose is "to maintain international peace and security." The U.N. charter prohibits any member nation from using armed force except for self-defense. At the same time, the charter gives the organization's **Security Council** the authority to examine any international conflict, impose economic and political penalties on an aggressor, and "take such action by air, sea, or land forces as may be necessary to restore international peace and security." In theory, the Security Council

United Nations *Founded in 1945 as a resurrected League of Nations, its main purpose is to "maintain international peace and security."*

Security Council *The United Nations body that has the authority to examine international conflicts, impose economic and political penalties on an aggressor, and even use force, if necessary, to restore international peace and security.*

has the power to police the world. In practice, however, this power is severely restricted. The Security Council's five permanent members—China, Great Britain, France, Russia (formerly the Soviet Union), and the United States—have to agree on any peacekeeping action. But none of them, and certainly not the United States, is willing to surrender sovereign power to a global organization.

The United Nations charter affirms and reinforces the primacy of the national state in world politics. Every "peace-loving" state is eligible to join the organization and to participate in its **General Assembly.** Founded with 50 members, the General Assembly comprises 192 members in 2008. Each member state, whatever its size, has one voice and one vote on all General Assembly resolutions, but General Assembly resolutions become legally binding on states only if all five permanent members of the Security Council agree to them.

The founders of the United Nations acknowledged the expanded scope of government since the late nineteenth century and gave voice to an emerging vision of global interdependence. According to its charter, the United Nations is "to achieve international cooperation in solving international problems of an economic, social, cultural, or humanitarian character, and in promoting and encouraging respect for human rights and for fundamental freedom for all without distinction as to race, sex, language, or religion."

During the cold war, the original hopes for the creation of an effective world body were stymied by Security Council members, most often the Soviet Union, using their veto power to block actions they felt would harm their own or their allies' national interests. With the Security Council often deadlocked, the General Assembly claimed ever-greater authority. As decolonization picked up speed and the number of member states grew, a nonaligned, anticolonial African-Asian bloc emerged. Reinforced by sympathetic Latin American countries, by the mid-1960s the bloc succeeded in organizing within the General Assembly a Third World majority that concentrated on economic and social issues.

With a large numerical majority, the developing nations succeeded in broadening the organization's economic, social, and cultural mission. By the 1970s an alphabet soup of United Nations committees, specialized agencies, and affiliated international organizations were studying and promoting health, labor, agriculture, industrial development, and world trade, not to mention disarmament, control of narcotics, and preservation of the great whales and other endangered species. Today, these United Nations agencies continue to serve their main constituency—the overwhelming majority of developing nations in both the General Assembly and the world's total population. Without directly challenging national sovereignty, they exert a steady pressure for international cooperation in dealing with specific global issues, and the world's major powers sometimes go along.

Chronology

1945	United Nations founded
1945–1960s	Decolonization in Africa and Asia
1945–present	Explosive growth of cities; rapid urbanization; increasing gap in wealth between rich and poor nations
1950s	Beginning of Green Revolution
1970	Non-Proliferation of Nuclear Weapons treaty
1973	OPEC raises price of crude oil and causes panic in industrialized countries
1980s–present	HIV/AIDS global epidemic
1989	United Nations Convention on the Rights of the Child; fall of communism in eastern Europe
1997	Asian currencies collapse; International Monetary Fund provides emergency loans; Kyoto Protocol on global warming
1998	India and Pakistan explode nuclear weapons
2000	United Nations Millennium Project initiated
2001	Al-Qaeda attacks on World Trade Center and U.S. Pentagon
2003	North Korea withdraws from 1970 nonproliferation treaty; U.S.-led coalition invades Iraq; Human Genome Project completes sequencing of human genome
2004	Bombing of train station in Madrid; tsunami kills thousands in South Asia
2005	Bombing of London subway and bus systems
2007	Assassination of Pakistani politician Benazir Bhutto

General Assembly *The second main body of the United Nations; each "peace-loving" state is eligible to join and participate in it.*

● **The United Nations in Action** These soldiers are part of a French battalion serving in a United Nations peacekeeping operation in Cambodia (Kampuchea), a country wracked by war and civil conflict since 1970. United Nations forces usually provide humanitarian aid as they try to preserve fragile cease-fires after warring armies agree to stop fighting. *(J. F. Roussier/Sipa Press)*

The United Nations became the central forum for the ongoing debate about the relations between rich and poor countries. In 2000, the United Nations issued the "Millennium Declaration," which created the Millennium Project, a plan of action identifying eight goals for the United Nations and member nations to reach by 2015. Millennium goals focus on global poverty and hunger, disease, education, the environment, maternal health, child mortality, gender equality, and global partnerships. (See the feature "Listening to the Past: The United Nations Millennium Project Report" on pages 1068–1069.)

Throughout the 1970s and 1980s the United Nations played a role in establishing peace in conflicts that did not directly involve the superpowers. Then, as the cold war ended, the United Nations participated in the largest joint military action taken since the Korean conflict in the early 1950s. In 1990 the five permanent members of the Security Council agreed to repel the Iraqi invasion of Kuwait, and in 1991 they required the defeated Saddam Hussein to destroy all his weapons of mass destruction. Success in Iraq led some leaders and observers to believe the United Nations could fulfill its original purpose and guarantee peace throughout the world.

Such hopes were immediately tested in 1992, when American armed forces landed on the beaches of Somalia to stop a savage civil war and allow United Nations soldiers to maintain peace thereafter. The operation failed, as Somali fighters attacked and killed some of their would-be benefactors. United Nations negotiators also failed to stop the savage civil war in Bosnia in the mid-1990s. In response to these and other setbacks, the United Nations scaled back its peacekeeping ambitions and concentrated on helping warring factions that wanted to make peace. Even this proved to be an awesome task. On average since the mid-1990s, around sixty-seven thousand United

Nations soldiers have been stationed in hot spots around the world. United Nations peacekeeping efforts have been imperfect, but they have also been indispensable.

In 2002 another crisis over Iraq brought the United Nations to the center of the world's political stage. U.S. president George W. Bush accused Iraq of rebuilding its weapons of mass destruction and ominously warned that Saddam Hussein might give them to anti-American terrorists, although he produced no evidence linking the secular Iraqi dictator with Osama bin Laden or other Islamic extremists. Bush made clear his intention to drive Saddam Hussein from power, claiming this outcome would promote democracy in Iraq and peace in the Middle East. He legitimized his attack against Hussein by claiming that the United States had the right to act preemptively to forestall or prevent a hostile attack. This claim, however, was at odds with the United Nations charter, which grants the Security Council the sole authority to use armed force except in self-defense; and Iraq, impoverished by a decade of tough United Nations sanctions, gave no indication of plans to attack any of its neighbors or the United States. Moreover, large numbers of Americans shared the world's doubts about the legality—and wisdom—of a U.S. attack on Iraq. Thus the Bush administration reluctantly agreed to new Security Council resolutions requiring Iraq to destroy any remaining prohibited weapons and to agree to the return of United Nations weapons inspectors. Iraq accepted, declaring it had destroyed all prohibited weapons.

As 2002 ended, UN inspectors operated freely in Iraq and found no weapons of mass destruction. The United States and Britain denounced Iraq's lukewarm cooperation, however, dismissed the inspections as a fraud, moved armies to the Middle East, and lobbied for a new resolution authorizing immediate military action against Iraq. France, Russia, China, Germany, and a majority of the smaller states argued for continued weapons inspections, and France in particular threatened to veto any resolution authorizing an invasion of Iraq. Rather than risk this veto, the United States and Britain claimed that earlier Security Council resolutions provided ample authorization and, with the almost token aid of about thirty other countries, they invaded Iraq.

Although all parties in the crisis recognized the United Nations as a key source of international legality, in the end American and British leaders and their coalition allies ignored the wishes of the majority of the international community and large numbers of their own populations, and went to war. What is more, America's declaration of its right to stage a unilateral "preemptive strike" to prevent attack seemed to set a dangerous precedent. It also raised questions about when and how the United Nations charter's stipulations about the use of armed force for self-defense apply.

The Iraq invasion began on March 20, 2003. President Bush announced an "end" to the war on May 1, 2003. Saddam Hussein was captured in December 2003. Although the war brought an end to Saddam's brutal rule, Iraq remained one of the most dangerous places on earth. Relatively free national elections were held in January 2005, but they were boycotted by one of the three main groups in Iraq, the Sunni Muslims. The other two groups, the Shi'ite Muslims and the Kurds, formed a government and tried, with mixed success, to include the Sunnis. Civil war remained a very real possibility. So-called insurgents carried out daily attacks on Iraqi police, members of the military, government officials, religious leaders, and civilians. Estimates of Iraqi deaths since the war began ranged from one hundred thousand to over 1 million. Many observers warned that Iraq was becoming a breeding ground for terrorists.

Meanwhile, the United States, Britain, and their coalition allies maintained their forces in Iraq. In the spring of 2004 stories and photographs surfaced in the world press of American soldiers abusing and torturing prisoners and even causing their deaths at Abu Ghraib and other detention centers in Iraq, at the Guantánamo Bay naval base in Cuba, and at prisons in Afghanistan. Some soldiers were prosecuted, but no high-ranking U.S. military officers or government officials were implicated. Questions were raised about the willingness of the United States to abide by the Geneva Convention on prisoners of war and by the United Nations convention against torture.

● **U.S. Army Humvee Burning in Baghdad** Although President Bush declared an end to the Iraq War with his "mission accomplished" speech on May 1, 2003, attacks on U.S. soldiers increased, resulting in over 4,100 U.S. deaths and over 60,000 wounded by July 2008. Here an Iraqi man throws gasoline on a destroyed Army Humvee. *(AP Photo/Wide World Photos)*

Disregarding opposition to the Iraq War in the United States and around the world, President Bush and the U.S. Congress by July 2008 had spent nearly $650 billion in Iraq, a number that roughly equaled the entire cost of the Vietnam War. An earthquake in world affairs, the Iraqi war split the West and seemed likely to reorient relations between Western and Islamic peoples in new and unpredictable directions.

Complexity and Violence in a Multipolar World

Alongside territorial nation-states and international organizations that focus on specific problems stretch a wide range of alliances, blocs, and partnerships. For several reasons, it is often difficult to make sense of this tangle of associations.

First, the end of the cold war removed one of the planet's most enduring political realities. During the cold war the hostile superpowers dominated and curbed their allies and clients and were in turn restrained by them. The sudden end of the cold war shattered these interlocking restraints, removing a basic principle of global organization and order.

Second, the cold war division had contributed to the ideology of Third World solidarity (see Chapter 32). Then in the 1980s and 1990s wide differences in economic performance in countries and regions undermined the whole idea of Third World solidarity, and developing countries increasingly went their own ways.

A striking third development was the growing "multipolar" nature of world politics. Calling on nationalism as a mobilizing force, increasingly assertive **middle powers** jockeyed for regional leadership and sometimes came into conflict. Brazil, with more than 140 million people, vast territory and resources, and a rapidly industrializing economy, emerged as the dominant nation-state in South America. Mexico emerged as the natural leader of the Spanish-speaking Americas. France and West Germany had re-emerged as strong regional powers in western Europe by the early 1960s. Nigeria and South Africa were unquestionably the leading powers in sub-Saharan Africa. Heavily populated Egypt and much smaller Israel were also regional powerhouses. Iran and Iraq competed and fought for dominance in the Persian Gulf. China, India, and Japan

Primary Source:
Selection from a Roundtable Discussion of Globalization and Its Impact on Arab Culture, October 26, 2000
An Arab intellectual discusses the challenges and opportunities of globalization for Arab culture.

middle powers *Those countries not considered part of either the First World or the developing world; they became increasingly assertive after the cold war.*

were all leading regional powers, and several other Asian countries—notably South Korea, Indonesia, Vietnam, and Pakistan—were determined to join them. The rise of these middle powers reflected the fact that most countries were small and weak, with fewer than 20 million people. Very few countries had the resources necessary to wield real power on even a regional scale.

Conflict and violence often bedeviled the emerging multipolar political system, leading to several major wars and many small ones. In the 1990s civil wars in Bosnia, Kosovo, Rwanda, and Afghanistan killed over a million people and sent many hundreds of thousands of refugees running for their lives. Since the new century began, new or continuing wars have caused millions more deaths and new refugees, particularly in Sierra Leone, Liberia, the Democratic Republic of the Congo, Uganda, Afghanistan, Burundi, Somalia, Iraq, Sudan, and Angola.

Rivalries between ethnic groups are often at the heart of the civil wars that produce so many deaths and refugees. Different ethnic groups compete among themselves for power, or they fight against a majority population to overturn entrenched discrimination and oppression. Ethnic competition can turn violent and lead to **separatism**— radical demands for ethnic autonomy or political independence.

Only about twenty states, representing about 10 percent of the world's population, are truly homogeneous. If common language were the only basis for national identity—and, of course, it is not—the number of countries in the world could explode to six thousand.[2] The goal of a separate state for each self-defined people—the classic nationalist goal—could lead to endless battles and to tragedy on a global scale. The peaceful reconciliation of existing states with widespread separatist aspirations stood as a mighty challenge in the early twenty-first century. The challenge of separatism seemed especially great in light of the fact that civil war and terrorism often had gone hand in hand in the previous century.

separatism *Radical demands for ethnic autonomy or political independence.*

terrorism *The use of force or violence by a person or organized group with the intention of intimidating societies or governments, often for political purposes.*

The Terrorist Threat

Beginning in the 1920s and peaking in the 1960s, many nationalist movements used **terrorism** to win nationhood and political independence. This was the case in Ireland, Israel, Cyprus, Yemen, and Algeria.[3] Those fighting for independence often targeted police forces for assassination campaigns, thereby breaking down confidence in colonial governments and provoking counteratrocities that generated increased support for independence.

In the Vietnam War era, some far-left supporters of the communist Vietnamese, such as the Weathermen in the United States, the Red Army Faction in West Germany, and the Red Brigades in Italy, engaged in "revolutionary terror" in an effort to cripple the United States and western Europe. These groups carried out deadly bombings, assassinations, plane hijackings, and kidnappings. This wave of terrorism receded in the 1980s as painstaking police work and international cooperation defeated the "revolutionaries" in country after country.

● **A Casualty of the Rwandan Civil War** A Red Cross worker helps an injured victim of the Rwandan civil war between Hutu and Tutsis, the two major ethnic groups in the country. In a three-month period beginning in April 1994, five hundred thousand to 1 million Tutsis were slaughtered by the majority Hutu, while up to 2 million Hutu became refugees, fleeing to Zaire (the Congo) or Tanzania. *(David Turnley/Corbis)*

Generally successful in keeping ethnic nationalism under control in the West in the 1990s, many Europeans and most Americans believed that terrorism was primarily a problem for the developing countries of Asia, Africa, and Latin America. In fact, terrorism had become part of a complex global pattern of violence and political conflict. In northwestern Spain the Basque separatist organization used assassinations and car bombings in its bloody campaign to obtain a breakaway state from the Spanish government. In Northern Ireland Protestant and Catholic extremists turned to bombs and killings in their bitter conflict. As the new century opened, the global dimension of terrorism was revealed most dramatically in the United States.

On the morning of September 11, 2001, two hijacked passenger planes from Boston crashed into and destroyed the World Trade Center in New York City. Shortly thereafter a third plane crashed into the Pentagon, and a fourth, believed to be headed for the White House or the U.S. Capitol, crashed into a field in rural Pennsylvania. These terrorist attacks took the lives of almost three thousand people from many countries. The United States, led by President George W. Bush, launched a military campaign to destroy the perpetrators of the crime, Saudi-born millionaire Osama bin Laden's **al-Qaeda** network of terrorists and Afghanistan's reactionary Muslim government, the Taliban. Building a broad international coalition that included western Europe, Russia, and Pakistan, the United States joined its tremendous airpower with the faltering Northern Alliance in Afghanistan, which had been fighting the Taliban for years. In mid-November 2001 the Taliban collapsed, and jubilant crowds in the capital of Kabul welcomed Northern Alliance soldiers as liberators.

In trying to make sense of this latest wave of terrorism, many commentators were quick to stress the role of extreme Islamic fundamentalism as a motivating factor. But the most perceptive scholars noted that recent heinous crimes had been committed by terrorists inspired by several religious faiths and sects and were by no means limited to Islamic extremists.[4] These scholars also noted that different terrorist movements needed to be examined in the context of underlying political conflicts and civil wars for meaningful understanding.

When this perspective is brought to the study of Osama bin Laden and al-Qaeda members, two stages of their activities stand out. First, in the long, bitter fighting against the Soviet Union and the local communists in Afghanistan, bin Laden and like-minded "holy warriors" developed terrorist skills and a narrow-minded, fanatical Islamic puritanism. They also developed a hatred of most existing Arab governments, which they viewed as corrupt, un-Islamic, and unresponsive to the needs of ordinary Muslims. The objects of their hostility included the absolute monarchy of oil-rich Saudi Arabia (bin Laden's own country of origin), pro-Western but undemocratic Egypt, and the secular, one-party dictatorship of Saddam Hussein.

Second, when these Islamic extremists returned home and began to organize, they met the fate of many earlier Islamic extremists and were jailed or forced into exile, often in tolerant Europe. There they blamed the United States for being the supporter and corrupter of existing Arab governments, and they organized murderous plots against the United States—a despised proxy for the Arab rulers they could not reach. Bin Laden's network also blamed the United States for steadfastly supporting Israel and denying the claims of the Palestinians, although attempts to exploit the Israeli-Palestinian tragedy generally came later and operated mainly as a recruiting tool. These developments set the stage for the 1998 bombing of the U.S. embassy in Nairobi, Kenya, which claimed nearly two hundred lives, and for the September 11 atrocity in 2001.

Although U.S.-led forces subsequently decimated al-Qaeda camps in Afghanistan and overthrew the Taliban government that protected them, many analysts have since argued that the war on terrorism may have become more difficult as a result. On March 11, 2004, multiple bombs were set off in a Madrid train station, killing 191 people and wounding over 1,800. The Madrid bombings were carried out by Islamic extremists with only loose ties to al-Qaeda. In London on July 7, 2005, 56 people

al-Qaeda *A terrorist network led by Osama bin Laden; it claimed responsibility for the September 11 attacks and other terrorist acts.*

Primary Source:
Islamic Fundamentalist Osama Bin Laden Calls on Muslims to Take Up Arms Against America, 1998
Learn why Osama bin Laden and his associates declared war against the United States.

were killed and more than 700 were injured by bombs detonated on three subway trains and a double-decker bus. In this instance, at least three of the bombers were British citizens of Pakistani descent with some unclear links to al-Qaeda. Since then terrorist acts linked in some way to al-Qaeda have killed dozens of people in Indonesia, Jordan, Iraq, Pakistan, Algeria, Scotland, and elsewhere. A suicide bomber perhaps with links to Al-Qaeda has also been blamed for the most significant terrorist act since the London bombing: the assassination of Pakistani presidential candidate, Benazir Bhutto, on December 27, 2007. Thus, the war on terrorism is no longer against just one global network—al-Qaeda. Many loosely connected cells and movements have emerged around the world, and these groups share many of the same goals but are not answerable to Osama bin Laden or to anyone else.

Weapons of Mass Destruction

President George W. Bush justified the U.S.-led attack on Iraq by saying that the world needed to disarm Saddam Hussein and destroy his stockpiles of weapons of mass destruction. As it turned out, Hussein had no weapons of mass destruction. Still, the fear that terrorists or rogue governments might acquire such weapons reflects global concern about the enduring menace of nuclear proliferation and nuclear war, as well as the danger of chemical and biological attacks. How did this frightening situation arise? And what is being done to find solutions? (See the feature "Global Trade: Arms" on pages 1030–1031.)

Having let the atomic genie out of the bottle at Hiroshima and Nagasaki in 1945, a troubled United States immediately proposed that it be recaptured through effective international control of all atomic weapons. The Soviets rejected the American idea and exploded their first atomic bomb in 1949. The United States responded by exploding its first hydrogen bomb in 1952, and within ten months the Soviet Union did the same. Further American, Soviet, and then British tests aroused worldwide fear that radioactive fallout

● **New York, September 11, 2001** Pedestrians race for safety as the World Trade Center towers collapse after being hit by jet airliners. Al-Qaeda terrorists with box cutters hijacked four aircraft and used three of them as suicide missiles to perpetrate their unthinkable crime. Heroic passengers on the fourth plane realized what was happening and forced their hijackers to crash the plane in a field. *(AP Photo/Wide World Photos)*

would enter the food chain and cause leukemia, bone cancer, and genetic damage. Concerned scientists called for an international agreement to stop all testing of atomic bombs.

Partly in response to worldwide public pressure, the United States, the Soviet Union, and Great Britain agreed in 1958 to stop testing for three years. In 1963 these three powers signed an agreement, eventually signed by more than 150 countries, banning nuclear tests in the atmosphere. A second step toward control was the 1970 Treaty on the Non-Proliferation of Nuclear Weapons, designed to halt their spread to non-nuclear states and to reduce stockpiles of existing bombs held by the nuclear powers. It seemed that the nuclear arms race might yet be reversed.

This outcome did not come to pass. De Gaulle's France and Mao's China, seeing themselves as great world powers, simply disregarded the test ban and continued their development of nuclear weapons, although they later signed the nonproliferation

ARMS

On April 16, 1953, U.S. president Dwight Eisenhower spoke about the tremendous sums the Soviet Union and the United States were spending on cold war weapons:

Every gun that is made, every warship launched, every rocket fired signifies, in the final sense, a theft from those who hunger and are not fed, those who are cold and are not clothed. The world in arms is not spending money alone. It is spending the sweat of its laborers, the genius of its scientists, the hopes of its children. . . . This is not a way of life at all, in any true sense. Under the cloud of threatening war, it is humanity hanging from a cross of iron.

In the fifty-plus years since Eisenhower's speech, the spending has never stopped, not even after the cold war's end. In 2004 global military spending exceeded $1 trillion; the United States accounted for nearly half of that total. Globally, in 2003, the value of all conventional arms transfer agreements was more than $25.6 billion, and deliveries totaled $28.7 billion. Although both of those numbers have been dropping since the early 1990s, global arms manufacturing and trade remains big business.

Three different categories of arms are available on the world market. The category that generally receives the most attention is nuclear, biological, and chemical weapons. After the Soviet Union collapsed, there was widespread fear that former Soviet scientists would sell nuclear technology, toxic chemicals, or harmful biological agents from old, poorly guarded Soviet labs and stockpiles to the highest bidders. Recognizing the horrific danger such weapons represent, the world's nations have passed numerous treaties and agreements limiting their production, use, and stockpiling. The most important of these are the Treaty on the Non-Proliferation of Nuclear Weapons (1970), the Biological and Toxin Weapons Convention (1972), and the Chemical Weapons Conventions (1993).

A second category of arms is so-called heavy conventional weapons, such as tanks, heavy artillery, jet planes, missiles, and warships. In general, worldwide demand for these weapons declined significantly after the cold

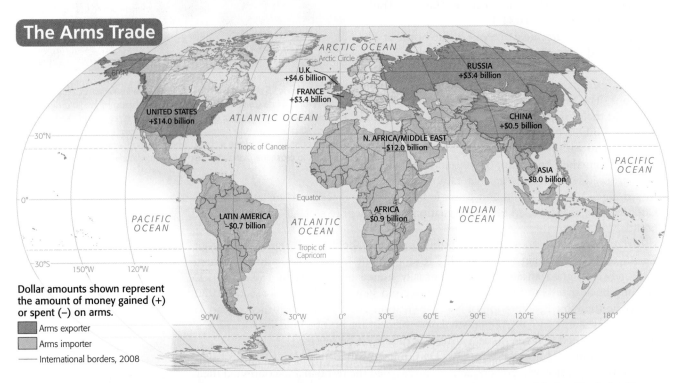

The Arms Trade

U.K. +$4.6 billion
FRANCE +$3.4 billion
RUSSIA +$3.4 billion
UNITED STATES +$14.0 billion
CHINA +$0.5 billion
N. AFRICA/MIDDLE EAST −$12.0 billion
ASIA −$8.0 billion
LATIN AMERICA −$0.7 billion
AFRICA −$0.9 billion

Dollar amounts shown represent the amount of money gained (+) or spent (−) on arms.

▮ Arms exporter
▮ Arms importer
— International borders, 2008

Source: Map and data from www.controlarms.org/the_issues/movers_shakers.htm, reproduced with the permission of Oxfam GB, Oxfam House, John Smith Drive, Cowley, Oxford OX4 2JY, UK, www.oxfam.org.uk. Oxfam GB does not necessarily endorse any text or activities that accompany the materials.

war ended. Only a few companies, located in the largest industrialized nations, have the scientists, the funding, and the capacity to produce them. Because the major Soviet- and Western-bloc nations had large weapon surpluses in 1991, most of the new weapons produced in this category have been made for export. In 1995 the United States for the first time produced more combat aircraft for export sales than for U.S. military use. New demand comes mainly from developing nations that are not technologically or financially capable of producing such weapons, such as Chile, which purchased ten F-16 jet aircraft worth $660 million from the United States in 2002, and Pakistan, which announced plans in March 2005 to buy a minimum of twenty-four F-16s. Another significant market for the United States, Great Britain, France, and Germany has been new or potential NATO member states. In 2003, for example, the United States sold forty-eight F-16 fighter aircraft worth $3.5 billion to Poland, while Germany received $1 billion from Greece for 170 battle tanks. Many of the former Soviet-bloc countries of eastern Europe have illegally served as points of origin or transfer points for sales to embargoed nations such as North Korea and to terrorist groups such as al-Qaeda.

The third category is small arms and light conventional weapons (SALWs). These are almost any remotely portable weapon including automatic rifles, machine guns, pistols, antitank weapons, small howitzers and mortars, Stinger missiles and other shoulder-fired weapons, grenades, plastic explosives, land mines, machetes, small bombs, and ammunition. SALWs make up the majority of weapons exchanged in the global arms trade. They also do the most harm. In the 1990s, the weapons of choice in forty-seven of forty-nine major conflicts were small arms. Every year, they are responsible for over a half million deaths.

SALWs are popular because they have relatively long lives and are low-maintenance, cheap, easily available, highly portable, and easily concealable. Many can be used by child soldiers. Globally, there are around 650 million guns, about 60 percent of them owned by private citizens. Fifteen billion to twenty billion or more rounds of ammunition are produced annually. Despite widespread concern about terrorists obtaining nuclear or chemical weapons, terrorists on the whole favor such small conventional weapons as truck and car bombs and automatic rifles and pistols for assassinations, sniping, armed attacks, and massacres. One of the most deadly SALWs is the land mine. Over 110 million of them still lie buried in Afghanistan, Angola, Iran, and other former war zones, and they continue to kill or injure fifteen thousand to twenty thousand people a year.

Over ninety countries manufacture and sell SALWs, but the five permanent members of the UN Security Council—France, Britain, the United States, China, and Russia—dominate. The United States and Britain account for nearly two-thirds of all conventional arms deliveries, and these two nations plus France sometimes earn more income from arms sales to developing countries than they provide in aid. The total legal international trade in SALWs is estimated at about $8 billion a year; the illegal total is about $1 billion. Of course, every legal weapon can easily become an illegal one.

In 2000 UN Secretary-General Kofi Annan observed that "the death toll from small arms dwarfs that of all other weapons systems—and in most years greatly exceeds the toll of the atomic bombs that devastated Hiroshima and Nagasaki. In terms of the carnage they cause, small arms, indeed, could well be described as 'weapons of mass destruction.'"*

*Kofi A. Annan, "Freedom from Fear," in *"We the Peoples": The Role of the United Nations in the 21st Century*, ch. 4, p. 52.

treaty. By 1968 they too had hydrogen bombs. Reversing its previous commitment to nuclear arms limitations, India also developed weapons and in 1974 exploded an atomic device. Meanwhile, the nuclear arms race between the Soviet Union and the United States surged ahead after 1968. The Strategic Arms Limitation Talks (SALT) in the 1970s only limited the rate at which the two superpowers produced more nuclear warheads. As of 2008 these two nations possess 95 percent of the world's nuclear warheads.

India developed its atomic capability partly out of fear of China, which had manhandled India in a savage border war in 1962. India's nuclear blast in 1974 in turn frightened Pakistan, which after 1947 regarded India as a bitter enemy. Pakistan's president Zulfikar Ali Bhutto (1928–1979) set up a nuclear weapons program after having reportedly said that Pakistan must have the bomb even if its people had to eat grass. By the mid-1980s Pakistan had the ability to produce nuclear weapons. In 1998 both India and Pakistan set off nuclear devices within weeks of each other, becoming the world's sixth and seventh nuclear powers. The two countries came to the brink of full-scale war in 2002, and there was some official and popular support on both sides for the use of nuclear weapons. Pakistan did not sign the nonproliferation treaty, nor did it accept the "no-first-use doctrine," by which it would agree not to be the first to use a nuclear weapon. Just as ominously, the father of Pakistan's nuclear weapons program, Abdul Qadeer Khan, was charged in 2004 with passing on nuclear weapons expertise and technology to Iran, Libya, and North Korea. An agreement in April 2005 to normalize political and trade relations between the two nuclear powers and to negotiate a peaceful solution to the Kashmir problem eased tensions somewhat.

As of 2008, Israel had never confirmed or denied having nuclear weapons. In the 1950s, however, Israel began a nuclear weapons development program, and it was generally believed that Israel had had an arsenal of nuclear weapons since the 1980s. Israel's apparent nuclear superiority was profoundly humiliating and threatening to the Arabs. When Iraq attempted, with help from France, to develop nuclear capability in the 1980s, Israel responded suddenly, attacking and destroying the Iraqi nuclear reactor in June 1981.

Fortunately, Israel's attack on Iraq was an isolated event, but the possibility of other similar attacks and the continuing proliferation of nuclear weapons helped mobilize the international community and contributed to positive developments through the 1980s and 1990s. Argentina (1983), Romania (1989), Brazil (1998), South Africa (1990s), and Libya (2003) all abandoned their nuclear weapons programs. Several of the former Soviet republics possessing nuclear arsenals, including Belarus and Kazakhstan, returned their nuclear weapons to Russia. Nuclear watch-guard agencies monitored exports of nuclear material, technology, and missiles that could carry atomic bombs. These measures encouraged confidence in global cooperation and in the nonproliferation treaty, which was extended indefinitely in 1995. The treaty has been signed by 189 countries as of 2008, including America, France, Russia, China, and the United Kingdom. Pakistan, India, and Israel, all of whom have the bomb, have not signed it. North Korea ratified the treaty in 1985 but withdrew in January 2003, making it the first nation ever to withdraw from the agreement.

Still, serious challenges remained in the early twenty-first century besides the nuclear confrontation between India and Pakistan. First, top-secret efforts by Iraq to build a bomb before the Gulf War almost succeeded, highlighting the need for better ways to detect cheating. Second, Russia and the United States had promised vaguely to cut their nuclear weapons drastically, but in 2002 they were stalled at about six thousand each, with no hope of quick progress. In May 2005 a month-long meeting of the nonproliferation treaty members failed to make any progress in strengthening the treaty. Members were particularly concerned that the Bush administration talked of modernizing the U.S. nuclear forces and that America would not reaffirm its commitment to disarmament as promised at the 1995 and 2000 meetings. Third, although Iran is a signatory to the 1970 treaty, it developed a nuclear energy program

● **South Korean Protests Against North Korea** North Korea's development of nuclear weapons has sparked angry demonstrations in the major cities of its Asian neighbors. Here a South Korean protester burns a North Korean flag and a mock atomic bomb during a rally in Seoul. *(Reuters/Corbis)*

to generate power. In 2003 the United States demanded that Iran be held accountable for seeking to produce nuclear weapons and also accused Iran of building nuclear missiles. Despite intense scrutiny, as of July 2008 no country, including the United States, had produced any evidence to support the claim that Iran had a nuclear weapons program.

Fourth, there is the threat that enriched nuclear materials will fall into the hands of terrorist organizations. In 2001, three Pakistani nuclear scientists were arrested following allegations they had met with Taliban and al-Qaeda representatives. And in early 2005 it was estimated that half of Russia's nuclear materials could not be accounted for because of widespread corruption in that country and its inability to guard its nuclear arsenal.

Finally, in early 2003 long-standing tensions between North Korea and the United States, which had never signed a peace treaty ending the 1950–1953 Korean War, reached crisis proportions over the question of nuclear arms on the Korean peninsula. As each side accused the other of failing to live up to a 1994 agreement, North Korea announced its intention to withdraw from the 1970 nonproliferation treaty, and in October 2006 North Korea tested its first nuclear device. George W. Bush insisted on six-party talks (rather than one-on-one) involving North Korea and the United States, China, Japan, South Korea, and Russia to get the North Koreans to abandon their nuclear program. In February 2007 North Korea agreed to shut down its major nuclear facility at Yŏngbyŏn in exchange for thousands of tons of heavy fuel oil from the West, and the release of $25 million in frozen North Korean funds, and it fulfilled its promise in July 2007. U.S., Russian, and Chinese inspectors toured the site in September 2007, and America's top Korean specialist, Sung Kim, was given eighteen thousand secret papers about activities at the reactor during a visit to North Korea in May 2008. As negotiations continue, this confrontation, like the one between India and Pakistan, illustrates the danger of atomic war in a multipolar world of intense regional rivalries.

Chemical and biological weapons of mass destruction created similar anxieties. For many years the use of chemical weapons had been outlawed by international agreement, but the manufacture of these terrible weapons was nonetheless permitted. In 1997 most of the world's nations signed a convention banning the production of chemical weapons and requiring the destruction of those in existence. Inspectors received the right to make surprise searches "anytime, anywhere." But complex practical questions relating to effective verification remained unanswered. Moreover, most Arab countries refused to sign the treaty, pointing to Israel's long-standing refusal to join the nuclear nonproliferation agreement. As of 2008, at least seventeen countries had active chemical weapons programs.

Building credible verification was an even greater problem for the experts monitoring the 1972 Biological and Toxin Weapons Convention, which outlawed the production of the tiny quantities sufficient to poison large populations. Iraq's attempts to develop biological weapons, discovered after the Gulf War, gave new urgency to formulating rules for surprise inspections and trade controls. Negotiations were held through the 1990s to develop a verification mechanism to carry out these inspections. In 2001, however, the Bush administration declared that the United States would not agree to any such protocol. Talks to develop a verification protocol acceptable to the United States were ongoing in 2008.

As far as terrorism was concerned, most weapons experts through the 1990s believed that terrorists were more likely to use chemical and biological weapons than to acquire and use nuclear arms because of the great complexity of construction of the latter and the need for missiles to deliver them. But there was growing concern that these experts might have underestimated the ability and willingness of terrorist groups to make and use nuclear devices. As early as 1978, Brian Jenkins, a RAND Corporation scholar, observed that

we are approaching an age in which national governments may no longer monopolize the instruments of major destruction. The instruments of warfare once possessed only by armies will be available to gangs. It will not be possible to satisfy the real or imagined grievances of all the little groups that will be capable of large-scale disruption and destruction, or to defend everyone against them. . . . In the future, warfare—highly destructive warfare—may be waged without the necessity for armies and governments, by people with little to lose.[5]

Jenkins's prescient vision appears more a possibility than ever before. Nations think in terms of preserving themselves while destroying their enemies. But terrorists willing to become martyrs with pounds of explosives strapped to their bodies have no need for a missile to deliver a nuclear device. They will deliver it personally.

In short, the terrible doomsday scenario of human-made plagues, lethal nerve gases, and mushroom clouds still haunts humanity, which seeks in turn to escape the threat of self-inflicted cataclysm.

GLOBAL INTERDEPENDENCE

How are the United Nations and multinational corporations representative of increasing globalization?

Alongside the political competition, war, and civil conflict in the twentieth century, a contradictory phenomenon unfolded: the nations of our small planet became increasingly interdependent both economically and technologically. Even the great continental states with the largest landmasses and populations and the richest natural resources found that they could not depend only on themselves. The United States required foreign oil, China needed foreign markets, and Russia needed foreign grain. All countries and peoples had need of each other.

Mutual dependence in economic affairs was often interpreted as a promising sign for the human race. Dependence promoted peaceful cooperation and limited the scope of violence. Yet the existing framework of global interdependence also came under intense attack. The poor countries of the developing world—frequently referred to now as the South—charged that the North (the industrialized countries) continued to receive far more than their rightful share from existing economic relationships, which had been forged unjustly to the South's disadvantage in the era of European political domination. The South demanded a new international economic order. Critics also saw strong evidence of neocolonialism in the growing importance of the North's huge global business corporations—the so-called multinationals—in world economic development. Thus global interdependence was widely acknowledged in principle and hotly debated in practice.

Multinational Corporations

A striking feature of global interdependence beginning in the early 1950s was the rapid emergence of **multinational corporations,** business firms that operate in a number of different countries and tend to adopt a global rather than a national perspective. Multinational corporations themselves were not new, but by 1971 they accounted for fully one-fifth of the noncommunist world's annual income, and they grew to be even more important in the 1980s and 1990s.

The rise of the multinationals was partly due to the general revival of capitalism after the Second World War (see Figure 33.1), relatively free international economic relations, and the worldwide drive for rapid industrialization. The multinationals also had three specific assets, which they used to their advantage. First, "pure" scientific knowledge unrelated to the military was freely available, but profitable industrial applications generally remained in the hands of the world's largest business firms. Second, the multinationals knew how to sell, as well as how to innovate and produce. They used modern advertising and marketing skills to push their products. Third, the multinationals developed new techniques to escape from political controls and

multinational corporations
Business firms that operate in a number of different countries and tend to adopt a global rather than a national perspective.

● **The Ubiquitous Multinational Corporations** Under one of the most recognized advertising symbols in the world, the Marlboro Man, Buddhist monks line up to wait for daily donations in Phnom Penh, Cambodia. *(AP Photo/ Wide World Photos)*

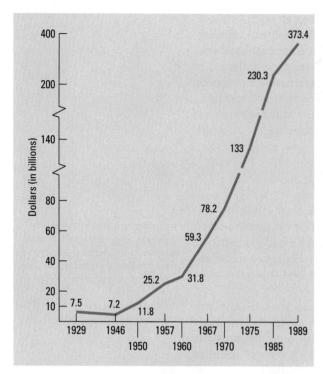

●FIGURE 33.1 **Total Investment by American Corporations in Foreign Subsidiaries, 1929–1989** (Source: Data from U.S. Department of Commerce, *Survey of Current Business*)

national policies. They treated the world as one big market, coordinating complex activities across many political boundaries.

The impact of multinational corporations, especially on Third World countries, was heatedly debated. From an economic point of view, the effects were mixed. The giant firms provided advanced technology, but the technology was expensive and often inappropriate for poor countries with widespread unemployment.

The social consequences were quite striking. The multinationals helped spread the products and values of consumer society to the developing world's elites. They fostered the creation of growing islands of Western wealth, management, and consumer culture around the world. After buying up local companies, multinational corporations often hired local business leaders to manage their operations abroad. Critics considered this practice an integral part of the process of neocolonialism, whereby local elites abandoned the national interest and made themselves willing tools of continued foreign domination. Global corporations often used aggressive techniques of modern marketing to sell products that were not well suited to Third World conditions, and they frequently came into sharp conflict with host countries.

Far from acting helpless in such conflicts, some poor countries found ways to assert their sovereign rights over the foreign multinationals. Many foreign mining companies, such as the extremely profitable U.S. oil companies in the Middle East, were simply nationalized by the host countries. More important, governments in the developing countries learned how to play Americans, Europeans, and Japanese off against each other and to make foreign manufacturing companies conform to some of their plans and desires. Increasingly, multinationals had to share ownership with local investors, hire more local managers, provide technology on better terms, and accept a variety of controls. Finally, having been denied the right to build manufacturing plants and industry as colonies, some newly independent countries also began to industrialize.

Industrialization and Modernization

industrialization strategy
The belief that the masses were impoverished because they were living in a primitive agricultural economy and that only modern factory industry would raise standards of living.

Throughout the 1950s and 1960s African, Asian, and Latin American leaders, pressed on by their European, American, and Soviet advisers, believed a vigorous **industrialization strategy** was the only answer to poverty and population growth. The masses, they concluded, were poor because they were imprisoned in a primitive, inefficient agricultural economy. Only modern factory industry appeared capable of creating wealth quickly enough to raise standards of living.

To Third World elites, the economic history of the West, Japan, and the Soviet Union seemed to validate this faith in industrialization. The wealthy countries had also been agricultural and "underdeveloped" until, one by one, the Industrial Revolution had lifted them out of poverty. It seemed this uneven progress of industrialization was primarily responsible for the great income gap between rich and poor countries in 1950.

modernization *A theory, popular in the 1960s, that assumed that all countries were following the path already taken by the industrialized nations and that the elites' task was to speed the trip.*

Modernization theories, popular in the 1960s, assumed that all countries were following the path already taken by the industrialized nations and that the elites' task was to speed the trip. Marxism, with its industrial and urban bias, preached a similar gospel. These ideas reinforced the desire of the newly independent countries to industrialize.

Nationalist leaders believed a successful industrialization strategy required state action and enterprise along socialist lines. Many were impressed by Stalin's forced industrialization in particular for its having won the Soviet Union international power and prominence. In Asia and Africa capitalists and private enterprise were often equated with the old rulers and colonial servitude. The reasoning was practical as well as ideological: socialism meant an expansion of steady government jobs for political and ethnic allies, and modern industry meant ports, roads, schools, and hospitals as well as factories. Only the state could afford such expensive investments.

The degree of state involvement varied considerably. A few governments, such as communist China, tried to control all aspects of economic life. A few one-party states in Africa, notably Zambia, Ghana, and Ethiopia, mixed Marxist-Leninist ideology and peasant communes in an attempt to construct a special "African socialism." At the other extreme the British colony of Hong Kong downgraded government control of the economy and emphasized private enterprise and the export of manufactured goods. Most governments assigned the state an important, even leading, role, but they also recognized private property and tolerated native (and foreign) business people. The **mixed economy**—part socialist, part capitalist—became the general rule in Africa and Asia.

mixed economy *An economy that is part socialist and part capitalist.*

Political leaders concentrated state investment in big, highly visible projects that proclaimed the country's independence and stimulated national pride. Enormous dams for irrigation and hydroelectric power were favored undertakings. Nasser's stupendous Aswan Dam harnessed the Nile, demonstrating that modern Egyptians could surpass even the pyramids of their ancient ancestors. These big projects testified to the prevailing faith in expensive advanced technology and modernization along European lines.

In many ways the Third World's first great industrialization drive was a success. Industry grew faster than ever before, though from an admittedly low base in Africa and most of Asia. Nevertheless, by the late 1960s disillusionment with relatively rapid industrialization was spreading. Asian, African, and Latin American countries did not as a whole match the "miraculous" concurrent advances of western Europe and Japan, and the great economic gap between rich and poor nations continued to widen.

Also, most leaders in the developing countries had genuinely believed that rapid industrial development would help the rural masses. Yet careful studies showed increasingly that the main beneficiaries of industrialization were business people, bureaucrats, skilled workers, and urban professionals. Peasants and agricultural laborers gained little or nothing. Moreover, the poorest countries—such as India and Indonesia in Asia, and Ethiopia and Sudan in Africa—were growing most slowly in per capita terms. Industrialization appeared least effective where poverty was most intense. Economic dislocations in the global economy after the 1973 OPEC oil embargo (see pages 946 and 949) accentuated this trend, visiting particularly devastating effects on the poorest countries.

Perhaps most serious, between 1950 and 1970, industrialization had provided jobs for only about one-fifth of the 200 million young men and women who had entered the exploding labor force in the developing countries in the same period. For the foreseeable future, it seemed, most people in these countries would have to remain on the farm or work in traditional handicrafts and service occupations. All-out modern industrialization had failed as a panacea. By the late 1960s widespread dissatisfaction with policies of all-out industrialization prompted a greater emphasis on rural development.

Agriculture and the Green Revolution

From the late 1960s onward the limitations of industrial development forced governments in the developing nations to take renewed interest in rural people and village life. At best this attention meant giving agriculture its due and coordinating rural development with industrialization and urbanization. At worst, especially in the very poorest countries, it deflated the optimistic vision that living standards would approach those of the wealthy industrialized nations.

Nationalist elites had neglected agriculture for various reasons. An agricultural economy represented colonial servitude, which they symbolically repudiated by embracing industrialization. To provide capital for industry, they squeezed agriculture and peasant producers, establishing artificially low food prices, which also subsidized their volatile urban supporters at the farmers' expense. In addition, the obstacles to more productive farming seemed overwhelming to unsympathetic urban elites and condescending foreign experts: farms were too small and fragmented for mechanization, peasants were too stubborn and ignorant to change their ways, and so on. Little wonder that only big farmers and some plantations received much government support. Wherever large estates and absentee landlords predominated—in large parts of Asia and in most of Latin America excluding Mexico, though not in sub-Saharan Africa—landless laborers and poor peasants who had no choice other than to rent land simply lacked the incentive to work harder. Any increased profits from larger crops went mainly to the absentee landowners.

Most honest observers were convinced that improved farm performance required land reform. Yet ever since the French Revolution, genuine land reform had been viewed as a profoundly radical measure, frequently bringing violence and civil war. Powerful landowners and their allies generally succeeded in blocking or subverting redistribution of land to benefit the poor. Land reform, unlike industrialization, was generally too hot for most politicians to handle.

Governments also neglected agriculture because feeding the masses was deceptively easy in the 1950s and early 1960s. Before 1939 the countries of Asia, Africa, and Latin America had collectively produced more grain than they consumed. After 1945, as their populations soared, they began importing ever-increasing but readily available quantities. Very poor countries, for example, received food from the United States at giveaway prices as part of a U.S. effort to dispose of enormous grain surpluses and help American farmers.

Although crops might fail in poor countries, starvation seemed a thing of the past. In 1965, when India was urged to build up its food reserves, one top Indian official expressed a widespread attitude: "Why should we bother? Our reserves are the wheat fields of Kansas."[6] In the short run, the Indian official was right. In 1966 and again in 1967, when famine gripped the land, the United States gave India one-fifth of the U.S. wheat crop. More than 60 million Indians lived exclusively on American grain. The effort required a food armada of six hundred ships, the largest fleet assembled since the Normandy invasion of 1944. The famine was ultimately contained, and instead of millions of deaths, there were only a few thousand.

That close brush with mass starvation sent a shiver down the world's spine. Complacency dissolved in Asia and Africa, and neo-Malthusian prophecies of disaster multiplied in wealthy nations. Paul Ehrlich, an American scientist, envisioned a grisly future in his polemical 1968 bestseller *The Population Bomb:*

The battle to feed all of humanity is over. In the 1970s the world will undergo famines— hundreds of millions of people are going to starve to death in spite of any crash programs embarked upon now. At this stage nothing can prevent a substantial increase in the world death rate.[7]

Countering such nightmarish visions was the hope offered by technological improvements. Plant scientists and agricultural research stations had already set out to develop new hybrid seeds genetically engineered to suit the growing conditions of tropical agriculture. Their model was the extraordinarily productive hybrid corn developed for the American Midwest in the 1940s. The first breakthrough came in Mexico in the 1950s, when an American-led team developed new strains of high-yielding dwarf wheat. These varieties enabled farmers to double their yields, though they demanded greater amounts of fertilizer and water for irrigation. Mexican wheat production soared. Thus began the transformation of agriculture in some poor countries—the so-called **Green Revolution.**

In the 1960s an American-backed team of scientists in the Philippines developed a new hybrid "miracle rice" that required more fertilizer and water but yielded more and grew much faster than ordinary rice. It permitted the revolutionary advent of year-round farming on irrigated land, making possible two, three, or even four crops a year. Asian scientists, financed by their governments, developed similar hybrids to meet local conditions.

Some Asian countries experienced rapid and dramatic increases in grain production. Farmers in India upped production more than 60 percent in fifteen years. By 1980 thousands of new grain bins dotted the Indian countryside, symbols of the agricultural revolution and the country's newfound ability to feed all its people. China followed with its own highly successful version of the Green Revolution under Deng Xiaoping.

The Green Revolution offered new hope to the developing nations, but it was no cure-all. Initially most of it benefits seemed to flow to large landowners and to substantial peasant farmers who could afford the necessary investments in irrigation and fertilizer. Subsequent experience in China and other Asian countries showed, however, that even peasant families with tiny farms could gain substantially. Indeed, the Green Revolution's greatest successes occurred in Asian countries with broad-based peasant ownership of land.

The technological revolution, however, shared relatively few of its benefits with the poorest villagers, who almost never owned the land. This helps explain why the Green Revolution failed to spread from Mexico throughout Latin America. As long as 3 to 4 percent of the rural population owned 60 to 80 percent of the land, as was still the case in many Latin American countries, the Green Revolution usually remained stillborn.

As the practice of genetically engineering or modifying foods grew in the late twentieth and early twenty-first centuries, global opposition to the practice and the foods also grew. Many people feared that such foods would have still-unknown effects on the human body. Several European and other countries placed bans on imports of genetically modified corn and soybeans from the United States, where the practice was most common.

The loss of biodiversity was also of growing concern. When one or two genetically engineered seeds replaced all of the local, naturally occurring seeds in a given area, as frequently happened when Green Revolution technologies became the norm, food security was threatened. As the world experiences a shrinking diversity of plants and animals, farmers will find it more difficult to respond and find alternatives if the dominant hybrid seed in use becomes susceptible to a particular disease or pest or there is a significant climate change. Corporate ownership of seeds through patents is another worrisome outcome of this shrinking diversity—farmers will be dependent on a few giant multinational agribusinesses for their seeds. And because seeds are being engineered that can be used for only one year, farmers will have to return to these companies each planting season for a complete stock of new seeds. Finally, economists worried that yet another gap would develop between the world's rich and poor over food. As mass-produced, genetically modified foods became cheaper, they would be eaten by the poor, while the rich would be able to afford organically grown, chemically free, but more expensive foods.

Green Revolution *The increase in food production stemming from the introduction of high-yielding wheat, hybrid seeds, and other advancements.*

The Economics and Politics of Globalization

After the 1960s there was dissatisfaction in Asia, Africa, and Latin America not only with the fruits of the industrialization drive but also with the world's economic system.

Scholars imbued with a Third World perspective and spokesmen for the United Nations majority declared that the international system was unjust and in need of radical change. Mahbub ul Haq, a Pakistani World Bank official and member of the international bureaucratic elite, sympathetically articulated this position in 1976:

The vastly unequal relationship between the rich and the poor nations is fast becoming the central issue of our time. The poor nations are beginning to question the basic premises of an international order which leads to ever-widening disparities between the rich and the poor countries and to a persistent denial of equality of opportunity to many poor nations. They are, in fact, arguing that in international order—just as much as within national orders—all distribution of benefits, credit, services, and decision-making becomes warped in favor of a privileged minority and that this situation cannot be changed except through fundamental institutional reforms.[8]

The subsequent demand of the developing nations for a "new international economic order" had many causes, both distant and immediate. Critics of imperialism such as J. A. Hobson (see page 724) and Third World writers on decolonization such as Frantz Fanon (see page 1014) had long charged that the colonial powers grew rich exploiting Asia, Africa, and Latin America. Beginning in the 1950s a number of writers, many of them Latin American Marxists, breathed new life into these ideas with their "theory of dependency."

The poverty and so-called underdevelopment of the South, they argued, were not the starting points but the deliberate and permanent results of exploitation by the capitalist industrialized nations in the modern era. Poor countries produced cheap raw materials for wealthy, industrialized countries and were conditioned to buy their expensive manufactured goods. As in the case of Latin America since the nineteenth

● **An International Labor Force** Since 2003 China has been the number one destination for foreign direct investment, with France and the United States ranking second and third. Although Chinese consumer goods—such as clothing or toys—dominate many world markets, China is also rapidly becoming a global leader in the production of high-tech products, such as personal computers. Here Chinese women assemble precision made parts on a factory production line. Beginning in 2007, problems with Chinese-made products—ranging from adulterated pharmaceuticals to tainted dog food to toys with high lead content—raised health and safety concerns in the United States and Europe. *(Peerpoint/Alamy)*

● **Indifference of Rich Nations to Poor** This cartoon expresses the opinion of many in the developing world that their suffering is being ignored by the more well-off residents of the developed world. The focus of their anger in 2005 was the huge debts of billions of dollars owed the rich nations. These debts were so large that many countries were paying more on their debts to the wealthiest nations than they were receiving in aid. European Union and G8 members pledged during the year to reduce the debts, but it remains to be seen what will come of the pledges. (The G8 consists of the original G6 members plus Canada and Russia.) *(Cam Cardow/The Ottawa Citizen)*

century, the industrialized nations perpetuated this neocolonial pattern after Third World countries gained political independence. Thus the prevailing economic interdependence was the unequal, unjust interdependence of dominant and subordinate, of master and peon. The international order needed a radical restructuring.

The OPEC oil coup of 1973–1974 ignited hopes in the developing countries of actually achieving a new system of economic interdependence. But generally the industrialized countries proved very tough bargainers when it came to basic changes. For example, in the late 1970s the developing nations hoped to formulate a new **Law of the Sea.** The proposed law was based on the principle that the world's oceans are "a common heritage of mankind" and should be exploited only for the benefit of all nations. In practice this would mean that a United Nations–sponsored authority would regulate and tax use of the sea. Some wealthy countries and their business firms were reluctant to accept such an infringement on what they judged to be their economic sovereignty and scope of action. The United States refused to sign the final draft of the law in 1982.

Law of the Sea *A proposed law based on the principle that the world's oceans are "a common heritage of mankind"; it would have allowed only a United Nations–sponsored authority to regulate and tax use of the sea.*

The great gap between the richest and poorest nations resulted from the coercive power of Western imperialism as well as from the wealth-creating effects of continuous technological improvement since the Industrial Revolution. In the face of bitter poverty, unbalanced economies, and local elites that often catered to Western interests, people of the developing countries had reason for frustration and anger.

But close examination of our small planet reveals a much more complex configuration than simply two sharply defined economic camps, a "North" and a "South." By the early 1990s there were several distinct classes of nations in terms of wealth and income (see Map 33.1). The former communist countries of eastern Europe formed something of a middle-income group, as did the major oil-exporting states, which still lagged behind the wealthier countries of western Europe and North America. Latin America was much better off than sub-Saharan Africa but contained a wide range of national per capita incomes. Some of the largest and fastest-growing economies, as well as highest standards of living, were found in South and East Asia. When one added global differences in culture, religion, politics, and historical development, the supposed clear-cut split between the rich North and the poor South broke down further. Moreover, the solidarity of the South had always been fragile, resting largely on the ideas of some Third World intellectuals and their supporters.

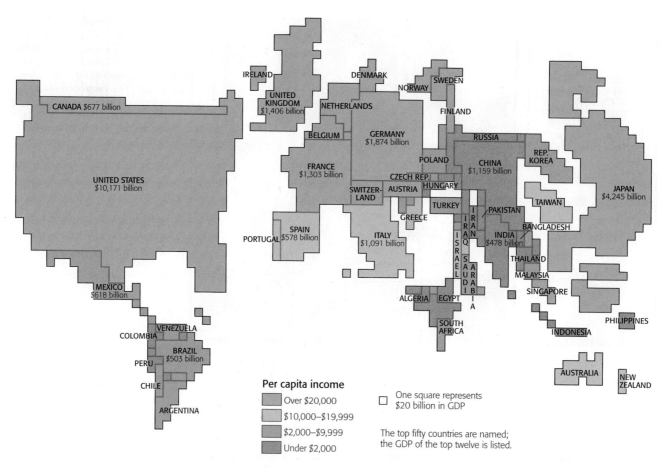

MAP 33.1 **The Global Distribution of Wealth** This size-comparison map, arranged according to global wealth distribution, vividly illustrates the gap in wealth between the Northern and Southern Hemispheres. The two small island nations of Japan and the United Kingdom have more wealth than all the nations of the Southern Hemisphere combined. As market capitalism expands in China, Vietnam and other Asian countries, and in Latin America and Africa, the relative size-ratios on the map will continue to change and evolve.

Thus a continuation of the global collective bargaining that first emerged in the 1970s seemed more likely than an international class war. The recurring international debt crisis illustrates the process of global bargaining. The economic dislocations of the 1970s and early 1980s worsened the problems of many developing countries, especially those that had to import oil. Growing unemployment, unbalanced budgets, and large trade deficits forced many poor countries to borrow rapidly from the wealthy industrialized nations. By the early 1980s much of the debt was short-term and could not be repaid as it came due, so it continued to build. By 2005 the world's poorest countries were spending more on debt repayments—$100 million a day—than on health care.

The wealthy lender nations generally were unwilling to cancel the debts. Seemingly only a major economic crisis that immediately threatened the lender nations themselves could get them to act. Such a crisis occurred in 1982 when Mexico appeared ready to default on its debts. The Reagan administration, consistently opposed to calls from the developing countries for a new international system, quickly organized a gigantic rescue operation to pump new money into Mexico. The reason was simple: Mexico's failure to service its foreign debt would cripple large American banks that had lent Mexico money and possibly cause a global financial panic and depression.

● **Run on the Banks**   A security guard at Indonesia's Bank Harapan Santosa blocks the way of hundreds of depositors trying to get into the closed bank in Jakarta in November 1997. Most of Asia suffered a severe economic crisis in the late 1990s that had damaging ripple effects on the entire world economy. Indonesia closed ten banks during the crisis, setting off runs on banks by panicked depositors reminiscent of the Great Depression. *(AP Photo/Wide World Photos)*

Thus a series of international negotiations beginning in the 1980s reduced the debts of some developing countries, granted new loans, and encouraged economic liberalization. In 2000 the United Nations Millennium Project Report made debt relief a major goal.

While debt relief highlights the great wealth gap between the have and have-not countries, financial crises in the world's financial markets and networks threaten everyone. After the United States again saved Mexico (and American banks) from default in 1995, the world saw a new round of global financial crisis. In 1997 the rapidly growing economies of Thailand, Malaysia, South Korea, and Indonesia experienced a "run on the bank" when previously enthusiastic foreign investors panicked and withdrew their funds. As a result, the currencies of these Asian countries plunged, many Asian banks and companies could not repay their debts, and prices and unemployment soared. As in the 1980s, the industrialized countries and the International Monetary Fund (IMF) tried to stem the crisis with emergency loans and prescriptions for recovery. Yet the "Asian contagion" spread, bringing financial collapse in Russia and threatening to destroy Latin America's hard-won financial stability. Worried increasingly about the fate of their own economies, in late 1998 Japan, the United States, and the European Union, working with the IMF, redoubled their rescue operations and managed to stabilize international finances. The outcome benefited rich and poor countries. Global interdependence was clearly a fact of life.

Pressure on Vital Resources and Economic Development

A common theme in world history is the constant struggle of all living organisms to acquire the vital resources necessary for life. Indeed, one approach to studying any event in world history is simply to ask what, if any, vital resources were involved. Was a war fought over oil? Over land? Was a human migration in search of water or better grazing land for livestock? Were ocean voyages made in search of spices?

● **Gathering Firewood** These African women in Burkina Faso bring home headloads of wood, requiring a journey of one hour each way. In developing countries women (rarely men) make two or more such trips a week to provide fuel for cooking and heating, illustrating what has been called the "other energy crisis." As nearby forests are depleted they must travel farther and farther to find available wood, while the denuded land becomes open to soil erosion. Women and children spend another two to three hours every day or two hauling water. *(Mark Edwards/Peter Arnold, Inc.)*

During the postwar economic boom of the 1950s and 1960s nations became increasingly dependent on each other for vital resources. Yet resources also seemed abundant, and rapid industrialization was a worldwide article of faith. The situation changed suddenly in the 1970s. In a famous study aptly titled *The Limits to Growth* (1972), a group of American and European scholars argued that unlimited economic development is impossible on a finite planet. In the early twenty-first century, they predicted, the ever-increasing demands of too many people and factories would exhaust the world's mineral resources and destroy the fragile biosphere with pollution. Meanwhile, Japan imported 99 percent of its petroleum, western Europe 96 percent. When the Organization of Petroleum Exporting Countries (OPEC) increased the price of crude oil fourfold in 1973, there was panic in many industrial countries. Skyrocketing prices for oil and other raw materials in the 1970s seemed to confirm grim predictions that the world was exhausting its vital resources.

Of all the pressures on global resources, many observers believed that population growth was the most serious. Here recent experience offered room for optimism: population growth in the industrialized countries fell dramatically. In the 1950s women there had 2.8 children on average; in the late 1990s they had only 1.5. This level was not enough to maintain a stable population, and if that trend continued, total numbers in the developed countries would decline in the next generation. More important, equally dramatic declines in population growth were occurring throughout the developing world, and it was estimated that the world's population would level off at about 10 billion by 2100 (see pages 1054–1055).

Whatever the case may be, efforts to bring living standards in developing countries to levels approaching those in rich industrialized countries will put tremendous pressure on global resources. Jared Diamond, in his study of how societies succeed or fail, says it is therefore incumbent to ask how much of the traditional industrialized countries' consumer values and living standards we can afford to retain. He recognizes the seeming political impossibility of inducing consumer societies to lower their impact on the world's resources. But, he argues, "the alternative, of continuing our current impact, is more impossible." Diamond remains optimistic, however. He notes the decline in human fertility rates, and he argues that the strain on global resources could be lessened significantly if those with the highest standards of living accepted only a minimal reduction in their daily consumption of these resources. He is also encouraged because today humans have the advantage of a global communications network and a knowledge of human history that were not available to earlier generations.[9] Throughout its history, the human race has exhibited considerable skill in finding new resources and inventing new technologies. Perhaps we can learn from the achievements and mistakes made in the human past, and in the future share our finite global resources more equitably and wisely.

THE GROWTH OF CITIES (1945 TO THE PRESENT)

What factors spurred the growth of cities in Africa, Asia, and Latin America, and what were some of the main consequences of urbanization in the late twentieth century?

Perhaps no single phenomenon in the last hundred years has had a greater impact on individuals, families, and communities than the mass movement of peoples from rural areas to cities. The reasons for this migration are numerous, and the consequences for life on earth are profound.

Many of the most severe problems and most wonderful pleasures that humans experience are found in cities. Cities represent modernity, progress, and civilization. Countries newly free from colonial rule built shiny airports, international hotels, and massive government buildings, often next to tarpaper slums, as evidence of political independence and ongoing industrial development. Cities were also testimonials to increasing population, limited opportunities in the countryside, and neocolonial influence.

Rapid Urbanization

In 1945 when one thought of large cities, New York and London came to mind, followed by Tokyo and Paris. They were all soon overtaken, however, by cities in the developing world. Cities in Africa, Asia, and Latin America expanded at an astonishing pace after the Second World War. Many doubled or even tripled in size in a single decade. The population of the Algerian city of Algiers jumped from 300,000 to 900,000 between 1950 and 1960; Accra in Ghana, Lima in Peru, and Nairobi in Kenya grew just as fast. Moreover, rapid urban growth continued. In 1950 there were only eight **megacities** (5 million or more inhabitants), and just two were in developing countries. Estimates are that by 2015 there will be fifty-nine megacities, and forty-eight of them will be outside North America and Europe.

megacities *Cities with population of 5 million people or more.*

The urban explosion continued in the 1980s and 1990s, so that by 2000 more than 60 percent of the planet's city dwellers lived in the cities of Africa, Asia, and Latin America, according to United Nations estimates. Still, in Africa's and Asia's poorest countries urbanization is in its early stages. Thus if United Nations projections hold true, the urban population will triple from 1.4 billion persons in 1990 to 4.4 billion in 2025. Rapid urbanization in the developing countries represents a tremendous historical change. As recently as 1920, three out of every four of the world's urban inhabitants were concentrated in Europe and North America.

In the developing world, the capital city often emerged as an all-powerful urban center, encompassing all the important elite groups and dwarfing smaller cities as well as villages. Mexico City, for example, grew from 3 million to 12 million people between 1950 and 1975 and had an estimated 22 million people in 2000. In the 1980s and 1990s, an estimated 1.4 million Brazilian peasants were migrating annually to São Paulo, which also has over 20 million inhabitants, and to other Brazilian cities. The

● **Juan O'Gorman: Credit Transforms Mexico (1965)** Emerging as an important architect in the 1930s, O'Gorman championed practical buildings and then led the movement to integrate architecture with art in postrevolutionary Mexico. These panels from a fresco for a bank interior combine an optimistic view of economic development with many Mexican motifs. O'Gorman believed that Mexico had to preserve its cultural values in order to preserve its independence. *(Photos: Enrique Franco-Torrijos. Courtesy, Banco Bital, S.A., Mexico City)*

pattern of a dominant megalopolis has continued to spread from Latin America to Africa and Asia. Tokyo, in Japan, remains the largest city in the world with over 30 million inhabitants.

What caused this **urban explosion?** First, the general growth of population in the developing nations was critical. Urban residents gained substantially from a medical revolution that provided improved health care but only gradually began to reduce the size of their families. At the same time, the pressure of numbers in the countryside encouraged millions to set out for the nearest city. More than half of all urban growth has been due to rural migration.

Another factor was the desire to find jobs. Manufacturing jobs in the developing nations were concentrated in cities. In 1980 half of all the industrial jobs in Mexico were located in Mexico City, and the same kind of extreme concentration of industry occurred in many poor countries. Yet industrialization accounted for only part of the urban explosion.

Newcomers streamed to the cities even when there were no industrial jobs available, seeking any type of employment. Sociologists call this **urbanization without industrialization.** Many were pushed: they simply lacked enough land to survive. Large landowners found it more profitable to produce export crops, such as sugar or coffee, for wealthy industrialized countries, and their increasingly mechanized operations provided few jobs for agricultural laborers. The push factor was particularly strong in

urban explosion *A rapid increase in the populations of world cities such as Mexico City.*

urbanization without industrialization *A sociological phenomenon in which newcomers stream to cities seeking work even when no industrial jobs are available.*

Latin America, with its neocolonial pattern of large landowners and foreign companies exporting food and raw materials. More generally, much migration was seasonal or temporary. Many young people left home for the city to work in construction or serve as maids, expecting higher wages and steadier work and planning to return shortly with a modest nest egg.

Of course the magnetic attraction of cities was more than economic. It rested on the services and opportunities they offered, as well as on changing attitudes and the urge to escape from the traditional restraints of village life. Most of the modern hospitals, secondary schools, and transportation systems in less-developed countries were in the cities. So were most banks, libraries, movie houses, and basic conveniences. Safe piped water and processed food, for instance, were rare in rural areas, and village women by necessity spent much of their time carrying water and grinding grain.

Many of these developments were mirrored in the industrialized countries as well. But because industrialization had advanced in Europe and North America in the nineteenth and early twentieth centuries, people there had been drawn to urban areas at a much earlier date. By 1920, more Americans were already living in cities than in rural areas.

Overcrowding and Shantytowns

The late twentieth century saw a repeat of the problems associated with urbanization that had arisen in the cities of Europe and North America in an earlier era, but on a larger scale. Rapid population growth threatened to overwhelm urban social services; local authorities in many cities in the developing countries could not keep up with the demand. New neighborhoods often lacked running water, paved streets, electricity, and police and fire protection. As in the early days of Europe's industrialization, sanitation was minimal in poor sections of town. Outdoor toilets were shared by many, and raw sewage often flowed down streets and into streams.

Surging population growth had particularly severe consequences for housing. As in western Europe in the early nineteenth century, overcrowding reached staggering proportions in a great many Third World cities. Many old buildings were divided and redivided until population density reached the absolute saturation point.

Makeshift squatter settlements were another striking manifestation of the urban housing problem. These **shantytowns,** also known more positively as **self-help housing,** sprang up continuously, almost overnight, on the worst possible urban land. Typically, a group of urban poor "invaded" unoccupied land and quickly threw up tents or huts. Often beaten off by the police, they invaded again and again until the authorities gave up and a new squatter beachhead had been secured.

Shantytowns grew much faster than more prosperous urban areas. In the giant Brazilian city of Rio de Janeiro, for example, the population of the shantytowns grew four times faster than the rest of the city's population in the 1950s and 1960s. In most developing countries, self-help settlements came to house up to two-fifths of the urban population. Such settlements had occasionally grown up in American mining towns and in Europe, but never to the extent they did in Latin America, Asia, and Africa.

In the 1960s and 1970s efforts to bulldoze spontaneous communities out of existence were generally abandoned. Responding to pressure from these still-primitive neighborhoods and activists, some governments, particularly in Asia, agreed to make improvements—gradually installing piped water, public toilets, lighting, and some paved streets. Eventually, centrally located slums and old shantytowns attracted the attention of government planners and capitalists, who, under the guise of "urban renewal," sometimes joined forces to evict the poor and build new housing for the middle and upper classes. New self-help settlements continued to spring up on the urban fringes, but in the largest cities these settlements were less desirable because poor public transportation made getting to and from work a nightmare.

shantytowns *Areas of makeshift squatter settlements created by a group of the urban poor.*

self-help housing *A euphemism for shantytowns.*

Rich and Poor

At the beginning of the twenty-first century, differences in wealth between rich and poor countries, and often between rich and poor individuals within those countries, were truly staggering (see Table 33.1). American basketball star Michael Jordan received roughly $300,000 per game, as much as $10,000 per minute, when he played professionally in the late 1990s. Dividing his yearly income by the number of days in the year revealed that he earned about $178,000 per day whether he played or not. Still, he was far down on the list of the richest Americans. Microsoft founder and CEO Bill Gates had a net worth roughly 120 times greater than Jordan's in 2005. At the other end of the global income spectrum, there were sixty-one countries where the average person made less than $750 a year; half of the world's population—3 billion people—lived on less than $2 a day. The wealth of the world's three richest people was greater than the GDP of the poorest forty-eight nations combined.

Such disparities were not new. After World War II the gap in real income—income adjusted for differences in prices—between the industrialized world and the former colonies and dependencies of Africa, Asia, and Latin America was enormous. According to a leading historian, in 1950, when war-scarred Europe was in the early phase of postwar reconstruction,

● **Rich and Poor in Hong Kong** Global inequalities in wealth are evident in this photo of Hong Kong that shows refugee squatter housing in the foreground and modern, affluent apartment blocks behind. As a result of rapid urbanization and peasants' having to leave their land, this stark contrast between desperately poor and comfortably wealthy is found throughout the developing world. *(Brian Brake/Photo Researchers, Inc.)*

the real income per capita of the Third World was five or six times lower than that of the developed countries.... In the developed countries, a century and a half of Industrial Revolution had resulted in a multiplication by more than five of the average standard of living in 1950.... For the average Third World countries the 1950s level was practically that of 1800 or, at best, only 10–20 percent above.[10]

The poor of these Third World countries were overwhelmingly concentrated in the countryside as small farmers and landless laborers.

Poverty meant, above all, not having enough to eat. For millions hunger and malnutrition were harsh facts of life. And in both developed and developing nations, even poor people who consumed enough calories often suffered from the effects of unbalanced high-starch diets and inadequate protein. Severe protein deficiency stunts the brain as well as the body, so many of the poorest children grew up mentally retarded.

Poor housing—crowded, often damp, and exposed to the elements—also contributed significantly to the less-developed world's high incidence of chronic ill health. So too did scanty education and lack of the fundamentals of modern public health: adequate and safe water, sewage disposal, immunizations, prenatal care, and control of communicable diseases. Infant mortality was savage, and chronic illness weakened and demoralized many adults, making them unfit for the hard labor their lives required. Generally speaking, people's health was better in Asia and Latin America than in the new states of sub-Saharan Africa.

After the developing countries achieved political independence, massive inequality continued, with few exceptions, to be the reality of life. A monumental gap separated rich and poor; it was most pronounced in the

Table 33.1 Urban Population as a Percentage of Total Population in the World and in Eight Major Areas, 1925–2025

AREA	1925	1950	1975	2000	2025 (EST.)
World Total	21	28	39	50	63
North America	54	64	77	86	93
Europe	48	55	67	79	88
Soviet Union	18	39	61	76	87
East Asia	10	15	30	46	63
Latin America	25	41	60	74	85
Africa	8	13	24	37	54

Note: Little more than one-fifth of the world's population was urban in 1925. In 2000 the urban proportion in the world total was about 50 percent. According to United Nations experts, the proportion should reach two-thirds by about 2025. The most rapid urban growth will occur in Africa and Asia, where the move to cities is still in its early stages.

exploding towns and cities. In Asia and Africa the rich often moved into the luxurious sections previously reserved for colonial administrators and foreign business people. Particularly in Latin America, upper-class and upper-middle-class people built fine mansions in exclusive suburbs, where they lived behind high walls with many servants and were protected from intruders by armed guards and fierce dogs.

Education also distinguished the wealthy from the masses. Children of the elite often attended expensive private schools, where classes were taught in English or French, and they had little in common with children in overcrowded public school classes taught in the national language. Subsequently, they often studied abroad at leading European and North American universities, or they monopolized openings at local universities. While absorbing the latest knowledge in prestigious fields such as civil engineering or economics, they also absorbed foreign customs and values. They mastered the fluent English or French that is indispensable for many top-paying jobs, especially with international agencies and giant multinational corporations. Thus elites in the developing countries often had more in common with the power brokers of the industrialized nations than with their own people, and they seemed willing tools of neocolonial penetration and globalization.

Too often the partnership formed among the wealthy elite of a developing country, multinational companies, and First World nations resulted in a developing country's experiencing **economic growth without economic development**. Enormous profits were being made from cash crop production or from industrial manufacturing, but few of these profits were used to build roads, schools, hospitals, or a more viable infrastructure, or to raise the standard of living of the common people. Multinational companies took the majority of the profits out of the country. The remainder often went directly into the private bank accounts of the wealthy elite, who also ruled the country, in return for their maintaining stability, keeping wages low and unions out, and allowing the companies to exploit the land and people as they wished.

In general, the majority of the exploding population of urban poor earned precarious livings in a modern yet traditional **bazaar economy** of petty traders and unskilled labor. Here regular salaried jobs were rare and highly prized, and a complex world of

economic growth without economic development *When large profits are made from cash crop production or from industrial manufacturing, few of these profits are put back into the construction of infrastructure or other efforts to raise the standard of living of the common people.*

bazaar economy *An economy with few salaried jobs and an abundance of tiny, unregulated businesses such as peddlers and pushcart operators.*

● **The Underground Economy** This Mexican woman sells fruit and other items along the roadside. In Latin America up to 60 percent of the workforce is part of the underground, or informal, economy. Throughout the developing world, millions of people eke out a daily living by selling their labor or crops. The government loses money because it receives no taxes from them. They nearly always earn less than a worker in the formal economy, and they are constantly harassed by corrupt police and government officials, blackmailers, and extortionists. *(Eric Nathan/Alamy Images)*

tiny, unregulated businesses and service occupations predominated. Peddlers and pushcart operators hawked their wares, and sweatshops and home-based workers manufactured cheap goods for popular consumption. This old-yet-new bazaar economy continued to grow prodigiously as migrants streamed to the cities, as modern industry provided too few jobs, and as the wide gap between rich and poor persisted.

Urban Migration and the Family

After 1945, large-scale urban migration had a massive impact on traditional family patterns in the developing countries, just as it had on families in industrialized countries earlier. Particularly in Africa and Asia, the great majority of migrants to the city were young men, married and unmarried; women tended to stay in the villages. The result was a sexual imbalance in both places. There were several reasons for this pattern. Much of the movement to cities (and to mines) remained temporary or seasonal. At least at first, young men left home to earn hard cash to bring back to their villages. Moreover, the cities were expensive, and prospects there were uncertain. Only after a man secured a genuine foothold did he marry or send for his wife and children.

For rural women the consequences of male out-migration were mixed. Asian and African women had long been treated as subordinates, if not inferiors, by their fathers and husbands. Rather suddenly, such women found themselves heads of households, faced with managing the farm, feeding the children, and running their own lives. In the East African country of Kenya, for instance, one-third of all rural households were headed by women in the late 1970s. African and Asian village women had to become unprecedentedly self-reliant and independent. As a result, the real beginnings of more equal rights and opportunities, of "women's liberation," became readily visible in Africa and Asia.

In Latin America the pattern of migration was different. Whole families migrated, very often to squatter settlements, much more commonly than in Asia and Africa. These families frequently belonged to the class of landless laborers, which was generally larger in Latin America than in Africa and Asia. Migration was also more likely to be once and for all. Another difference was that single women were as likely as single men to move to the cities, in part because women were in high demand there as domestic servants. The situation in Mexico in the late 1970s was typical:

They [women] leave the village seeking employment, often as domestic servants. When they do not find work in the cities, they have few alternatives. If they are young, they frequently turn to prostitution; if not, they often resort to begging in the streets. Homeless peasant women, often carrying small children, roam every quarter of Mexico City.[11]

Some women also left to escape the narrow, male-dominated villages. Even so, in Latin America urban migration seemed to have less impact on traditional family patterns and on women's attitudes than it did in Asia and Africa.

Urbanization and Agriculture

As we saw above, multinational agribusinesses, the Green Revolution, and various patterns of land transfer have dramatically altered the methods of global food production, the types of foods produced, and who produces it. These changes have also caused millions of small farmers and peasants to leave their land and migrate to the city. This is a global phenomenon, affecting farmers in developed and developing countries alike. The decline of the family farm in the United States is as representative as any of the consequences of modern agricultural production on small farmers.

A family farm is on land owned by the family; the majority of labor is done by family members; and the business is managed by the family in an open market system. In the United States, the number of family farms decreased from 7 million in the 1930s to fewer than 2 million in 2000. Since 1981, 750,000 farms and over a million jobs have been lost. Every week 330 farm operators leave the land. While the total number of farmers has decreased, total acreage under cultivation has increased. The average farm size increased from under 200 acres in 1940 to over 500 acres in 2000.

This transfer of land, from small family farmers to large operations owned by factory farmers or corporate agribusinesses, has dramatically altered the American labor force. Since the 1930s, the percentage of farmers in the workforce has shrunk from 21 percent to 2 percent. One half of all family farms now depend on off-farm income. Local economies and communities have also suffered because small farmers bought from local vendors, sold to local markets, received loans from local bankers, and shopped at local stores. The result has been the death of many small towns in America and the loss of many farm-related businesses and jobs.

Why has this happened? One simple reason is that the younger generation wants to move to the city—only 6 percent of American family farmers are under thirty-five. But there are other reasons as well. In 1980 an American farmer received 37 cents of every dollar spent on food; by 2000 he or she got only 20 cents. Even in the early 1980s, nominal net income, adjusted for inflation, was the same as during the Great Depression. As farm-related costs—land, equipment, fuel, seeds, fertilizer, irrigation—rise, it becomes more difficult for small farmers to compete with the large operations. Agribusinesses have the advantages of economy of scale and can afford larger machines to farm larger acreages as agriculture is industrialized. And, while the family farmer focuses simply on planting and harvesting a crop, the agribusiness is vertically integrated to control all phases of the process, from producing the hybrid seeds to marketing the final product, and can take advantage of international markets.

Peasants in developing countries leave the land for many of the same reasons. The major difference in developing countries, though, is that these peasant farmers, usually illiterate, are often producing subsistence crops and are simply forced off the land by government troops or thugs hired by large landowners or companies to make way for large cash crop production. The loss of land can also result from peasant families' possessing no documents proving ownership of the fields they have worked for generations. This inability to produce proof of ownership allows wealthy landowners, who obtain the proper documents, to claim the land and have the peasants legally evicted.

As we begin the twenty-first century, a few large agribusinesses threaten to fully industrialize, and then monopolize, global food production. At the same time, millions of small farmers around the world are leaving the land, willingly or unwillingly, and heading for the cities. In industrialized countries like the United States, the farmers and their children have educational and employment options. In developing countries, few options are available for illiterate peasants with no skills other than farming.

SCIENCE AND TECHNOLOGY: CHANGES AND CHALLENGES

What key technological and scientific developments have had the greatest impact on life at the beginning of the new millennium?

The twentieth century was a time of rapid urbanization, but it was equally an era of amazing advances in science and technology. These advances were not always positive. The great excitement over the telephone, the automobile, electricity, and the airplane was quickly tempered in 1914 by the killing machines invented and used in the Great War. Totalitarian regimes exploited new developments in mass communication for mass propaganda. And no sooner had the atom been harnessed than the United States released atomic bombs over Hiroshima and Nagasaki. Yet since the Enlightenment, scientists have believed that progress is possible and that no problem is unsolvable; whether their discoveries are used for good or evil is often out of their hands.

The Medical Revolution

medical revolution *The discovery of vaccines for many of the most deadly diseases during a period from the late 1800s through post–World War II.*

The **medical revolution** began in the late 1800s when Louis Pasteur made the case for a germ theory of disease and developed techniques for vaccine inoculation. The revolution continued after World War II. Scientists discovered vaccines for many of the most deadly diseases. Jonas Salk's development of the polio vaccine in 1952 was followed by the first oral polio vaccine (1962) and vaccines for measles (1964), mumps (1967), rubella (1970), chickenpox (1974), and hepatitis B (1981). Globally, these vaccines have saved millions of lives, especially those of children. According to the United Nations World Health Organization, medical advances reduced deaths from smallpox, cholera, and plague by more than 95 percent worldwide between 1951 and 1966.

Following independence, Asian and African countries increased the small numbers of hospitals, doctors, and nurses they had inherited from the colonial past. Sophisticated medical facilities became symbols of the commitment to a better life. In addition, local people were successfully trained as paramedics to staff rural outpatient clinics that offered medical treatment, health education, and prenatal and postnatal care. Many paramedics were women, for many health problems involved childbirth and infancy, and villagers the world over considered it improper for a man to examine a woman's body.

The medical revolution significantly lowered death rates and lengthened life expectancies. In particular, children became increasingly likely to survive their early years, although infant and juvenile mortality remained far higher in poor countries than in rich ones. By 1980 the average inhabitant of the developing countries could expect to live about fifty-four years; life expectancy at birth varied from forty to sixty-four years depending on the country. In industrialized countries life expectancy at birth averaged seventy-one years.

● **The Medical Revolution**   A woman doctor in Yemen on the Arabian peninsula makes house calls by motorcycle, thereby carrying modern medicine to women in isolated desert communities. The doctor wears the veil traditionally required of women in public throughout parts of the Arab world. *(© Hans Bollinger/Pictures Press/Hamburg)*

Since the 1980s medical science has continued to make remarkable advances. In 1979 the World Health Organization announced the worldwide eradication of smallpox. By this time, transplants of such organs as hearts, lungs, eyes, and kidneys had become routine, and in 1982 an American man became the first recipient of an artificial heart. Also important were advances in our understanding of DNA made in the 1940s, 1950s, and 1960s that led to the Human Genome Project in the 1980s. Teams of scientists worked on this project until April 2003, when they announced they had successfully identified, mapped, and sequenced the entire genome, or hereditary information, of human beings. This knowledge gives health care providers immense new powers for preventing, treating, and curing diseases and makes the completion of the project one of the most important scientific developments in history. Embryonic stem cell research remains one of the most controversial areas of research in the early twenty-first century, but also one of the most promising. Proponents argue that it may offer cures for a range of illnesses from Parkinson's and Alzheimer's diseases to diabetes.

Still, despite these advances, the world continues to face a health care crisis because of the wide gap in health care availability and affordability between the rich and poor. Of the roughly $75 billion spent annually on health research, less than 10 percent is directed at 90 percent of the world's health problems. Thousands of people die every day from diseases and illnesses that are curable and easily treated. Between 1980 and 2000 the number of children under the age of five dying annually of diarrhea dropped by 60 percent, from 4.6 million to 1.8 million, through the global distribution of a cheap sugar-salt solution mixed in water. Still, over 1.5 million children worldwide continue to die each year from diarrhea. Malaria and tuberculosis also continue to be major killers of young and old alike, while deaths worldwide from HIV/AIDS are reaching epic proportions.

Population Change: Balancing the Numbers

A less favorable consequence of the medical revolution was the acceleration of population growth. As in nineteenth-century Europe, a rapid decline in death rates was not immediately accompanied by a similar decline in birthrates. Women in developing countries continued to bear five to seven children each, as their mothers and grandmothers had done. The combined populations of Asia, Africa, and Latin America, which had grown relatively modestly from 1925 to 1950, increased between 1950 and 1975 from 1.7 billion to 3 billion. It was an unprecedented explosion that promised to continue for many years.

The population explosion aroused fears of approaching famine and starvation. Thomas Malthus's gloomy late-eighteenth-century conclusion that population always tends to grow faster than the food supply (see page 655) was revived and updated by **neo-Malthusian** social scientists. Some governments began pushing family planning and birth control to slow population growth. These measures were not very successful in the 1950s and 1960s. In many countries Islamic and Catholic religious teachings were hostile to birth control. Moreover, widespread cultural attitudes dictated that a "real" man keep his wife pregnant. There were also economic reasons for preferring large families. Farmers needed the help of plenty of children at planting and harvest times, and sons and daughters were a sort of social security system for their elders. Thus a prudent couple wanted several children because some would surely die young. By the 1970s and 1980s, however, population growth in the industrialized countries had already begun to fall significantly. By the 1990s, some European leaders were bemoaning a birthrate in their countries that was below the 2.1 level needed to maintain a stable population.

Of much greater importance from a global perspective, the world's poor women began to bear fewer children. Small countries such as Barbados, Chile, Costa Rica, South Korea, Taiwan, and Tunisia led the way. Between 1970 and 1975 China followed, registering the fastest five-year birthrate decline in recorded history. Then other big countries, especially in Latin America and East Asia, experienced large declines in fertility. In 1970 the average Brazilian woman had close to 6 children; by 2005 she had 1.9. In 1970 the average woman in Bangladesh had more than 7 children; in 2005 she had 3.1.

There were several reasons for this decline in fertility among women in the developing world. Fewer babies were dying of disease or malnutrition, so couples needed fewer births to guarantee the survival of the number of children they wanted. Also, better living conditions, urbanization, and more education encouraged women to have fewer children. No wonder the most rapidly industrializing countries, such as Taiwan and South Korea, led the way in declining birthrates.

neo-Malthusian *Social science belief, based on the late-eighteenth-century works of Thomas Malthus, that population tends to grow faster than the food supply.*

● **Five Generations of the Yang Family** This group portrait suggests the enduring Chinese commitment to close family ties. It also puts a human face on social transformation, for the great-great-grandmother has bound feet and the baby she holds will be an only child. In the 1980s the Chinese government prohibited couples from having more than one child, a major factor in China's falling birthrate. *(Dermot Tatlow/Panos Pictures)*

In the early 1960s, the introduction of the birth control pill marked a revolution not only in birth control techniques but also in women taking control of their own fertility. "Family planning" was now truly possible; couples could make private decisions about how many children to have and when. In the early twenty-first century more than half of the world's couples practiced birth control, up from one in eight just forty years earlier, and that proportion continued to rise. Male chauvinism, religious teachings, and conservative government leaders combined in many countries to control the availability and distribution of birth control methods and abortion. Birth control and abortion were generally banned in predominately Roman Catholic countries, such as Ireland, Italy, Spain, and the countries of Latin America, and also in most Muslim countries. The practices were most accepted in North America, Protestant Europe, the Soviet Union, and East Asia, which explains why these regions had the lowest birthrates and population growth.

Although significant differences still exist between regions, projections of world population growth have declined sharply. By 2005 global birthrates had fallen to the lowest level in recorded history. The average woman in the developing world had 2.9 children, down from an average of nearly 6 babies in the 1970s. Fertility in most of the developing world could fall below the replacement level (2.1 children per woman) before 2100. The most recent estimates are that the world's population will "only" grow by 50 percent between 2000 and 2050, when it will reach about 9 billion. Over the next century it is then expected to level off at about 10 billion.

Global Epidemics

One of humanity's gravest fears in the early years of the new millennium comes from the threat posed by epidemic diseases. Outbreaks in Africa of the deadly Ebola and Marburg viruses; a worldwide outbreak of severe acute respiratory syndrome, or SARS, which began in 2002; ongoing avian, or bird, flu in Asia; and "mad-cow" disease, which has wreaked havoc with meat production in several countries, have all raised the frightening specter of a global recurrence of a modern Black Death. Tuberculosis (TB) has also made a comeback and kills one person every fifteen seconds, thus claiming millions of lives every year even though it is a curable disease. Malaria kills a million people a year worldwide, 90 percent of them in Africa.

But few diseases in world history have been more frightening, or caused more disruption of human society, than **HIV/AIDS**. In 2007 the Population Division of the United Nations calculated that 36 million persons globally were infected with HIV, the virus that causes AIDS. AIDS was the world's fourth-leading cause of death.

HIV/AIDS *A virus and a disease that infected more than 40 million persons worldwide by 2004; now the world's fourth leading cause of death.*

The global distribution of AIDS testifies to the existence of a lopsided, unequal world. About 90 percent of all persons who die from AIDS and 86 percent of those currently infected with HIV live in sub-Saharan Africa (see Map 33.2). In Africa HIV/AIDS has most commonly spread through heterosexual sex, and men and women frequently have failed to protect themselves against the disease in casual sexual relations. Widespread disease and poverty are also significant factors in that Africans already suffering from other illnesses such as malaria or tuberculosis have less resistance to HIV and less access to health care for treatment.

Another critical factor contributing to the spread of AIDS in Africa is the continued political instability of many countries—particularly those in the corridor running from Uganda to South Africa. This corridor was the scene of brutal civil or liberation wars that resulted in massive numbers of refugees, a breakdown in basic health care services, and the destruction of family and cultural networks. The countries along this corridor—Uganda, Rwanda, Burundi, Zaire/Congo, Angola, Zimbabwe, Mozambique, and South Africa—have had their populations decimated by HIV/AIDS. South Africa currently has the largest number of HIV/AIDS cases in the world. In 2007 around 10 percent of the South African population, about 5 million people, were

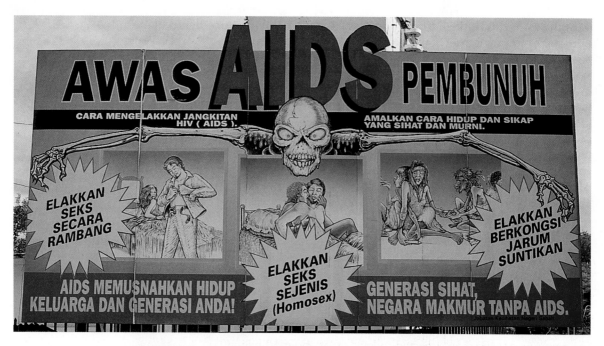

● **Fighting the AIDS Epidemic in Asia** A dramatic billboard warns people in Malaysia about the deadly dangers of AIDS. The billboard offers sound advice, focusing on the three primary ways by which the AIDS virus is spread. Can you "read" the three-part message? *(Robert Francis/The Hutchison Library/Eye Ubiquitous)*

living with HIV. Of these, 230,000 were children under fifteen years of age. An estimated 519,000 South Africans died of AIDS in 2005. As of 2005 medical health experts expected that Russia, India, China, Japan, and other countries in Asia might soon overtake South Africa in reported HIV/AIDS cases.

Although HIV/AIDS has had a devastating impact on Africa, globally the epidemic is still at a relatively early stage. Changes in behavior will be critical to slowing the spread of AIDS in the developing world. Although complicated treatments to contain the epidemic were available in 2008 in the wealthy industrialized countries, these treatments were still too expensive and too complicated for most national health services in the poor countries. Global interdependence increased in monitoring the spread of AIDS, but profound inequalities remained in its treatment.

Environmentalism

Many observers consider the publication in 1962 of Rachel Carson's *Silent Spring* as marking the beginning of the modern environmental movement. In the first pages, Carson (1907–1964) describes a "silent spring" in a nameless small American town. All the vegetation withers and turns brown. The townsfolk begin to fall ill. Birds make no sounds and are too weak to fly. No chicks hatch. Pig litters are small and soon die. There are no blossoms on the apple trees and no droning bees. Fishermen can catch no fish. Although her account is fictitious, Carson pointed out that some of these disasters had already befallen many real communities, and she warned that new chemicals released into the environment every year were responsible:

Along with the possibility of the extinction of mankind by nuclear war, the central problem of our age has therefore become the contamination of man's total environment with such substances of incredible potential for harm—substances that accumulate in the tissues of plants and animals and even penetrate the germ cells to shatter or alter the very material of heredity upon which the shape of the future depends.[12]

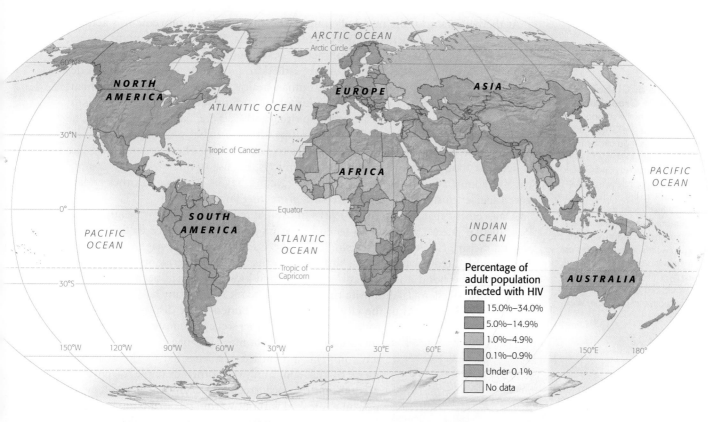

MAP 33.2 **People Living with HIV/AIDS Worldwide, 2007**   As this map illustrates, Africa has been hit the hardest by the HIV/AIDS epidemic. It currently has fifteen to twenty times more identified cases than any other region of the world. AIDS researchers expect that in the coming decade, however, Russia and South and East Asia will overtake and then far surpass Africa in the number of infected people. (*Source: Data from World Health Organization,* www.whosea.org)

Carson was particularly concerned about pesticides, especially DDT, which was being utilized extensively and with much success to eradicate malaria. Her writings and campaigning, more than any other single cause, brought about the ban on DDT. Her work was a clarion call alerting people to the hazards present in all the chemicals they were using around their homes. Difficult decisions had to be made when weighing the advantages and disadvantages of using these often effective but highly toxic chemicals. At the time DDT was banned, for example, malaria had largely been wiped out; since the banning it has been making a deadly comeback.

Environmental history is one of the fastest-growing fields of study. Like disease, the environment knows no boundaries and therefore is an ideal topic for world historians. There have always been some voices expressing concern for the environment. In the eighteenth century, for example, governments became increasingly concerned about their forests as the great demand for lumber to build ships nearly destroyed the forests of Britain, Europe, the eastern United States, and later India. The United States created the first national park in the nineteenth century. "Wilderness areas" were viewed as refuges from industrialization and urbanization. The Sierra Club, today one of America's most famous environmental organizations, was founded in 1892. The modern environmental movement began with concerns about chemical waste, rapid consumption of energy and food supplies, massive global deforestation, environmental degradation caused in part by sprawling megacities, and threats to wildlife. By the 1970s citizens had begun joining together in organizations such as Greenpeace and Friends of the Earth to try to preserve, restore, or enhance the natural environment.

At the beginning of the new millennium, the environmental movement is actually several different movements, each with its own agenda. Rachel Carson might be seen as an early proponent of the environmental health movement. She and others were concerned about the effects of chemicals, radiation, pollution, waste, and urban development on the environment and on human health. The conservation movement, represented by the Sierra Club and the Audubon Society, seeks to protect the biodiversity of the planet and emphasizes the spiritual and aesthetic qualities of nature. The ecology movement consists of different groups with somewhat similar agendas, ranging from the politically active Green parties to Greenpeace. These organizations are concerned about global warming, toxic chemicals, the use of nuclear energy and nuclear weapons, genetically modified food, recycling, saving whales and other endangered species, sustainable agriculture, and protecting ancient forests.

A movement that began in the 1980s in the United States is the campaign for environmental justice, which seeks to end what its supporters consider to be environmental racism, classism, and sexism. The Love Canal tragedy in Niagara Falls, New York, highlighted environmental justice concerns. In 1978, residents of the Love Canal neighborhood learned that their houses and local school had been built on top of an industrial chemical dumpsite that Hooker Chemical Company had covered with earth in 1953 and sold to the city for a dollar. As buried waste disposal drums corroded, benzene and other toxic chemicals seeped through the ground and into homes. The negative effects on the environment and on the residents led to the abandonment of the community. Another example of environmental injustice occurred on December 3, 1984, when poison gas leaked without warning from a Union Carbide factory in Bhopal, India, while people were sleeping. The plant's safety systems were not working, so no warning sounded, and thousands soon died horrible deaths from breathing in the gas. Years after this tragedy, toxic chemicals abandoned at the plant continued to poison local drinking water. In 2004 the Indian Supreme Court ordered a cleanup. In 1986 the worst nuclear accident occurred: the explosion of a nuclear power plant at Chernobyl, in Ukraine. Estimated deaths from the accident range from hundreds to hundreds of thousands, and over two hundred thousand people had to be evacuated. Nuclear fallout landed in several European countries, and scientists are still studying the ongoing effects of the event.

At the beginning of the twenty-first century environmentalists are especially concerned about **global warming,** the increase of global temperatures over time. The 1990s was the warmest decade in recorded history. The majority of the world's scientists believe the increase began with the Industrial Revolution in the 1700s. The subsequent human-generated hydrocarbons produced through the burning of fossil fuels—coal, oil, natural gas—have caused a greenhouse effect.

Possible effects of global warming over the next century include a catastrophic rise in sea levels that would put many coastal cities and islands under water; ecosystem changes that may threaten various species of plants and animals; extreme and abnormal weather patterns; destruction of the earth's ozone layer, which shields the planet from harmful solar radiation; and a decline in agriculture

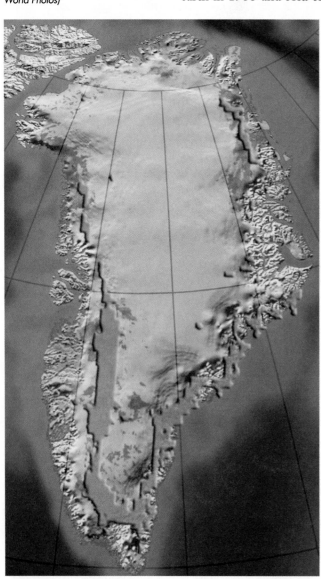

● **Evidence of Global Warming in Greenland** This graphic indicates the seasonal melt extent, in red, of the Greenland ice sheet in 2002. Of greatest immediate concern to scientists is that melting polar icecaps and Greenland glaciers are releasing cold, fresh water into the northern Atlantic Ocean, which could shut down the Gulf Stream that warms Europe and northeastern North America by bringing warm ocean currents up from the equator. This could produce an ice age in the northern Atlantic that would drastically affect global weather patterns. *(AP Photo/Wide World Photos)*

production. Although the exact causes and consequences of global warming are being debated, the world community is so concerned that in 1997 an amendment, the Kyoto Protocol, was added to the United Nations Framework Convention on Climate Change. Countries that ratify the protocol agree to try to reduce their emissions of carbon dioxide and five other greenhouse gases. Each country is assigned a certain limit of emission for each of these six gases, but countries may also trade emission amounts with one another if they want to maintain or increase gas emission for a particular gas. As of early 2008, 174 countries had ratified the protocol, including Russia in November 2004 and Australia in December 2007. The most notable exception was the United States.

global warming *The belief of the majority of the world's scientists that hydrocarbons produced through the burning of fossil fuels have caused a greenhouse effect that has increased global temperatures over time.*

Mass Communication

Between 1875 and 1900 the world witnessed the invention of the phonograph, the first moving pictures, the Kodak camera, the first dial telephone, the radio, magnetic recordings, and loudspeakers. These revolutionary new technologies prepared the way for a twentieth century of mass communications and the "information age." The radio and moving pictures dominated entertainment for the first half of the century and also served as propaganda tools for the era's dictators.

The global availability and affordability of transistorized radios and television sets in the 1950s introduced a second communications revolution. The transistor radio penetrated the most isolated hamlets of the developing world. Governments universally embraced radio broadcasting as a means of power, propaganda, and education. Relentlessly, the transistor radio propagated the outlooks and attitudes of urban elites and challenged old values.

Though less common, television use expanded into nearly every country, even if there was just one television in a village. Governments recognized the power of the visual image to promote their ideology or leader, and a state television network became a source of national pride. By the beginning of the twenty-first century, television was bringing the whole planet into the bars and meetinghouses of the world's villages and was having a profound, even revolutionary, impact everywhere. At the very least, alluring television images of high living standards and the excitement of urban life stirred powerful desires in young people, who copied Western materialism, migrated to the cities, and created a global youth culture.

The third, and perhaps greatest, communications revolution occurred with the first Apple personal computers in 1976. Mass communications have exploded since then. Some new technologies are obsolete by the time they reach the market. The computer and the cell phone have effected the greatest change in people's lives.

The first cell phones, in 1985, freed users from land lines and allowed individuals and nations in the developing world to bypass most of the stages of twentieth-century telephone development. Telephone lines, installation, and numerous other traditional obstacles to telephone use can be avoided with cell phones. Africa now has over 85 million cell phone users; equivalent land-line phone use would be impossible. Cell phone use has to overcome no barriers of gender, age, income, education, or even access to electricity. Cell phones have become one of the most widely owned consumer products worldwide.

Computers have revolutionized so many areas of human endeavor that it is impossible to enumerate them all. The Internet, or World Wide Web, has had the greatest impact on human communication. First made available in 1994 to the general public, the Internet and e-mail provide all human beings with the possibility of instantaneous communication with each other. They create a global coffeehouse where anything and everything may be discussed and debated. The possibilities for global access to information and knowledge are seemingly infinite. In the tradition of authoritarian regimes throughout history, dictators have quickly realized the threat the Internet poses to their power and control. The governments of China and North Korea have

● **Educational TV in South Africa**   A South African TV crew films *Soul Buddyz,* a popular show for children that grapples honestly with everything from sexuality and AIDS to child abuse and physical disabilities. This show was inspired by *Soul City,* an award-winning soap opera for teenagers and young adults that includes practical information on safe sex and HIV infection. *(Louise Gubb/Corbis Saba)*

spent millions of dollars trying to restrict information traveling in and out of their countries over the Internet. For the first time in history, this type of censorship may prove impossible.

SOCIAL REFORM AND PROGRESS

What social problems are the focus of reformers in the new millennium?

Just as an end to slavery became the rallying cry for social reformers in the nineteenth century, modern social reformers have sought to end global inequality, racism, and sexism, and to improve human and civil rights for all. We have already described many of these developments, such as the victory of the democratic movement in eastern Europe and the end of the racist apartheid system in South Africa. Much remains to be achieved, however, and nowhere is more worldwide attention being focused than on the advancement of human and civil rights for women and children. Although significant progress has been made since 1945, women and children continue to enjoy fewer rights than men worldwide in nearly every category that might be measured.

Women: The Right to Equality

In September 1995 delegates from around the world met in Beijing, China, for the United Nations Fourth World Conference on Women. The meeting's final report called on the world community to take strategic action in twelve areas of critical concern to women: poverty, access to education and training, access to health care, violence against women, women and war, economic inequality with men, political inequality with men, creation of institutions for women's advancement, lack of

The Dalai Lama

His Holiness the Dalai Lama in Germany promoting freedom for Tibet. (*AP Photo/ Wide World Photos*)

Shortly before he died in 1933, Thupten Gyatso (1876–1933), the "Great Thirteenth" Dalai Lama of Tibet, had a vision of the future. He predicted that if the Tibetans did not protect their territory, their spiritual leaders would be exterminated, their property and authority would be taken away, their political system would vanish, and their people would become slaves. For fifty-seven years he had ruled over a country treated like a pawn in the "Great Game" played by Russia, Britain, and China for territory and power. He feared the Chinese the most.

After his death, a mission of high officials went in search of his successor. Tibetans believe that each succeeding Dalai Lama is the reincarnation of the previous one. In 1937 the mission came to a peasant village in northeastern Tibet to question a two-year-old boy, Tenzin Gyatso. When he passed all their tests, they took him and his family to Lhasa, the Tibetan capital. There, in 1940, he was enthroned as His Holiness the Fourteenth Dalai Lama.

In Lhasa the boy spent much of his time studying, eventually earning a doctorate in Buddhist philosophy at age twenty-five. His youth ended abruptly in October 1950 when the thirteenth Dalai Lama's vision came true: eighty thousand Chinese soldiers invaded Tibet. In November the fifteen-year-old Dalai Lama assumed full political power. In 1954 he traveled to Beijing to meet for peace talks with Mao Zedong. Although he was impressed by Mao's promise to modernize Tibet and intrigued by socialism, he was stunned by Mao's last words to him: "But of course, religion is poison."*

This remark was deeply troubling because the Tibetans are an intensely religious people. For centuries they lived in near isolation, practiced Buddhism, and looked to the Dalai Lama as both their political and their spiritual leader. After returning to Tibet, the Dalai Lama tried to negotiate a peaceful settlement with the Chinese, to no avail. In March 1959 the Chinese army crushed a massive demonstration in Lhasa, and the Dalai Lama had to flee for his life. The Indian prime minister, Jawaharlal Nehru, gave him political asylum, and he established a Tibetan government-in-exile at Dharamsala, India. More than 120,000 Tibetan refugees live there today.

Since the Chinese occupation began, all but twelve of more than six thousand monasteries in Tibet have been destroyed, and thousands of sacred treasures have been stolen or sold. An estimated three thousand political or religious prisoners are in labor camps in Tibet, and the Chinese have been directly responsible for the deaths of 1.2 million Tibetans. Over 7 million Chinese settlers have poured into Tibet. Tibetan women are routinely forced to undergo sterilization or have abortions.

To counter this destruction, His Holiness the Dalai Lama has campaigned for Tibetan self-determination and basic human rights. He has established programs abroad to save the Tibetan culture and language and to shelter the refugees. There is a Tibetan educational system for refugee children, a Tibetan Institute of Performing Arts, and a university for Tibetan Studies. There are also agricultural settlements for refugees and over two hundred new monasteries to preserve Tibetan Buddhism and to train new monks. In his quest for justice, the Dalai Lama travels around the world seeking support from world leaders, institutions, and common citizens. Although he describes himself as a simple Buddhist monk, few individuals in human history have spoken for the downtrodden and oppressed and for universal justice and human dignity with such moral authority.

In December 1989 the Dalai Lama received the Nobel Peace Prize. In accepting, he said that he did so on behalf of all oppressed peoples—those who struggle for freedom and work for world peace—as well as for the people of Tibet. The prize, he said, "reaffirms our conviction that with truth, courage and determination as our weapons, Tibet will be liberated. Our struggle must remain nonviolent and free of hatred."†

Questions for Analysis

1. In what ways do Tibet's history and the Dalai Lama's life reflect many of the major issues and events of the twentieth century?

2. The world's response to China's occupation reflects what political and economic factors?

Source: Freedom in Exile: The Autobiography of the Dalai Lama (London: Little, Brown), 1990.

†http://nobelprize.org/peace/laureates/1989/lama-acceptance.html.

*Tenzin Gyatso, the Dalai Lama, *My Land and My People* (New York: McGraw-Hill, 1962), p. 117.

● **Kuwait's First Female Minister** Maasuma al-Mubarak, a leading women's rights activist and professor of international relations at Kuwait University, gives a thumbs-up during a session of the Kuwaiti parliament in June 2005. Al-Mubarak was the first woman in Kuwaiti history to be appointed as a cabinet minister in the government. She served as Health Minister until August 2007, when she resigned following a fire at a Kuwaiti hospital that killed two people. *(Yasser Al-Zayvat/AFP/Getty Images)*

feminization of poverty *The issue that those living in extreme poverty are disproportionately women.*

respect for women's rights, stereotyping of women, gender inequalities and the environment, and violation of girl children's rights.[13]

These are concerns that all women share, although degrees of inequality vary greatly from one country to another. Concerns over political inequality in the United States, for example, might focus on electing a woman president or electing as many women as men to the U.S. Senate. In countries where women are not allowed to vote, let alone hold political office, the concerns would be different. The type and extent of inequality varies greatly, and global progress in lessening it has been uneven. Generally the greatest advances have been in the leading industrialized nations, and there is some correlation between women's equality and economic prosperity.

The **feminization of poverty,** women living disproportionately in extreme poverty, is one of the greatest concerns among women activists in the new millennium. Unlike many other issues, it is as great a problem in the developed world as elsewhere. Even in the most developed countries, two out of every three poor adults are women. In the United States half of all poor families are supported by single mothers, who earn an average income 23 percent below the poverty line. There are many causes for this phenomenon. Having principal responsibility for child care, women have less time and opportunity for work, and because they have less access to health care they are often unable to work. As male labor migration worldwide increases, the number of households headed by women increases and thus the number of families living in poverty. Job restrictions and discrimination, plus limited education, result in women having few job options except in the "informal economy" as maids, street vendors, or prostitutes. These are generally the lowest-paid jobs; they require long hours to earn even a small amount of money; and they frequently involve violent and abusive treatment.

It is true that the declining global birthrate means that more women and couples are gaining control over their fertility through access to birth control. Women also benefit through improved overall health, longer life, and healthier children when they have fewer pregnancies. Even within developed countries, however, birthrates remain high among poor women, especially among poor adolescents, who make up an inordinate number of the estimated 585,000 women who die every year during pregnancy and childbirth. And it is the poorest women who usually suffer most from government policies, usually legislated by men, that restrict their access to reproductive health care.

Women have made some modest gains in the workplace, making up 38 percent of the nonfarm-sector global workforce in the early 2000s, as compared to 35 percent in 1990. But segregated labor markets remain the rule, with higher-paying jobs reserved for men. Gender equality in the workforce is critical if women are to become financially independent, have some financial security as they age, and contribute to the overall improvement of a country's economy. In the farm sector, women globally produce more than half of all the food that is grown, and up to 80 percent of subsistence crops grown in Africa. Because this is informal labor, and often unpaid, these women laborers are denied access to loans, and many of them cannot own the land they farm.

Some observers believe that violence against women is becoming worse rather than better. Although rape has always been a part of war, during the wars in the former Yugoslavia and in Rwanda in the early 1990s, rape and sexual violence became weapons of war. Both have been subsequently labeled crimes against humanity and are considered forms of torture and genocide. Still, rape and sexual violence have continued to be used as weapons of war in conflicts in Sierra Leone, Kosovo, Afghanistan, the Democratic Republic of the Congo, East Timor, and elsewhere. Domestic violence appears to be on the increase in many countries, including Russia, Pakistan, Peru, Uzbekistan, and South Africa. Forced prostitution and international female slave traffic is carried on by traffickers from such countries as Ukraine, Moldova, Nigeria, Burma, and Thailand. Perhaps five thousand women a year are killed in "honor killings," which occur when men kill their female relatives for bringing dishonor on the family's reputation, frequently because of some perceived misuse of their sexuality.

Some progress has been made toward equality for women. Just the fact that UN member nations have signed various human rights accords pertaining to women is a positive development. (See the feature "Listening to the Past: The United Nations Millennium Project Report" on pages 1068–1069.) New laws have been enacted, and more girls than ever before worldwide are receiving an education. More women are now allowed to vote and to hold office, and half of all the female heads of state elected since 1900 were elected after 1990. Women also are moving across and up in the workplace—holding a wider variety of jobs and more senior positions.

Children: The Right to Childhood

In 1989 the United Nations General Assembly adopted the Convention on the Rights of the Child, which spelled out a number of rights that member nations believed are due every child. These include civil and human rights and economic, social, and cultural rights. The convention has been ratified by more countries than any other human rights treaty in world history—192 countries as of 2005. The United States and Somalia are the only two countries that have not ratified it.

It is not difficult to see why such a document was necessary. Globally, a billion children live in poverty—one in every two children in the world. In the United States, 16 percent of children, more than 11 million girls and boys, live in poor families with parents who earn at or below the poverty line. Worldwide, 640 million children do not have adequate shelter, 400 million do not have safe water, and 270 million receive no health care. From 10 million to 11 million children die each year before age five.

Besides poverty, the convention addresses a number of other concerns. These include children making up half of the world's refugees, child labor and exploitation, sexual violence and sex trafficking, police abuse of street children, HIV/AIDS orphans, lack of access to education, and lack of access to adequate health care. Increasingly in the last decade, children have been recruited or kidnapped to become child soldiers, as many as 300,000 worldwide, 120,000 in Africa alone. Child sexual abuse and child soldiers have become such widespread problems that the United Nations wrote two additional protocols—one on the involvement of children in armed conflicts and the other on the sale of children, child pornography, and child prostitution—that were attached to the original convention and adopted in 2000.

● **Child Soldier in Sierra Leone** This eleven-year-old boy, with a rifle slung over his shoulder, is a member of the Sierra Leone army and stands guard at a checkpoint during his country's civil war. Tens of thousands of boys and girls under eighteen have been used by the militaries in more than sixty countries since 2000, either as armed combatants or informally in tasks such as spying, scouting, carrying messages, and cooking. *(AP Photo/Wide World Photos)*

Education

As the twenty-first century began, nearly a billion people were unable to read a book or sign their names. Of these, more than two-thirds were women. Of the 100 million children without access to primary education, 60 percent or more were girls. If less than 1 percent of the money allocated worldwide to military weapons every year were spent on education, every child in the world would be able to go to school.

There is a direct correlation between national rates of literacy and economic prosperity. Most of the global literacy problems are found in the developing world. The democracy movement of the early 1990s and increasing economic globalization have put pressure on all governments to improve literacy rates and to improve educational opportunities for young people. Since the 1990s more and more countries have recognized the importance of providing a minimum level of basic education and have made it compulsory. Globally, four in five children now participate in lower secondary education (U.S. ninth and tenth grades), but discrepancies remain wide. Many countries have 90 to 100 percent participation in at least lower secondary education, but in Africa the rate is closer to 45 percent and only 29 percent for upper secondary (U.S. eleventh and twelfth grades). Only when countries are stable and have prosperous economies will all children receive the education they deserve.

The most revolutionary advances in education in the developing world will come through access to the Internet. Despite the initial costs—significant for many countries—the benefits obtained from having even one computer connected to the Internet in each school are incalculable. Instantaneously, children get access to all the world's libraries, art galleries, museums, educational sites, and knowledge bases. Internet access does not make the playing field between rich and poor students exactly level, but it comes closer to doing so than any other development in history.

Chapter Summary

To assess your mastery of this chapter, go to
bedfordstmartins.com/mckayworld

• *What is the global political situation in the early twenty-first century, and how do competing nation-states address common problems?*

After forty years of superpower confrontation, the cold war's end brought renewed hope for global peace and prosperity. If we have learned anything since 1991, however, it is that neither peace nor prosperity come easily for the human race. New rifts and old animosities have set us at odds in ways that are just as dangerous and lethal as the cold war differences they replaced. Nation-states remained the primary building blocks of political organization as the world entered the twenty-first century. But increasing interdependency and globalization were forcing nations and peoples to come together, negotiate, and make joint global decisions more frequently than at any time in human history.

• *How are the United Nations and multinational corporations representative of increasing globalization?*

Increased globalization has created the need for public and private international organizations, such as the United Nations, to provide a forum and a vehicle for nation-states to come together to solve global problems. These organizations exert a steady pressure for international cooperation when dealing with global issues. Multinational corporations, however, have become perhaps the most important symbol of globalization. With capitalism's revival after World War II, relatively free international economic relations, and the need globally for swift industrialization, multinational corporations rapidly emerged in the early 1950s. They used advanced marketing and sales techniques to push their products around the world; they put huge sums of money into research and development; and they operated across political boundaries to create a single global marketplace.

• *What factors spurred the growth of cities in Africa, Asia, and Latin America, and what were some of the main consequences of urbanization in the late twentieth century?*

The phenomenal growth of cities over the past fifty years has had a tremendous impact on individuals, families, and communities. Megacities, in particular, have evolved at an astonishing pace. The reasons for this urban explosion include a tremendous spurt in population growth and people's desire to find jobs, particularly manufacturing jobs that were concentrated in the cities. People also left the countryside because they were pushed off their land or, if they were young, also for the excitement of the city.

The consequences of this rapid urbanization are similar to those associated with early-twentieth-century urbanization in Europe and North America, but on a larger scale. Overcrowding and shantytowns have been some of the most visible problems. Urban social services have been overwhelmed, and cities have been unable to provide the necessary police and fire protection and adequate sanitation, running water, and electricity services.

Key Terms

United Nations
Security Council
General Assembly
middle powers
separatism
terrorism
al-Qaeda
multinational corporations
industrialization strategy
modernization
mixed economy
Green Revolution
Law of the Sea
megacities
urban explosion
urbanization without
  industrialization
shantytowns
self-help housing
economic growth without
  economic development
bazaar economy
medical revolution
neo-Malthusian
HIV/AIDS
global warming
feminization of poverty

• What key technological and scientific developments have had the greatest impact on life at the beginning of the new millennium?

Science and technology also significantly changed global society in the twentieth century. A medical revolution has discovered vaccines to treat some of history's most deadly diseases; artificial hearts and organ transplants have become routine. The successful mapping of human DNA offers unimaginable possibilities for the prevention, treatment, and cure of diseases. As we learn more about the environment, global warming has drawn more attention from government leaders and private citizens. Mass communication is another area where advances have been revolutionary. Many people around the world now carry hand-held computers, phones, and other devices that make information exchange almost instantaneous.

• What social problems are the focus of reformers in the new millennium?

Social reformers continue to identify problems and inequalities in human society that need to be addressed. During the past hundred years these reformers have had some success in bringing an end to racial injustice in terms of political freedom, human and civil rights, and social and political equality. At the end of the twentieth century and the beginning of the twenty-first, social reformers have turned their attention to the advancement of human and civil rights for women and children.

The study of world history will put these and future events in perspective. Future developments on this small planet will surely build on the many-layered foundations hammered out in the past. Moreover, the study of world history, of mighty struggles and fearsome challenges, of shining achievements and tragic failures, imparts a strong sense of life's essence: the process of change over time. Again and again we have seen how peoples and societies evolve, influenced by ideas, human passions, and material conditions. Armed with the ability to think historically, students of history are prepared to comprehend this inexorable process of change in their own lifetimes, as the world races forward toward an uncertain destiny.

Suggested Reading

Allison, Graham. *Nuclear Terrorism: The Ultimate Preventable Catastrophe.* 2004. An assessment of the global nuclear threat.

Bales, Kevin. *Disposable People: New Slavery in the Global Economy.* 2004. Analysis of the economic exploitation of the world's poor.

Caircross, Frances. *The Death of Distance: How the Communications Revolution Is Changing Our Lives.* 2001. Discusses the global consequences of cell phones, satellites, and the Internet.

Chandler, Alfred D., and Bruce Mazlish. *Leviathans: Multinational Corporations and the New Global History.* 2005. A stimulating global perspective on multinational corporations and how they affect everyone's lives.

Das, Gurcharan. *India Unbound: The Social and Economic Revolution from Independence to the Global Information Age.* 2002. India's leap into the age of modern technology and computers and the consequences for its population and the world.

Drexler, Maeline. *Secret Agents: The Menace of Emerging Infections.* 2003. Provides an overview of the global threat from infectious diseases, old and new.

Fishman, Ted C. *China, Inc.: How the Rise of the Next Superpower Challenges America and the World.* 2006. Explains the profound consequences of China's becoming the next economic superpower.

Foer, Franklin. *How Soccer Explains the World: An Unlikely Theory of Globalization.* 2005. A unique but fascinating interpretation of globalization.

Friedman, Thomas L. *The Lexus and the Olive Tree: Understanding Globalization.* 2000. An interesting look at globalization and multinationals.

Gareis, Sven Bernhard, and Johannes Varwick. *The United Nations: An Introduction.* 2005. An up-to-date introduction to the United Nations.

Gore, Al. *An Inconvenient Truth: The Planetary Emergency of Global Warming and What We Can Do About It.* 2006. Reasoned discussion of the greatest threat to the planet in the twenty-first century, for which Gore won the Nobel Peace Prize.

Hobsbawm, Eric J. *On the Edge of the New Century: In Conversation with Antonio Polito.* 2000. An extraordinarily prescient commentary on the recent past and the near future by one of the premier historians of our time.

Johnson-Odim, Cheryl, and Margaret Strobel, eds. *Expanding the Boundaries of Women's History: Essays on Women in the Third World.* 1992. Groundbreaking essays on women's history outside of Europe and North America.

Jones, Geoffrey. *Multinationals and Global Capitalism: From the Nineteenth to the Twenty-first Century.* 2005. A historical overview of the development of multinational corporations and a global capitalist economy.

Kasarda, John, and Allan Parnell, eds. *Third World Cities: Problems, Policies and Prospects.* 1993. Discusses the prodigious growth of Third World cities in the second half of the twentieth century.

Kenney, Padraic, and Max Paul Friedman, eds. *Partisan Histories: The Past in Contemporary Global Politics.*

2005. An intriguing analysis of how nations are revising their histories to shape modern identities.

Klare, Michael T. *Resource Wars: The New Landscape of Global Conflict.* 2002. Analyzes the conflict over vital resources and the impact on national military and economic policies.

Moaddel, Mansoor. *Islamic Modernism, Nationalism, and Fundamentalism.* 2005. A scholarly historical introduction to society and politics in the Middle East.

O'Neill, Bard. E. *Insurgency and Terrorism: From Revolution to Apocalypse,* 2d ed. rev. 2005. An excellent introduction to the nature of modern war.

O'Neill, John Terence, and Nicholas Rees. *United Nations Peacekeeping in the Post–Cold War Era.* 2005. Discusses the problems associated with United Nations peacekeeping efforts.

Price, Monroe E. *Media and Sovereignty: The Global Information Revolution and Its Challenge to State Power.* 2004. Considers the challenges and threats posed by media and the communications revolution to the sovereignty of nation-states.

Notes

1. A. Toynbee, *Mankind and Mother Earth* (New York: Oxford University Press, 1976), pp. 576–577.

2. B. Barber, *Jihad vs. McWorld* (New York: Times Books, 1995), p. 9.

3. D. Rappaport, "The Fourth Wave: September 11 in the History of Terrorism," *Current History,* December 2001, pp. 419–424.

4. Ibid.

5. Quoted in J. Fallows, "Success Without Victory," in *The Atlantic Monthly* 295 (January/February 2005): 80.

6. Quoted in L. R. Brown, *Seeds of Change: The Green Revolution and Development in the 1970s* (New York: Praeger, 1970), p. 16.

7. P. Ehrlich, *The Population Bomb* (New York: Ballantine, 1968), p. 11.

8. M. ul Haq, *The Poverty Curtain: Choices for the Third World* (New York: Columbia University Press, 1976), p. 152.

9. J. Diamond, *Collapse: How Societies Choose to Fail or Survive* (New York: Viking, 2004), pp. 524–525.

10. P. Bairoch, *Economics and World History: Myths and Paradoxes* (Chicago: University of Chicago Press, 1993), p. 95.

11. P. Huston, *Third World Women Speak Out: Interviews in Six Countries on Change, Development, and Basic Needs* (New York: Praeger, 1979), p. 11.

12. R. Carson, *Silent Spring* (1962; repr., New York: Houghton Mifflin, 1994), pp. 1–3, 7–8.

13. United Nations, "Critical Areas of Concern," *Report of the Fourth World Conference on Women* (New York: United Nations Department for Policy Coordination and Sustainable Development, 1995), ch. 1, annex II, ch. 3, pp. 41–44; available at http://www.un.org/esa/gopher-data/conf/fwcw/off/a—20.en. See also Population Reference Bureau, *Women of Our World 2005* (Washington, D.C.: Population Reference Bureau, 2005), for the latest data and ten-year follow-up to the Beijing meeting.

Listening to the PAST

The United Nations Millennium Project Report

In September 2000, the United Nations issued a "Millennium Declaration"—a bold statement of values and an agenda of actions to be undertaken by the United Nations and its member nations to reach eight major goals relating to global poverty and hunger, disease, education, the environment, maternal health, child mortality, gender equality, and global partnerships by 2015. In the following speech delivered the previous April, Secretary-General Kofi Annan set out the broad framework for this plan of action, which became the United Nations Millennium Project. In January 2005, the United Nations issued a five-year report that summarized the results to date and offered strategies for meeting the goals by 2015.

If one word encapsulates the changes we are living through, it is "globalisation." We live in a world that is interconnected as never before. . . . This has its dangers, of course. Crime, narcotics, terrorism, disease, weapons—all these move back and forth faster, and in greater numbers, than in the past. . . .

But the *benefits* of globalisation are obvious too: faster growth, higher living standards, and new opportunities—not only for individuals but also for better understanding between nations, and for common action.

One problem is that, at present, these opportunities are far from equally distributed. . . . A second problem is that, even where the global market does reach, it is not yet underpinned, as national markets are, by rules based on shared social objectives. . . .

So, . . . the overarching challenge of our times is to make globalisation mean more than bigger markets. To make a success of this great upheaval we must learn how to govern better, and—above all—how to govern better together.

We need to make our States stronger and more effective at the national level. And we need to get them working together on global issues—all pulling their weight and all having their say.

What are these global issues? I have grouped them under three headings, each of which I relate to a fundamental human freedom—freedom from want, freedom from fear, and the freedom of future generations to sustain their lives on this planet.

First, *freedom from want.* How can we call human beings free and equal in dignity when over a billion of them are struggling to survive on less than one dollar a day, without safe drinking water, and when half of all humanity lacks adequate sanitation? Some of us are worrying about whether the stock market will crash, or struggling to master our latest computer, while more than half our fellow men and women have much more basic worries, such as where their children's next meal is coming from. . . .

Many of these problems are worst in sub-Saharan Africa, where extreme poverty affects a higher proportion of the population than anywhere else, and is compounded by a higher incidence of conflict, HIV/AIDS, and other ills. I am asking the world community to make special provision for Africa's needs, and give full support to Africans in their struggle to overcome these problems. . . .

Within the next fifteen years, I believe we can halve the population of people living in extreme poverty; ensure that all children—girls and boys alike, particularly the girls—receive a full primary education; and halt the spread of HIV/AIDS. In twenty years, we can also transform the lives of one hundred million slum dwellers around the world. And I believe we should be able to offer all young people between 15 and 24 the chance of decent work. . . .

The second main heading in the Report is *freedom from fear.* Wars between States are mercifully less frequent than they used to be. But in the last decade *internal* wars have claimed more than five million lives, and driven many times that number of people from their homes. Moreover, we still live under the shadow of weapons of mass destruction.

Both these threats, I believe, require us to think of security less in terms of merely defending territory, and more in terms of protecting *people.* That means we must tackle the threat of deadly conflict at every stage in the process. . . .

A child is immunized against disease in a remote village in Thailand, advancing one of the United Nations Millennium Project's goals. *(Peter Charlesworth/OnAsia Images)*

[T]he best way to prevent conflict is to promote political arrangements in which all groups are fairly represented, combined with human rights, minority rights, and broad-based economic development. Also, illicit transfers of weapons, money or natural resources must be forced into the limelight, so we can control them better.

We must protect vulnerable people by finding better ways to enforce humanitarian and human rights law, and to ensure that gross violations do not go unpunished. National sovereignty offers vital protection to small and weak States, but it should not be a shield for crimes against humanity. In extreme cases the clash of these two principles confronts us with a real dilemma, and the Security Council may have a moral duty to act on behalf of the international community. . . .

Finally, we must pursue our disarmament agenda more vigorously. Since 1995 it has lost momentum in an alarming way. That means controlling the traffic in small arms much more tightly, but also returning to the vexed issue of nuclear weapons. . . .

The third fundamental freedom my Report addresses is one that is not clearly identified in the Charter, because in 1945 our founders could scarcely imagine that it would ever be threatened. I mean the freedom of future generations to sustain their lives on this planet. . . .

If I could sum it up in one sentence, I should say we are plundering our children's heritage to pay for our present unsustainable practices.

This must stop. We must reduce emissions of carbon and other "greenhouse gases," to put a stop to global warming. Implementing the Kyoto Protocol is a vital first step. . . .

We must face the implications of a steadily shrinking surface of cultivable land, at a time when every year brings many millions of new mouths to feed. Biotechnology may offer the best hope, but only if we can resolve the controversies and allay the fears surrounding it. . . .

We must preserve our forests, fisheries, and the diversity of living species, all of which are close to collapsing under the pressure of human consumption and destruction. In short, we need a new ethic of stewardship. We need a much better informed public, and we need to take environmental costs and benefits fully into account in our economic policy decisions. We need regulations and incentives to discourage pollution and overconsumption of nonrenewable resources, and to encourage environment-friendly practices. And we need more accurate scientific data. . . .

But, you may be asking by now, what about the United Nations? . . .

[My] Report contains a further section on renewing the United Nations. . . . But let us not forget *why* the United Nations matters. It matters only to the extent that it can make a useful contribution to solving the problems and accomplishing the tasks I have just outlined.

Those are the problems and the tasks which affect the everyday lives of our peoples. It is on how we handle *them* that the utility of the United Nations will be judged. If we lose sight of that point, the United Nations will have little or no role to play in the twenty-first century.

Let us never forget . . . that our Organisation was founded in the name of "We, the Peoples." . . . We are at the service of the world's peoples, and we must listen to them. They are telling us that our past achievements are not enough. They are telling us we must do more, and do it better.

Source: Millennium Report, presented to the United Nations by Secretary-General Kofi Annan, April 3, 2000. Copyright © 2000 by the United Nations. Reproduced by permission.

epilogue

THE MIDDLE EAST IN TODAY'S WORLD

Roger B. Beck

The focus of this update essay is a broad examination of the various crises in the Middle East and their global consequences.

ISRAEL, LEBANON, AND THE ISRAEL-HEZBOLLAH WAR

Following the collapse of the Ottoman Empire after World War I, the French designated Lebanon as one of several ethnic enclaves within a larger area that became part of the French mandate of Syria. Maronite Catholic Christians made up the majority of Lebanon's population, but there were also significant numbers of Muslims and Druzes. In 1926 Lebanon became a separate republic but remained under the control of the French mandate. During World War II, the French Vichy government allowed Germany to transport war materials and aircraft through Syria to Iraq to use against the British. The British then invaded Syria and Lebanon, and the Allies regained control, turning the area over to Charles de Gaulle and the Free French government in exile. In 1943 the Free French granted Lebanon independence.

In the ensuing decades, Lebanon has vacillated between periods of peace and prosperity and periods with wars of catastrophic destruction and death. Initially, despite its involvement in the 1948 Arab-Israeli War and a civil conflict in 1958, Lebanon prospered. In the 1950s, 1960s, and early 1970s, it was a favorite tourist destination; Beirut was referred to as the "Paris of the Middle East." The country became a regional center of banking and trade, and the economy thrived. A model primary, secondary, and university education system produced a population with one of the highest literacy rates in the Arab world.

In spring 1975, however, long-simmering dissatisfaction and anger over the dispersal of political power erupted into violence, setting off an utterly devastating fifteen-year civil war. A brief review of the civil war sheds light on events fifteen years after its end.

When Lebanon became an independent nation in 1943, the unwritten National Pact included agreement that the Lebanese president would be a Christian and the prime minister a Muslim. This arrangement was based on a 1932 census (still the last one taken in Lebanon) that showed a Christian majority. By the late 1960s, however, the Lebanese Muslim population had grown significantly, and Muslims were no longer content with a Christian-controlled government and military. The situation was exacerbated by the arrival after 1970 of thousands of Palestinian refugees into southern Lebanon following their expulsion by Jordan's King Hussein in an event known in the Arab world as Black September. Tensions came to a head in early 1975, starting with armed scrimmages between Christian and Muslim factions that resulted in the slaughter of many innocent civilians, and the escalating violence and reprisals led to all-out civil war.

In the course of the war the Lebanese army, whose soldiers represented all the various political and religious factions in the country, disintegrated as soldiers switched their allegiance from the national government to various sectarian militias. Eventually, besides the Lebanese army, there were five main militias. Four of them, the Christians, Sunnis, Shi'ites, and Druzes, were based on religious identity. In the early 1980s a hard-line faction broke away from the main Shi'ite militia to form a separate group known as Hezbollah, or Party of God, which had as one of its stated objectives the complete destruction of the state of Israel. A fifth group, the Palestinians, fought for a nationalist cause. In addition to these five militias, a number of loosely organized nonreligious groups fought for various causes, such as communism or a Greater Syria. The final major players in the civil war were Syria and Israel. Syria, which entered the war in 1976, eventually had over forty thousand soldiers stationed in the east and north of the country. The Arab League legitimized Syria's presence by giving Syria a mandate to provide the bulk of an Arab Deterrent Force charged with restoring peace. Concern over the Palestine Liberation Organization's control of southern Lebanon, and cross-border attacks that led to some Israeli civilian and military deaths, provoked Israel's first invasion of Lebanon in 1978. Although Israel withdrew later that year, the threat remained. In 1982 Israel invaded Lebanon again under the direction of the defense minister, Ariel Sharon. Israeli forces pushed deep into southern Lebanon to the outskirts of Beirut, intending to completely destroy the PLO and to establish southern Lebanon as a buffer zone to prevent future attacks against northern Israel.

The Lebanese civil war was brutal, massively destructive, and characterized by an utter disregard for human rights and human decency. War crimes and terrorist acts were committed by all sides. Car bombs became a particularly favorite weapon, and their perceived effectiveness has encouraged their continued use in terrorist acts to the present day. Extortion and mistreatment of civilians were common as militias set up Mafia-like control over their territories and supported their causes financially through smuggling—particularly of drugs as Lebanon became a major hashish producer—theft, ransom payments, and forcing travelers to pay "customs" as they passed through checkpoints. Altogether an estimated one hundred thousand people were killed and a like number injured. Close to a million people were forced out of their homes, and an estimated two hundred fifty thousand Lebanese left the country permanently. Tens of thousands of Lebanese, victims of kidnapping and wartime violence, are still missing. Lebanon's entire infrastructure was destroyed, and Beirut in 1990 looked like the bombed-out cities of Europe after World War II.

The beginning of the end to the civil war came with the Taif Agreement of 1989. The agreement provided for political reform, specifically a more balanced sharing of power between Lebanon's Maronite Christian and Muslim communities, provisions for a special cooperative relationship between Lebanon and Syria, and a framework for the complete withdrawal of Syrian troops from Lebanon. Maronite Christian general Michel Aoun, who directed a large militia in East Beirut and had been appointed prime minister illegally (the position was supposed to go to a Muslim), refused to recognize the agreement. As the violence continued into 1990, Syria launched a major offensive against Aoun's forces, destroying them and driving him into exile in France. By May 1991 the sectarian violence had generally ceased. With the critical exception of Hezbollah, all the militias were dissolved, and the Lebanese military tried to re-establish control over the country.

This proved an impossible task, however, as thousands of Syrian troops remained in the north and east of the country and Israel retained a large military presence in the south. Hezbollah, with significant diplomatic and financial backing from Iran, continued to attract thousands of followers, particularly among the rural and urban poor. Israeli forces finally left Lebanon in May 2000, but Syrian forces soon moved south to take their place. Following the assassinations of several prominent Lebanese politicians and journalists and massive protests in Beirut against the Syrian presence and influence in Lebanon, Syria was forced to withdraw its fifteen thousand troops from Lebanon. Thus a new beginning in Lebanon's history began on April 27, 2005, when the last Syrian troops departed, two months after Lebanon's Syrian-backed prime minister and cabinet were forced to resign. Lebanon was now free of Syrian occupiers for the first time in decades.

From the end of the civil war in 2006, Lebanon had slowly rebuilt its infrastructure. Schools and universities reopened; thousands of new buildings arose out of the war rubble; and new roads, bridges, hospitals, hotels, and restaurants served an increasingly prosperous population and foreign tourists who returned to the country once known as the "Switzerland of the Middle East."

But after the Israeli withdrawal in 2000, Hezbollah set about establishing a power base among the many villages and towns of the south and by 2004 had established virtual control over much of southern Beirut and southern Lebanon. Although it had abandoned its goal of transforming Lebanon into an Islamic republic, it continued to call for the complete destruction of Israel. Much to the chagrin of Washington and other Western capitals, Hezbollah won fourteen seats in the Lebanese legislature in parliamentary elections held in June 2005. It broadcast its message on its own radio and satellite television stations, and it set up massive charity and social programs that rivaled anything the government could provide. Hezbollah also developed a highly trained paramilitary army possessing some of the most advanced and sophisticated military hardware available through the international arms market. Hezbollah members adhere to a distinct brand of Islamic Shi'ite theology and ideology developed by the Shi'ite ayatollah Ruhollah Khomeini, leader of the Iranian Islamic Revolution in 1979. This connection explains the significant financial and military support that Iran provides and its powerful influence in shaping Hezbollah's policies, particularly toward Israel. Since coming to power in 2005 Iranian president Mahmoud Ahmadinejad has repeatedly called for the total annihilation of Israel, which is Hezbollah's primary goal.

That was the situation in July 2006, when Lebanon's years of reconstruction and hopes for peace were shattered once again. On July 12, 2006, Hezbollah began bombardment of northern Israeli military installations and towns while carrying out a cross-border raid that resulted in the capture of two Israeli soldiers and the killing of three others. An immediate rescue effort by Israel resulted in the deaths of five more Israelis. Hezbollah's intentions were to obtain Israeli prisoners to swap for Arab prisoners held by Israel. Israel responded with massive air strikes and artillery fire directed at what the Israeli military claimed were Hezbollah positions in southern and central Lebanon. Israel also instituted an air and naval blockade of the entire country and bombed runways at Beirut International Airport to render it impossible for planes to land or depart. Hezbollah retaliated with a rocket barrage launched into northern Israel, which Israel answered by invading southern Lebanon and thereby setting off a vicious war called the July War in Lebanon and the Second Lebanon War in Israel.

Israeli prime minister Ehud Olmert declared Hezbollah's attack an "act of war" and promised a "very painful and far-reaching response." In the ensuing weeks, Israeli

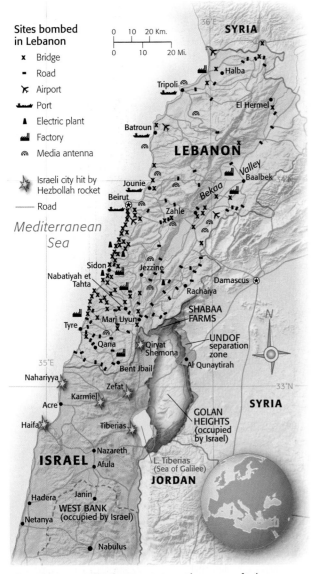

Sites bombed in Lebanon

✕ Bridge
− Road
✕ Airport
⚓ Port
▲ Electric plant
⚙ Factory
📡 Media antenna
★ Israeli city hit by Hezbollah rocket
—— Road

The 2006 Israel-Lebanon War The nation of Lebanon became the unwilling site of Israeli attacks directed at the political-religious movement Hezbollah following Hezbollah's shelling of northern Israel, abduction of two Israeli soldiers, and killing of eight others on July 12, 2006. In this Israel-Hezbollah war, the nation and people of Lebanon were the ones who suffered. This map shows the villages and cities in northern Israel struck by Hezbollah rockets and mortars, and the widespread damage done to Lebanon's infrastructure by Israeli shelling from the sea, land, and air.

forces hammered Lebanon from the land, sea, and air in what appeared to some as indiscriminate attacks on Hezbollah and non-Hezbollah targets alike. These attacks resulted in the destruction of large parts of Lebanon's civilian infrastructure, including schools, hospitals, sewage treatment plants, electrical facilities, roads, fuel stations and depots, commercial buildings, and homes. One attack by the Israeli air force on the Jiyeh power plant south of Beirut in mid-July ruptured oil tanks that spilled up to 110,000 barrels of fuel oil into the Mediterranean Sea, comparable in size to the 1989 *Exxon Valdez* oil spill in Alaska. The Jiyeh oil spill massively polluted beaches along the entire Lebanese coast, where the local economy is heavily dependent on the tourist and fishing industries.

Lebanese prime minister Fouad Siniora denied any knowledge of the Hezbollah raid, condemned it, and called for United Nations intervention. He and his government were forced to watch helplessly over the next few weeks, however, as Hezbollah and Israel fought. Hezbollah proved itself a formidable opponent to the much-vaunted Israeli Defense Force. Equipped with modern weaponry from Iran, China, Syria, and Russia, Hezbollah's well-organized and well-trained paramilitary units inflicted significant death and destruction on the invading Israeli forces. They also carried the attack into Israel itself, bombing more than eleven major cities in northern Israel along with dozens of kibbutzim and Druze and Arab villages. Over a half million civilians in northern Israel were forced to flee. Hezbollah forces destroyed at least twenty Israeli tanks, damaged an Israeli warship so severely that it had to be towed back to port, claimed credit for bringing down an Israeli helicopter, and on August 12 killed twenty-four Israeli soldiers, marking Israel's worst single-day loss. Environmentally, Hezbollah rockets ignited forest fires across northern Israel that are estimated to have destroyed as much as nine thousand acres of Israel's few forests.

United Nations organizations and various humanitarian agencies accused both sides of committing war crimes. Israel stood accused of indiscriminate and intentional attacks against civilians, the use of cluster bombs (that left more than one hundred thousand lethal unexploded bomblets) near civilian areas, and the reported use of white phosphorus, which is considered a chemical weapon when used in civilian areas. Hezbollah was condemned for indiscriminate and intentional shelling of civilian populations in cities and filling its shells with ball bearings to maximize harm to civilians. While Israeli forces dropped leaflets warning civilians to leave the southern Lebanon war zone, their destruction of roads and bridges into and out of the area made this impossible for many. Israel justified these attacks by claiming they were to prevent Hezbollah from rearming through Syria and Iran and smuggling out the captured Israeli soldiers. For its part, and as frequently happens in guerrilla wars, Hezbollah appeared to locate its rocket launchers and troops within populated residential areas. Israeli and some neutral reports charged that Hezbollah purposefully sought to draw Israeli fire on civilian targets in order to maximize civilian casualties and earn more sympathy for its cause.

● **Environmental Consequences of War**   Israeli attacks on the Jiyeh power plant south of Beirut during the Israel-Hezbollah war in July 2006 caused a massive oil spill of 10,000 to 15,000 barrels of oil, the worst environmental disaster in Lebanon's history. A hundred-mile stretch of Lebanon's shoreline was seriously affected, severely damaging the ecology and the local tourism economy. *(Ben Curtis/AP Images)*

Besides the release of the two captured Israeli soldiers, Israel appeared to have two goals: first, to destroy Hezbollah as a viable organization; and second, to send a clear signal to the Lebanese population and government that they would pay dearly if they continued to allow Hezbollah to control southern Lebanon and maintain a paramilitary presence that threatened Israel's peace and security. For its part, Hezbollah's leader, Hassan Nasrallah, said at one point during the war that Hezbollah would probably not have invaded Israel and captured the two soldiers if its leaders had known Israel's response would be so massive and destructive. Once at war, however, Hezbollah soldiers fought tenaciously and clearly did not intend to just slip away, abandoning Hezbollah's power base in southern Lebanon.

Diplomatic efforts to end the war involved, as is often the case, a flurry of diplomatic messages, diplomats shuttling back and forth between world capitals, solemn world leaders expressing profound concern, and little action. As the war intensified and civilian casualties mounted, there were calls from all quarters for an immediate and unconditional cease-fire—particularly from the Lebanese prime minister Fouad Siniora, who pleaded with the United States, Israel's closest ally, and with the United Nations to put an immediate stop to the war. Because the United States considers Hezbollah a terrorist organization, however, President George W. Bush and Secretary of State Condoleezza Rice continually refused to call for an immediate cease-fire, arguing that any agreement had to include the return of the two Israeli soldiers and Hezbollah's surrender of its weapons and return of control of southern Lebanon to the Lebanese government. Some observers argued that the U.S. refusal to demand an immediate and unconditional cease-fire was motivated by its desire to give Israel time to completely destroy Hezbollah.

Two events during the war drew particular condemnation from the world community and put greater pressure on Israel to end its invasion. First, there was what the

Israeli military described as a nondeliberate bombing of a UN observation post on July 26, 2006, that killed three UN observers. The Israelis argued that they were targeting Hezbollah fighters in the area. The second incident occurred on July 30, 2006, during an Israeli Air Force attack on a building in al'Khuraybah, near the village of Qana in southern Lebanon. The building collapsed, burying many Lebanese refugees who were sheltered in the basement. Although initial reports listed more than fifty casualties, the final count showed that at least twenty-eight people were killed, including sixteen children, and thirteen were missing. Although Israel argued it was responding to rockets launched from the village, the high number of women and children killed sparked outrage against Israel across the Muslim world and set off worldwide demonstrations protesting Israel's action and calling for peace.

Hezbollah's continued shelling of northern Israel and Israel's seeming inability to gain a quick military victory, while sustaining increasing numbers of civilian and military deaths itself, generated mounting discontent in Israel among soldiers and civilians alike about the handling and course of the war. By early August all sides clearly desired a way out, and on August 11, 2006, the United Nations Security Council unanimously approved UN Resolution 1701, which led to a cease-fire on August 14, 2006.

The resolution called for a full cessation of all hostilities. Israel was to withdraw its forces from southern Lebanon while Lebanese and UN forces took their place. Hezbollah was to be disarmed, and no paramilitary forces would be allowed in southern Lebanon. The Lebanese government was to have full control over the entire country, and the two Israeli soldiers were to be released. Hezbollah declared, however, that it would not disarm; Lebanon announced that it would not disarm Hezbollah; and Israel said it would not withdraw its forces until Hezbollah had been disarmed. Matters seemed at a stalemate, and Israel maintained its air and sea blockade of Lebanon, ostensibly to block illegal shipments of arms from Syria and Iran to resupply Hezbollah. Only four days after the cease-fire, on August 18, Hezbollah's famed network of humanitarian services attracted worldwide notice as the organization began distributing $12,000 (U.S. dollars) cash to every family in southern Beirut whose home had been destroyed. Hezbollah's largesse was an embarrassment to the Lebanese government, which could not match such funding, and to the international community, which was slow in responding to the war with humanitarian aid. Hezbollah's funds were thought to come from Syria and Iran.

As discontent with his conduct of the war continued to grow in Israel, Prime Minister Olmert lifted the aviation blockade on September 7 and the naval blockade the following day, and Israeli forces began to withdraw from southern Lebanon. On October 1, 2006, the last remaining Israeli soldiers in Lebanon crossed the border back into Israel. Hezbollah fighters had melted back into the population.

Opinions vary as to who won and who lost the war. Both the Syrian and Iranian presidents claimed victory for Hezbollah, although their countries may have gained more from the war than did Hezbollah. Certainly many in the Muslim world felt pride in Hezbollah's ability to stand up to the Israeli military machine and fight it toe to toe for thirty-four days. Many were also happy to see Israel under attack. This renewed Islamic pride would certainly rub off on the two leaders, Syrian president Bashar Assad and Iranian president Ahmadinejad, both of whom are seen as Islamic leaders in the forefront of the battle against Israel and its closest, and most unpopular, ally, the United States. Although Hezbollah's leaders declared victory over Israel, there can be no doubt that, other than perhaps the propaganda war, Hezbollah paid dearly. Even its leader, Hasan Nasrallah, admitted that given the opportunity he would not do it again. Hezbollah lost the elaborate infrastructure it had taken years to build in the south. Large amounts of its weaponry were used up, destroyed, or captured, and hundreds of its best fighters killed. The organization also lost the support of hundreds of thousands of Lebanese whose homes, lives, and livelihoods—and decades of painstaking rebuilding after the civil war—were destroyed by Hezbollah's actions. These

Lebanese deeply resented Hezbollah's crying "victory!" as they themselves sat among the rubble.

For its part, Israel claimed victory but was no better off. The two missing Israeli soldiers, Ehud Goldwasser and Eldad Regev, whose capture had sparked Israel's initial invasion of Lebanon, were not returned until July 16, 2008, in coffins. Many Israelis believe that Olmert's indecisive leadership cost Israel a rare opportunity to destroy Hezbollah, thereby ending its threat to Israeli security and its influence in Lebanese politics, and frustrating Iran's foreign policy. Israelis emerged from the war deeply troubled by a new sense of vulnerability. The Israeli government's Winograd Commission, tasked with investigating the war, issued reports in April 2007 and January 2008 highly critical of Olmert and his government's handling of the war. On July 30, 2008, Olmert announced he would resign as prime minister as soon as his Kadima Party picked his successor. His resignation has shaken up the peace process and created concern that Israeli hardliners, such as former prime minister and opposition Likud Party chair Benjamin Netanyahu, would win the next election. Netanyahu could be expected to take a much tougher stand against Hamas, Hezbollah, and Iran.

Meanwhile in Lebanon efforts have been ongoing to rebuild the country once again. The majority of Lebanese people appear to want nothing but peace. But in the last two years, Hezbollah has rearmed and reemerged as a political and military power. In May and June 2008 Hezbollah militia attacked Lebanese army units in Beirut and the Beqaa Valley. Furthermore, in May 2007 the worst internal fighting since the civil war broke out with a battle between the Lebanese armed forces and the militia of the Sunni extremist group Fatah al-Islam near Tripoli and the enormous Palestinian refugee camp of Nahr al-Bared in northern Lebanon. The fighting ended with the Lebanese army regaining control, but only after the death of several hundred soldiers, civilians, and Islamic militia members.

Lebanon perhaps pulled back from the brink of another civil war, however, when its politicians finally chose a successor to President Emile Lahoud, who had resigned in November 2007. On May 25, 2008, Lebanon's parliament elected army chief Michel Suleiman as the new head of state, ending months of government paralysis. Suleiman is expected to work for national unity, seek equal political relations with Syria, and try to integrate Hezbollah's militia into the Lebanese army.

ISRAEL AND PALESTINE

While Israel was busy fighting Hezbollah in the north, the Israeli-Palestinian conflict remained unresolved. Prime Minister Ariel Sharon's successful execution of his unilateral plan for withdrawal of all Israeli settlers from the Gaza Strip in August and September 2005 resulted in a split in his ruling Likud party. Sharon left the party in November 2005 to found his own political party, Kadima, Hebrew for "forward." Despite changing his political allegiance, Sharon continued pressing for the completion of the West Bank barrier, or wall, which ostensibly is intended to protect Israel from attacks by armed Palestinian groups and suicide bombers. Despite worldwide criticism, the wall continues to be built, effectively annexing 9.5 percent of West Bank territory originally given to the Palestinians in the United Nations Partition Plan in 1947. Sharon also proceeded with his plan to build thirty-five hundred new Jewish settler homes in the West Bank, but his plans were cut short when he suffered a massive hemorrhagic stroke on January 4, 2006, that left him completely incapacitated and in a vegetative state with little hope of recovery. His place was taken by Ehud Olmert, who became acting prime minister and leader of the Kadima party. He and his party won national legislative elections in their own right in April 2006.

For their part, the Palestinians held legislative elections for the Palestinian National

Authority government in January 2006. To everyone's surprise, Hamas, a Sunni Muslim political party considered by many in the West to be a terrorist organization, won 76 of the 132 seats. Using suicide bombers as its primary weapon, Hamas has been best known for its attacks on Israeli civilians and military and security forces. Formed in 1987, its charter calls for Israel's destruction and its replacement with a Palestinian Islamic state. Not only does it share with Iran and Hezbollah a desire to destroy Israel, but like Hezbollah, Hamas has gained widespread support from many Palestinians for the extensive welfare programs it has established in the West Bank and Gaza Strip. While many Palestinians view the old ruling Palestine Liberation Organization as increasingly corrupt and impotent, they have watched as Hamas built health-care clinics, orphanages, shelters, and schools throughout the Gaza Strip and West Bank.

For President George Bush and other Western leaders who have called for the spread of democracy in the Middle East, the parliamentary victories in relatively free and fair elections by Hezbollah in Lebanon and Hamas among the Palestinians have caused embarrassment and concern. Immediately after the Hamas victory, Israel, the United States, the European Union, and several other leading European and Western donor nations cut off all aid to the Palestinian Authority. The United States and EU outlined "three principles" that they said Hamas and the Palestinians had to accept for funding to be renewed and diplomatic relations established. First, Hamas had to revise its charter and recognize Israel's right to exist as a sovereign nation, something Hamas has adamantly refused, through 2008, to do. Second, Hamas had to renounce violence and cease its support of suicide bombings. Third, it must fully support the Middle East peace process as outlined in the 1993 Oslo Accords. Hamas rejected these principles out of hand, calling them unfair and suggesting that it might agree to recognize Israel if Israel withdrew to its pre-1967 borders, which would mean pulling out of the West Bank, the Gaza Strip, the Golan Heights, and, most important, East Jerusalem. Hamas also demanded the right of return to their old homes and lands of all Palestinian refugees and their descendants.

Many political observers felt that once the Hamas members took their seats in the Palestinian legislature and formed a cabinet, the political realities of actually being responsible for the running of a government and the welfare of its citizens would force its leaders to abandon their most extreme positions. The new cabinet was announced on March 20, 2006. The old ruling PLO party, Fatah, refused to accept positions in the new cabinet, leaving the majority of the seats to Hamas and a few independents. It soon became clear that the new Hamas government would not back away from its call for the destruction of Israel.

The one moderate voice in the Palestinian Authority remains the president, Mahmoud Abbas, who is the chairman of the PLO Executive Committee. Elected president of the Palestinian Authority in January 2005 after the death of Yasir Arafat in November 2004. Abbas has found himself in a nearly impossible position. He has been blamed by the Israelis for not doing enough to stop attacks on Israeli civilians and military forces. Many of these attacks have been carried out by members of Hamas or by their allies in the Islamic Jihad movement. He has also failed in his efforts to form a government of national unity. Hamas refuses to join a coalition government if it means recognizing Israel and rejecting violence. In frustration, in December 2006 Abbas called for new elections for early 2007. Prime Minister Ismail Haniya, representing Hamas, dismissed the proposal, saying Abbas had no authority to call elections. In June 2007 Hamas seized control of the Gaza Strip, forcing Abbas and his followers out. Abbas then established an emergency Palestinian Authority government, which has been officially recognized by Israel and the West, in the West Bank. Abbas and Israeli prime minister Olmert met in Annapolis, Maryland, in November 2007 and set themselves the goal of reaching a final peace settlement by late 2008. Outbreaks of violence between the two sides continue, however, and little progress had been made through July 2008. Recent public opinion surveys of citizens on both sides suggest that attitudes are hardening against any compromise peace settlement.

If outgoing Prime Minister Ehud Olmert is succeeded by someone from the Likud Party, as appears likely, it will almost certainly mean Israel will take a more hardline stand toward any peace settlement with the Palestinians.

Meanwhile, economic and humanitarian conditions for average Palestinians, particularly in the Gaza Strip, continue to decline. The Palestinian Authority has no mechanism to raise tax revenues, but is dependent on Israel to forward an estimated $60 million in monthly tax revenues so that the government can pay its 165,000 civil employees. Israel stopped making these payments after Hamas took power and has only sporadically released some of these funds to Abbas and the West Bank Palestinian authorities. By late 2006, surveys suggested that more than 70 percent of the civil employees could no longer make ends meet and that more than 20 percent were considering emigrating. Health care has also deteriorated sharply, with drugs and medical supplies in critically short supply. Some hospitals and clinics have closed, and healthcare providers, teachers, and other public employees have gone on strike, protesting having worked for months without pay or pay raises. The infrastructure in the Gaza Strip, already crippled by years of war, continues to deteriorate, with electrical power low and unreliable and water supplies irregular. Without reliable electricity, sewage treatment plants cannot operate efficiently, increasing the risk of disease spreading. Sixty-seven percent of Gazans live below the poverty line, and general lawlessness has risen sharply.

Making life even more difficult for average Palestinians, Hamas and Israel began an exchange of attacks in early June 2006 that have continued through early 2008. The refusal of Hamas to recognize Israel's right to exist has brought peace negotiations to a standstill and has delayed the formation of a viable, operative Palestinian government that will focus on protecting its citizens and providing for their needs. Nearly all the world powers have refused to recognize Hamas as a legitimate government until it renounces violence and recognizes Israel. It remains to be seen whether Hamas can continue to hold out, particularly as living and working conditions in the Gaza Strip and West Bank continue to deteriorate. Of course, the leaders of Hamas face the same problem that has caused many more-moderate leaders in the Middle East to hesitate to recognize Israel; when the Egyptian president Anwar Sadat formally recognized Israel in the late 1970s, he was assassinated by the Egyptian Islamic Jihad. Members of various radical groups have already threatened violence against the Hamas leaders if they back away from their call for Israel's destruction.

Thus, despite years of diplomacy, war, and stalemate, the main differences between the Israelis and the Palestinians remain unresolved. These include the nature of a future Palestinian state; the fate of Palestinian refugees and their "right of return"; Israel's establishment of Jewish settlements in the occupied territories and their ultimate fate; the status and future of the West Bank, East Jerusalem, and the Gaza Strip, which are the designated areas for a future Palestinian state; Israeli security and the recognition by all parties of Israel's right to exist; and, perhaps the most difficult question of all, who is to have sovereignty over Jerusalem and its holy sites, including the Temple Mount and Western Wall complex. For the moment at least, there appears to be no light at the end of the tunnel for one of the most complex human, religious, and ethnic dilemmas in world history.

• • • • • •

IRAQ

One of the rationales for the overthrow of Saddam Hussein still put forward by the Bush administration is the desire to establish a stable democratic government in Iraq. To that goal, the Coalition Provisional Authority, established as a transitional government following Saddam Hussein's ouster, held executive, legislative, and judicial authority over the country from April 2003 to June 2004. On June 28 it handed over

● **Protecting Iraqi Oil** A U.S. soldier stands guard over an Iraqi oil field. Although Iraq is estimated to have the world's second largest oil deposits, about 11 percent of the world's total deposits, its oil production has been severely limited since the early 1990s—due first to UN sanctions and, from 2003, to the Iraqi war. Peak production of Iraqi oil was about 3.5 million barrels per day (bpd) in the late 1980s. In spring 2008 oil production was around 2 million bpd. Saudia Arabia's oil production, by comparison, was about 10 million bpd in May 2008. Still, with world oil prices at record levels, members of the U.S. Senate and House are pressing Iraq to accept a larger share of the war's costs. *(D. Hurst/Alamy)*

sovereignty to an Iraqi interim government, with Iyad Allawi serving as Iraq's acting prime minister until elections could be held in January 2005. Allawi immediately reintroduced capital punishment and, after assuming legal custody of Saddam Hussein, set in motion the trial of the former dictator. Insurgent attacks against coalition forces continued to mount, however, and the interim government failed to gain the support of large portions of the population, who viewed Allawi as a puppet of the United States. These factors, together with disputes and disorganization within the interim government itself, made the organizing of elections difficult at best.

Elections to select a 275-member Iraqi National Assembly that would draft a permanent Iraqi constitution were finally held on January 30, 2005. Many Sunni Arabs boycotted the elections, but most of the eligible Shi'ite and Kurdish population voted. Somewhat to Washington's embarrassment, the party of Prime Minister Allawi came in third, with just 14 percent of the vote. A party backed by the leading Shi'ite cleric, Ayatollah Ali al-Sistani, a frequent critic of the American-led war, received 48 percent of the votes, reflecting the Shi'ite majority in the country. A Kurdish party came in second with 26 percent of the votes.

After several delays, the draft of the new Iraqi constitution was approved in a nationwide referendum held on October 15, 2005. By permitting a compromise that allowed the first government working under the new constitution to make amendments to it at any time during the first four months, which would then have to be ratified by a similar referendum, the constitution received the important backing of the Sunni-majority Iraqi Islamic party. A new election was then held on December 15, 2005, to elect a permanent Iraqi National Assembly.

Disputes over vote rigging meant that the elections were not officially certified until February 10, 2006. Disagreements between all the various factions and parties in the legislative assembly over who should be the speaker, as well as who would be the first president and first prime minister, continued through the spring.

The current Iraqi government finally took office on May 20, 2006. The Kurdish leader Jalal Talabani was elected president, and the prime minister was Nouri al-Maliki, a Shi'ite Muslim whose Islamic Dawa party was a member of the United Iraqi Alliance, a coalition of primarily Shi'ite parties that had received the most votes in the election. Although by spring 2008 they had managed to hold a government together for two years, Iraq's leaders still faced essentially the same daunting problems as when they first took office. The most important challenge is to train national military and police forces that will restore order to the country and put an end to insurgency and sectarian violence without continued U.S. support. The government must also determine what the ongoing relationship will be with the United States and with a continued allied military presence that some Iraqis consider an occupation force. Government corruption must be ended, particularly relating to the illegal sale of Iraqi oil. Iraq's leaders have to convince all Iraqis that they are not favoring one faction—religious or ethnic—over another. Finally, the government must determine how the new constitution is to be

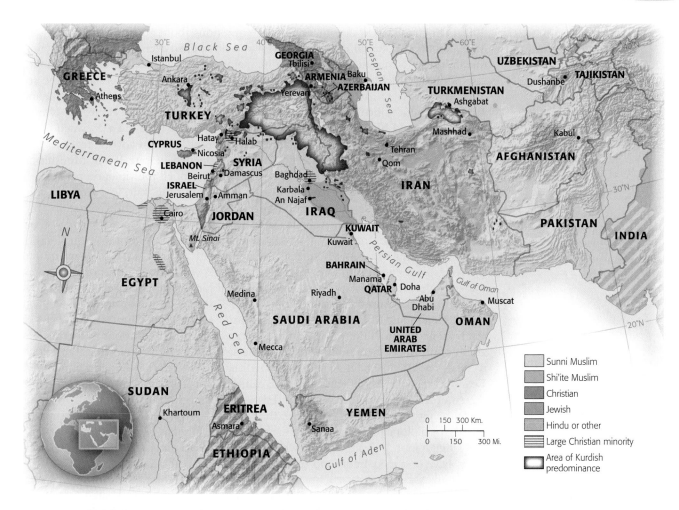

Abrahamic Religions in the Middle East and Surrounding Regions   Although Islam is the majority religion throughout the Middle East, Judaism and Christianity, which also trace their origins back to the patriarch Abraham, still have significant populations, particularly in the modern Jewish state of Israel and in Lebanon. Though the Sunni branch of Islam has always dominated the Shi'ite branch, since the 1979 Iranian revolution Shi'ites throughout the region have become more strident in their demands for equality and power, and more militant. The Kurds, one of the largest stateless ethnic groups, who follow various religions, have become a major player in the politics of the region, especially in Iraq and Turkey, where they seek Kurdish independence.

implemented, whether it needs to be amended, and how much autonomy will be given to the various regions and factions within the country, especially the Kurds in the north.

As Iraqi politicians were writing a new constitution and attempting to form a new government, Iraqi judges and lawyers were trying Saddam Hussein for crimes against humanity. Specifically, Hussein was charged with the murder of 148 Shi'ite men in the town of Dujail after a 1982 assassination attempt against him. The trial began on October 19, 2005, with the defiant Hussein pleading not guilty, and adjourned in June 2006. On August 21 a second trial began, this time charging Hussein with war crimes against Iraqi Kurds, specifically for ordering poison gas to be dropped on Kurdish mountain villages. On September 19, 2006, the government appointed a new chief judge, Mohammed al-Ureybi, after sacking the old one, Abdullah al-Amin, allegedly for saying that Hussein was not a dictator. This action raised doubts in some legal circles about the freedom of the court from government interference in the trial.

On November 5, 2006, the court found Hussein guilty of crimes against humanity and condemned him to death by hanging. Rather than take the available thirty days to consider the Appeals Court decision, the Iraqi government determined that Hussein should be executed immediately, and the hanging took place on December 30,

2006. This "rush to execution" again raised questions about government impartiality. Many Sunnis considered Hussein a martyr and threatened even more reprisals against the Shi'ite-led government and the Shi'ite majority in the country. While these political and judicial deliberations were being held within the secure confines of the so-called Green Zone in downtown Baghdad, the violence in Baghdad's streets and across the country increased dramatically. In July and August 2006 alone, the United Nations reported, almost sixty-six hundred Iraqis, nearly a hundred a day, died in the sectarian violence. Attacks were averaging nearly eight hundred a week, up nearly 24 percent from the beginning of 2006. All this happened despite Prime Minister al-Maliki's repeated announcements of new initiatives to quell the violence, particularly in Baghdad. Instead, the violence increased throughout the year, with entire neighborhoods coming under the control of private militias. As the security situation grew worse, so too did the supply of basic services, such as sewage, electricity, and potable water, which remain intermittent at best. Outside Baghdad there were large areas of the country over which the Iraqi government had no control at all. In August 2006 the chief of intelligence for the U.S. Marine Corps concluded in a report that there was only a remote possibility that U.S. and Iraqi forces could secure al-Anbar Province, the heart of Sunni resistance.

The United States also seemed to be losing the battle for the "hearts and minds" of the Iraqi people in 2006. Most damaging were the various allegations of torture and abuse of prisoners, beginning with incidents at Abu Ghraib prison. American troops were also accused of killing civilians at Haditha in November 2005, and four of five U.S. soldiers accused of raping and then murdering a fourteen-year-old Iraqi girl and then murdering her mother, father, and sister on March 12, 2006, have pleaded guilty, while the fifth awaits trial. Blackwater, the American private security firm that supplies guards for diplomatic convoys and other security details, has been accused of harming and killing innocent Iraqi civilians while carrying out its duties. These and other incidents have outraged Iraqis and made innocent American soldiers the targets of revenge attacks.

At the same time, antiwar sentiment, always high outside the United States, has grown significantly within the United States since 2006 as the dollar cost of the war, estimated in spring 2008 at over $600 billion, mounts and the death toll continues to climb. On September 22, 2006, the number of U.S. soldiers killed in the Iraq and Afghanistan wars marked one more death than the 2,973 killed in the World Trade Center towers on September 11, 2001. U.S. deaths in Iraq passed 4,000 in March 2008. As the violence continues, the specter of an Iraqi civil war remains ever present—and some argue that Iraq is already experiencing a civil war. The Iraq War has also had a negative effect on the centerpiece of President Bush's foreign policy, the war on terror. A leaked U.S. intelligence report from April 2006, which pulled together intelligence information from sixteen American spy agencies, concluded that Islamic radicalism had mushroomed worldwide and that the Iraq War had contributed to a growth in the overall terrorist threat since 9/11.

Following the Republican loss of both houses of the U.S. Congress in the November 2006 elections, partly due to the unpopularity of the Iraq War, President Bush in January 2007 announced a new American strategy of sending an additional 20,000 American troops to Iraq and deploying the majority around Baghdad and in al-Anbar province. This new strategy has been called colloquially the "troop surge" (antiwar opponents refer to it as a "troop escalation") and has resulted in an increase of the American military presence in Iraq from 130,000 to over 160,000 troops. Whether this new strategy has been a success remains a matter of heated debate. Politically, most of the benchmarks set for the Iraqi government by the U.S. Congress have gone unmet. Militarily, there has been a decrease in violence across the country, but it is unclear whether this is due to the increased troop presence. Some mixed Sunni-Shi'ite neighborhoods that had experienced extreme factional violence have since been taken over by one or the other side, forcing the losers to flee from their homes. The Iraqi economy has shown some signs of recovery, with oil revenues increasing significantly, which has prompted both Democratic and Republican members of Congress to ask why Iraq is not paying a larger share of the cost of the war.

The Iraq War, as it has since its beginning in 2003, remains a complex affair that displays aspects of civil war, military occupation, religious and ethnic conflict, and holy war. With no end in sight after five long years, it appears that Bush's successor will have to find a solution that will bring peace and prosperity to Iraq while disengaging American troops and bringing them home.

• • • • • •

IRAN

Prior to Iran's June 2005 elections many political observers felt that moderates were gaining an upper hand in revolutionary Iran and that Akbar Hashemi Rafsanjani, a relatively more moderate candidate in Iranian politics, would win the election. Certainly there was no expectation that he would be challenged by Mahmoud Ahmadinejad, the ultraconservative hard-line mayor of Tehran. Despite a series of protests prior to the election about the power of the Guardian Council, which has veto power over all political candidates in Iran and used that power to disqualify a number of more moderate ones, the elections went smoothly, with nearly 60 percent of eligible voters casting ballots. In a runoff, Ahmadinejad defeated Rafsanjani, winning 61 percent of the vote.

Mahmoud Ahmadinejad (b. 1956) holds bachelor's and master's degrees in civil engineering and a Ph.D. in traffic and transportation engineering and planning, which he received in 1987, after which he taught civil engineering at the prestigious Iran University of Science and Technology. He was appointed mayor of Tehran in May 2003 and served for three years before running for president. As mayor he reversed many of the more moderate and reformist regulations instituted by previous mayors, while implementing various social and welfare programs to help the poor. It is thought that this populist element in his governing style and rhetoric appeals to the masses and is partly responsible for his winning the presidency. Ahmadinejad has also enjoyed wide support among religious hardliners for his hostility to secular reforms and attacks on Western culture.

During the Iran-Iraq War in the 1980s Ahmadinejad was a member of the Revolutionary Guard, which operates parallel to the regular Iranian army. He served in the security and intelligence branch, and his role was to suppress dissidents in Iran and abroad. Although the evidence remains murky, a number of reports charge Ahmadinejad with involvement in the interrogation and execution of prisoners. He is also alleged to have been involved in a number of extraterritorial operations as part of an elite force that carried out assassinations in the Middle East and Europe.

Ahmadinejad is the sixth president of the Islamic Republic of Iran. He took office on August 3, 2005. During his campaign Ahmadinejad emphasized both his religious conservative views and his plans for helping the poorer economic classes, including a proposed monthly stipend to each citizen. He calls himself a "principalist" in reference to his strict adherence to his perceived version of the principles of Islam and of the Iranian Islamic Revolution. His most popular economic goal is a more even distribution of Iran's oil wealth among all its people, particularly the poor. After three years in office, however, Ahmadinejad has failed to repair Iran's ailing economy, and his support, even among conservatives, has eroded. In the March 2008 legislative elections, some reformers who want more democracy and closer ties with the West were allowed to run and won a few seats, but Ahmadinejad's party retained a large majority.

Ahmadinejad had not been in office long before he became the center of worldwide controversy. The debate over Iran's nuclear power program has stirred the most intense discussion, but Ahmadinejad's comments in speeches and interviews, particularly about Israel and the Holocaust, have also drawn sharp criticism from many world political and religious leaders outside the Muslim world. Ahmadinejad has criticized the arrangement of the United Nations Security Council and the veto power of the five permanent members (Great Britain, United States, France, Russia, and China), arguing that the world's 1.5 billion Muslims are thereby denied a vote in the global policymaking process. Ahmadinejad is not staking out a particularly new or unusual position here. All five veto-holding members of the Security Council are nuclear powers and have blocked any efforts to give other countries membership in this privileged club. Germany, Japan, Brazil, and India have all sought permanent, veto-holding membership on the Security Council.

Ahmadinejad's remarks regarding Israel have created a firestorm of controversy. In a speech in October 2005 at a "World Without Zionism" conference held for students in Tehran, he said that he accepted the position taken by the Ayatollah Khomeini that Israel should be "wiped off the map" and that he expected Palestinians to soon "wipe this disgraceful stain from the face of the Islamic world." Despite worldwide condemnation of these remarks, he has not backed away from them. Nor has he backed away from statements first made on December 15, 2005, that seemed to deny the Holocaust. In subsequent remarks he has continued to voice doubts that the Holocaust ever happened. In August 2006 a contest was held in Tehran to determine the best Holocaust caricatures; the contest was presented as retaliation for the publication of caricatures of Muhammad first published in Denmark in September 2005. In December 2006 a state-sponsored conference held in Tehran openly challenged the scale and even the reality of the Holocaust.

Ahmadinejad has backed up his anti-Israel rhetoric with action. Iran's Shi'ite clergy have long supported the Shi'ite population in Lebanon, and many Lebanese Shi'ite clergy were trained in Iran before the 1979 revolution. After the revolution, Lebanon was one of the first countries to which Iran's Shi'ite revolutionaries looked to export their revolution. As we have seen, the immediate outcome of these efforts was the formation of Hezbollah, whose stated goals were the creation of an Islamic Lebanese state and the destruction of Israel. Lebanon is on the western end of what is becoming known as the Shi'ite Crescent, a regional axis that stretches from Iran in the east through Shi'ite communities in Bahrain, Iraq, eastern Saudi Arabia, and Syria (see the map on page 1081). In Lebanon, Iran has provided both military and humanitarian supplies and was probably responsible for the handout of $12,000 to each family that lost its home after the war. There were even reports that some Iranian Revolutionary Guard soldiers were training Hezbollah fighters in southern Lebanon. On June 16, 2006, a month before the Israel-Hezbollah war, Syria signed a defense pact with Iran that would allow the stationing of Iranian troops in Syria and perhaps other support from Iran if Syria were attacked. Iran has also supported Hamas with money, war materials, and humanitarian supplies.

The issue that has set Iran most at odds with the world's major powers, however, is its determination to continue its nuclear energy program. The United States, the European Community, and other nations have accused Iran of developing nuclear power in order to form a nuclear weapons arsenal. Iran has consistently denied that this is its intention.

The Iranian nuclear technology program began during the reign of the Shah of Iran in the 1950s with the help and support of the United States. It was abandoned temporarily after the 1979 revolution, but then revived. Although they have received only limited Western assistance since then, primarily from Russia, the Iranians seem to have developed a very sophisticated program and have several research sites. Iran has a uranium mine and uranium-processing facilities, including a uranium enrichment plant. It also has a nuclear reactor. Russia is building Iran's first nuclear plant, Bushehr I, which is expected to be operational by fall 2008. This program is the result of a compromise whereby Russia provides nuclear fuel and expertise to build the plant, thus

● **Iranian Nuclear Energy Program** Despite threats of sanctions from the United States, France, Germany, Great Britain, and Russia, Iran continues to develop its nuclear energy program. Here Iranian scientists move a container of radioactive uranium. Whether the uranium is being used for peaceful purposes, as Iran staunchly maintains, or to develop nuclear weapons, as the West argues, remains to be seen. *(Behrouz Mehri/AFP/Getty Images)*

alleviating international concerns over Iran's nuclear program, while still allowing Iran access to nuclear energy.

There is currently no evidence that Iran possesses any weapons of mass destruction, and the country is a signatory to most of the major agreements banning such weapons, such as the Biological Weapons Convention, the Chemical Weapons Convention, and the Nuclear Non-Proliferation Treaty. On March 6, 2006, despite continued accusations from the United States, Great Britain, France, Germany, and Russia, the International Atomic Energy Agency (IAEA) director general, Mohamed ElBaradei, stated that the agency had not found any evidence that Iran was diverting nuclear material to the production of weapons or nuclear explosive devices. The United Nations Security Council, however, passed a resolution on July 31, 2006, that demanded the suspension of Iran's uranium enrichment program by August 31 or face sanctions. These and later demands and ultimatums have had few teeth, however, as the world powers cannot agree on appropriate sanctions. Iran continues to take a hard line. On April 20, 2008, Ahmadinejad said he rejected any new incentives the world powers might offer in return for Iran's suspending its uranium enrichment program.

The debate over Iran's nuclear energy program has become a global issue that reaches far beyond the question of simply whether Iran has the ability to make, or intends to make, a nuclear weapon. By standing up to the West on this issue, Iran has garnered the support of many other nations that see the prohibition as another example of how the nations of the West want to deny to the rest of the world what they already enjoy—nuclear power and nuclear weapons. This support was most powerfully expressed in a resolution passed on September 16, 2006, at the meeting of the 118

Non-Aligned Movement members in Havana, Cuba. The resolution stated the developed countries should allow developing countries to participate in the development of nuclear energy for peaceful purposes, and that all countries had the inalienable right to produce and use nuclear energy for peaceful purposes without discrimination. In the Muslim world there is also the perception of hypocrisy on the part of the Western powers in allowing Israel to develop nuclear power and, it is generally agreed, possess nuclear weapons, while denying Iraq, Iran, and other Middle East countries that right.

Experts generally agree, however, that it will be at least ten to fifteen years before Iran has the capability to produce even one nuclear weapon. Thus, the immediate question of whether Iran intends to use its nuclear program to produce nuclear weapons is still open to debate. The larger question of who will determine which countries can produce nuclear energy programs in the future remains one to which the world community will have to return.

AFGHANISTAN

After the 2001 attack on the World Trade Center towers and the Pentagon, the United States declared a war on terrorism. Its first target was Afghanistan, where the accused mastermind of the September 11 attack, al-Qaeda leader Osama bin Laden, was being sheltered by the ultra-fundamentalist Sunni Muslim Taliban, which had ruled Afghanistan since 1996. With the help of the Afghan Northern Alliance, a loose coalition of Afghan groups that had been fighting the Taliban for some time, and U.S. and NATO member troops, the United States began Operation Enduring Freedom.

Taliban forces abandoned Kandahar, the birthplace of the movement and the last Taliban-controlled city, on December 7, 2001. The Taliban's leader, Mullah Mohammad Omar, managed to escape, however, with many of his troops and their weapons. Al-Qaeda forces meanwhile, with some Taliban allies, had concentrated their positions in a cave complex known as Tora Bora located to the southeast of the capital Kabul near the Pakistan border. The U.S.-led forces made a last assault on the al-Qaeda strongholds in the caves, where it is believed Osama bin Laden was also hiding. A temporary truce, however, appears to have allowed bin Laden, many other top al-Qaeda leaders, and many of their troops to escape across the mountains into Pakistan. This is the closest U.S. forces have ever been to capturing bin Laden. Through July 2008, bin Laden's whereabouts remain unknown.

When the fighting appeared to have ended, a grand council of the major Afghan factions and tribal leaders met in June 2002 to form an interim Afghan government. They selected Hamid Karzai, a politician almost from his birth in Kandahar in 1957. Karzai belongs to the influential Popalzai clan of the ethnic Pashtun, the second-largest ethnic group in Afghanistan. His father was a member of the Afghanistan parliament under the former king Mohammad Zahir Shah. Karzai was taking a postgraduate course in political science at a university in Shimla, India, when the Soviet Union invaded and occupied Afghanistan in 1979. During the resistance he served as an adviser, fundraiser, and diplomat. After the Soviets pulled out in 1989, Karzai was deputy foreign minister in the postwar government, but he resigned his post in 1994 as the country fell into civil war. When the Taliban came to power in 1996, Karzai went into exile in Pakistan, from where he organized anti-Taliban opposition.

After his father was murdered in Pakistan in July 1999, presumably by Taliban assassins, Karzai succeeded his father as clan chief, or khan, of the half-million Popalzai. He then organized a procession of tribal mourners that carried his father's body back to Kandahar, the Taliban stronghold but also the Popalzai home. The Taliban did not dare to halt the funeral or harm Karzai. This single act of courage and defiance earned Karzai recognition as the leader of Pashtun resistance to the Taliban.

When Karzai took power in 2002 his political base in the country was quite limited—so much so that people sometimes derided him as just the mayor of Kabul—and he ruled only through the presence of the coalition forces. When presidential elections were held in October 2004, however, Karzai won twenty-one of the thirty-four provinces to become the first democratically elected Afghanistani leader. After taking office, Karzai was expected to immediately set about initiating democratic and modernizing reforms in the country, but that has not been the case. In December 2004 he made major changes in his cabinet, removing many of the former Northern Alliance warlords but, reflecting his desire to proceed very cautiously, also fired his finance minister, Ashraf Ghani, who had instituted extensive economic, banking, credit, and customs reforms between 2002 and 2004 and had been recognized as the best finance minister in Asia in 2003.

Although the economy has been growing and government revenues increasing, this is partly the result of the harvest of the main crop in Afghanistan, the opium poppy, which in 2007 reached the highest levels ever recorded, up almost 60 percent from the 2005 harvest. The 2008 crop is already expected to be nearly as high. Total production was around sixty-five hundred metric tons of opium for the 2007 growing season, which equals 93 percent of the world's supply. Its estimated export value was $4 billion. Thirty-five percent of the country's gross domestic product now comes from the opium trade. This is despite the millions of dollars poured into eradication of the poppy crop by the Afghan government and international agencies.

Large areas of the country still under the control of warlords are increasingly coming back under the control of the Taliban, and the record harvest can be attributed in part to the resurgence of Taliban rebels in the prime opium-growing region in the

● **Afghanistan's Opium Poppy Fields**   An impoverished Afghan farmer inspects his opium poppy crop, which will bring him far greater profits than any other crop he can produce. The government's eradication program, poorly funded and facing much opposition from farmers and local officials, has had little success. The 2007 opium poppy harvest was the largest ever recorded, up nearly 60 percent from the 2005 harvest. (Ahmad Sear/Corbis)

south. The Karzai government exercises almost no control over these areas, and farmers have received virtually no incentives to plant alternative crops. The Taliban have stepped in, distributing seeds and fertilizers for new poppy crops and offering farmers protection, while receiving increased support, new recruits, and profits from the drug trade to fund their military operations.

The Bush administration has made opium poppy eradication one of the primary targets of its aid to Afghanistan, and it has been critical of the Karzai administration for not doing more. Karzai has been inconsistent in his efforts to deal with the opium problem. He rejected a U.S. proposal to eradicate production by aerial spraying with chemical herbicides, but he continues to reiterate his determination to eradicate the crops. He must tread a fine line, however, because he has neither the funds nor the worker capacity to effect much change or to initiate reforms beyond a very limited region around the capital of Kabul. Aerial spraying might get rid of the opium poppy, but it would win Karzai few allies among the warlords who profit from the drug trade and little political support from the farmers who depend on poppy production for their livelihood.

In a speech before the United Nations General Assembly on September 2006, Karzai said that terrorism is rebounding in Afghanistan, both from terrorists acting from within the country and from terrorists coming across from other countries to attack Afghanistani civilians. Since his speech, the situation has deteriorated even further. One estimate in February 2008 suggested that the Karzai government controlled only about 30 percent of the country and the Taliban about 10 percent, and that the remainder was under local tribal control. Suicide bombings have soared, and hundreds of civilians, aid workers, and Afghan security personnel have been killed despite an increased allied military presence. The United States has raised its troop level in Afghanistan from twenty-five thousand in 2004 to fifty thousand in 2008. Still, casualty figures have risen sharply in the last two years, and by August 2008 over 900 coalition troops, including over 500 Americans, had died since October 2001. Without the coalition forces, it is generally agreed that the Taliban would be in control of Kabul within a week, so ill-trained and ill-organized is the Afghanistani military. This would likely lead to another civil war as the warlords of the old Northern Alliance would defend their fiefdoms once again.

As the violence and death toll mount, President Karzai and the U.S.-led coalition are becoming increasingly unpopular. In 2007 and early 2008 the Bush administration took steps to more strongly support the war in Afghanistan, such as raising American troop levels there and encouraging other members of the coalition to do the same, but these efforts are still far short of U.S. military and monetary support for the Iraq War.

- - - - - - - - - - - - - -

TURKEY

Turkey remains a country on the border—seeking membership in the European Union of the West, while acknowledging its Islamic heritage and historical connections with the East. It is a secular country, not ruled by Islamic law. Many of its citizens lead Western lifestyles, although the population is overwhelmingly Sunni Muslim. Despite concerted efforts by leaders to meet the economic, legal, and humanitarian standards set by the EU, Turkey's pace of reform has met with heavy EU criticism. The 1915–1917 Armenian massacres remain a major point of contention. In September 2006 a Turkish court acquitted a prizewinning Turkish author, Elif Shafak, of charges that she denigrated Turkish national identity by having characters in her novel *The Bastard of Istanbul* make statements about the Armenian massacres. Although this ruling saved Turkey short-term embarrassment, it did not seem to satisfy EU officials, who warned Turkey that it should purge its penal code of all restrictions on freedom of speech as a firm demonstration of its commitment to human rights and democracy.

The European Commission evaluating Turkey's application to join the EU has been highly critical of Turkey's accession progress, expressing concern over issues of access to ports and airports for EU member Cyprus, freedom of expression (especially in cases dealing with writers and journalists), and Kurdish minority rights. On December 7, 2006, Turkey announced it was opening one port and one airport to trade with Cyprus. It will be at least 2013, and the next round of EU membership admissions, before Turkey can be admitted into the EU, provided that it meets all of the EU's demands.

Although it is a major concern for Turkey's politicians and people, EU membership is not the only issue troubling the country. Turks are also deeply divided over the future of the secular state in Turkey, as well as the Kurdish question. To understand the first concern, we must remember that Turkey is the most secular of Islamic countries, going back to the presidency of Mustafa Kemal in the 1920s and 30s (see pages 853–854). Since that time Turks have closely guarded their secularism and maintained a strict separation of state and religion. In 2002 elections, however, the newly formed (1991) Justice and Development Party (or AKP) scored a stunning victory. Abdullah Gul became president of Turkey, and Recep Erdogan, head of the AKP, became prime minister. Although the AKP campaigned as a moderate, conservative, pro-Western party, supporting liberal market economics, many Turks are concerned that the AKP is really intent on doing away with Turkey's secular constitution and establishing an Islamic state. Although Erdogan has adamantly denied any secret agenda, laws such as the banning of alcoholic beverages, the lifting of the headscarf ban in all universities, the placing of antisecular individuals in government offices, the awarding of government contracts to Islamic businesses, and the arrest of several secular opponents of the government have been criticized by secular parties. Although the AKP won the 2007 elections by an even wider margin over its opponents, Turkey's chief prosecutor filed a lawsuit in March 2008, seeking to close down the AKP and ban Erdogan and Gul from holding any political office for five years. The AKP was charged with committing antisecularist actions that were banned by the constitution. On July 30, 2008, Turkey's Supreme Court fell one vote short of disbanding the party. The Court did, however, sharply criticize the party for its actions, and halved state funding for the party.

The second major problem facing Turkey is its handling of its minority Kurdish population, a problem that closely relates to the Iraq War. Many observers view the landslide victory of the AKP in the 2007 elections as prompted by a surge in Turkish nationalism and a resurgence of conservative Muslim influence since September 11, when the West, particularly the Bush administration in the United States, demanded an either-or, "with us or against us" position from Turkey, Pakistan, and other allies in the Middle East. When Turkey refused to participate in the invasion of Iraq in 2003 because it worried about destabilizing fragile relations with its Kurdish citizens, many in the Bush administration labeled the Turks as "against" the United States and the war on terrorism. As the situation in Iraq has continued to deteriorate and as the Kurds in northern Iraq continue to push for more autonomy, Kurdish nationalists within Turkey have increased their attacks against Turkish targets. In February and March 2008 the Turkish army began a military offensive against Kurds in eastern Turkey and also across the border in northern Iraq. These attacks have increased tensions between Turkey and the West.

Index